D1264621

THE "E" FACTOR

THE "E" FACTOR

E = ERGOGENIC (er-go-jen'-ik)
—performance enhancing substance or technique

DR. BOB GOLDMAN
and DR. RONALD KLATZ

■

THE SECRETS OF NEW TECH TRAINING
AND
FITNESS FOR THE WINNING EDGE

William Morrow and Company, Inc.
New York

Library of Congress Cataloging-in-Publication Data

Goldman, Bob, Dr., 1955–
    The "E" factor : the secrets of new tech training and fitness for the winning edge / by Dr. Bob Goldman and Dr. Ronald Klatz
      p.   cm.
    Bibliography: p.
    ISBN 0-688-06468-X
    1. Sports—Physiological aspects. 2. Physical fitness. 3. Sports medicine—Technological innovations.   I. Title.
RC1235.G65 1987   87-21326
613.7'1—dc19   CIP

Printed in the United States of America

First Edition

1 2 3 4 5 6 7 8 9 10

BOOK DESIGN BY M 'N O PRODUCTION SERVICES INC.

To the athletes of the world.
I hope they will seek their goals via ethical and fair paths,
and preserve the beauty and brotherhood
that sports competition breeds.
I also dedicate this book to my parents, Alice and Arnold,
and my grandmother Rose,
who have taught me that truth and belief in one's self
are first and foremost—nothing is impossible!

ACKNOWLEDGMENTS

There have been many people who were vital to the completion of this book. I want to thank those who have aided me in this goal.

First, my collaborator, Dr. Ron Klatz, who endured my inhuman around-the-clock working habits and served as a sounding board; Dr. Thomas Allen, Department of Sports Medicine at the Chicago College of Osteopathic Medicine, who provided me with the progressive sports medicine time schedule milieu to work on the text; Dr. Larry Haspel and Dr. Fred Schwartz for their belief in this project; Ben Weider, CM, president of the International Federation of Body Builders, who strives to eliminate drug use from the sport of body building; Dr. Ronald Lawrence for his guidance and friendship; my literary agent, Jed Mattes; friend and adviser Eric Roper; and my editor, Doug Stumpf.

Many of the following people shared knowledge and experiences: Peter Carl (NBC-TV); Nick Jannes; Bud Moon; Doris Barrilleaux; Dr. Pat Bush (George Washington University School of Medicine); Dr. Ken Bretts; June Colbert and Sam Lamensdorf; Denie Walters; John Husar, Rich Philips, and Ron Kotulak (*Chicago Tribune*), Dr. Don Catlin (UCLA Olympic Drug Testing Lab); Professor Manfred Donike (West Germany Olympic Drug Testing Lab); Perris Calderon; Jennifer Colbert Lane; Dr. Richard Strauss, Dr. Alan Ryan, and Fran Munnings (*Physician and Sports Medicine*); Randy Minkoff (United Press International); Claudia Brodsky; Dr. Don Cooper (Oklahoma University); Les Cohen; Don Rutz (CNN); Mark Kramm (*Detroit Free Press*); Karen Dennis; Mary Dietz; Dr. Mark Dollard (Secretary, AAU Sports Medicine Committee); Robert Echales; Jeff Everson (*Muscle and Fitness* magazine); Cory Everson (Ms. Olympia); Carole Page (*Boston Globe*); Ed Pitts (*Fitness Management*); Grahm and Katherine Putnam; Steven Groshek and Bob Arndtt (Ciba Pharmaceuticals); Mitch Kaufman; Phil Gumby (*Journal of the American Medical Association*); Dan Gable (U.S. Olympic wrestling-team coach); Becky Green; Alfreda Green; Susan J. Greenberg, PT; David Groves (*Health Magazine*); Dr. Ed Grog (Carle Clinic); Dr. Robert Hackman (University of Oregon); Robert Helmick (president of the U.S. Olympic Committee); Randy Harvey, Julie Cart (*Los Angeles Times*); Dr. Art Hafner (American Medical Association chief of Library Services); Ira Hurley; Ralph Hittman (BBR); Rich Harkins (President, AAU); Tom Hagler; Lee Harris; Lisa Hildebrand; Dr. James Nicholas, Dr. Tony Maddalo (Institute of Sports Medicine and Trauma); Mike Interator; Lisa Chodof, Amy Allision (International Racquet and Sports Association); John Jeansonne (*Newsday*); Robert Jolliff; Cris McIntyre, Carole Jacobs, and Joe Weider (*Shape* magazine); Susan Jacobs; Dr. Ernst Jokl (University of Berlin); Dr. Peter Jokl (Orthopedics, Yale University); Dr. Alan Jacobs; Dr. Karen Gayda; Bob Gayda; Ken Kontor (National Strength and Conditioning Assoc.); Dr. Charles Kochakin; Larry Kuhel, Bob Kelley; Dr. Robert Kappler; Dr. Thad-

deus Kawalek; Dr. Paul Keill (*American Medical Athletic Association Journal*);
Claudia Kreiss; Keith and Wendy Bennett; Elbert Hunter; John Lombardo
(Cleveland Clinic); Leon Locke (*Wave Publications*); Kenneth Scott; Amy
Munice; Bill Lumas; Russ Stewart; Drs. Masse and Degaulle of the Montreal
Olympic Drug Testing Laboratory; Debbie Losure (*Inside Chicago* magazine);
Dr. Ljiljana Ostojic; Kathy Lynch (California division of Athletes Against Drug
Abuse); Drs. Gabe Mirkin and Mona Shangold (Sports Medicine Institute,
Georgetown University School of Medicine); Claudia Miller; Rainer Martens
(Human Kinetics Publishers), Bob Carr, Mark Klionski (*Sporting Goods Busi-
ness*); Todd Logan (*Club Industry* magazine); Sandy Lerner (*Fitness Industry*);
Karre Slafkin, Steve Warner (*Home Gym and Fitness*); Dr. Alan Mintz
(Unimed Inc.); Marlene Tuattrocchi; Dr. Tom Miller (Sports Medicine Con-
gress); Gary Vogel; Sandy Merle, Larry Strickler; Steve Neul; Dick Nuzzo
(Medical Communications); Dan Neidermyer; Dr. Art Nahas; Tom Doyle, Bob
Rader (National Sporting Goods Trade Association); Dr. Richard Ornstein;
Tim Basting (*Osteopathic Medical News*); Jeffrey Plitt; Brenda Payne; Bob Dee
(Point West Typesetters); Dr. Keith Peterson (The Sports Medicine Clinic);
Ellen Rosen; Dr. Mike Liang; Dr. Jerry Rodos; Porter Schimer (*Rodale Press*);
Bill Reynolds, Ben Pesta (*Muscle and Fitness*); Ricky Wayne (*Flex* magazine);
Amy Sklar; Marty Silverberg; Mark Mulvoy, Walter Bingham (*Sports Illus-
trated*); Arnold Schwarzenegger; Barry Shapiro (*Sport Magazine*); Brian
Hewitt, Teresa Barker (*Chicago Sun Times*); Dick Schapp (ABC-TV); Lee
Siegle (Associated Press); Dr. Gary Slick; Joe Schultz; Steve Sokol; Jim
Sarland; Sana Siwolop (*Business Week*); George Snyder; Dr. William Taylor;
Dr. Terry Todd, Jan Todd (University Texas, Austin); Wally Tokarz (*American
Medical Association News*); Henry Freeman, Tom Weir (*USA Today*); Roy
Cartin, Al Sanoff, Adam Weisman (*U.S. News & World Report*); Pat McKor-
mack (UPI); Colonel George Miller (USOC); Dr. Robert Voy (Chief Medical
Officer, Olympic Training Center); Carole Weidman; Pat Walker; Alison
Dowson (*Women's Sports* magazine); Sandra Wahl; Brenda Winkle (NBC-TV);
Harris and Pamela Kagan (IFBB Administration); Michael Zucker; the Ad-
visory Board of the American Longevity Research Institute: Dr. Steve Bern-
stein, Dr. Richard Beik; Dr. Carole Claycomb, Dr. Kirby Hotchner, Dr. Ward
Dean, and Dr. Brian Rothstein; Linda Gioni; Goldie Klatz; Susan Ellis (*Lon-
gevity Newsletter*); Kari Granger, Karen Peterson, John Alevizos.

The following equipment companies and associated individuals have
been a pleasure to work with: Jerry Brentham (Hydra-Fitness); Jim Trisler and
Steve Rhodes (Paramount Fitness); Mark Siegle, Bob Bowen (Cybex/Eagle);
Parker Mahnke (Marcy); Jim Flanagan and Arthur Jones (Nautilus); Joe Con-
naughton and Frank Smith (Universal); Phil Scotte (Polaris); Arno Paviainen
and Ed Eisen (David Fitness); Dan Woods and Kelly Ellis (Tunturi); Greg
Monsey and Sean Harrington (Heart Mate); David Smith, Bill Potts and Paul
Byrne (Precor USA); Dennis Keiser (Keiser Sports); Dave Primeau (Biocy-
cle/EDC Corp); Debra Kumm (West Bend); Randy Peterson (Stairmaster); Dick
Cremer, Mike Hoffman (Bally Life cycle); Dick Charniski (Versa-Climber);
Brian Lewallen, Mike Stima, and Greg Evans (Myotech/Muscle Dynamics);
Tom Lincir (Ivanko); William Farrell (Monark); Gary Hecht (Hecht Communi-
cations/Vitamaster); Stu Warner (Hunk); Paul Briggs, Joe Ress, and Nancy
Basilicato (Bosch Medical); Jerry O'Keefe and Al Fritz (Schwinn/Excelsior);
Burt Birnbaum (Computer Instruments Corp.); Kevin Cummings (Saunatone);
Warren Cuzzens (Marquette Electronics); Jim and Frank Trulaski (True
Sports); Dave Ringer (Pro-Gym Systems); Marty Dupont (Tygr USA); Greg
Lekhtman (Biosig Instruments); Brian Jones (Zeus Supermats); and Carl Tow-
ley (Serious Lifting Systems). I hope I have not forgotten anyone. My deep
thanks to all for their help.
                                                                —B. G.

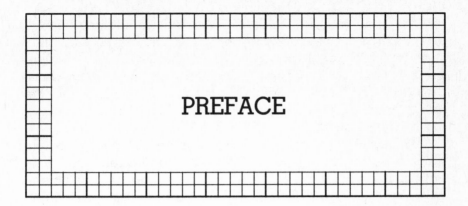

PREFACE

There are many techniques employed by champion athletes to get the winning edge. Some of them are safe and beneficial, while others may be hazardous, even deadly. Up until now, the "total athletic environment" has not been explored with an eye to showing how to attain optimum physical performance for each individual.

What is "the ergogenic factor," long known to elite athletes but unknown to the general public? It is the whole array of substances and techniques used to enhance athletic potential. Everything—from ions in the air to the food you eat, from drugs and vitamins to exercise devices—can affect your abilities. In *The "E" Factor* we will explore these potential tools in depth in order to help you find the special combination that will provide your personal winning edge.

The age of high tech is here: devices now available in medical research centers can speed recovery from injuries to a rate faster than anyone would have thought possible ten years ago. Electrical stimulating packs the size of a Sony Walkman can contract and work chosen muscle groups harder than any weight training. Combinations of substances right off the grocery shelves can be combined within the body to achieve far more potent nutritional benefit than most consumers are aware of.

At the same time, the spread of drug dependency is only the most obvious example from among a wide range of socially induced maladies in which the patient's own life-style is the key pathogen. Fast pace and fast foods contribute to the high levels of heart disease among Americans.

Many are now asking how we can reverse these trends and improve the quality of life in a way that will contribute to the health and well-being of the population. As we approach 1988 and beyond, there is a growing demand for health research that generates objective data on the alternatives to such life-style–induced pathologies and possible remedies. For this reason I joined with a group of research scientists and medical professionals who consistently try to provide leadership in the health and fitness field—the High Technology Fitness Research Institute it is called.

The Institute is intended to serve as an objective research laboratory, providing medically reliable and scientifically sophisticated evaluations of the safety and health benefits potentially available for all health and fitness products marketed in the United States. Institute staff will investigate ways this technology can be utilized to modify or reverse the health risks statistically associated with so-called life-style–induced diseases. Eventually, the Institute hopes to become the authoritative nucleus in the scientific community on the periodic controversies that cloud the health and fitness field, e.g., improper use of hormone drugs (steroids) by athletes; use of optimal-level exercise, dietary supplemental calcium, or estrogen supplements for prevention or reversal of osteoporosis in women; high-impact aerobics versus nonballistic low-impact exercise training; etc.

The Institute's first research project is to establish protocols and standards for fitness-technology evaluation, producing objective medical guidelines on both potential health risks and efficiency levels of various fitness devices. To follow will be specific research on fitness-technology applications in treatment and prevention of life-style–induced pathologies.

Much of the information in this book is derived from my work with the Institute, as well as from my research on the effects of high-dose anabolic steroids and high-protein intake on athletes, conducted at the Chicago Osteopathic Medical Center. But I have tried to go beyond these specialties to extract the information, which up to now has mostly been buried in stacks of complex medical data, on everything you need to know about the effects of food and drugs (including such common substances as caffeine and aspirin as well as steroids and other "exotics"), exercise machines, subliminal and psychological training—in other words, the entire range of what I call The "E" Factor. Overall health and longevity should not and need not be sacrificed to immediate athletic performance. Peak fitness can be attained safely to prolong life and augment competitive ability at the same time. Here is how to do it.

CONTENTS

ACKNOWLEDGMENTS   vii
PREFACE   **PART I**   ix

I.   **NUTRITIONAL ERGOGENIC AIDS**   3
      Carbohydrate Loading   4
      Water   5
      Sports Drinks   6
      Baking Soda   8
      Sodium Phosphate   9
      Vitamin and Mineral Supplementation   9
      Amino-Acid Supplements   13
      Potential Fat Burners   13
      Neurotransmitter Precursors   14
      Conclusion   15
      For Further Reading   15

II.   **NUTRITIONAL AIDS, CONTINUED**   17
      Pantothenic Acid (Vitamin B_5)   17
      Selenium   18
      Niacin   19
      Oil of Evening Primrose   19
      PABA   19
      Arginine/Ornithine   20
      The Placebo Effect   22
      A Note to Pregnant Women   22

III. **KEEPING THE EDGE/LONGEVITY AND THE
      ATHLETE**   24
      Free-Radical Theory of Aging   25
      Death-Hormone Theory of Aging   25
      Thymosyns, Thymic-Stimulating Hormones, and Aging   25
      Hayflick Constant and Aging   26
      DHEA and Aging Theory   26
      DNA Repair Theory   27
      Cortisol and Aging   27
      MHC As a Mechanism of Aging   28
      The Little Pills of Longevity   28

IV.   DRUGS, HORMONES, AND OTHER
       NONNUTRITIONAL ERGOGENICS   36
       Ergogenic Drugs Down Through the Ages   36
       Anabolic Androgenic Steroids   37
       Testosterone—The Male Hormone   41
       Cancer's Warning Signs   42
       Heart Disease   45
       Other Side Effects   46
       Steroid Effects on Women   47
       Psychological Effects of Steroids   48
       Human Growth Hormone   49
       Beta-Adrenergic Blockers   54
       DMSO   55
       Alkalies   56
       Phosphates   57
       Gelatin and Glycine   57
       Caffeine   58
       Blood Doping   61
       Oxygen   63
       Altitude Training   65

V.   RECREATIONAL DRUGS   66
       Marijuana   66
       Sedatives   68
       Amphetamines   68
       Nicotine   70
       Alcohol   71
       Cocaine   82

VI.   DRUG-DETECTION TECHNIQUES   86
       How Long Do Drugs Stay in the System?   86
       Instrumentation   88
       IOC Drug Testing Labs (North America)   90
       Procedures for Drug-Testing   90

VII.   DON'T DRINK THE WATER, AND OTHER
       HAZARDS TO YOUR HELATH   93
       Aluminum Toxicity   93
       Water Pollution   94
       What's in the Water Anyway?   95
       Airborne Attack!   96

VIII. BODY COMPOSITION   98
       Body Composition Analyzers   100

PART II

IX.   GUIDELINES FOR EQUIPMENT EVALUATION
       AND DEFINITIONS   105
       Biomechanic Evaluations of Equipment   108

Terminology Overview   109
Types of Muscle-Training Systems   111

X.   THE PHYSIOLOGY OF TRAINING SYSTEMS   115
      The Energy Systems—Their Role in Muscular Work   119
      Principles of Training   129
      Muscular Endurance   132
      Muscular Power   134

XI.   ROWING MACHINES   136
      Checklist for Selecting a Unit   137
      Rowing Technique   138
      Precor   140
      Tunturi   142
      West Bend   143
      Universal ComputeRow   144
      Bally Fitness   146
      Coffey   148
      Concept 2   150
      Hydra-Fitness   151
      Heart Mate   152

XII. EXERCISE CYCLES   154
      Notes on Exercise Cycling   155
      Precor   156
      Tunturi   157
      Bodyguard/Oglaend   160
      Monark   161
      Bosch   162
      Universal   164
      Biocycle   164
      Bally Fitness   166
      Schwinn   167
      Exercycle   168
      Fitnron Cycle Ergometer   169
      Cateye Ergometer   169
      Paramount Fitness   170
      Protec Sports   171
      Cybex UBE   172
      Uppercycle by EDC   172

XIII. TREADMILLS AND OTHER AEROBIC
      TRAINING DEVICES   173
      Precor   173
      Universal   175
      True Sports   176
      Landice   177
      Marquette Electronics   177
      Quinton   178
      Cross-Country Skiers   179
      Other Aerobic Training Devices   180

XIV. **INSTITUTIONAL-LEVEL EXERCISE
      EQUIPMENT**   **183**
      Eagle/Cybex   183
      Paramount Fitness   184
      Hydra-Fitness   188
      David Fitness   193
      Myotech/Muscle Dynamics   194
      Nautilus   198
      Tygr USA   201
      Hunk Fitness   202
      Serious Lifting Systems   203
      Polaris   204
      Universal   205
      Kinesi-Arc   207
      Keiser   208
      Bally Fitness   209

XV.   **DIAGNOSTIC MUSCLE-TRAINING SYSTEMS   211**
      Hydra-Fitness   211
      Universal   211
      Cybex   213
      Kin-Com   213
      Isotechnologies   215
      Loredan   215
      Biodex   216
      Microfit   217

PART III

XVI.   **THINK TO WIN: SPORTS PSYCHOLOGY   221**
       Maximum Performance   222
       Taking It to the Limit   225
       Mental Imagery—Visualization   226
       Relaxation   226

XVII. **SUBLIMINAL TRAINING   229**
       Auditory Subliminals   230
       Do-It-Yourself Subliminal Training   233
       Physician's Note   234

XVIII. **BIOFEEDBACK   235**

XIX.   **HIGH-TECH PULSE MONITORING   240**
       Pulse Meters   244

XX.   **FLOTATION—THE RELAXING ART   248**
       Flotation-Tank Manufacturers   261

XXI.   **HIGH TECH/ELECTRONICS IN THE
        TREATMENT OF SPORTS INJURIES**   **262**
        Heat Packs   262
        Fluidotherapy   263
        Shortwave Diathermy (SWD)   263
        Transcutaneous Electrical Nerve Stimulation (TENS)   263
        Electrical Stimulation   264
        Ultrasound and Galvanic Stimulation   264
        Interferential Current   264

APPENDICES   **267**
        1: Organizations   268
        2: Additional Information on Life Extension, Longevity,
           Toxicology, and Drug Abuse   283
        3: Suggested Magazines and Journals for the Fitness
           Trade   287
        4: Normal Hormonal Levels in Blood and Urine 288
        5: Norms of Principal Blood-Chemistry Tests and
           Interpretation   292
        6: American College of Sports Medicine Position Stand on
           *The Recommended Quantity and Quality of Exercise
           for Developing and Maintaining Fitness in Healthy
           Adults*   307
        7: American College of Sports Medicine Position Stand on
           Proper and Improper Weight Loss Programs 317
        8: National Strength and Conditioning Association
           Position Paper on *Prepubescent Strength Training* 328
        9: American College of Sports Medicine Position Stand on
           The Use of Alcohol in Sports   341
       10: American College of Sports Medicine Position Stand on
           The Use of Anabolic-Androgenic Steroids in Sports 347
       11: National Strength and Conditioning Association
           Position Paper on *Anabolic Drug Use by Athletes* 361
       12: *A Self-Screening Examination for the Male Athlete
           Taking Anabolic Steroids*   404
       13: Normal Blood Composition   414
       14: NCAA Drug-Testing Program   416
       15: International Olympic Committee Banned-Drugs List 429
       16: United States Olympic Committee Banned Drugs 434
       17: Commonly Used Anabolic Steroids, with Chemical
           Structures, Normal Dosages, and Trade Names 502
       18: Structures, Names, and Manufacturers of Anabolic
           Steroids   505
       19: Medical References and Bibliographies   514

INDEX   **559**

■

PART 1

CHAPTER I

■

NUTRITIONAL ERGOGENIC AIDS*

Many athletes operate under the mistaken assumption that quality training procedures are sufficient to optimize their athletic performance. Evidence accumulates that nutritional status can significantly influence performance, and therefore nutrition is an essential component of training. While optimal nutrition is essential for maximum physiological and biochemical functioning, routine dietary practices generally do not further enhance a person's physiology beyond hereditarily determined limits. In other words, no matter what one eats or what supplements are used, not everyone can run a mile under four minutes, a marathon under two and a half hours, or win a power-lifting competition. However, nutrition ergogenics may be beneficial in helping the athlete approach his or her upper limit. Nutritional ergogenics include compounds that can promote both long-term and short-term optimization of function. Such "fine tuning" of one's body may produce significant improvement for a few days or weeks, but may not be suitable for long-term or daily practice. This review considers many of the common nutritional ergogenic aids, outlining the existing knowledge and speculating about future use. The reader is encouraged to keep abreast of the latest research, which may change some of the concepts contained in this chapter. Athletes should also experiment with the concepts presented in this chapter as part of their training program, to determine which strategies are best suited for their own unique biochemistry.

*The information on pages 3–16 was contributed by Robert M. Hackman, Ph.D., University of Oregon.

3

CARBOHYDRATE LOADING

More than twenty years ago, it was determined that eating a large amount of carbohydrates (starch) might improve long-distance aerobic performance. In endurance events usually lasting longer than ninety minutes, the athlete may have an edge if a high-carbohydrate diet has been eaten. High-carbohydrate intake stimulates skeletal muscle to superload with glycogen, a storage form of glucose and the body's preferred energy source.

Initial research suggested that carbohydrate loading could be achieved by first depleting the muscles of glycogen seven days before an event. This was done with a low-carbohydrate, high-protein diet coupled with exhaustive exercise during days seven to four before an event. For the final three days, a high-carbohydrate diet (approximately 70 percent of calories) coupled with tapering of training was used. Subsequent research indicates that the depletion phase is unnecessary for muscle-glycogen superloading and may make one feel lethargic, dizzy, and sometimes nauseated. A high-carbohydrate intake coupled with the tapering of training for three days before an event is now suggested as most effective in producing glycogen supercompensation.

Carbohydrates are glucose chains. Complex carbohydrates occur naturally in foods such as whole grains, dried beans, and starchy vegetables (potatoes, winter squash, etc.). Refined carbohydrates have been processed, removing most of the original fiber and many vitamins and minerals. They are found in foods such as white bread, white rice, and white pasta. In general, a complex-carbohydrate diet is recommended for the athlete. A normal training diet would include 55 to 65 percent of total calories coming from the various forms of complex carbohydrates. Under the carbohydrate-loading regimen, the percentage of calories from carbohydrate is increased to 70 to 75 percent for the three days prior to an event. For day three prior to an event, complex carbohydrates are recommended. For the two days prior to an event, refined carbohydrates may be more helpful. The lack of fiber in refined carbohydrates reduces the likelihood of food residue in the bowel (less chance of a bowel movement) during a competition.

When fat is consumed with carbohydrate, the pyloric valve at the bottom of the stomach constricts, slowing digestion by holding the food in the stomach for a longer time. This is undesirable for carbohydrate loading, where a large amount of digested carbohydrate is needed to enter the bloodstream. A low-fat intake is best during the three-day carbohydrate-loading period. Consuming pasta is fine, but when a butter sauce or cheese (both high in fat) is added to the pasta, the fat slows the digestion of the carbohydrate and reduces the amount of glycogen loaded into muscle. When eaten before a race, pasta, bread, or other carbohydrates should be prepared with little or no fat.

The endurance athlete is advised to experiment with a carbohydrate-loading plan during the training phase, maybe one month before an event. Bloating and muscle pain have been reported during carbohydrate loading, due to a retention of water which accompanies the stored glycogen. Waiting until three days before a big race to first try carbohydrate loading may not produce the desired outcome.

Lastly, carbohydrates are as important after a long race or workout as they are before. Leg-muscle fatigue and pain may be associated with a depletion of glycogen, which may drop in concentration ten times after a long, hard workout. The best time to reload those muscles is immediately after such an effort, when one's legs hunger for carbohydrates and glycogen.

WATER

Perhaps the most effective nutritional ergogenic aid is the forgotten nutrient. The body is approximately 65 percent water, and during exercise a well-hydrated body will perform better than one that is marginally dehydrated. Water is needed to cool the body, taking heat from the deep muscle tissue and organs to the body surface for conduction or evaporation, where water is also needed for sweat. Water keeps the blood thinned, allowing efficient cardiovascular function and transport of oxygen and nutrients to exercising muscle. Another critical role of water is its vital function in keeping the brain adequately hydrated. Even a slightly dehydrated body can produce a small but critical shrinkage of the brain, thereby impairing neuromuscular coordination, concentration, and thinking. A well-hydrated body provides the basis for high-level training and maximal functioning.

In addition to the health-promoting practice of consuming eight to ten glasses of water daily, people who exercise are advised to consume water (one to two glasses) fifteen to twenty minutes before a workout or competition. In the ensuing fifteen minutes, while a person is getting dressed and warming up, the water is usually absorbed from the stomach (assuming minimal food is in the stomach), and little chance of "sloshing" is likely. If a long workout or competition occurs, small quantities of water should be ingested every fifteen to twenty minutes during exercise. This may be only a few sips or a small glass, but the fluid is vital for maintaining normal body temperature and cardiovascular function. The water is best at a cool, not cold, temperature, for cold water is more slowly absorbed than cool. Again, one is advised to experiment with this practice during the training period rather than waiting until a competition.

Drinking water after a workout or competition is also crucial for recovery of both muscles and the brain. Drink cool water in quantities beyond thirst needs. Studies of marching soldiers have shown quite clearly that thirst is not a good indicator of the body's water needs. When soldiers were taken on a march and either given no water or allowed to drink water to their own desire, body temperatures rose dangerously after a period of time. When soldiers were marched and consumed water that equaled their body weight loss, which was a larger amount of water than consumed by free choice, body temperatures stayed in a normal range for over five hours. This suggests that drinking beyond one's thirst needs is most beneficial for maintaining a well-cooled and highly functional body.

SPORTS DRINKS

Since 1965, products have been available that are promoted to replace the electrolytes and glucose thought to be lost during exercise. The minerals in these preparations are primarily sodium, chlorine, and potassium, with some products containing phosphate, magnesium, and other electrolytes. It was initially thought that replacement of minerals lost in sweat was beneficial to long-term stamina and recovery from exercise. Studies since then have shown that body adaptation to heat and sweating occurs, thus conserving body electrolytes. Unless one exercises heavily during a high heat period and is not adjusted to the environmental conditions, electrolyte losses in sweat are generally not likely to exceed those available from body stores.

Most sports drinks also contain sugar in some form as well as electrolytes. Sugar gets absorbed as glucose, and may help to maintain a relatively elevated blood-glucose level in the face of glycogen depletion. This would conserve glycogen stores while fueling muscle tissue with some glucose energy. If sugar levels in the drinks are too high relative to the body glucose concentration, there will occur an influx of water into the stomach in order to dilute the ingested fluid and normalize it for absorption. Sports drinks with a high glucose concentration actually may impair athletic performance as the solution draws vital body water away from the bloodstream and into the stomach.

Some glucose intake during aerobic exercise may be beneficial. Studies done on Gatorade, a well-known sports drink, showed that runners did have greater stamina after consuming it compared to those who consumed only water. Cyclists were also found to have improved endurance during the sports-drink trial compared to those taking water only. In any sports drink, a maximum of 2.5 g of glucose per 100 ml of water is recommended. If electrolytes are also consumed, 0.2 g of table salt is advised for every 100 ml of water, which provides sodium and chloride. Less than 5 mEq of potassium per liter is recommended. Fluids are best taken cool ($5°$ C; $41°$ F) in volumes of 100 ml to 300 ml every 10 to 15 minutes.

Some of the newer sports drinks contain a polymerized-glucose solution in addition to a combination of electrolytes. These products are isotonic (at the same concentration as body tissue), do not draw fluid into the stomach, and empty from the stomach at a rate similar to that of water. Polymerized glucose, derived from cornstarch, has a chemical composition that allows it to empty rapidly from the stomach into the small intestine, promoting quick absorption, maintaining blood-glucose levels, and reducing the depletion of glycogen stores. This may enable an athlete to perform longer before the onset of fatigue, particularly in long-term endurance sports. When well-trained male endurance runners ran on an exercise treadmill and drank either no fluid, water only, or a water and glucose-polymer solution every 15 minutes, there were striking differences. When the runners received no fluid, they ran an average of 56 minutes, but when they drank water every 15 minutes during the run, they went an average of 78 minutes. When the same runners drank the glucose-polymer solution, they ran an average of 102 minutes. The results show not only the benefits of drinking water but also of maintaining blood-glucose levels during exercise.

Additional research may indicate whether polymerized glucose is beneficial for short-term intensive events such as football, basketball, and weight-lifting competitions.

BAKING SODA

When muscles exercise intensively, they produce lactic acid, a waste by-product of short-term anaerobic (no oxygen) activity. Lactic acid eventually decreases muscle efficiency by altering the acid-base balance, and may produce muscle pain. If lactic acid accumulation could be buffered, muscles might continue working better and longer. It is not that lactic acid is bad. In fact, more lactic acid is better, for it shows that one's muscles can produce and tolerate longer anaerobic activity. High-intensity exercise is one way to increase the body's natural ability to deal with lactic acid, as the body adjusts over time to this accumulation. Taking sodium bicarbonate may be another way to neutralize the lactic-acid buildup.

When highly trained half-milers took sodium bicarbonate shortly before their time trials, their times improved by almost three seconds, a statistically significant change relative to when they did their time trials and took only a placebo. Other studies have not shown such a convincing effect on improved performance but do suggest that taking baking soda after a hard, intense workout may speed muscle recovery by helping the lactic-acid-loaded blood to return to its normal neutral condition.

Since anaerobic exercise is generally sustained for a maximum of ten to twelve minutes, baking soda is best taken right before a workout or competition. However, swigging baking soda may be unpleasant. In most studies, subjects have taken between two hundred and three hundred milligrams of sodium bicarbonate for every kilogram (2.2 lbs.) of body weight, and some reported diarrhea. Again, it is suggested that the athlete experiment with taking baking soda a number of weeks before an event to determine the effects it might have, if any.

SODIUM PHOSPHATE

Success in long-distance aerobic endurance events depends on the delivery of oxygen to the exercising muscles. Recent research suggests that consuming sodium phosphate may increase maximum oxygen uptake by as much as 20 percent. This improvement would turn a three-hour marathoner into a 2:35 runner, for example. The potential benefit of sodium phosphate lies in its ability to affect a key enzyme (2,3-DPG) in the blood. Hemoglobin, a part of red blood cells, carries oxygen to the exercising muscles. High levels of 2,3-DPG in the red-blood-cell hemoglobin facilitates the release of oxygen into muscle. When ten highly trained runners took one gram of sodium phosphate four times a day for three days, they had greater endurance and exhibited a 6 to 12 percent increase in their maximum oxygen consumption during treadmill running compared to times when they took a placebo. Other studies with athletes riding a stationary bicycle for up to three hours found an improvement in maximum oxygen consumption of about 20 percent. The sodium phosphate also reduced the athletes' relative perceived exertion.

Other research with sodium phosphate has been far less convincing. In one five-mile bicycle time trial, nine subjects averaged only three seconds' improvement when sodium phosphate was given rather than a placebo. The phosphate-loaded riders did have higher levels of blood hemoglobin and 2,3-DPG, but the differences were minor.

Sodium phosphate certainly does not make up for the effects of improper training, but it may produce an effect and allow for better performance. Here again, the athlete is advised to experiment with this compound a few weeks before an event.

VITAMIN AND MINERAL SUPPLEMENTATION

Opinions vary regarding the potential benefits of supplementation for enhancing athletic performance. Unfortunately, however, research knowledge lags far behind popular opinions. One of the difficulties involved in assessing the true physiological benefits of vitamin and mineral supplementation is distinguishing the effect of the biochemicals from the placebo effect. Simply believing that a pill will improve one's ability to perform may be one of the strongest types of supplementation available. Another difficulty in assessing the validity of nutrient supplementation involves biochemical individuality. Supplements that might improve performance in one person may not necessarily have the same effect on other people. If a person's enzymatic and biochemical processes are functioning at or close to 100 percent efficiency, it is unlikely that supplementation will make much difference, but marginal vitamin and/or mineral status, even 10 to 20 percent below optimum levels, may have a significant effect on performance.

The B vitamins (e.g., thiamine, riboflavin, niacin, pyridoxine) are involved in the efficient metabolic production of energy. With the large energy consumption that occurs during athletic performance, additional supplementation of the energy-related vitamins may be beneficial, particularly when taken together.

The most convincing work in this regard has been with riboflavin. College women were assessed for their biochemical riboflavin status while they were either sedentary or running twenty to fifty minutes per day. The riboflavin requirements increased significantly when the women were exercising compared to when they were sedentary. Even when the women were consuming 100 percent of their recommended dietary allowance (RDA) of riboflavin, their riboflavin needs still were not met.

A variety of diffuse neurological symptoms, such as loss of appetite, lethargy, excessive fatigue, depression, and irritability, may have a nutritional component relevant to athletes. In twenty individuals reporting such symptoms with no apparent pathological basis, a common theme among them was their excessive sugar intake, primarily in sweetened beverages. Upon further biochemical investigation, it was found that thiamine levels were extremely depleted. This explains the neurological problems, since thiamine is integrally involved in nerve-cell physiology. Upon thiamine supplementation, the patients showed dramatic improvements, most returning to normal within a period of weeks. This is not to imply that all fatigue, irritability, depression, and loss of appetite can be overcome with thiamine supplementation. The research has relevance to exercisers who consume large amounts of sugar. While sugar does provide an easily available source of energy without the bulk associated with complex carbohydrates or fruits, the potential of sugar to deplete thiamine and other nutrients must be considered. A low intake of sugar is strongly recommended for long-term health and increasing athletic performance.

The role of vitamin C (ascorbic acid) in boosting immune-system function is controversial. While opinions vary, a number of reports do suggest that vitamin C may be beneficial in boosting a lagging immune system. Since many athletes complain of lingering colds, sore throats, infections, and lethargy, all of which suggest a depressed immune system, additional ascorbic acid may be helpful. Vitamin C intake in the range of 2,000 mg (2 g) per day may be a reasonable prophylactic amount to boost a lagging immune system. If a person's immune system is already functioning at a very high level, it is doubtful that additional vitamin C supplementation would have much effect.

Ascorbic acid acts as an antioxidant, and may be very beneficial in protecting the athlete from free-radical damage. Free radicals are extremely caustic, highly reactive compounds which easily damage cell membranes and DNA, the cell's genetic code. Damaged cell membranes impair the normal influx of oxygen and essential nutrients and hinder the normal efflux of carbon dioxide and metabolic wastes. This damage to cell membranes may significantly impair physiological performance on a cellular level, as cells hunger for oxygen and fuel while swimming in wastes.

One way in which free radicals are formed is by breathing oxygen. People who exercise, particularly for extended periods of time, inhale abundant quantities of oxygen, and this can substantially increase the production of free radicals. Inhaling ozone and carbon monoxide further promotes free-radical damage. These air pollutants are generally found in metropolitan areas. Iron also promotes free-radical formation, and iron supplementation is a common practice among active people. To combat free-radical damage, antioxidants are needed. The body has an extensive array of enzyme systems which serve as antioxidants, scavenging free radicals before they do much damage. Additionally, vitamin E, vitamin C, beta-carotene, and selenium, all essential nutrients, serve as antioxidants. Supplementation of these nutrients in moderate amounts may be advantageous in reducing damage to cell membranes and DNA. Vitamin E intake in the range of 400–800 IU per day, vitamin C intake in the range of 2,000 mg per day, and selenium intake in the range of 50 to 100 micrograms per day are general recommendations. Selenium can be toxic in amounts above 150 micrograms daily, so caution is advised.

Iron status has been found to vary with exercise, although the need for a large intake of iron is questionable. For women, particularly those whose beef intake is low, a moderate (18 mg daily) iron supplement may be a standard health-promoting practice. Male long-distance runners sometimes display marginal iron status, possibly due to excessive iron loss in sweat. Optimal iron status is essential for maximum performance, since iron is the part of the hemoglobin that sends and carries oxygen to the exercising cells. Beef and pork are rich sources of iron but may be undesirable in some athletes' diets. A supplement of 18 mg daily of a chelated iron is a good general recommendation. Amounts twice this much may be taken on a short-term therapeutic basis, but quantities of iron greater than 50 mg daily may antagonize the absorption of other essential trace minerals.

Zinc is involved in more than one hundred different biochemical reactions in the body, and plays a crucial role in the immune system, healing of injuries, protection from free radicals, and muscle function. Some male long-distance runners are reported to have lower serum zinc levels than those of sedentary men, and even of the standard clinical lower limits. Although serum zinc levels may not be completely indicative of total body-zinc status, the serum values in some male runners are so low that marginal zinc deficiency may be present. Dietary intake of zinc was lower than the RDA in a large number of runners surveyed in Eugene, Oregon, and Honolulu, Hawaii. The best dietary sources of zinc are oysters, beef, and pork, which may not be staples in a health-promoting diet. Supplemental zinc beyond 15–30 mg daily may antagonize the absorption of iron and copper and is not recommended.

Vitamin and mineral supplements are just that—supplements to a healthful diet of whole foods, and not a substitute for them. A high-quality multiple vitamin/mineral formulation is probably a good insurance strategy. Spending large amounts of money on a multitude of tablets to be taken every day is probably a waste of money. The athlete is again advised to experiment with different formulations, finding a regimen that works best for his or her own individual biochemistry.

AMINO-ACID SUPPLEMENTS

Amino acids are the building blocks of proteins. Essential amino acids must be supplied by the diet, while nonessential amino acids can be synthesized within the body from other sources. Pure amino-acid supplementation is a currently popular strategy for a growing number of athletes, primarily weight lifters. This expensive practice is touted by a number of weight lifters who have won major competitions, usually spending five to six hundred dollars each month on their amino-acid supplements. Unfortunately, objective research is unavailable to support this practice, and one is hard pressed to base amino-acid supplementation on much more than testimonials and beliefs. It is true that particular amino acids, specifically L-arginine and L-ornithine, have been shown to stimulate the release of human growth hormone (HGH) in animal models. Human growth hormone stimulates muscular development in rats, but no useful studies have yet been done in humans. These amino-acids supplements have been used as an alternative to anabolic steroids for weight lifters and others desiring increased muscle mass. Individuals who consume them are participating in a large and uncontrolled human experiment to determine the effects and side effects of these compounds. Some companies market ten to fifteen amino acids in one pill or powder, contending that the balance is important for promoting optimal absorption. Generally, the body's intestinal absorption system recognizes the L form of amino acids from high-quality protein sources as well as it does from the isolated amino acids. An egg white, therefore, may be just as effective and far cheaper than taking hundreds of dollars of amino-acid supplements each month.

POTENTIAL FAT BURNERS

Substances that enhance the uptake and metabolism of fatty acids into muscle might be important in preserving glycogen stores and in facilitating the ease of aerobic activity. Long-term exercise depends on fat and oxygen for fuel. Two potential ergogenic compounds for helping to supply fat to the muscles are octacosanol and L-carnitine. Octacosanol, a wheat-germ-oil extract, has been found to improve worktime until exhaustion, the speed with which a person can run half a mile, and coordination responses during exercise. It is suggested that octacosanol aids in the uptake of fatty acids into the muscle cell, thereby making a highly concentrated source of fuel (fat) available while sparing muscle glycogen, although the exact mechanism by which octacosanol might be effective has not been described. A number of studies over the past two decades have not found octacosanol to be of any benefit in long-term exercise. Additional research needs to be conducted to assess the potential benefit of this compound.

L-carnitine is also a substance that might facilitate the uptake and combustion of fatty acids in skeletal muscle, thereby preserving glycogen stores for later use. Studies in Italy have found that L-carnitine supplementation prolongs worktime until exhaustion during aerobic exercise. Carnitine is also available in the D, L form, but the D isomer impairs the absorption and utilization of the L isomer, thereby making the D, L form much less biologically potent than the pure L form. L-carnitine is a substance that has potential as a nutritional ergogenic, and future research is likely to clarify this issue.

NEUROTRANSMITTER PRECURSORS

Substances that can maintain the level of neurochemicals at the junction between nerves and muscles, and within the nervous system itself, have a potential for reducing fatigue and improving performance. In studies of highly trained college swimmers, runners, and weight throwers, half took a placebo while the others took D-amphetamine. An improvement of 0.6 to 4 percent in performance was found when the athletes took the amphetamine. Amphetamine is dangerous, producing deleterious side effects, and its use is both unhealthy and illegal.

The best candidate in this regard is phosphatidycholine, a substance typically marketed as lecithin. Phosphatidycholine may also maintain neurotransmitter levels similar to the effect of amphetamines, and therefore might be beneficial to athletes. Dogs have shown dramatic improvement in neuromuscular coordination after choline loading, and while these case studies done on animals do not definitively represent the effect of this chemical on humans, such positive reports suggest the possibility that choline may be beneficial in reducing fatigue and improving coordination.

CONCLUSION

Nutrition is an essential component of optimal athletic performance, requiring the same precision and commitment the athlete uses for other parts of his or her training program. Because so many athletes ignore the value of nutrition, those who have tailored a diet and supplement program to their unique biochemistry may have a substantial edge. Nutritional ergogenics may support an athlete during a competition or during and after an exhaustive workout. Knowledge of effective nutritional ergogenics is growing rapidly, and many new developments are anticipated in the near future. These may include improved sports drinks, more refined supplements oriented to specific types of sports, and dietary manipulations designed to maximize performance and help the athlete to recover quickly from training. In implementing any new nutritional factor, the athlete is advised to experiment with it well before a competition to determine its effects.

FOR FURTHER READING

Belko, A. Z., Obarzanek, E., Kalkwarf, H. J., Rotter, M. A., Bogusz, S., Miller, D., Haas, J. D., and Roe, D. A. Effects of exercise on riboflavin requirements of young women. *American Journal of Clinical Nutrition*, 1983, 37, 509–517.

Benson, H., and McCallie, D. P. Angina pectoris and the placebo effect. *New England Journal of Medicine*, 1979, 300, 1,424–1,429.

Cureton, T. K. *The physiological effects of wheatgerm oil on humans in exercise*. Springfield: Thomas, 1972.

Demopoulos, H. B., Santomier, J. T., Seligman, M. L., Hogan, P. I., and Peitronigro, D. D. Free radicalpathology: rationale and toxicology of antioxidants and other supplements in sports medicine and exercise science. In *Sport, Health and Nutrition*, 1984 Olympic Scientific Congress Proceedings, F. I. Katch (Ed.), Human Kinetics, Champaign, IL, 1986.

Hackman, R. M. The leading edge: Nutrition and athletic performance. In *Sport, Health, and Nutrition*, 1984 Olympic Scientific Congress Proceedings, F. I. Katch (Ed.), Human Kinetics, Champaign, IL, 1986.

Harless, S. J., and Turbes, C. C. Choline-loading: Specific dietary supplementation for modifying neurologic and behavioral disorders in dogs and cats. *Veterinary Medicine/Small Animal Clinician*, August 1982, 1,223–1,231.

Haskell, W., Scala, J., and Whittam, J. (Eds.) *Nutrition and Athletic Performance*, Palo Alto, CA: Bull Publications, 1982.

Keen, C. L., and Hackman, R. M. Trace elements in athletic performance. In *Sport, Health, and Nutrition*, 1984 Olympic Scientific Congress Proceedings, F. I. Katch (Ed.), Human Kinetics, Champaign, IL, 1986.

Lonsdale, D., and Shamberger, R. J. Red cell transketolase as an indicator of nutritional deficiency. *American Journal of Clinical Nutrition, 1980, 33*, 205–211.

Macaraeg, P.V.J. Influence of carbohydrate electrolyte ingestion on running endurance. In E. L. Fox (Ed.), *Nutrient hydration during exercise*, Ross Symposium. Columbus, OH: Ross Laboratories, 1983, 91–98.

Williams, M. H. (Ed.) *Ergogenic aids in sport*. Human Kinetics, Champaign, IL, 1983.

■

CHAPTER II

■

NUTRITIONAL AIDS, CONTINUED*

With a large percentage of the population taking daily nutritional supplements, the question of real value and safety must be addressed. There are many new nutrients that are under closer investigation for their antioxidant properties and effects on longevity. How much is too much? At what levels do nutrients become toxic?

PANTOTHENIC ACID (VITAMIN B₅)

Pantothenic acid is fast emerging as the superstar of longevity nutrients. As a matter of fact, more antiaging effects have been imputed to this nutrient than for any other vitamin. It is said to have the ability to aid the body in dealing with stress. Early studies revealed that rats given high dosages were able to swim in ice-cold water twice as long and with less harm than those who were not given the nutrient. It has long been associated with endurance, and is now being investigated for its memory-enhancing properties. Pantothenic acid is found in a wide variety of foods: whole-wheat flour, oatmeal, egg yolks, brewers' yeast, cauliflower, and broccoli, among others.

One of the richest sources of naturally occurring pantothenic acid is royal jelly, the substance produced by worker bees and fed to the queen bee to keep her alive and fertile. There is basically no difference between the queen bee and any other female worker bee other than the addition of royal jelly to her diet, yet her life expectancy can be as long as eight years, compared to the average life-span of the worker bees, which is approximately thirty days.

*The information on pages 17–23 was contributed by Dr. Ronald Klatz.

Experiments with pantothenic acid conducted on mice as early as 1950 produced an increase of 19 percent (18 percent in males and 20 percent in females) in life-span over the control group. The mice in the control group lived an average of 550 days, compared to the 653 days of those given 0.3 mg of pantothenic acid in their drinking water.

There is even hope that pantothenic acid may have a positive effect on reversal of rheumatoid arthritis. Barton-Weight and Elliot discovered that patients with rheumatoid arthritis had a significantly lower-than-normal level of pantothenic acid in their bloodstreams.

In a double-blind study, ninety-four patients with varying forms of arthritis, including rheumatoid, were tested. Dosages were increased gradually from 500 mg to 2 g per day for a period of two months. A significant improvement was seen in those patients suffering from rheumatoid arthritis. They felt less pain and stiffness than those given a placebo.

The suggested dosage for this nutrient is divided dosages of 500 mg to 2 g daily. As always, consult your physician before taking any nutrients.

SELENIUM

Selenium is a very powerful antioxidant mineral that when combined with other substances forms a barrier protecting the body from free-radical damage. The role of selenium is similar to that of vitamin E—both are antioxidants. Selenium deficiencies can cause impaired immune-system function, brain damage, and weakening of muscles, especially the heart. In certain areas in China that have soil sorely lacking in selenium, there is a high incidence of a disease called Kenshan, which is fatal in many cases. Patients suffering from Kenshan die of sudden heart failure.

Investigations into this nutrient have been scarce in the past due to the potential health hazard of selenium. It is extremely toxic in high dosages, causing elevated serum cholesterol levels and an increased number of malignant tumors and premature death. Toxic symptoms have been observed at 1,000 mg per day. The generally agreed-upon level for safety is 50–100 mg per day. In proper dosages it has proven effective in extending the life-span of laboratory rats. One particular rat lived an incredible 1,830 days, the equivalent of 160 years for a human—40 years longer than any recorded human life.

NIACIN

Niacin may prove to be effective in cholesterol control. The American Heart Association has issued a report on the control of hyperlipidemia in adults that discusses the use of niacin for both hypercholesterolemia and hypertriglyceridemia. The side effects of niacin are short-lived and may be overcome with time. Nonetheless, they may be alarming if you are not expecting them: the skin flushes, often quite dramatically; the heart palpitates; and an itchy feeling can be felt in some cases. Yet it has also been reported that niacin has been used to enhance sexual pleasure when taken half an hour prior to intercourse.

OIL OF EVENING PRIMROSE

This supplement has been anecdotally held responsible for increased libido and decreased symptoms of PMS. The true power of this herb is most likely due to its 72 percent linoleic-acid content. Linoleic acid is the most important of the fatty acids essential for human metabolism. When converted by the body, these substances play a significant role in the function of the immune system, and have been shown to inhibit the formation of blood clots.

PABA

Para-aminobenzoic acid (PABA), a B vitamin, serves as a great protection against ultraviolet-light damage. With our ozone layer in jeopardy, we must take greater care to protect ourselves from the damaging rays of the sun. This should be done all year round, not only in the summer months.

PABA has similar side effects to niacin, only in a much milder fashion. It should be avoided while taking any medication containing sulfa, as it will render the drug ineffective.

ARGININE/ORNITHINE

Arnold Schwarzenegger kept a bucket by his workout station when he was a youth. He said that if he did not work out hard enough to vomit, he was not working out hard enough to build muscles. The nausea he experienced was due to his body's natural release of large amounts of growth hormone. This side effect disappeared as he matured, probably due to the reduced levels of growth hormone in his body. One look at Arnold can tell you his formula worked.

Growth-hormone levels are high in athletic persons in their late teens and early twenties. It is possible, with the assistance of nutritional supplementation, to maintain these high levels of growth hormones. However, strict guidelines must be followed for optimum benefits and safety. By maintaining these levels, you can have the body beautiful for many years.

High levels of growth hormone allow you to exercise less and profit more. Your metabolism will be faster, thus allowing you to eat more and gain less weight. Your body is actually tricked into thinking it is still in a growth phase.

Growth-hormone (GH) releasers are produced by the body and are found in many foods. Chicken and turkey are two good sources of the amino acid arginine, which in turn produces the amino acid ornithine. Arginine and ornithine can be taken as supplements rather than obtained from natural-food sources, if preferred.

The primary biological effect of arginine is its ability to induce the release of growth hormone from the pituitary gland, and ornithine stimulates an even higher release than that of arginine. It is now believed by researchers that one of the functions of growth hormones is to conserve muscles at the expense of fat, that they actually "mobilize" fat from the cells. This research could prove to be a tremendous breakthrough for body builders who are trying to get "cut" as well as for the average dieter.

Studies have been conducted on the effects of a lack of growth hormones. The results were quite startling: patients could look as much as fifteen years older than their actual chronological age if growth hormones were deficient.

Two of the conditions associated with a growth-hormonal deficiency are an increased disposition to develop fat instead of muscle and a premature wrinkling of the skin. Although these conditions will eventually appear with age, studies indicate that they may be delayed dramatically by these growth hormones.

Dosages

Before undertaking *any* program, you should always consult your private physician. Arginine should be started with 2 g, taken on an empty stomach 30 minutes before a workout or just before bedtime. Ornithine should be taken in the same manner, only half the dosage, that is, 1 g. Dosages should never exceed 6 to 12 g of arginine, or 3 to 6 g of ornithine, per day, depending on your body weight.

Who Should Not Take GH Releasers

These therapies are not suitable for persons having:

- hyperglycemia
- diabetes
- any form of cancer
- arthritis

The above conditions will be aggravated by the use of growth-hormone releasers.

Precautions

Following are some side effects of growth-hormone use:

- Increased libido and irritability, especially in males
- Nausea and weakness when dosages are too high
- Excessive levels of GH have caused skin growth to accelerate, causing roughening and thickening (This side effect sometimes reverses in a few months with discontinuation.
- Extremely high levels of growth hormones taken over an extended period of time will cause such *irreversible* conditions as joint growth and larynx growth (causing voice levels to lower).

THE PLACEBO EFFECT

During a world championship the team physician came upon one of his athletes shivering and cowering in the corner of the locker room. After questioning the massive brute, the doc learned that the jock could not fight without the special blue vitamin pills he had just run out of. The team doc frantically searched through his bag to find a pill of the same color. He came up with one, but it was twice the size the athlete was used to taking. The doc told him that it was twice as big because it was twice as strong. Renewed, the athlete went out and just about murdered his competition. Upon returning victorious, he told the doc the pill was great and asked if he could get a whole bottle. The team physician realized he would have a hard time justifying prescribing pills for vaginal itching to a healthy male.

This modification of a true story depicts how the placebo effect works on the mind. If you believe something will help you, even if it is just an empty capsule, it will. The placebo effect can be triggered by a medicine, food substance, or any device that the athlete feels will help when in reality it has no inherent benefits.

A NOTE TO PREGNANT WOMEN

It is important to make sure you are getting proper nutrition as it is vital to your health as well as to the health of your baby. It is also important to remember that as your requirements for certain nutrients increase during pregnancy. It is, however, strongly advised that your physician be aware of all nutrients and dosages taken during your pregnancy. A seemingly harmless nutrient may pose a threat to your health as well as to that of your baby.

Vitamin A

This nutrient becomes toxic at levels of 100,000 IU and can cause headaches and lethargy.

Vitamin B$_6$

High dosages over a period of four months can damage the nervous system, resulting in numb limbs and loss of muscle coordination.

Vitamin C

If you are taking megadoses of vitamin C (3–10 g per day), it can lead to "rebound" scurvy in your baby after birth.

Vitamin D

This nutrient should be handled with extra care in high doses (10,000–25,000 IUs). It can lead to calcification of the blood vessels and the kidneys.

Vitamin K

This nutrient can increase the severity of jaundice in children born with this condition if the mother takes it during her last trimester.

Minerals

Certain minerals such as iodine may adversely affect the thyroid of the unborn baby, especially if taken during the second or third trimester.

■

CHAPTER III

■

KEEPING THE EDGE/ LONGEVITY AND THE ATHLETE*

Some people try to achieve immortality through their offspring or their works. I prefer to achieve immortality by not dying.

—Woody Allen

After sacrificing ten or twenty years of effort and painful training to develop your abilities to their peak, it seems somehow unfair to let the gradual decline of age take from you that which you have worked so long and hard to achieve. We are fortunate to live in an age of science and medicine when great strides are being made in the eradication of infectious and cardiovascular diseases. Action can be taken to slow the detrimental effects of aging and extend your time in the game as a winner a while longer.

The average life expectancy of any organism is the age at which one half of its population will be dead. In humans this figure has changed dramatically in the past century. In 1900 the average individual could expect to live to the ripe old age of 46. Today, men can look forward to an average life-span of approximately 76 years, and women slightly more. For many years it was thought that women lived longer because of genetic superiority. We now know that such longevity may be more a factor of environment and learned behavior patterns than genetics. As more women enter the once male-dominated workplace, diseases that previously seemed primarily to affect males are now appearing in women, who are subject to the same stress levels as men.

Even though we are seeing an increased "span" of life, one thing has remained constant: the "top-end." The longest-lived humans seem always to hover somewhere around the 110-year mark. It is hoped that with modern medical discoveries we will

*The material on pages 24–35 was contributed by Dr. Ronald Klatz.

24

be able to inch this figure upward to the 121-year level and beyond. Who would want to live that long? The obvious answer is the 120-year-old, but most life-extension advocates support the theory that the quality "middle years" will be extended in addition to the years of senility and infirmity.

To reach these goals, the mechanisms of aging must be found. For all of our knowledge of disease prevention and cure, we still have not concluded exactly what causes a body to begin the process of aging, and what can be done to slow down this catabolic process. There are several plausible theories at the moment, however:

FREE-RADICAL THEORY OF AGING

Free radicals are highly reactive chemicals created as by-products of oxygen metabolism. They are negatively charged, electrically unbalanced, and therefore reactive enough to combine with any available healthy cell and form a "cross-linked" complex: a deformed large cell unable to perform its primary functions. Cross-linked cells are responsible for wrinkled skin and weak, stiff muscles. Possible antidotes to the problem of free radicals may be such antioxidants as vitamins C and E, the drug Hydergine, and even the preservatives BHA and BHT, which combine with free radicals and neutralize them before they can attack a healthy cell.

DEATH-HORMONE THEORY OF AGING

DECO (decreasing oxygen consumption hormone), also called the death hormone is supposedly created in the pituitary gland and is responsible for the aging proces. It was discovered by Dr. W. D. Dencla, who removed the pituitary glands from laboratory rats and noticed a corresponding decrease in the rate of aging. Recent studies, however, are focusing more on the absence of cellular growth factors than on the presence of a death hormone.

THYMOSYNS, THYMIC-STIMULATING HORMONES, AND AGING

Thymosyns are a family of hormones produced by the thymus, a small but important gland located in the upper chest cavity.

"The thymus is the master gland of the immune system," says biochemist Alan Goldstein, chairman of the biochemistry department at George Washington University. "Twenty-five years ago no one even knew what the thymus gland was. . . . We only knew that it weighs two hundred to two hundred fifty grams at birth and then shrinks throughout puberty until it becomes three grams of grizzled, clumped cells by the sixtieth year." Now he and other scientists are investigating whether the disappearance of the thymus contributes to the aging process by decreasing the body's immune response.

Studies have shown that thymic factors are helpful in restoring the immune systems of children born without them as well as rejuvenating the poorly functioning immune systems of the elderly. In the future, these immunostimulators may be used in the fight against AIDS. New research indicates that thymic hormones even play a role in stimulating and controlling the production of neurotransmitters and brain and endocrine-system hormones, which means they may in fact be the pacemakers of aging itself as well as key regulators responsible for immunity.

HAYFLICK CONSTANT AND AGING

Dr. Leonard Hayflick theorizes that the aging process is controlled by a biological clock contained within each living cell. His 1961 study showed that human cells are mortal. They divide approximately 50 times over a period of years and then suddenly stop. Nutrition seems to have an effect on the rate of cell division: overfed cells can make 50 divisions in a year while cells that are underfed can take up to three times as long as normal cells to make their divisions.

Vincent Cristofallo from the University of Pennsylvania has found a relation between certain cell protein levels and the rate at which organisms age. According to Cristofallo, as humans age, levels of proteins that prevent DNA synthesis increase. A serum that inhibits production of this senescent protein might drastically increase the longevity of body cells.

DHEA AND AGING THEORY

Dr. Arthur Schwartz of the Temple University Fells Institute Cancer Research Center has linked low levels of DHEA (dehydroepiandrosterone) to an increased risk of developing malignant growths. The human body produces high levels of DHEA until age 25. Production then drops off; by age 70 the body's levels are five percent of what they were at 25.

Dr. Schwartz is now working on a DHEA analogue that he says may be ten times as strong as the naturally occurring DHEA. It could be important for its supposed anticancer, anti-aging properties as well as for its potential as a weight-reduction aid—DHEA alters metabolism by causing the body to shift glucose metabolism from the production of fat to the production of energy. Schwartz warns against the use of natural DHEA by athletes at this time because exogenous DHEA in the human body can be converted into either testosterone or estrogen through specialized metabolic pathways. The new analogues presumably do not possess steroid activity, but serious testing has not yet been carried out.

DNA REPAIR THEORY

DNA is the master blueprint of life on which all the plans for the tens of thousands of different types of body cells are encoded. Many scientists believe that as humans age their DNA becomes less and less able to repair damages to itself. Accumulated errors create suboptimal cells, which leads eventually to the destruction of the entire organism. Dr. Joan Sonneborn of the University of Wyoming has proven that stimulation of DNA-repair mechanisms in lower animals can lead to their rejuvenation and an extended life-span.

CORTISOL AND AGING

Hans Selye, M.D., has shown that high levels of stress lead to many of the diseases of aging by increasing levels of adrenal steroids (cortisol). A vivid demonstration of this phenomenon can be seen in salmon whose adrenal glands produce massive amounts of steroid hormones to help them handle the Herculean task of swimming upstream to spawn. This outpouring of hormones needed to convert proteins to carbohydrates, which the fish utilize for energy, results in their literally burning themselves up.

In humans, prolonged high levels of cortisol have been

shown to damage brain cells. Studies on prisoners of war and concentration-camp prisoners from World War II have shown them to have an accelerated rate of aging and a higher incidence of Alzheimer's disease, arthritis, and cancer.

MHC AS A MECHANISM OF AGING

Major histocompatability complex (MHC) is a supergene responsible for a wide variety of the human body's immune mechanisms, including the rejection of foreign tissues as in a kidney or heart transplant. It also appears to control the body's own mechanisms for the production of the free-radical scavengers, including superoxide dismutase (SOD)—one of the body's most powerful antioxidants—and possibly even cellular DNA-repair mechanisms. It has also been found that MHC analysis can predict one's susceptibility to developing many diseases associated with aging, including Alzheimer's. A better understanding of MHC might lead to solutions to the puzzle of human aging.

Even if we aren't certain what causes aging—any one or combination of these eight theories may yield the answer—we do know of a number of marvelous drugs that have been shown to have significant effects in the treatment of age-related diseases as well as possible antiaging properties. Remember, not all of these drugs are available and FDA approved in the United States, you should ask your physician if they are viable therapies for you.

THE LITTLE PILLS OF LONGEVITY

Aspirin can be listed in the category of wonder drugs. It relieves muscle aches, offers relief from arthritis pain and headaches, and has been a mainstay of medical practice since the turn of the century. Now recent studies indicate that it may even extend life-span, because it acts as a blood-thinning agent, which when taken in low doses—1/2 to 1 aspirin (5 grams) daily—has been shown to decrease the risk of heart attack and stroke in men by as much as 50 percent due to its action of reducing platelet activity in blood clotting.

Excessive use—far more than 1 tablet daily—can cause

ringing in the ears, which usually disappears within a few days after its use has been discontinued, and nausea. In very high doses it can lead to gastritis and bleeding disorders due to the combination of platelet inhibition and its acid effects.

Coenzyme Q_{10}

Coenzyme Q_{10} (also known as CoQ or ubiquinone), a relatively new substance now in the United States, has been used in Japan for over 10 years in the treatment of cardiac patients—approximately six million people take it annually. It is also one of the substances responsible for generating approximately 95 percent of the energy the body extracts from food. CoQ is an essential part of the mitochondria, the respiration centers of our bodies; without it we would literally not have the energy to breathe. As we age, our natural levels of CoQ decline—by as much as 80 percent—which could help explain why so many older people experience a lack of energy.

CoQ is reported to have antiaging properties, among which are increased energy levels, stimulation of the immunological system, positive effects in the treatment of periodontal diseases, and antioxidant properties. Recent testing has shown CoQ is effective in treating high blood pressure and cardiac arrhythmias. Because CoQ supposedly strengthens the heart muscles, its value in the prevention of congestive heart failure is also being examined.

Evidence from Japanese studies has shown there are no side efects from dosages of 10 mg three times daily, nor from dosages as high as 100 mg per day. Tests are still under way in the United States. Coenzyme Q_{10} has not yet received FDA approval, but it is presently available as a nutrient in many health-food stores and through vitamin distributors.

DMAE (Deanol)

Several experiments have shown that DMAE-treated lab animals of advanced age (approximately 70 years old in human terms), had a mean life-span of almost 50 percent longer, a maximum survival rate of approximately 36 percent longer, and a maximum life-span of approximately 11 percent longer than those of untreated animals. These studies indicated that

DMAE reverses the aging process, which had already produced physical deterioration. DMAE, a precursor of acetylcholine, has also been used effectively to improve memory and intelligence.

High doses have produced headaches and muscle tension, and in some cases cardiac abnormalities. DMAE was available as the prescription drug Deaner in the United States until 1983, when it was removed from the market because of a "lack of evidence" of its efficacy. It is currently available as a nutrient.

Hydergine

Hydergine, a nonhallucinogenic derivative of lysergic acid diethylamide (LSD), is one of the three most prescribed drugs in the world today. Its major function is to stabilize the neurotransmissions of brain cells by regulating the electrical activity in the brain. Hydergine is also a powerful antioxidant, preventing the damage to brain and liver cells caused by drinking and smoking. It is usually prescribed for elderly people experiencing disorientation, depression, memory loss, lack of concentration, and aberrant behavior, but recent clinical studies have revealed that hydergine therapy has also benefited normal, healthy college students by increasing their memory capacity.

Although hydergine is a popular drug in the United States, it enjoys far greater usage in Europe. (The average dosage in the U.S. is 3 mg per day, where in Europe it can be as high as 9 mg per day.) Studies have shown that lab animals given dosage levels of hydergine similar to those given to Europeans have experienced a 60 percent reduction in the occurrence of breast cancers. In Europe hydergine is used to treat strokes, heart attacks, and traumas in accident victims.

Hydergine has been known to produce some degree of nausea, headaches, and psychosis in very rare and extreme cases. It is available by prescription only.

Gerovital

The Rumanian Dr. Aslan has developed a formula called Gerovital (GH-3) that apparently has great rejuvenation properties. Its supposed main ingredient is procaine (novocaine).

However, investigations have found large amounts of para-aminobenzoic acid (PABA) in the formula, which when combined with diethylaminoethanol (DEA) form the products that result from metabolism of procaine in the body. It should be emphasized, however, that PABA is not the same substance as procaine. Testing at UCLA has revealed that Gerovital helps relieve depression, improve intelligence and concentration, and produce a feeling of well-being in the elderly. It may also be able to slow the aging process by virtue of cortisol antagonist functions (it reduces the intensity of the body's reaction to stress). Additionally, GH-3 may possess a mild antiinflammatory property, which would account for the relief of arthritis symptoms reported in some studies.

Gerovital has been used internationally for more than 25 years, and no major side effects have been reported. In this country, it is available in eleven states, including Nevada, by prescription only. Full testing has not yet been completed.

Vasopressin

Vasopressin (Diapid) is a prescription drug that comes in the form of a nasal spray. As a pituitary peptide hormone, its main functions are to control the body's carbohydrate metabolism and to regulate water balance via the kidneys. It also appears to be necessary to the process of encoding memory into the brain and also to the ability to recall these data. Several studies on Vasopressin have been conducted in Europe using amnesia patients, and have yielded impressive results. Current studies on the effects of Vasopressin seem to indicate that the best results are to be found with generally healthy individuals; young or old, who do not have any major brain damage.

In clinical European trials, dosages of as high as 50 USP units have been used daily without serious effects. Recent clinical reports in the United States, however, have not supported European data. At best, memory enhancement remains an experimental application for Vasopressin. One of the chief complaints of those people using Vasopressin is nasal congestion and irritation. Headaches, nausea, and tremors have also been reported. Vasopressin is a powerful drug. It can have serious effects on your heart. It should be handled with the utmost respect, and then only under the constant supervision of a knowledgeable physician. At present, Vasopressin is available by prescription only for the treatment of Diabetes insipidus.

Ritalin (Methylphenidate Hydrochloride)

Ritalin, a prescription drug manufactured by the CIBA corporation, is a mild central-nervous-system stimulant that has effects similar to those of amphetamines. Although it is not extremely addictive, it should only be used under the strict supervision of a physician.

It works by stimulating the reticular activating system in the brain, the area of the brain responsible for alertness and arousal. Ritalin is traditionally prescribed for hyperkinetic children and children with learning disabilities, attention-deficit disorder, cerebral dysfunction, narcolepsy, mild depression, and apathetic withdrawal associated with senility (although these latter two conditions are listed as "possibly" improved by Ritalin therapy). It's possible that Ritalin releases vasopressin in the body. It also has an effect on metabolism and appetite, making it somewhat useful as a weight-control aid, and it is occasionally effective in treating mild depression.

It is not suggested for use in individuals who have marked anxiety, glaucoma, motor tics, or family histories of Tourette's syndrome. It also should not be used for the prevention of naturally caused fatigue. Drug dependency can occur with severe withdrawal symptoms of depression and/or psychotic episodes. Ritalin is a class II drug (controlled), and should be closely monitored during therapy.

L-Dopa

L-Dopa is currently marketed by Roche Laboratories under the brand name Larodopa, and is utilized primarily in the treatment of Parkinson's disease. It is a precursor of the amino acid dopamine, a powerful antioxidant. It also encourages the release of growth hormones by stimulating the pituitary gland, and has been used by athletes in training programs because of its effects on movement and coordination, (although we do not recommend this practice). In its capacity as a growth-hormone releaser, it has also been credited with stimulating the generation of muscle and the loss of fat.

As the body ages, the levels of dopamine decrease, and in

research studies on aged laboratory rats, results showed old animals who had previously demonstrated bad form and a general inability to swim well performed as well as young animals when injected with L-Dopa. Dopamine is also responsible for neurotransmissions in the brain, and a decreased level accounts for some of the loss of mental acuity associated with age.

Low dosages of L-Dopa are recommended for life-extension therapies. 1/4 to 1/2 gram at bedtime. It is an extremely powerful drug that should be handled very carefully, and only under the care of a knowledgeable physician. Patients suffering from Parkinson's disease should avoid taking vitamin B_6, as it renders L-Dopa ineffective and may worsen the condition. In some cases, it has been shown to cause some preexisting forms of skin cancers to grow more rapidly. It can also cause cardiac irregularities, palpitations, and in some cases paranoia, depression, and suicidal tendencies. Rarely seen side effects are ulcers and hypertension. L-Dopa should be avoided by anyone having a history of cardiac disease, broncial asthma, kidney disorders, liver disorders, and any form of endocrine disease. It is available by prescription only.

Warning: The use of L-Dopa and MAO inhibitors together can lead to severe, life-threatening drug reactions.

Centrophenoxine

Centrophenoxine is a chemical compound that was developed in France at the National Scientific Research Center in 1959. The compound consists of two ingredients: P-chlorophenoxy-acetic acid (a synthetic formula similar to the naturally occurring plant-growth hormone auxin), and dimedthylaminsesthanol (DMAE). Centrophenoxine has been used to improve learning abilities in both humans and animals. Clinical studies have been conducted to examine its effect on memory disturbances, intellectual impairment, and confusion. It is also known for its ability to eliminate age pigmentation. In Europe this drug is also used to treat mental deterioration in the elderly.

Researcher Richard Hachschild has experimented using centrophenoxine as a life-extension therapy on fruit flies, and certain strains of mice. The overall result has been an extension of mean and maximum life-spans by approximately 30 percent.

It is believed that centraphenoxine has the ability to rejuvenate the synaptic structures in the brains of old laboratory animals. This is an important finding since brain cells do not maintain themselves by division but by constant regeneration.

Other scientists have been able to reproduce Hachschild's results. Current dosages in Europe are 200—600 mg per day. Side effects like headaches, dizziness, nausea, and in some cases stiffness have been reported. It is presently available in Europe only by prescription.

Cell Therapy

Perhaps one of the most prestigious longevity clinics in the world is Clinique Paul Niehans in Switzerland, whose clientele list sounds like a page from *Who's Who*. The clinic conducts a treatment known as cell therapy, which is based on the simple assumption that if you are injected with young vital cells, these cells will in turn "rejuvenate your entire system." The clinic recommends cell therapy for people who suffer from a loss of vitality, mental and physical exhaustion, premature aging, and a weakened immunity to infection.

Clients are injected with cells from sheep especially bred to produce cells that will be readily accepted by the human body (although not all are). The treatment consists of two to six injections, followed by a day or two of bed rest. Patients may begin to see some results almost immediately, but the full impact is supposedly felt in three to four weeks, and lasts up to six months.

Although the clinic has an excellent reputation, scientific evidence for the efficacy of cell therapy is seriously lacking. There are dangers too: Live-cell injections can cause abscesses, as a result of the immune system's rejection of foreign biological material. For more information on this therapy, contact Clinique Paul Niehans SA, Switzerland.

Zumba-Forte

This tonic in pill form claims to strengthen the male system and restore sexual vitality. It contains damiana, yohimbine, and homeopathic levels of the steroid testosterone. Many Europeans claim that Zumba-Forte restores vigor and sexual prowess.

Zumba-Forte does have side effects: Yohimbine is contraindicated for people with heart disease, and testosterone in large dosages has been proven to be extremely dangerous. It is available at many specialty health-food stores.

Although anecdotal reports claim that human longevity can be as high as 160 years, the confirmed and documented maximum human life-span now stands at 120 years—an age reached by Yasuhisa Uemura of Japan, who attributed his long life and vitality to regular exercise, a simple nonstressful lifestyle, and multiple daily doses of 60-proof sake. Many experts in the field of longevity believe that the average human lifespan will continue to climb from the 76-year mark to an estimated 85 years early in the next century. If you doubt the predictions made by these experts, consider this: The doubling time for scientific knowledge hovers somewhere around five to ten years. This means that we will know twice as much about science and medicine in 1991 as we do today, and even more by 2000.

One place where this quest for knowledge is being carried out is at the newly established American Longevity Institute, Inc. (A.L.I), which was founded to provide a clinical antiaging and maximum-human-performance facility for individuals interested in realizing their greatest potential for peak performance and extended life-span. The institute is located in Chicago, Illinois, and interested athletes are encouraged to call 312-929-8700.

Whether the task of life extension is fighting difficult battles against biological enemies or merely slowing down the inevitable biological clock, a vast shift is taking place in the way we all look at our mortality. Certainly in the not-too-distant future, our basic understanding of the mechanisms of aging and our abilities to counteract the aging process will increase to the point where we may all be able to enjoy an active, productive century of life.

■

CHAPTER IV

■

DRUGS, HORMONES, AND OTHER NONNUTRITIONAL ERGOGENICS

The merciless rigor of modern competitive sports, especially at the international level, the glory of victory, and the growing social and economic rewards of sporting success (in no way any longer related to reality) increasingly forces athletes to improve their performance by any means possible.

—*Manual on Doping*
Medical Commission—International Olympic Committee

There are two classes of sports drugs. One is the restorative drugs, which **aid** the **recovery** to health. They may enable the athlete to compete despite being injured, and attempt to restore her or him to optimal performance even when in a weakened condition. Some drugs in this class are pain-killers, aspirin, morphine, muscle relaxants, topical anesthetics, and anti-inflammatories.

The other class of sports drugs is the ergogenic substances. These are **additive,** and in some cases enable performance to go beyond what would normally be possible. They may be pharmacological, physiological, or nutritional. Examples of such substances are anabolic steroids, speed and amphetamines, cocaine, caffeine, and blood doping.

ERGOGENIC DRUGS DOWN THROUGH THE AGES

Drug use by the athletic community is not a contemporary phenomenon. It has been a common occurrence throughout the history of sport. Cocaine, amphetamines, strychnine, caffeine, muscle relaxants, tranquillizers, barbiturates, narcotics, as well as a host of other goodies, have all been hot items at one time or another.

Drug doping comes from the Dutch word *Dop,* which goes back more than one hundred years. The word *doping* first appeared in the English dictionary in 1889, and was defined as a narcotic mixture of opium used for racehorses. In the dialect of the Kaffirs of southern Africa, *dop* refers to the stimulating hard liquor used in religious ceremonies. When the Boers adopted the word, the final e was added, making it *dope*.

The earliest reports of drug taking by athletes in competition were in Amsterdam in 1865, when swimmers in canal races were charged with taking dope. It was also about this time that the first evidence of doping among cyclists appeared. In 1869, the coaches of teams of bicycle racers were widely known to be administering the heroin-and-cocaine mixture now known as speedball to increase the endurance of their racers. The practice caught the attention of the sports world when the first recorded drug-related death in sports occurred to a cyclist in a race in 1886.

Drug taking in sports cropped up repeatedly through the end of the nineteenth century and on into the twentieth. The Belgians were said to be taking sugar tablets soaked in ether, the French to be taking caffeine tablets, and the British to be breathing oxygen and taking cocaine, heroin, strychnine, and brandy, all in frantic attempts to gain competitive edges that would capture the coveted laurel wreaths of victory.

ANABOLIC ANDROGENIC STEROIDS

Some of the most controversial ergogenics are anabolic steroids. These derivatives of male hormones have an interesting history.

Steroid hormones are secreted through the endocrine system, and vary with the needs of the body. To meet these requirements, different hormones are constantly secreted, inactivated, produced, and excreted. These hormones go to the target organ, where they induce specific effects.

As far back as 1849, Berthold performed experiments on the growth of the combs and wattles of fowl that predated the science of endocrinology by half a century. The famous scientist Brown-Séquard injected himself with a homemade ground-up testicle soup and felt a supposed new vigor. He died of old age a short time later.

Back in the forties, at the University of Chicago, Dr. Fred Koch and his students had the pleasure of collecting tons of bull testicles in order to extract male-hormone components. At the time, one pessimistic doctor claimed there weren't enough bulls in the world to revive the lustiness of more than a handful of old men for more than one evening.

During World War II, the Germans were thought to be giving steroids to their troops and SS units to induce aggressiveness and hostility. Ironically, these same drugs were later given to concentration-camp survivors to help them build up muscle mass and strength.

The Russians began to experiment with anabolic steroids on their athletes in the 1950s. During an international weight-lifting championship, the American team physician, Dr. John Ziegler, observed some peculiarities in the Russian athletes. He noted how some of the male athletes had to be catheterized in order to urinate (this occurred because steroids cause the prostate gland to enlarge, and when it obstructs the urinary canal a tube has to be inserted up the urethra to get the urine out) as well as how masculinized the female athletes were. In addition, he noted how the Eastern Bloc athletes would burn out after a year or two and not be seen again. With these things in mind he approached the Soviet team physician and they became friendly. Over a drink in a bar, the Soviet team doc confided in Dr. Ziegler that they (the Soviets) were trying out new male hormones on their athletes to make them stronger. A photo of the two doctors appeared together in the foreign newspapers, and Dr. Ziegler never saw or heard from the Soviet doc again.

Ziegler came back to the United States and, in conjunction with Ciba Pharmaceutical Corporation, came up with the "old gold standard" in anabolic steroids—Dianabol. He took the drug to the York Barbell Gym, which in the 1960s was the mecca of American strength athletes, and began the athletes on low dosages. Dr. Ziegler could not understand how on such low dosages the athletes were having physical problems such as elevated liver enzymes and prostatic enlargement.

What happened was that the jocks liked the drugs so much, they found a local pharmacist who would give them as much as they could pay for, and the steroid epidemic was born in this country. Ziegler could not deal with such obsessive personalities, so he withdrew his support of drug taking.

It had been Dr. Ziegler's intention to help preserve our winning ways in sports, but it turned into a nightmare for him. John Ziegler was one of the finest men I have ever known. I had the honor of studying under him for eight years. He died in

November 1983, several days before his sixtieth birthday. The last time we spoke he told me he wished he could wipe that whole chapter from his life. Since then the steroid epidemic has spread through the entire sports world.

I performed a survey where I asked 198 world-class athletes the following question: If I had a magic drug that was so fantastic if you took it once you would win every competition you entered, from the Olympic decathlon to Mr. Universe, for the next five years, but it had one minor drawback—it would kill you five years after you took it—would you still take the drug?

Of those asked, 103 (52 percent) said yes, winning was so attractive they would not only be willing to achieve it by taking a pill (in other words, through an outlawed, unfair method that is, in effect, cheating), but they would give their lives to do it. It can be argued that it is only because the athletes knew there was no such magic medicine that they indicated their willingness to commit Olympic hara-kiri, that faced with such real-world magic medicine they would have second thoughts. But evidence suggests that athletes will take anything, or do anything to their bodies, to win, even with no real assurance of winning.

Since I wrote about this in my last book *Death in the Locker Room: Steroids & Sports*, I have been astonished at how correct this survey has proven. I have a steroid-research program, where I monitor athletes long term. We do not give them any steroids but just follow them medically in an attempt to pick up serious health dysfunction early, document it, and in some cases save the athlete's life. A mistake the medical community made initially was to take the position that anabolic steroids do not enhance athletic performance. They went so far as to place this in position statements and in drug information inserts. Well, the athletes knew they worked, so when the medical and sports communities came along and told the athletes these drugs would hurt them, the jocks laughed and said, "You lied to us about them working, so why should we believe you about this." This credibility gap is still haunting drug-education programs.

Steroid Effects on the Body

Anabolic steroids are male hormones. The full term is *androgenic anabolic steroid: androgenic*—meaning male hormone—like; *anabolic*—to build up; and *steroid*—the class of drugs these are, derivatives of cholesterol. They are, in essence, hormones that aid the building process.

There is a ratio between the androgenic (male characteristics) and the anabolic (growth-producing) qualities of steroid preparations. The androgenic factor is defined as the steroid's ability to stimulate the growth of rat prostate gland and seminal vesicles (sex-gland components). The anabolic factor is the growth noted in the rat levator ani muscle. Testosterone is given the Therapeutic Index value of T-1. The higher the Therapeutic Index (TI), the more anabolic the compound. Some anabolic steroid drugs have had their chemical structure modified to decrease the androgenic properties while increasing the anabolic or building qualities.

The Therapeutic Index can be calculated by this example: The levator ani muscle has grown 6 times the standard, and the seminal vesicles have grown 2 times the standard, which would equal 6 divided by 2, for a TI of 3.

There are a number of ways the drugs are taken, and there is significant polypharmacy (large combinations of different drugs taken simultaneously). Some common methods are:

1 Stacking: using more than one drug at the same time
2 Shotgunning: a hit-or-miss technique
3 Tapering: gradually decreasing intake
4 Plateauing: when one drug is no longer effective at a certain level
5 Blending: mixing of different drugs
6 Cycling: for example, going on for a six- to eight-week period and then off for the same time and repeating

Hormones can alter cellular activity by:

- inactivating or activating enzyme systems.
- changing the rates of reactions.
- altering the permeability of cell membranes to certain substances.
- causing an increase or decrease in specific enzyme production.
- changing the rate and quality of reactions by varying the amounts of one or more reactants.

One point of confusion is that there are two basic classes of steroids—the male hormone androgens we are discussing, and the anti-inflammatory steroids, which reduce inflammation and are used in such disorders as chronic obstructive lung disease (i.e., prednisone) and injected into joints (i.e., cortisone). These are different from the anabolic steroids (they are anti-inflammatory and not anabolic), and do not carry identical side effects.

TESTOSTERONE—THE MALE HORMONE

Testosterone has the following effects on the body:

1 Associated with the mental disposition of the libido, sexual desires, and aggressiveness
2 Stimulates growth of target organs
3 Promotes protein anabolism (building)
4 Sexual characteristics: at puberty—larynx enlargement, vocal-cord thickening, increase in body hair, increase in muscle mass, increase in oil-gland secretion by skin (this in some cases leads to acne)
5 Reduction in protein catabolism (breakdown, degradation)
6 Stimulates spermatogenesis (sperm production)
7 Metabolic effects on muscle, skin, and bone
8 Closure of epiphyses in long bones (growth potential)
9 Increases size of seminiferous tubules and testes
10 Aids in the development and maintenance of accessory sex organs, including secretory functions, and increase in external genitalia and tubule structures. With decreased androgen, these structures begin to atrophy (shrink).

There is a carefully calibrated balance of hormones in the body that serve as an internal protective system. If this system is disturbed, problems may arise. When this antitumoral (anti-cancer) system is shut off, mutant cells that the body normally produces and eliminates may be allowed to reproduce and grow.

A theory that carcinogenic hydrocarbons might come from steroids that occur naturally was formulated [by Cook Dodds and Kennwaay]. . . . There is a considerable body of evidence to be presented at this conference that steroids are directly implicated in the cancer problem.
—Ciba Foundation Colloquia on Endocrinology, 1956

In other research along these same lines, Dobriner, Rhoads, and colleagues (1974) noted that adrenocortical hormone production and metabolism were disturbed in neoplastic (cancer) disease. The five theories of cancer-hormone disturbances are:

1 They may provide growth of tissue upon which other mechanisms act.

2 They act in conjunction with other agents as co-factors or promoters.
3 They cause the tissues themselves to produce carcinogens (cancer cells).
4 They may initiate the neoplastic change (cancer).
5 They may give rise to neoplasia-inciting metabolites.

CANCER'S WARNING SIGNS

1 A sore that does not heal
2 A change in bowel or bladder habits
3 Unusual bleeding or discharge
4 Thickening or lump in breast or elsewhere (males included)
5 A nagging cough or hoarseness
6 Obvious change in a wart or a mole
7 Indigestion or difficulty in swallowing

Cancers associated with androgenic anabolic steroids target such organs as the prostate, liver, and, according to some research, possibly the testicles and the kidney.

The Liver

The association of tumors of the liver with the use of anabolic steroids has been increasingly documented in recent years.
—Doctors Pat, Gray, Stolley, and Coleman of the Cornell Medical Center,
Journal of the American Medical Association

The liver is the major detoxifying organ in the body. It is where the steroids are metabolized, conjugated (broken down and joined with other body substances), secreted, and excreted. Among the liver's many vital functions are:

- excretion of bile pigments
- destruction of old red blood cells
- conversion of amino acids—transamination and deamination (transfer and removal of amino-acid groups, respectively)
- storage of glycogen and metabolism of carbohydrates
- conversion of nitrogenous wastes into urea so that the kidney can excrete them
- regulation of blood glucose

Liver cancer is an androgen-dependent tumor. In some cases, when the steroids are withdrawn the tumor will shrink and disappear, but once it has reached a certain size it will have already spread (metastasis) through the body with fatal outcome. Of all liver cancers, 80 to 90 percent are hepatoma or hepatocellular tumors. Typically, the clinical presentation is an increase in the size of the liver (hepatomegaly), and there is pain and tenderness in the upper right quadrant (just below the right rib cage). Laboratory findings may show anemia and elevated alkaline phosphatase levels (liver enzymes). Lab tests that will aid in the diagnosis are:

- alpha-fetoprotein (AFP), which will be elevated in 70 percent of cases
- liver biopsy
- ultrasound
- CT scan
- gallium-67 scan
- exploratory surgery

Some physical signs the athlete should look out for are:

- jaundice, a yellow discoloration of the skin and mucous membranes due to staining by bile pigments. This occurs when the serum bilirubin exceeds 2 mg/dl. Jaundice is first noted in the scleras (whites) of the eyes. This may also be accompanied by xanthoma, which is the deposition of fat globules around the eyes. The skin begins to itch (pruritus).
- an increase in the size of the liver (hepatomegaly), and increased nodularity. The general texture of the liver surface may increase in hardness, and it may become tender to palpation. Tenderness to ballottement (pushing to and fro) can occur.
- a visceral type of abdominal pain, increased by coughing and/or movement
- a change in mental state or neurologic function
- weight loss
- spider angiomas, which are brown spiderlike blemishes on the skin, and palmar erythema (red palm). These changes may be indicative of acute or chronic liver disease.
- finger clubbing, which is a swelling of the flesh at the base of the nail bed on the fingers.
- darkened urine, not to be confused with urine color changes that can occur with high intake of vitamins

There have been almost three dozen cases of androgen-induced liver cancer documented in the scientific literature, but these were of "sick" patients who had been treated with anabolic steroids for anemias and other disease states. None of these patients had had any previous history of liver disease. In some of the cases when the drugs were withdrawn the tumors regressed, but when the steroids were again used, the tumors came back.

Two cases of liver cancer in otherwise healthy athletes are of particular interest. If the physicians involved had not been acutely aware of possible drug associations, these cases would probably not have been reported. This suggests that numerous other cases have gone undocumented due to a lack of familiarity with this link. As the population of steroid-taking athletes increases, as do the dosages and combinations of drugs taken, more cases will undoubtedly surface.

The first case was reported in the January 1984 issue of *Annals of Internal Medicine* by Overly and colleagues. This case described a twenty-six-year-old white male who had been taking steroids for about four years. He had no previous history of liver disease. His presenting complaints were malaise and weight loss. The patient's body weight decreased from a well-muscled 210 pounds down to about 130 pounds at the time of his death two months later.

The second case is one that I reported in the November 1985 *Journal of the American Osteopathic Association*. This was a thirty-seven-year-old weight lifter who was taking steroids just to "look better." He had been taking 50 mg of Anadrol for nearly five years. He was not even aware he had a problem until he became ill one evening after going out to dinner. The patient was taken to a hospital emergency room, and the sonogram showed a massive tumor in his liver. He was rushed to emergency surgery and a four-pound malignant tumor was removed.

The frightening aspect of liver cancer is that by the time liver enzymes elevate and weight loss begins to occur, the cancer has already spread and the prognosis is grave.

Another condition that occurs is peliosis hepatitis. This is a pathological condition that is characterized by widespread cystic sinusoidal dilations, which can form "blood pools" or "blood lakes" in the liver substance. The Greek word *peliosis* means extravasation of blood.

Prostate and Kidney Cancer

Two other cancer-risk areas are the prostate gland and the kidney. The prostate, which is a small gland that lies below the bladder, enlarges as men grow older. If it enlarges too much, it can obstruct urine flow. When a cancer occurs there, it is androgen dependent, which means that male hormones quicken the spread and growth of the cancer. The treatment is removal of the gland and the testicles (the producers of male hormone), and the administration of female hormones as therapy.

We now are seeing young athletes with grossly enlarged prostate glands (in some cases the size of a senior citizen's). Some may eventually develop prostatic cancer—although, in fact, we do not yet know what the ultimate effects will be.

In reference to the kidney, Wilms's tumor (nephroblastoma), common in children but quite rare in adults, has occurred in several athletes taking steroids. Early warning signs for this are:

hematuria (blood in the urine)

pain and fever

hypertension

a palpable mass

flank, lumbar, or abdominal pain

HEART DISEASE

Probably one of the most common side effects experienced by steroid-taking athletes will be cardiovascular disease. Anabolic steroids cause the body to retain sodium, calcium, nitrogen, and fluid, which in turn increases blood pressure. It is not uncommon for systolic blood pressure to rise 20 points.

High-density lipoproteins (HDLs) are protective components in the blood that help to strip the arteries clean and decrease plaque buildup. Steroids drastically decrease the HDLs from a norm of about 45 to as low as 5, which dramatically increases cardiovascular risks. On the other hand, low-density lipoproteins (LDLs), are increased by steroids to unwanted levels, which in turn increases cholesterol-plaque buildup.

Between the increase in unwanted LDLs, the decrease in wanted HDLs, and increased blood pressure, there occurs a significant heart risk. This is further aggravated by the high-fat and -protein diets of some athletes and the fact that some of them take amphetamines because they get depressed from the withdrawal effects of steroids.

In my research with athletes I have noted many cardiovascular changes even in young people with no family history of heart disease. Some of them are in their early twenties and have already had heart-surgery catheterization. Physicians should follow up on so-called sudden-death cases that occur on the playing field and look into possible drug history to better document them.

OTHER SIDE EFFECTS

A number of my patients have experienced testicular atrophy (shrinking of the testicles). Their bodies are telling them they need not produce as much male hormone. Sperm counts drop dramatically, frequently down to the sterile level.

Gynecomastia, the formation of female breast tissue in the male, is also common. This occurs because there is so much of the male hormone testosterone in the body, it is converted into the female hormone estrogen. Athletes should be made aware that just because they stop the drugs does not mean the gynecomastia will regress. Often surgery is required. In addition, just because the drugs are stopped does not mean the body will ever return to its normal hormone levels, and the former steroid user may still note the onset of female characteristics.

In young athletes, full growth potential may be impaired because the steroids cause the ends of the long bones to ossify (close off) earlier, which is known as premature epiphyseal closure. In addition, severe acne may be noted on the face, shoulders, and back, and odd hair-growth patterns can occur in such places as between the eyebrows and in the ears and nose. Premature baldness is seen in both men and women.

There are some drugs that male athletes take in an attempt to counteract the feminizing and sterility factors. One is human chorionic gonadotropin (HCG). This substance is secreted from the trophoblastic cells of the placenta and excreted in the urine. The HCG secreted in the urine of pregnant females is composed of two subunits, the highest secretion of which is during the first three weeks of pregnancy. The alpha subunit is akin in structure to LH (luteinizing hormone) and FSH (follicle-stimulating hormone). Male athletes take HCG in order to stimulate their failing testes. Since their endogenous (originating in the body) production of sperm and testosterone is depressed, the LH stimulation aids the interstitial cells of the testes in producing testosterone. As side effects these men may experience what it feels like to be pregnant, suffering morning sickness, nausea, changes in fat distribution, and gynecomastia production.

Nolvadex and Danocrine (Danazol) are antiestrogens used to cut down on the feminizing effects that occur when testosterone is converted to estrogen and stored in the peripheral adipose tissue. Another such drug is Clomid (chlomiphene citrate), which is a fertility drug used to aid women in becoming pregnant. It does so by enhancing the secretion of LH and FSH. This drug has been tried on men who had a normally low endogenous production of testosterone. Clomid has no ergogenic effect in women, for it needs the testes to effect its action.

STEROID EFFECTS ON WOMEN

For women, the effects of steroids are even more severe. They develop permanent deepening of the voice due to vocal-cord thickening, facial hair, male pattern baldness, upset in menstrual cycle, and clitoral hypertropy (increase in size of female genitals). The masculinization process can be very rapid and permanent. The long-term effects on fertility, reproductive-organ cancer, child-bearing potential, and birth defects in offspring are yet unknown. Women athletes are especially tempted, for even small doses of anabolic steroids can make significant changes in strength and size. One popular story from the 1976 Montreal Olympics told of the East German women's swimming-team coach, who was asked why so many of their women had such deep voices. He replied, "We have come here to swim, not sing."

There is no way in the world a woman nowadays, in the throwing events—at least in the shot put and the discus—I'm not sure about the javelin—can break the record unless she is on steroids. These awful drugs have changed the complexion of track and field. It's a terrible thing, but it's true. Once a girl

has developed her natural powers to the upmost, she has to start taking
something that will alter her natural endowments of strength in order to continue the quest for a world record. She sees these big balloons competing,
and she thinks she must become a balloon too.
                    —Olga Fikotova Connolly, winner of the 1956 Olympic Gold Medal for discus

Some people say they are no more dangerous than birth-
control pills. What do you think would happen if a woman took
a full month's supply of birth-control pills every day? We are
talking about micrograms of female hormones versus many
hundreds of milligrams of powerful male hormones in oral, as
well as injectable, forms in mind-blowing combinations.

PSYCHOLOGICAL EFFECTS OF STEROIDS

There was a case reported in *The New York Times* on March
19, 1986, of a twenty-six-year-old navy man who broke into six
homes, stole cash and jewelry, and set three of the houses on
fire. The court found that the defendant was "suffering from an
organic personality syndrome caused by toxic levels of anabolic steroids taken to enhance his ability to win body building
contests, and . . . this disorder substantially impaired his ability to appreciate the criminality of his acts."

Testosterone is the male "aggression" hormone. Documentation of steroid-induced aggressive and even violent behavior
has been increasing. As the above case report illustrates, actual litigation has been won on the premise that steroids are
the cause of violence.

It is well documented and widely known that estrogens,
progesterones, and corticosteroids have among their side
effects various mental disturbances that can mimic manic-
depressive psychosis and forms of schizophrenia. Classic examples would include the agitated psychosis of Cushing's
disease, the schizophreniform psychosis of lupus cerebritis,
and the "iatrogenic" depressive illness found with the use of
contraceptives.

There is a documented case of a seventeen-year-old athlete
who suffered acute schizophrenic episodes each time he took
anabolic steroids. The drug he was taking was Dianabol. During his hospitalization, he informed the physician that he had
been using anabolic steroids in 1977 and 1978 while weight lifting to "gain weight." The drugs were obtained on the black
market and used without medical supervision. He noted that

six months after initiating this self-medication he began to feel uncomfortable, sleep poorly, and have thought confusion, ruminations, paranoid ideation, and audible thoughts.

We feel that with the widespread use of illicit anabolic steroids by athletes, and their unwillingness to offer this information to consulting physicians, the possibility of such an exogenous etiology for severe psychotic disturbances going unnoticed is very high.

Journal of Clinical Psychiatry, April 1980

Some additional mechanisms of these mind changes are that steroids serve as a sort of "hormonal upper." The body feels as if it has been supercharged. When the steroids are stopped, the feeling is the opposite. The athlete becomes very depressed. Not only does he watch helplessly as the size and strength of his muscles melt away, but as the in-body production of hormones and other stimulating products is decreased, there occurs depression, sometimes reaching suicidal proportions.

Uwe Beyer, the West German hammer thrower who won the European championships in 1971 while setting a world record that same year, was so dependent on anabolic steroids that he said after stopping them, "I was listless, depressed and despaired of winning anything . . . I suffered withdrawal symptoms like a drug addict."

On a parting note, there was the case of a 125-pound woman who suffered repeated physical beatings from her 250-pound weight-lifting husband. Every time he would start his new steroid cycle, the violence was sure to follow. It reached a point where she had to fight back, so she proceeded to fill his abdomen with lead bullets. In this case it can be said that steroids were fatal due to lead poisoning.

HUMAN GROWTH HORMONE

The new big boy on the block, the "hormonal manipulator" of the 1980s, is Human Growth Hormone (HGH). HGH is a polypeptide hormone with a molecular weight of 21,000 (composed of 191 amino acids), and is produced by the pituitary gland (a small gland located right behind the eyes). Numerous hormones are secreted by this gland and it has many complex functions.

In the early 1920s, H. M. Evans and J. A. Long found that following an injection of alkaline extracts from ox pituitary glands, normal rats reached abnormally large proportions. In conjunction with the skeletal muscle growth, they also noted visceromegaly and organomegaly (increase in size of the viscera and other organs). The growth induced by the pituitary gland seemed to affect almost all the cells of the body.

Other names for this hormone extracted from the pituitary gland are somatotrophin and somatotrophic hormone (STH). It comes from the anterior division of the glands constituting 10 percent of the dry weight of the pituitary (8 milligrams).

During the past three decades, growth hormone has been used to treat children who are deficient in it. It used to be difficult and expensive to extract this vital hormone from the pituitary gland to aid pituitary dwarf children. (It can now be produced synthetically.) The National Pituitary Association and several private companies controlled the pituitary-derived sources. Due to the tightly controlled supply, numerous clinical trials had to wait patiently for their turn or postpone work in this area.

An event that shook the medical community was the theft of hundreds of vials by some athlete or black-market sports-drug dealer. Although the HGH vials were eventually recovered, the drug had by that time entered the athletes' underground hot line.

The quest for this drug was no doubt fired by the desire to grow bigger. Perhaps we should ponder the short H. G. Wells novel *Food of the Gods*. In this story, a chemical substance known as Herakleophorbia (named for the food of Hercules) falls into the hands of some young people who then form a small colony of giants that squares off against the establishment of England in a war. Wells eloquently shows man's inability to deal with such scientific advances. He wrote, "In the record of the rocks [fossils] it is always the gigantic individuals who appear at the end of the chapter."

A further blow to the production of pituitary-derived HGH occurred when some of the drug was shown to be transmitting a fatal slow virus disease that remained viable in the final drug form.

But as medicine marches on, so does the production of an unlimited supply of genetically manufactured HGH. The October 1983 issue of *Hospital Practice* noted that E. coli (a bacterium in the gut) could be reprogrammed to manufacture HGH synthetically. It is virtually identical to the natural pituitary-derived human-growth hormone, except that it contains an additional methionine amino-acid terminal. There is the possibility that the additional methionine residue may cause some significant antibody formation within the body, as suggested by early clinical trials. This could mean that the body may react to, and destroy, the synthetic HGH, and possibly over a long period of time even react to the endogenous, naturally produced HGH in the body. This synthetic HGH will be marketed under the trade name of Protropin by Genentech Inc. Another corporation, Biotechnology General, is claiming the successful production of "authentic" HGH produced by recombinant DNA techniques but further purified by the removal of the extra methionine amino-acid terminal.

So now, with the capability of synthetically producing 10 g of HGH from a 10-liter bacterial suspension, a limitless supply of growth hormone has arrived. This is very promising for the young children that need the drug to lead a normal life, but in the sports community it means the prohibitive costs of abusing this substance (five to fifteen hundred dollars for a six- to ten-week course) will be drastically reduced.

One of the abuse factors is that the half-life of HGH is so short it is at this time undetectable by present drug-testing methods. It has been proposed that the formula for synthetic production be modified so that it can be detected but still be physiologically utilizable.

Physiology of Human Growth Hormone

Human Growth Hormone affects many body tissues. In preadults it stimulates linear growth and aging of the bone. It also stimulates intracellular transport of amino acids and causes nitrogen retention, which is a supposed marker of protein anabolism. The activity of messenger RNA is affected, which increases protein synthesis in specific cells. In addition, HGH stimulates the intracellular breakdown of body fat so that more fat is used for energy. This has a protein-sparing effect. The synthesis of collagen (the sticky stuff that is the glue of the body) is stimulated, which is necessary for strengthening of cartilage, bones, tendons, and ligaments. Finally, HGH stimulates the liver to produce somatomedins, which are messenger molecules sometimes referred to as growth factors.

There are numerous factors that can affect the endogenous secretion of HGH. A while back, there were advertisements for a growth-hormone diet that would enable you to lose weight while you slept. It was based on the fact that certain amino acids, such as arginine and ornithine, have been known to stimulate secretion of HGH. But this is self-limiting, since you can only abuse the pituitary gland so much.

One drug that some athletes have used in conjunction with HGH is levodopa (L-dopa). This drug has been used in the treatment of Parkinson's disease. However, this is not a benign medication, as the side effects it can cause are:

- phlebitis (inflammation of the veins)
- gastrointestinal bleeding
- cardiac arrythmia and other heart irregularities
- activation of melanoma (skin cancer)
- hemolytic anemia
- headaches, blurred vision, insomnia
- narrow-angle glaucoma worsening
- abdominal distress
- vertigo
- agranulocytosis
- orthostatic hypotension (drop in blood pressure)
- mental changes such as depression, paranoia, and dementive episodes
- anorexia
- nausea and vomiting

Dangers of Growth-Hormone Excess

Procustes in modern dress, the scientist will prepare the bed on which mankind must lie; and if mankind doesn't fit—well, that will be just too bad for mankind. There will have to be some stretching and amputations as have been going on ever since applied science really got into stride, only this time they will be a good deal more drastic than in the past. . . . In "Brave New World" this standardization of the human product has been pushed to fantastic, though not impossible extremes.

—Aldous Huxley,
Brave New World (1932)

The side effects of excess HGH are numerous and complex, two of which are gigantism (larger physical stature) and acromegaly. The term *acromegaly* was first used in the 1880s in an attempt to define certain clinical observations. The word itself comes from the roots *arc*, which refers to the peripheral parts of the body, such as the hands, toes, nose, and so on, and *megol*, meaning large.

Commonly, this disorder occurs in cases where there is a metabolic or tumor condition that causes the pituitary to kick out inordinate quantities of HGH. The bones of the hands, feet, and jaw, and the cartilage and soft tissues of the nose, forehead, face, lips, nasolabial fold, and tongue grow, to induce what I call the Frankenstein Syndrome.

The first symptom may be a progressive increase in ring, shoe, or hat size. Then there is the coarsening of facial features, with increased size of the nose, lips, tongue, and the soft facial tissues. An underbite is noted, with enlargement of the mandible and the jaw. The forehead becomes more prominent as the orbital ridges and frontal sinuses enlarge. The voice develops a deep, husky, cavernous quality, and the fingers and toes widen into a spadelike shape. There is an increase in sweating and sebaceous-gland activity, along with small patches of increased skin pigmentation, known as *fibromata mollusca*. The skin takes on a very rough, thick, coarse appearance. An increase in coarse body hair may occur. The growth of the cartilage and soft tissues causes the joint spaces to widen, leading to significant joint pain. There is distortion of the bony structures, leading to disfigurement. The organomegaly and increased heart size can lead to congestive heart failure. People with this condition age very rapidly and are usually dead by the age of forty.

Unfortunately, young people tend to believe what is written in underground drug literature or other nonscientific sources. One individual who sells HGH to athletes wrote in a bodybuilding magazine that athletes who take this drug can "put on 40 pounds of muscle, with no change in waist size, and that they would increase in height, as well as increase the size of their penis." Well, needless to say they came from all over to visit this man.

A series of pamphlets that prey on young people is the anonymously authored *Underground Steroid Handbook*. The data provided is so incorrect and hazardous that body-building magazines now refuse ad space to the pamphlets.

A colleague and friend of mine, Dr. Bill Taylor, has been very outspoken on the abuse of human-growth hormone and fears its advent will change the face of sports forever. He sees "athletic acromegaly" and "selective gigantism" as a wave of the future and he has been pushing for reclassification of HGH as well as steroids to be controlled substances.

BETA-ADRENERGIC BLOCKERS

Beta blockers are drugs that result in vasodilation (dilated blood vessels) and relaxation of the nonvascular smooth muscle of the bronchioles and gut, cause cardiac stimulation, and stimulate lipolysis and glycolysis (breakdown of fat and starch for energy).

There are two types of beta (β) receptors: Beta-1 (β1) and Beta-2 (β2). The beta blockers can block either of these, depending on what they are specific for. Beta-1 receptors are specific for the kidneys, heart, and adipose tissue; Beta-2 receptors are located in the liver, bronchi, and arteries.

Propanolol (Inderal) is a popular beta blocker. Its original therapeutic use was for angina, which is a condition where the coronary arteries that surround the heart are not getting enough blood to the heart muscle. This causes chest pain. Propanolol decreases the heart rate and, thus, oxygen needs of the heart muscle.

Other uses for beta blockers are for hypertension, arrythmia, anxiety states, migraine headaches, drug-withdrawal syndromes, and thyrotoxicosis. When the level of Beta-1 blockade gets high, it crosses over to Beta-2 cells and blocks them also.

Athletes who desire to decrease anxiety and heart rate, such as those needing concentrated control (for pistol and rifle shooting or archery), have turned to these drugs. However, the negative side effects tend to deter athletes from these supposed ergogenics. Athletes needing endurance may find that energy pathways are disrupted. The more B1 selective the drug, the less the side effects. In those athletes with a history of asthma, bronchospasm can result. Some unwanted cardiovascular effects noted are congestive heart failure (fluid in the heart), bradycardia (slowed heart rate), hypotension (low blood pressure), and atrioventricular block. Peripherally, the vasoconstriction may cause a Raynaud's syndrome, which occurs when constriction of the small blood vessels causes the fingers to become white, blue, and painful due to ischemia (poor blood supply). The glycogenolysis can cause hypoglycemia, and due to the lowered blood pressure, male impotence is a risk. Some additional unwanted side effects can be reversible alopecia (hair loss) and gastrointestinal disturbances.

Withdrawal symptoms can occur when the drugs are stopped, such as anxiety, sweating, palpitations, angina, and headaches, so the dose should be decreased slowly. These drugs now appear on the banned list of the International Olympic Committee.

DMSO

Dimethyl sulfoxide (DMSO) is a drug that has been used by athletes for some time now to aid in the healing of musculoskeletal injuries due to its ability to penetrate the skin and enter the cellular tissue.

DMSO was first synthesized in 1866 by Russian scientist Alexander Saytzeff in Kazan, on the Volga River in Central Russia. He discovered that the substance was colorless, had a garliclike odor, felt oily to the touch, looked like mineral oil when poured from the test tube, and left an aftertaste similar to clams or oysters. For eighty years Dr. Saytzeff's paper, which was published in an obscure 1867 edition of a German chemistry journal, was the only scientific work on the substance.

It was not until after World War II that chemists became interested in DMSO. In 1947 it was found to be an excellent solvent. A British group in 1959 demonstrated that DMSO could protect red blood cells and other tissues against freezing conditions.

In 1964, Jacob and colleagues published the first report on the clinical pharmacological use of DMSO. As M. Walker and U. C. Douglass wrote in their book *DMSO: The New Healing Power* (Devin-Adair, 1983), "It caused a flood of trials and wild enthusiasm over the new "miracle" drug that carried other substances through the skin and into all the organs of the body. It was soon obvious that the chemical could relieve inflammation and pain in many conditions, some previously untreatable.

"The first investigational new drug (IND) application for the clinical study of DMSO in humans was submitted to the FDA on October 25, 1963, and was subsequently approved. Enormous interest developed rapidly, and it began to be used extensively, especially for the treatment of sprains, bruises, and minor burns. The drug was supplied at no charge to great numbers of investigators in general medicine, specialty medi-

cine, and to paramedical professionals, including phys-
iotherapists, a few dentists, and nurses.

"By 1965, an estimated one hundred thousand patients had
received the medication. Studies were conducted, but the FDA
did not consider them well-enough controlled to document
clearly which observed benefits were actually due to the drug.
The *New York Times* in a lead editorial on April 3, 1965, called
DMSO 'the closest thing to a wonder drug produced in the
1960's.' An international symposium of medical scientists in
Berlin, West Germany, in July 1965, was held to exchange information of the effects of DMSO."

In the last twenty-five years, many studies have been performed with a variety of results. An underground supply of
DMSO appeared because originally it could be purchased in-
expensively by the gallon—pharmacies sell the pure medical
grade on a doctor's prescription for fifteen to twenty dollars for
four ounces. The black market sells it off the backs of trucks, in
parking lots, in ice-cream parlors, and even via mail order.

DMSO is widely available as an over-the-counter preparation in pharmacies
throughout this country, and it is widely used by athletes of all ages because
of its alleged anti-inflammatory properties. Athletes rub it on an injured area
in the belief that the inflammation (and therefore the pain and discomfort)
will be relieved sooner than by such traditional methods as rest and heat.
The pungent odor of the breath, which occurs within minutes of its being
applied to the skin, makes double-blind placebo-controlled studies difficult.
However, one recent study compared the effectiveness against elbow ten-
dinitis of the standard 70 percent solution with a 5 percent DMSO placebo,
and no benefit could be ascertained.

The Problem with DMSO is that its human toxicity has not been fully
explored. Its early use in humans as a treatment for arthritis was stopped
when the FDA withdrew the drug from clinical use because of reports of eye
toxicity in animals. It has since been reapproved only for the instillation into
the bladder in the treatment of interstitial cystitis. The principal worry about
the compound is that it is both an excellent solvent and an extremely effective
skin penetrant. It will therefore carry into the body any substance con-
taminating the solution being used. As the industrial grade of DMSO is presumably the one being used by the athlete, its standard of purity does not
approach that which would be required of a manufacturer if the chemical
were a drug approved for human use. Its use should be discouraged until
human research indicates that it is both safe and effective.

—from "Overuse Syndromes in Young Athletes,"
by John Harvey, Jr., M.D., Pediatric Clinics of North America, December 1982

ALKALIES

Alkalies are buffers to help neutralize the accumulation of
acids in the bloodstream during exercise and muscular exertion. It was observed in some studies that sodium bicarbonate

might allow greater oxygen depth or capacity, but there were no significant improvements in muscular performance.

Although the following theory has provided conflicting reports, Dennig and his co-workers found an increase in endurance with the following alkali intake:

sodium bicarbonate...3.5 g

sodium citrate..5.0 g

potassium citrate ....1.5 g

These prescribed doses are taken once daily after a meal for two days before a contest and two days after. The dosage is continued for the two days after competition to avoid an acidotic reaction. However, if the athlete was to take the alkalies for a longer period of time, it might hinder his or her performance.

PHOSPHATES

Phosphates are very important compounds that are necessary in order to furnish energy for muscular contraction. They also act as a buffer in the blood. Researchers have noted increases in ergogenic tests with the administration of sodium phosphate in the form of Recresal. A dose of 3 grams can provide feelings of euphoria and well-being, but too much will cause insomnia. Some researchers also found phosphates to be good laxatives and to aid in recovering from fatigue more quickly. However, there are some studies that show little or no benefit with the use of phosphates. On the whole, there is no definite proof that phosphate ingestion will lead to improved athletic ability.

GELATIN AND GLYCINE

These substances are rich in amino-acetic acid and are considered incomplete proteins. The amino-acetic acid comprises 25 percent of the weight of gelatin and glycine. Creatine and glycine are chemically related, and creatine is very important in muscular contraction. For this reason glycine and, later on, gelatin have been used therapeutically to aid and improve muscular action. Several studies have pointed to the positive

effects glycine has had on work performances in terms of decreased fatigue and work-output increases, sometimes as high
as 240 percent. But the results have been conflicting, aside
from the psychological factors (placebo effect). There is no
proof that adding gelatin to a diet will improve strength.

CAFFEINE

Caffeine is a plant alkaloid, a naturally occurring compound
found in the extracts of Coffea arabica and Cola acuminata. It
is also found in several dozen plant species, as the Cola mates
with many other plants.

It is amazing to realize that more than half of the world's
production of coffee is consumed in American homes, which
averages out to sixteen pounds per person per year!

Some of the general actions of caffeine are:

- stimulation of the central nervous system
- stimulation of the kidneys, inducing diuresis
- stimulation of the heart and skeletal muscle (increased contractility)
- increased oxygen consumption and metabolic rate
- tachycardia, both ventricular and atrial
- increased heart rate, cardiac output, blood pressure at rest, and increased stroke volume
- increased lipolysis (breakdown of fat for energy)
- possible stimulation of the adrenal glands

These stimulating actions of coffee and coca are caused by
methyl derivatives of xanthine, and they may also induce relaxation of smooth muscle, elevate plasma-free fatty acid and
glucose concentrations, and increase gastric secretions.

There was an uproar in the sports medical community
when one scientist recommended caffeine pills to make "a marathon a fun run." Following such statements in the 1970s, athletes of all ages began to pop caffeine pills even before high
school track competitions. In 1971 the Medical Commission of
the British Commonwealth Games reported that the caffeine in
coffee was not regarded as a doping agent. In 1972 the International Olympic Committee removed caffeine from the doping
list. However, it has been placed back on the list and banned
at high levels.

Caffeine As an Ergogenic Aid

It is felt that xanthines and caffeine derivatives work to enhance performance due to their direct action on the heart and skeletal muscle, hormonal activity, the central nervous system, and chemical shifts or mobilization of different body enzymes and substrates. Since caffeine distributes evenly through the body fluids, its total effects depend on the individual's body composition, state of hydration, and the quantity ingested. Just as people have different tolerances to alcohol, so it is with caffeine.

When ingested, caffeine is rapidly emptied from the stomach and absorbed into the gastrointestinal tract. Peak effects are reached in about one hour, regardless of the dose. As calibrated by some researchers (Burg, 1975), the half-life of this drug was determined to be 2.0–2.8 hours, so they surmised that at the end of a twenty-four-hour period, no significant portion remained. Other scientists differed and found the half-life to be 3.5 hours (Axelrod, 1953), while others (Robertson, 1981) found it to be nearly 10 hours for elimination.

When used as an ergogenic, the two areas where caffeine has been found to yield positive results are in endurance events and in those events requiring increased alertness and decreased reaction times as well as lowered anxiety levels. The bradycardia (slowed heart beat) and the factors just mentioned may come in handy in archery and shooting, where relaxed concentration is essential. Dose levels were critical for positive study results, as Cheney (1935) found that the dose had to exceed 3.0 mg/kg of body weight, while much higher levels impaired performance.

The Price to Pay

Those athletes who are "hooked" on coffee and coffeelike products suffer anxiety and nervousness when withdrawn from them. The adverse withdrawal effects are dose related. Some of these are:

- headaches
- tremors, nervousness
- tachycardias—abnormally fast heart rate (a common sign is paroxysmal atrial tachycardia [PAT])

- central-nervous-system irregularities (tremulousness, hyperactivity, dry mouth, irritability, restlessness, tinnitus [ringing in ears], scotoma [black spot in visual field], insomnia, and depression, to name a few)

THE CONCENTRATION OF CAFFEINE IN COMMON BEVERAGES AND PHARMACEUTICALS

Beverage or Product	Caffeine Concentration (mg/dl)	Quantity per Standard Serving Dose (mg)
Cocoa	25–30	50
Coffee	55–85	100–150
Cola drinks (other sodas also contain caffeine in smaller amounts)	10–15	35–55
Tea	55–85	100–150
Prescription Medications and Over-the-Counter Preparations	**(mg/tablet)**	
APC (aspirin/phenacetin/caffeine)	32	
Anacin	32	
Anacin—aspirin compound	32	
Cafergot	100	
Coricidin	30	
Darran compound	32	
Dristan	15	
Empirin compound, Midol	32	
Excedrin	60–65	
Fiorinal	40	
Many cold preparations	40	
Migral	50	
NōDōz	100	
Ordrinex	50	
PreMens	66	
Prolamine	140	
Spantrol	150	
Vanquish	32	
Diet Medications (Over-the-Counter)	**(mg/tablet)**	Usually also contain phenylpro-panolamine (a sympathomimetic agent)
Anorexan	100	
Appedrine	100	
Appress	100	
Caldrin Reducing Plan	100	
Dexa Diet II	200	
Dexatrim	200	
Dietac	200	
Permathene 12	140	
Others		
Small chocolate bar	30	

From Goldfrank L, Lewin N, Melinek M, et al: Caffeine. Hosp Phys 43:42–59, 1981. Reprints with permission.

There is a five-symptom complex described by Goldfrank and colleagues:

1 Anxiety-like presentation
2 Hypochondriasis-like presentation (a recurrent feeling of coming down with illnesses)
3 Insomnia and/or headache
4 Withdrawal symptoms
5 Depressive presentation

These effects show up in the 200–500 mg range and increase as the levels top 700 mg.

This drug is not a problem if the athlete is just having a Coke or a Pepsi or a cup of coffee here or there, but if taken in pill form, or if there is chronic use of caffeinated products, problems may arise. Two cups of coffee, for example, may contain 3–6 µg/ml caffeine, with a half-life of 2–3 hours. One NōDōz tablet contains about the same amount as those two cups, while two colas contain about half as much: 1.5–3 µg/ml. One aspirin, Empirin, or Anacin tablet contains 2–3 µg/ml. Caffeine has been banned by the International Olympic Committee in amounts greater than 15 µg/ml in the urine. Due to its chemical makeup, it is easily detected by today's advanced instrumentation.

BLOOD DOPING

At a world championship, the winner was disqualified for having steroids in his blood sample. He claimed that it was a mistake, that he had not taken steroids for more than a year. But he had his blood doped for the competition, and when they retransfused his old blood, he claimed, there must have still been some steroids in it. Well, now the officials had two reasons to disqualify him: Blood doping is also banned.

Some athletes will go to any length to boost their endurance, increase their maximal oxygen uptake (VO_2 max), and prevent physiological fatigue during prolonged aerobic exercise. Blood plays a key factor in this. If 500–1,000 ml of blood were to be removed, along with the concomitant loss of hemoglobin and thereby a loss in the blood's oxygen-carrying capacity, the VO_2 max would decrease. Along opposite lines, if someone were to train at elevated altitudes, they would produce more red blood cells due to the thinner air and would have enhanced performance upon returning to normal sea-level altitude.

It was inevitable that the athletic community would discern that if total blood volume and hemoglobin levels could be increased, so would endurance capacity and VO_2 max. This is how blood doping was born. It seemed to be a way to mimic training at elevated altitudes.

With blood doping, the blood is withdrawn from the athlete five to six weeks before a competition, and then retransfused just prior to the event. It usually is the athlete's own blood, or properly crossed matched blood, but autologous blood is strongly preferred.

It is rumored that blood doping first came on the scene in 1971, but it has moved rapidly into endurance sports since that time. The way blood doping appears to work is possibly by altering gas transport in the blood, which may be a limiting factor in VO_2 max. The increase in red-blood-cell mass (polythycemia) and hemoglobin (Hb) may alter the amount of oxygen that can be transferred. In 1967, Levy and Berne theorized that "a 500 ml blood transfusion would result in an efflux of approximately 250 ml of the plasma within one hour of transfusion. Thus, infusion of 500 ml whole blood, or packed RBC (red blood cells) in normal saline to an equivalent of 500 ml whole blood, would result primarily in an elevated Hb concentration, RBC count, and hematocrit (Hct—number of RBCs) with little change in total blood volume."

In 1977 Williams and Ward noted a 4 percent and a 9 percent increase in Hb and Hct, respectively, following a one-mile run. Thus, it appears that nature attempts to increase the O_2 transport capacity during exercise via an increased Hb concentration and Hct level. It is known that the Hct and Hb increase when whole blood or packed RBCs are infused, thus the belief in increased O_2 carrying capacity. Another benefit proposed is that blood doping may decrease the lowering of blood pH, which occurs in fatigue states (blood becomes acidotic as it lowers) as infused RBCs act as an acid-base buffer. In fact, some researchers believe that RBCs are responsible for 70 percent of the buffering in whole blood.

However, it can work in a negative way as well. When the blood viscosity (thickness) increases due to the extra infused blood, this can actually hamper oxygen transport in the blood. Another drawback is that the storage process of blood will decrease its oxygen-carrying capacity. It has been found that blood stored in acid-citrate-dextrose (ACD) will lose 60 percent of its 2,3-DPG in one week, and 90 percent in two weeks. Another anticoagulant, citrate-phosphate-dextrose (CPD), has been shown to be a better preservative.

In summary, studies in which 500–1,000 ml of blood were removed from the athlete on several occasions (200–300 ml each sitting) and then retransfused did in some cases show an increase in work output until exhaustion set in. In these cases, the athlete needed at least five weeks to replenish the lost Hb and Hct. When only 500 ml or less were utilized, results were much poorer. It appears that the amount of blood reinfused and the timing are critical factors. If the blood is frozen, there is no problem, but if it is stored by conventional means, it must be used in less than twenty-one days, which does not give the athlete enough time for rejuvenation.

There was quite a scandal when a group of American cyclists were found to be retransfusing before a world championship. Someone entered a room and saw all the bikers laid out on their backs with IV needles in their arms and blood dripping in. One athlete was even taking a live transfusion from his own mother!

This is a very dangerous practice and is now banned in Olympic competition. Some of the problems that can arise are infection, hepatitis, improperly transferred blood, the risk of AIDS, and transfusion reactions. I can see the newspaper headlines now: VAMPIRES GO TO THE OLYMPICS, DRACULA WINS GOLD MEDAL.

OXYGEN

A common sight on the sidelines of football games is a player sucking oxygen. Mask in hand, the athlete becomes renewed and ready to go out again to do battle. The jury is divided on how effective supplemental oxygen is. Two possible limiting factors involved in oxygen delivery are getting enough of it to the working muscles and disruptions in transport. Another is in what form the oxygen is delivered: as pure O_2 at normal atmospheric pressure versus as hyperoxygenated air.

Another matter of dispute is whether it is more beneficial to give the oxygen before, during, or after an athletic trial. It is possible that O_2 could aid performance by increasing transport of it in the cardiorespiratory complex. Increased concentration of O_2 could aid transport by supplying a richer source of oxygen to the blood. Some researchers have found pulmonary diffusion to be the most significant factor relating increased performance with O_2 supplementation. It has been found that inhaling oxygen prior to an event was not significantly effective, but taken during an event it did have some positive effects. The exact mechanisms for this are yet to be determined. For the most part it is of little advantage to athletes.

Another odd use of oxygen was reported after the 1976 Olympics, when it was revealed that the West German swimming team had used rectal injections of air in an attempt to improve their performance by increasing buoyancy. E. C. Percy, in *Medicine and Science in Sports*, wrote, "You are aware, of course, that there are four basic strokes in swimming, and it would appear that the West Germans have now added a fifth stroke—the 'floater or Zeppelin' stroke. One might truly say that their athletes have attempted to join the jet set."

ALTITUDE TRAINING

Research has shown that training at elevated altitudes does not have adverse effects on the heart. In fact, it may serve to strengthen cardiovascular function, as pointed out by several studies at the Fifty-ninth Scientific Sessions of the American Heart Association. The project was known as Operation Everest Two, and for it seven men between the ages of twenty-one and thirty-one were placed in hypobaric chambers and taken progressively over a forty-day period to the simulated altitude of 29,000 feet, which is the height of Mount Everest. All the subjects were well-trained athletes, and they were monitored by echocardiographic studies of the heart at rest and while exercising in order to examine physical acclimation to the low-oxygen concentrations at high altitudes.

Dr. James K. Alexander at the Baylor College of Medicine in Houston found "that the volume of the left ventricular pumping chamber tended to shrink with increasing altitude and lower barometric pressures . . . and that the pumping capacity of the left ventrical remained intact even to the very highest altitude. In fact pumping capacity seemed to be somewhat enhanced." Similar shrinkage in pumping volume has been reported by other researchers at lower altitudes.

Further, Dr. Alexander found that several of the indices

(measurements) of the heart's pumping capacity were "well preserved all the way to 29,000 feet. In two of the indices, there were some suggestions of an improvement in performance, which took us quite by surprise."

It was theorized that some of this improvement may have been due to increased activity of the sympathetic nervous system, which is commonly activated by hypoxic (poor oxygen supply to the blood and tissues) conditions.

Due to these observations, the researchers felt that the heart was able to perform normally under hypoxic conditions, so that the reduction in exercise tolerance "did not appear to be related to heart muscle dysfunction." The researchers then suggested that if a physician notes abnormalities in heart function under hypoxic conditions, some underlying cardiac pathological explanation should be sought. During sleep at elevated altitudes, changes were noted in breathing patterns. These factors had some real-life applications at the summer Olympics in Mexico City, where the variance in altitude played a part in athletic performance. Some athletes try to arrive early in regions with unusual climate or atmospheric conditions so that they can adapt to the different environment.

■

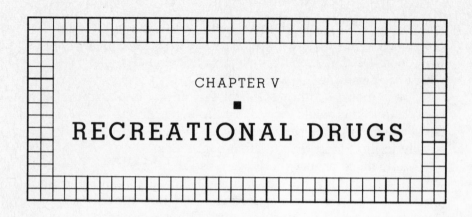

CHAPTER V

■

RECREATIONAL DRUGS

MARIJUANA

Everybody must get stoned.
—Bob Dylan

First reported in 2737 B.C. by Shen Nung, the Chinese emperor, marijuana is an ancient medicinal herb. Its uses for centuries in Asia, South America, and Africa were as a topical anesthetic, muscle relaxant, bronchodilator, analgesic, sedative-hypnotic, and anticonvulsant.

Marijuana found its way to Europe and America in the nineteenth century. Then, with new synthetic drugs replacing its medicinal uses, it was outlawed by Congress in 1937 with the Marijuana Tax Act. In the 1960s, the Vietnam War and the hippie era brought about a resurgence of marijuana smoking. The National Institute of Drug Abuse came up with some interesting findings in their 1982 survey: They found 6.3 percent of high school seniors to be daily users, and daily use among young adults (ages 18–25) to be 21 percent for months at a time. A governmental study in 1970 found that more than 20 million people had tried marijuana, which was 10 percent of the U.S. population at the time. Another 1970 survey found decreased marijuana use by athletes, but a 1975 study by Corder and colleagues found that nonathletes and athletes used the drug with the same frequency.

Marijuana is derived from the leaves of the easily grown *Cannabis sativa* hemp plant. It can be grown anywhere, from open fields to indoor planters. The active ingredient in marijuana is tetrahydrocannabinol (THC), and is very difficult to synthesize in the lab. Some black-market drugs purported to be

THC are in actuality phencyclidine, a sedative. Rapidly absorbed and lipid soluble, THC gives a fairly rapid high and has a half-life of about five days, but due to the lipid solubility, it can remain in the system six weeks or more.

Some effects of marijuana are:

- anesthesia (Some patients request it to ease pain.)
- excitement
- disinhibition
- vasomotor and respiratory depression
- ataxia
- sedation
- decreases in intraocular pressure (lowering of pressure in the eyeball. Some patients request the right to smoke marijuana to control glaucoma.)
- increased appetite

Marijuana has also been known as a disinhibiting aphrodisiac, for much of sexual dysfunction is due to inhibitions and lack of interest. The action of marijuana is similar to that of alcohol and barbiturates, whereby the central nervous system is depressed.

Marijuana As an Ergogenic

This drug is one substance you do not want in your body if you are training seriously. It is dose related, so the more you take, the more it may take to give a similar high. It remains in the body for an extended period of time, and in drug-tested competitions it is detectable for some time. It can unknowingly be spiked with dangerous additives such as PCP. It slows reaction time, and time, space, and depth perception are altered by it. Your short-term and immediate memory can be hampered, you can be more susceptible to suggestion, and judgment is significantly affected. An amotivational syndrome described by O'Brien shows that the athlete can become lazy and apathetic, experience frustration and unrealistic thinking, and exhibit increased introversion. Finally, you are placing toxic smoke in the lung tissue and damaging alveoli. This can cut down on pulmonary capacity.

SEDATIVES

Along these same lines, sedatives, which are synthetic drugs used to induce sleep and relieve anxiety, will also cut down on performance. Sedative-class drugs include:

1 Barbiturates (such as pentobarbital [Nembutal])
2 Benzodiazepines (such as diazepam [Valium])
3 Monoureides (such as carbromal)
4 Piperidinedione (such as glutethimide [Doriden])
5 Carbamates and dicarbamates (such as methocarbamol [Robaxin])

These drugs significantly depress the central nervous system, and the drive to win is strongly affected in a negative way. For the winning athlete, sedatives and marijuana are bad news. The greatest danger is accidental death, which can occur when sedatives are combined with alcohol and marijuana.

AMPHETAMINES

According to Al Davis, head coach of the Oakland Raiders in the mid-sixties, amphetamines were used by the special teams to counteract fear. But high doses of amphetamine can engender a nearly psychotic paranoid rage. Comparable doses are used by the "pillhead" and intravenously by the "speed freaks." Linemen who had taken very high doses of amphetamine had difficulty adjusting their play; one game film showed a veteran defensive end on high levels of amphetamine going inside on every play, disregarding the linebacker's signals. The opposing offense consistently aimed its running attack at the region he could be counted on to leave, and no amount of shouting by the defensive-line coach during the game could change the defensive end's behavior; he said he was always playing a sweep to the other side. One might speculate that his brain had been driven to a limit cycle by the drug.

Stimulants have been used as ergogenics for many years. The first ones were of plant origin, such as the leaves of the coca plant and the African plant Catha edulis. These contain the psychomotor stimulant drugs cocaine and norisoephedrine, respectively. Natives of the regions of the world where these plants grow believe that these substances increase strength and endurance.

Amphetamine (2-phenylisopropylamine) is very similar to the naturally occurring stimulants. It was first synthesized in 1887 as a crystalline, white, odorless powder. Its derivative, N-methamphetamine, was first produced in 1919. Both of these drugs were used extensively by troops during World War II to fend off fatigue. The soldiers carried the drug from the battlefield to the athletic field—athletes have turned to speed to fight fatigue and to get psyched up for competition.

Common amphetamines are benzedrine and dexedrine. Some of the effects of this class of drug are:

- rise in blood pressure
- increase in heart rate
- constriction of blood vessels
- mydriasis (pupil dilation)
- intestinal muscle relaxation
- increase in blood sugar
- dilation of bronchi
- shorter blood-coagulation time
- increased muscle tone
- stimulation of the adrenal glands

Some people use these drugs as appetite depressants to lose weight. Amphetamines work by stimulating the release of epinephrine and norepinephrine from the adrenal glands and nervous system, respectively.

There is overwhelming evidence that amphetamines extend aerobic endurance and quicken recovery from fatigue. However, with high concentrations of the drug, endurance capacity can drop to a quasi-paralytic state (neuromuscular blockade). Amphetamines may not improve the reflexes and reaction time of the alert, nonfatigued athlete, but may aid the fatigued athlete. On the whole, though, it is a losing proposition. Amphetamines cause irritability, dizziness, disorientation, confusion, and, much worse, can lead to addiction and death.

It is felt that there is less amphetamine abuse today than in the 1960s and 1970s.

This decrease can be attributed to a growing awareness by youth that "speed kills," and to the liability concerns of professional teams and their physicians who have been sued by athletes injured while playing under the influence of these drugs. Use of amphetamines had been the major drug-related problem in athletics, so its decline is encouraging. . . . Obscuring an athlete's physiologic fatigue level may allow him to exceed his limits and precipitate a sudden collapse, eliminating him from the event. Football players on amphetamines seem to be able to ignore pain from injuries, thus allowing further play and thus even more damage. Such drugs can also make an athlete more aggressive, resulting in unnecessary brutality and rough play in contact sports, causing even more injuries. High doses may induce a paranoid, prepsychotic state or a paranoid schizophrenic syndrome, both of these apparently dose related.

—John Harvey, M.D.

NICOTINE

Following its discovery in the New World, tobacco swept its way through Europe. There are historical indications that as early as 3500 B.C. tobacco was an article of established value to the inhabitants of Mexico and Peru. It appears that people who frequently lacked sufficient food alleviated their hunger pains by chewing tobacco. Native Americans used tobacco to alleviate toothaches, relieve the effects of spider, snake, and insect bites, and disinfect cuts. During the nineteenth and early twentieth centuries in the Americas, dental snuff was advertised to relieve toothache pain, to cure bleeding gums, neuralgia, and scurvy, and, as odd as it sounds, to whiten teeth and prevent dental decay. Even the Australian aborigines chew the leaves to get the nicotine jolt.

However, The Surgeon General was not the first person to speak out against tobacco:

- In Japan in the 1500s, tobacco was outlawed, with users having their property confiscated and then given a jail term.

- King James VI of Scotland increased taxes on tobacco 4,000 percent during the 1600s to cut down on tobacco imports to England.

- The use of tobacco was a capital offense in Turkey under Sultan Murad IV. To break the law meant death by hanging, beheading, or starvation. It was his feeling that smoking ruined the fighting ability of troops and caused infertility.

- In Russia in the 1600s, Czar Fedorovich prohibited the sale of tobacco, with users being physically punished and persistent users executed.

- A Chinese law of 1683 declared that the punishment for possession of tobacco was beheading. (The Imperial Smoking Cessation Programs proved 100 percent effective at that time.)

According to the National Institute of Drug Abuse, more than 70 percent of high school seniors have tried cigarettes and more than 20 percent smoke regularly. Fortunately, in the last twenty years the male smoking population has decreased by 17 percent, although the female group has decreased only a fourth as much. There has been an alarming increase in female lung cancer and heart disease, which can in part be attributed to smoking. In addition, smokeless tobacco use has increased and is very popular among baseball and football players.

Nicotine, the active ingredient in tobacco smoke, is an alkaloid that affects both the parasympathetic and sympathetic nervous systems. A norepinephrine release is stimulated from the adrenals, leading to increased heart rate and high blood pressure. There are also increases in peristaltic movements and gastrointestinal muscle tone. Decreased urine output is noted, due to the release of antidiuretic hormone from the pituitary. In addition, nicotine hits the satiety center and decreases appetite, which is why people tend to put on weight when they stop smoking. The absence of nicotine causes increased hunger.

Smoking significantly decreases endurance and athletic performance, and the nicotine, although calming to some athletes, is very addictive. Smokeless chewing tobacco has been linked to cancer of the pharynx, throat, mouth, and lip. Smoking is one of the strongest links to serious heart and lung disease and therefore a suicidal habit.

ALCOHOL

Drink! for you know not whence you came, nor why: Drink! for you know not why you go, nor where.

—Omar Khayyám, *Rubáiyát*

One of the most popular drinks of champions is alcohol. Ethyl alcohol has been around for centuries and utilized in potions, beverages, anesthetics, and ceremonial drinks. Its strength can range from 2 to 4 percent in beer, 12 to 20 percent in wine, and 80 proof or more in "the hard stuff."

In a 1982 study, virtually all high school students said yes when asked if they had tried alcohol in the past month, and this beverage is one of the most popular druglike substances used for entertainment.

Alcohol was once thought to improve athletic performance, but in truth it detracts from peak work potentials. A series of testing procedures in which a Johansson ergograph was used (a device where the subject uses both hands to determine pull strength) showed significant decreases in power and activity after an initial boost. Decreases in oxygen consumption have also been noted by some studies.

A fallacy many people believe is that alcohol warms them during a game. Actually, alcohol acts as a mild dilator on the vascular system, affecting the peripheral blood vessels, which are the tiny blood vessels at the surface of the skin. This in turn results in a small drop in blood pressure. This vasodilation occurs as a result of the depressive action on the vasoconstrictor centers in the medulla. Higher brain centers, such as the hypothalamus, may mediate this action. These cells are normally in a state of vessel vasoconstriction. Alcohol dulls the cells, which then emit constrictive impulses. With this stimulus gone, the vessels become relaxed and enlarged, allowing more blood flow to the surface of the skin that is in contact with the external environment, which is cooler than the body's temperature. This in turn leads to an increase in loss of body heat. So the next time you take an alcoholic drink during competition in cold weather, remember you will be decreasing your body temperature.

Another effect of alcohol on performance is decreased hand-eye coordination and reaction time. Balance and accuracy are also severely hampered. The athlete may think he is doing well, and may feel very strong, but tests show otherwise.

Up to 20 percent of the alcohol you drink is absorbed in the stomach and small intestines. Ninety percent of the first dose of alcohol is absorbed in the first hour, with peak blood levels in three quarters of an hour. It is then distributed throughout the body tissues and oxidized to acetaldehyde in the liver. Aldehyde dehydrogenase then converts it even further. There is a drug called Antabuse (Disulfiram) that is given to alcoholics to prevent them from drinking. It interferes with the oxygenation of acetaldehyde, which leads to increased levels of this byproduct. The acetaldehyde toxicity causes severe headaches, nausea, and abdominal cramps and makes drinking a very unpleasant affair.

■

FACT SHEET: SELECTED STATISTICS ON ALCOHOL AND ALCOHOLISM*

Drink Equivalents

The following typical drinks have about the same alcohol content—one-half ounce of ethanol (absolute alcohol):

- a 12 ounce can of beer
- a 5 ounce glass of wine
- a cocktail (1½ ounce shot of 86-proof liquor)

Drinking Problems

- Of all adults who drink, approximately 1 adult drinker in 10 is likely to be a problem drinker (includes alcoholics).

  Definitions of adult problem drinking and alcoholism include consideration of one or more of the following: alcohol consumption level, adverse social and physical consequences of alcohol use, evidence of alcohol dependence.

- In addition to adult problem drinkers, it is estimated by the National Institute on Alcohol Abuse and Alcoholism that 19 percent of adolescents (14 to 17 years of age) or 3.3 million youth are problem drinkers.

  Youth problem drinking is defined differently than for adults because youth problems tend to be acute rather than chronic. For example, they usually involve drinking-driving episodes and belligerence, rather than alcohol-related medical illnesses and addiction.

Mortality

- The mortality rate for alcoholics has been reported as 2.5 times greater than that expected.

*The information on pages 73–81 has been reprinted with permission from the National Institute of Alcohol Abuse and Alcoholism/Division of Public Health Service, U.S. Dept. of Health and Human Services.

- The total number of deaths in 1977 directly related to alcohol (alcoholism, alcoholic psychosis, cirrhosis of the liver) was between 18,066 and 34,724. (see also chart on page 75)

- The total number of deaths in 1977 where alcohol was a contributing factor (accidents, homicides, suicides) was between 42,949 and 60,487. (see also chart on page 75)

Social Implications of Alcohol Abuse

- Between 35 and 64 percent of drivers in fatal accidents had been drinking prior to the accident.

- Between 45 and 60 percent of all fatal crashes with a young driver were alcohol related.

- Between 50 and 68 percent of drowning victims had been drinking.

- Between 25 and 37 percent of successful suicides involved alcohol.

- A divorce rate of 40 percent occurs among families experiencing alcohol problems.

- Almost 26 percent of adult fire deaths involved alcohol.

- Almost 45 percent of deaths from falls involved alcohol.

- Estimates suggest that alcohol may play a role in as many as one third of all reported cases of child abuse.

- It is estimated that between 3,000 and 6,000 births in 1980 (1 in 500—1 in 1,000 births) will evidence the full fetal alcohol syndrome (characterized by mental retardation, slow growth rate, small head, distinctive facial features, heart and genital organ defects).

- Although there are no overall statistics linking alcohol use with spouse abuse, studies estimate that between 6 percent and 50 percent of cases of marital violence involve alcohol use.

Treatment

- Person treated in both private and public facilities for alcoholism and problem drinking rose from 1.384 million in 1976 to 1.712 million in 1977.

- Recovery rates for alcoholism and problem drinking vary considerably according to various studies. A study conducted for the National Institute on Alcohol Abuse and Alcoholism by the Rand Corporation followed the same problem drinking population over a four year period. This study showed that the rate of problem drinking decreased from 90 percent at admission to treatment to 54 percent at the 4 year followup. The speed with which alcohol brings drunkenness and drunken behavior depends upon the rate of absorption into the

ESTIMATED DEATHS RELATED TO ALCOHOL IN THE UNITED STATES, 1977, FOR SELECTED CAUSES

Cause of Death	Number of Deaths 1977	Percent Related to Alcohol	Estimated No. Related to Alcohol
Alcohol as a Direct Cause			
Alcoholism	5,100	100%	5,100
Alcoholic psychosis	318	100%	318
Cirrhosis	30,848	41%–95%	12,648–29,306
Alcohol as an Indirect Cause			
Accidents			
Motor vehicle	49,510	30%–50%	14,853–24,755
Falls	13,773	44.4%	6,115
Fires	6,357	25.9%	1,646
Other[1]	30,455	11.1%	3,381
Homicides	19,968	49%–70%	9,784–13,978
Suicides	28,681	25%–37%	7,170–10,612
Total for Direct Causes	36,266		18,066–34,724
Total for Indirect Causes	148,744		42,949–60,487
TOTAL	185,010		61,015–95,211

[1] Includes all accidents not listed above, but excludes accidents incurred in medical and surgical procedures.

Source: Malin, H.; Coakley, J.; Kaelber, C.; Munch, N.; and Holland, W. An Epidemiologic Perspective on Alcohol Use and Abuse in the United States. Draft report prepared for the National Institute on Alcohol Abuse and Alcoholism under Contract No. (ADM) 281-79-0022. 1980.

blood stream, the individual's drinking behavior and what he/she wants or expects to happen.

The body takes in alcohol quickly and gets rid of it slowly. Alcohol enters the bloodstream through absorption and is distributed to body tissues and cells. This absorption can be slowed down a little if there is food in the stomach. Water in food slows alcohol's entry into the blood. The bloodstream carries alcohol throughout the body. Behavior is affected when alcohol reaches the brain.

The human body can burn up about ½ ounce of alcohol in one hour. Elimination through urine, perspiration and breath account for the other 10%. The body gets rid of alcohol through oxidation and elimination. Oxidation is simply the burning up of alcohol. Oxidation is necessary to sober up. The burning of alcohol takes place in the liver. It is the liver that gets rid of 90% of the alcohol consumed. One half ounce of alcohol is contained in about ¾ of a standard serving of beer, wine or liquor. Home remedies do not help one sober up faster. In fact, a cold shower results in a cold drunk, coffee results in a wide awake drunk, exercise leads to a tired drunk. The only cure that helps in "sobering up" is TIME.

If oxidation could stay ahead of the amount drunk, you would never get smashed. The problem is, no matter how much you drink, the liver just plugs along at the same old rate. Both absorption and oxidation are very stubborn characters. Absorption won't slow down very much and oxidation can't speed up. When you drink more alcohol than your liver can oxidize, the percentage of alcohol in your blood increases. In other words, you are becoming more intoxicated. The greater the percentage of alcohol in the blood, the more intoxicated the person is.

The amount of alcohol in the body can be measured. The percentage of alcohol in the body fluids can be determined by using a breath, urine or blood sample. Alcohol in the blood is called the *Blood Alcohol Concentration* or *BAC*. The amount of alcohol is expressed as a percentage. The measure is very accurate—it indicates so many parts of alcohol to so many parts of blood.

The percentage of alcohol in the blood depends on body weight, the amount of alcohol and drinking time. To a lesser degree, food in the stomach makes a difference because the alcohol is absorbed more slowly. Thinking that you can keep from getting drunk by drinking on a full stomach may just result in an unhungry drunk.

No matter what you weigh or eat, the more you drink in a fixed amount of time, the greater your BAC will be. This is true no matter what you drink. Beer, wine and liquor can all be thought of as a drink. Why? Because of the one common element—ALCOHOL. In standard amounts, all drinks have the same amount of alcohol. 12 ounces of beer, 5 ounces of wine and 1½ ounces of liquor are considered standard servings.

Whichever kind of alcohol you choose to drink the alcohol reaches the brain and affects behavior. The effects are present with as little as one drink. When the drinker has trouble talking or walking, it is not because the muscles controlling the speech and movement are impaired but rather because the control center, the brain, is affected. The first area of the brain affected controls social inhibitions and other things that we learn. We learn to do or say things when we are with friends as well as what not to say and do. Eventually alcohol affects all behaviors and body processes. Alcohol works in this way usually if the suggested number of drinks are consumed in one hour:

1 drink—inhibitions are lessened, less critical of self and others, judgment begins to be affected

2 drinks—reaction time slower, less critical of self and others, appears relaxed and friendly

3 drinks—judgment is not sound, not thinking clearly, reasoning less reliable, may be rude and unreasonable

4 drinks—hearing, speech, vision and balance are affected

5 drinks—most behavior is affected, body parts seem not to work together, performing any task is difficult, walking is difficult

A blood alcohol concentration (BAC) of one tenth of one percent is legally drunk. If 12 drinks were consumed the BAC would be about three tenths of one percent. At this level the person would probably be in a deep sleep or coma. A BAC of higher than .30% can result in death.

Myths—The Insidious "Enabler"

We have come to consider the word "enabler" in the field of alcoholism as an individual who, although motivated by the best of intentions, enables the alcoholic to continue his addiction and to further his disease. Another area where the word "enabler" should be used and, as a matter of fact, has greater input in the field of enabling are the myths perpetuated by those with good intentions and extraordinary sympathy that serve only to harm rather than help.

There are myths surrounding alcohol that are accepted as fact simply because of their longevity. No reference is made to any clinical research and they are the foundation for a non-productive approach to the subject of alcoholism. They can be divided into two major sections. One we will call the medical myths, and the other, the social myths.

The medical myths are the most dangerous for they frequently stem from the medical field, often taken out of context, or more often, exist simply because the individual doing the quoting has not done the research to warrant the statements.

Myth

Alcohol is a food. There is even some literature that extols the virtue of various forms of alcohol as being nutritious, as being helpful to one's health.

Fact:

Alcohol is often referred to as a ready source of calories and energy. It is true that it is a ready source of calories, but not of energy. The energizing effect that people experience from alcohol is due to the effect on the central nervous system, in which alcohol doesn't give energy, it actually disinhibits various portions of the central nervous system and people feel they have more energy when in fact, the central nervous system is depressed.

Myth:

It is a source of calories.

Fact:

There are many calories in a gram of alcohol. However, they have been labeled by others as naked calories because they in fact do not contribute to the metabolism of carbohydrates, lipids or proteins in a positive way. There have been a number of experiments done on alcohol as a foodstuff. The most recent I can recall was done with rats. They gave them nothing but water, which had no calories, and a hundred rats had nothing but alcohol. The ones getting the alcohol died infinitely sooner than the ones who were drinking the water, so the caloric content of alcohol is a naked calorie. Instead of doing anything positive to the metabolism of food, it actually produces a number of negative impacts.

Myth:

Alcohol is a source of vitamins.

Fact:

You can read that wine and beer contain vitamins, particularly the B-complex group. Allow me to indicate that for you to receive the daily minimum requirements of Vitamin B_1, you would have to drink approximately eighteen quarts of beer in one day. So, alcohol is a source of vitamins, but it is not a ready source of vitamins; there are much better sources.

Myth:

Alcohol helps metabolism.

Fact:

People often say "A couple of drinks before dinner will excite your appetite." There are whole countries of people that say "A few drinks before dinner are good for your appetite and help you to digest your food." What are the facts? Alcohol has no protein in it, but the effects that alcohol has on protein metabolism is most interesting. It decreases absorption of protein from the gastrointestinal tract. In other words, if you are eating a steak and drinking a martini, the protein from that steak is not all absorbed because the alcohol impairs the breakdown of protein; you don't get the amino acids you should from the proteins you have digested and this causes some drastic effects on the central nervous system.

Myth:

Alcohol is a carbohydrate.

Fact:

Alcohol is actually more of a lipid, more of a fat. Because of the medical complications caused by alcohol in the metabolism of carbohydrates or sugar, we get a resulting low blood sugar or high blood sugar count in those who are utilizing alcohol on any regular basis. Therefore, many who are being treated for a low sugar content or a high sugar content are being treated for something that does not really exist. It is actually the result of alcohol ingestion and its effect on metabolism of the carbohydrates.

Myth:

Alcohol can be used to overcome a feeling of malaise (a feeling of not feeling well).

Fact:

Alcohol creates the very situation that contributes to the feeling of malaise.

Myth:

Alcohol stimulates the appetite.

Fact:

It has been shown that one and one half ounces of wine will increase the stomach secretion of acid, although it does not necessarily stimulate appetite. Anything above that amount suppresses it. Two or three martinis before dinner actually suppresses the release of gastric juices and suppresses initial metabolism and absorption and does nothing to stimulate appetite.

Myth:

Wine contains essential minerals and is drunk for that purpose.

Fact:

I have not met the individual yet who consumes quantities of wine so that he can get from that wine the necessary zinc, cobalt and iron his system requires.

Myth:

Alcohol calms your nerves.

Fact:

The opposite would be true. There is a great deal of research in the area of the effects of alcohol on the central nervous system, the peripheral nervous system, but not as much as should and could be done to determine the entire effects of alcohol in relationship with this vital area of the human system. There is no question that the nervous system is most sensitive to alcohol. People drink because of the effect of alcohol on the nervous system. It is actually a factor in the degeneration of the nerves and the sheath around the nerves. It is treatable only with the absence of alcohol and usually with vitamin therapy.

Myth:

Alcohol is good for the heart patient.

Fact:

One of the direct results of alcohol consumption is a diagnosis of hypertension (high blood pressure). A significant proportion of people being treated for hypertension are being treated because they are drinking. Alcohol does not lower blood pressure. It is not good for a hypertensive patient.

Now to some of the social myths.

Myth:

Alcohol indicates a lack of willpower.

Fact:

Research done at Yale University, Johns Hopkins, and the New Jersey Department of Health indicate that willpower has nothing to do with acquiring the disease of alcoholism.

Myth:

Alcohol sedates the feeling of anxiety and depression.

Fact:

Alcohol sedates your ability to feel the results of anxiety and depression and by itself is a major cause of the alcoholic-depressed individual. Anxiety and depression can be caused by drinking. Pharmacologically, alcohol, due to its effect on the central nervous system, can lead to a chronic anxiety depressive state.

Myth:

One or two beers won't hurt you, or switch to beer.

Fact:

Ten ounces of beer or three or four ounces of wine or one and one-half ounces of eighty proof whiskey are all equal in alcoholic content.

Myth:

One or two drinks don't affect me.

Fact:

You have learned to control your functions while under minor sedation. There is no way you can consume a sedative without it acting as a sedative.

Myth:

A few drinks won't hurt you.

Fact:

The American Medical Association, in a recent article, released information as a result of their research stating: "Any form of regular consumption of alcoholic beverages reduces life expectancy. The degree of such reduction depends on the consistency of the consumption."

Myth:

The alcoholic is a homeless individual with no visible means of support and makes no contribution to society, but must be supported by society.

Fact:

Only five percent of our alcoholics fit this category. The other ninety-five percent are your neighbors, your professional workers, your tradesmen and the people you meet in your normal daily living.

Myth:

There is a difference between the social drinker, the heavy drinker and the alcoholic.

Fact:

They are all drinking ethyl alcohol and the only difference that does exist is the amount being consumed. The effect of the amount being consumed on a given individual will vary in each individual and, therefore, no criteria as to amount can be established on a cause and effect basis.

Myth:

Alcohol gives me a high.

Fact:

Alcohol is a sedative and acts only as a sedative within the human system. It releases the inhibitions (controls) that would stop you from doing certain things and permits you to do them. This illusion is called a "high."

Although knowledge by itself will not stop alcoholism, there is no question in my mind that knowledge will at least stop those who have been enabling others to continue their addiction to a point where the disease becomes irreversible. These are not all the myths regarding alcohol, but then the list would be too long and we would have to include rubbing whiskey on a wart to get rid of the wart, having a drink of gin early in the morning to cleanse your kidneys (ad infinitum, or perhaps it should be ad nauseam).

COCAINE

Cocaine is an old drug that is now very popular. It is derived naturally from the leaf of the *Erythorxylon coca* plant, which was used in ancient rituals by the Incas. The first coca extract was isolated by Gaedcke in the nineteenth century, and the principal active ingredient was isolated by Niemann. Sigmund Freud used it on his patients for asthma, other drug addictions, as a stimulant and a local anesthetic, and even for digestive disorders, and became addicted to the drug himself. The Corsican chemist Angelo Mariani came up with a coca-containing elixir known as Vin Mariani, and administered this magic potion to H. G. Wells, Auguste Rodin, Pope Leo XIII, Thomas Edison, and Jules Verne. Cocaine was an original ingredient in earlier Coca-Cola drinks, but was removed from it in 1903. Today, as a recreational drug, it brings in billions of dollars to the black market.

Cocaine is a very powerful stimulant and affects the circulatory rate and the central nervous system. It increases muscular tension as well as having a direct sympathomimetic effect. It can serve as an anesthetic as well as a stimulant.

Cocaine can be taken in a number of fashions:

- *Smoking:* A less-pure form of cocaine (coca paste) gives a rapid onset high of short duration. To smoke free-base, the extract of cocaine is prepared with the use of a volatile solvent such as ether. This method has been known to set people's faces on fire. Richard Pryor got a chemical face-lift from free-basing.

- *Sniffing:* The white powder crystals are inhaled through the nose via a straw or a rolled up piece of paper. The drug is rapidly absorbed through the nasal mucosa for a rapid euphoria. With repeated nasal ingestion, the mucosa is severely damaged in regular users.

- *Intravenous:* The high peaks out in three to five minutes and the user is vulnerable to all the risks of intravenous drug abuse (hepatitis, AIDS, etc.).

- *Crack:* This is the most serious threat to society this drug presents. It can get a new victim on the way to addiction for less than ten bucks. Crack is a very pure form of cocaine that can be smoked or mixed with tobacco. Its effects are similar to intravenous cocaine ingestion. Due to the purity of the drug, it can have devastating effects.

The drive for cocaine is so strong that lab animals will forego food and water in lieu of it and actually starve to death.

The cocaine and crack problem has been described as one of the most frightening problems facing America today. Some studies have estimated that almost a third of all adults between twenty and forty years of age have tried cocaine.

With its great allure to pro athletes, all sports are engulfed with the drug. Addiction is such a problem in pro sports that many leagues now have drug-treatment programs.

The Killer of Athletes

The tragedy and loss of great athletes in their prime is typified by the deaths of Don Rodgers and Len Bias, who were both in their early twenties. In the same time frame, Willie Smith, a 1986 draft choice, was arrested on cocaine and weapons charges.

Len Bias had the world at his feet as the twenty-two-year-old number-one draft choice of the world champion Boston Celtics— his dream team. He was picked in the draft on Tuesday, and pronounced dead on Thursday at 8:50 A.M. The autopsy of Bias indicated he was not a chronic cocaine abuser—in fact, it may have been one of the only times he had tried the drug.

Rodgers was to be married the day following his bachelor party. He never did make it to the wedding.

With more than 6 million regular cocaine users (by National Institute on Drug Abuse [NIDA] estimates) and 45 metric tons of this killer white powder snorted or ingested each year, we have a serious problem. Total worldwide consumption was a mere 500 kg per year in the mid-1960s.

Cocaine-related emergency-room visits have increased by 500 percent in the last decade, and the number of deaths related to this drug has tripled, with more than seven hundred deaths reported by the NIDA in 1984. Reports have surfaced in the medical literature associating cocaine intoxication with numerous cardiovascular deaths in young people. It appears that cocaine interferes with the electrical system of the brain and heart, causing ventricular fibrillation (uncontrolled spasms and twitching at a rapid and irregular rate). If left uncontrolled, this can, and has, resulted in cardiac death.

Cocaine Treatments

Cocaine addicts are very difficult to cure, and the severity and variation of abuse may be wider than with other forms of drug abuse. Utilization may vary from the occasional recreational abuser to the heavy intravenous or free-base cocaine abuser. The latter are in some ways similar to the intravenous methamphetamine addicts of ten years earlier. The route of administration does not necessarily denote the level and severity of abuse. Most important, the patient must first be made aware of the addiction before treatment can begin.

There are three major areas of acute psychiatric complications with cocaine abuse:

1 Acute severe postuse depression
2 Dysphoric agitation
3 Psychotic symptoms

Warning Signs:

1 Severe disruption of sleep cycles; difficulty sleeping
2 Nightmares
3 Worn-out physical appearance
4 Nerves on edge and jittery
5 Concomitant use of barbiturates to aid sleeping difficulties
6 Rapid addiction phase and endurance to medication with escalations in dose

When the subject begins to "crash," depressive symptomology and suicidal ideation may occur, so the patient should be watched carefully.

For cocaine patients, treatment is approached from three dimensions:

1 Supportive
2 Behavioral
3 Psychodynamic

Supportive treatment is where an attempt is made to separate the abuser from his or her drug source. Psychotherapy sessions, exercise therapy, and self-control strategies are employed. The patient should be encouraged to be in contact with friends who are not drug users, and any contact with drug-abusing partners or dealers is forbidden. All mood-altering drugs should be stopped. The organization Cocaine Anonymous, similar in structure to AA (Alcoholics Anonymous), should be contacted.

Behavioral treatment is where an attempt is made to make the patient aware of just how destructive his or her habit is. Pressure from family, friends, and the law contribute to engaging the subject in a treatment program. Drug detection via urinalysis has become commonplace in industry as well as in the sporting world. If there is great risk of financial and career penalties, the individual may seek rehabilitation more quickly.

Psychodynamic treatment involves exploring aspects of the patient's life that may have inclined him or her toward drug abuse.

A combination of all three approaches must be employed simultaneously for a comprehensive medical program. If psychotic symptoms or depression continue for more than one to three days post crash, inpatient care may be required.

Washton and others have summarized reasons for hospitalization:

1 Chronic free-base or intravenous use, because such use is usually out of control
2 Concurrent dependence on alcohol or other drugs
3 Psychiatric or medical problems of a serious nature
4 Psychosocial impairment of a severe nature
5 Lack of motivation
6 Lack of family or social supports
7 Repeated outpatient failures

Cocaine Hot line: 1-800-COCAINE
Drug Hot line: 1-800-662-HELP

CHAPTER VI

■

DRUG-DETECTION TECHNIQUES

Interest in drug-testing began in the late 1950s and early 1960s when drug abuse by athletes became public knowledge. Belgium and France passed antidoping laws in 1965. Although all international federations now outlaw doping, the International Cycling Federation was the first to employ it. A medical committee under the direction of chairman Prince de Merode of Belgium was established by the International Olympic Committee (IOC) in 1967. Doping is the primary concern of the committee.

In 1965, Dr. Beckett introduced sensitive gas chromatography test procedures. Dr. Brooks developed Radioimmunoassays (RIA), making steroid testing a reality. There was IOC testing at the 1968 games, but a comprehensive testing program was not employed until the 1972 games in Munich under Dr. Manfred Donike. Since that time, gas chromatographs and mass spectrometers have been required for IOC testing. Anabolic steroids were added to the list at the 1976 Montreal Olympics. During the 1984 Olympics in Los Angeles, the UCLA lab, under the direction of Dr. Don Catlin, performed steroid testing on all fifteen hundred samples.

HOW LONG DO DRUGS STAY IN THE SYSTEM?

Drug detection has become very sophisticated. Injectable oil-based steroids have been detected up to nine months after administration, and in rare cases even up to a year. Oral steroid medications remain detectable for two to four weeks or more. This all depends on the type of drugs, combinations taken, for how long, by what route, and, of course, the body's metabolic rate and the amount stored in the adipose tissue.

Drugs such as marijuana can with chronic use remain in

the system for six weeks or more. Amphetamines, and in some cases cocaine, can have a short half-life. Growth hormone has a very short half-life, so it is at this time still undetectable, but due to the antibody formation occurring with synthetic HGH, a test may be in the wings.

Some athletes attempt to use catheters to take urine from one person and, using a tube, insert it up the urethra of another person. These people should be aware that urine is individually specific, like a fingerprint. In addition, the body is always producing new urine, so a mixing will occur with catheterized urine.

When I was running the drug-testing for the Mr. Universe contest in Japan, I was called in to look at a sample. It was not warm like urine, very clear, and had oil droplets floating at the surface. I had the athlete disrobe and pulled out a suntan-lotion bottle he had stuck between his legs. He would squeeze his legs together to force the urine out of the bottle.

Another interesting story tells of a male athlete who cathetered urine from his girlfriend into himself. The test officials called him in and told him not only was he really a woman, but he was also pregnant—and disqualified!

Another technique is to take a lot of diuretics to dilute the sample, but if the sample is too dilute (specific gravity less than 1.005), the athlete must provide another sample. There is no way of beating the test—you must simply be off the drugs for a long enough period of time.

I am very much in favor of drug-testing because it is an excellent deterrent. It is not a cure, but it is a first and vital step. But it must be performed by the strict protocols, and by IOC-level accredited labs. I have a great fear of individual schools and private industry using inferior and inaccurate home kits handled by untrained personnel, opening the system to error and abuse.

One story that sums up this problem actually happened to me. I was to lecture on drugs at a prominent southwestern sports school. Two weeks prior to my lecture, the school decided to perform their own drug-testing on their athletes. They used inexpensive home kits run by their athletic trainers, and came up with 2 percent cocaine use and 5 percent marijuana use among their student athletic body. They then proceeded to claim they had no drug problems at their school. When called by the local newspaper to comment, I could only state that this was unrealistic for a school that was rated by *Playboy* as one

of the top-ten party schools in the country and located on the
Mexican border—drug-traffic heaven. Their figures were better suited to a monastery. I proceeded to say they were no different from any other school, and that to perform improper
testing was not correctly addressing the problem.

Well, when this hit the papers the school officials were very
angry: "We don't need his kind of expertise here!" My seminar
canceled, I was amused to read in the newspaper the following week that one of the biggest cocaine busts in history (hundreds of millions of dollars' worth) occurred one block from the
school the same week I was to have lectured.

INSTRUMENTATION

Anabolic steroids are processed by the body in the same manner as other drugs. The body modifies the chemical structure of
the steroid molecule to make it more soluble in water. This
means that anabolic steroids and their metabolites are present
in the urine. The most common metabolic change of steroid
molecules is the formation of a conjugate with glucuronic acid.
The first step in the analysis of steroids in urine is to break up
the conjugate to extract the original steroid molecule. This is
done by treating the urine with a chemical called beta-
glucuronidase.

Gas chromatography-mass spectrometry (GC-MS) does the
basic screening for stimulants and narcotic analgesics and requires confirmation on the GC-MS. Small amounts of a sample
are measured into four test tubes, each portion of which under-
goes a specific chemical workup so that it will be pure enough
to be injected into the GC or GC-MS.

The chemical workup for the anabolic steroids is as follows:
The urine is dripped slowly through a resin, which catches the
steroids but allows the water, salt, and other chemicals to pass
through and be discarded. Then the steroids are chemically
removed from the resin. The procedure includes drying, adding
a buffer, and shaking. The result is then centrifuged, becoming
a two-layered liquid. The top clear layer includes free steroids
and is ready for the final steps, but the bottom layer contains
steroid conjugates and needs to be processed further to free the
steroids. The liquid that contains free steroids is evaporated to
dryness. At this point only a thin film is visible at the bottom of
the test tube. This is the evaporation procedure. The steroid

molecules are not yet suitable for the gas chromatography. They must first be reacted with chemicals called "derivatizing reagents" to change their molecular structure to one that is suitable for gas chromatography. Only then is one microliter of the resulting solution injected into the GC-MS.

As long as the known standards are treated the same way as the unknown samples, there are no problems using derivatizing reagents. This small amount of material goes through a 25-meter-long tube in the GC-MS called the capillary column, which is heated to over 200 degrees Celsius. The molecules pass through in an order determined by their volatility. The long glass tube is coated with a chemical. Helium carrier gas constantly flows through the tube, where the temperature is carefully controlled. The mass spectrometer (MS) is attached to the end of the gas chromatograph column.

Next, the sample passes into the MS, where an electron gun splits each molecule into fragments which are propelled into a detector to measure their mass-to-charge ratio. Each fragment has a characteristic-retention time, that is, the length of time it takes to pass through the column. The detector picks them up and the printout comes out of the GC.

The final result is a specific graph which can be compared with the graph readouts of known substances. After these fragments are measured and counted by the mass spectrometer, the results are calculated and tabulated by a computer. The result is analogous to a fingerprint; each substance fragments in a similar manner and can be compared with the graph of the known substance.

The GC-MS is calibrated by taking a pure steroid and adding it to urine that is steroid-free. This is then run through the extraction and derivatizing process. The standard is then injected into the GC-MS, and the time required to pass through the column and the fragmentation pattern are recorded. Urine from a suspected steroid user is processed in an identical fashion and injected into the GC-MS. If it peaks at the same time and with the same fragmentation pattern as the standard, the steroid is confirmed to be present. If it doesn't peak at the same time with the right fragmentation pattern the sample is negative.

There is some degree of subjective evaluation of the sample by the reviewing scientist, to determine if there have been attempts at "masking" or if various combinations of drugs have been employed to "fool" the test. In addition, the ratio of epi-testosterone to testosterone is evaluated, and if it is greater than 1 to 6, the athlete is disqualified.

To achieve greater sensitivity, a technique called Selective Ion Monitoring (SIM) may be used. With this method, only three or four larger fragments that are present in the pattern of the steroid of interest are looked for. If the fragments are present at the right time, the steroid is present. This technique is at least ten times more sensitive than scanning the whole fragment pattern.

IOC DRUG-TESTING LABS (NORTH AMERICA)

Dr. Donald Catlin
UCLA School of Medicine
CH S-23-278
Los Angeles, CA 90024
213-825-2789

Dr. Robert Voy
U.S. Olympic Training Center
1750 East Boulder Street
Colorado Springs, CO 80909
United States Olympic
Comittee Drug Hotline
1 800-233-0393

Dr. John Barnziger
Indiana University School
of Medicine
Riley Hospital
Room A 20
Indianapolis, IN 46223
317-274-4345

Canadian Olympic Lab
245 Hymus
Pontclaire, Quebec
Canada 89 R I G6
514-630-880

PROCEDURES FOR DRUG-TESTING

Due to the abuse of androgenic-anabolic steroids and associated compounds as well as other banned substances, drug-testing is instituted at specified competitions.

The following is an example of drug-collection procedures for the International Federation of Body Builders and may be used as a guideline for collection of samples.

Points

1 Athletes will be made aware that testing will take place prior to the competition. They will sign in (time, place, and date) on test-

verification forms, which should include the athlete's name, address, phone number, medical and drug history, and any other pertinent information.

2 Athletes will report to the test station at the determined times.

3 Any athlete refusing to be tested for said competition will not be allowed to compete.

4 It is suggested the athlete wear shorts and pullover shirt for ease of disrobing. Only authorized personnel may be at the test station.

5 Any attempt by an athlete to conceal urine or drug samples or ampules vaginally, rectally, or on their person is grounds for immediate disqualification and disciplinary action by the IFBB.

6 The athlete will be accompanied into the lavatory by a guard or official of the same sex and will be observed throughout the voiding process. Any coach, aide, or assistant who is shown to have aided or abetted any offense is also subject to disciplinary action.

7 A sterile, disposable plastic beaker will be used to catch the midstream urine catch. The athlete will pick his own beaker for voiding, and break the plastic seal on it, after which the sample will be presented to the test officials who, in the presence of the athlete, will split the sample into two (2) portions, which will then be distributed into two (2) sterile specimen bottles. The A and B specimen bottles will be selected by the athlete, and they will break the seals on them. The glass bottles for final sample collection should have the athlete's name scratched into the glass or a label adhered to it (with the athlete's name printed and signed by the competitor). Both the A and B samples will then be sealed within separate *Envopak* zipper-locked transport cases, along with verification forms. (The *Envopak* system was created by scientists in Great Britain to prevent tampering. These are individual carrying cases that enclose and protect the samples.) These will be locked, and special coded nonrepeating numbered seals will be affixed to prevent tampering. The seal must be broken for the *Envopak* to be opened. The athlete will place his signature on both bottle labels, and verification forms will be placed in each *Envopak*. Both samples (A and B) will then be placed in a special transport case for collected-samples transport and not examined until the samples are in the laboratory for testing. The athlete will sign verification forms attesting to the fact that there were no irregularities in the collection process. Any irregularities should be recorded at that time. A urine pH and specific gravity test [must be greater than 1.005] check may be provided by the testing team. If the pH of the urine in the collection beaker is alkaline, the athlete will be detained until a strongly acidic specimen is provided. The athlete will be photographed, and this will go on permanent record with verification materials.

8 Only the A sample will be tested. Both the A and B bottles will

remain on refrigerated file should there be athlete disputes.

9 If there is a positive test, the sample will be reverified again from the A sample. The sealed B sample will remain untouched and on file. If an athlete wishes to dispute the results, he may at his own expense have the sample retested in his presence. If he wishes another laboratory to perform the test on the B sample, he will bear all costs of chain-of-custody transport and testing procedures.

   It is requested that the athlete be present when the sample is retested, although he may send a surrogate representative. It is necessary that the testing be performed on state-of-the-art gas chromatographs and mass spectrometers at a certified International Olympic Committee laboratory.

10 Comments on chain of custody:

A The athlete will be observed throughout the voiding process.

B An official will be stationed at the sample testing area at all times. No one is to enter the restricted area without official permission from the testing team.

C No one but the collecting team is to touch sample collections without express permission.

D Athletes who attempt to provide dilute samples by taking diuretic medications will be required to repeat the voiding process until an acceptably concentrated sample is provided. Specific gravity of the sample may be tested at the test site and should not exceed 1.005. An acceptable sample must be provided prior to the close of collection time period. Athletes are to drink fluids only from sealed containers to aid the voiding process.

E It is requested that a 100 ml sample be provided.

F The samples will be transported by drug-testing-team personnel or special courier to the laboratory testing site within a twenty-four-hour period following collection.

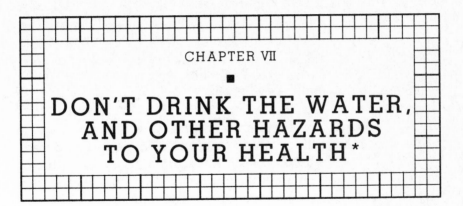

CHAPTER VII

■

DON'T DRINK THE WATER, AND OTHER HAZARDS TO YOUR HEALTH*

One man's meat is another man's poison.
—Anonymous

In today's increasingly complex world, the athlete must be ever alert to protect his or her body, which took such effort to develop. The air is often not safe to breathe and the water not safe to drink, but the picture is not quite as bleak as it seems. There are many things you can do to protect yourself, and knowing where the dangers lie is the first step.

ALUMINUM TOXICITY

There have long been suspicions regarding the link between certain pollutants and age-related diseases. One substance under suspicion is common aluminum, which occurs in medications as a binding agent, as the active ingredient in underarm antiperspirants, and even in the foods we eat. Many researchers now believe that a good deal of the mental disorders seen in the elderly can be linked to the use of products containing aluminum.

For years it was believed that the aluminum in deodorants, soda cans, and cooking utensils was not absorbed by the body. This has proved to be an expensive error. Today, chronic excess-aluminum absorption has been linked to Alzheimer's disease. Since 1965, researchers have reported that the destruction of neurons in the brain leads to shriveled tangles of cells, all with molecules of aluminum at their core.

Patients on long-term dialysis (where their blood is washed

*The material on pages 93–97 was contributed by Dr. Ronald Klatz.

by fluids high in aluminum content) run a significantly increased risk of contracting Alzheimer's disease. Today we know that the danger is not just restricted to kidney patients.

Aluminum is found in household baking powder, nondairy creamers, and even processed cheese (one slice of individually wrapped cheese could contain as much as 50 mg of aluminum). Cookware has come under attack as well. The key factor to bear in mind is that nothing acidic or alkaline (coffee or tea, for example) should be prepared in aluminum. A good rule of thumb is don't use aluminum to prepare anything that leaves marks, stains, or appears to corrode the aluminum. The safest solution obviously is not to use aluminum cookware at all.

It therefore seems prudent for the longevity-minded athlete to avoid excess aluminum by refraining from the use of aluminum pots, pans, and other cooking utensils. Avoid aluminum-canned foods and drinks (especially soda, which is acidic and will leach greater amounts of aluminum from the walls of cans), antiperspirants, antacids containing aluminum, and aspirin products (many use aluminum as a binder). In order to enjoy top physical and mental performance into your sixth decade and beyond, your best line of defense is to *read all labels carefully before you make a purchase.*

The good news is that new research indicates that supplemental calcium and fluoride in the diet can chelate, or bind, the aluminum in the intestine to prevent its absorption.

WATER POLLUTION

Almost 70 percent of the human body is composed of water. The cells of our bodies thrive in an ocean of living vital fluids. Perhaps this is why pollution of our nation's water seems so insidious. Despite stringent EPA guidelines, mostly unenforced and unmonitored thanks to a 31 percent cut in the clean-water program budget after the 99th Congress failed to pass the Clean Water Act of 1986 over President Reagan's veto, our nation's water supply is of an increasingly inferior quality.

Ten billion gallons of sewage, radioactive waste, and toxic chemicals are deposited deep into the earth each year. Four hundred million pounds of industrial toxic waste enter the nation's waterways annually. A 1982 report by the EPA found that 45 percent of all public water systems were contaminated with organic chemicals, some of which are known carcinogens.

A 1986 report from the Centers for Disease Control in At-
lanta indicates that more than four thousand reported cases of
human maladies are linked directly with contaminated water
in the United States each year. With so many toxins showing
their harmful results only after a prolonged period of time, this
is clearly just the tip of the iceberg.

It is important to note that some individuals are more susceptible than others to the effects of toxins in the water. Children, due to their lower body weight, growing body organs,
and faster respiratory rate, are at a higher risk, as are those
with certain genetic factors or weaker body constitutions,
smokers, and dieters. In general, it may be advisable for anyone who is concerned about these hazards to drink only distilled or bottled water, or tap water that has been run through
an activated charcoal filter.

WHAT'S IN THE WATER ANYWAY?

Arsenic

Improperly disposed-of chemicals in groundwater carry this
toxin into the water system. Large quantities can cause lung
cancer, skin cancer, brain damage, liver and kidney disease,
and birth defects.

Asbestos

Asbestos is not limited to insulation and fireproofing in old
buildings. Asbestos dust from landfills, particles from brake lin-
ings, and even parts of car tires are washed away from the
roads and end up in the water system. Asbestos has been
shown to cause lung cancer and has been banned from construction.

DDT

Although this pesticide was banned in 1972, the residues of this
long-lasting chemical are still prevalent in agricultural waters.
These toxins accumulate in body tissue, where they can cause
liver damage, and have recently been linked to cancer. Trace
levels of DDT can still be found today in human breast milk,
and even in ice samples from Antarctica.

Dioxin

Dioxin is a defoliant that was used in the manufacture of Agent Orange in Vietnam. It is found in rural areas around farmland that has been sprayed with herbicides containing the chemical. Dioxin is extremely toxic even at low levels, and extremely persistent in the environment.

Mercury

Although a naturally occurring substance, mercury when entering the water system becomes a hazard to your health. It is converted to methyl mercury by microorganisms. Mercury is particularly dangerous because its toxicity levels increase as it is passed along the food chain. Fish, which pass this substance on to man, have a much higher level of concentration than the water. The resulting diseases from mercury have ranged from brain damage to birth defects and, in some cases, death.

Nitrates

We thought that if we avoided processed meats, bacon, and other foods containing nitrates, we were safe. Unfortunately this is not true: We can obtain significant amounts of the carcinogen nitrosamine directly from our water supply.

PCBs (Polychlorinated Biphenyls)

This industrial compound is another substance that has been banned in the United States, but we are still feeling the damage. PCBs are still found in our fresh-water supplies, and are accumulated in the body producing symptoms ranging from chronic fatigue to birth defects and liver disease.

AIRBORNE ATTACK!

Secondhand Smoke

We all know the dangers of smoking, and that the effects can cut a productive life short. What we did not know until recently is that secondhand smoke, which comes from someone in your vicinity, has far greater health implications than actually smoking yourself! The estimates are that secondhand-smoke inhalation in closed-room situations such as offices or the smoking sections of bars or airplanes may be equivalent to smoking as much as three packs of cigarettes per day. Reports from the U.S. Surgeon General indicate that "sidestream smoke" can increase nonsmokers' risk of developing cancer by as much as 300 percent.

Radon

Radon is a naturally occurring odorless, colorless gas that has been found to be a killer. It is formed by the natural breakdown of radioactive substances in the earth, such as carbon and uranium, and is estimated to seep into approximately 15 percent of our nation's homes. Radon is itself radioactive and may account for thirty thousand deaths from lung cancer each year.

However, even if all four of your surrounding neighbors' homes are contaminated with radon, it does not necessarily mean that yours is. Presently, the only accurate method of determining if your home, workplace, health club, etc., is contaminated with radon gas is by the use of an air-sampling test kit (usually twenty-five dollars per test). A home need only be tested once.

■

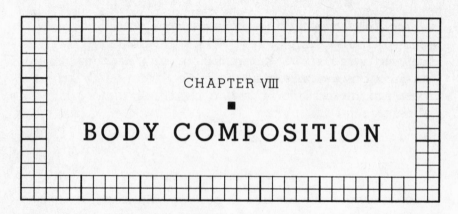

CHAPTER VIII

■

BODY COMPOSITION

Obviously, certain body types are better suited to certain sports than others; for example, a tall, lean person will make a better basketball player than a short, stocky one. The practice of visually evaluating athletes has evolved into a sophisticated science—anthropometrics—which is used in sports programs around the world. Anyone can see that a Porsche is faster than a pickup truck, and that the truck, though slower, is stronger. But you cannot see inside the body of an athlete to tell how fast he is or how much stamina he has.

Anthropometric measurements are genetically determined. They include weight, height, width, length, fat stores, lean body mass (that part of the body that is not body fat, i.e., nerve sheaths, the brain, cell membranes, and other vital lipids), and circumference of all body segments. These measurements are used as an index to determine the body somatotype. The three basic somatotypes are: endomorph—burly or stocky people; mesomorph—muscular or sinewy people; and ectomorph—lean or skinny people. Endomorphy refers to fatness or leanness, while ectomorphy has to do with the skeleton. Mesomorphy refers to the degree of muscularity.

To somatotype an individual, he or she is given a score of 1 to 6 in relation to the body types described. Of course, other factors also count in determining athletic ability. Capacity of the heart and lungs, coordination—the consideration of all these qualities has evolved into the science of kinanthropometry.

In the early and mid 1960s, East Germany began to select swimmers scientifically. Czechoslovakia did the same for tennis players, and Rumania for gymnasts. In 1968, East Germany came away with nine gold medals in the Olympics, even though it was the first time it had competed as an independent country. In the 1976 Olympics it won 47 gold medals—an astonishing achievement for a small country. When a virtually unknown East German runner beat America's champion Frank Shorter in the marathon, the U.S. began to realize it could no longer depend on unguided athletic selection.

Now athletes undergo a number of evaluation procedures. One of the most important is determining percentage of body fat. In terms of athletics, extra fat decreases speed and jumping height, and lowers endurance.

Men and women differ with regard to fat distribution. Women tend to have larger skinfolds in the limbs, while men have more skinfold fat at the chest, axilla (armpit), and suprailium (upper hip). Men tend to accumulate fat around the waist, while women, in the thighs and the buttocks.

Usually suggested as healthy parameters are 10 to 22 percent body fat for men, and for women, 20 to 33 percent. Athletes, however, tend toward considerably lower fat ratios—in the 10 to 15 percent range. Competitive body builders, who must have low body fat in order to display muscular definition, may have as low as 4 percent, as do some long-distance runners and triathletes.

In the past, body fat was measured using height-to-weight ratios. However these have not been found to be very accurate. Currently, three methods are generally in use: hydrostatic weighting, in which the subject is weighed and then lowered into a tank of water—after noting how much water is displaced, a formula is used to calibrate body fat; measuring skinfold thicknesses using a caliper that clamps onto the skin—the results are then used in conjunction with special charts; and computerized devices that utilize ultrasound (sound waves) and electrical impedance (electric currents), which determines not only body fat but also water content.

In order to measure skinfold thickness a Lange (Cambridge Scientific Instruments, Cambridge, Maryland) or other caliper may be utilized. There are less expensive plastic calipers, but they may yield somewhat less accurate measurements.

Here are the regions to measure:

1. Chest: a diagonal fold taken half the distance between the anterior axillary line and nipple for men, and one-third the distance from the anterior axillary line to the nipple for women.

2. Axilla: a vertical fold on the mid-axillary line at the level of the xiphoid process of the sternum.
3. Triceps: a vertical fold on the posterior midline of the upper arm (over the triceps muscle), halfway between the acromion and olecranon processes. The elbow should be extended and relaxed.
4. Subscapular: a fold taken on a diagonal line coming from the vertebral border to 1 to 2 cm from the inferior angle of the scapula.
5. Abdominal: a vertical fold taken at a lateral distance of approximately 2 cm from the umbilicus.
6. Suprailium: a diagonal fold above the crest of the ilium at the spot where an imaginary line would come down from the anterior axillary line. Many recommend that the measure be taken more laterally at the anterior axillary line.
7. Thigh: a vertical fold on the anterior aspect of the thigh midway between hip and knee joints.

To measure skinfold thickness, grasp the skinfold firmly by the index finger and thumb. Hold the caliper perpendicular to the fold at about 1 cm (1/4 in.) from the thumb and forefinger. Then release the caliper grip so that full tension is exerted on the skinfold. Use the pads at the tip of the thumb and finger to grasp the skinfold. The tester should not have long nails—they may scratch the skin. The dial should be read to the nearest 0.5 mm 1 to 2 seconds after the grip has been released. Measurements should be taken several times.

If measurements begin to decrease the fat may be getting compressed. Do not take measurements after exercise or when skin is hot or sweaty. It is best to have the skin dry. The tester may have to perform this technique on 50 to 100 subjects before he feels truly confident with it.

BODY COMPOSITION ANALYZERS

There are new computerized wonder devices that use either electrical impedance or ultrasound to measure body fat. Much controversy surrounds these devices. Just as the charts giving ideal body weight may be irrelevant to certain physiques, so too do these devices have computation problems. Dr. Mike Pollock, a noted researcher in this field, notes that "you can have two people with the same height and weight, but with a wide difference of 15% to 30% fat."

The *Physician and Sportsmedicine* has reported on two types of Bioelectrical impedance Analyzers (BIA): The portable

BIA, and the 17-foot-long, $60,000 total body electrical conductivity unit (TOBEC). Although the BIA and TOBEC are based on the same principle, they are as different as night and day.

The BIA consists of a small computer and an impedance analyzer packaged in a briefcase-sized case. The unit can either be plugged in or powered by batteries. To get a reading from BIA you attach two rubber-based ECG electrodes to the wrist and two to the ankle of the supine subject. Then a barely perceptible 800-μ charge at 50 KHz is introduced to measure the resistance of fat in the body. That value in ohms is then put into a formula (height squared divided by resistance) to get a breakdown of lean body mass and body fat.

With TOBEC, the person lies on a table that slides into a chamber. The chamber is wrapped by an electromagnetic coil, which induces an electromagnetic force. The person disturbs the electromagnetic field by passing through it; the size of the disturbance is proportional to the electrical conductivity of the individual. TOBEC takes 64 readings of lean-body-mass conductivity within a 10-second period (the BIA takes only 1 reading).

Percentage readouts can vary by as much as 30 percent when compared to skin-caliper measurements. The technology and accuracy for BIA units is ever-improving, although the degree to which the person is dehydrated or overhydrated may significantly affect the final readings.

RJL has been producing a portable body comp analyzer since 1981 which noninvasively measures and assesses total body water (TBW), lean body mass (LBM), and body fat.

The *Valhalla Scientific 1990A* is a Bio-resistance Body Composition Analyzer, and uses a low-leverl electrical signal frequency of 50 KHz which penetrates the body's deep tissues. It reads out fat body mass, lean body, body water, suggested optimum weight, and basal metabolism.

The *SomaTech*, uses ultrasound to determine body parameters. The *SomaTech Ultrasonic Bodyanalyzer* reveals body-fat percentage and weight, lean-body percentage and weight, total body water, total extracellular water, total intracellular water, body cell mass, body bones and mineral percentage, and a series of other measurements.

Valhalla Scientific
  9955 Mesa Rim Road
  San Diego, CA 92121
  619-457-5576

RJL Systems Inc.
  9930 Whittier
  Detroit, MI 48224
  313-881-2030

SomaTech
  17022 Montanero
  Carson, CA 90746
  213-637-6836

■

PART 2

CHAPTER IX

■

GUIDELINES FOR EQUIPMENT EVALUATION AND DEFINITIONS

Exercise machines are a relatively new development as a fitness and training aid—fifty years ago they were practically nonexistent. But these days the athlete is faced with a bewildering variety of such machines and the number increases each year.

Why bother with exercise machines at all? the purist might ask. If the ancient Greeks got along without them . . . ? But the truth is that exercise machines provide a number of very real benefits, especially for the serious athlete. Such machines as stationary bicycles and rowers allow the athlete to train comfortably and safely indoors when the weather outdoors is not good enough for regular training. Even more interesting are the newer machines for building strength. The design of these takes into account new discoveries in sports medicine and the development of new technologies to take advantage of them. Now, with these machines, it is possible to train in ways that were never before dreamed of.

Before delving too deeply into the new types of machines available today, it must be noted that advances have been made in training systems without machines, too. Everyone knows about "new" systems such as interval training. But more exotic developments are on the horizon. For example, plyometrics is a method of developing explosive power through exercises that require powerful muscular contractions which are in response to dynamic, rapid stretching or loading of the muscles. The word *plyometrics* is derived from the Greek word *pleythyein*, which means "to increase." The great Russian coach Yuri Veroshanski trained his jumpers with this principle because he believed that training designed to augment the athlete's ability to react aided in developing the neuromuscular system of the athlete.

The physiologic basis of plyometrics is the so called stretch reflex, which integrates both voluntary and involuntary processes. When a load is placed on them, muscles undergo a stretching phenomenon sort of like cocking back a spring, which then generates the swing and recoil. Stimuli via the muscle spindles to the spinal cord cause the muscles to contract strongly. Training the muscles to react explosively is helpful for those athletes who need to produce high speed or have the ability to change direction quickly.

All you need to begin your plyometric training is some jump boxes that can be constructed of plywood. The training involves jumping onto and off of the boxes quickly. The heights can be adjusted as you become accustomed to the movements so that you will be jumping up onto higher and higher levels. Medicine balls, sandbags, or weights can be used to increase the difficulty of the exercise, but remember to use caution: Any forceful bounding and jumping movements can cause serious injury.

Through the efforts of the High Technology Fitness Research Institute a series of data-evaluation mechanisms have been established to discern which of the new equipment is best for an individual's needs. All things are taken into account— service and dependability of the manufacturer are just as vital in the long run as the equipment itself.

Here are some of the things we look for, and things you may wish to take note of yourself (they are derived from the twenty-page checklist established by the Institute):

- On initial contact with the company, is there a toll-free number? How courteous is the person answering the phone? What is that person's position and status in the company? If the president answers the phone, this may indicate the size and manpower of the company.

- Just because a company is small does not mean they give inferior service. On the contrary, because they are smaller they may be more apt to please and to care about keeping your business. In fact, it is usually easier to have custom work performed by smaller companies.

- How much does the person answering the phone know? Are you referred quickly to the proper individual to have your questions answered, or placed forever on hold and repeatedly disconnected? We usually give a series of five calls before forming an opinion about this. There is always the possibility of catching a company on a bad day.

- How is the equipment shipped? If by truck, does the company have its own fleet or use a private independent line? Do the truckers have a working knowledge of how to move such machines? Some units are very large and heavy yet fragile. Always check to see if it can be delivered by a dealer. At least then you will have a contact person and a professional setting it all up.

- Note how equipment is packaged for shipment. Some common materials used to encase the units are wood frames and skids (flat wooden bases); Styrofoam; crushed paper; paper board (corrugated); metal frames with bolts; heavy nylon wraps and strips; plastic tape; rope; bubble plastic wrap; and blankets. A good method is to wrap the unit in Styrofoam or bubble plastic wrap, which is taped around the metal sections; this is all placed in a wood-framed box filled with Styrofoam or crushed paper, placed on wood skids and bolted down.

- Always check your shipment before signing for it. Once you have signed the trucker's sheet, broken parts and repairs can be a headache. Dealing with a problem after this point will determine the real quality of service the company provides.

- A local dealer is preferred, especially where assembly is required. Some units, although they appear simple in the showroom, can be hell on earth if assembly is unguided. If a dealer assembles it, note the procedure—should you move, you may have to do it yourself.

- Check for missing parts or damaged sections. A good company will replace parts rapidly; however, some equipment is manufactured overseas, and waiting for parts can be a nightmare.

- What type of metal is used in the frame? Is it square or circular? Some mechanics feel that square is more stable. Inspect the ends to determine the thickness of the metal. How are the pieces bolted or welded together? Note connecting joints and metal unions. Often poor tooling and loose-fitting parts are covered over with a sloppy, heavy weld. This can wear down and break under continued torsion. Metal heats up as it is used, and can eventually snap if stressed enough.

- Note the covering materials on the benches and accessories. A strong Naugahyde is recommended rather than thin plastic coverings. Poor-quality vinyl coverings can tear and split. A high-density foam cushion is preferred over soft break-apart foam. Foam will wear out where you position yourself if not of sufficient density.

- Check out the pulley system in each section of the machine. Any grinding or catching is a bad sign.

- Chroming (the silver gloss metallic look) is very popular. Ask if they do their chroming in-house or have it shipped out. Find out which process they use, and look at demo models to see if chrome is chipping off. You do not want chrome chips to get into your eyes.

- On painted surfaces many companies are now using electrostatic processes, in which an electric charge fuses the paint and metal together. This tends to hold up better than just spray-painting it on. Make sure they follow it up by baking the metal sections in the heat-drying units. Hand-painted sections are not preferred.

- Look for rusting potential and sharp edges. Sometimes the insides of holes are not properly filed or drilled out, and clumps of sharp metal remain. This is not only dangerous but may also make proper assembly of nuts and bolts difficult.

- Take note of warning decals and signs. What was once the exception is now a common sight on most units sold today. These warning instructions are there for your safety, so be aware of and obey them.

- Review instruction manuals and information sheets. All units should be accompanied by detailed parts information and explanations. It is a plus if follow-up educational seminars are held by the manufacturer for consumers to attend.

BIOMECHANIC EVALUATIONS OF EQUIPMENT

- How adaptable is the unit to the individual's body type? Are there height, torso-width, and body-weight adjustments for different body frames? Can the resistance or weight stacks be easily reached by the user in the exercise position? Can it adapt to extremity length and biomechanics? (Many units are in a fixed mode and force the user to adapt to the machine, even to the point of discomfort.)

- Are the electronics and computer microprocessor components "user friendly"? Some machines, although exceptional in design and graphics, are just too complicated to use.

- Placement of the unit is very important. One should know in advance the total floor space available and where each unit will go. Floor-strength supports are very important. Typical institutional buildings can support 150–250 pounds per square foot. Some apartments may be limited to under 100 pounds per square foot of static (nonmoving) poundage. Square footage is figured by taking the total floor space that would be used and dividing it by the weight of the machine. For instance, if you have a multiexercise unit that is 4 feet long by 3 feet wide, it will take up 12 feet of floor space. If the unit weighs 1,000 pounds, that is 83.3 pounds per square foot (1,000 divided by 12). If you are concerned, attempt to place the unit near support beams or at the wall edges of the room for extra support.

TERMINOLOGY OVERVIEW

Work: the product of force times the distance through which the force acts: $W = F \times D$ (work equals force times distance).

Power: the work performed per unit of time: $P = F \times D/T$ (power equals force times distance/time).

Watt: a measure of the power involving a known force, time frame, and distance. One watt equals 6.12 kg per minute. Cardiorespiratory response is monitored in association with power outputs to determine aerobic fitness.

Calorie (C): the measure used to express energy expenditure associated with physical activity. By definition it is the amount of heat necessary to raise the temperature of 1 kg (liter) of water 1 degree C. It is also known as a kilocalorie.

VO_2 max: the maximum amount of oxygen that can be transported to the body tissues from the lungs. This provides a means by which one can assess a person's capacity for aerobic-energy transfer and performance. VO_2 max is also known as maximal oxygen uptake, or maximal aerobic power, and can be used to determine a person's level of physical fitness.

The limiting factor in sports performance is how much oxygen one's system can effectively utilize. This depends on a number of physiologic factors:

1 The movement (ventilation) of air in and out
2 The movement (diffusion) of oxygen from the lungs to the blood
3 The blood taking up the oxygen, which in some ways depends on the amount of hemoglobin in the blood
4 The heart pumping the blood
5 The delivery of blood to the muscles via the arteries, capillaries, and arterioles
6 The cell's ability to utilize the oxygen in the blood

METS: In order to get the maximum benefit out of training, the duration and intensity of the workout must achieve a certain level. To quantify the difficulty of a work effort, there is a ratio determined by the amount of energy required for the task in relation to the resting basal metabolic rate (basal living energy requirements):

Moderate work—the intensity of a task that elicits an oxygen consumption (or energy expenditure) of up to three times the resting basal metabolic rate

Hard work—categorizd as that requiring three to eight times the resting metabolism

Maximal work—that degree of intense work that requires a metabolic rate that is nine times or greater above the resting basal rate

The term *MET* is used to define some multiple of the basal resting rate. A MET is equal to 3.5 ml of oxygen per kg of body weight per minute. If a certain physical challenge is 5 METS, this would mean it requires 5 times the energy of basal metabolism. The MET is individualized in that it takes the person's body weight into account. A bigger man will use more energy to perform a task than a smaller one. He has a greater load to carry.

Kilogram-meter: a measure of work involving a known force and distance. As an example, if one were to lift 50 pounds to a height of 2 meters, that would equal 50 kg × 2 m, or 100 kg-m, of work.

Muscular strength: defined as the amount of force that a specific muscle at a specific joint angle can exert in the isometric mode. An isometric force is exerted against an immovable resistance. The forces of muscular strength can be measured in a number of ways. Some methods of quantification are free-weight lifting, cable tensiometry, and hydraulic readout gauges.

Muscular endurance: defined as the ability of a muscle to contract continuously and/or repeatedly against a resistance while moving through a full range of motion. The more movements or repetitions made, the greater the muscular endurance indicated. The endurance factors are dependent on the body's ability to deliver energy to a working muscle.

Muscular power: the ability to use strength dynamically, for instance by exerting strength against resistance. The level of muscular power is determined by the number of muscle fibers, the size of the fibers, the recruitment ability of the fibers, the amount of energy resources available, the rate at which the resources can be converted to utilizable energy forms, and the ratio of slow-twitch to fast-twitch muscle fibers.

Torque: that which produces torsion or rotation. Muscular power is dependent on torque.

Flexibility: the ability of a muscle to stretch and relax, thus allowing proper joint motion/action. There are two paired muscle groups at various regions of the body. These serve as antagonist (opposing) and agonist (teamed-up, helper) muscles. One group shortens (flexes, tightens) while the other lengthens, thereby making joint motion possible. This is why it is so critical to train muscles to be balanced.

Some basic terms of muscle movement are:

Concentric contraction—the muscle is flexed and contracted. The muscle-contraction force overcomes resistance and the muscle shortens.

Eccentric contraction—the muscle is fully extended. Resistance overcomes the muscle-contraction force and the muscle lengthens.

Static—in the fully contracted flexed muscle state, the joint can move no farther.

Negatives—a form of eccentric contraction where a group of muscles is forced to contract continuously while attempting to prevent a weight or force from moving in the direction of gravity.

TYPES OF MUSCLE-TRAINING SYSTEMS
Isometric Contractions

These occur when a resistance is equal to or greater than the force the muscle is exerting upon it. As a result there is no movement. *Iso* means same and *metric* means measure or length—together they mean *same length.* The muscle contracts but remains the same length. This form of a static contraction involves no change in joint motion. There is no movement, for the resistance is too great, which gives 100 percent intensity at a specific joint angle. Since developing strength at just an isolated angle is not physiologically advantageous in sports, this is not the ideal form of training.

Isotonic Contraction

Iso means same and *tonic* means tone—the muscle keeps the *same muscle tone*. This is the principle employed in most weight training. Here the muscles generate a greater force than the resistance, so that the limb goes through a range of motion. The factors that limit or regulate one's potential are:

1 Fatigue status
2 Summation of joint forces
3 Muscle-fiber recruitment
4 Injury factors
5 Changes in biomechanical leverage due to changes in joint angles
6 Type of muscle contraction (eccentric versus concentric)

This is why many exercise machines attempt to adapt to the biomechanical force curves of muscle action with variable-resistance devices as well as the addition of cams (conch-shaped pully holders that vary the forces on the pulley cable).

Isokinetic Contractions

These occur against a load that allows movement at a mechanically fixed rate of speed and offers resistance proportional to the muscle's dynamic tension-developing capacity at some optimal shortening speed and at every point in its shortening range. This provides for the controlled rate of shortening of muscle by a constant-rate-of-motion device. This form of training movement has some control over the motion that is being performed, and the control is present at every joint angle during a range of motion.

By integrating speed factors into muscle training, one can mimic the faster forces the muscles must perform against in sports. With conventional isotonic weight training, the limb speed rarely exceeds 60 degrees per second, while most functional movements in sports may require limb speeds in excess of 90 degrees per second, in some cases even exceeding 200 degrees per second.

Isokinetics have become a means of testing and rehabilitating muscles and joints. Some performance measurements include the maximum load lifted, the number of repetitions completed during submaximal isotonic exercises, and the time-based position changes and torques exerted during isokinetic exercises.

By virtue of the construction of the machines, they inhibit joint freedom of motion, for in order to test a specific joint system, it must be isolated from the rest of the body. The rotary characteristics of a joint can be described by the relative angular displacements of those body sections involved, the torques used to produce these movements, and the time during which these displacements occur. These factors can aid in the evaluation of muscular performance. The isokinetic device attempts to restrain the movement about the joint to a constant velocity. This does not truly correspond to actual sports motion. Biomechanical research has noted that actual body-segment motion consists primarily of about 82 to 84 percent acceleration and deceleration, with only 16 to 18 percent of the motion being isokinetic.

The forces of torque and lifting can be explained in relation to isokinetics with the following example. If you have an object on the floor, it is acted upon by two forces. One is its weight (W), and the other is the upward supporting force of the floor (F). This places the object in a state of static equilibrium, and it remains motionless because the sum of both of these forces gives a torque-force value sum of zero. As described by McIntyre and Sawhill, in order to lift this object and describe the motion, one must assume an axis of rotation at the center of the elbow joint and a system comprising the forearm plus hand and the object. The turning effects produced by torques generated by the user are opposed by the turning effects produced by the weight of the object and the weight of the forearm plus hand. Prior to the onset of movement, efforts by the user result in equivalent reductions in the torques produced by the user. This results in equivalent reductions in the torques produced by the upward supporting force, thereby maintaining the conditions for static equilibrium.

Rotary movement occurs when the torques produced by the user exceed the torques due to both the weight of the object and the weight of the forearm plus hand. This initial movement must be an acceleration. The magnitude of acceleration is determined by both the moment of inertia of the system and the difference between the counterclockwise torques and clockwise torques. (The moment of inertia of an object is the angular analogue to mass. It takes into consideration both the mass of the object and how that mass is distributed relative to the axis of rotation.) The system will travel at a constant angular velocity if the counterclockwise and clockwise torques are equal in magnitude (when the system is in a state of dynamic equilibrium).

Isometric equipment can only simulate static tasks. Isokinetic units monitor the efforts of the user against either an immovable resistance or a resistance traveling at a constant speed. The resulting movement patterns are not determined by the efforts of the user but by the preselected levels determined by the isokinetic machine.

Omnikinetics (developed by Hydra-Fitness) provides a self-accommodating, variable isokinetic overload resistance at any joint angle throughout a range of motion and at whatever speed the user is capable of generating.

■

CHAPTER X

THE PHYSIOLOGY OF TRINING SYSTEMS*

Strength, power, speed, and endurance may be developed and performance may be improved by any one or a combination of four training methods. These four methods are called, respectively, *Isometrics, Isotonics, Isokinetics,* and *Omnikinetics.* Each method offers a specific way in which the muscles are trained and fitness is achieved.

Before we review these four training methods, we should first review the physiological processes of muscle contraction, so that we can fully appreciate the differences between the four types of training.

Skeletal muscle is made up of muscle cells, usually called "fibers" instead of "cells" because of their threadlike appearance. These fibers also have different names for their component parts than those usually associated with cells. Thus, the plasma membrane is called the *sarcolemma,* the cytoplasm is called *sarcoplasm,* and the network of internal cellular structures is called the *sarcoplasmic reticulum* instead of the endoplasmic reticulum.

Muscle cells have some structures in common with other body cells, such as mitochondria and other "organelles." However, muscle fibers have structures that are peculiar to them, and which enable them to contract upon receiving a signal through the nervous system to do so.

Each muscle contains bundles of fibers called *myofibrils.* These myofibrils run lengthwise in the muscle fibers, and are made up of extremely fine "thick filaments" and "thin filaments." The thick filaments consist almost entirely of the protein molecule, *myosin.* Thin filaments consist of an intricate arrangement of the three protein compounds, *actin, tropomyosin,*

*The information on pages 115–135 has been reprinted with permission from Hydra-Fitness, Inc.

115

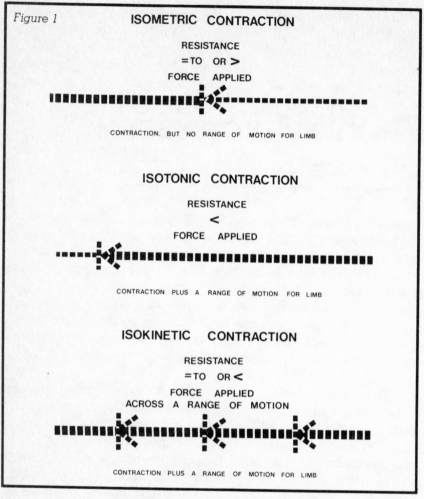

Figure 1

ISOMETRIC CONTRACTION

RESISTANCE
=TO OR >
FORCE APPLIED

CONTRACTION. BUT NO RANGE OF MOTION FOR LIMB

ISOTONIC CONTRACTION

RESISTANCE
<
FORCE APPLIED

CONTRACTION PLUS A RANGE OF MOTION FOR LIMB

ISOKINETIC CONTRACTION

RESISTANCE
=TO OR <
FORCE APPLIED
ACROSS A RANGE OF MOTION

CONTRACTION PLUS A RANGE OF MOTION FOR LIMB

THREE TYPES OF CONTRACTIONS

In the case of an isometric contraction, the resistance is equal to (or, if you are pushing against an immovable object, greater than) the force applied. There is no range of motion for the limb whose muscles are contracting. The joint angle is not a consideration.

In the case of an isotonic contraction, the resistance is less than the force applied, so that the limb whose muscles are contracting proceeds through a range of motion.

In the case of an isokinetic contraction, the resistance is equal to or (more accurately) only slightly less than the force being applied, so that the speed of the movement through a range of motion is regulated.

and troponin. It is the interaction among these four protein compounds that produces muscle contraction.

Thick and thin filaments within the myofibrils are arranged into *sarcomeres*, which are distinct units of thick and thin filaments, located between "Z" lines (a further myofibrillar division). The thick filaments have cross bridges between themselves and the thin filaments. The cross bridges are believed to point at 60-degree angles toward six thin filaments. When a nerve impulse triggers the process of contraction, myosin interacts with actin to bond the cross bridges to the thin filaments, thus sliding them toward the center of the sarcomere. This is the specific mechanism of muscle fiber contraction. Each sarcomere is a single contractile unit.

Each sarcomere also has cross striae (thus giving rise to the name, "striated muscle tissue"), and a structure called a *T System*, a system of tubules that extend transversely through the sarcoplasm. These tubules enter the sarcoplasm at the site of the "Z" lines. They open to the outside of the muscle fiber, since it is indentations in the sarcolemma that form the tubules of another system of tubules within muscle fibers. The T-System tubules and the sarcoplasmic reticulum sacs are sandwiched between each other to form what is called a *triad*.

Muscle fibers are basically of two types, fast-twitch or white fibers and slow-twitch or red fibers. These two types of fibers develop different tensions because they exhibit differences in contractile properties. Fast-twitch fibers are usually associated with explosive displays of strength (power) and with the anaerobic energy system. Slow-twitch fibers are usually associated with slower contraction times, sustained effort over a long period of time, and with the aerobic energy system.

Each fiber is connected to the central nervous system so that it can both transmit and receive nerve impulses. Data concerning loads and velocities are transmitted to the brain (or to the spinal cord in the case of a reflex arc) by proprioceptors in muscles, tendons and joints. These proprioceptors are of four main types, (a) *muscle spindles*, (b) *Golgi corpuscles*, (c) *Pacinian corpuscles*, and (d) *free nerve endings*. Information concerning potential loads and velocities is transmitted by the external senses of touch, sight, and hearing. When a person prepares to lift a weight or move a limb against a resistance, all of these information sources transmit the data necessary for a proper contractile response.

On the receiving end, muscle fibers are stimulated by the axon of a nerve cell called a *somatic neuron*. Each such neuron, plus the muscle fibers that it stimulates (or into which its axon terminates), is called a motor unit. The area where the motoneuron contacts the muscle fiber is called the *motor end plate* or *neuromotor junction.*

When nerve impulses reach the ends of the axons, tiny vesicles in the axon terminals release acetylcholine into the neuromotor junction. The acetylcholine diffuses across this microscopic space, comes in contact with the sarcolemma, and initiates muscle fiber contraction. The following is a step-by-step outline of what happens in the fiber as contraction occurs:

1 Upon reception of the nerve impulse, Ca + + is released from the sacs of sarcoplasmic reticulum into the sarcoplasm of the muscle fiber.
2 Ca + + is bound to the thin filaments' troponin molecules, and CA + + bound troponin then "activates" the thin filaments which allows the cross bridges on the thick filaments to attach to the thin filaments at a specific angle.
3 The cross bridges rotate to a different angle, thus sliding the thin filaments towards the center of the sarcomeres, thus causing a shortening of the myofibrils and the muscle fibers they constitute.

When these processes occur within the muscle fibers, and the fibers contract in sufficient number, the muscles which are composed of the many tiny fibers themselves shorten and the limb moves. If the limb is moving against a light resistance, fewer contracting fibers are needed to complete a successful movement than would be necessary if the resistance were greater. Proprioceptors as well as external stimuli provide the central nervous system with the data it needs to signal the contraction of a greater or a lesser number of fibers. This is true regardless of the type of resistance that the limb is trying to overcome, whether it be isometric, isotonic, isokinetic, or omnikinetic.

On one level, then, the strength of a contraction is dependent on at least four factors:

1 The initial length of the fibers involved in the contraction
2 The metabolic condition of the fibers in terms of available ATP and oxygen, calcium and troponin
3 The number of fibers that are activated during any given muscle contraction
4 The load that is being placed on the limb whose muscles are contracting

The amount of force generated within a muscle cell is dependent upon the number of cross bridges that are formed and attendant sliding of thin filaments that goes with the interaction of actin and myosin and the rotation of the cross bridges. The total amount of force generated by a muscle is a product both of the processes within individual fibers and the number of fibers that are recruited for the action.

Further, the speed with which an individual fiber shortens is dependent on the speed with which the actin and myosin filaments can slide by each other. If many cross bridges are formed, the speed of the contraction decreases. To generate maximum force, many cross bridges must be formed, and contraction will be slow. On the other hand, if rapid contraction is desired, few cross bridges must be formed and the force will be low.

Force and velocity, therefore, are related such that if force increases, velocity decreases; but as force decreases, velocity can be increased. However, it must be remembered that fast-twitch fibers are able to generate more force and higher velocities than slow-twitch fibers. Fast-twitch fibers contain more actin and myosin than slow-twitch fibers, and therefore are capable of forming more cross bridges per fiber.

The faster speeds of the fast-twitch fibers result from their ability to release and remove more $Ca + +$ at a faster rate, and from faster action of ATPase, which allows the cross bridges to make and break at a higher rate of speed.

Now, let us turn to a careful review of the four methods of training, to see the direct applications of our discussion of the physiology of muscle contraction.

THE ENERGY SYSTEMS—THEIR ROLE IN MUSCULAR WORK

For muscle contraction (shortening) to occur, ATP-CP must be combusted to produce free energy. There is a supply of ATP-CP located in the muscle cell where it is readily available. However, for muscular contraction to continue, the pool of ATP-CP in the muscle cell must be replenished. (Figure 2.)

The generation of ATP occurs in the muscle cell. Some nutrients (glycogen and fats) are stored in the muscle cell where they are readily available for conversion into ATP via the metabolic pathways. The circulatory system is responsible for bringing additional nutrients (glucose, F.F.A.) and oxygen to

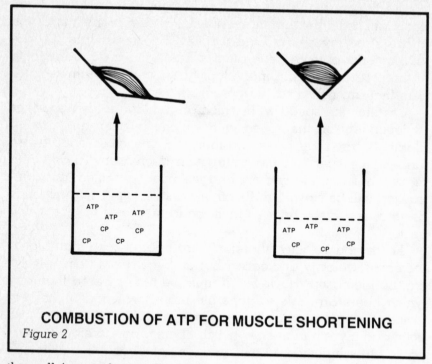

COMBUSTION OF ATP FOR MUSCLE SHORTENING
Figure 2

the cell (upon demand) plus removing the metabolic by-products (CO_2, lactic acid) from the cell to be excreted from the body or reconverted by the liver into metabolic fuels.

The generation of ATP, for muscular work, occurs through three pathways:

1 alactate—immediate
2 glycolysis (lactic acid)—short term
3 citric acid or Krebs cycle and oxidative phosphorylation (aerobic)—long term

Which pathway is used depends upon the intensity and duration of muscular work as well as the fitness level of the participant. Since Hydra-Fitness Omnikinetic training produces best results with superexertion or maximal intensity effort, the contributions of each energy system or pathway are determined by the duration of the effort and physical abilities of the participant.

From Figure 3 one can see that activities requiring an immediate source of ATP, the most powerful source of energy (alac-

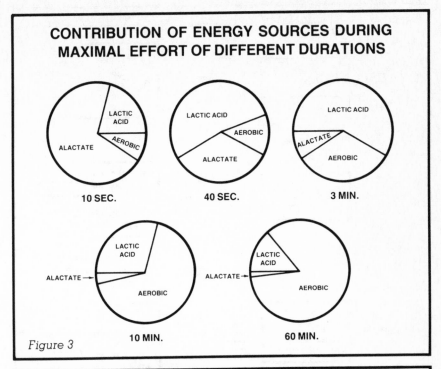

CONTRIBUTION OF ENERGY SOURCES DURING MAXIMAL EFFORT OF DIFFERENT DURATIONS

Figure 3

Figure 4 **Minute per Mile Pace For Various Distances**

(Based on Men's 1982 world record times)

Distance (meters)	Time (hours: min:sec)	Pace (min: Sec)
100	9.95	2:40.2
200	19.72	2:38.4
400	43.86	2:56.4
800	1:41.8	3:24.6
1500	3:31.36	3:46.8
3000	7:32.1	4:02.4
5000	13:00.42	4:10.8
10,000	27:22.4	4:24.0
20,000	57:24.2	4:37.2
30,000	1:29:18.2	4:47.4
Marathon	2:08.13	4:53.4
(42,168)		

tate) contributes the most, while for long term activities, the system with the greatest capacity (aerobic) contributes the most. The short term source of energy is the lactic acid system. Thus, the implication is that the three systems vary in their power and capacity. Figures 4 and 5 should better clarify these differences.

Since the times given in Figure 4 are world records the assumption is that maximal effort was given over all distances.

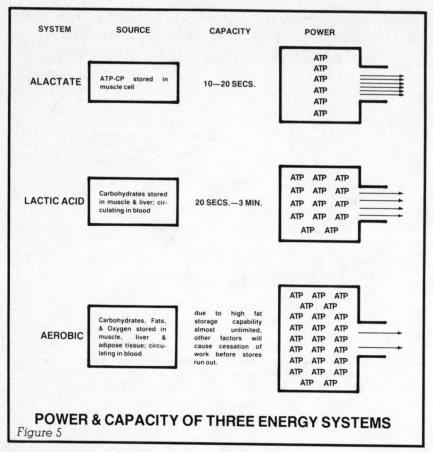

POWER & CAPACITY OF THREE ENERGY SYSTEMS
Figure 5

Thus, since the Alactate system has the greatest power but the least capacity it is easy to understand why the 100 meter and 200 meter distances can be run at basically the same pace (slight differences likely due to the time factor coming out of the blocks). The 400 meter distance cannot be run at the same pace as the 100 or 200 meter distances due to the longer duration (40 seconds compared to 10 and 20). Remember, the alactate source nearly exhausts its supply after 20 seconds and now the less powerful lactic acid system becomes the major supplier of ATP for continued muscular activity. As the distance covered, and therefore the duration, increases the pace becomes slower. Again this is due to the lactic acid system being less powerful than the alactate system and the aerobic system being less powerful than the lactic acid system. However, it is interesting to note that the difference in pace between 10,000 meters and the Marathon (more than four times the distance and duration) is not that great (29.4 sec. per mile). This is because both these distances get the majority of ATP from the aerobic system. Thus, the *capacity* of the system becomes the limiting factor as the *power* is similar. Since the aerobic system has an almost unlimited capacity it is not unreasonable to assume the pace for these distances should be similar. In contrast, if we look at the difference in pace between 400 meters and 1500 meters (less than four times the distance but more than four times the duration) we see that it is 50.4 seconds per mile. It appears then, that the difference in pace indicates the division points (duration) between the three suppliers of ATP; up to 20 seconds the alactate system plays the predominant role, from 20 seconds to 3 minutes the lactic acid system is the major supplier, and more than 3 minutes the aerobic system becomes king.

How do the three pathways produce the ATP necessary for continued muscular contraction? Figure 6 graphically depicts the sources of muscular energy.

Alactate Energy (anaerobic)

ATP and CP are stored in limited capacities in the muscle cell. The ATP is combusted (ATP—ADP + Pi + Heat) for muscle contraction. The by-products (ADP + Pi) can be used to rapidly re-synthesize ATP for continued muscle contraction. Two en-

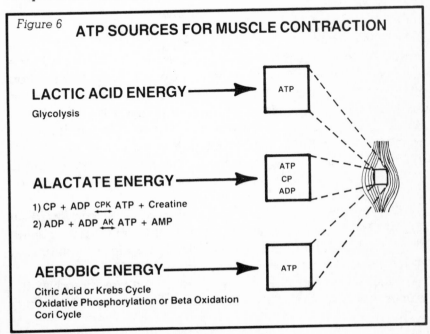

Figure 6   **ATP SOURCES FOR MUSCLE CONTRACTION**

LACTIC ACID ENERGY ⟶ ATP

Glycolysis

ALACTATE ENERGY ⟶ ATP / CP / ADP

1) CP + ADP $\xrightleftharpoons{CPK}$ ATP + Creatine

2) ADP + ADP $\xrightleftharpoons{AK}$ ATP + AMP

AEROBIC ENERGY ⟶ ATP

Citric Acid or Krebs Cycle
Oxidative Phosphorylation or Beta Oxidation
Cori Cycle

zymes present in the muscle cell (creatine phosphokinase—CPK, and adenylate kinase—AK) catalyze the following two reactions:

1 CP + ADP CPK ATP + creatine—this reaction continues until the supply of CP (creatine phosphate) is exhausted.
2 ADP + ADP AK ATP + AMP—this reaction's primary function is to provide a source of AMP, which serves as a stimulus for the initiation of glycolysis by activating the enzymes phosphorylase and phosphofructokinase.

Glycolysis—Lactic Acid Energy (anaerobic)

The breakdown of carbohydrate (CHO) in the absence of oxygen supplies the energy for muscle contraction or for the re-synthesis of ATP. The CHO utilized in glycolysis is either stored intramuscular glycogen, circulating blood glucose, or glycogen stored in the liver that is converted to glucose and then enters the bloodstream to be carried to the muscle. Glycogen is a readily mobilized storage-form of glucose. The first step is in the reaction to convert glucose to glucose $-6-$phosphate. The last step is to convert pyruvate to lactate. The net reaction is:

Glucose + 2Pi + 2ADP $\rightarrow$ 2 lactate + 2ATP + $2H_2O$.

Citric Acid or Krebs Cycle (aerobic)

The breakdown of stored carbohydrates (CHO's) and fats in the presence of oxygen supplies the energy for muscle contraction or for the re-synthesis of ATP. The CHO comes from the same sources as for glycolysis—intramuscular glycogen, circulating blood glucose and liver glycogen. The fats come from the adipose sites and, to a small extent, from fat globules found in the muscle cell. Under certain conditions lactic acid, amino acids, and ketone bodies can be used as fuels in the presence of oxygen to generate ATP.

The pyruvate formed during glycolysis is converted to Acetyl CoA when sufficient amounts of oxygen are present. The Acetyl CoA then enters the Citric acid cycle by condensing with oxaloacetate to form citrate (see Figure 7).

Fats, in the form of triacylglycerol, that are stored in the adipose sites are hydrolyzed to produce Glycerol and Free Fatty

Acids (F.F.A.) which are carried by the blood to the working muscle. The F.F.A.'s enter the citric Acid Cycle as Acetyl CoA.

Oxidative phosporylation or beta oxidation (aerobic)

The major source of ATP during aerobic activities comes from this process which occurs in the mitochondria of the muscle cell. The NADH and $FADH_2$ required for this transfer process are formed during glycolysis, fatty acid oxidation and the citric acid cycle.

By now you may be wondering what all this means. Hopefully, some of you may be sufficiently curious to refer to the numerous textbooks that describe these energy pathways in more detail.

All muscular work, be it for strength, power, or endurance, requires energy. This energy comes from the foodstuffs we ingest. As well, the energy necessary for protein synthesis (the building of muscle) comes from the stores in our body. The three storage forms of foodstuffs are proteins, carbohydrates, and fats. Our muscles are the largest source of protein storage. Glycogen in the liver and muscle is the major storage form of the starch and sugar we ingest. Subcutaneous adipose pads (under the skin) are the major storage sites of the saturated and unsaturated fats we ingest. Proteins, carbohydrates and fats can all produce ATP for energy use by being hydrolyzed to amino acids, glycogen and glucose, and glycerol and free fatty acids, which can enter the citric acid cycle in the form of Acetyl CoA (see Figure 7). However, for this to occur, sufficient oxygen has to be available to the exercising muscle. During a Hydra-Fitness workout this is not possible, as maximal muscular effort is recommended. When you think about it, most athletic activities require bursts of maximal muscular effort—just like the work-intervals in a typical Hydra-Fitness workout. Now, remembering what we've learned about the three sources of ATP, we can see that, during the exercise bout (from 20 to 40 seconds), one is overloading the alactate and lactic acid sources while, during the recovery bout (10 to 50 seconds), one is overloading the lactic acid and aerobic sources. The shorter the recovery bout the greater the stress on the lactic acid system as the major source of ATP re-synthesis.

You have seen someone get light-headed and possibly sick to the stomach during or after their first workout. This hap-

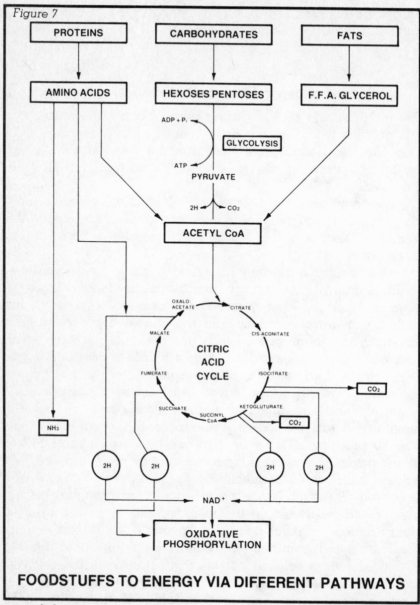

Figure 7

FOODSTUFFS TO ENERGY VIA DIFFERENT PATHWAYS

pened because the exercising muscles were demanding a great amount of oxygen due to the extreme energy demand. The circulatory system, working at maximum heart rate, was pumping the blood past the exercising muscles at great speeds. Unfortunately, as a result of improper breathing (holding breath while exercising rather than breathing normally) and an inability of the muscle cell to extract the oxygen from the blood, the muscle cell was getting very little oxygen. Thus,

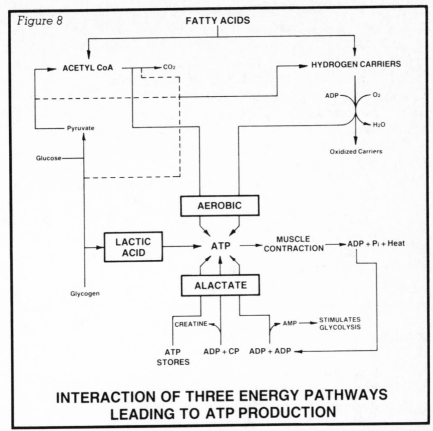

Figure 8

**INTERACTION OF THREE ENERGY PATHWAYS
LEADING TO ATP PRODUCTION**

the individual was working almost exclusively anaerobically.
Now, during the recovery bout, when the oxygen debt should
be repaid, this individual, because of his/her poor physical
condition, was still generating ATP anaerobically (through
glycolysis) rather than aerobically. This created a greater oxygen debt and a large buildup of lactic acid, which finally resulted in the cessation of exercise due to dizziness and an upset
stomach. A very fit individual, breathing properly, would not
experience this problem as his/her muscle would be capable of
extracting more oxygen during the recovery bout. You should
now be able to see the importance of having a high aerobic
base.

In summary then, the immediate source of ATP needed for
muscular work comes from the Alactate system; the stored ATP
being hydrolyzed to ADP plus free energy with the ADP then
combining with CP to form additional ATP plus creatine (ADP
+ CP CPK ATP + creatine) or with the ADP combining with
another ADP to form additional ATP plus AMP (ADP + ADP

AK ATP + AMP). These reactions are catalyzed by the enzymes creatine phosphokinase (CPK) and adenylate kinase (AK). Once the CP is used up and once levels of AMP increase, then additional ATP for continued muscular work must come through glycolysis. The cyclic AMP stimulates the hormones epinephrene and glucagon, which in turn stimulate glycogen breakdown (for use in glycolysis) in the muscle and liver, respectively. Elevated concentrations of Ca + (a result of muscle contraction), plus low energy levels in the muscle cell (lack of ATP), also stimulate glycogen breakdown. Cyclic AMP also regulates the lipases. The lipases, which are also stimulated by hormones (epinephrine, norepinephrine, glucagon, and adrenocorticotrophic hormone), catalyze the hydrolysis of fat to yield glycerol and free fatty acids which are used in the citric acid cycle (along with the pyruvate from glycolysis) and oxidative phosphorylation to re-synthesize ATP for continued muscular activity. It becomes apparent, then, that the energy demand (power) on the muscle cell (determined by the intensity and duration of exercise) dictates the substrate and the pathway.

Basically, low-intensity long-duration exercise preferentially utilizes fats first and carbohydrates second through the citric acid cycle and oxidative phosphorylation. High-intensity, very short-duration exercise utilizes stored ATP and CP through the alactate pathway. High-intensity short-to-intermediate-duration exercise first exhausts the Alactate ATP and CP and then utilizes carbohydrates through glycolysis. High-intensity intermediate-to-long-duration exercise first exhausts the Alac-

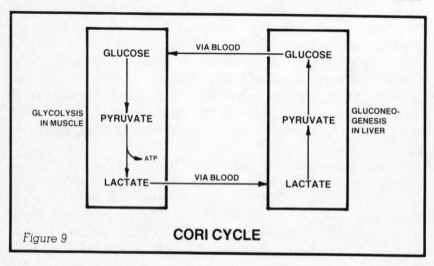

Figure 9   **CORI CYCLE**

tate ATP and CP, then exhausts the glycolytic pathway, then utilizes carbohydrates and fats through citric acid cycle and oxidative phosphorylation. During recovery bouts in interval training, ATP is re-synthesized via glycolysis, citric acid cycle and oxidative phosphorylation. Figure 8 visualizes the interaction of these pathways.

There is one other pathway which deserves brief mention— the Cori Cycle; only because a typical workout produces high levels of lactic acid from glycolysis. This lactic acid is metabolized in the liver, during recovery, back to glucose for use again as a fuel during exercise. This process is called gluconeogenesis. (Figure 9.)

PRINCIPLES OF TRAINING

Intensity

For any body system to improve, it must be stressed or made to work harder than it does normally. This principle is called **"overload."** "Intensity" refers to the extent that a system is overloaded. The amount of overload greatly influences the rate at which physiological improvement occurs. Generally speaking, the greater the intensity, the greater the physiological improvement of the system being stressed. The amount of intensity which produces optimal physiological adaptation varies according to the system being exercised, as well as to the fitness level of the person doing the exercise.

Duration

In order to achieve optimal physiological improvement in any body system, the intensity must be repeated within the same exercise bout. The "duration" of exercise refers to the amount of time necessary to provide sufficient overload stimulus to the system being stressed to produce optimal physiological improvement. The duration required for such improvement varies from individual to individual, according to the system being exercised and the person's fitness level.

Frequency

After a body system has been overloaded, it must be allowed to rest. Rest is essential, because it is during rest that body

mechanisms rebuild the overloaded system to a higher physiological level than before overloading. "Frequency of exercise" is defined within the context of rest periods between
exercise bouts. Again, the frequency of exercise necessary for
optimal physiological improvement varies according to the system being exercised and the fitness level of the individual.

Specificity of Training

For optimal physiological improvement in a specific sports activity (for example, vertical jumping in basketball), training
should be directed toward the specific muscular system used in
such activities. For the best results, the training movements
should simulate the actual movement that is done in the sports
activity. If a basketball player wants to improve his ability in
the vertical jump, he must exercise the extensors of the lower
body in a vertical position and at rapid limb speed. This exercise will simulate the rapid vertical movements that the sport
activity actually calls for.

Impulse

"Impulse" refers to the amount of time in any specific movement in which the muscles have the opportunity to generate
force against a resistance. The greater the impulse, the slower
the limb movement and the greater the force generation. Further, the greater the impulse, the more time the muscles have
to recruit muscle fibers to generate force through a range of
motion. For example, on the Series II-295 Jump Squat, more
force can be generated at a #6 setting than at a #1 setting,
although the distance traveled is identical. This is because the
impulse is greater at the #6 setting (much slower limb speed),
thus allowing for greater muscle fiber recruitment.

Timing

Muscle fibers contract when their motor neurons fire. "Timing"
refers to the firing of many motor neurons at the same time.
This is called "synchronous firing." When motor neurons fire
synchronously, muscle fibers contract at the same time, thus

combining their force. Timing is a learned response, and can be practiced and trained. Specificity of training is relevant here. In training for the vertical jump, for example, although the athlete might bend his knees enough to achieve a large impulse, without timing, the potential force generated may already be dissipated before the player's feet leave the ground. It is timing that ties specificity of training and impulse together. By training for a specific movement and striving for the greatest impulse possible within the range of motion of that movement, timing focuses these two variables into the maximum performance level.

Improving Performance

When a coach plans his season and his practice sessions, he has three major objectives in mind. These objectives are both immediate and long-range:

1 To improve the skill level of his athletes
2 To improve the physiological level of his athletes
3 To motivate his athletes so that they will achieve and maintain an optimal level of mental and emotional readiness to perform

A wise coach will emphasize all three of these objectives during each practice session. He will organize the sessions so that his athletes will peak at the critical portion of his season, bringing all three objectives together when each is at its optimum.

The successful coach will be the one who understands and uses the principles and concepts discussed previously, which are: strength, power, endurance, flexibility; aerobic, anaerobic, alactic and lactic acid energy systems; concentric and eccentric movements; fast- and slow-twitch muscle fibers; and the concepts of intensity, duration, frequency, specificity, impulse and timing.

To improve athletic performance from a physiological perspective, the athlete must improve in the following areas:

1 **The delivery system:** the cardiovascular/cardiopulmonary system that supplies fuel for energy production and which removes the waste byproducts of energy production.
2 **The energy production systems:** aerobic, alactic, and lactic acid.
3 **The muscular system,** and its ability to generate force (power) as determined by its mechanisms and contractile properties.

4 **The flexibility of the skeletal system:** flexibility around the joints as controlled by the muscles, ligaments and tendons.
5 **The neuromuscular interplay,** which controls muscle fiber recruitment and "firing," the process that is essential for execution of skilled athletic movements.

As previously stated, optimal improvement is determined by intensity, duration, and frequency of training. In pursuing his short and long-range goals, the wise coach will be able to translate these goals and principles into practical advice on "how much, how long, and how often." He can do this both by understanding the specifics of the sport he coaches in terms of the five physiological considerations listed above, and by determining the fitness levels of all his athletes in terms of the same five considerations. These five physiological considerations constitute the primary variables of performance and performance improvement.

MUSCULAR ENDURANCE

Muscular endurance is determined to a large extent by the ability of the body to deliver energy to a working muscle, and by the speed with which a particular movement is performed.

At slow contraction speeds and less than maximal intensity, the muscle's energy requirements come from the aerobic system. This is the case with walking or jogging. Under these conditions, many repetitions can be performed before exhaustion. In this type of exercise, the aerobic system supplies most of the required energy. The large number of contractions is possible because of the great capacity of the aerobic system to supply energy.

On the other hand, if we perform the actions at maximal speed and at the same setting, an individual can perform considerably fewer repetitions before fatigue forces him to stop. This is because under such circumstances, it is the anaerobic system that is supplying the energy, with the limited capacity that the anaerobic system implies. This system also produces lactic acid, which hastens the fatigue of the contracting muscle.

It is for these reasons that it is possible to perform (for example) more situps at a reasonable steady pace than at the fastest pace possible.

Muscular endurance can be measured in two ways:

1 By counting the total number of repetitions of a particular exercise that is performed without rest between movements, until it is no longer possible to perform the movement.

2 By counting the total number of repetitions of a particular exercise that is performed with a rest interval between the movements or between sets of the movements, until it is no longer possible to perform the movement.

In the performance of any sport, movements are specific. For example, throwing a baseball involves specific movements of the arm, with specific muscles and muscle groups being used in specific ways. To be able to perform successfully in a given sport, the athlete must be able to perform the various movements of that sport with skill, strength, speed, and endurance.

Consequently, **measurements of endurance in athletic activities must be made in terms of specific performance requirements for particular sports.** This fact follows what is called the **principle of specificity.** This principle must be the determinant of any measurement of athletic endurance.

The ability to perform large numbers of situps or pushups, while perhaps an indicator of general muscular endurance, is not necessarily a good indicator (for example) of a wide receiver's ability to run sixty pass routes at full speed during a sixty-minute football game. Unfortunately, many coaches make this oversimplification.

Let's look for a moment at the wide receiver's endurance requirements during a typical game:

1 He must be capable of running every pass pattern at his optimal speed, even if ten patterns are called successively in the same series.

2 He must be able to maintain this high performance level, whether the patterns are called in the same series or the call is for two runs, a pass and a punt for the entire game.

Consequently, instead of attempting to measure a wide receiver's game-specific endurance by counting the number of situps he can do, a better measure of muscular endurance would be to pre-test the athlete with game-specific activities. This means that he should be timed at the beginning of practice (when he is fresh) on how long it takes him to run the pass pattern to a specific spot on the field. If he runs ten different patterns, he can be timed on ten separate days.

When such timing is completed, the coach should determine the duration of the rest intervals (or rest periods) between plays in an actual game situation, then time the player as follows:

1 Have the wide receiver run the ten pass routes in succession.
2 Allow time for the appropriate rest interval between each pass route run.

MUSCULAR POWER

We can define muscular power as **the ability to use strength dynamically, that is, to exhibit strength while moving against a resistance.** Remember, strength is defined in this manual *statically*. Power, on the other hand, is defined in terms of dynamic movement. For the coach, power is defined practically as the ability to use strength in competition.

By defining these terms (strength and power) precisely, it is possible to see that they represent two different aspects of muscular activity. It is possible for a person to be strong, but not powerful. It is also possible for a person to be powerful, but not excessively strong. To be strong means to be able to maintain a specific joint angle against a force. To be powerful means to be able to move a limb or the torso through a range of motion against a resistance. The more powerful you are, the faster you will be able to move against the resistance. The greater the strength base, the greater the potential for power.

Because of the difference between strength and power, it is difficult to correlate the two in terms of measurements. This difficulty is further complicated by the fact that when a person is being measured for strength, the body is capable of recruiting all available fast- and slow-twitch muscle fibers. By contrast, when a person is being measured for power, the body is not capable of recruiting all available fibers of both types. This difference is true because muscular power measurements are made dynamically, and the fiber recruitment impulse is decreased.

Muscular power is dependent on the same elements as muscular strength: the number of muscle fibers, the size of the muscle fibers, and the recruitment ability of the nervous system. However, muscular power also depends, to a large extent, on:

1 The ratio of fast- to slow-twitch fibers present in the muscles
2 The amount of ATP and CP available for immediate energy supply
3 The rate that ATP can be hydrolized to produce the energy necessary for movement to occur.

Measurements of muscular power are affected by the speed at which the fibers contract (or by the speed at which the particular limb is moved).

In measuring muscular power, it is appropriate to talk in terms of *torque*. **Torque** is defined as **that which produces, or tends to produce, rotation or torsion.** Two measures of muscular power, therefore, are:

1 The peak torque output of the muscles in the range of motion
2 The total torque output through an entire range of motion

■

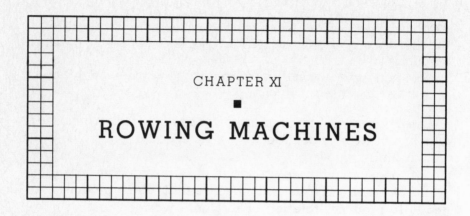

CHAPTER XI

ROWING MACHINES

Although boat rowing goes back to ancient times, it was not until the early 1980s that land rowing, or rowing machines, came to be popular. Back in the early 1980s there were just a few rowing machines on the market; now there are hundreds of models available.

Why rowing machines? They give a full body workout, they are very compact and can be easily stored in a closet; inclement weather is no hindrance to the workout, and listening to music or watching TV helps the time pass. In fact, there are even special videos that simulate rowing in an Olympic-level race. The ballistic pounding that the hips, knees, and weight-supporting joints take from outdoor running are significantly decreased by training in the seated position. Rowing uses more muscle groups than stationary cycling, and provides an exceptional aerobic workout. It trains the arms, shoulders, abdominal muscles, lower and upper back, and legs. The strain on the lower back may be a deterrent for some people, but for the healthy athlete rowing is a great workout. I think some of the distress over back problems arises because people row at too high a resistance level. Rowing should be mainly an aerobic exercise, but some people put the resistance higher than they should in an attempt to build muscle.

The basis of the machine is a chassis frame constructed of steel, aluminum, wood, or high-density plastic. Aircraft aluminum and/or heavy-gauge steel tubing is suggested for strength. Some units have stabilizer bars on the sides. Nonskid pads on the underside provide stability by preventing the machine from moving back and forth on the floor. On the center chassis are the seat (which glides on low-friction wheels or ball bearings), lever-pull rowing arms, and, at the far end, foot-pad holders and straps. Make sure the machine you use suits you—if you're tall (especially if you're six feet two inches or taller) you may need a unit with a longer chassis.

Resistance is provided by shock-absorber–like cylinders that have oil encased in them, and under compression the oil passes through a small opening within the cylinder. In other units, a type of gas-assisted mechanism (such as freon or nitrogen) in the form of a bag attached to the shock absorber keeps air bubbles out of it, helping to protect the resistance integrity of the cylinder, since air bubbles can impair the proper workings of the cylinder.

The larger the diameter of the shock-absorber cylinder the better, for it will have more resistance power and may last longer. The rocker-rowing arms work like levers. The higher up you position the arm-locking mechanism, the more difficult the resistance and stroke force you must exert. This is basic physics of torque mechanics—when you lengthen the lever arm you increase the force needed to move.

Another mechanism for providing resistance is a fan-like wheel device that utilizes wind resistance. The harder and faster you pull, the greater the resistance. Some of the more expensive units use microprocessors in conjunction with electronics to provide resistance electrically.

CHECKLIST FOR SELECTING A UNIT

- First and foremost, try the unit out for comfort and biomechanics.
- Is the seat comfortable, and does it slide smoothly back and forth?
- Look under the seat and examine the glide wheels that attach it to the frame. Sit on it and sway to and fro to test its torsion stability.
- Hold the frame on its side to make sure it's straight and has no bends or warping in construction. Metal heats up as it bends, so if the frame is off by even a small degree you could end up with two halves of a machine.
- Are the lever-pull arms strong and stably locked in? Sometimes the point where they attach is loose and the play in that focal point, combined with the torque of your pull, can be the end of the unit. Some rower arms are so weak they can break off in your hand.
- Note if the resistance levels are marked off clearly on the lever row arms so that your pull will be even. It is best when they are etched

in. If you set one level higher than the other, injury can occur due to uneven pull biomechanics. The force provided can be anywhere from 5 to 300 pounds of resistance.

- There should be some type of condensed foam covering on the handle-grip sections to aid in gripping. You may wish to wear workout gloves to avoid getting painful blisters on your palms.

- There are three different types of arm-pull mechanisms—the double-arm rowers, a central arm pull, and a long side-arm rower.

- Foot pads are best when they sway with the to-and-fro motion of strokes and feet. They should be smooth moving, and lock the feet in with either Velcro straps or a bucklelike mechanism.

- If there are electronics as motivational feedback, the panel should be easily accessible while in the locked-in position. Some LCD (Liquid Crystal Display) crystal readouts are difficult to see, especially in poorly lit rooms. Some readout terms noted are time (in minutes and seconds), total cumulative strokes, average strokes per minute, work rate in terms of calories, and total calories.

- Check for sharp edges and metal burrs to avoid laceration.

- Pay attention to warning decals—they are there for your safety.

ROWING TECHNIQUE

There are three basic phases of rowing:

Phase One: The Catch

While seated on the rowing machine, slide forward, drawing your knees up to your chest. Your upper body should be slightly forward, with your back firm and muscles flexed, keeping your head up and arms straight. Use an overhand grip on the oars. At this point your chest should be up against your knees. You are now in position.

Phase Two: The Power Stroke or Drive

As you exhale, push back against the foot pedals. Lean back slowly as you extend your legs, and continue the stroke as you draw your arms in. Shoulders should remain at the same height. With your legs fully extended, your hands should reach your chest. The power stroke should be fluid in motion.

Phase Three: The Recovery

At the completion of the power stroke, you come forward by "feathering" (rolling hands) on the roller grips forward. Push your palms forward and thrust your wrists forward. As your wrists twist, push the rowing arms ahead of your chest to focus on the muscles of your forearms.

ROWING TECHNIQUES*

1. CATCH
- Raise only the hands.
- Do not "open."
- Enter the water before beginning the leg drive.

2. DRIVE No. 1
- Almost no change in the body position.
- The body is "hanging" on the oar and footstretcher.
- Work is done exclusively by the legs.

3. DRIVE No. 2
- Upper body slowly takes over the leg drive.
- The body starts to "uncoil" in a natural way.

4. DRIVE No. 3
- Legs almost finish their work.
- The upper body still continues its swing.
- The arms begin their work.

5. DRIVE No. 4
- End of the "layback."
- The arms move quickly and strongly to the body.

6. FINISH
- Forearms and outside hand move oar handle down and around in fluid and continuous manner.

7. RECOVERY No. 1
- Hands move away from the body at a constant speed.

8. RECOVERY No. 2
- At the beginning of the slide, arms are past the knees.
- There is early forward body angle preparation.

9. RECOVERY No. 3
- The slide is halfway through.
- The arms and upper body have finished reaching out.

10. BEFORE CATCH
- Last part of the slide.
- All movements are finished except continuation of slide with concentration on a direct catch.

*Reprinted with permission from *Home, Gym & Fitness* magazine.

PRECOR

The *612 Dual Piston Rower* has two resistance pistons.
    Length: 50" Width: 30" Weight 35 lbs.
    Price: $285

The *620 Dual Piston Professional Rower* is the largest in the Precor line, with dual stabilizer bars for maximum frame strength and stability. Coupled with a larger seat and heavy duty cylinders, the 620 is ideal for larger people.
    Length: 53" Width: 32" Weight: 45 lbs.
    Price: $350

Precor 620e

The *620e Dual Piston Professional Rower* with electronics gives digital readout displays of time, strokes per minute, total strokes (during workout), average strokes per minute, maximum strokes per minute, and total cumulative strokes.
    Length: 53" Width: 32" Weight: 45 lbs.
    Price: $415

Precor has also come out with a new group of rowers known as the M Series. These feature a one-piece internal track made from aircraft aluminum alloy with a deep protective finish. The track is supported by a monocoque box frame designed for increased strength and balance. The frame was chosen for its favorable weight-to-strength ratio. Pivoting foot pedals aid correct body-to-foot alignment during the total rowing cycle. The resistance on the rowing arms has been profiled to the strength curve of the bicep. This means maximum resistance comes in the midstroke where all muscles are being used, not at the end or beginning of the stroke, to reduce strain on the lower back.

The Precor M rowers utilize Delrin bushings, made by Dupont, that join the rowing arms to the frame. These are one of the most sophisticated engineering resins (plastic) available. The Delrin bushings have a high tensile and yield strength, and low coefficient of friction (the lower the coefficient of friction, the easier two parts move when they come together). And because the bushings are self-lubricating, they are quieter, smoother, and won't dry out. Delrin bushings retain their shape, won't rust, and, unlike bearings, allow tighter tolerances on assembly. These tighter tolerances mean there's no free play, or "slop," in the rower arm.

Each rower in the M Series is fitted with a specially designed ribbed seat that is fitted onto a maintenance-free seat carriage that glides on sealed bearings.

The 6.2 has three positions of elevation (where the back end of the rower can be elevated to vary the exercise resistance), electronics, and an internal track.

Electronics: elapsed time, strokes per minute, total strokes per workout, average strokes per minute, maximum strokes per minute, scan (time, strokes per minute, total strokes), cumulative strokes, and continuous strokes per minute
   Height: 8.5" Length: 51.5" Width: 30" Weight: 40 lbs.
   Power: 2 AA batteries
   Price: $365

The 6.4 is suitable for institutional use, and is a larger and stronger version of the 6.2.
   Height: 8.5" Length: 54.5" Width: 32" Weight: 42 lbs.
   Power: 2 AA Batteries
   It has the same electronics features as the 6.2.
   Price: $450

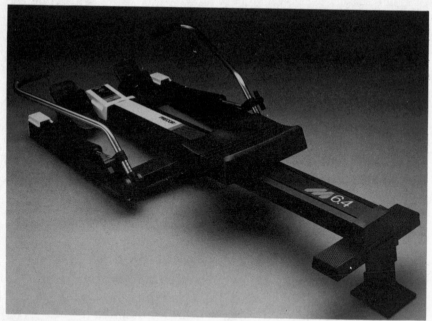

Precor M Series 6.4

The 6.5 monitors both calories per minute and total calories, in addition to stroke rate, total strokes, and elapsed time.

Electronics: time, rpm, distance, calories per minute, and calories
    Height: 8.5"   Length: 51.5"   Width: 30"   Weight: 39 lbs.
    Power: 9-volt alkaline battery
    Price: $600

Precor USA
    20001 North Creek Parkway North
    P.O. Box 3004
    Bothell, WA 98041-3004
    800-662-0606

TUNTURI

The top of their line, the *Tunturi 2* rowing machine unit has hydraulic cylinders and independent rowing arms. A patented snap-lock load adjustment gives an accurate selection of resistance levels. (This is an excellent way of assuring equal re-

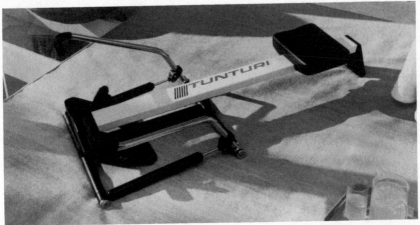

Tunturi 2

sistance in the rower-arm level pull.) Wide padded foot plates and pedal straps provide foot support.

    Height: 9″ Length: 58″ Width: 30″ Weight: 47 lbs.
    Price: $249

Tunturi/Amerec
    P.O. Box 3825
    Bellevue, WA 98009
    800-426-0858

WEST BEND

The *West Bend 5100* has a one-piece molded high-density plastic frame, with a five-year guarantee on the frame.
    Price: $249

The step up, the *West Bend 5200* features extra-long anodized aluminum rails for taller people. The seat roller track is internal, along with the chrome-plated steel base which has an extended support crosspiece. The number of strokes is automatically recorded on a resettable stroke counter. Resistance is supplied by dual hydraulic cylinders. The rower arms are made of chrome-plated steel. An electronic timer/stopwatch counts down from 100 minutes, counts up to 60 minutes, and recycles automatically.
    Price: $279

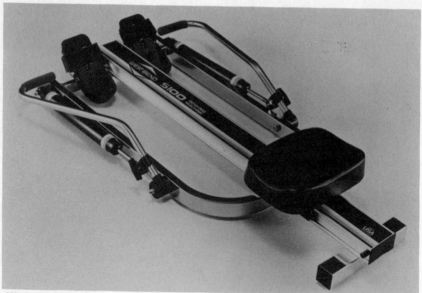

West Bend 5100

The top of their line, the *West Bend 5300* is the electronically monitored unit. It displays strokes, calories, time, and distance.
   Price: $329

West Bend Company
   P.O. Box 278
   West Bend, WI 53095
   414-334-6909

UNIVERSAL COMPUTEROW

This state-of-the-art computerized rowing machine has numerous programs and data functions. The LED console reads out the following:

Time mode: to preset the length of the workout

Distance mode: to preset the distance to be rowed

Competitive racing mode: an imaginary opponent is racing as a pacer; the rower's progress is monitored by relative racing positions on the console as the race progresses

Caloric expenditure monitor: indicates the number of calories burned

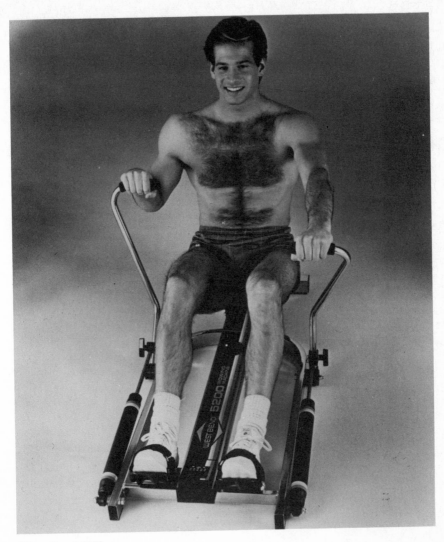

West Bend 5200

Variable exercise time: may be adjusted from 1 to 99.59 minutes

Variable distance monitor: to program the distance to be rowed from 100 to 9999 meters, or .10 to 99.9 miles

Variable stroke resistance: set for aerobic or high-strength benefits. Both range from lowest (1) to highest (9)

Variable stroke cadence: the adjustable rhythmic tone keeps stroke-pace consistent.

Size: 16" wide by 100" long by 38" high, and seat travels 48" backward from foot pedals

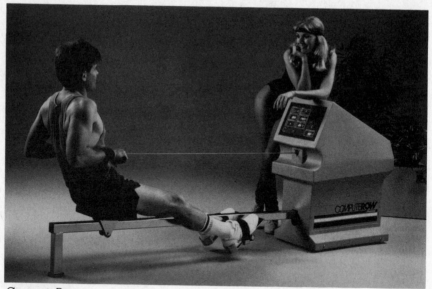

ComputeRow

Construction: 120" wall, tubular steel frame and rail with polyethylene Roto-mold housing

Electronics: fully computerized control console with microprocessor

Drive system: 14¾" diameter, 13-pound flywheel connected by industrial-rated chain and sprocket mechanism to the 7" × 19" aviation-grade nylon-sheathed cable. Infinitely variable electromagnetic resistance to simulate actual rowing motion. Self-powered unit utilizing an 8-volt rubber battery.

Seat: Molded foam-rubber racing seat with Nylatron rollers. Swiveling foot pedals equipped with adjustable Velcro straps.

Price: $1,440

Universal Corp.
P.O. Box 1270
930 27th Ave. S.W.
Cedar Rapids, IA 52406
800-553-7901

BALLY FITNESS

From the company that created Pac Man and instigated America's love affair with video games comes a rowing machine

Bally Liferower

with unmatched visuals. A 13-inch video color screen presents not LED readouts but full-color graphics. The machine takes you through a color-assisted programming protocol and allows you to code in the desired program. First it teaches you the proper techniques of rowing. Once programmed, the *Liferower* automatically selects the proper strokes-per-minute rate. Then the race begins with "On your mark, get set, go." As a starting gun sounds, the race is under way. As you race the computer-image pacer, the Liferower continues to give advice (such as "Keep your back straight," or "Use your legs"). If you are victorious, you'll hear the crowd whistle and cheer at the finish. Afterward, all the statistics of your competition are stored and may be presented on the screen for the next opponent.

This rower requires an electrical outlet. A sophisticated mechanism creates gliding action and the sound of whooshing water with each pull stroke. A center pull bar on a cable is present instead of lever arms. The parts are modular so that they can be repaired more easily. The 13-inch screen displays user versus pace boat, recommended stroke rate, actual stroke rate, distance ahead or behind pace boat, total distance traveled, total time remaining, and total calories burned. There are 15 workout levels from beginning to advanced (Olympic level), with 90 possible programs.

Height: 35"   Length: 90"   Width: 22¼"   Weight: 180 lbs.
Price: $2,700

Bally Fitness Products Corp.
   9601 Jeronimo Rd.
   Irvine, CA 92718
   800-542-2925
   714-859-1011

COFFEY

Coffey rowing machines are the only ones that were designed and built by a leading racing-shell manufacturer. Calvin Coffey, former Olympic silver medalist, has been building medal-winning elite racing shells for more than fifteen years.

Coffey units attempt to simulate real water rowing. The seat is contoured and on a double track to prevent tipping. The resistance is provided by a quiet draft-free flywheel located under the seat so that the line of vision is unobstructed. The ball-bearing pulleys are sealed for durable wear. The flywheel is covered with a molded fiberglass cover.

Electronic readout measures these functions: miles per hour (speed in miles or kilometers), instant speed, peak speed, average speed, maximum miles per hour, odometer, trip odometer (total distance and target distance), time of workout, clock/stopwatch (12-hour clock, AM and PM, stopwatch in hours, minutes, and seconds), and an audible tone that goes off after

Coffey Indoor Rower

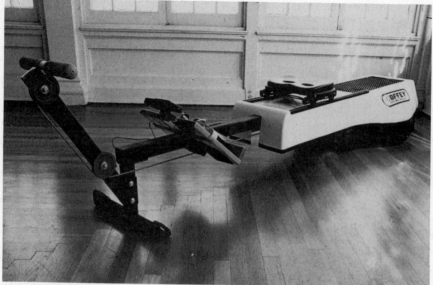

Coffey Sweep Simulator

Coffey Sculling Simulator

every quarter of the target trip. An exercise monitor computes calories consumed by using the rower's body weight. A stroke-pacer tone gives a clear tone in two speeds. Optional computer software is available for biofeedback and rowing-games simulations.

Approximate size:
Height: 22" Length: 97" Width: 27" Weight: 91 lbs.
Prices:
Coffey Indoor Rower—$595
Sweep Simulator—$695; Weight: 138 lbs.

Sculling Simulator—$795

Coffey Racing Shells
48 East Fifth St.
Corning, NY 14830
607-962-1982

CONCEPT 2

The *Concept 2 Rowing Ergometer* is popular among professional and scholastic rowing athletes. The resistance is provided by a flywheel via a wind-resistance mechanism. The older model had a spoked wheel, which has been replaced with a molded solid-metal flywheel. An electronic performance

Concept 2 Rowing Ergometer

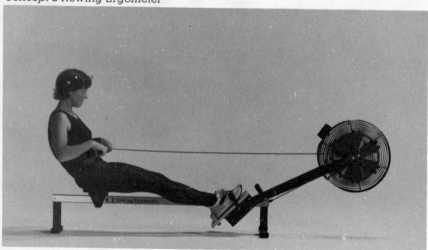

monitor has been added to aid computation of stroke, time, distance, etc. The motion of the machine mimics water rowing.

Height: 31″   Length: 94″   Width: 18″   Weight: 65 lbs.
Price: $650
Concept 2 Inc.
RR1, Box 1100
Morrisville, VT 05661
802-888-7971

HYDRA-FITNESS

Hydra-Fitness ProRow 2000 is one of the most powerful rowers made. Hydra-Fitness has a reputation for the use of heavy-steel construction, and uses the largest hydraulic cylinders in the fitness industry. The *ProRow 2000* weighs almost 200 pounds, has a solid stainless-steel glide chassis for the seat, and is built to withstand any institutional use. Six levels of resistance are available to choose from in the turnstile hydraulic mechanism. The machine can also double as a seated chest press. Force

Hydra-Fitness ProRow

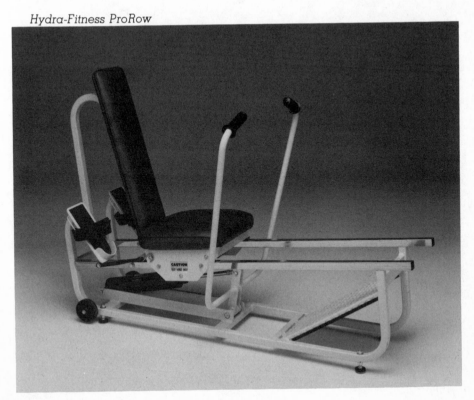

output is exhibited on a readout needle gauge. Everything about this unit is heavy duty.

     Length: 62"   Width: 30"   Weight: 217 lbs.

     Price: $995

Hydra-Fitness Industries
     P.O. Box 599
     2121 Industrial Blvd
     Belton, TX 76513
     800-792-3013

HEART MATE

The *Heart Mate Windracer Rower* attempts to duplicate the feel of water rowing. The Windracer has 7 different programs, with

Heart Mate Windracer

the resistance generated by a torque converter. Every turn of the torque converter requires the same amount of energy. The on-board computer counts the revolutions and converts them into watts, calories, and speed. The Windracer has 100 levels of intensity, so that small 1 percent jumps can be made. The Heart Mate prompter measures heart rate. The seven programs to choose from are:

1 Computer Race Program
2 Interval Training Program
3 Exercise Physiology Program
4 Self-design Program
5 Match Race Program, with which you can race a friend
6 Group Race Program, with which up to 10 people can race each other on a big-screen TV. Each individual screen displays each racer's information.
7 Just exercise

The electronic panel reads out strokes per minute, speed, power, calories, time, and matches a video opponent. The LCD is large—4" by 9.5".
  Length: 96"   Width: 14"   Weight: 150 lbs.
  Price: $1,995

Heart Mate
    260 West Beach Ave.
    Inglewood, CA 90302
    213-677-8131

■

CHAPTER XII

■

EXERCISE CYCLES

One piece of exercise equipment that has remained popular for a long time is the stationary exercise cycle. A 1984 survey of home-fitness products indicated that the sales of stationary bicycles jumped 70 percent over the previous two years, going from 1.5 million units to nearly 2.5 million units, and the numbers just keep escalating. Quality of construction, sophistication, and durability have all improved. Back in the 1960s there were just a few quality stationary cycles, but now there are many good models to choose from.

There are numerous benefits to indoor stationary cycling:

- It is safer than outdoor cycling. After all, it is very difficult to fall off a stationary cycle or to get hit by a car in your living room.
- Weather has no effect. You are in a safe, climate-controlled environment and can train at any hour of the day or night.
- It is a nonballistic form of training. The pounding and shock waves that result from running on hard pavement are eliminated.
- The controlled environment aids the accuracy of pulse-detecting mechanisms. Many of these devices record the light passing through the blood vessels. With indoor cycling, the changing light patterns of outdoors are replaced with consistent indoor lighting.
- Computerized resistance mechanisms challenge and inspire you to push harder, and give data feedback of performance for record keeping.

Most cycles on the market today are ergometers. An ergometer gives feedback and data on what you are doing (how much work you have performed). Some values that are calibrated are rpm (rotations of the pedal per minute), tension or resistance level, calories burned, time, and distance. An odometer (distance) and a speedometer are standard functions.

A stationary bike is simply a cycle with one wheel removed mounted inside a frame that is usually constructed of some form of tubular steel. The older bikes had pedals that turned a sprocket chain to drive a wheel. Some of the new cycles use electrical resistance, but the older ones used a caliperlike device that clamped on to the wheel and increased the friction between the wheel and brake pads. Some other units have a flat nylon band that wraps around the front wheel, and with its connection to a turnstile mechanism tightens the band, thereby increasing friction and tension resistance.

NOTES ON EXERCISE CYCLING

- One common mistake is to cycle at too high a level of resistance. This can cause knee and leg pain. Attempt to keep your legs spinning between 50 and 100 rpm. Pedal in smooth circles.

- Make sure the seat is comfortable. One of the most common causes for cutting short a workout is buttock pain and numbness in the lower extremities. You may want to place a towel on the seat for extra cushioning.

- If the bike has spokes on the wheel, make sure children and pets are at a safe distance.

- Both seat and handlebars should be adjustable to suit your individual body biomechanics.

- You should keep 10 to 15 degrees of flexion in the knee, and not fully extend your legs when the pedal is at the lowest point.

- Proper tracking pattern (path of motion) of knees and legs is important to avoid injury.

- Pedals should be wide and molded to the feet. Be sure to wear athletic shoes when riding. Toe clips are recommended as they allow one not only to push but also to pull up as they pedal. The ball of the foot should be on top of the pedal, preferably on top of the pedal spindle. This maximizes the workout on the lower leg muscles (gastrocnemius and soleus).

SEMIRECUMBANT CYCLES

This is a new breed of exercise cycle that has become very popular in the last few years. As mentioned previously, one of the things that can end an exercise session is a pain in the buttocks. What happens is that the pressure of the upper body weight on the buttocks compresses the sciatic nerve as well as compromising the blood supply that feeds down from that region to the legs. The lower extremities become numb, with tingling and even painful sensations. The buttocks even become numb. Going from an upright seated posture, where all the weight is on the buttocks, to a semirecumbant one, where the weight is more evenly distributed between that body part and the lower back, gives some people the ability to train longer. By varying the body position, different regions of the lower-extremity muscles can be exercised.

In addition, due to the fact that the heart is now on almost an equal level with the legs (versus above them), people with compromised leg veins or cardiovascular status may be able to exercise better. Also, the blood pressure may tend not to elevate as much as it is always lower in the supine posture than in the upright posture.

PRECOR

The *Precor 820e* stationary cycle utilizes a V-belt instead of greasy chains. The internal drive system is enclosed and moves with sealed bearings, and the 25-pound flywheel rotates faster than traditional flywheels for smoother action. Increases in tension are controlled by a turnstile knob. Microprocessors calibrate and display elapsed time, pedal rpm, and distance.
Height: 42" Length: 12.5" Width: 16" Weight: 55 lbs.
Price: $500

The *Precor 825e* is advanced in electronics and design.
Price: $650

The *Precor 8.4* and *8.5* stationary M Series cycles are each built around a custom monocoque aluminum frame designed to minimize size and weight and yet maximize strength. The M Series cycles incorporate CMOS microprocessor electronics.

The *8.4* has a unique V-belt drive system, with a front-mounted precision flywheel and sealed ball bearings. Electronic features are elapsed time, pedal rpm, distance (miles), average rpm, maximum rpm, scan (time, rpm, distance), and continuous analog rpm.
Height: 42" Length: 25.5" Width: 16" Weight: 60 lbs.
Price: $500

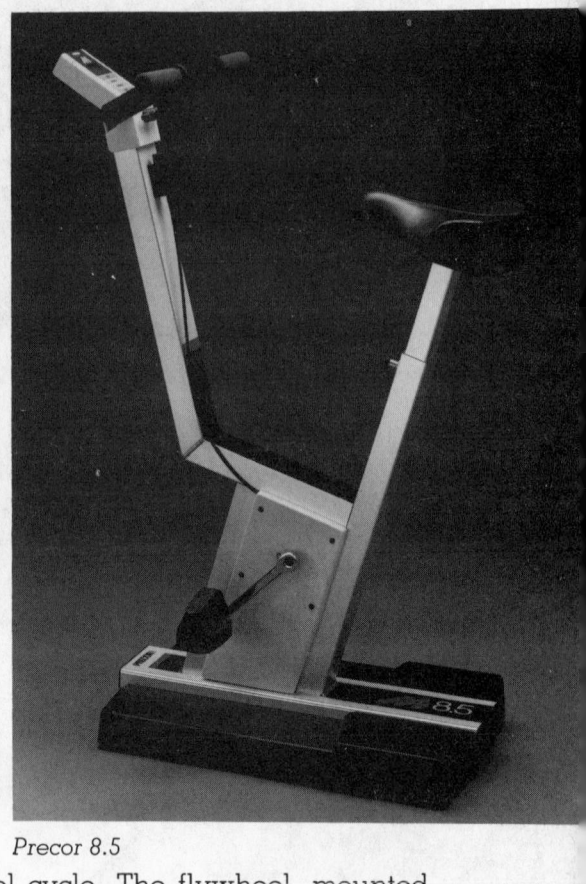

Precor 8.4   *Precor 8.5*

The 8.5 is the institutional-level cycle. The flywheel, mounted horizontally into the base giving a low center of gravity, is connected to an internal direct-drive gear box, producing an accurate simulation of cycling.

   Height: 42″   Length: 25.5″   Width: 16″   Weight: 65 lbs.
   Price: $850

Precor USA
20001 North Creek Parkway North
P.O. Box 3004
Bothell, WA 98041-3004
800-662-0606

TUNTURI

Tunturi, the Scandinavian equipment importer, has a large line of cycles. Their electronic ergometer, the *EL 400*, is a medi-

cal testing cycle. Pedal resistance is regulated by means of an electronically controlled current brake. The ergometer will automatically regulate the pedaling efficiency to the watt value seen. This results in a constant workload, no matter how fast or slow the pedal speed. A pulsemeter built into the control panel is tied into an earlobe sensor clip and displays the reading via LED. The control panel features a stopwatch, pedaling-speed indicator, pedal-efficiency control setting, and a metronome timer. The pedal speed LED display goes from 30 to 120 rpm. The handlebar setting rotates 360 degrees.

Height: 46.9″   Length: 40.2″   Width: 21.7″   Weight: 120 lbs.
Price: $1995

The *Tunturi Professional Ergometer* has a 51-pound front flywheel. The control panel contains a tachometer, a stepless tension control, and an energy-expenditure scale to determine calories burned.

Height: 48″   Length: 43″   Width: 20″   Weight: 126 lbs.
Price: $799

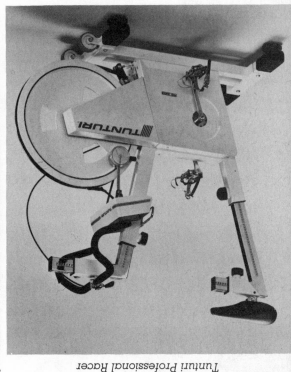

Tunturi Professional Racer

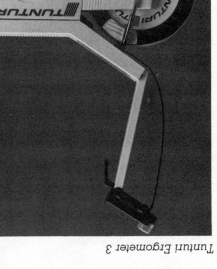

Tunturi Ergometer 3

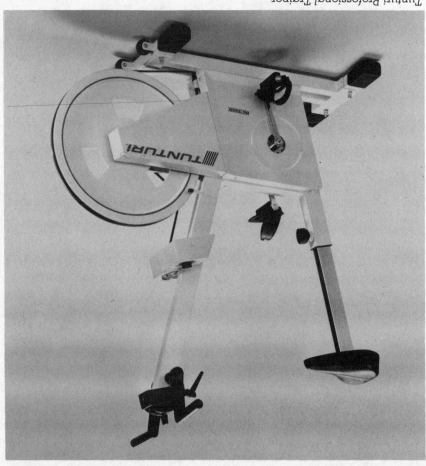

Tunturi Professional Trainer

The *Tunturi Professional Racer* has similar features, except for the racing design of seat and handlebars.

Price: $899

The *Tunturi Ergometer 2 and 3 (TE2* and *TE3)* are new electronic home models. Electronic displays report pedal rpm, distance, and time. A scan feature is also present. A 40-pound flywheel gives a smooth, stable ride.

Height: 42"   Length: 37"   Width: 23"   Weight: 90 lbs.

Price: TE 2—$475, TE 3—$650

The *Tunturi Professional Trainer* is the heavy-duty model with a low center of gravity due to 20-inch-wide legs. The 51-pound flywheel adds to the stability, and it has a built-in tachometer and timer.

Height: 47" Length: 43" Width: 19.5" Weight: 126 lbs.
Price: $599

The *Executive Ergometer* has a 40-pound flywheel and re-
sistance from free-wheeling to 450 watts.
Height: 42.5" Length: 37.5" Width: 20" Weight: 73 lbs.
Price: $349

Tunturi
P.O. Box 3825
Bellevue, WA 98009
800-426-0858

BODYGUARD/OGLAEND

Another Scandinavian import cycle company, Bodyguard/
Oglaend is housed in Sandnes, a small town near the west coast
of Norway. They entered the bicycle business in 1906, and due to
a demand by the medical community for stationary exercise
cycles, they entered that market in the 1970s.

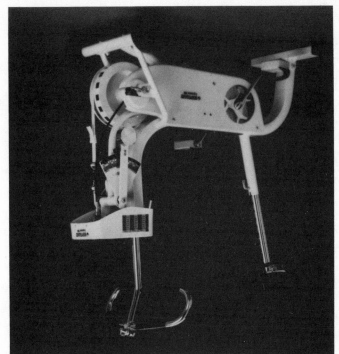

Bodyguard 990

The *Bodyguard 990* has a dual chain/sprocket drive system with a sprocket-to-sprocket ratio of 8.3 to 1, increasing the kinetic energy of the wheel 400 percent. This gives a smoother ride. The workload is indicated in kilopounds, kpm (kilometers per minute), and watts, with a workload range up to 1,800 kpm, or 300 watts. Other indicator panels give rpm, distance, and speed, plus timer and alarm. Floor space required: 21" × 40" Weight: 95 lbs. Price: $795

Bodyguard 980 ERG Cycle

The top line for Bodyguard is the *980* model. This unit has a Histogram that provides visual feedback on 10 separate colored LED (Light Emitting Display) bars. The progressive electronic instrument panel features three separate computerized LED bar graphs that show speed, RPM, instantaneous workload in watts, and accumulated calories expended. In addition distance and numerous modes can be called up. Price: $1,495

Bodyguard
    40 Radio Circle
    Mt. Kisco, NY 10549-0096
    800-828-1186

MONARK

Monark, also manufactured in Scandinavia, has a full line of stationary cycles. The *Monark 819 Electronic Ergometer* is their top-of-the-line cardiac-testing ergometer. Its features present a constant workload independent of pedal speed. Work may be set in watts, kpm, newtons, or kp (unit used by European companies). It has a built-in digital timer. Heart rate is measured with ECG electrodes, chest belt, optical ear clip, or direct input from an external ECG instrument. It has a heart-rate meter and a maximum heart-rate alarm. Speed is indicated in miles per hour and kilometers per hour, with distance traveled calculated in miles and kilometers. There is a computer interface for computer control of the ergometer as well as built-in protocols and calculators for oxygen consumption: Astrand, Bruce, Naughton and YMCA cardiac-testing protocols.

Monark 819

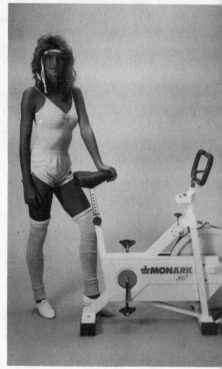

Monark 817

Height: 39" Length: 44" Width: 23.2" Weight: 68.2 lbs.
Price: $2,995

The *Monark 817* exercise cycle has been remodeled. It has
electronic readouts of time, speed, and distance.
Height: 35" Length: 44" Width: 21" Weight: 65 lbs.
Price: $520

Universal Corp.
P.O. Box 1270
930 27th Ave. S.W.
Cedar Rapids, IA 52406
800-553-7901

BOSCH

Robert Bosch Medical Electronics is a well-known West German manufacturer of precision medical diagnostic and
treatment machines. Cycle ergometry for cardiac testing is far

Bosch Erg 551

more popular in Europe than in the United States. One problem with treadmill stress-testing is that sometimes the person may stop because of the ballistic pounding the knees and legs take upon running. With cycle ergometry, the pounding of lower extremities is eliminated, and the heart remains in the physiologic position.

Bosch's *ERG 551* is a compact cycle ergometer for speed and/or loading examination in the sedentary position. The integrated microprocessor ensures ease of operation during the load examination. Digital displays are time/pulse (switchable), rotational speed, and output (in watts). The 551 has an integrated load programmer for automatically controlled step loading. The performance range is from 25 to 400 watts, the speed indicator from 0 to 100 rpm; time from 0 to 60 minutes in 10-second steps, and the pulse indicator from 30 to 240 per minute. The LED readouts and construction of the units are exceptional, as is common with West German engineering.

Height: 48″ Length: 34″ Width: 16″
Price: $2,500

The Bosch *ERG 550* is a more competitively priced ergometer, but its construction is of the same high standards as the 551.
    Price: $2,000

Bosch Medical Electronics
    359 Turnpike St.
    North Andover, MA 01845
    800-MEDLINE

UNIVERSAL

The *Universal Aerobicycle* is an electronic exercise cycle with 5 distinct preprogrammed exercise modes that visually monitor progress. There are monitors for pulse rate, caloric expenditure, and workload selection (resistance). The programs are:

Steady Climb: provides a constant resistance similar to pedaling up a long hill

Rolling Hills: resistance varies, the equivalent of pedaling down hills of different lengths and elevations

Pulse Training: the microprocessor automatically readjusts workload to maintain the established target pulse rate

Constant RPM: the user is encouraged to maintain a predetermined rpm rate by drastically increasing the workload when the rpm rate is exceeded, and decrease the workload when the rpm falls below its predetermined rate

Fitness Test: after adjusting for age and sex, this mode furnishes the user with his or her aerobic fitness level, in percentile ranking according to national YMCA norms

Price: $2,000 to $2,500, depending on features.

Universal Corp.
    P.O. Box 1270
    930 27th Ave. S.W.
    Cedar Rapids, IA 52406
    800-553-7901

BIOCYCLE

Biocycle, by Engineering Dynamics Corp., is a computer cycle with 12 different programs. Pulse rate is monitored via re-

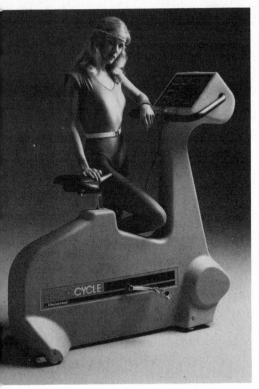
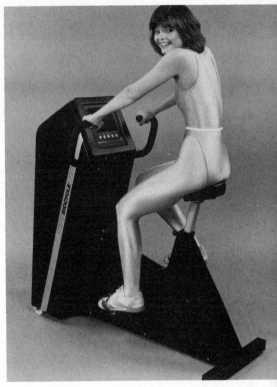

AerobiCycle II   *Biocycle*

ceivers in handlebars, along with rate of calories per hour, speed, time remaining in program, cycle image on video screen to serve as motivator, rpm pedal speed, percentage score of performance on a particular program, and exercise profile. The programs include Daily Short Workout, Daily Long Workout, Endurance Training, Interval Training, Boston Marathon, Rocky Mountain Ride, New England Hills, San Francisco Tour, Surfside Beach Run, Olympic Bike Trails, and additional customized programs. The bike interfaces with a computer for exercise testing, and the body is constructed of sturdy ABS plastic.

Height: 48.5″ Length: 52″ Width: 26″ Weight: 180 lbs.
Price: $3,200 and up, depending on options.

The *Biocycle 931* is the second-generation Biocycle, but at a lower price. An LCD display reveals heartbeats per minute (via a fingertip probe), calories burned, watts, time remaining, speed, distance, and miles per hour. There are 7 computer profiles to choose from, with time ranges from 4 to 64 minutes.

Biocycle 931   *Lifestyle 9000 Aerobic Trainer*

Height: 49" Length: 42" Width: 21" Weight: 110 lbs.
Price: $1,850

Biocycle/Engineering Dynamics Corp.
120 Stedman St.
Lowell, MA 01851
800-225-9020

BALLY FITNESS

Lifecycle was the first computerized exercycle to hit the health-club market. The flashing LED lights of the computer panel are still a very common sight in fitness clubs. Lifecycle attempts to simulate riding up and down imaginary hills by varying the resistance. It takes the user through a warm-up period, on to a testing period, through interval training, and then finally to a cool-down period. Displayed are calories per hour, pedal rpm, an LED matrix of graphics to present upcoming effort levels, hill profile, elapsed time/stopwatch, and a multiple-function data entry display which depicts program time, exercise levels, and fitness score computations. The RAN (Random) program gives an immeasurable number of preprogrammed random accessed training combinations. The Manual program gives a preselected fixed load of resistance, and the Maximum Oxygen Uptake gives an approximate measure of ml of oxygen consumed per minute. There are 12 resistance programs available on this unit. The *Lifecycle Aerobic Trainer* is priced at just under $2,000.

The *Lifecycle 9000 Aerobic Trainer* has some design changes, such as a new V-belt system that reduces noise levels. The bell-shaped hill profile gives smoother transitions of hills/resistance. The time of training periods has been expanded to up to an additional 24-minute ride.

Price: under $1,500.

Bally Lifecycle Fitness Products Corp.
 9601 Jeronimo Rd.
 Irvine, CA 92718
 800-543-2925
 714-859-1011

SCHWINN

The *Schwinn Air Dyne* cycle is very popular for cardiac rehabilitation because you can train the upper body at the same time as the lower body. Upper-arm rowers are gripped in the hands and go back and forth for a total body workout. The gauge panel reads out time, speed, distance, and power. Specialty dealers hand-deliver the unit to the buyer and service it.
 Price: $650.

Schwinn
 Excelsior Fitness Co.
 615 Landwehr Rd.
 Northbrook, IL 60062
 312-291-9105

Schwinn Air Dyne   *Exercycle Executive*

EXERCYCLE

One of the oldest exercise cycle companies is Exercycle Corp.,
which was founded in the 1930s. The *Exercycle* was designed
as an "all body action" training device, and is the only model
on the market that has a motorized gearbox. The motor provides the user with a programmed regimen, now a feature in
the company's three models. The Exercycle's range of motor-
driven movements are intended to duplicate seven distinct exercises: push-pull, swimming, rowing, sit-up, chin-up, stretch,
and cycling. The electronic Personal Exercise Planner (PEP)
aids the informational needs of the user. The PEP elements include relative exercise-level adjuster; work-level meter; warm-
up/cool-down signal; digital and exercise program clocks; and
an on-off switch. The three models to choose from are:

Executive: features 2 speeds (60 and 90 pedal rpm), weight adjustment and ½ hp motor, and PEP system.

Senior: has all the features of the Executive, but goes at slower speeds (30 and 45 pedal rpm)

Therapeutic: has all the features of the Executive, but offers a fully variable speed motor which enables the user to pedal at anywhere from 0 to 90 rpm. The length of the pedal crank can be adjusted.

The PEP is not available for this unit.

Prices range from $2,200 to $3,500, depending on options.

Exercycle Corp.
  667 Providence Street
  P.O. Box 1349
  Woonsocket, RI 02895
  401-769-7160

FITNRON CYCLE ERGOMETER

The Fitnron is one of the only isokinetic cycles on the market. Due to the makeup of the unit, even one-legged cycling is smooth, which can be ideal for specific patients. The unit can be made accessible to nonambulatory patients. A digital timer/stopwatch monitors exercise sessions, and the pedal RPM adjustment gauge sets the resistance speed and force levels. Since the Fitnron is a hydraulic ergometer, no electrical outlet is required. It takes up only 2' by 3½' of floor space.
  Width: 36" Length: 48" Weight: 145 lbs.
  Price: $1,495

Fitnron by Cybex
  2100 Smithtown Ave.
  Ronkonkoma, NY 11779
  800-645-5392

CATEYE ERGOMETER

The *Cateye Ergocisor* is an electronic cycle with a number of microprocessor functions printing out right off the cycle's instru-

Cateye Ergociser   *The Chair*

ment panel. An earlobe pulse sensor records heart rate, and the unit monitors energy consumption, elapsed time, current workload (kilograms per meter), cadence, work rate (watts), and maximal oxygen uptake. This data is displayed on an LCD screen. The cycle will retain your data by code number (up to nine people can have their personal data stored), and it also has an automatic safety alarm system, should the user exceed workload safety limits.

    Price: $995

Cateye Ergometer/Maximum Fitness Products
    P.O. Box 277
    La Habra, CA 90633-0277
    213-694-0800

PARAMOUNT FITNESS

Paramount produces a semirecumbant exercise cycle—*The Chair*—that utilizes an encased fluid system as pedal resistance. It is very quiet, and can be used as an upper-body, as well as a lower-body, ergometer. The seat slides all the way forward so that the upper body and arms can also be trained. Other upper-body ergometers are produced by Cybex (the UBE), Biocycle (the Uppercycle), and Monark (Rehab Trainer 881).

Paramount Fitness
    6636 E. 26th
    Los Angeles, CA 90040
    800-854-0183

PROTEC SPORTS

Another semirecumbant cycle is the *PTS Turbo 1000* by ProTec Sports. This unit is structured so that any bicycle shop can perform repairs, as the gears are so similar to a regular racing cycle. The seat can adjust to people of various heights, and an electronic microprocessor panel reads out distance, speed, and rpms. One real plus of the unit is the comfortable, cushioned, and contoured seat. The frame is welded steel, and the unit is shipped assembled.
    Unfolded dimensions: 84″ × 26″ × 32″
    Folded dimensions: 66″ × 26″ × 32″   Weight: 52 lbs.
    Price: $795

ProTec Sports
    1965 E. Blair
    Santa Ana, CA 92705
    800-453-5332

UPPER-BODY ERGOMETERS

Upper-body ergometers exercise the muscles and joints of the upper body. Rhythmic, continuous movement and variable work rates train the shoulders, arms, and wrists. One can exercise elbow extension/flexion and shoulder extension/flexion, abduction/adduction, circumduction, and protraction/retraction patterns, with variable amounts of torso rotation. This can be performed in both the forward and reverse directions.

CYBEX UBE

The Cybex UBE has an epoxy-coated steel frame with a durable scratch-resistant, molded polystyrene cover. The unit comes with a built-in digital timer. This is an isokinetic device with numerous force readouts. An institutional, strongly constructed unit, the UBE is very popular in physical-medical-rehab units, as well as sports medicine centers and health clubs.

Height: 52"   Length: 29"   Weight: 250 lbs.
Price: $2,295

Cybex
2100 Smithtown Ave.
Ronkonkoma, NY 11779
800-645-5392

UPPERCYCLE BY EDC

An electronic upper-body training unit is produced by EDC. An electronic computer panel reads out digital levels of calories burned, time, rpm, and workout load in both watts and kilopounds. The pivoting ergometer head can be adjusted to minus 45 degrees to plus 45 degrees to better focus on specific muscle areas. The workload can be varied from 20 to 300 watts in 5-watt increments.

Height: 52"   Width: 30"   Length: 58"
Weight: 125 lbs.   Power: 110 watts
Price: $2,195

Uppercycle by EDC
120 Stedman St.
Lowell, MA 01851
800-225-9020

CHAPTER XIII

■

TREADMILLS AND OTHER AEROBIC TRAINING DEVICES

One elderly athlete was known to proclaim, "I don't care what the weather is outside, even if it's thirty below zero and two feet of snow—I get in my five mile run! However, I do it on a treadmill in my basement. Only nuts run outdoors." Indoor running treadmills free the athlete from weather conditions. You can train any time of the day or night and avoid all the hazards of running outdoors, from stray dogs to lightning and muggers. Treadmill tracks have more give in them, and are not as ballistic as outdoor running on cement. The electronic motorized models with their speed controls and visual LEDs will not only spur you on but also will give you a more accurate account of the day's exercise, and the controlled environment of indoor running will give a more accurate heart-rate account.

PRECOR

Precor produces an exceptional line of treadmills. The Precor 910e and 935e have running beds designed with "flex" to reduce foot-plant shock, minimizing the stress on joints and vertebrae. The microprocessor-controlled DC drive motor provides smooth running action. The Precor treadmills are constructed from aircraft-grade anodized aluminum, TIG welded into a strong frame. The actual running surface is a woven poly-elastomer belt. The low-friction combination of belt and running bed keeps the running surface from getting too hot.

The *Precor 910ei* has steel side handrails for user safety, and a gas-assisted arm inclines the unit from a 0- to a 15-percent grade. It goes from a speed of 1 to 8 mph in $\frac{1}{10}$-mile incre-

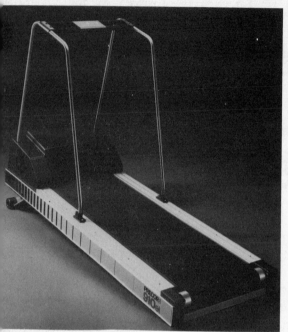

Precor 910ei   *Precor 935e*

ments, displayed on the LED monitor along with time and distance.

    Height: 43″   Length: 72″   Width: 26″   Weight: 155 lbs.
    Price: $2,400

The *Precor 935e* runs up to speeds of 10 mph and displays speed, calories, time, and distance. There is no elevation mechanism.

    Height: 46″   Length: 75″   Width: 28″   Weight: 165 lbs.
    Price: $2,800

The Precor M Series includes the 9.4 and 9.5 institutional-level treadmills. The 9.5 uses a monocoque aluminum frame, running platform with built-in shock absorption, and a durable running surface. The unit can be inclined electronically from a 0- to a 15-percent grade with the touch of a button. The 9.5 electronic treadmill has speeds that range from 1 to 12 mph. CMOS electronics sends information to the three LED displays, which read out percentage of incline, calories per minute, total calories, speed, time, and distance. An industrial 2 hp motor handles the power needs. A unique system known as Inte-

grated Foot Plant (IFP) has been developed for consistent surface speed control. The IFP divides each foot plant into
segments, with each segment being read by the microprocessor, which adjusts the belt speed to eliminate sticking
and jerking motions.

Height: 46"   Length: 80"   Width: 28.5"   Weight: 230 lbs.
Price: Precor 9.4—$3,400; Precor 9.5—$4,200

Precor USA
20001 North Creek Parkway North
P.O. Box 3004
Bothell, WA 98041-3004
800-662-0606

UNIVERSAL

The *Universal Tredex 2924* treadmill features a microprocessor-
controlled 14-digit LED display panel, depicting distance (miles
and kilometers), time (minutes/seconds and hours/minutes),
speed (miles per hour and kilometers per hour), pace (minutes
per mile and minutes per kilometer), and pause and reset buttons. Speed jumps can be made in fast (5 mph) or slow (1 mph)
accelerations and decelerations. The readouts and motor

Precor 9.5

Universal Tredex 2924

speed automatically return to zero when the machine is turned off. Front handrails are a safety feature for emergency shutoff.
    Height: 50"   Length: 81"   Width: 25"   Weight: 230 lbs.
    Price: $2,500 to $3,500, depending on features.

Universal Corp.
    P.O. Box 1270
    930 27th Ave. S.W.
    Cedar Rapids, IA 52406
    800-553-7901

TRUE SPORTS

True Sports treadmills have a flex-frame system to decrease the ballistics of running. A side view of a runner on the True units shows the give of the running bed as it flexes with the runner. Energy from each shoe impact is transferred into the machine rather than into the person's body. The instrument panel displays, via individual LCDs, kilometers per hour, miles per

True 1-E

Landice T-8400

hour, elapsed time, distance in miles or kilometers, percentage of grade, and heart rate. A cushioned handrail on the console is present to aid balance. An electronic breaking system is a standard feature on all True units.

	True 1-E	True 1
Speed range	.5–9 mph	.5–9 mph
Horsepower	1.5 hp	1.5 hp
Length	73″	73″
Width	24″	23.5″
Height	47.25″	46″
Weight	250 lbs.	200 lbs.
Price	$2,500	$2,000

True Sports Inc.
P.O. Box 1115
Maryland Heights, MO 63043
314-739-3770

LANDICE

The *Landice T-8400* motorized treadmill by BodyGuard features a 15-percent elevation and an LED display of speed, distance, time, elevation, calories burned, and METS. Speed runs from 0 to 10 mph. The frame is constructed of welded anodized aluminum.
Height: 40″   Length: 70″   Width: 24″   Weight: 200 lbs.
Price: $2,500 to $5,000, depending on features

Landice/BodyGuard
40 Radio Circle
Mt. Kisco, NY 10549-0096
800-828-1186

MARQUETTE ELECTRONICS

One of the leaders in cardiac-testing treadmills is Marquette Electronics. Their *Series 1800* treadmill sports a 2hp drive motor protected by a sound-absorbing shroud. Speed can be varied

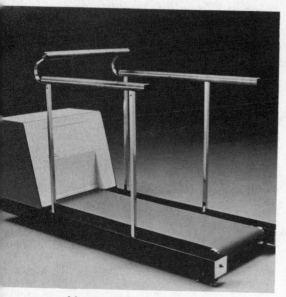

Marquette Series 1800   *Precor 515e*

from 0.6 to 13 mph, with an adjustable grade from 0 to 25 percent.

Height: 40"   Length: 81"   Width: 30"   Weight: 400 lbs.
Price: $6,450

Marquette Electronics, Inc.
8200 W. Tower Ave.
Milwaukee, WI 53223
414-355-5000

QUINTON

Quinton treadmills are a staple of medical cardiac-testing labs. The *Quinton 645* is a programmable treadmill that can store up to 10 user-programmed protocols, and can calculate METS, VO_2 max, and calories per minute.

Price: $8,000 and up

Quinton
2121 Terry Ave.
Seattle, WA 98121
800-426-0347

CROSS-COUNTRY SKIERS

One sport that requires the ultimate in cardiovascular fitness is cross-country skiing. Here the arms and legs work in tandem for a heart-pumping challenge. A number of different cross-country-ski–like devices are available. They provide a good nonballistic form of cardiovascular training.

Precor USA has developed a sleek-looking cross-country-ski device known as the *Precision Ski Machine 515e*. Its assembly is simple, and the intelligent Precor design makes it a functional attractive training device.

Price: $600

Precor USA
20001 North Creek Parkway North
P.O. Box 3004
Bothell, WA 98041-3004
800-662-0606

NordicTrack PRO Model 530   *Fitness Master*

One of the first devices of this type was the *NordicTrack* unit. Constructed of a hardwood base, heavy front flywheel, and elevation ability, this unit will withstand institutional use. It requires 2' by 7' of operating space, but can be stored in 17" by 23" of floor space.

Price: $600

PSI NordicTrack Co.
141 Jonathan Blvd. No.
Chaska, MN 55318
800-328-5888

Fitness Master produces three ski training devices. The *LT-35* and *XC-1* train the upper and lower body in cross-country-skiing movements. They also produce a ski bounder (*Sno-Bound'r*), which trains the athlete for the side-to-side torsions of the snowplowing of downhill skiing.

	LT-35	XC-1	Snobounder
Price	$420	$550	$320

Fitness Master Inc.
1260 Park Rd.
Chanhassen, MN 55317
800-328-8995

OTHER AEROBIC TRAINING DEVICES

You may remember seeing the *VersaClimber* in the Russian training camp in the movie *Rocky IV*, but it has been a common sight in serious health clubs for some time. It is a total-body climbing device that vigorously trains the arms and legs in a cardiovascular workout. The specialized ECG heart-rate sensing system provides a display of the actual heart rate, present heart-rate goal, exercise time, step height, and work performance measured in feet per minute. The microprocessor has a personalized heart-rate control mode (using sensing technology originally developed for NASA) and 15 preprogrammed workout modes with increasing levels of difficulty. This information is programmed in via a dial. The computer acts as a biofeedback speedometer, and during the workout the workload is recalculated every 30 seconds. The LCD read-

Fitness Master SnoBound'r   *VersaClimber*

outs display actual climbing speed in feet per minute (0 to 240 feet), total accumulated exercise time up to 99 minutes, 15 different programs, a total of accumulated feet climbed, two modes (Preprogrammed or Heart-Rate Control), selector for desired heart rate (120 to 190 beats per minute), and selector for standard time, rate, distance, and step height.

Models range in height from 93" to 106" and start at $2,000.

VersaClimber/Heart Rate Inc.
   3186-G Airway Ave.
   Costa Mesa, CA 92626-6601
   714-850-9716

Another unique device is the StairMaster by Tritech. This machine simulates the action of walking up stairs, accompanied by a rotating series of stairs with varying speed controls. The user's performance is monitored by an eye-level TV console that measures heart rate, caloric expenditure, VO_2 max, METS, watts, kilograms per meter, rate of exercise, and time of exer-

Tritech StairMaster

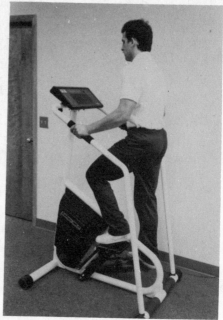

StairMaster 4000-PT

cise. This data is recorded with a thermal printer to provide a permanent record of performance. The primary electronic components of the *StairMaster 6000* are: monochromatic monitor, microcomputer, heart monitor, and thermal printer. The speed of the unit is checked every 1/60 of a second, so calculations are constantly updated. The climbing speeds vary from 45 to 115 steps per minute.

    Height: 75" Length: 51" Width: 32" Weight: 350 lbs.
    Price: $3,000 to $3,500, depending on features.

A smaller version of this unit is the *StairMaster 4000PT*. Weighing 80 pounds, this machine utilizes an LED dot matrix system to take the user through a series of interval training sessions.

StairMaster Sports/Medical Products
    259 Route 17K
    Newburgh, NY 12550
    800-722-0089

CHAPTER XIV

INSTITUTIONAL-LEVEL EXERCISE EQUIPMENT

The sophistication of upper-level exercise equipment has reached heights unforeseen by fitness buffs of the past. Just a decade or so ago, the only people who had a gym in their home were either very wealthy, eccentric, or fitness fanatics. A gym back then may have meant a few dumbbells and free weights and a stationary cycle. Since then the sporting-goods industry has grown into a $16-billion-dollar market, with more than 30 million Americans claiming to own some sort of exercise equipment. In 1984, $1 billion was spent on some form of equipment by home consumers. Americans purchased 1.5 million jogging trampolines; 750,000 multipurpose gyms; and 500,000 rowing machines. A Gallup poll noted that 59 percent of all adults exercised daily, which is 12 percent more than a 1982 figure and double the figure for 1961.

If you want to know where the home market is headed, just look at the institutional market. Just as computers that once filled a large room are now desk-top size, today's institutional exercise devices can be expected to go from the exclusive health clubs to your basement or living room in the near future.

EAGLE/CYBEX

One of the real emerging powers in the field of rehabilitation medicine is Eagle/Cybex. As most in the medical community know, Cybex pioneered the medical diagnostic muscle testing systems, and now with their selecterized weight training system (Eagle), they are taking a large share of the rehabilitation sports-medicine market. Their twenty-two different-single station selecterized units are manufactured in a two-hundred-thousand-square-foot facility. The pulleys are glass-reinforced nylon pulleys that cradle nylon coated aircraft cable with a breaking strength of over 4200 pounds. Precision-sealed bearings are maintenance free and sealed for smooth operation and to keep dirt out. The painted surface is electrostatically applied epoxy powder finish, and is scratch- and chip-resistant. The weight-stack guide rods are solid case-hardened steel with hard chrome finish, and the plate bushings are low friction for a smooth feel. The weight stacks are solid cold-rolled steel, and the wrinkle finish hides fingerprints and scuff marks.

The biomechanics on Eagle units are exceptional and can be individually adjusted to women and men, height 4'10" to 6'6".

Many of the units have a range-limiting mechanism so that for muscle rehabilitation the range of motion can be adjusted in 10 degree increments, with this being a standard feature on the leg curl, leg extension, pullover, and back extension units. A finishing touch are the 7" × 11" placards that visually illustrate each exercise step by step, and show body positioning.

Eagle/Cybex
2100 Smithtown Ave.
Ronkonkoma, NY 11779
800-645-5392

PARAMOUNT*

Computer technology has been making inroads into the fitness industry for several years. The first machines to use this technology were sophisticated units designed primarily for physical therapy and user evaluation. Such machines usually require technicians to operate them and, for most institutions, their cost is prohibitive.

Paramount Fitness Equipment Corporation has been an innovator of quality fitness equipment since the days of the barbell. Paramount has recently introduced a line of affordable, safe, easy-to-use computer-controlled exercise equipment. The Computer Fitness Systems features include "user friendly" graphics, resistance programmable in one-pound increments,

*The information on pages 184–188 has been reprinted with permission from Paramount Fitness Equipment Corp., Inc.

microprocessor-controlled variable resistance that follows the isometric power curves for the muscles exercised, and also performance information. This allows the users to gauge their progress and identify their deficiencies.

Paramount's research has found that the most reliable electronic means of resistance is the electromagnetic brake. The electromagnetic brake provides infinite variable resistance with a minimum of electronics (as compared to a DC motor). It has a proven history in industry operating under severe use conditions. These brakes also can supply resistance in both directions, allowing for the design of dual-function machines. Paramount coupled the electronic brake with a chain-drive gearbox to achieve a quiet, smooth-running, high-torque unit.

A sophisticated yet simple microprocessor circuit and keyboard allows for resistance adjustment in one-pound increments. This resistance is the maximum force exerted during the exercise movement. The point at which the maximum occurs is determined by the isometric power curve for the muscles being exercised. The microprocessor varies the resistance to the brake in accordance with a power curve stored in its memory. Some machines feature resistance in both the inward and outward direction. On these machines a different resistance may be selected for each direction. Each resistance is displayed on the electronics panel as it is selected.

If a user selects a resistance greater than the machine is capable of accepting, the electronics will automatically default to the maximum for that machine. Likewise, the lifting mechanisms for each machine contribute resistance of their own, so if a user selects a resistance that is less than the minimum for the machine, the electronics will default to the minimum for that machine.

Information is available from the electronics panel to provide the user with feedback both during and after the exercise set. In addition to the weight resistance selected, the number of repetitions, the time spent exercising, and the average range of motion for the set (in percent) are all displayed numerically. As the user goes through the movement, a light bar graph indicates the range of motion from 0 to 100 percent. If the individual only moves through a portion of the exercise range, the bar graph will indicate that limited movement as a percent of the whole range.

After the set is complete, a performance rating is calculated, based on the average range of motion and the speed of

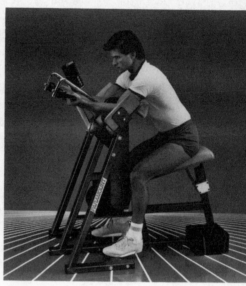
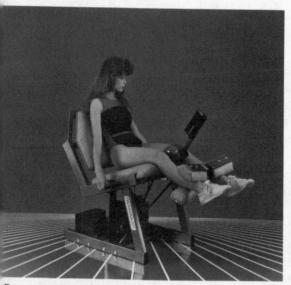
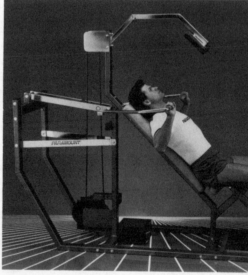

Paramount exercise machines

movement. This rating (from 0 to 10.0) gives the user a number by which she can gauge her performance. Analysis lights also illuminate at this time to further help the user improve. These lights tell the user to increase his/her range of motion (if the average is below 90 percent), and/or to vary the speed of movement or weight chosen.

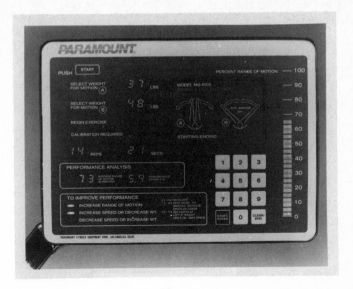

Paramount's System incorporates a number of safety features into the basic design of each unit. User fatigue has always been a source of possible injury. These machines have
no gravitational forces, thus if the user stops mid-movement,
nothing will happen. Also, if the user is struggling to complete
the last repetition and stops moving for two seconds, the power
to the brake will be decreased gradually and therefore decrease the resistance.

A constantly charging battery system will maintain electrical power to the circuit in the event of a power failure. This
will prevent injury if someone is working out and power to the
machine is disrupted.

All frames are constructed from 1.5″ × 3″ × .120″ wall structural steel tubing for integrity and durability. These frames are
coated with a tough epoxy powder coating for long-lasting
good looks and low maintenance.

All pivot points feature bronze bushings or ball bearings for
smooth movement.

Steel gears and sprockets are used wherever power transmission is required. Number 40 roller chain with a tensile
strength of 3,700 pounds is used on each unit.

The upholstered pads use high-density foam (in many
places 2½″ thick), ¾″ plywood and commercial-grade Nau-

gahyde. This combination provides for comfort and long-lasting good looks.

Paramount Fitness
    6636 E. 26th St.
    Los Angeles, CA 90046
    800-854-0184

HYDRA-FITNESS*

Each Hydra-Fitness omnikinetic machine provides resistance that is determined by the contractile capabilities of the muscle being exercised. This is made possible by the use of hydraulic cylinders instead of plates, weights, or inertia-reel mechanisms. The SERIES III machines feature hydraulic cylinders with settings of "1" through "6" so you can adjust them to vary the impulse and thus the resistance. At any one of these settings, the user, by exerting a maximal effort, will optimally overload the contractile and energy production capabilities of the muscle fibers at the limb speed these fibers are capable of producing.

This is true because, although the valve on the cylinder is pre-set, the rate of speed required for perfect self-accommodating resistance is not pre-set to an invariable value. The valves establish the machine's resistance to lever arm movements. They do this by changing the aperture size through which hydraulic fluid must flow as the lever arm moves. The faster you move the lever arm, the more resistance you will meet.

However, as your muscles fatigue, you will not be able to move the lever arm as fast as you did when you started the exercise bout. On Hydra-Fitness omnikinetic machines, you will find that the resistance will follow you as you slow your movements because of muscle fatigue, and will continue to accommodate itself to your movements until you can no longer do the movements. In short, although you may slow down as a result of fatigue, your fatigued muscles will be receiving an optimal accommodating resistance automatically as long as you continue to move the lever arms with maximal effort.

The uniqueness of Hydra-Fitness omnikinetic machines lies partly in the fact that while the valve is pre-set, the rate at which the limb moves against the resistance of the cylinder is determined so much by the machine as it is by the contractile

*The information on pages 188–191 has been reprinted with permission from Hydra-Fitness, Inc.

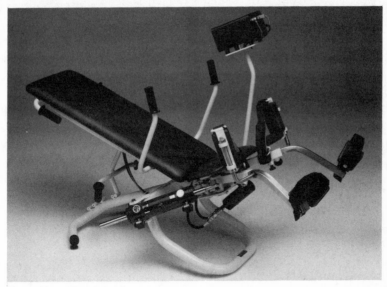

Omni-Tron Hip Ad/Ab

Omni-Tron Knee Machine   *Total Power Unit*

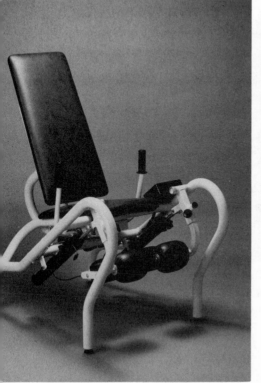

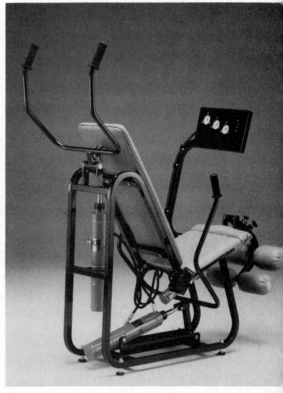

properties of the user's muscle fibers and the muscle groups
that those fibers constitute.

Consequently, at a given valve setting, the user receives
optimal resistance overload with each repetition performed,
even as the muscle fatigues. Although the speed of the movement may decrease as the muscle fatigues, the *effective*
resistance overload remains the same. Thus, the user achieves
optimal resistance overload at the beginning of the set when
his muscles are at their peak energy level, and also at the end
of the set when his muscles are fatigued.

The stronger the user, the faster he will be able to perform
the movement at a given valve setting. As his muscles fatigue,
he will not be able to move the lever arm as fast as he did
when he began the set. As he fatigues more and more, he will
move the lever arm more and more slowly.

But as he moves the lever arm more slowly, those muscle
fibers that were contributing less at the fast speeds now increase their involvement—and therefore their contribution—to
the total force pool.

Consequently, as the muscles being exercised fatigue, the
resistance offered by the machine does not decrease as dramatically as with isokinetic devices. Further, contrary to the operation of isotonic devices, the self-accommodating variable
resistance allows continued movements, instead of precluding
movement after a few repetitions.

HYDRA's machines also feature unique, unilateral and bilateral double-positive action, which allows alternating contractions of opposing muscle groups. The agonist shortens
while the antagonist lengthens; then the opposing muscles are
activated, with the original agonist becoming the antagonist
and the original antagonist becoming the agonist. Let's look at
the muscles of the upper leg as an example. As the quadriceps
contract, they are the agonist in the leg extension at the knee,
while the hamstring group is the antagonist. Then, when the
leg flexes and begins its movement away from full extension,
the hamstrings become the agonist and the quads, the antagonists. This alternating contraction and relaxation of opposing
muscle groups simulates the action of actual sports movements
such as running and assures proper balance in development.

Bilateral Muscle Action

Bilateral muscle action occurs on HYDRA-FITNESS OM-
NIKINETIC machines when they allow both limbs to move

against the same lever arm in the same direction at the same time. An example would be the action of the SERIES III Quad/Hamstring machine, in which both legs can be extended or flexed at the same time. Another example would be the SERIES III Bench Press/Row.

Unilateral Muscle Action

Unilateral muscle action occurs on HYDRA-FITNESS OM-NIKINETIC machines when they allow the movement of a limb or pair of limbs independently of each other, in opposite directions or in the same direction, against separate resistances, separately or alternately. This movement is possible, for example, on the SERIES III Unilateral Quad/Hamstring machine. For unilateral movement on this machine (for example), one leg extends while the other flexes. On one leg the quads contract while the hamstrings relax, while at the same time on the other leg, the hamstrings contract while the quads relax. It is also possible, of course, to work only one leg at a time on the Unilateral Quad/Hamstring, since resistance and linkages for each leg are independent. Further, both legs can be worked in the same direction at the same time.

Hydra-Fitness
   P.O. Box 599
   2121 Industrial Blvd.
   Belton, TX 76513
   800-792-3013

David 200   *David 300*

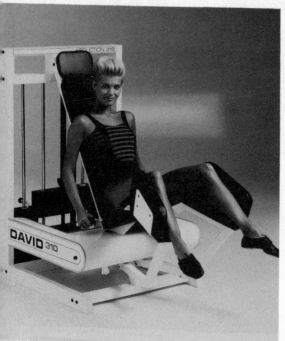

David 310

David 500

David 510

David 700

David 800

David 900

DAVID FITNESS

David Fitness is a Scandinavian-designed series of single-station units that have some unique features. Traditionally, exercise equipment has been designed to provide variable resistance. Tension increases throughout each movement until the muscles are fully contracted. By placing the greatest stress on muscles in their fully contracted state, variable resistance demands the most of muscles when they are least able to adapt. David feels this not only prevents efficient physical functioning but can also cause injury.

David Fitness equipment does exactly the opposite. It demands the most of your muscles when they are strongest, and when they can benefit most. A cam system balances resistance with muscle strength, providing light resistance at the beginning of the movement, heavy in the midrange, and lightest at the point of maximum contraction. Not only does the equipment work you hardest when your potential strength is greatest but it also takes fatigue into account. As you complete successive repetitions of a movement, your motion slows. David matches your pace gradually, adjusting resistance as necessary to provide premium exercise benefit.

David reports that those using this scientifically designed system have been able to increase their total workload, the weight lifted, and the distance through which it is lifted by 30 to 40 percent from what they could accomplish with variable-resistance equipment. David's appealing functional design reflects European styling—no exposed chains or sprockets, no hydraulics, no extra pads are needed to fit smaller frames. A unique weight stack doubles available resistance and weight functions. You can increase your lifts in 11-pound increments rather than the 25-pound shifts required by some traditional exercise machines. Top weights range between 308 and 660 pounds. The cam is connected to the weight stack by a maintenance-free polyamide belt. Needle and roller bearings provide smooth action but require no lubrication.

There are 12 new machines in David's second generation of units, with an entire line costing from $30,650 to $34,000. David's Finnish founder, 30-year old Arno Parviainen, has taken his company from a novel breed of equipment to one of the leading companies in the field internationally.

David Fitness Equipment, Inc.
177 Main Street
Suite 202
Fort Lee, NJ 07024
800-843-8577

MYOTECH/MUSCLE DYNAMICS

Myotech, a division of Muscle Dynamics, has developed a microprocessor-controlled electro-hydraulic exercise system. Their design features include:

1 A low mass system that eliminates high acceleration or shock forces.
2 The addition of a damping factor that provides smooth movement and eliminates jerkiness.
3 Mechanically rigid components and a fast-acting control system that provide a quick, tight response to movement and force changes and also eliminate sponginess, backlash, and play in the machine.

Conventional machines without these capabilities have sticking points, regions of too high or too low resistance, or

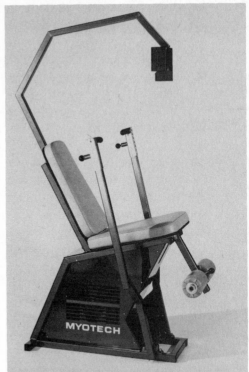

Myotech exercise machines

jerkiness. This can give the sensation of the machine controlling you, or of hitting a brick wall in the middle of a movement.
Myotech's machines are antiballistic and inertially compen-
sated, serving to prevent possible hazardous reactions as you
accelerate from one transition point to another.

Feel is very important in evaluating these machines. The
Myotech machines give the sensation of providing continuous
tension on the muscle without the weak or jagged points so
often found in some units. The resistance is infinitely adjustable, so that true positive (concentric) and negative training
(eccentric) can be performed.

The resistance through the full range of motion is fully accommodating to the specific strength curve of the individual.
The muscle can be preloaded at any desired level or start position. These choices are known as Volitionally Operant Exercise
(VOEX), and the resistance mode is called Polyphasic because
it offers the features of both isotonic and isokinetic exercise.
Mike Stima, president of Myotech, explains, "The end result to
the users is that they experience fully accommodating resistance while under the continuous tension, the effect of which
virtually eliminates any discontinuities associated with acceleration and deceleration that occur with weight machines.

"Exercise should be defined in terms of both movement and
resistance. The resistance provided on the Myotech unit is always positive and unidirectional, but in terms of movement, the
physiology of the muscle is such that it contracts concentrically
(fibers lengthen with negative movement and work). In both
cases, the muscle is contracting, although the direction of movement is opposite. The Myotech design results in the muscle
getting a level of resistance set by the user. Therefore, the fric-
tional compensation component allows for equal loading in both
muscle contractile conditions. This function is called Equi-
Positive/Negative Resistance, and allows for precise resistance
application during any format selected. The format choices:

1 Positive only
2 Negative only
3 Negative Accentuated (more resistance on negative portion than
   on positive)
4 Hyper Negative (negative motion forces you down even if you are
   exerting your maximal effort)
5 Hypo Negative (less resistance on the negative portion)

Movement velocity can be varied infinitely within the range
of inertial compensation. This gives users the ability to select

any speed they need, for the kind of training they want. The resistance will adjust itself to the force applied—automatically and instantaneously. Mr. Stima goes on to say in the *National Fitness Trade Journal* that "Myotech offers, in addition to all the features currently provided by cam/weight stack machines, these additional features:

1 Continuous tension
2 Accommodating resistance
3 Antiballistic action
4 Inertial compensation
5 Friction compensation
6 Polyphasic resistance
7 Volitionally Operant Exercise (VOEX)
8 Infinite adjustment of preload and positive/negative resistance
9 Multimodal contraction
10 Variable velocity
11 Automatically sensed force

"All units will allow option enhancement, including the ability to link to micro-, mini- or main-frame computers for data acquisition and evaluation."

Muscle Dynamics, the parent company for Myotech, is a producer of top-quality selectorized single and multistation weight-training machines. Their Maxicam line is unique in design since the machines are customized to suit the client. A product of Muscle Dynamics that has made significant impact on the home market is a series of modular single-station units that can be attached to each other to suit the shape of the room. For this they have teamed up with Ivanko Barbell, probably one of the finest manufacturers of barbells and dumbbells, to tool the metal plates. The modular single-station units, instead of just having painted-on weight numbers, have individual miniplates of inlayed brass and black enamel with the weight number clearly displayed implanted right into the front of the larger chromed weight plates. Ivanko is the top-quality source for well-calibrated and finely constructed free weights.

Muscle Dynamics/Myotech
    17022 Montanero St.
    Carson, CA 90746-4606
    213-637-9500

Ivanko Barbell Company
    P.O. Box 1470
    San Pedro, CA 90733
    213-514-1155

NAUTILUS

In 1948, Arthur Jones built the first prototype Nautilus machine. It was a pullover model designed to apply rotary and direct resistance to the upper arms and against muscles that work around the axis of the shoulders. This prototype was a major design breakthrough. It solved the problems of rotary and direct resistance, and exposed other deficiencies of the barbell. One of these is the requirement for variable resistance.

As a muscle contracts, its effective strength changes. Optimum exercise provides correct variable resistance in every possible position.

Because of changing leverage and directions of movement, the resistance supplied by a barbell changes, but it varies arbitrarily, not according to the need of the muscle. Jones believed efficient exercise required variable and balanced resistance—resistance that is properly balanced to the potential strength of the muscle in every position.

The requirements for variable and balanced resistance led

Nautilus exercise machines

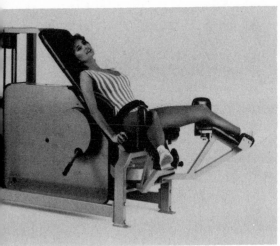

Nautilus exercise machines

to the concept of a cam. A Nautilus cam is a pulley with an off-center axis. Placing a cam appropriately in an exercise machine alters the trainee's leverage.

The cam configuration was designed to vary the resistance properly throughout the range of movement. Since the profile of one of the early cams resembled the silhouette of the chambered nautilus shell, Nautilus became the name for the exercise tool named after it.

Nautilus is constantly updating its line of institutional machines, has increased the number of units, and has added free plate loading leverage machines. With these units there is no need to balance the weight plates. They have also developed a line of machines on a slightly smaller scale specifically for women. Still in the prototype stage is a series of medical diagnostic units for the medical community called Tensiometers.

Nautilus Sports/Medical Industries
    P.O. Box 1783
    Deland, FL 32721
    800-874-8941

TYGR USA

Tygr USA produces a series of 11 single-station units that utilize an electromagnetic break and computer interfaces to provide a wide variety of training protocols. Tygr units can generate forces of up to 750 pounds, and can be calibrated to 0.03 pounds. Personalized force curves can be programmed in as well as positive and negative curves. Via electronic technology, 2 separate force profiles for each phase of the exercise motion are possible. The Pyramid program takes the user on a linear progression of increased resistance step by step, up to maximum resistance potential.

TYGR USA
    1775 38th St.
    Boulder, CO 80301
    303-443-7127

Tygr USA exercise machines

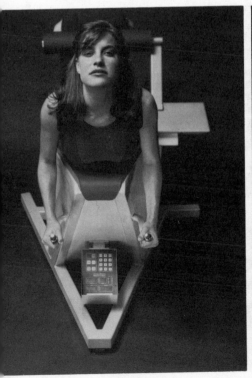 

HUNK FITNESS

Hunk Fitness manufactures a unique pulley system that is re-
defining training for the handicapped. Their VVF (Variable
Vector Force) pulley system reduces risk of joint wear while
broadening the range of muscle development. The machine's
pulley is mounted on a chassis that slides on a guide rod, so
that the pulley mechanism moves with the user. In this way,
the cable never touches the body.

Hunk is also well known for powerfully built institutional-
level body-building equipment, and places pieces in "hard-
core" gyms to aid in the redesigning process. They tend to use
extra steel freely to make powerful equipment. The equipment
is "overengineered," constructed with extra-heavy-gauge steel
with gussets (which are 45-degree arched additional support
pieces). Stress points are "stress-relieved" (heating after the
welding process). All parts are deburred for tighter fit in

Hunk Fitness variable vector machines

the welded points, and cut to .007 of an inch for precision fit. The high-tensile, high-silicone content of the welding wire gives it a 93,000-pound tensile strength.

Welds are done on all 4 sides of the tubing, and square tubing gives more surface-steel thickness for greater strength than just circular tubing (which has less surface area). Hunk uses 3 different types of foam for better support. All fasteners are locking aircraft fasteners, and all equipment is acid-etched for better paint retention. It is also rust-proofed inside and out. There is a lifetime warranty on all metal structures, and they are built under compressive loading, not shear mechanics, so that torsion factors have less effect.

Hunk Fitness
    3030 W. Carroll Ave.
    Chicago, IL 60612
    312-722-HUNK

Range-adjustment mechanisms are now seeing popular use in institutional-level pieces made by Universal, Polaris, and Eagle fitness equipment. These utilize a holding pin to limit the range of motion by a specific joint rotatory movement on the machine.

SERIOUS LIFTING SYSTEMS

Serious Lifting Systems uses an advanced enclosed design of weight stacks with ball-bearing supported load devices in combination with a belt coupling made of nylon/Kevlar. Using the nylon/Kevlar combo on the belts instead of just chains or cables gives a tensile strength of more than 5,000 pounds, with less than 1 percent stretch coefficient. Since there are no chains, the machines are silent. They use self-locking safety catches, not cotter pins, to hold the weight. A hardened and ground shaft is used in all the pressing machines. The company provides a choice of 15 premier electrostatically coated colors, and can even build machines in stainless steel upon request. Their leg extension is a 275-pound stock resistance unit, and continues maximum resistance through 100 degrees via the cam effect. The weight can be adjusted while in the seated position.

Serious Lifting Systems Enclosed Leg Extension

Serious Lifting Systems
   2120 Chanticleer
   Santa Cruz, CA 95062
   408-724-7727

Each of the following companies are well known for quality institutional-level single-station and multi-station weight-based equipment:

POLARIS

Polaris produces more than 25 different variable-resistance machines, 10 multi-jungles, and more than 20 different benches and pulleys. Their equipment is built with solid-welded framework, hardwood, powder-fused coatings, aircraft cable (nylon coated), and steel cam systems. Pulley wheels are constructed with aluminum alloy, and the cables have a breaking strength of 2 tons. The bearings are made of self-lubricating Turcite,

Polaris Pullover   *Polaris Lying Leg Curl*

and press fit into seamless tubing. Weight stacks are steel, not cast iron, in 5-, 10-, and 15-pound increments.

Polaris/Iron Co.
    P.O. Box 1458
    Spring Valley, CA 92077
    800-858-0300

UNIVERSAL

Universal Fitness Equipment began in 1957, when the company developed a special weight-training unit that incorporated several resistance exercise stations with selectorized weight stacks. They were the first to develop a patented Dynamic Variable Resistance (DVR) mechanism, which automatically and progressively adjusts the machine's weight resistance to accommodate the body's changing leverage during each lifting stroke.

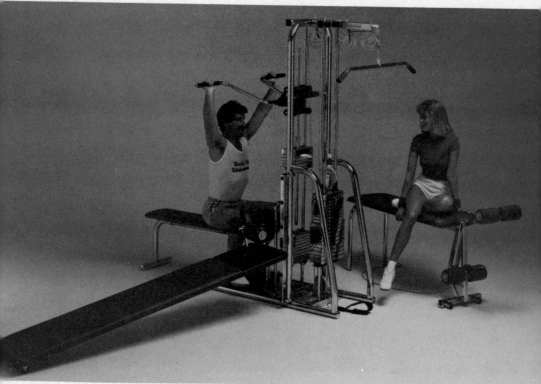

Universal Power-Pak 400

Universal is one of the few companies that do their chroming in-house, and has an extensive research and design department to develop new concepts. Their equipment is made of 2-inch-diameter tubular steel that is welded and bolted into a strong integral unit. All Universal equipment has a tough duplex nickel-chrome finish. The weight stacks feature self-lubricating inserts (Capron Nylon 6), which float and self-align as the stack moves up and down on runner guides. In addition, Universal has an extensive educational network, to keep customers informed and updated long after the equipment is in place.

Universal Fitnet System

Fitnet is a network of computerized electronic resistance exercise machines and aerobic devices that are controlled by a host computer. The speed and position are registered 30 times/degrees of movement. Force or torque is accurate to [+]

or [−] 1 foot 1/10 pound according to Universal, and the resistance can change 285 times/sec.

The user is given immediate feedback, and post-exercise printouts can be produced, as well as a permanent data base formed. The computer used is an IBM-AT compatible, with high resolution color graphics with a 640K memory. The terminal screen is three and a half times sharper than a TV screen. Each Fitnet user is given a computer card to gain access to and operate the system. This special card allows the user to get his personalized exercise prescription from the host computer. The eleven exercise machines in the system are shoulder press/pulldown, low pulley, total hip, arm curl/triceps extension, chest press/seated row, abdominal/back extension, vertical chest/reverse fly, leg press/hip flexion, rotary oblique, leg extension/leg curl, and high pulley. Positive resistance is used in both directions. Each machine has four customized high-speed microprocessors, which can handle one million instructions per second and up to four billion operations per second. The Fitnet networking system communicates at 375,000 bytes of information per second. This is about 120 times faster than normal modem communications.

The types of training that can be utilized are IDVR (own individual force curve); Isokinetics (at a prescribed speed); Pyramid (4 types—climb, descend, hill, and valley [resistance getting easier or harder]).

Universal Corp.
    P.O. Box 1270
    930 27th Ave. S.W.
    Cedar Rapids, IA 52406
    800-553-7901

KINESI-ARC

Kinesi-Arc attempts to simulate the feel of free-weight lifting by not locking in the lifting fulcrum, as is typical with many of the units now on the market. They attempt to be the compromise between free weights and selectorized machines. Their machine chain hookup is positioned right where the weight would be with a barbell or dumbbell, giving a natural feel to the exercise. The Kinesi-Arc machines allow a full range of motion, including a deep stretch. They employ dual stack action so that each arm can train independent of the other, as would be the case with free weights. They designed their machines by filming the action and biomechanics of free-weight lifting and then modeling the construction after these movements.

Kinesi-Arc/Pro Gym Systems
P.O. Box 10
13 Ilene Ct.
Belle Mead, NJ 08502
201-874-4544

KEISER

The Cam II system developed by Keiser Sports Health Equipment is the forerunner of a new breed of low-inertia variable-resistance machines. Pressurizing pneumatic cylinders with compressed air creates the resistance, rather than the high-inertia iron weights used in other machines. A pressure regulator located on each machine is controlled by the user to select the exact air pressure supplied to the pneumatic cylinders. The only moving mass (inertia) involved in this system is the piston and rod, which weigh approximately 3 pounds. This is a significant reduction when compared to 491 pounds of moving mass in an equivalent iron-weight stack, enabling a strength curve to be programmed into the machines and have that curve remain consistent over a wide range of speeds. Automatic closing of a valve as the arm leaves the starting position traps the air in the cylinder and further compresses it. While moving through the positive stroke (or concentric contraction), this allows for storage of the energy expended on that positive stroke so that it can be delivered back on the negative stroke (or eccentric contraction). This, in turn, provides an eccentric contraction equal to the concentric contraction, which is impossible with a high-inertia system except at extremely slow speeds. Also, as the air is further compressed in the cylinder, its pressure increases, thus increasing the force output on the cylinder. This, plus the changes in leverage by the linkages, is how the variable-resistance curve is programmed, eliminating the use of cams and chains. This is the exact method by which the human body carries its forces. The contractive effort of the

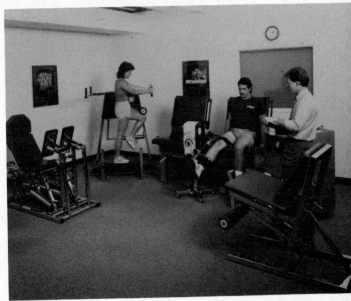

Keiser Cam II Systems

muscle changes as it shortens, and the muscular leverage changes as the joint passes through its range of movement.

Keiser Sports Health Equipment
   411 S. West Ave.
   Fresno, CA 93706
   209-266-2715

BALLY FITNESS

Makers of the highly motivating and visual Lifecycle and Life-rower have made their entrance into the institutional single-station-unit market with the Lifecircuit. This system carries a three-year warranty and consists of three minicircuits of four machines each. A video training program called the Lifecenter provides touch-screen access to instruction on the machines. The Lifecircuit simulates the feel and intensity of free-weight lifting, but instead of weight stacks is a simple touch-control console.

   The heart of every Lifecircuit machine is a self-instructing touch-sensitive console that walks the user through both beginner and advanced weight-lifting routines. In addition to a first-time-user strength test, Lifecircuit machines provide standard constant-weight resistance programs and variable-resistance strength curves.

Lifecircuit also utilizes the accepted pyramid concept that warms up the muscles before generating a level of resistance that varies for beginners, intermediate, and advanced users, then ends with a cool-down phase. The advanced pyramid program provides peak-effort training and adjustable negative resistance for maximum strength and muscle-size building. Range of motion is adjustable so that Lifecircuit machines can be used in therapeutic programs.

Instructions appear in lighted word commands; resistance appears in lighted numerals; each repetition is monitored by rising and descending colored lights. Cumulative repetitions are displayed to eliminate bothersome counting. Instant visual feedback is a Bally Fitness product trademark. A graphic instruction chart is also attached to the surface of every Lifecircuit machine.

Weight resistance is provided by a quiet electronic-belt-drive system. Modular construction makes service simple. Bally Fitness is considering a wiring package which will help club owners reconfigure the outlet access necessary to operate the complete 12-machine Lifecircuit system.

The self-instructing design of Lifecircuit equipment is targeted at cutting down the often-extensive club personnel time required with some weight-training equipment.

Open-port design in Lifecircuit equipment permits software updates for more advanced exercise programs, cardreader capability for monitoring trainee use, and the addition of color CRT screens as well as IBM PC interface for extensive record keeping and program analysis.

Bally Fitness
 9601 Jeronimo Rd.
 Irvine, CA 92718
 714-859-1011

■

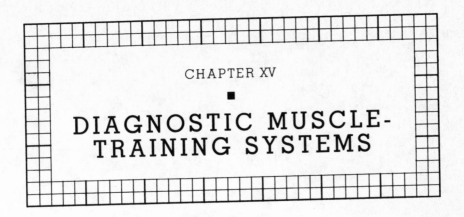

CHAPTER XV

■

DIAGNOSTIC MUSCLE-TRAINING SYSTEMS

These systems go a step beyond standard exercise equipment by isolating particular muscle groups in order to evaluate and increase their output.

HYDRA-FITNESS

The *Omni-Tron* by Hydra-Fitness utilizes Omnikinetics, which means variable resistance at a variable speed of movement. It was designed to give an accommodating resistance back to whatever force one applies. The Omni-Tron features Omnikinetic exercise, double concentric variable extension/flexion controls, and multiple-plane exercise. The individual Omni-Tron machines include the total power, knee, shoulder, and hip units.

Hydra-Fitness
  P.O. Box 599
  Belton, TX 76513-0599
  800-792-3013

UNIVERSAL

Universal has come out with the MERAC (Musculoskeletal Evaluation, Rehabilitation, and Conditioning) system, which offers six testing modes for the knee, ankle, shoulder, hip, wrist, and elbow; a single bench system with attachments for all planes and testing protocols; speeds up to 500 degrees per

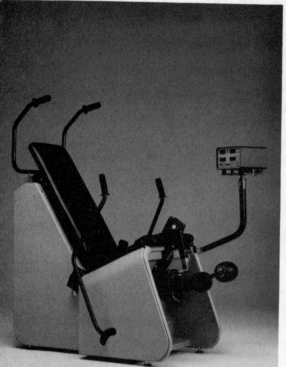
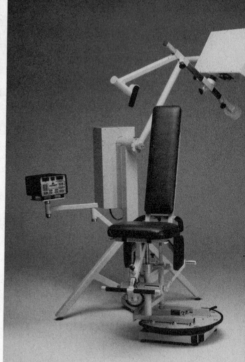

Omni-Tron Shoulder Machine   *Omni-Tron Total Power*

second and torque to 500 foot-pounds; protocol set-up and storage; and automatic data calculations for work, power, fatigue, and exertion.

In addition to isokinetic training, MERAC offers isokinetic fatigue, isotonic fatigue, isometric, individualized dynamic variable resistance (IDVR) testing, and conditioning modes.

Time measurements are in milliseconds, work measurements in joules, power in watts, exertion in torque-seconds, strength in foot-pounds, and torque in newton-meters. The unit self-monitors torque 1,000 times per second, speed up to 11,333 times per second, and position 32,400 times per second.

MERAC
    Universal Corp.
    P.O. 1270
    930 27th Ave. S.W.
    Cedar Rapids, IA 52406
    800-553-7901

CYBEX

Cybex was the first company to develop isokinetic-testing devices. Their Cybex 2+ is a passive-resistance system. The accommodation is patient-activated (not computer-controlled robotic). Limb velocities may be tested and treated up to 300 degrees per second. A Dual-Channel Recorder produces high-resolution real-time printouts (up to 360 ft-lb) and range of motion (up to 300 degrees).

Some of the torque measurements and calculations possible are maximum gravity effect torque, where all torque ratio effects are considered with gravity calculated in. Peak torque and angle of occurrence aid in measuring muscular-tension intensity. Opposing muscle-group torque ratios and maximum range of motion are also tested. Cybex also has a back-testing and -training unit.

Cybex
2100 Smithtown Ave.
Ronkonkoma, NY 11779
516-585-9000

KIN-COM

Kin-Com produces a unit that tests all the major muscle groups—in the wrist, elbow, shoulder, back, abdominals, hip,

MERAC

Cybex

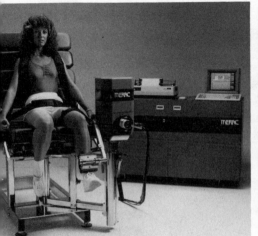

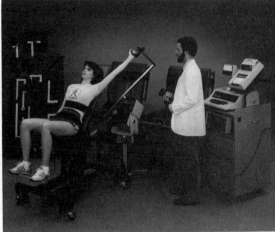

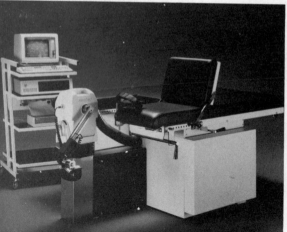

Kin-Com

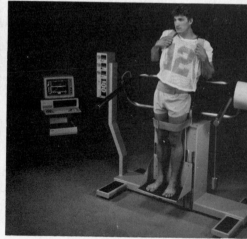

Isotechnologies back-testing unit

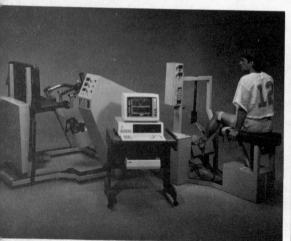

Isotechnologies knee-testing and
ankle-testing units

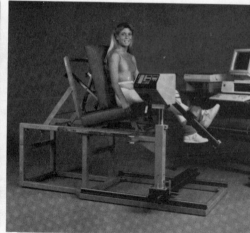

Loredan Lido

knee, and ankle. Available testing and training modes are
isometric, isokinetic (max eccentric testing, accelera-
tion/deceleration controls), the Force Mode (isotonic) to test normal muscular activity of acceleration and deceleration, and the
Passive Mode for patients needing assistance. Kim-Com integrates EMG (electromyography) with the testing procedures.
The force resistances are supplied by hydraulics.

Kin-Com/Chattecx Corp.
   P.O. Box 4287

101 Memorial Dr.
Chattanooga, TN 37405
615-870-2281

ISOTECHNOLOGIES

Isotechnologies has developed a series of joint diag-
nostic/rehabilitation machines. They are performance-testing
tools that accommodate natural acceleration, constant speed,
and deceleration over the full range of complex movements.
Each of these machines allows three dimensions of motion,
with the resistance module for each axis of rotation remotely
and independently controlled. Light-emitting diodes display
the established resistance that must be overcome for angular
acceleration to occur. The units available from Isotechnologies
are for training the back, knee, and ankle. The back unit is
three-dimensional to measure flexion/extension, rotation, and
lateral flexion.

Isotechnologies
    P.O. Box 1239
    Hillsborough, NC 27278
    919-732-5961

LOREDAN

Loredan has developed the LIDO, a digital isokinetic rehabilitation system. These units are multijoint systems. Their
accommodating technology accounts for "moment arm" torque
changes by patients. The torque generated depends in part on
the distance between the biological axis of rotation and the
point at which the force is applied. Variability of dynamic flex-
ion-extension movements is accounted for by the employment
of a sliding chest carriage. The sliding lever arm compensates
for the normal change of the joint axis. Speed-based ramping
is internally controlled by an on-board electronic processor to
reduce impulse loading. Loredan also has knee- and back-
testing systems available.

LIDO/Loredan Biomedical, Inc.
   P.O. Box 1154
   Davis, CA 95617
   916-758-3622

BIODEX

The Biodex isokinetic system is utilized for muscle testing and rehabilitation. A joint-angle motion of 450 degrees per second is the maximum velocity. The maximum torque is 450 ft-lb, and the modes available are eccentric, continuous passive, iso-kinetic, and concentric/concentric loading modes.

Biodex
   P.O. Box S
   Shirley, NY 11967
   516-924-9300

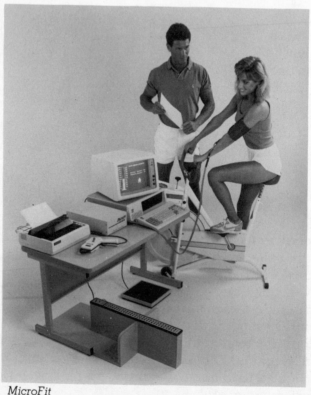

MicroFit

MICROFIT

MicroFit is a fully computerized fitness-evaluation system allowing for immediate graphic display of performance and automatic data collection. MicroFit evaluates all major components of fitness, including body weight, body fat, heart rate, blood pressure, flexibility, strength, and aerobic fitness. MicroFit compares test results to national standards and provides recommendations for improving fitness. The computer can also save test results and produce individual test-retest or group-analysis reports.

MicroFit
    P.O. Box 2107
    Menlo Park, CA 94025
    800-822-0405
    415-322-6738

■

PART 3

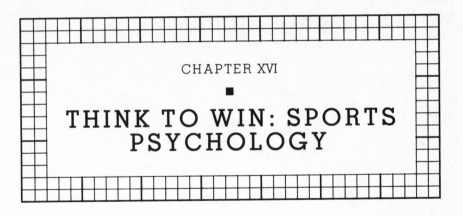

CHAPTER XVI

■

THINK TO WIN: SPORTS PSYCHOLOGY

Do or not do. There is no trying
—The Yoda,
from *The Empire Strikes Back*

The difference between the champion and the also-ran is the desire to win. Winning begets more winning. The science of sports psychology has come a long way. Many teams now have sports psychologists on staff, and some professional athletes even have their own personal psycher-uppers.

A sports psychologist can do many things, the first of which is to aid us in finding out what our true needs are. One of the pioneers in psychology, Abraham Maslow, outlined a series of basic human needs. In order to satisfy the higher needs in his hierarchy, lower order needs must first be met. Some of the lower-order needs are food, shelter, water, heat, clothes, and security, then traveling up to self-respect, love, etc. The culmination of these needs leads to "self-actualization," that is, living to our full capabilities and potentials.

Another psychologist, Andras Angyal, pointed out two basic categories of human needs: mastery and participation. Not only do we wish to become competent and successful but also part of the group. Thus arises the great camaraderie in team sports.

In their book *Psychological Foundations of Sports:* Mahoney and colleagues have summarized some techniques for augmenting the self-efficacy expectations of athletes:

1 Response-induction aids—devices that may reduce the perceived discrepancy between the athlete's current and desired performance

2 Modeling—having the athlete observe another individual who is successfully executing the skill

221

3 Self-efficacy statements—having an athlete practice saying positive statements to himself/herself prior to the performance
4 Imagery—having the athlete imagine him/herself performing the desired response
5 Verbal persuasion—reassuring and encouraging the athlete that he/she is capable of performing the desired response
6 Performance accomplishments—structuring the environment to create a successful experience. Avoid focusing solely on the outcome of the event without considering the process or level of performance exhibited.

MAXIMUM PERFORMANCE

The Soviets and East Germans have developed the field of "anthropomaximology," which is the study of human maximums. They view their athletes under pressure with a critical eye toward making modifications to augment performance, rather than correcting psychological imbalances. They feel time is better spent developing skills than worrying over who may be gaining on you. If you don't look over your shoulder, you won't waste time worrying about who is coming up on you.

There are those great moments in sports history when everything just seems to click for an athlete. Did you ever hit a tennis ball or have a game of bowling that just flowed perfectly from you. The Maslow term for this is a peak experience. He saw such experiences as those rare times in which we transcend our limitations to achieve states of beauty, wonder, bliss, clarity, calm, and wisdom, to use a few descriptive adjectives. These unplanned, unpredictable quantum-leap experiences were also described by Murphy and White (1978): "In hundreds of reports from athletes we have found that the sport experience produces many unusual feelings and ideas. We have noted sixty or more kinds of sensations in the sports, from a simple sense of well-being to exotic movements when the body seemed to stop time, or change shape, or free the self to travel out of the body.

"Their accounts support each other: Men and women in very different sports tell stories that are quite similar. Their experiences range from surges of speed and power to movements of mystery and awe, from ecstasy to peace and calm, from intrinsic right action to intimations of immortality, from detachment and perfect freedom to a sense of unity with all things, from a comfortable feeling of being at home to uncanny

incidents when the body, as if weightless, tells the brain that it
has taken up floating or flying."

As odd as this may sound, people in totally unrelated pro-
fessions—the salesman who just smoothly closed a major sale
and was astonished at the flow of words from his mouth—also
report similar experiences.

I have personally had a few of these experiences, the most
memorable being my high school New York Championship
wrestling match. I had dropped twenty-five pounds for the
match, and after defeating my first three opponents, I was to
go to the final championship match. By this time I was severely
dehydrated, spiking a fever, and not capable of even a brisk
walk let alone wrestling three time periods. I tried to capture
my feelings in the preface to my last book, *Death in the Locker
Room:*

"The air is thick and musty, as the boom of the heavy bass
of inner-city disco music reverberated through the large gym-
nasium, teeming with bodies covered in skin-tight, sleek nylon
wrestling gear. I have a sick feeling in the pit of my stomach,
after having not eaten for three days, in order to make weight
for the New York Wrestling Championships. Having to lose
twenty-five pounds in the last five days, my guts feel as if they
had been bound with wire and dropped down an elevator
shaft. Daydreaming for a minute, and blocking out the sound
of grunts and thuds as bodies clash in battle on the mats, I
reflect on this past week: The wearing of three layers of sweat
suits so I'd sweat more; running and wrestling until I passed
out in puddles of sweat-laden garb in a pool of body perspiration; the countless flights of stairs climbed; the tonnage of
weight moved in endless repetitions until muscle fibers
screamed for relief as the weights clanged to the floor. What
am I doing here? And why do I want to win this tournament so
badly?

"Three weeks ago, in an accident, I separated my wrestling
coach's shoulder going over moves together. Was this the
drive? To win, for him? Like a twig snapping, I am removed
from this dazed state by a teammate's tapping on my shoulder.
'Your name's been called,' he says slowly. I had won my first
three matches decidedly, but not without incident. I can taste
the dried blood in my mouth from the elbow that conveniently
found its way there. I think two of my fingers are broken, but
the white tape is hiding most of the swelling that is peeking out
from the uneven cracks. I'm so dehydrated, my lips keep stick-

ing together and my tongue cleaves to the roof of my mouth. My lips cracked, I retort, 'So soon?'

"I begin to feel the adrenaline, what's left of it, surge in my body as I walk past the judge's table, and in the corner of my eye I catch a glitter of the trophy's reflections, the award we are all fighting for. What seems like only an instant later, the whistle sounds, as my muscles are again interlocked in battle. I feel my muscles swell as the fatigue is replaced by rage and desire to win. Seconds of combat feel like minutes. My opponent makes the fatal mistake, and I clamp on him like a vice.

"It's over. As the referee holds up my arm, the room begins to spin and darken, my legs go to soft rubber, and I fall, like a loose sack of potatoes, to the floor. I ache all over, bloodied and sweat-laden—yet it feels so warm and wonderful inside. I won, and that was all I cared about."

I remember the event as though it were yesterday. I can still taste the blood in my mouth and feel those body aches. I was astonished at the power and strength that seemed to come from thin air. The event still mystifies me to this day.

Tom Kubistant, in his book *Performing Your Best*, wrote about achieving peak performance:

"1-Time seems to shift into slow motion, yet the event seems to go by so quickly. Golfers, bowlers, and baseball pitchers and batters have all reported that during such times, they seem to have all the time in the world to make last minute adjustments, and attend to all the details of their actions. Endurance radically improves. Marathon runners and triathletes have reported how they seem to have vast storehouses of energy, feeling as if they could go on for days. Writers, composers, and artists have noted how they achieved extreme levels of concentration for hours when they were creating something outstanding.

"2-Shapes and colors change. Martial arts students and football defensive backs have reported how their opponents seemed to change shape to elude them. Observers of figure skating have noted how sometimes a performer was just a blur that seemed to cover unbelievable distances during jumps and leaps. Those experiencing peak performances also reported how familiar colors seem to strangely alter or change altogether. These alterations almost always coincide with shifts in time perspectives.

"3-Sizes and weights change. Weight and power lifters and shot put, javelin, and discus throwers have reported times when their objects seemed so light that they felt they could lift or throw any weight any distance. Golfers, tennis and racquetball players, and baseball hitters said that there were times when their implements became so light and diffuse that they almost seemed to become a natural extension of their arms, so much so that they could not distinguish where their hands left off and the implement began.

"4-The senses became super alert and acute. Batters and tennis players have reported how they could see the seams of the ball, orchestra conductors have experienced times when they could hear every note from every instrument, football defensive players have stated that there were times when they could hear the play being called in the opponent's huddle 15 yards away, and many various athletes and business people could actually taste victory or smell fear in their opponents!"

TAKING IT TO THE LIMIT

Argue for your limitations and, sure enough, they're yours.
—Richard Bach

You are your own limit setter. It is well known that the world of track had a mental barrier against breaking the four-minute mile. But once Roger Bannister, the British physician, broke the four-minute mile by smashing his "mental barrier," no less than six other runners also broke the unreachable mark of four minutes soon thereafter. Bannister's achievement served as a mold maker even more than a mold breaker. As Kubistant notes, "A more productive perspective is to replace the word limitation with the word 'frontier.' . . . As limitations focus on what I cannot do or achieve, frontiers focus on what I eventually do and achieve."

A successful approach is to set goals, and to do them right now! These goals should be reasonable but challenging and progressive, pointing the way to new frontiers. Think of it as being like climbing a ladder. As you take each step, the next rung is not so far away that you cannot reach it, but enables you to ascend in a smooth, progressive fashion. But don't get so wrapped up in short-range goals that the full picture and long-range goals are lost. Set up a time-line schedule of goals according to priority, and keep the final one in mind. Write these out on separate sheets of paper, and even on your personal calendar. The goals should be specific, and all efforts should be made to achieve step B before jumping to step C. But if you get stuck at one step, perhaps some modification is in order. Don't stagnate on a stumbling block. If you have a bad play, forget it until the competition is over. When the play is done, it's done. Use the time that remains to your advantage. If you are playing basketball and your average from the foul line is 70 percent and you miss a shot, that just means your odds of making the next nine shots are so much better. Turn a negative into a positive.

MENTAL IMAGERY—VISUALIZATION

Much of the winning and losing has already occurred before the competition even begins. Champion athletes spend much time visualizing what they are going to do. They imagine their bodies to be light as a feather and moving at great speed, or visualize the weight they are about to lift as a fraction of its true poundage.

Pain is a large barrier to overcome, whether you're a runner "hitting the wall," or a body builder fighting the muscle burn. This is where disassociative imagery may serve as a form of mental anesthesia. Daydreaming or thinking of something else may help one to overcome the barriers. Did you ever sit in a dentist's chair with the drill humming in the background and attempt to think of being on a tropical island? I remember setting world records in endurance exercises. On the way to a world sit-up record, I went to a different tropical island every one thousand sit-ups. I must have visited half the Caribbean. Top-level athletes train instinctively, mentally planning for the day's training period and focusing on how much their body can deal with on a particular day. Sometimes actually talking to their muscles to give them strength to continue, while the average athlete blasts loud music in the background and methodically goes through a routine.

RELAXATION

One of the most important techniques to mind training is learning to relax. The combination of visualization and mind-relaxation techniques is one of the foundations of mind training. The following is a basic relaxation technique.

To perform this exercise find a quiet dark place where you can concentrate. Take the phone off the hook, wear as few clothes as you feel comfortable with, but if you have a belt on, make sure that it is not tight. You should be flat on your back, with your arms and legs uncrossed so as not to restrict any blood flow. You can make an audio tape of the following material and speak in a soft, calm voice, or have someone you trust read this data to you and guide you through the relaxation exercise:

Note where you are, then close your eyes and attempt to get in touch with your other senses. Begin by breathing in deeply and hold for a count of 3 . . . 1 . . . 2 . . . 3 . . . then blow out slowly . . . 1 . . . 2 . . . 3 . . . (repeat five times). Note any sounds, no matter how slight. Try to feel your body's presence. If you begin to lose your concentration, catch yourself. See if any odd smells are present . . . the taste in your mouth . . . the taste of your saliva . . . can you feel the tiny taste-bud bumps on your tongue? . . . And then scope out the shape and contour of your inner mouth . . . rub your tongue along the roof of your mouth. . . . Can you feel any air or breezes brushing against your skin? Is one part of your body hotter or colder than another? Do you feel fatigue or pain anywhere in your body?

Now that you are relaxed (this process should have so far taken less than 3 minutes), begin from your head down and attempt to feel the different parts of your body with your mind . . . your hairline and scalp . . . forehead . . . face, nose . . . jaw . . . neck, throat . . . down to your shoulders . . . and then down to your arms . . . forearms and hands . . . each individual finger . . . attempt to feel sensation up and down each finger and then up your arms and back. Now go up and down your back and attempt to feel each vertebra and muscle . . . now move around to the front of your body to your abdomen and groin area . . . to your buttocks . . . and then down your legs . . . to your calves and feet . . . now to each toe individually. Make sure you have scanned your entire body and can go at will to any part of it.

Now shift your attention to your breathing . . . feel your chest raise and fall . . . feel the air glide in and out through your nose and mouth . . . in and out . . . with each deep breath in and out . . . you blow out more tension . . . it is leav-

ing your body . . . each breath should feel like a wave going in
and out . . . taking tension with it . . . see the seashore in your
mind's eye. Again begin the deep breathing . . . hold for a
count of three . . . 1 . . . 2 . . . 3 . . . then out . . . 1 . . . 2 . . . 3
(repeat 3 times). Try to imagine your third eye . . . this is located on your forehead . . . open it . . . and feel your heart
beating . . . feel the blood rushing through your veins and arteries . . . feel yourself sinking lower and deeper into the bed
. . . deeper . . . deeper . . . feel your heartbeat slowing down
. . . slower . . . breath deeper . . . let yourself drift . . . deeper
and farther . . . let yourself drift (15-second period).

You are now totally relaxed . . . begin to feel again your
awareness in the room . . . back to your senses . . . begin to
slowly move . . . stretch . . . move your extremities . . . on the
count of 4 you will open your eyes . . . 1 . . . 2 . . . 3 . . . 4 . . .
awaken.

This is a very effective exercise to perform at least once a
week during heavy training. After a handful of sessions you
can perform it by yourself and work it in with your visualization
exercises when you go to sleep in the evening. It is really a
form of self-hypnosis. If you are a runner, go to sleep each evening dreaming of your body moving at a blurring speed; if you
are a weight lifter, imagine the weight to be feather-light and
visualize yourself lifting it right up, and so on, for whatever you
challenge.

Practice seeing yourself standing in your uniform, running,
jumping . . . winning!

Another technique is to write out your thoughts. There is
something about seeing your goals or needs on paper that
makes them more real. In addition, speaking your desires out
loud or quietly to yourself can serve to guide you through the
competition. Process or positive affirmations can help to push
you through the barriers.

Some examples are:

Go	Flow	Intensity	Do it
Yes	Stroke	Focus	Bust it
Smooth	Pump up	Kill	Soft
Go for it	Now	Keep form	Explode
Relax	C'mon	Push	Win
Easy	Best	Strong	Power

■

CHAPTER XVII

■

SUBLIMINAL TRAINING *

Anything the mind of man can conceive and believe, it will achieve.
—Andrew Carnegie

Does the *smell* of bacon and coffee make you think of Sundays at home? Does the *sound* of sleigh bells make you think of Christmas? Does the *sight* of a puppy make you want to smile? Your responses to all these sensations have been programmed into your subconscious mind. Your responses are all there waiting to be triggered by some stimuli in the environment.

"It's the real thing," "You deserve a break today," "Aren't you hungry for Burger King now?" Today we are barraged with more images and sounds in one day than our grandparents experienced in five. We are constantly responding to stimuli, much of which we are totally "unconscious" about. About 1950 an innovative marketing technique was discovered—subliminal marketing. This was really a new application of a discovery made in the early part of the nineteenth century, namely hypnosis. Almost 140 years later, when it was discovered that if you flashed the words *popcorn* or *I'd like a Coke* on a movie screen at a speed just fast enough not to be registered by the conscious mind, studies noted that popcorn and soda sales increased by almost 60 percent. Without inducing a trancelike state, it was possible to bypass the conscious mind and access the subconscious mind, much in the same way as hypnosis had in the past.

Federal agencies have established policies prohibiting the public broadcasting of subliminal suggestions, and there is a United Nations agreement stating that air recording and transmitting may not use subliminal-suggestion techniques. Yet there are no federal or state laws currently outlawing its use.

*The material on pages 229–234 was contributed by Dr. Ronald Klatz.

We may be subject to many more subliminal messages each day than one might think. Subliminals are even appearing in computer-software packages. New Life Institute in California has developed a product for your computer called Self-hypnosis. It enables you to have a self-help image flash across your computer terminal at speeds that you are unable to recognize, but it nonetheless makes an impact on your subconscious mind.

AUDITORY SUBLIMINALS

A good deal of the research on subliminals has been conducted on audio subliminals. These work in much the same way that visual subliminals do: the message is recorded just below the audible range of hearing, thereby bypassing the conscious mind and going directly to the subconscious. The most popular masking sounds have been natural ones such as ocean waves, as they may be listened to many times and also facilitate multiple tapes being run at the same time.

An important factor in the study of auditory subliminals is the brain's hemisphericity factor, which means that each hemisphere of the brain is responsible for a separate specialized form of mental processing. The left side is responsible for language and sequential skill, while the right side controls spatial relations.

In 1976, Mykel found that subliminal messages to the right ear were accepted significantly better than the same messages to the left, with or without alternative ear masking. In his experiments words were used as stimuli. Words tend to be processed in the left hemisphere of the brain, which receives messages from the right ear. Apparently, the left side of the brain is accessed via the right side of the body, and the right hemisphere of the brain is accessed by the left side of the body.

Each person's brain is dominated by either the right hemisphere or the left hemisphere. Right-brain persons are intuitive and spontaneous, while left brain people are more structured, tending to follow set formulas.

Additional studies in 1977 by Sackeim, Packer, and Gur revealed that hemisphericity and cognitive sets were correlated with the subliminal response. Right-brain persons showed a subliminal effect when the messages and cognitive sets were

holistic and intuitive, whereas left-brain persons showed a subliminal effect when encouraged to think in an organized and
logical manner. The researchers postulated that the hemisphericity factor may account for the discrepancies found in literature on subliminal stimulation.

Recent insights into human sports psychology have given
us new tools with which to reprogram our subconscious minds.
These methods promise to allow you to reprogram your behavior by enhancing your desirable traits while eliminating
those traits which do not serve your goals. Auditory subliminals are now being employed in conjunction with sensory deprivation tanks, which provide a profound state of relaxation
and calm, making the subject more receptive to the subliminal
messages.

Research studies conducted at both United States and Canadian universities have provided us with significant statistical
results indicating a positive effect from subliminal-training
methods on actual behavior. Audio subliminal messages in
controlled studies have proven 37 percent more effective than a
control placebo white-noise group in the prevention of shoplift-
ing in a major national department store.

Lynn Stitz, president of Midwest Research, the largest producer of subliminal audio-training tapes in the world, reports
the following: ". . . our company in just the past six years has
increased sales of SCWL [subconscious to conscious way of
learning] method subliminal tapes to over seven million dollars
a year . . . and although we feel that we have the best quality
product on the market at this time, we surely are not alone in
the field of manufacturing subliminal audio training tapes.

"I believe that subliminal training works by getting positive
messages or affirmations past the conscious mind, where they
can impact positively on the subconscious mind, leading the
listener to make desired changes in their behavior or performance. Our training tapes are being used by professional athletic teams across the United States and overseas. We are
supporting scientific research at major universities, and are
working with professional sports teams to develop, improve,
and develop more effective methods of subliminal training. The
true potential for subliminal training is as vast as the subconscious mind itself (which by best estimates comprises almost 90
percent of our mental function)."

The positive effects of subliminal training on athletic perfor-

mance are borne out in a controlled study that was done by
Donna Capka, Ph.D., on the U.S. Figure Skating Association
members. Dr. Capka reported that in objective psychological
testing, anxiety levels in test subjects dropped significantly,
with 52 percent of the test subjects reporting that their skating
performance had improved, and 32 percent reporting that their
confidence levels had improved.

Subliminal training has been used by both professional
and amateur athletes to improve concentration, confidence,
and actual athletic performance on the playing field. Subliminal audio-training methods are today in use to enhance performance for almost every athletic competition imaginable.

Don Morgan, Ph.D., director of the Center for Independent
Research, Triangle Park, North Carolina, an expert in subliminal research, helped develop the SCWL training technique
marketed by Midwest Research. He is now engaged in multiple
studies to determine the effectiveness of subliminal training in
the field of education and maximum sports performance. It is
his belief that "armed with this breakthrough technology, we
are for the first time in history able to actually take control and
change our lives on the subconscious level. The possibilities for
application are only limited by our imagination."

The SCWL programs have developed a formula for recording positive affirmation at the precise frequencies and the right
tones to be readily accepted by the subconscious mind. These
messages are being delivered to the subconscious mind while
the conscious mind is being occupied with the pleasant sounds
of the seashore.

You do not need to concentrate on the tapes to have them
work. Technology has taken much of the suffering out of
changing our behavior by enabling us to transform the very
basis of how we think. This is achieved by going back and
undoing behavior patterns that were ingrained in youth and
had heretofore been considered permanently fixed in the personality. The formula is simple: Put a tape on and go about
your business; forget about it; when you notice it is not on, simply turn the tape over. Hearing-impaired people may lose
some of the upper- and lower-frequency messages, yet they
will still receive value from the programs. Some studies have
shown results in approximately twenty-one days, and even
earlier in some cases. (Results from SCWL's subliminal tape on
procrastination can be seen almost immediately in some
cases.)

DO-IT-YOURSELF SUBLIMINAL TRAINING

With custom-designed subliminal-training tapes costing as much as $250, it is not an inexpensive affair. But there is a way to test their effectiveness in your own training program before investing in the top-quality technology, which cannot be duplicated by the individual. Here is a simple and inexpensive method that has produced limited results in a group of my patients.

Be sure to use a clear *positive* message for your affirmation. Often, it is even better if someone you love and respect records a message for you, as it seems easier to accept positive suggestions from others than from yourself. An auto-reverse cassette-tape player is required, and the suggested tape is a C-20 dictation tape, with ten minutes of playing time per side. Play a soothing instrumental or natural sound, such as rain or a waterfall, ocean waves, or any sound that you will not mind listening to repeatedly.

While your background music is playing (approximately 6 inches from the microphone), speak in a soft, distinct monotone voice (holding the microphone approximately 12 inches from your mouth). You may say something like "I feel more vital, more energetic than ever before. I feel great and look great. I enjoy eating healthful foods. I enjoy my athletic workout every day. I am stronger and more powerful, alive and well every day in every way I am getting better and better."

You may pause for a few seconds, then repeat this message (12 times on each side of the tape). If all has gone well, you should have your own custom-made subliminal tape.

Play back your tape, and you should have a soft background sound, with a barely audible voice urging you on to a healthier and more high-performance life-style. At night, when ready to retire, put the headphones under your pillow and play your tape, placing the tape recorder under your bed to dull the click of the auto-reverse mechanism. During the course of the evening it will deliver approximately 576 inspirational messages to your subconscious per each 8 hours of sleep.

To avoid boredom and the occasional side effect of hearing that melody in your head throughout the next day, I recommend making three or four tapes and rotating them. You will soon find that you have successfully programmed your inner self with stronger beliefs which will beget healthier behaviors, and as your inner self changes for the better, the external self will soon follow.

PHYSICIAN'S NOTE

Positive subliminal suggestions have not been reported to be associated with adverse psychological or physical effects and appear to be completely safe. However, a word of caution is in order. Be sure that the subliminal-training method used is produced by a reputable company and that its content is reviewed by physicians and psychologists for safety and efficacy. Negative subliminal messages may be detrimental to the user. Unfortunately, the user may not wish to know the content of the subliminal message, as some researchers in this field suggest that subliminal training works best when the affirmations are unknown to the subject. Effectiveness of subliminal training has not been completely demonstrated, although there have been many positive studies done by researchers with respected credentials. Many thousands of anecdotal reports attest to the effectiveness of subliminal training, and it appears to be a powerful technique for self-improvement, but as with all powerful therapies, caution and restraint are in order.

■

CHAPTER XVIII

■

BIOFEEDBACK*

The word *biofeedback* has been used extensively during the last fifteen years among professionals and the public. But it is surprising to see how few people really know the meaning of the word. Feedback is the major element in any regulatory process. A system of regulation can be described as follows:

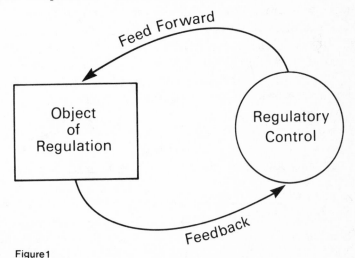

Figure 1

For example: You can't drive the car safely without seeing the road. The visual information about the road is feedback that enables us to control the steering. In this case, according to Figure 1, the driver is the regulatory control. Proper steering is the object of regulation. The visual information we receive is a feedback.

Biofeedback is feedback of biological information to the person whose biology is sensed. It is an essential element in the body-regulatory processes. A simple example of biofeedback is

*The material on pages 235–239 was contributed by Gregory Lekhtman.

the performance of any manual task or body coordination. The sensory information about the movement and positioning enables us to control coordination of the movement.

A biofeedback instrument is a device that enhances our natural biofeedback sensors. A simple example of a biofeedback instrument is a mirror, which provides a reflection of ourselves, therefore providing the feedback information for proper control and precision movements such as shaving and combing the hair.

A biofeedback device enables the high nervous system to get additional sensory information in an easy, recognizable form for proper regulatory control. For example, if we could provide information about tension to our high nervous system, we would be able to control relaxation. In order to do so, we should identify an adequate physiological indicator of tension, then provide that information to the brain via existing sensory systems. The EMG (electromyograph) level in the frontalis muscle is one good physiological indicator of tension. The biofeedback instruments should monitor the EMG level from the frontalis and convert it into a visual or audio pattern. But here arises a problem: The visual system cannot be used because eye concentration or movement disturbs the EMG level in the frontalis and causes interference with accurate sensing of tension. Taking this phenomenon into consideration, we should provide audio feedback rather than visual. Now we can measure the EMG level in the frontalis and provide the biofeedback via sound without causing disturbances to the measured parameter.

When biofeedback information is adequately presented in a form of modulated pitch of the sound, it becomes a part of a natural regulatory system. The brain learns how to change the pitch of the tone, and so far controls the EMG level in the frontalis, and in turn controls the relaxation.

Another example of a biofeedback system that uses the principle just described is EMG biofeedback for muscle rehabilitation after paralysis. The sensory system provides natural biofeedback to the brain. In a case where the sensory system is impaired, the biofeedback instrument can provide a feedback to another sensory system, for instance visual, that has not been damaged, thus providing biofeedback to the brain. The muscle tension is measured by an EMG monitor, and the EMG level is converted to a deflection of a needle of an analogue display. The person uses the deflection of the needle

as guidance, and learns how to control muscle tension and relaxation. This technique is successfully used in muscle rehabilitation.

The same principle is used to control cardiac disturbances,
such as arrythmia and tachycardia. In these cases, the beat-to-
beat measurements of heart rate are used as a feedback.

The following parameters could be monitored as physiological information for the purpose of biofeedback:

EEG   (electroencephalogram)

ECG   (electrocardiogram)

EMG   (electromyogram)

GSR   (galvanic skin resistance)

Temperature

Heart Rate

Different problems will require different choices of physiological parameters for biofeedback purposes. Tension,
headaches, anxiety, backaches, muscle cramps, and spasms
can use EMG monitoring from the different groups of muscles
associated with each problem. Temperature biofeedback can
be used to regulate blood volume in different parts of the body.

Biofeedback information should be continuous. Interrup-
tions will not produce optimum regulation. It would be like
driving a car and looking at the road once every 10 seconds.
Biofeedback instrumentation that is unable to provide an uninterrupted flow of information should be considered ineffective.
One example is the stress-card device, which uses liquid crystal to change color with temperature. This device doesn't provide an uninterrupted flow of biofeedback because the subject
has to lift his finger and then replace it for each reading.

Biofeedback should not be disturbed by interferences from
the body and its ambient environment. For example, a GSR
(galvanic skin resistance) should not be used to monitor relaxation, because it is easily disturbed by ambient temperatures,
humidity, and food chemistry. The EMG biofeedback more adequately represents a state of relaxation because it is not disturbed by those parameters.

Biofeedback requires systematic training and should be
practiced on a daily basis. That is why a short biofeedback-
training course provided in an institutional environment is of
limited value.

In order to use biofeedback successfully, we have to follow these steps:

1 Identify the problem.
2 Find adequate physiological parameters that express this problem.
3 Measure this parameter and present it in a form understandable to the brain using existing sensory systems.
4 Convert physiological data into an easy, recognizable pattern.
5 Provide biofeedback to a sensory system that doesn't interfere with measuring parameters.
6 Present the biofeedback information continuously to the brain.
7 By using biofeedback information, the brain quickly learns how to control sensory-understandable interpretations, and in turn controls the initial parameters.
8 Biofeedback should initially be practiced on a daily basis in a comfortable private environment with minimum ambient or psychological disturbances.

The result is a self-regulatory process which can be described using the accompanying diagram (Figure 2).

Biofeedback is a very powerful tool when properly used and understood and can be an essential technique in sports when enhanced mind-body link is required for better coordina-

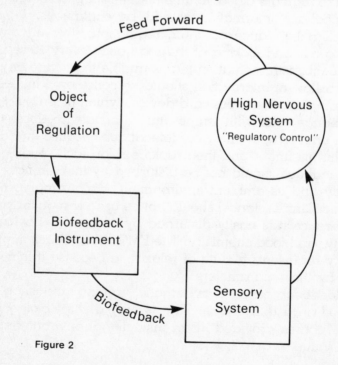

Figure 2

tion, physical strength, endurance, and reduction of stress levels before or during competition.

Just 20 years ago, the biofeedback technique was considered impossible because of a physiological belief that it was impossible to establish control of the autonomic nervous system; in other words, change of the body temperature, heart rate, blood pressure, etc., were considered impossible. In recent years, with the application of biofeedback, that myth was destroyed. Biofeedback has found successful application in the treatment of chronic headaches, tension headaches, migraines, phobias, anxiety, insomnia, alcoholism, depression, asthma, hypertension, ulcers, colitis, menstrual distress, muscle spasms with pain, and stress.

The biofeedback field is growing, but progress could be faster with more cooperation between biofeedback specialists and fitness professionals. In general, specialists are not promoting the biofeedback technique adequately to either the fitness community or the public, with the result that skepticism exists about its effectiveness. Since biofeedback treatment is generally done in an institutional environment, the effectiveness of the training is reduced because of psychological tension associated with that environment.

Biosig Instruments has developed and produced a variety of home-practice, dedicated, self-contained biofeedback instruments such as ANTACHE (antiheadache device), ANTENSE (antitension device) EMG biofeedback systems, and INSTA-PULSE heart-rate monitors.

The future of biofeedback will depend on good quality, affordable instruments that can be operated by nontechnical personnel. Many people strongly believe that continued research and development of new instrumentation will lead to a situation where biofeedback will become a drugless alternative in the treatment of many ailments and to enhance body conditioning.

Biosig Instruments
    5471 Royal Mountain Ave.
    Montreal, Quebec
    Canada HY8 153
    514-733-3362

CHAPTER XIX

■

HIGH-TECH PULSE MONITORING *

The volume of blood pumped by the heart per minute is proportional to heart rate and stroke volume and is called cardiac output. Stroke volume is the amount of blood pumped with each beat of the heart, and is proportional to the size of the heart. The cardiac output is an essential parameter for evaluation of cardiovascular exertion. The heart receives blood at a low pressure and sends it out at a high pressure. The relaxed state between beats of the heart is called diastole. Contraction of the heart is called systole. Because of mechanical restraints in the heart's ventricle construction, heart rates above 180 BPM make performance of the heart inefficient. In order to maintain cardiovascular fitness, the training zone of the heart rate should be maintained below the maximum heart rate, which equals 220 minus the age and determines ineffective dangerous heart rate. Usually the average training heart rate is from 70 to 85 percent of the maximum heart rate and is called the target zone (Figure 1).

Heart rate is a medical term for *pulse*. It is not a stable parameter, and is largely under reflex control by the autonomic nervous system. Cardioaccelerator and cardioinhibitor centers cause the increase and decrease of the heart rate. The stimulation of any cutaneous nerve will elicit a change in it. Pain, heat, cold, blood pressure, touch, joy, exhilaration, fear, anxiety, respiration, and any other activity may cause a variation in the heart rate. Any body or brain demand for oxygen will affect the cardiac output, and in turn will change the heart rate and its regularity. It is well known that stimulation of certain areas of the brain can reproduce the pattern of cardiac re-

*The material on pages 240–247 was contributed by Gregory Lekhtman.

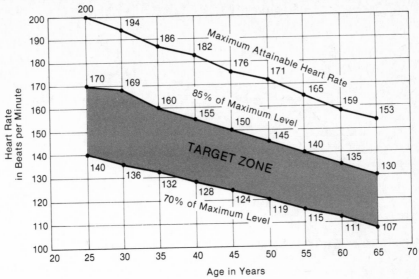

Figure 1

sponse associated with physiological activities such as exercise. In other words, the physiological condition of the individual is an important factor in heart rate. The fitness level can be evaluated just by analyzing the instant changes in heart rate when going from a sitting to a standing position. The fluctuation of the heart rate is sometimes more important than heart rate itself, and should always be monitored during sports training.

The following techniques are used to monitor heart rate:

1 Manual pulse-taking, based on intervals of 10–15 seconds, can produce an average error from + 16 to − 18 beats per minute, and is totally inaccurate in estimating the fluctuation of the heart rate in response to exercise or psychological stress.

2 Photo-electric pickups from earlobe or finger sensors, or other techniques using peripheral blood pulse pickup, are also inaccurate, because there is inconsistent time delay between heart contraction and propagation of the blood pulse to the periphery (Figure 2). This delay is a function of the condition of the blood vessels, body temperature, gravitation, and acceleration forces during physical activities. Another problem in this method is susceptibility to the mechanical interference from body movement, and that is why this method cannot be used for accurate pulse monitoring, especially during physical activity. Nevertheless, some manufacturers and distributors of devices using this method of pickup were successful in penetrating the fitness market.

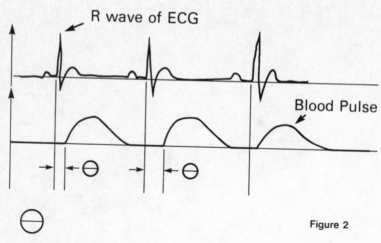

Figure 2

Time delay between heart contraction and peripheral blood pulse.

3 ECG pickup from the chest or peripheries is the most reliable and most accurate method of pickup because each R wave (represented by the "spike" portion of the printout) of ECG signal represents precise timing in heart contraction and is totally unaffected by physical conditions of the body, gravity, and physical movement. The technology involved in monitoring ECG without special preparation of the skin is very sophisticated, and that is why many manufacturers try to avoid this method.

The following techniques are used to calculate the heart rate:

1 Average calculation is the oldest and best-known technique. Average pulse calculations are done by counting the number of pulses per given time.
For example:

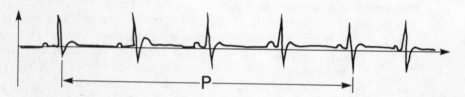

Figure 3

P = Time; N = number of pulses; BPM = Beats/Min.
Example: N=5; P=6 seconds = 1/10 minute = .1 min.
BPM = N/P = 5/.1 min. = 50 BPM

The longer the period, the less fluctuation of the heart rate will be shown. But the calculation will not represent the true picture, especially for people with unstable heart rates, and also athletes with fast recovery time; i.e., if your average is based on 15-second intervals, the calculation of heart rate will show, for instance, 150 beats per minute, but the trained athlete's actual pulse will recover at this time to 120 beats per minute. The discrepancy of 30 beats per minute occurs because of this technique of calculation.

The average method of calculation doesn't show the changes in time between one beat of the heart to another (fluctuation), and doesn't represent the true picture of the heart's response to exercise, stress, and environment.

In the past, when the electrocardiogram and beat-to-beat measurements of the heart rate were not available, heart rate was perceived as a stable parameter. This error is still common, even among those medical and fitness professionals who have never studied the physiology of the heart.

2 Beat-to-beat calculations are done by counting the time between two pulses and converting this time into BPM using the formula BPM = 60.

For example:

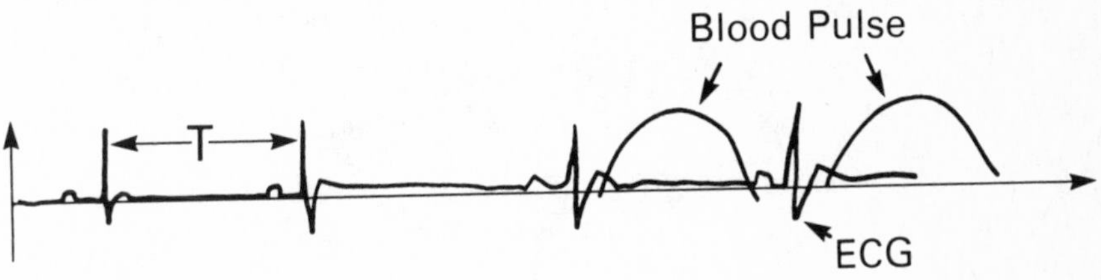

Figure 4

T = Time between pulses in seconds
T = 1 second; BPM = 60/1 = 60 BPM
T = 0.983 second; BPM = 60/0.983 = 61 BPM

This technique is the most accurate and represents the true picture of the heart rate and heart-rate response. Beat-to-beat calculation cannot be performed with earlobe or finger detectors because they pick up the mechanical pulse of the blood wave, which is generated by heart contractions, but this wave is 40 times wider than the R wave of the EKG, and the fronts of it cannot be identified. Some monitors combine beat-to-beat calculation with computer averaging based on 4 or 6 beats.

Based on evaluation of the techniques of pickup calculation, let me present a verbal picture of the heart-rate monitor that would be most valuable for sports training:

1 The heart-rate monitor should be a guide in exercise, a personal motivator, a preventive diagnostic tool, a biofeedback instrument, all in one. This is why it should be ECG-type beat-to-beat, or a maximum 4–6 beats average.

2 No alarms or beeping features should be presented to the user, because, as was mentioned before, the heart rate is altered by any psychological stimuli. The heart monitor should be a passive measuring device only.

3 The heart-rate monitors should be "user friendly," which means that any multiple-functions knobs, dials, and push buttons will distract the person from concentrating on exercise and will produce psychological stress, which results in a change in the heart-rate response.

PULSE METERS

Biosig

Biosig Instruments has developed a variety of heart-rate monitors for professional and home use. All the monitors use the ECG principle of pickup from the hands and chest. The type of calculation is beat-to-beat or 2-, 4-, and 6-beat average.

Insta-Pulse 105 on floor stand

The *Insta-Pulse 105* looks like a rally baton, and can be used during running and other activities. It has a 4-beat average ECG pickup from the hand; it is watertight and comes with an optional wall bracket or floor stand.

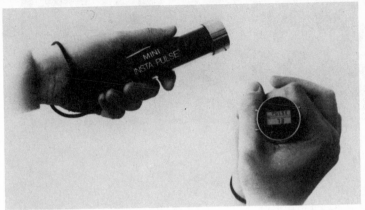

Mini Insta-Pulse 107

The *Mini Insta-Pulse 107* has similar functions, but is half the size and features a 2-beat ECG pickup.

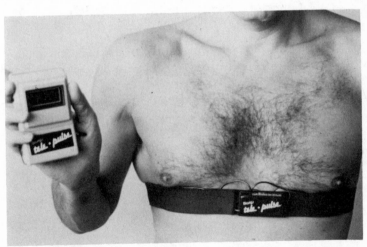

Tele-Pulse 801

The *Tele-Pulse 801* wireless pulse meter uses a small transmitter with a chest-belt ECG pickup through the short. It transmits heart rate by radio up to 30 feet away from the receiver, which can be mounted on treadmills, rowing machines, etc.

The *Insta-Pulse 302* bicycle pulse meter fits on all types of exercise bikes. It has ECG pickup from the handlebars and a 6-beat average.

Insta-Pulse 302

Biosig Instruments
5471 Royal Mountain Ave.
Montreal, Quebec
Canada HY8 153
514-733-3362

Computer Instruments Corp. (CIC)

The *Exersentry* heart-rate monitor operates through skin moisture and requires no messy gels. The lightweight harness is placed around the chest so that body motion is not hindered. The electrodes are built into the chest belt and will record from

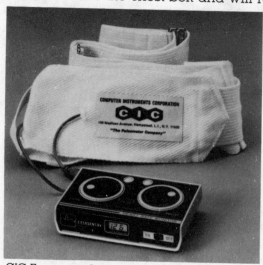

CIC Exersentry heart-rate monitor

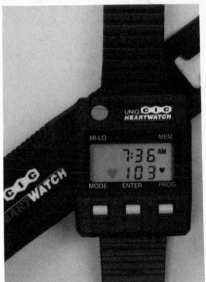

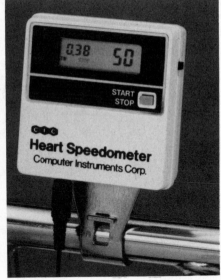

CIC Heartwatch

CIC Heart Speedometer clip-on
pulse meter

40 to 200 beats per minute. As long as you train within ten beats of your target heart-training zone (high or low), the unit will remain quiet. If you go beyond that range, the Exersentry will sound a warning beep.

Price: $180

The *Heartwatch 8799* and *8799S* monitor exercise and also give a monitor of heart rate and training target zones. They are capable of wireless transmission from the chest-strap ECG sensor to the wristwatch display, and will store the information for recall. They also function as full sports watches, with stopwatch, time functions, etc.

Price: under $400

CIC also has a series of clip-on pulse meters (models *8519* and *8629*) that can be attached to exercise cycles and rowing machines.

Price: from $120 to $160

Computer Instruments Corp.
  100 Madison Ave.
  Hempstead, NY 11550
  800-227-1314

CHAPTER XX

FLOTATION—
THE RELAXING ART *

It is easier to sail many thousands of miles through cold and storm, and cannibals, in a government ship, with five hundred men and boys to assist one, than it is to explore the private sea, the Atlantic and Pacific Ocean of one's being alone.

—H. D. Thoreau, *Walden*

Stress surrounds us, and to be alone is sometimes heavenly. Floating, isolated in a sound-proof tank, is one such escape.

What Is Flotation?

In this type of relaxation-training therapy, a flotation tank or pool is filled with a saline solution and enclosed in a light-proof, sound-insulated shell. The filtered solution is kept at skin temperature. The subject feels as if he is floating in deep, dark space, with the tank providing a restricted environment. Researchers have been exploring restricted environmental stimulation therapy (REST) for more than thirty years.

What Happens When You Float?

A growing body of scientific evidence supports floating as a means to relieve stress. Floating lowers blood pressure, lowers levels of stress-related biochemicals (ACTH and cortisol), and, perhaps most important, removes feelings of tension and stress. In addition, floating works to reduce pain by stimulating the body's production of beta endorphins (a natural pain killer)

*The information on pages 248–256 was contributed by Michell Hutchinson, one of the most well-known authors on floatation. His books include *Floating/Exploring the Private Sea* and *Megabrain: New Tools and Techniques for Brain Growth and Mind Expansion* (both published by William Morrow and Co., Inc.).

and by accelerating the removal of lactic acid (one of the cell's waste products). The result is a profound feeling of relaxation and well-being that can last for weeks.

How Does Flotation Compare with Other Relaxation Techniques?

The Flotation REST Response is similar to the Relaxation Response in that the same physical systems are activated and similar goals of mind/body relaxation are achieved. However, the Relaxation Response must be actively achieved through *effort*, on the part of the patient. He or she must try to relax. Acquiring this skill (for example, meditation or progressive relaxation or biofeedback) can be difficult and for some people impossible. The activation of the Flotation REST Response is passive and *universally* achieved. Also, the level of relaxation achieved during Flotation REST is generally much deeper and the effects longer lasting.

How Often Does One Float?

People often ask how frequently they should float in order to stay relaxed and achieve the maximum benefits of floating. The answer varies with the individual. Whether you float three times a week or once a month depends on the amount of stress you are experiencing in your life and on the coping strategies you are already using. When faced with periods of high stress, you may want to float more often. Even when you are pressed for time, the occasional float will improve your efficiency and help you make the best use of your time. Some people have learned to plan float sessions at crucial points during their creative or problem-solving projects.

Are Tanks Used for Behavior Modification?

REST in combination with various behavioral and cognitive techniques has proven extremely effective in the treatment of weight problems, smoking problems, hypertension, and phobias. In addition, athletes and stage performers have used REST to enhance their skills, increase their confidence, and re-

duce performance anxieties. One of the most impressive findings is the occurrence of a *maintenance effect;* REST builds
perseverance and a lasting motivation to achieve personal
goals.

The flotation tank is the ideal place for achieving relaxation for
several reasons:

1 The darkness, silence, and warmth of floating are soothing and
  naturally conducive to relaxation.
2 Floating removes outside stimulation so that the mind is relieved
  of having to monitor excessive stressors. This begins the process
  by which the mind becomes clear and at ease with itself.
3 The flotation tank provides a natural biofeedback, resulting in an
  increased awareness and control of heart rate, breathing, and
  muscle tension.
4 The float experience becomes part of the body's conditioned relaxation response. Later, when you return to your normal environment, your mind and body can recall the profound
  relaxation achieved while floating and bring back the same
  soothing sensations.

The virtues of floating are many. For example, each day,
Dallas Cowboy kicker Rafael Septien climbs into a chamber in
the Cowboy training room that looks like a small space capsule. The chamber contains a 10-inch-deep pool of water
warmed to body temperature and saturated with over 800
pounds of Epsom salts—a solution so dense that when Septien
lies back he bobs atop the water like a cork. With the door
closed, floating motionlessly in total darkness and silence, Septien begins his practice. When he emerges, deeply relaxed,
Septien has executed hundreds of perfect kicks. Though the
kicks have only taken place in his mind, he is convinced, and
his conviction is supported not only by his own kicking statistics
but by a growing number of scientific studies, that the mental
practice has improved his actual kicking abilities. An hour of
practice in the tank, Septien claims, is the equivalent of 10
hours of practice on the playing field. "They say that practice
makes perfect," he says, "but actually it's *perfect* practice that
makes perfect. That's what goes on in the tank—perfect practice."

What can be so beneficial in floating in an enclosed tub of
water? A recent surge of research by scientists is now producing a flood of hard evidence that the float tank is a powerful

tool for a variety of purposes, including pain relief, stress reduction, relaxation, increasing mental powers and facilitating
communication between body and mind. Among the beneficial effects of floating that have been documented:

Injury prevention: Sports medicine authorities agree that many
sports injuries result from inappropriate muscular tension, and
could have been prevented by deep musculoskeletal relaxation. Now several studies have measured muscular tension in
both float and non-float groups before and after floating or
equivalent periods of progressive relaxation. *In every study*
floaters show a dramatic, whole-body reduction of muscular
tension, and reach a state of relaxation far deeper than the
non-float groups. Significantly, the studies find that this absolute reduction in tension persists for days and even *weeks* after
a one hour float. Clearly floating can help eliminate a lot of
tension-related injuries.

Pain relief: Several laboratory and clinical studies have
proven that floating has a powerful analgesic effect. St. Elizabeth's Hospital in Appleton, Wisconsin, made a statistical
study of people who used the hospital float tank, and found
that 100 percent of pain sufferers experienced reductions in
pain. One explanation for this (aside from the obvious benefits
of floating in a 93.5 degree Epsom salt solution with the musculoskeletal system freed from the pressures of gravity) has
emerged from experiments performed by researcher Thomas
Fine, who heads up a behavioral medicine and stress management clinic at the Medical College of Ohio. Fine has found
evidence that floating triggers the release of the body's own
opiates, the *endorphins*. These natural painkillers, thought to
be one cause of the "runner's high," also create pleasure and
could explain the euphoria noted by many floaters. Fine,
whose clinic uses floating to help sufferers of severe chronic
pain, says, "Virtually all of our chronic pain patients have said
that during the flotation period they have lost awareness of
their pain."

Enhanced recovery, speeded growth: After intense workouts,
lactic acid, adrenaline and other biochemicals released during
exercise linger in the body to produce fatigue, pain, irritability,
depression, anxiety. Full recovery can take days. Now there is
evidence that floating can speed up this process in several

ways. First, floating has been found to have a *vasodilatory* effect, causing blood vessels to relax and dilate, thereby lowering blood pressure and allowing the bloodstream to carry more healing nutrients to all cells, as well as speeding up the elimination of lactic acid and other wastes. Second, studies by Thomas Fine, and neuroendocrinologist Dr. John Turner show that floating directly reduces the amount of the stress-related biochemicals the body secretes, and keeps the levels lower for days, even weeks, after floating. In these ways, floating quickly reduces fatigue and speeds healing.

There are also indications that due to the speeded flow of nutrients to muscle cells and the reduced gravity and stress experienced in the tank, floating allows for more rapid protein synthesis, resulting in faster and greater muscle growth. Among many athletes profiting from this aspect of floating was the 1984 U.S. Olympic weightlifting team, which incorporated frequent floats into its training schedule.

Improved performance through relaxation: The stress of exercise (as well as the stresses of daily life) can cause an instinctive "fight-or-flight" response, triggering floods of adrenaline and other stress-biochemicals, resulting in tense muscles, rapid and shallow breathing, elevated pulse and blood pressure—clearly not good for the whole-body coordination needed in athletic performance and training, or for dealing with the stress of daily life. If continued for too long, this state of arousal can lead to exhaustion and increase susceptibility to a host of stress-related illnesses.

However, an equally powerful and automatic reaction, the *relaxation response*, counteracts the effects of stress. Unfortunately, the relaxation response is not easy to produce: The most effective techniques have been meditation, self-hypnosis, progressive relaxation, and biofeedback, which require training, discipline and repeated efforts.

Now, however, a number of studies have concluded that flotation automatically triggers a powerful relaxation response, reducing heart rate, blood pressure, oxygen consumption, tension, and so on. Statistical analysis of floaters shows that they experience significant reductions in levels of perceived stress, and in stress-related illness. These effects persist for days and even weeks after floating—so an hour in the tank can carry over into more relaxed exercise and training, and reduced stress in general, throughout the entire week.

Heightened suggestibility: There is now overwhelming evidence that floating enormously increases suggestibility; that is, much as in a deep hypnotic trance, whatever the floater is told or tells himself while in the tank is accepted by his subconscious mind as being true. New York City sports psychologist Dr. Lloyd Glauberman, an experienced hypnotherapist now using a float tank to train athletes, believes that "the float tank is much more powerful than hypnosis—simply floating, without inducing a trance, makes you more suggestible than hypnosis." Among the ways athletes like Rafael Septien and the U.S. Olympic weightlifting team profit from the tank's enhancement of suggestibility is to use part of their float session to play tapes to themselves that offer positive suggestions for improving their fitness and competitive abilities, assuring themselves they can kick farther, run faster, grow stronger.

Visualization: Visualization makes use of the fact that "seeing is believing"—whatever image you hold in your mind tends to be accepted by your subconscious, and your body, as being real. Sensors attached to your body as you visualize yourself jumping hurdles, say, will register minute muscular contractions of the same type that would take place if you were actually jumping hurdles. In one study, a group of boys who only visualized themselves practicing shooting free throws improved as much over a month period as a second group which actually practiced free throw shooting every day.

In the total darkness of the tank, with most other stimuli eliminated, mental images gain intensity and clarity. Says hypnotherapist Glauberman: "From my experience, the ability to visualize is much more powerful while you're floating than it is in hypnotic trance. It seems more real, more dreamlike. Most of the time you're actually *in* the experience." When floating athletes visualize themselves performing perfectly, their body accepts this perfect performance, "imprints" it by a sort of muscle memory. An example of how strong this imprinting can be is javelin thrower David Schmeltzer of the New York Pioneer Club. After beginning to use float tank visualization under the direction of Glauberman, Schmeltzer made a throw that beat his personal record by several feet. He recalls that "When I released the javelin on that day it was like *deja vu*. At that point of release, I said, '*I know this throw*, I've thrown this throw before.' And I never experienced that before I began floating."

The above are just a few of the effects of floating documented by solid scientific studies. Clearly there are many ways
flotation tanks can be profitably incorporated into a health club
or gym. Those who will make frequent use of the tank include
clients seeking pain relief from injuries ranging from simple
aches and pains to broken bones, athletes who train at high
intensity and want to use floating in a hard-easy training
schedule (alternating their days of high-intensity work with a
day during which they float, profiting from the enhanced recovery and protein synthesis effects of the float), those who simply like to end their workouts by climbing into the tank for an
hour of deep relaxation, and the increasing numbers of athletes who are discovering how effective it is to precede their
training with float sessions during which they work on their
"inner game," and visualize themselves performing their workouts or their athletic specialties perfectly.

For this last purpose, tank manufacturers now produce
tanks fitted with roof-mounted video systems that enable the
floater to view videotapes; and a variety of tapes are now
available that show computer-enhanced images of professional athletes performing perfectly (sports include golf, tennis,
skiing, racquetball, bowling, baseball, and cross-country skiing). Studies at Stanford and elsewhere show that as a floater
watches the repeated performances on videotape, his nervous
system reacts as if it were physically performing the skill. Thus
the skill becomes imprinted or assimilated by the user in what
scientists call "neuro-muscular programming," resulting in improved skills and performance.

For those who belong to a gym or spa as part of a total
health program that includes losing weight, stopping smoking
or altering other behavioral patterns, tanks are equipped with
underwater in-tank speakers so that tapes can be played to the
floater to make use of the relaxed hypersuggestibility induced
by the tank. Commercially made audio and videotapes are
available that use subliminal or other techniques for a variety
of purposes, including sports training, breaking habits, lowering blood pressure, eliminating pain, relieving anxiety, etc.

While scientists have been studying the benefits of floating
for years, the commercial use of tanks has only recently begun
to flourish. And it is flourishing in a big way—tank sales are
increasing so rapidly that *Entrepreneur* magazine was moved
to rate a tank manufacturer "one of the 500 best business investment opportunities in the world," and in recent years over

150 commercial flotation centers have opened throughout the U.S. However, very few of these have made the logical and obvious step of combining tanks with sports training facilities, so gyms and spas that provide floating as part of their program will profit from being on the leading edge of what will be an increasing trend. John Dietrich, past president and director of the New York Health & Racquet Clubs, consultant to fitness facilities, and author of *The Complete Health Club Handbook*, says that "As people grow more sophisticated in their knowledge of health, they are understanding that physical fitness absolutely depends on relaxation and mental fitness. In the future, tanks will be essential equipment in every health club."

Tanks are also clear profit-makers. They are comparatively inexpensive (ranging from basic tanks at around $3,500 to the top-of-the-line model with in-tank controls operating such features as video and audio systems, intercom, volume control, and even Jacuzzi™ jets, costing about $5,500), and are easy to install—they simply plug into a 110-volt outlet (the pump and heater systems consume about as much electricity as a 150-watt bulb). Maintenance is no problem—the tank's pump and filter system cleans the water after each use; the dense salt solution is an anti-bacterial agent itself, and its purity is insured by the addition of chlorine, so that the salt solution can be used for a year or more.

To provide the most relaxing and silent float, it's advisable to place the tank in a room separate from other activities of the gym. However, the tanks are a little larger than a single bed (dimensions average about eight feet long by five feet wide and four feet high) so a simple private float room can be constructed at little cost.

After these initial expenses, the cost of operating a float tank is minimal: Combining the costs of chemicals, electricity, maintenance, towels, and foam ear plugs, the cost-per-float for a one-hour session is far less than one dollar. At commercial float centers, fees range from $15 to $40 per hour. Based on a modest float fee of $25, and an estimated eight float sessions per day (many commercial centers rent 12 or more sessions), one could forecast a potential gross income from one tank of $70,000 for one year.

In many ways the key to advances in sports and fitness training, and to the dramatic growth of modern health facilities, has been new and improved tools. Tools for intensified physical training, like Nautilus machines, and computerized treadmills and cycles; tools for mental training, like hypnosis, visualization, and subliminal audio and videotapes; tools to speed recovery and treat pain and injuries, like hot tubs, electrotherapy and ultrasonic devices. Perhaps the most exciting thing about the flotation tank is that it can perform *all* these functions, simultaneously providing an ideal environment for physical and mental training as well as enhancing recovery, speeding healing and eliminating pain. As popular interest in floating expands rapidly, and growing numbers of world-class athletes make floating an integral part of their training, it seems clear that increasing numbers of people will choose to join those health clubs or gyms that provide a float tank as part of the fitness equipment.

ATHLETIC FLOATERS*

Frank Zane

Perhaps the finest all-around bodybuilder of our time, Frank Zane has won every major honor in that sport: Mr. America, Mr. World, Mr. Universe (3 times) and the highest title in professional bodybuilding, Mr. Olympia (3 times). In addition to his immense natural gifts—fellow bodybuilders and other experts invariably single him out as having the "ideal" or "perfect" physique for bodybuilding—Zane has brought his keen intelligence (he has degrees in both psychology and education) to bear on all aspects of bodybuilding, particularly in the area of sports psychology and physiology. While many bodybuilders focus simply on the endless pumping of iron, Zane, in a series of popular books (the latest: *Zane Nutrition,* Simon & Schuster, 1986) and highly original training courses, has emerged as an influential teacher and thinker, pioneering the concept that *mental* training is the key to bodybuilding, and emphasizing that through mental development, bodybuilding can be not just an end in itself but can produce dramatic personal growth and self-mastery. Says Zane, "When you discover how your mind affects your training, you actually gain considerable insight into other areas of your life as well." As a result of this emphasis on mental attitude, "the Zane Way" of training emphasizes such things as concentration exercises, deep relaxation and meditation techniques, positive self-suggestion and hypnosis, visualization and guided imagery.

All these mental training techniques require the ability to become relaxed, to "turn off" external distractions and direct attention inward, so it's little wonder that with his first float Zane immediately recognized that the tank was a potentially revolutionary training device for bodybuilding. Says Zane, "The deepest form of relaxation that I've experienced was achieved while floating, and I can achieve it much more quickly than through meditation, because I lose my body right away. All that's there is my consciousness."

Zane points out that entering this state of "deep peace and total relaxation," is "a tremendous way to change your attitude. Although I obviously don't know what dying really feels like," he says, "floating turns off all sensory reception, so that you experience a mini-death. When you come out of the tank, it's almost as though you have just been born. You're very mentally receptive—a tremendous

*This article has been reprinted with permission from *Fitness Management,* Leisure Publications, Inc., 3923 W. Sixth St., Los Angeles, CA 90020.

time to positively program your mind." Convinced of the value of flotation, Zane wasted no time in installing a tank at Zane Haven, his own state-of-the-art training facility in Palm Springs, California. Here throughout the year Zane guides selected small groups through a 5-day 4-night live-in training program that includes weight training and aerobics, and seminars in nutrition, deep relaxation, visualization, workout organization, posing and contest preparation. The flotation tank, in Zane's opinion, is a key to the success of his program: all participants intersperse their training with float sessions, that speed their recovery from high-intensity workouts and enable them to practice the relaxation and mental training techniques they are learning.

Floating, says Zane, "can release all the negativity in your mind, giving you a completely fresh start. After spending one or two hours in a tank, I have the power to put anything I want into my mind. I always choose something positive— such as a clear visual image of how I want my physique to appear at the next Mr. Olympia."

Bob Said

Bob Said is a race driver—a champion driver in the 50s, he won European Grand Prix races and set a speed record at Daytona Beach. For over 20 years he has focused on driving a four-man bobsled down an icy course, and has been on two Olympic teams and captained five U.S. World Cup Teams. In 1984, at the age of 50, he was still driving hard, preparing his team, his sled and himself for the Olympic trials. Each morning he would rise before dawn and climb into his flotation tank, where he mentally piloted his bobsled through the run: "In the sled," he told me, "you know where you want to be in each corner but often you find yourself someplace else. So you try to visualize all the different ways you can get into each corner, so that when you get into the corner you're already programmed for coming out." By the time he emerged from the tank ready to make his actual practice runs, Said claims he had assimilated the real experience and "muscle memory" of scores of runs.

In sports, with rapid-fire volleys at the net or screaming line drives, we need to act automatically. But too often we're paralyzed by the need to think. For Said, the muscle memory that comes from visualization frees him from that need: "If you have to *think* a reaction in the sled, even if you have the world's fastest reactions, you're too slow. You have to function subconsciously, automatically. The 'cleaner' you are, the faster you are. So if you float in the morning and get rid of the pressures of the phone and the rent and the sore shoulder, and you get in the sled, it's just easier to let it all pop out there. There's just no doubt in my mind at all that I'm sharper from floating. But it's not a sharpening of abilities so much as it's allowing one's abilities to function the way they're supposed to function by getting rid of clutter."

Said values the physical benefits of floating as much as the mental effects. He compares each rattling bobsled run comparable to "falling down a long flight of stairs," and the stress of five or six practice runs a day "the equivalent of running a marathon."

He says, "I'm 50 years old, a little long in the tooth to be doing this, but I found that I would come out of that tank at 7:30 every morning feeling *just great.* I mean loose and ready for it, and morning after morning for about six weeks!" Even after a sled crash left him severely injured, Said found the tank enabled him to continue training: "Basically, the thing I liked about it was specifically in the physical sense. It blotted out a lot of aches and pains. As for speeding of healing, I don't think there's any question about it, you heal faster if you let go of it—I think I healed faster, simply because I didn't limp, I didn't favor the injury. I could recognize the injury for what it was, and let it get on with its own healing, and it didn't drag the rest of me down. I mean, you hurt your ankle and you limp for weeks, just simply 'cause you get used to limping. In fact, you don't have to limp at all, and while you're limping you're using muscles you haven't used before and *they* begin to hurt. But in the tank, what pains I *had* became very local. That tank—I'd like to figure out some way to take the damn thing to the Olympics with me!"

His overall assessment of the float tank after using it for more than a year: "I think that the more you relax, the more you're open when you start to race, the better you can do it. To that extent, the tank really works. The tank improved my performance and certainly made my life better. It's sensational and it works, what more can you ask? It's just a wonder drug that nobody knows about!"

John Dietrich

New Yorker John Dietrich is a successful businessman and a Type A personality. Past president and director of the New York Health & Racquet Clubs, he is founder and head of American International Health Industries, serving as a consultant to fitness facilities and corporations throughout the country. He has written (with Susan Waggoner) *The Complete Health Club Handbook* (Simon & Schuster).

A key to his ability to maintain a business schedule and training regimen that would burn out many is regular floating. With his first float, he said, "I realized the tank was one of the most marvelous tools for *fitness* I had ever come across. My definition of fitness includes four essentials: strength, flexibility, cardiovascular fitness, and the one most people forget, relaxation to combat stress.

"I look upon a health club as an adult playground, a Coney Island for the body. Well, the tank is an adult *mind* playground. So the gym and the tank are alike—a gym stimulates people to exercise in a way they wouldn't at home, and when I float, I *have* to shut myself away and relax. There are no phones, no input. And with my Type A behavior, that was the only thing that could get me totally relaxed. For the executive, it's like a doctor's appointment—it forces the Type A personality to build a commitment to relax into his schedule."

Another important consideration for executives: "The last time I flew back from California I booked myself right from the airport into a tank, and normally where I might feel a bit of jet lag, after the float I'm immediately up and ready to go. I'm sure that in the near future we'll see tanks in airports."

The future of float tanks. "In one word," says Dietrich, "limitless." We know that for superlearning, relaxation, problem solving, visualization, behavior modification, the deeper the state of relaxation, the more you're going to learn, the more you're going to get done, and the more beneficial it's going to be for you. The tank has gotten me into the deepest states of relaxation I've ever experienced. I think in the future they'll be essential equipment in every health club."

Rafael Septien

As the 1981 NFL season began, Dallas cowboy kicker Rafael Septien had an undiagnosed hernia that spread such pain and stiffness throughout his legs, abdomen and back that Coach Tom Landry thought he might have to find a new kicker. However, the Cowboys had just acquired a float tank, and Rafael discovered that floating not only relaxed him and helped him relieve the pain, but also increased his ability to concentrate.

Kicking demands total concentration and confidence, and Rafael had begun reading books on positive thinking and visualization. He found that the tank increased his ability to visualize and the power of his positive suggestions. As he floated, he saw himself kicking perfect field goals, and repeated, "I am my own authority, I only let the finest thoughts enter my mind and spirit . . . I have done it over and over. I **know** if I put my left foot in the right position and keep my head down and follow through I will kick all my field goals, or at least 90 percent of the time."

Despite his injury, Septien opened the season with a string of perfect field goals, at one point had kicked 22 out of 24, and capped a spectacular season by being selected All-Pro.

Since then, Septien has incorporated audio and videotapes into his float. The audio tapes play relaxation and positive thinking messages; the videotapes show him kicking perfect field goals, played over and over through a video monitor attached to the top of the tank. He believes his daily floats are the key to his success: "No doubt about it," he says, "If you conquer doubt and fear, you conquer failure. If you don't doubt, if you know you're going to do it, it's easier. Your muscles are more relaxed, and then you perform what you have practiced in the tank."

■

FLOTATION-TANK MANUFACTURERS

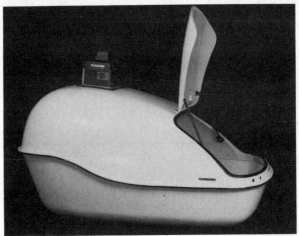

Floatarium

The *Floatarium* unit measures 105″ in length, 67″ in width, and 53″ in height. It can be converted into a Jacuzzi, has a video switch and volume controls, and may be purchased with a video unit.
    Price: $6,000 to $10,000, depending on options.

Enrichment Enterprises Inc.
    175 West Carver Street
    Huntington, NY 11743
    516-549-9740

The Samadhi Tank Co.'s unit may also double as a bed when closed up.
    Prices: $3,500 to $6,000, depending on options

Samadhi Tank Co.
    1655 N. Bonnie Beach Place
    Los Angeles, CA 90063
    213-264-3615

For those budget-conscious people who will self-assemble, there is Tank Alternatives, at $2,500 to $3,500 per unit.

Tank Alternatives
    141 Fifth Ave.
    New York, NY 10010

CHAPTER XXI

■

HIGH TECH/ELECTRONICS IN TREATMENT OF SPORTS INJURIES

For the athlete it is vital to distinguish among different kinds of pain. The deep muscle-ache pain experienced with training is necessary for muscle building. However, a sharp, radiating, burning, or stinging pain may be an early warning sign of impending injury—damage to the nerves, tendons, muscles, or bone. Your body has these warning signals for protection, and they must be listened to. When injury occurs, physical therapists and physicians have many means of relief at their disposal, ranging from hot packs or compressors to ice packs, infrared radiation to electrical stimulation and diathermy. The basic prescription after an injury is RICE:

R-Rest

I-Ice in the first 24–48 hours (a good ice holder can be made by filling a Styrofoam cup with water, freezing it, and then just peeling off the top of the cup, and having the Styrofoam portion as a handholder

C-Compression

E-Elevation of the injured body part

HEAT PACKS

Hydrocollators (heat packs) are units that produce heat. They are made from a combination of sand and silicone, which enhances heat retention. These packs are stored in 126-degree water. Since this is very hot, at least 8 layers of towels are first placed on the skin surface, then the pack is placed on top. A typical therapy session is about 20 minutes, with heat diffusing into the subcutaneous tissues and superficial muscle layers, thereby increasing blood supply to the damaged area. The increase in temperature tends to relax and soothe the muscles, and decreases nerve excitability.

Moist heat has been found to penetrate better than dry heat. Dry heat, like that produced by infrared lamps, penetrates only the top layer of skin.

FLUIDOTHERAPY

Another form of heat-related therapy is fluidotherapy. This high-intensity dry-heat modality works by transferring heat to the submerged part of the body by a swirling mixture of air and small cellulose particles. The bed of fine solid particles through which a stream of heated gas is slowly pressed upward serves as the thermotherapeutic agent. Automatic temperature controls and an automatic timer enable the therapist to control the heat level and duration of treatment. The body part to be treated is inserted into a glovelike receptacle in the machine and remains there for about twenty minutes.

SHORTWAVE DIATHERMY (SWD)

Shortwave diathermy is a physical-therapy modality that has deep-heating effects. The high-frequency waves of diathermy penetrate up to several inches into the body tissues. One caution for those with heart problems: The waves emitted may be disruptive to pacemakers. For acute as well as chronic musculoskeletal injuries, diathermy can promote the healing process and decrease pain. It does this via the heat vasodilating the blood vessels and lymph vessels, which results in increased blood flow, which in turn provides necessary oxygen and nutrition for improved metabolism. The increase in circulating white blood cells causes a greater phagocytic effect in damaged tissues, and waste products are more readily removed. The conduction velocity increases in the peripheral nerve fibers, relieving pain and relaxing the muscles.

TRANSCUTANEOUS ELECTRICAL NERVE STIMULATION (TENS)

This method of pain treatment was developed in the 1950s. The TENS unit is battery-operated and has either 2 or 4 carbon electrodes. By emitting a low-voltage electrical stimulus, it bombards the sensory nerve endings in the treated area. The brain picks up these impulses instead of the pain signals. TENS stimulation may aid in the release of the body's own natural opiates (pain-killers), known as endorphins.

It is recommended that the small unit (which can be clipped to a belt) be used intermittently (on 30 to 60 minutes and then off again).

ELECTRICAL STIMULATION

Some athletes feel that they can get a whole workout by using electrical currents to stimulate the muscles. The low-level current will not damage the skin, and even a small battery-operated unit can strongly contract the muscles. It feels like a tiny pinprick at the skin surface. In some new techniques, an electrical device can be implanted into the body at the region of a bone break or fracture to aid bone healing. However, it is doubtful that an electrical device will fully replace proper resistance training, for the neuromuscular coordination required in sports is unaffected by this technique. But electrical stimulation may be useful in rehabilitating a muscle or attempting to decrease (atrophy) during nonuse, or when a body part has been or is immobilized for a long period of time.

Caution should be exercised when using electrical stimulation, for if the current is not carefully controlled, the force generated can be strong enough to tear the muscle and tendon right off the bone.

ULTRASOUND AND GALVANIC STIMULATION

Ultrasound involves the use of high-frequency sound waves to penetrate the skin and deep soft tissues. The waves cause the skin to vibrate, which in turn makes the body tissues more accepting to the needed nutrients in the blood. This also aids in the elimination of waste products. This is achieved by increasing cellular membrane permeability (the ease with which substances pass through the cell membrane). To treat sprains and strains, apply 6 to 10 doses of 5 to 10 minutes, effecting proper rehabilitation of the body region. If you feel too much heat, the dose should be decreased. High-voltage galvanic stimulation can be found on some ultrasound units. A moist towel and the electrode pads are placed on the skin. The galvanic stimulator can be set either at a constant level or in a pulse manner so that it will be released in timed spurts.

Caution: Ultrasound should not be used on the ears, eyes, spinal cord, testes, ovaries or a fertilized uterus, or in any region of active infection.

INTERFERENTIAL CURRENT

Interferential current involves a higher frequency than galvanic stimulation. It is used regularly by athletes as a treatment that increases flexibility and accelerates healing time. It is used for muscle reeducation, increased local blood flow, reduction of edema, relaxation of muscle spasms, prevention of nonuse atrophy, and increased joint flexibility. Interferential current units have cup transmitters that are placed at three different axes within a body region. In this manner the current is able to saturate a body section from all angles, into the very deep tissues.

■

APPENDICES

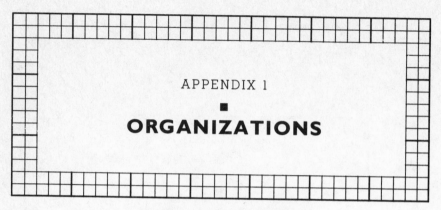

APPENDIX 1

■

ORGANIZATIONS

THE AMATEUR
ATHLETIC UNION

AAU

The Amateur Athletic Union of the United States is the largest non-profit volunteer service organization in the U.S. dedicated to the promotion and development of amateur sports and physical fitness programs.

PHYSICAL FITNESS PROGRAM

The Amateur Athletic Union's Physical Fitness Program represents a major element of the AAU's overall dedication to the health and well being of the American people. The AAU developed and put into operation a testing program to examine the physical capabilities of America's youth in 1943. Modifications in the test and standards have been made in 1968, 1978, and 1981. The scoring system has been continually updated to simplify test administration and record keeping.

The tests, which form the basis of the AAU Physical Fitness Program and are now being used in over 17,000 schools, provide the means of determining the present physical capabilities of young people between the ages of 6 and 17. The standards listed are designed to motivate boys and girls to increase sports participation for the development of physical fitness.

Junior Olympics

A major program of the Amateur Athletic Union is the AAU/USA Junior Olympics with over 3 million young athletes, ages 8 to 18, participating in sports. Founded in 1948, the AAU Junior Olympics teaches young athletes to set goals for themselves, and then strive to reach and exceed those goals. The AAU is joined by several national youth organizations, community service organizations, and amateur sport National Governing Bodies in the development of activities at the local, state, regional and national levels, culminating in the AAU/USA Junior Olympic Games. Sears, Roebuck, and Co., has been the sole national corporate sponsor since 1977. The following sports challenge young athletes to qualify for the AAU/USA Junior Olympic National Championships each year:

Baseball	Judo	Trampoline & Tumbling
Basketball	Soccer	Volleyball
Cross Country	Swimming	Water Polo
Decathlon/Hepthalon	Synchronized Swimming	Weightlifting
Diving	Table Tennis	Winter Sports
Field Hockey	Taekwondo	Wrestling
Gymnastics Sports	Track & Field	

AMATEUR ATHLETIC UNION

The Amateur Athletic Union of the United States of America was formed in 1888 by sports leaders who defined amateurism and established standards and guidelines for amateur athletes.

The AAU consists of many Associations and several thousand member clubs encompassing all of the United States and its territories. In addition to local, state, regional, and national competition, the AAU's more than 200,000 volunteers sponsor general athletic programs for all amateurs ages 8 to 80. The AAU is the only sports organization in the nation with programs for all people, all ages, all year long.

For many, AAU programs offer an opportunity to keep physically fit. For others, the AAU is the path to national and international competition. At the 1984 LA Olympic Games, former AAU Junior Olympians won 18 individual gold medals and contributed to 12 team gold medals while comprising only 11 percent of the team.

The Amateur Athletic Union continues to grow and has been successful in securing major private enterprise support for amateur sport and physical fitness programs from Corporations like Sears, Roebuck and Co., and The NutraSweet Company. "Building American Athletes the American Way" is a fact of life for the AAU and its volunteers.

If you are interested in participating in any of the sports and fitness programs of the AAU, contact your local AAU Association or the AAU National Office. The programs of the AAU could not survive without volunteers. Millions of people, young and old, participate in the programs of the AAU each year. In order to maintain and increase these programs, the AAU always needs new volunteers, meet directors, planners, coaches, typists, timers, and many others. You are invited to join with the AAU in promoting amateur sports and physical fitness in America. Contact your local AAU Association or write the AAU directly:

AAU HOUSE
    3400 West 86th Street
    Indianapolis, IN 46268
    (317) 872-2900

AMERICAN COLLEGE OF SPORTS MEDICINE

The American College of Sports Medicine was founded on April 22, 1954, in New York City. A brief history of the association follows:

In the early 1930s, Joseph B. Wolffe, a prominent physician from Philadelphia, and Grover W. Mueller, director of physical education in the public schools of Philadelphia, discussed the desirability and importance of establishing closer cooperation among physicians, physical educators, and physiologists. Dr. Albert S. Hyman, a cardiologist from New York, later participated in these discussions, which included the establishment of a national organization for the exchange of ideas and knowledge among members of various disciplines.

In 1953, Dr. Ernst Jokl, who had been associated with sports medicine in Europe, joined Dr. Wolffe at the Valley Forge Hospital and Research Institute and the discussion continued more frequently among the small group of men. The result was the organizational meeting in April 1954, held in conjunction with the annual convention of the American Academy of Health, Physical Education and Recreation.

At the first business session, it was voted: 1) to establish a college; 2) to elect officers, including Joseph B. Wolffe as president; and 3) to empower these men to proceed with the establishment of a permanent organization and the drafting of a constitution.

On February 8, 1955, the college was incorporated as a nonprofit organization. The first regional scientific meeting was arranged by Joseph B. Wolffe in conjunction with an administrative council meeting at the Valley Forge Heart Hospital.

The founders recognized that members of the college would no doubt hold membership in other professional organizations. However, the strength of the college, and, in fact, its reason for being, lies in the interdisciplinary nature of the organization and the common forum it provides for the dissemination of ideas, which occurs when members of various groups come into contact. For example, the physiologist may learn about heat stress and physical activity, but the physician, coach, and physical educator must be informed if the health of the young athlete is to be safeguarded. For this reason also, the ACSM was conceived as a college in the true sense of the word.

Administrative policies of the ACSM are determined by its elected officers and board of trustees, both of which reflect the diversified interests of the college. Membership has grown from fifty-four members in 1954 to almost eleven thousand in 1986. The college publishes its own quarterly newsletter (*Sports Medicine Bulletin*) and provides a bimonthly scientific journal *(Medicine and Science in Sports and Exercise)*.

The central office of the American College of Sports Medicine is now located at 401 West Michigan Street, Indianapolis, Indiana 46206. Mailing address is PO Box 1440, Indianapolis, Indiana 46206. Executive director is currently John A. Miller. The phone number is 317-637-9200.

■

NATIONAL STRENGTH AND CONDITIONING ASSOCIATION

AN INTRODUCTION TO THE NATIONAL STRENGTH AND CONDITIONING ASSOCIATION (VERSION A)

The National Strength and Conditioning Association is the non-profit professional membership organization of persons involved in the conditioning of athletes to optimum physical performance. Professionals in the United States and 34 other countries share the commitment to total conditioning of athletes, and represent such various disciplines as strength and conditioning coach, athletic trainer, physical therapist, sports medicine physician, sports science researcher and the athletes themselves.

A NON-PROFIT EDUCATIONAL ASSOCIATION

Founded in 1978 in Lincoln, Nebraska, the National Strength and Conditioning Association was recognized by the Internal Revenue Service in July, 1982, as meeting qualifications for exemption from Federal income tax under section 501 (c) (3) of the Internal Revenue Code and assigned Federal Identification Number 47-06-11-479.

In March, 1983, the NSCA was granted the permit for special mailing rates reserved for publishers of educational materials. The association was, therefore, recognized by the U.S. Postal Service as primarily educational in the nature of its activities and fully in compliance with Section 423.1, Domestic Mail Manual.

PUBLISHER OF THE NSCA JOURNAL

The peer-reviewed NSCA Journal is a bi-monthly scientific publication featuring the latest research and practical application methodology in the profession of athletic strength and conditioning. The NSCA Journal is received by all members, among them representatives of U.S. high schools, institutions of higher learning, students in graduate and undergraduate programs and others in varied professional and educational settings.

A resource to the world, articles from the NSCA Journal have been translated into Japanese, Bulgarian and Russian. An additional Journal of Sports Science Research is published quarterly.

PROVIDING EDUCATIONAL AIDS

Videotapes, audiotapes, instructional brochures and posters complement the educational library of NSCA materials predicated on the NSCA Journal. New materials are reviewed for technical accuracy, clarity and practical applicability.

Educational videotapes available through the NSCA have been produced from original materials written and taped in the United States, as well as from translations of Russian and Polish master tapes.

PROFESSIONAL CERTIFICATION PROGRAM

In June, 1985, the NSCA conducted its first certification examination for strength and conditioning professionals. Developed with the assistance of Professional Examination Services and a select committee of NSCA members, the certification program offers a comprehensive evaluation of academic preparation and practical ability. The designation awarded upon such successful completion of both sections of the examination is C.S.C.S. (Certified Strength and Conditioning Specialist).

NATIONAL CONVENTION

The certification examination is held in conjunction with the annual National Convention of the association. Utilizing a multi-track approach, professionals of many disciplines benefit from the lectures, discussions, demonstrations and free communications presented by the top names in the field. The NSCA, in conjunction with Creighton University, awards college credit for continuing adult education to persons attending the national convention, as well as NSCA-conducted state clinics.

Approved clinics of NSCA state divisions present curriculum which closely follows NSCA-developed guidelines. Special seminars and in-service opportunities are offered by NSCA professionals at colleges, universities, junior and community colleges and high schools. These same learning experiences may be tailored to the specific needs of any age group, to emphasize the value of total conditioning for all sports. All such services are localized through NSCA state divisions. Member coaches are available to conduct such clinics for municipalities, particularly in the context of youth and adult recreational programs.

AWARDING RESEARCH GRANTS AND SCHOLARSHIPS

NSCA grants fund practical sports research at U.S. universities, including Creighton University, the University of Wyoming, Ohio University, Kent State University and the University of Illinois. NSCA Challenge Scholarships provide financial support to graduate and undergraduate student members of the association. Advanced education is important to its members. A 1986 survey indicates that over 50% of members hold an advanced academic degree. About 65 percent of the membership are employed by educational institutions at the secondary or post-secondary levels.

LIFTAMERICA FOR SPECIAL OLYMPICS

State and national programs of Special Olympics, world's largest sports organization serving over 1,000,000 retarded individuals, receive financial support through the LiftAmerica fundraising effort of the NSCA. The association has also compiled a guide for strength training. Used by the Special Olympics coach in the training school setting. LiftAmerica funding also supports the grant and scholarship programs of the association, and underwrites the cost of important position papers issued to clarify issues vital to the sport community.

Two such papers are currently available: Strength Training for the Prepubescent and Use of Anabolic Steroids.

The NSCA helps coaches and athletes share the latest information and methods for improving athletic performance through strength training and total conditioning. The association welcomes coaches, trainers, athletes and anyone interested in athletic conditioning to become a member. For a membership brochure, write:

NSCA
P.O. Box 81410
Lincoln, NE 68501

The NSCA is a non-profit, educational association.

INTERNATIONAL DANCE-EXERCISE ASSOCIATION (IDEA) FACT SHEET

WHAT:

The International Dance-Exercise Association (IDEA) is the only organization dedicated to meeting the needs of professionals in aerobics, jazz exercise, slimnastics and all forms of dance exercise to music.

The IDEA has rapidly become the largest organization of dance-exercise professionals, with more than 12,000 members forming an international network throughout the 50 United States and in 34 countries. The membership also elects regional and state representatives to serve IDEA members on the local level.

IDEA members are entitled to a number of services, including the annual International Industry Convention, offering advanced workshops, panel discussions, in-depth lectures with industry notables, business how-to's, industry awards and a major trade show; regional educational conferences; *Dance Exercise Today* magazine; the IDEA Annual Industry Directory; reduced rates on insurance; professional discounts and participation in IDEA-sponsored events.

The IDEA is the national sponsor of the American Heart Association's "Dance for Heart" program and the official sanctioning body of the Crystal Light National Aerobic Championship.

WHEN:

Founded by Peter and Kathie Davis in 1982 to enhance the professionalism and raise the standards of the flourishing dance-exercise industry.

WHY:

With 24 million participants, of which 5.9 million were new participants in 1985, aerobic dance-exercise is continuing to expand its appeal. But with this growth, today's dance exercise instructors are becoming aware of the need for a network of peers to share updated information on research in new exercise techniques and injury prevention. They are also aware of the benefits of developing professional contacts and of instructor certification for the overall enhancement and growth of the sport. The IDEA was created to provide a supportive community and leadership within the industry, as well as to promote safe dance exercise.

275

WHERE:

4501 Mission Bay Drive
Suite 2-F
San Diego, CA 92109
(619) 274-2770

■

IRSA
(INTERNATIONAL RACKET
SPORTS ASSOCIATION)

. . . Serving the owners, manufacturers, suppliers and developers in the racquet sports industry.

IRSA is an active, not-for-profit professional association dedicated to helping ensure the long-term profitability of the fitness and racquet sports club investment. IRSA's primary goal is to help the commercial club owner profit through the dissemination of responsible, reliable information in the form of statistics, reports, seminars, magazines, newsletters, regional meetings and IRSA's annual National Convention/Trade Show.

Every industry needs a strong national organization to provide the leadership necessary to maintain the flow of valuable information to the key segments of that industry. IRSA performs this service for the club industry.

IRSA was formed in the summer of 1981 as a joint effort of its two predecessor organizations, the National Tennis Association (NTA) and the National Court Club Association (NCCA), the national organizations of tennis club owners and racquetball club owners respectively. Recognizing that both groups were traveling parallel paths, the two joined forces to bring those paths together. Today IRSA includes non-racquet fitness facilities as well.

IRSA represents over 1,200 dues-paying sports facilities, with membership growing every day. In addition, over 200 manufacturers and suppliers also support IRSA's efforts as Associate Members.

Another role IRSA has continued to perform is the providing of accurate and reliable information to potential developers of new facilities, warning them of the hazards of building in already developed areas, while at the same time helping them "do their homework" to ensure that if they do build, that their club is properly developed, financed, located and marketed.

The benefits of IRSA Club Membership are great; the cost is small. We encourage you to review the programs and benefits described in this brochure and invite you to join forces with your colleagues to help solidify the club industry's future.

We look forward to welcoming you into IRSA . . . serving the owners, manufacturers, suppliers and developers in the club industry.

IRSA
132 Brookline Avenue
Boston, Massachusetts 02215
1-800-232-4772

In Canada 1-800-228-4772
In Mass. 617-236-1500

BENEFITS AND SERVICES

Some of the membership benefits and services offered by IRSA are clearly measurable in dollars and cents. Others pay off in more subtle but no less important ways.

1 IRSA CLUB BUSINESS

    Published 11 times a year, *IRSA Club Business* is a magazine that concentrates on the "nuts & bolts" of the club business. Preferring to cut away the "glitter," *IRSA Club Business* gets right down to real numbers, real situations and real issues confronting today's club owner.

2 NATIONAL CONVENTION/TRADE SHOW

    Once a year IRSA conducts its National Convention & Trade Show, the only time that club owners from across North America and internationally as well congregate at the same time and place for the purpose of sharing ideas, working together and conducting business. It is a profitably-spent 4-day series of case studies, seminars, small group discussions and presentations, utilizing the real experts in the field. IRSA presents, without question, one of the most significant events in the club industry.

3 INDUSTRY DATA SURVEY

    Each year IRSA sends its members a questionnaire covering virtually every aspect of club operations, financial structure, personnel and P&L. Hundreds of clubs respond in total confidence to a nationally known CPA firm for analysis of these reports. The result is the most complete statistical information available in the club industry. You can measure yourself against the average of TOP FIVE CLUBS, help determine fees and salaries, make important savings, focus on profit centers and much more. The report is especially useful when you are considering expansion or diversification.

4 RECIPROCAL ACCESS (THE "PASSPORT")

    When you join IRSA you are automatically entitled to an important membership service, IRSA's Reciprocal Play Program. This is an optional program that entitles your members to play at other participating clubs. The "Passport" Kit is a great sales tool for your club. It lists the participating clubs with their phone numbers and amenities, and includes a stand-up display with instructions for your members.

5 THE IRSA INSTITUTE

    The IRSA Institute for Professional Club Management responds to the need for further professional training for club managers. Taught by both practitioners and academic faculty, this two-year training program equips the club manager with the skills necessary to properly manage the investor-owned club.

■

NSGA
(NATIONAL SPORTING
GOODS ASSOCIATION)

NSGA

The National Sporting Goods Association (NSGA) was founded in 1929 by sporting goods retailers and distributors. With headquarters in the Chicago area, NSGA has a staff which includes more than 45 full- and part-time employees.

NSGA was created to provide efficient and effective communication among all members of the sporting goods industry. NSGA brings the latest in marketing techniques to its members and stresses service to consumers.

MEMBERSHIP

NSGA membership consists of suppliers, retailers, wholesalers and sales agents in the sporting goods industry. NSGA supplier members number more than 2,000; retailer members operate more than 18,000 retail outlets for sports equipment, footwear and clothing. NSGA is the largest sporting goods trade association in the United States.

TRADE SHOWS

NSGA produces two of the sporting goods industry's major trade shows each year.

NSGA World Sports Expo, held in the fall in Chicago, is the largest sporting goods trade show in North America. Approximately 1,200 companies exhibit at this show and more than 45,000 industry members attend.

The NSGA Fall Market, also held in the fall in Anaheim, California, serves the western U.S. market—the largest and most concentrated sporting goods market in the U.S. This major show attracts 900 exhibitors and 24,000 industry members.

PUBLICATIONS

Sports Retailer is a monthly trade magazine circulated to chief executives of sporting goods retail buying outlets. The publication, geared to the management needs of chain and independent sporting goods retailers, features the latest information on products and retailing advice. Articles on market data and industry outlooks for specific sporting goods categories assist buyers in planning ahead. The magazine also includes a Merchandising and Advertising Guide. A special section called "Team Outfitter," which is targeted to retailers serving the institutional market, is published quarterly as part of the magazine.

NSGA Cost-of-Doing Business Survey, compiled by Dr. E. Laird Landon of the University of Houston, provides income statements and productivity ratios for various types of sporting goods stores.

The 500-page *NSGA Buying Guide* lists more than 9,000 suppliers of sporting goods products. Products are listed by more than 70 major categories and 1,200 sub-categories. In addition, the Buying Guide contains the names, addresses and telephone numbers of major sporting goods associations.

Market Watch, a newsletter for NSGA members, provides data on market trends, trade shows, statistics and interpretations of government rulings that may affect the sporting goods industry.

The Sporting Goods Market, based on an annual consumer survey of 80,000 U.S. households, is the most comprehensive original research available on consumer purchases of sports equipment, footwear and clothing. Using the National Family Opinion, Inc., panel, the report makes retail sales projections in more than 20 sport categories. The market study is published each spring.

Sports Participation: Series I & Series II provides data on total sports participation, "dropout" activity, new participation and frequency of participation. Demographic data on participation includes sex, age, age by sex, household income and region of the country. *Series I* surveys 27 activities using a 10,000-household sampling. *Series II* surveys 18 additional activities using a 35,000-household sampling. Special state-by-state data also are available.

SERVICES

The Supplier Services Department provides members research and counsel on governmental and community affairs, sports promotion, public relations, marketing and merchandising services.

For retailers NSGA services include:

Visa/MasterCard merchant discounts.

Low group insurance rates—low rates because of NSGA's enormous group buying power for: (1) Major Medical, (2) Worker's Compensation, (3) Business Casualty Insurance.

Store Location Analysis—provides demographic information on potential store locations at a rate previously available only to large retail chains.

Discount Services—discount prices available on store and office supplies and store fixtures.

EDUCATION

The NSGA Management Conference, held each spring, draws industry retailers, suppliers and agents together in a dialogue to address industry problems, increase communication and exchange ideas.

The NSGA Education Department also conducts regular seminar programs at NSGA's two trade shows. These strive to improve communication within the industry and update retailers on changing merchandising and marketing trends.

RESEARCH

The NSGA Information Center provides members with information on manufacturing, retailing, sports participation and other data useful in conducting their daily business. The Information Center currently handles an average of 20 calls a day from industry members and responds to more than 3,000 inquiries annually.

NSGA research provides industry data to its members through its annual "Sporting Goods Market" report, "Sports Participation" reports and its bi-annual "Cost-of-Doing-Business" Survey. These comprehensive studies are useful aids in judging the latest consumer sports interests and predicting future trends.

The NSGA *Sales Reporting Panel*, retail sporting goods stores with annual sales of more than $1 billion, provides monthly sales data to the Association so that buying trends can be quickly spotted.

The Research Department also prepares *Brand Share Reports* that indicate consumer brand preference by specific product line. These are available to members on a subscription basis.

TEAM DISTRIBUTORS

This active NSGA division, Athletic Goods Team Distributors, provides services to the athletic team distributor who specializes in supplying equipment to high schools, colleges and organized teams. The Division acts as a liaison with rule-making bodies and with national high school and college federations. *The Team Line-Up*, a quarterly news bulletin, is sent to members with up-to-date information important to this specialized industry segment.

SPORTS FOUNDATION

The Sports Foundation Inc. was originated in 1965 by leaders of the sporting goods industry to promote interest in active sports and to support worthy recreational activities. Among its programs are the annual Gold Medal Awards for parks and recreational districts. The Foundation, working with NSGA grants, honors those parks and recreational departments and programs that best serve their communities. Special Recreation awards also are presented annually to park and recreational districts that have outstanding programs serving the handicapped.

ASMI

Association and Show Management Inc. is an NSGA trade show and association management subsidiary. A variety of products and services needed by other associations and sporting goods organizations are met through this management/consulting service firm: NSGA, 1699 Wall St., Mount Prospect, IL 60056.

SGMA
(SPORTING GOODS
MANUFACTURERS
ASSOCIATION)

The Sporting Goods Manufacturers Association is a non-profit trade association representing both U.S. and Canadian *manufacturers* of sporting goods and *distributors* of U.S.-owned brand-name sports equipment. Since its founding in 1906, the Association has served as a forum for exchanging ideas and information as a means to build a better industry. The SGMA's success in achieving this goal is attributable to the leadership of the board of directors and president, the involvement of the membership, and work of the staff.

The goal of making the industry better is facilitated by a structure of thirteen standing committees, which report directly to the board of directors through the President and Chief Executive Officer, Howard J. Bruns. These committees, through their members' perseverance and their interaction with the board of directors and the CEO, conduct the work of the SGMA. This committee structure has enabled the SGMA to make considerable progress in expanding and improving programs beneficial to the industry.

The SGMA also provides numerous administrative services for a variety of affiliated sports organizations in an effort to provide maximum economy in operating costs and professional management expenses. This arrangement enables these sports organizations to draw upon other SGMA capabilities that can help them achieve their goals.

The affiliated organizations are: the Archery and Manufacturers Organization, the American Sports Education Institute/Booster Clubs of America, the Athletic Institute, the Billiard and Bowling Institute of America, the International Senior Athletics Association, the National Association of Police Athletic Leagues, the National Golf Foundation, the Golf Manufacturers Association, the Non-Powder Gun Products Association, the Racquetball Manufacturers Association, the Tennis Foundation of North America, the Tennis Manufacturers Association, and the Water Ski Industry Association.

SGMA
200 Castlewood Drive
North Palm Beach, FL 33408
305-842-4100

■

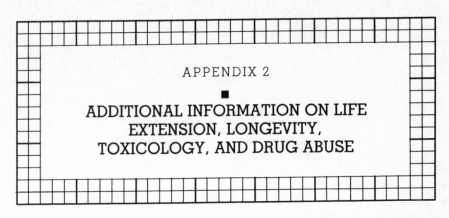

APPENDIX 2

■

ADDITIONAL INFORMATION ON LIFE
EXTENSION, LONGEVITY,
TOXICOLOGY, AND DRUG ABUSE

PUBLICATIONS

National Health and Medical Trends (The Official Journal of the
American Longevity Research Institute, the High Technology Fitness
Research Institute, and the National Centers for Health and Medical
Information)
1510 Montana St.
Chicago, IL 60614

This quarterly journal reports on the latest developments in elite
sports-performance training as well as providing clinically useful information on improving the quality of life. Must reading for anyone
interested in longevity and/or sports performance.

Life Extension Report (previously *Antiaging News*)
2835 Hollywood Blvd.
Hollywood, FL 33020

This newsletter is well documented, very timely, and clinically useful
with practical information.

Longevity Letter
American Longevity Association
330 S. Spalding Dr., Suite 304
Beverly Hills, CA 90212

Edited by Don Swanson, Ph.D., of the University of Chicago, this
publication usually covers one topic per month in great detail. It is
well written and useful for the professional.

Newsletter of The International Academy of Holistic Health and
Medicine
218 Ave. B
Redondo Beach, CA 90277

Edited by Hans J. Kugler, this monthly report is an enlightened editorial with unique information sources on timely issues.

Newsletter of the American Aging Association, Inc.
University of Nebraska Medical Center
Omaha, NE 68105

Edited by Denham Harmon, M.D., this newsletter provides useful information for professionals and laypersons.

New Medical Science
65 Lock Lane
Portsmouth, RI 20871
401-846-6670

Edited by Mark Kudinitz, Ph.D., this bimonthly magazine is an excellent source of information on breakthrough biotechnologies and new biotech companies that are bringing new products to market.

RESOURCES

Air Check—Alpha Energy Labs (Radon gas air-sampling reference laboratory)
P.O. Box 200-PH
Penrose, NC 28766

American Longevity Research Institute (Education and research on longevity and maximum human performance)
1510 Montana St., Suite 333
Chicago, IL 60614
312-871-7325

Watertest Corporation
33 S. Commercial St.
P.O. Box 6360
Manchester, NH 03108-6360
1-800-426-8378 (Ext. 1A)

Aqua Associates, Inc. (Independent water-analysis testing laboratory)
P.O. Box 1251
West Caldwell, NJ 07006
201-227-0422

National Testing Labs, Inc. (Independent water-analysis testing laboratory)
6151 Wilson Mills Rd.
Cleveland, OH 44143

AIDS Information Hotline
1-800-324-AIDS
1-800-221-7044

National public health service for AIDS information
404-329-1296

Cocaine Hotline (For information and resources on treatment and addiction)
1-800-COCAINE

National Institute on Drug Abuse
P.O. Box 2305
Rockville, MD 20852
301-443-4577

Environmental Defense Fund (Research information on toxic waste)
1525 18th St. N.W.
Washington, D.C. 20036
202-833-1484

Environmental Protection Agency
401 M St. S.W.
Washington, DC 20460
202-755-2700
202-755-0707 (Public inquiry center)
202-382-2090 (Switchboard)

National Centers for Health and Medical Information
944 Lexington Drive
Dunedin, FL 33528
813-734-9016

Computerized data-retrieval service for professionals and laypeople. Their system includes information from more than 200 national and international data banks on the topics of medicine, sports, wellness, new drugs, and therapies from around the world.

National Cancer Institute (Cancer research and education)
9000 Rockville Pike
Bethesda, MD 20014
301-496-5615

American College of Advancement in Medicine
6151 West Century Blvd.
Suite 1114
Los Angeles, CA 94115

Education and research on chelation therapy as a method of treating degenerative disease.

Suppliers

American Scientific Health and Fitness Products
P.O. Box 912
Wilmette, IL 60691

This company provides a complete line of top-quality vitamin/nutritional products as well as names of dealers for peak-performance athletic-training equipment.

Life Extension Foundation (Distributors of antiaging nutritional and vitamin products)
2835 Hollywood Blvd.
Hollywood, FL 33020
800-327-6110

■

APPENDIX 3

■

SUGGESTED MAGAZINES AND
JOURNALS FOR THE FITNESS TRADE

Club Industry
1415 Beacon St.
Brookline, MA 02146
617-277-3823

Sporting Goods Business
1515 Broadway
New York, NY 10036
212-869-1300

Fitness Industry
1545 NE 123rd St.
North Miami, FL 33161

City Sports
118 King Street
San Francisco, CA 94107
415-546-6150

Fitness Management
P.O. Box 1198
215 S. Highway 101
Suite 115
Solana Beach, CA 92075-0910
619-481-4155

*American Medical Athletic
Association Newsletter*
1397 Coles
Mountainside, NJ 07092

*Rodale Press
Publications/Runner's World*
33 East Minor St.
Emmaus, PA 18049
215-967-5171

Sports Illustrated
Time Life Inc.
Rockefeller Center
New York, NY 10020

Sport Magazine
119 West 40th St.
New York, NY 10018
212-869-4700

Women's Sports & Fitness
310 Town & Country Village
Palo Alto, CA 94301
415-321-5102

Muscle and Fitness/Shape/Flex
Weider Publications
21100 Erwin St.
Woodland Hills, CA 91367
818-704-6540

Physician and Sports Medicine
4530 West 77th St.
Minneapolis, MN 55435
612-835-3222

*National Strength & Conditioning
Association Journal*
251 Capitol Beach Blvd.
Lincoln, NE 68528
402-472-3000

IRSA Club Business
132 Brookline Ave.
Boston, MA 02215
800-232-IRSA

■

NORMAL HORMONAL LEVELS
IN BLOOD AND URINE

The chart below (reprinted with permission from *Interpretation of Diagnostic Tests*, Jacques Wallach, M.D., 3d edition, Little, Brown & Co., Publishers) lists the normal levels for many hormones found in the blood and urine, determined through laboratory tests. Your physician will decide which of the parameters to focus on. The ones of importance are starred here.

BLOOD AND URINE HORMONE LEVELS

Measure of Thyroid Function	Blood
T-3 (concentration)	50–210 ng/100 ml serum (radioimmunoassay)
T-4 (concentration)	4.8–13.2 µg/100 ml serum (mean = 8.6) (radioimmunoassay)
T-3/T-4 ratio	Average 1.3%
T-3 (resin sponge uptake)	24–36%
T-4 (resin sponge uptake)	4–11%
Free thyroxine index (T-3 uptake × T-4 uptake)	96–396
T-4 (thyroxine by column chromatography)	2.9–6.4 µg/100 ml
"Free thyroxine"	1.0–2.1 mµg/100 ml
Thyroxine-binding globulin (TBG)	10–26 µg/100 m. thyroxine
Thyroid-stimulating hormone (TSH)	$\leqq 0.2$ µU/ml
Long-acting thyroid stimulator (LATS)	None detectable

Measure of Thyroid Function	Blood
Radioactive iodine uptake (RAIU)	9–19% in 1 hour 7–25% in 6 hours 10–50% in 24 hours
Radioactive iodine excretion	40–70% of administered dose in 24 hours
Protein-bound iodine (PBI)	3.6–8.8 µg/100 ml

Hormone	Blood	Urine
Pregnanediol Male		<1.5 mg/24 hours
Female		
Proliferative phase		0.5–1.5 mg/24 hours
Luteal phase		2–7 mg/24 hours
Postmenopausal		0.2–1.0 mg/24 hours
Pregnanetriol		<4 mg/24 hours
*Estrogens (total)		Male: 4–25 µg/24 hours Female: 4–60 µg/24 hours (marked increase during pregnancy)
*Testosterone Male (adult)	0.30–1.0 µg/100 ml (average = 0.7)	47–156 µg/24 hours (average = 70)
Male (adolescent)	>0.10 µg/100 ml	
Female	0–0.1 µg/100 ml (average = 0.04)	0–15 µg/24 hours (average = <6)
*Pituitary gonadotropins (FSH)		6–50 mouse uterine units/24 hours
*Chorionic gonadotropin		0
Prolactin	<20 ng/ml	
Progesterone	<1.0 ng/ml during follicular phase	

Hormone	Blood	Urine
	>2.0 ng/ml during luteal phase	
*Luteinizing hormone	<70 mIU/ml during follicular phase > 70 mIU/ml during luteal phase	
*Growth hormone	≦ 6 ng/ml in men ≦ 10 ng/ml in women	
Aldosterone	0.015 μg/100 ml	3–32/24 hours
Catecholamines (adrenaline, noradrenaline)		Epinephrine <10 μg/24 hours Norepinephrine <100 μg/24 hours
Metanephrines, total		24–288 μg/24 hours
Metanephrine		24–95 μg/24 hours
Normetanephrine		72–288 μg/24 hours
Vanillylmandelic acid (VMA)		≦ 9 mg/24 hours
Homovanillic acid		<15 mg/24 hours
Serotonin (as 5-Hydroxyindole-acetic acid, 5-HIAA)	0.05–0.20 μg/ml	2–10 mg/24 hours (qualitative = 0)
*17-Hydroxycorticoids	(cortisol) 5–25 μg/100 ml at 8 A.M. <10 μg/100 ml at 8 P.M. Falls to μ10 μg/100 ml by 9 P.M.	3–8 mg/24 hours (lower in women)
Glenn-Nelson		Males: 3–10 mg/24 hours Females: 2–6 mg/24 hours
*17-Ketogenic steroids		Males: 5–23 mg/24 hours Females: 3–15 mg/24 hours

Hormone	Blood	Urine		
*17-Ketosteroids	25–125 µg/100 ml	Age (years)	Males (mg/24 hours)	Females (mg/24 hours)
		10	1–4	1–4
		20	6–21	4–16
		30	8–26	4–14
		50	5–18	3–9
		70	2–10	1–7
*ACTH	9 A.M.: 5–95 pg/ml Midnight: 0–35 pg/ml			
*Insulin	6–26 µU/ml (fasting) <20 µU/ml (during hypoglycemia) <150 µU/ml (after glucose load)			
Gastrin	0–200 pg/ml			
Calcitonin	Absent in normal (>100 pg/ml in medullary carcinoma)			

■

APPENDIX 5

■

NORMS OF PRINCIPAL
BLOOD-CHEMISTRY TESTS
AND INTERPRETATION

The basic tests that an athlete should undergo are the SMAC (serum chemistry profile), CBC (complete blood count), UA (urinalysis), and, for males, a sperm count.

The following chart and analyses concentrate on the SMAC. First there is a printout for the SMAC, showing normal ranges in serum-chemistry values. This is followed by a list of differential diagnoses that need to be evaluated to determine the cause of the patient complaint. These diagnoses are from Jacques Wallach, M.D., *Interpretation of Diagnostic Tests* (Boston: Little, Brown, & Co.). These lab tests also serve as an early-warning system to pick up problems before they become critical.

SMAC (SERUM CHEMISTRY)

Name	Test abbrev.	Normals	Units
glucose	GLUH	70–115	MG/DL
blood urinary nitrogen	*BUN	9–22	MG/DL
creatinine	*CREA	0.7–1.5	MG/DL
uric acid	*UA	3.9–9.0	MG/DL
phosphate	PO_4	2.5–4.5	MG/DL
calcium	*CA	8.5–10.5	MG/DL
sodium	*NA	135–145	MEQ/L
potassium	*K	3.5–5.0	MEQ/L
chloride	CL	99–110	MEQ/L
carbon dioxide	CO_2	24–30	MEQ/L
electrolyte balance	EBAL	5–17	MEQ/L
triglycerides	*TRIG	0–150	MG/DL
cholesterol	*CHOL	140–270	MG/DL
total bilirubin	*TBIL	0.2–1.2	MG/DL
direct bilirubin	DBIL	0.0–0.4	MG/DL
indirect bilirubin	IBIL	0.0–1.2	MG/DL
alkaline phosphatase	*ALK	30–101	U/L

Name	Test abbrev.	Normals	Units
gamma glutamyl transpep-tidase	*GGT	9–38	U/L
alanine aminotransferase	*SGPT (ALT)	0–45	U/L
aspartate aminotransferase	*SGOT (AST)	0–40	U/L
lactic dehydrogenase	*LDH	60–230	U/L
creatinine phosphokinase	CK	0–225	U/L
iron	IRON	35–200	MCG/DL
protein	PRO	6.0–8.0	G/DL
albumin	ALB	3.5–5.5	G/DL
globulin	GLOB	2.0–4.0	G/DL

The starred values are the ones to look for abnormalities in.

HEART	LIVER	ELECTROLYTE IMBALANCE
LDH	GGT	PO_4
CK	SGPT	CA
	SGOT	NA
	K	CL

The starred values (*) on the following diagnostic interpretations indicate symptoms to which particular attention should be paid for a steroid-taking athlete.

All from: *Interpretation of Diagnostic Tests* by Jacques Wallach, M.D. Pub. Little, Brown & Co.

Serum Urea Nitrogen (BUN)

Increased In

Impaired kidney function
Prerenal azotemia—any cause of reduced renal blood flow

Congestive heart failure

Salt and water depletion (vomiting, diarrhea, diuresis, sweating)

Shock

Etc.

Postrenal azotemia—any obstruction of urinary tract (ratio of BUN creatinine increases above normal of 10:1)
Increased protein catabolism (serum creatinine remains normal)

Hemorrhage into gastrointestinal tract

Acute myocardial infarction

Stress

Decreased In

*Severe liver damage (liver failure)

*Drugs
Poisoning
*Hepatitis
Other

Increased utilization of protein for synthesis

Late pregnancy
Infancy
*Acromegaly

Diet

Low-protein and high carbohydrate
IV feedings only
Impaired absorption (celiac disease)

Nephrotic syndrome (some patients)

A low BUN of 6–8 mg/100 ml is frequently associated with states of overhydration.

A BUN of 10–20 mg/100 ml almost always indicates normal glomerular function.

A BUN of 50–150 mg/100 ml implies serious impairment of renal function.

Markedly increased BUN (150–250 mg/100 mg) is virtually conclusive evidence of severely impaired glomerular function.

In chronic renal disease, BUN correlates better with symptoms of uremia than does the serum creatinine.

Serum Creatinine
Increased In

Diet

*Ingestion of creatinine (roast meat)

Muscle disease

*Gigantism

*Acromegaly

Prerenal azotemia
Postrenal azotemia
*Impaired kidney function

Ratio of BUN: creatinine >10:1
  *Excess intake of protein
  Blood in small bowel
  Excess tissue breakdown (cachexia, burns, high fever, cor-
  tiocosteroid therapy)
  Urinary tract obstruction (postrenal)
  Inadequate renal blood flow (e.g., prerenal congestive heart
  failure, dehydration, shock)
  Urine reabsorption (e.g., ureterocolostomy)

Ratio of BUN: creatinine <10:1
  Low protein intake
  Repeated dialysis
  Severe diarrhea or vomiting

*Hepatic insufficiency

Serum creatinine is a more specific and sensitive indicator of renal disease than BUN. Use of simultaneous BUN and creatinine
determinations provides more information.

Decreased In

Not clinically significant

Serum Creatine

Increased In

*High dietary intake (meat)
Destruction of muscle
Hyperthyroidism (this diagnosis almost excluded by normal serum
creatine)
Active rheumatoid arthritis
*Testosterone therapy

Decreased In

Not clinically significant

Serum Uric Acid

Levels are very labile and show day-to-day and seasonal variation in same person; also increased by emotional stress, total fasting.

Increased In

Gout
25% of relatives of patients with gout
Renal failure (does not correlate with severity of kidney damage; urea and creatinine should be used)
Increased destruction of nucleoproteins

Leukemia, multiole myeloma

Polycythemia

Lymphoma, especially postirradiation

Other disseminated neoplasms

Cancer chemotherapy (e.g., nitrogen mustards, vincristine, mercaptopurine)

Hemolytic anemia

Sickle cell anemia

Resolving pneumonia

Toxemia of pregnancy (serial determinations to follow therapeutic response and estimate prognosis)

Psoriasis (one-third of patients)

*Diet

*High-protein weight reduction diet
*Excess nucleoprotein (e.g., sweetbreads, liver)

Asymptomatic hyperuricemia (e.g., incidental finding with no evidence of gout; clinical significance not known but people so afflicted should be rechecked periodically for gout). The higher the level of serum uric acid, the greater the likelihood of an attack of acute gouty arthritis.

Miscellaneous

Von Gierke's disease

Lead poisoning

Lesch-Nyham syndrome

Maple syrup urine disease

Down's syndrome

Polycystic kidneys

Calcinosis universalis and circumscripta

*Some drugs (e.g., thiazides, furosemide, ethacrynic acid, small doses of salicylates)

Hypoparathyroidism

Primary hyperparathyroidism

Hypothyroidism

Sarcoidosis

Chronic berylliosis

Some patients with alcoholism

*Patients with arteriosclerosis and hypertension (Serum uric acid is increased in 80% of patients with elevated serum triglycerides.)

Certain population groups (e.g., Blackfoot and Pima Indians, Filipinos, New Zealand Maoris)

Decreased In

*Administration of ACTH
Administration of uricosuric drugs (e.g., high dose of salicylates, probenecid, cortisone, allopurinol, coumarins)
Wilson's disease
*Fanconi's syndrome
*Acromegaly (some patients)
Celiac disease (slightly)
Pernicious anemia in relapse (some patients)
Xanthinuria
Administration of various other drugs (x-ray contrast agents, glyceryl guaiacolate)
*Neoplasms (occasional cases) e.g., carcinomas, Hodgkin's disease
Healthy adults with isolated defect in tubular transport of uric acid (dalmation dog mutation)

Unchanged In

Colchicine administration

Serum Sodium

Increased In

Excess loss of water
    Conditions that cause loss via gastrointestinal tract (e.g., in vomiting), lung (hyperpnea), or skin (e.g., in excessive sweating)

Conditions that cause diuresis

Diabetes insipidus

Nephrogenic diabetes insipidus

Deabetes mellitus

Diuretic drugs

Diuretic phase of acute tubular necrosis

Diuresis following relief of urinary tract obstruction

Hypercalcemic nephropathy

Hypokalemic nephropathy

Excess administration of sodium (iatrogenic), e.g., incorrect re-placement following fluid loss

"Essential" hypernatremia due to hypothalamic lesions

Decreased In (serum osmolality is decreased)

Dilutional (e.g., congestive heart failure, nephrosis, cirrhosis with ascites)

Sodium depletion

Loss of body fluids (e.g., vomiting, diarrhea, excessive sweating) with incorrect or no therapeutic replacement, diuretic drugs (e.g., thiazides)

Adrenocortical insufficiency

Salt-losing nephropathy

Inappropriate secretion of antidiuretic hormone

Spurious (serum osmolality is normal or increased)

Hyperlipidemia

Hyperglycemia (serum sodium decreases 3 mEq/L for every in-crease of serum glucose of 100 mg/100 ml)

Serum Potassium

Increased In

Renal failure

Acute with oliguria or anuria

Chronic end-stage with oliguria (glomerular filtration rate (3-5 ml/minute)

Chronic nonoliguric associated with dehydration, obstruction, trauma, or excess potassium

Decreased mineralocorticoid activity

*Addison's disease
Hypofunction of renin-angiotensin-aldosterone system
Pseudohypoaldosteronism
Aldosterone antagonist (e.g., spironolactone)

Increased supply of potassium

Red blood cell hemolysis (transfusion reaction, hemolytic anemia)
*Excess dietary intake or rapid potassium infusion
Striated muscle (status epilepticus, periodic paralysis)
Potassium-retaining drugs (e.g., triamterene)
*Fluid-electrolyte imbalance (e.g., dehydration, acidosis)

Laboratory artifacts (e.g., hemolysis during venipuncture, conditions associated with thrombocytosis, incomplete separation of serum and clot)

Decreased In

Renal and adrenal conditions with metabolic alkalosis

*Administration of diuretics
Primary aldosteronism
Pseudoaldosteronism
Salt-losing nephropathy
*Cushing's syndrome

Renal conditions associated with metabolic acidosis

*Renal tubular acidosis
Diuretic phase of acute tubular necrosis
Chronic pyelonephritis
Diuresis following relief of urinary tract obstruction

Gastrointestinal conditions

Vomiting, gastric suctioning

Villous adenoma

Cancer of colon

Chronic laxative abuse

Zollinger-Ellison syndrome

Chronic diarrhea

Ureterosigmoidostomy

Serum Cholesterol

Increased In

*Idiopathic hypercholesterolemia
Biliary obstruction

Stone, carcinoma, etc., of duct

*Cholangiolitic cirrhosis

von Gierke's disease
Hypothyroidism
Nephrosis (due to chronic nephritis, renal vein thrombosis, amyloidosis, systemic lupus erythematosus, periarteritis, diabetic glomerulosclerosis
Pancreatic disease

Diabetes mellitus

Total pancreatectomy

Chronic pancreatitis (some patients)

Pregnancy

Decreased In

*Severe liver cell damage (due to chemicals, drugs, hepatitis)
Hyperthyroidism
Malnutrition (e.g., starvation, terminal neoplasm, uremia, malabsorption in steatorrhea)
Chronic anemia

Pernicious anemia in relapse

Hemolytic anemias

Marked hypochromic anemia

*Cortisone and ACTH therapy
Hypo-beta- and a-beta-lipoproteinemia
Tangier disease

Serum Alkaline Phosphatase
Increased In
Increased deposition of calcium in bone

Osteitis fibrosa cystica (hyperparathyroidism)

Paget's disease (osteitis deformans)

Healing fractures (slightly)

Osteoblastic bone tumors (osteogenic sarcoma, metastatic carcinoma)

Osteogenesis imperfecta

Familial osteoectasia

Osteomalacia

Rickets

Polyostotic fibrous dysplasia

Late pregnancy; reverts to normal level by 20th day postpartum

Children

*Administration of erogosterol

*Liver disease—any obstruction of biliary system
*Nodules in liver (metastatic tumor, abscess, cyst, parasite, amyloid, tuberculosis, sarcoid, or leukemia)
*Biliary duct obstruction (e.g., stone, carcinoma)
Cholangiolar obstruction in hepatitis
*Adverse reaction to therapeutic drug (e.g., chlorpropamide) (progressive elevation of serum alkaline phosphatase may be first indication that drug therapy should be halted)
Marked hyperthyroidism
Hyperphosphatasia
Primary hypophosphatemia (often increased)
Intravenous injection of albumin; sometimes marked increase (e.g., 10 times normal level) lasting for several days
Some patients with myocardial or pulmonary infarction, usually during phase of organization

Decreased In

*Excess vitamin D ingestion
  Milk-alkali (Burnett's) syndrome
  Scurvy
  Hypophosphatasia
  Hypothyroidism
  Pernicious anemia in one-third of patients
  Celiac disease
  Malnutrition
  Collection of blood in EDTA, fluoride, or oxalate anticoagulant
  Alkaline phosphatase isoenzyme determinations are not clinically useful; heat inactivation may be more useful to distinguish bone from liver source of increased alkaline phosphatase.

Serum Gamma-Glutamyl Transpeptidase
Increased In

*Liver disease. Generally parallels changes in serum alkaline phosphatase, LAP, and 5'-nucleotidase but is more sensitive.

*Acute hepatitis. Elevation is less marked than that of other liver enzymes, but it is the last to return to normal and therefore is useful to indicate recovery.

*Chronic hepatitis. Increased more than in acute hepatitis. More elevated than SGOT and SGPT. In dormant stage, may be the only enzyme elevated.

*Cirrhosis. In inactive cases, average values are lower than in chronic hepatitis. Increases greater than 10–20 times in cirrhotic patients suggest superimposed primary carcinoma of the liver.

Primary biliary cirrhosis. Elevation is marked.

*Fatty liver. Elevation parallels that of SGOT and SGPT but is greater.

Obstructive jaundice. Increase is faster and greater than that of serum alkaline phosphatase and LAP.

*Liver metastases. Parallels alkaline phosphatase; elevation precedes positive liver scans.

Pancreatitis. Always elevated in acute pancreatitis. In chronic pancreatitis is increased when there is involvement of the biliary tract or active inflammation.

Renal disease. Increased in lipoid nephrosis and some cases of renal carcinoma.

Acute myocardial infarction. Increased in 50% of the patients. Elevation begins on fourth to fifth day, reaches maximum at 8–12 days. With shock or acute right heart failure, may have early peak within 48 hours, with rapid decline followed by later rise.

Heavy use of alcohol, barbiturates, or phenytoin sodium (Dilantin). Is the most sensitive indicator of alcoholism, since elevation exceeds that of other commonly assayed liver enzymes.

Normal In

Women during pregnancy (in contrast to serum alkaline phosphatase and LAP) and children over 3 months of age; therefore may aid in differential diagnosis of hepatobiliary disease occurring during pregnancy and childhood.

Bone disease or patients with increased bone growth (children and adolescents); therefore useful in distinguishing bone disease from liver disease as a cause of increased serum alkaline phosphatase.

Renal failure.

Serum Transaminase (SGOT)

Increased In

Acute myocardial infarction
  Liver diseases, with active necrosis of parenchymal cells
  Musculoskeletal diseases, including trauma and intramuscular injections
  Acute pancreatitis
  Other

Myoglobinuria

Intestinal injury (e.g., surgery, infarction)

Local irradiation injury

Pulmonary infarction (relatively slight increase)

Cerebral infarction (increased in following week in 50% of patients)

Cerebral neoplasms (occasionally)

Renal infarction (occasionally)

"Pseudomyocardial infarction" pattern. Administration of opiates to patients with diseased biliary tract or previous cholecystectomy causes increase in LDH and especially SGOT. SGOT increases by

2–4 hours, peaks in 5–8 hours, and increase may persist for 24 hours; elevation may be 2½–65 times normal.

Falsely Increased In

(because enzymes are activated during test)
> Therapy with Prostaphlin, Polycillin, opiates, erythromycin
> Calcium dust in air (e.g., due to construction in laboratory)

Falsely Decreased In

(because of increased serum lactate-consuming enzyme during test)
> Diabetic ketoacidosis
> Beriberi
> *Severe liver disease
> Chronic hemodialysis (reason unknown)
> Uremia (proportional to BUN level) (reason unknown)

Normal In

Angina pectoris
> Coronary insufficiency
> Pericarditis
> Congestive heart failure without liver damage

Varies <10 units/day in the same person.

SGPT generally parallels SGOT, but the increase is less marked in myocardial necrosis, chronic hepatitis, cirrhosis, hepatic metastases, and congestive changes in liver, and is more marked in liver necrosis and acute hepatitis.

Serum Lactic Dehydrogenase (LDH)

Increased In

Acute myocardial infarction
> Serum LDH is almost always increased, beginning in 10–12 hours and reaching a peak (of about 3 times normal) in 48–72 hours. The prolonged elevation of 10–14 days is particularly useful for late diagnosis when the patient is first seen after sufficient time has elapsed

for CPK and SGOT to become normal. Levels >2000 units suggest a poorer prognosis. Because many other diseases may increase the LDH, isoenzyme studies should be performed. Increased serum LDH, with a ratio of $LDH_1/LDH_2 > 1$ ("flipped" LDH), occurs in acute renal infarction and hemolysis associated with hemolytic anemia or prosthetic heart valves as well as in acute myocardial infarction. In acute myocardial infarction, flipped LDH usually appears between 12 and 24 hours and is present within 48 hours in 80% of patients; after 1 week it is still present in <50% of patients, even though total serum LDH may still be elevated; flipped LDH never appears before CPK MB isoenzyme. LDH_1 may remain elevated after total LDH has returned to normal; with small infarcts, LDH_1 may be increased when total LDH remains normal.

Acute myocardial infarction with congestive heart failure. May show increase of LDH_1 and LDH_5.

Congestive heart failure alone. LDH isoenzymes are normal.

Insertion of intracardiac prosthetic valves consistently causes chronic hemolysis with increase of total LDH and of LDH_1 and LDH_2. This is also often present before surgery in patients with severe hemodynamic abnormalities of cardiac valves.

Cardiovascular surgery. LDH is increased up to 2 times normal without cardiopulmonary bypass and returns to normal in 3–4 days; with extracorporeal circulation, it may increase up to 4–6 times normal; increase is more marked when transfused blood is older.

*Hepatitis. Most marked increase is of LDH_5, which occurs during prodromal stage and is greatest at time of onset of jaundice. Total LDH is also increased in 50% of the cases. LDH_5 is also increased with other causes of liver damage (e.g., chlorpromazine hepatitis, carbon tetrachloride poisoning, exacerbation of cirrhosis, biliary obstruction) even when total LDH is normal.

Untreated pernicious anemia. Total LDH (chiefly LDH_1) is markedly increased, especially with hemoglobin <8 gm/100 ml. Only slightly increased in severe hemolytic anemia. Normal in iron-deficiency anemia, even when very severe.

*Malignant tumors. Increased in about 50% of patients with carcinoma, especially in advanced stages. Increased in $\cong$ 60% of patients with lymphomas and lymphomatic leukemias. Increased in $\cong$ 90% of patients with acute leukemia; degree of increase is not correlated with level of WBCs; relatively low levels in lymphatic type of leukemia. Increased in 95% of patients with myelogenous leukemia.

Diseases of muscle.

Pulmonary embolus and infarction.

Renal diseases. Occasional increase but to no clinically useful degree.

Other causes of hemolysis

Artifactual (e.g., poor venipuncture, failure to separate clot from serum, heating of blood)

Various hemolytic conditions in vivo (e.g., hemolytic anemias).

5'-Nucleotidase (5'-N)

This is a very sensitive test for liver problems.
   Increased Only In
   *Obstructive type of hepatobiliary disease

*May be an early indication of liver metastases in the cancer patient, especially if jaundice is absent.

Normal In

Pregnancy and postpartum period (in contrast to serum LAP and alkaline phosphatase); therefore may aid in differential diagnosis of hepatobiliary disease occurring during pregnancy.

*Whenever the alkaline phosphatase is elevated, a simultaneous elevation of 5'-N establishes biliary disease as the cause of the elevated alkaline phosphatase. If the 5'-N is not increased, the cause of the elevated alkaline phosphatase must be found elsewhere, e.g., bone disease.

■

Increasing numbers of persons are becoming involved in endurance training activities and thus, the need for guidelines for exercise prescription is apparent.

Based on the existing evidence concerning exercise prescription for healthy adults and the need for guidelines, the American College of Sports Medicine makes the following recommendations for the quantity and quality of training for developing and maintaining cardiorespiratory fitness and body composition in the healthy adult:

1 Frequency of training: 3 to 5 days per week.

2 Intensity of training: 60% to 90% of maximum heart rate reserve or, 50% to 85% of maximum oxygen uptake (VO_2 max).

3 Duration of training: 15 to 60 minutes of continuous aerobic activity. Duration is dependent on the intensity of the activity, thus lower intensity activity should be conducted over a longer period of time. Because of the importance of the "total fitness" effect and the fact that it is more readily attained in longer duration programs, and because of the potential hazards and compliance problems associated with high intensity activity, lower to moderate intensity activity of longer duration is recommended for the non-athletic adult.

4 Mode of activity: Any activity that uses large muscle groups, that can be maintained continuously, and is rhythmical and aerobic in nature, e.g., running-jogging, walking-hiking, swimming, skating, bicycling, rowing, cross-country skiing, rope skipping, and various endurance game activities.

RATIONALE AND RESEARCH BACKGROUND

The questions, "How much exercise is enough and what type of exercise is best for developing and maintaining fitness?" are frequently asked. It is recognized that the term "physical fitness" is composed of

*Reprinted with permission of the American College of Sports Medicine. Copyright © 1987 by the American College of Sports Medicine.

a wide variety of variables included in the broad categories of cardiovascular-respiratory fitness, physique and structure, motor function, and many histochemical and biochemical factors. It is also recognized that the adaptive response to training is complex and includes peripheral, central, structural, and functional factors. Although many such variables and their adaptive response to training have been documented, the lack of sufficient in-depth and comparative data relative to frequency, intensity, and duration of training make them inadequate to use as comparative models. Thus, in respect to the above questions, fitness will be limited to changes in VO_2 max, total body mass, fat weight (FW), and lean body weight (LBW) factors.

Exercise prescription is based upon the frequency, intensity, and duration of training, the mode of activity (aerobic in nature, e.g., listed under No. 4 above), and the initial level of fitness. In evaluating these factors, the following observations have been derived from studies conducted with endurance training programs.

1 Improvement in VO_2 max is directly related to frequency (2, 23, 32, 58, 59, 65, 77, 79), intensity (2, 10, 13, 26, 33, 37, 42, 56, 77), and duration (3, 14, 29, 49, 56, 77, 86) of training. Depending upon the quantity and quality of training, improvement in VO_2 max ranges from 5% to 25% (4, 13, 27, 31, 35, 36, 43, 45, 52, 53, 62, 71, 77, 78, 82, 86). Although changes in VO_2 max greater than 25% have been shown, they are usually associated with large total body mass and FW loss, or a low initial level of fitness. Also, as a result of leg fatigue or a lack of motivation, persons with low initial fitness may have spuriously low initial VO_2 max values.

2 The amount of improvement in VO_2 max tends to plateau when frequency of training is increased above 3 days per week (23, 62, 65). For the non-athlete, there is not enough information available at this time to speculate on the value of added improvement found in programs that are conducted more than 5 days per week. Participation of less than two days per week does not show an adequate change in VO_2 max (24, 56, 62).

3 Total body mass and FW are generally reduced with endurance training programs (67), while LBW remains constant (62, 67, 87) or increases slightly (54). Programs that are conducted at least 3 days per week (58, 59, 61, 62, 87), of at least 20 minutes duration (48, 62, 87) and of sufficient intensity and duration to expend approximately 300 kilocalories (Kcal) per exercise session are suggested as a threshold level for total body mass and FW loss (12, 29, 62, 67). An expenditure of 200 Kcal per session has also been shown to be useful in weight reduction if the exercise frequency is at least 4 days per week (80). Programs with less participation generally show little or no change in body composition (19, 25, 42, 62, 67, 84, 85, 87). Significant increases in VO_2 max have been shown with 10 to 15 minutes of high intensity training (34, 49, 56, 62, 77, 78), thus, if total body mass and FW reduction is not a consideration, then short duration, high intensity programs may be recommended for healthy, low risk (cardiovascular disease) persons.

4 The minimal threshold level for improvement in VO_2 max is approximately 60% of the maximum heart rate reserve (50% of VO_2 max) (33, 37).

Maximum heart rate reserve represents the percent difference between resting and maximum heart rate, added to the resting heart rate. The technique as described by Karvonen, Kentala, and Mustala (37), was validated by Davis and Convertino (14), and represents a heart rate of approximately 130 to 135 beats/minute for young persons. As a result of the aging curve for maximum heart rate, the absolute heart rate value (threshold level) is inversely related to age, and can be as low as 110 to 120 beats/minute for older persons. Initial level of fitness is another important consideration in prescribing exercise (10, 40, 46, 75, 77). The person with a low fitness level can get a significant training effect with a sustained training heart rate as low as 110 to 120 beats/minute, while persons of higher fitness levels need a higher threshold of stimulation (26).

5 Intensity and duration of training are interrelated with the total amount of work accomplished being an important factor in improvement in fitness (2, 7, 12, 40, 61, 62, 76, 78). Although more comprehensive inquiry is necessary, present evidence suggests that when exercise is performed above the minimal threshold of intensity, the total amount of work accomplished is the important factor in fitness development (2, 7, 12, 61, 62, 76, 79) and maintenance (68). That is, improvement will be similar for activities performed at a lower intensity/longer duration compared to higher intensity/shorter duration if the total energy cost of the activities is equal.

   If frequency, intensity, and duration of training are similar (total Kcal expenditure), the training result appears to be independent of the mode of aerobic activity (56, 60, 62, 64). Therefore, a variety of endurance activities, e.g., listed above, may be used to derive the same training effect.

6 In order to maintain the training effect, exercise must be continued on a regular basis (2, 6, 11, 21, 44, 73, 74). A significant reduction in working capacity occurs after two weeks of detraining (73) with participants returning to near pretraining levels of fitness after 10 weeks (21) to 8 months of detraining (44). Fifty percent reduction in improvement of cardiorespiratory fitness has been shown after 4 to 12 weeks of detraining (21, 41, 73). More investigation is necessary to evaluate the rate of increase and decrease of fitness with varying training loads and reduction in training in relation to level of fitness, age, and length of time in training. Also, more information is needed to better identify the minimal level of work necessary to maintain fitness.

7 Endurance activities that require running and jumping generally cause significantly more debilitating injuries to beginning exercisers than other non-weight bearing activities (42, 55, 69). One study showed that beginning joggers had increased foot, leg, and knee injuries when training was performed more than 3 days per week and longer than 30 minutes duration per exercise session (69). Thus, caution should be taken when recommending the type of activity and exercise prescription for the beginning exercise. Also, the increase of orthopedic injuries as related to overuse (marathon training) with chronic jogger-runners is apparent. Thus, there is a need for more inquiry into the affect that different types of activities and the quantity and quality of training has on short-term and long-term participation.

8 Most of the information concerning training described in this position stand has been conducted on men. The lack of information on women is apparent, but the available evidence indicates that women tend to adapt to endurance training in the same manner as men (8, 22, 89).

9 Age in itself does not appear to be a deterrent to endurance training. Although some earlier studies showed a lower training effect with middle-aged or elderly participants (4, 17, 34, 83, 86), more recent study shows the relative change in VO_2 max to be similar to younger age groups (3, 52, 66, 75, 86). Although more investigation is necessary concerning the rate of improvement in VO_2 max with age, at present it appears that elderly participants need longer periods of time to adapt to training (17, 66). Earlier studies showing moderate to no improvement in VO_2 max were conducted over a short time-span (4) or exercise was conducted at a moderate to low Kcal expenditure (17), thus making the interpretation of the results difficult.

Although VO_2 max decreases with age, and total body mass and FW increase with age, evidence suggests that this trend can be altered with endurance training (9, 12, 38, 39, 62). Also, 5- to-10 year follow-up studies where participants continued their training at a similar level showed maintenance of fitness (39, 70). A study of older competitive runners showed decreases in VO_2 max from the fourth to seventh decade of life, but also showed reductions in their training load (63). More inquiry into the relationship of long-term training (quantity and quality) for both competitors and non-competitors and physiological function with increasing age, is necessary before more definitive statements can be made.

10 An activity such as weight training should not be considered as a means of training for developing VO_2 max, but has significant value for increasing muscular strength and endurance, and LBW (16, 24, 47, 49, 88). Recent studies evaluating circuit weight training (weight training conducted almost continuously with moderate weights, using 10 to 15 repetitions per exercise session with 15 to 30 seconds rest between bouts of activity) showed little to no improvements in working capacity and VO_2 max (1,24,90).

Despite an abundance of information available concerning the training of the human organism, the lack of standardization of testing protocols and procedures, methodology in relation to training procedures and experimental design, a preciseness in the documentation and reporting of the quantity and quality of training prescribed, make interpretation difficult (62,67). Interpretation and comparison of results are also dependent on the initial level of fitness (18,74-76,81), length of time of the training experiment (20,57,58,61,62), and specificity of the testing and training (64). For example, data from training studies using subjects with varied levels of VO_2 max, total body mass and FW have found changes to occur in relation to their initial values (5,15,48,50,51), i.e., the lower the initial VO_2 max the larger the percent of improvement found, and the higher the FW the greater the reduction. Also, data evaluating trainability with age, comparison of the different magnitudes and quantities of effort, and comparison of the trainability of men and women may have been influenced by the initial fitness levels.

In view of the fact that improvement in the fitness variables discussed in this position stand continue over many months of training (12,38,39,62), it is reasonable to believe that short-term studies conducted over a few weeks have certain limitations. Middle-aged sedentary and older participants may take several weeks to adapt to the initial rigors of training, and thus need a longer adaptation period to get the full benefit from a program. How long a training experiment should be conducted is difficult to determine, but 15 to 20 weeks may be a good minimum standard. For example, two investigations conducted with middle-aged men who jogged either 2 or 4 days per week found both groups to improve in VO_2

max. Mid-test results of the 16 and 20 week programs showed no difference between groups, while subsequent final testing found the 4 day per week group to improve significantly more (58,59). In a similar study with young college men, no differences in VO_2 max were found among groups after 7 and 13 weeks of interval training (20). These latter findings and those of other investigators point to the limitations in interpreting results from investigations conducted over a short time-span (62,67).

In summary, frequency, intensity and duration of training have been found to be effective stimuli for producing a training effect. In general, the lower the stimuli, the lower the training effect (2,12,13,27,35,46,77,78,90), and the greater the stimuli, the greater the effect (2,12,13,27,58,77,78). It has also been shown that endurance training less than two days per week, less than 50% of maximum oxygen uptake, and less than 10 minutes per day is inadequate for developing and maintaining fitness for healthy adults.

REFERENCES

1 Allen, T. E., R. J. Byrd and D. P. Smith. Hemodynamic consequences of circuit weight training. *Res. Q.* 43:299–306, 1976.

2 American College of Sports Medicine. *Guidelines for Graded Exercise Testing and Exercise Prescription.* Philadelphia: Lea and Fibiger, 1976.

3 Barry, A. J., J. W. Daly, E.D.R. Pruett, J. R. Steinmetz, H. F. Page, N. C. Birkhead and K. Rodahl. The effects of physical conditioning on older individuals. I. Work capacity, circulatory-respiratory function, and work electrocardiogram. *J. Gerontol.* 21:182–191, 1966.

4 Bensetad, A. M. Trainability of old men. *Acta Med. Scandinav.* 178:321–327, 1965.

5 Boileau, R. A., E. R. Buskirk, D. H. Horstman, J. Mendez and W. C. Nicholas. Body composition changes in obese and lean men during physical conditioning. *Med. Sci. Sports* 3:183–189, 1971.

6 Brynteson, P. and W. E. Sinning. The effects of training frequencies on the retention of cardiovascular fitness. *Med. Sci. Sports* 5:29–33, 1973.

7 Burke, E. J. and B. D. Franks. Changes in VO_2 max resulting from bicycle training at different intensities holding total mechanical work constant. *Res. Q.* 46:31–37, 1975.

8 Burke, E. J. Phhysiologicl effects of similar training programs in males and females, *Res. Q.* 48:510–517, 1977.

9 Carter, J.E.L. and W. H. Phillips. Structural changes in exercising middle-aged males during a 2-year period. *J. Appl. Physiol.* 27:787–794, 1969

10 Crews, T. R. and J. A. Roberts. Effects of interaction of frequency and intensity of training. *Res. Q.* 47:48–55, 1976.

11 Cureton, T. K. and E. E. Phillips. Physical fitness changes in middle-aged men attributable to equal eight-week periods of training, non-training and retraining. *J. Sports Med. Phys. Fitness* 4:1–7, 1964.

12 Cureton, T. K. *The Physiological Effects of Exercise Programs upon Adults.* Springfield: C. Thomas Company, 1969

13 Davies, C.T.M. and A. V. Knibbs. The training stimulus, the effects of intensity, duration and frequency of effort on maximum aerobic power output. *Int. Z. Agnew. Physiol.* 29:299–305, 1971.

14 Davis, J. A. and V. A. Convertino. A comparison of heart rate methods for predicting endurance training intensity. *Med. Sci. Sports* 7:295–298, 1975.

15 Dempsey, J. A. Anthropometrical observations on obese and non-obese young men undergoing a program of vigorous physical exercise. *Res. Q.* 35:275–287, 1964.

16 Delorme, T. L. Restoration of muscle power by heavy resistance exercise. *J. Bone and Joint Surgery* 27:645–667, 1945.

17 DeVries, H. A. Physiological effects of an exercise training regimen upon men aged 52 to 88. *J. Gerontol.* 24:325–336, 1970.

18 Ekblom, B., P. O. Astrand, B. Saltin, J. Sternberg and B. Wallstrom. Effect of training on circulatory response to exercise. *J. Appl. Physiol.* 24:518–528, 1968.

19 Flint, M. M., B. L. Drinkwater and S. M. Horvath. Effects of training on women's response to submaximal exercise. *Med. Sci. Sports* 6:89–94, 1974.

20 Fox, E. L., R. L. Bartels, C. E. Billings, R. O'Brien, R. Bason and D. K. Mathews. Frequency and duration of interval training programs and changes in aerobic power. *J. Appl. Physiol.* 38:481–484, 1975.

21 Fringer, M. N. and A. G. Stull. Changes in cardiorespiratory parameters during periods of training and detraining in young female adults. *Med. Sci. Sports* 6:20–25, 1974.

22 Getchell, L. H. and J. C. Moore. Physical training: comparative responses of middle-aged adults. *Arch. Phys. Med. Rehab.* 56:250–254, 1975.

23 Gettman, L. R., M. L. Pollock, J. L. Durstine, A. Ward, J. Ayres and A. C. Linnerud. Physiological responses of men to 1, 3, and 5 day per week training programs. *Res. Q.* 47:638–646, 1976.

24 Gettman, L. R., J. Ayres, M. L. Pollock, J. L. Durstine and W. Grantham. Physiological effects of circuit strength training and jogging on adult men. *Arch. Phys. Med. Rehab.*, In press.

25 Girandola, R. N. Body composition changes in women: Effects of high and low exercise intensity. *Arch. Phys. Med. Rehab.* 57:297–300, 1976.

26 Gledhill, N. and R. B. Eynon. The intensity of training. In: A. W. Taylor and M. L. Howell (editors). *Training Scientific Basis and Application.* Springfield: Charles C. Thomas, pp. 97–102, 1972.

27 Golding, L. Effects of physical training upon total serum cholesterol levels. *Res. Q.* 32:499–505, 1961.

28 Goode, R. C., A. Virgin, T. T. Romet, P. Crawford, J. Duffin, T. Pallandi and Z. Woch. Effects of a short period of physical activity in adolescent boys and girls. *Canad. J. Appl. Sci.* 1:241–250, 1976.

29 Gwinup, G. Effect of exercise alone on the weight of obese women. *Arch. Int. Med.* 135:676–680, 1975.

30 Hanson, J. S., B. S. Tabakin, A. M. Levy and W. Nedde. Long-term physical training and cardiovascular dynamics in middle-aged men. *Circulation* 38:783–799, 1968.

31 Hartley, L. H., G. Grimby, A. Kilborn, N. J. Nilsson, I. Astrand, J. Bjure, B. Ekblom and B. Saltin. Physical training in sedentary middle-aged and older men. *Scand. J. Clin. Lab. Invest.* 24:335–344, 1969.

32 Hill, J. S. The effects of frequency in exercise on cardiorespiratory fitness of adult men. M. S. Thesis, Univ. of Western Ontario, London, 1969.

33 Hollmann, W. and H. Venrath. Experimentelle Untersuchungen zur be-dentung aines trainings unterhalb and oberhalb der dauerbeltz stungsgranze. In: Korbs (editor). *Carl Diem Festschrift*. W. u. a. Frankfurt/Wein, 1962.

34 Hollmann, W. Changes in the capacity for maximal and continuous effort in relation to age. *Int. Res. Sport Phys. Ed.*, (E. Joki and E. Simon, editors). Springfield: C.C. Thomas Co., 1964.

35 Huibregtse, W. H., H. H. Hartley, L. R. Jones, W. D. Doolittle and T. L. Criblez. Improvement of aerobic work capacity following non-strenuous exercise. *Arch. Env. Health*, 27:12–15, 1973.

36 Ismail, A. H., D. Corrigan and D. F. McLeod. Effect of an eight-month exercise program on selected physiological, biochemical, and audiological variables in adult men. *Brit. J. Sports Med.* 7:230–240, 1973.

37 Karvonen, M., K. Kentala and O. Mustala. The effects of training heart rate: a longitudinal study. *Ann. Med. Exptl. Biol. Fenn.* 35:307–315, 1957.

38 Kasch, F. W., W. H. Phillips, J.E.L. Carter and J. L. Boyer. Cardiovascular changes in middle-aged men during two years of training. *J. Appl. Physiol.* 314:53–57, 1972.

39 Kasch, F. W. and J. P. Wallace. Physiological variables during 10 years of endurance exercise. *Med. Sci. Sports* 8:5–8, 1976.

40 Kearney, J. T., A. G. Stull, J. L. Ewing and J. W. Strein. Cardiorespiratory responses of sedentary college women as a function of training intensity. *J. Appl. Physiol.* 41:822–825, 1976.

41 Kendrick, Z. B., M. L. Pollock, T. N. Hickman and H. S. Miller. Effects of training and detraining on cardiovascular efficiency. *Amer. Corr. Ther. J.* 25:79–83, 1971.

42 Kilborn, A., L. Hartley, B. Saltin, J. Bjure, G. Grimby and I. Astrand. Physical training in sedentary middle-aged and older men. *Scand. J. Clin. Lab. Invest.* 24:315–322, 1969.

43 Knehr, C. A., D. B. Dill and W. Neufeld. Training and its effect on man at rest and at work. *Amer. J. Physiol.* 136:148–156, 1942.

44 Knuttgen, H. G., L. O. Nordesjo, B. Ollander and B. Saltin. Physical conditioning through interval training with young male adults. *Med. Sci. Sports* 5:220–226, 1973.

45 Mann, G. V., L. H. Garrett, A. Farhi, H. Murray, T. F. Billings, F. Shute and S. E. Schwarten. Exercise to prevent coronary heart disease. *Amer. J. Med.* 46:12–27, 1969.

46 Marigold, E. A. The effect of training at predetermined heart rate levels for sedentary college women. *Med. Sci. Sports* 6:14–19, 1974.

47 Mayhew, J. L. and P. M. Gross. Body composition changes in young women with high resistance weight training. *Res. Q.* 45:433–439, 1974.

48 Milesis, C. A., M. L. Pollock, M. D. Bah, J. J. Ayres, A. Ward and A. C. Linnerud. Effects of different durations of training on cardiorespiratory function, body composition and serum lipids. *Res. Q.* 47:716–725, 1976.

49 Misner, J. E., R. A. Boileau, B. H. Massey and J. H. Mayhew. Alterations in body composition of adult men during selected physical training programs. *J. Amer. Geriatr. Soc.* 22:33–38, 1974.

50 Moody, D. L., J. Kollias and E. R. Buskirk. The effect of a moderate exercise program on body weight and skinfold thickness in overweight college women. *Med. Sci. Sports* 1:75–80, 1969.

51 Moody, D. L., J. H. Wilmore, R. N. Girandola and J. P. Royce. The effects of a jogging program on the body composition of normal and obese high school girls. *Med. Sci. Sports* 4:210–213, 1972.

52 Myrhe, L., S. Robinson, A. Brown and F. Pyke. Paper presented to the American College of Sports Medicine, Albuquerque, New Mexico, 1970.

53 Naughton, J. and F. Nagle. Peak oxygen intake during physical fitness and program for middle-aged men. *JAMA* 191:899–901, 1965.

54 O'Hara, W., C. Allen and R. J. Shephard. Loss of body weight and fat during exercise in a cold chamber. *Europ. J. Appl. Physiol.* 37:205–218, 1977.

55 Oja, P., P. Teraslinna, T. Partaner and R. Karava. Feasibility of an 18 months' physical training program for middle-aged men and its effect on physical fitness. *Am. J. Public Health* 64:459–465, 1975.

56 Olree, H. D., B. Corbin, J. Penrod and C. Smith. Methods of achieving and maintaining physical fitness for prolonged space flight. Final Progress Rep. to NASA, Grant No. NGR-04-002-004, 1969.

57 Oscai, L. B., T. Williams and B. Hertig. Effects of exercise on blood volume. *J. Appl. Physiol.* 24:622–624, 1968.

58 Pollock, M. L., T. K. Cureton and L. Greninger. Effects of frequency of training on working capacity, cardiovascular function, and body composition of adult men. *Med. Sci. Sports* 1:70–74, 1969.

59 Pollock, M. L., J. Tiffany, L. Gettman, R. Janeway and H. Lofland. Effects of frequency of training on serum lipids, cardiovascular function, and body composition. In: *Exercise and Fitness* (B.D. Franks, ed.), Chicago: Athletic Institute, 1969, pp. 161–178.

60 Pollock, M. L., H. Miller, R. Janeway, A. C. Linnerud, B. Robertson and R. Valentino. Effects on walking on body composition and cardiovascular function of middle-aged men. *J. Appl. Physiol.* 30:126–130, 1971.

61 Pollock, M. L., J. Broida, Z. Kendrick, H. S. Miller, R. Janeway and A. C. Linnerud. Effects of training two days per week at different intensities on middle-aged men. *Med. Sci. Sports* 4:192–197, 1972.

62 Pollock, M. L. The quantification of endurance training programs. *Exercise and Sport Sciences Reviews*, (J. Wilmore, editor). New York: Academic Press, pp. 155–188, 1973.

63 Pollock, M. L., H. S. Miller, Jr. and J. Wilmore. Physiological characteristics of champion American track athletes 40 to 70 years of age. *J. Gerontol.* 29:645–649, 1974.

64 Pollock, M. L., J. Dimmick, H. S. Miller, Z. Kendrick and A. C. Linnerud. Effects of mode of training on cardiovascular function and body composition of middle-aged men. *Med. Sci. Sports* 7:139–145, 1975.

65 Pollock, M. L., H. S. Miller, A. C. Linnerud and K. H. Cooper. Frequency of training as a determinant for improvement in cardiovascular function and body composition of middle-aged men. *Arch. Phys. Med. Rehab.* 56:141–145, 1975.

66 Pollock, M. L., G. A. Dawson, H. S. Miller, Jr., A. Ward, D. Cooper, W. Headly, A. C. Linnerud and M. M. Nomeir. Physiologic response of men 49 to 65 years of age to endurance training. *J. Amer. Geriatr. Soc.* 24:97–104, 1976.

67 Pollock, M. L. and A. Jackson. Body composition: measurement and

changes resulting from physical training. Proceedings National College Physical Education Association for Men and Women, pp. 125–137, January, 1977.

68 Pollock, M. L., J. Ayres and A. Ward. Cardiorespiratory fitness: Response to differing intensities and durations of training. *Arch. Phys. Med. Rehab.* 58:467–473, 1977.

69 Pollock, M. L., L. R. Gettman, C. A. Milesis, M. D. Bah, J. L. Durstine and R. B. Johnson. Effects of frequency and duration of training on attrition and incidence of injury. *Med. Sci. Sports* 9:31–36, 1977.

70 Pollock, M. L., H. S. Miller and P. M. Ribisl. Body composition and cardiorespiratory fitness in former athletes. *Phys. Sports Med.*, In press, 1978.

71 Ribisl, P. M. Effects of training upon the maximal oxygen uptake of middle-aged men. *Int. Z. Angew, Physiol.* 26:272–278, 1969.

72 Robinson, S. and P. M. Harmon. Lactic acid mechanism and certain properties of blood in relation to training. *Amer. J. Physiol.* 132:757–769, 1941.

73 Roskamm, H. Optimum patterns of exercise for healthy adults. *Canad. Med. Ass. J.* 96:895–899, 1967.

74 Saltin, B., G. Blomqvist, J. Mitchell, R. L. Johnson, K. Wildenthal and C. B. Chapman. Response to exercise after bed rest and after training. *Circulation* 37 and 38, Supp. 7, 1–78, 1968.

75 Saltin, B., L. Hartley, A. Kilborn and I. Astrand. Physical training in sedentary middle-aged and older men. *Scand. J. Clin. Lab. Invest.* 24:323–334, 1969.

76 Sharkey, B. J. Intensity and duration of training and the development of cardiorespiratory endurance. *Med. Sci. Sports* 2:197–202, 1970.

77 Shephard, R. J. Intensity, duration, and frequency of exercise as determinants of the response to a training regime. *Int. Z. Angew. Physiol.* 26:272–278, 1969.

78 Shephard, R. J. Future research on the quantifying of endurance training. *J. Human Ergology* 3:163–181, 1975.

79 Sidney, K. H., R. B. Eynon and D. A. Cunningham. Effect of frequency of training of exercise upon physical working performance and selected variables representative of cardiorespiratory fitness. In: *Training Scientific Basis and Application* (A. W. Taylor, ed.) Springfield: C. C. Thomas, Co., pp. 144–188, 1972.

80 Sidney, K. H., R. J. Shephard and J. Harrison. Endurance training and body composition of the elderly. *Amer. J. Clin. Nutr.* 30:326–333, 1977.

81 Siegel, W., G. Blomqvist and J. H. Mitchell. Effects of a quantitated physical training program on middle-aged sedentary males. *Circulation* 41:19, 1970.

82 Skinner, J., J. Holloszy and T. Cureton. Effects of a program of endurance exercise on physical work capacity and anthropometric measurements of fifteen middle-aged men. *Amer. J. Cardiol.* 14:747–752, 1964.

83 Skinner, J. The cardiovascular system with aging and exercise. In: Brunner, D. and E. Jokl (editors). *Physical Activity and Aging.* University Park Press, 1970, pp. 100–108.

84 Smith, D. P. and F. W. Stransky. The effect of training and detraining on the body composition and cardiovascular response of young women to

exercise. *J. Sports Med.* 16:112–120, 1976.

85 Terjung, R. L., K. M. Baldwin, J. Cooksey, B. Samson and R. A. Sutter. Cardiovascular adaptation to twelve minutes of mild daily exercise in middle-aged sedentary men. *J. Amer. Geriatr. Soc.* 21:164–168, 1973.

86 Wilmore, J. H., J. Royce, R. N. Girandola, F. I. Katch and V. L. Katch. Physiological alterations resulting from a 10-week jogging program. *Med. Sci. Sports* 2(1):7–14, 1970.

87 Wilmore, J. H., J. Royce, R. N. Girandola, F. I. Katch and V. L. Katch. Body composition changes with a 10-week jogging program. *Med. Sci. Sports* 2:113–117, 1970.

88 Wilmore, J. H. Alterations in strength, body composition, and anthropometric measurements consequent to a 10-week weight training program. *Med. Sci. Sports* 6:133–138, 1974.

89 Wilmore, J. Inferiority of female athletes: myth or reality. *J. Sports Med.* 3:1–6, 1974.

90 Wilmore, J., R. B. Parr, P. A. VOdak, T. J. Barstow, T. V. Pipes, A. Ward and P. Leslie. Strength, endurance, BMR, and body composition changes with circuit weight training. *Med. Sci. Sports* 8:58–60, 1976. (Abstract)

■

APPENDIX 7

∎

AMERICAN COLLEGE OF SPORTS MEDICINE
POSITION STAND ON
PROPER AND IMPROPER WEIGHT LOSS PROGRAMS*

Millions of individuals are involved in weight reduction programs. With the number of undesirable weight loss programs available and a general misconception by many about weight loss, the need for guidelines for proper weight loss programs is apparent.

Based on the existing evidence concerning the effects of weight loss on health status, physiologic processes and body composition parameters, the American College of Sports Medicine makes the following statements and recommendations for weight loss programs.

For the purposes of this position stand, body weight will be represented by two components, fat and fat-free (water, electrolytes, minerals, glycogen stores, muscular tissue, bone, etc.):

1 Prolonged fasting and diet programs that severely restrict caloric intake are scientifically undesirable and can be medically dangerous.

2 Fasting and diet programs that severely restrict caloric intake result in the loss of large amounts of water, electrolytes, minerals, glycogen stores, and other fat-free tissue (including proteins within fat-free tissues), with minimal amounts of fat loss.

3 Mild calorie restriction (500–1000 kcal less than the usual daily intake) results in a smaller loss of water, electrolytes, minerals, and other fat-free tissue, and is less likely to cause malnutrition.

4 Dynamic exercise of large muscles helps to maintain fat-free tissue, including muscle mass and bone density, and results in losses of body weight. Weight loss resulting from an increase in energy expenditure is primarily in the form of fat weight.

5 A nutritionally sound diet resulting in mild calorie restriction coupled with an endurance exercise program along with behavioral modification of existing eating habits is recommended for weight reduction. The rate of sustained weight loss should not exceed 1 kg (2 lb) per week.

6 To maintain proper weight control and optimal body fat levels, a lifetime commitment to proper eating habits and regular physical activity is required.

*Reprinted with permission of the American College of Sports Medicine. Copyright © 1987 by the American College of Sports Medicine.

RESEARCH BACKGROUND FOR THE POSITION STAND

Each year millions of individuals undertake weight loss programs for a variety of reasons. It is well known that obesity is associated with a number of health-related problems (3,4,57). These problems include impairment of cardiac function due to an increase in the work of the heart (2) and to left ventricular dysfunction (1,40); hypertension (6,22,80); diabetes (83,97); renal disease (95); gall bladder disease (55,72); respiratory dysfunction (19); joint diseases and gout (90); endometrial cancer (15); abnormal plasma lipid and lipoprotein concentrations (56,74); problems in the administration of anesthetics during surgery (93); and impairment of physical working capacity (49). As a result, weight reduction is frequently advised by physicians for medical reasons. In addition, there are a vast number of individuals who are on weight reduction programs for aesthetic reasons.

It is estimated that 60–70 million American adults and at least 10 million American teenagers are overfat (49). Because millions of Americans have adopted unsupervised weight loss programs, it is the opinion of the American College of Sports Medicine that guidelines are needed for safe and effective weight loss programs. This position stand deals with desirable and undesirable weight loss programs. Desirable weight loss programs are defined as those that are nutritionally sound and result in maximal losses in fat weight and minimal losses of fat-free tissue. Undesirable weight loss programs are defined as those that are not nutritionally sound, that result in large losses of fat-free tissue, that pose potential serious medical complications, and that cannot be followed for long-term weight maintenance.

Therefore, a desirable weight loss program is one that:

1 Provides a caloric intake not lower than 1200 kcal·d^{-1} for normal adults in order to get a proper blend of foods to meet nutritional requirements. (Note: this requirement may change for children, older individuals, athletes, etc.).

2 Includes foods acceptable to the dieter from the viewpoints of sociocultural background, usual habits, taste, cost, and ease in acquisition and preparation.

3 Provides a negative caloric balance (not to exceed 500–1000 kcal·d^{-1} lower than recommended), resulting in gradual weight loss without metabolic derangements. Maximal weight loss should be 1kg·wk^{-1}.

4 Includes the use of behavior modification techniques to identify and eliminate dieting habits that contribute to improper nutrition.

5 Includes an endurance exercise program of at least 3 d/wk, 20–30 min in duration, at a minimum intensity of 60% of maximum heart rate (refer to ACSM Position Stand on the Recommended Quantity and Quality of Ex-

ercise for Developing and Maintaining Fitness in Healthy Adults, *Med. Sci. Sports* 10:vii, 1978).

6 Provides that the new eating and physical activity habits can be continued for life in order to maintain the achieved lower body weight.

1. Since the early work of Keys et al. (50) and Bloom (16), which indicated that marked reduction in caloric intake or fasting (starvation or semistarvation) rapidly reduced body weight, numerous fasting, modified fasting, and fad diet and weight loss programs have emerged. While these programs promise and generally cause rapid weight loss, they are associated with significant medical risks.

The medical risks associated with these types of diet and weight loss programs are numerous. Blood glucose concentrations have been shown to be markedly reduced in obese subjects who undergo fasting (18,32,74,84). Further, in obese non-diabetic subjects, fasting may result in impairment of glucose tolerance (10,52). Ketonuria begins within a few hours after fasting or low-carbohydrate diets are begun (53) and hyperuricemia is common among subjects who fast to reduce body weight (18). Fasting also results in high serum uric acid levels with decreased urinary output (59). Fasting and low-calorie diets also result in urinary nitrogen loss and a significant decrease in fat-free tissue (7,11,17,42,101; see section 2). In comparison to ingestion of a normal diet, fasting substantially elevates urinary excretion of potassium (10,32,37,52,53,78). This, coupled with the aforementioned nitrogen loss, suggests that the potassium loss is due to a loss of lean tissue (78). Other electrolytes, including sodium (32,53), calcium (30,84), magnesium (30,84), and phosphate (84) have been shown to be elevated in urine during prolonged fasting. Reductions in blood volume and body fluids are also common with fasting and fad diets (18). This can be associated with weakness and fainting (32). Congestive heart failure and sudden death have been reported in subjects who fasted (48, 79, 80) or markedly restricted their caloric intake (79). Myocardial atrophy appears to contribute to sudden death (79). Sudden death may also occur during refeeding (25,79). Untreated fasting has also been reported to reduce serum iron binding capacity, resulting in anemia (47,73,89). Liver glycogen levels are depleted with fasting (38,60,63) and liver function (29,31,37,75,76,92) and gastrointestinal tract abnormalities (13,32,53,65,85,91) are associated with fasting. While fasting and calorically restricted diets have been shown to lower serum cholesterol levels (88,96), a large portion of the cholesterol reduction is a result of lowered HDL-cholesterol levels (88,96). Other risks associated with fasting and low-calorie diets include lactic acidosis (12,26), alopecia (73), hypoalaninemia (34), edema (23,78), anuria (101), hypotension (18,32,78), elevated serum bilirubin (8,9), nausea and vomiting (53), alterations in thyroxine metabolism (71,91), impaired serum triglyceride removal and production (86), and death (25,37,48,61,80).

2. The major objective of any weight reduction program is to lose body fat while maintaining fat-free tissue. The vast majority of research reveals that starvation and low-calorie diets result in large losses of water, electrolytes, and other fat-free tissue. One of the best controlled experiments was conducted from 1944 to 1946 at the Laboratory of Physiological Hygiene at the University of Minnesota (50). In this study subjects had their base-line caloric intake cut by 45% and body weight and body composition changes were followed for 24 wk. During the first 12 wk of semistarvation, body weight declined by 25.4 lb (11.5 kg) with only an 11.6-lb (5.3 kg) decline in body fat. During the second 12-wk period, body weight declined an additional 9.1 lb (4.1 kg) with only a 6.1-lb (2.8 kg) decrease in body fat. These data clearly demonstrate that fat-free tissue significantly contributes to weight loss from semistarvation. Similar results have been reported by several other investigators. Buskirk et al. (20) reported that the 13.5-kg weight loss in six subjects on a low-calorie mixed diet averaged 76% fat and 24% fat-free tissue. Similarly, Passmore et al. (64) reported results of 78% of weight loss (15.3 kg) as fat and 22% as fat-free tissue in seven women who consumed a 400-kcal·d^{-1} for 45 d. Yang and Van Itallie (101) followed weight loss and body composition changes for the first 5 d of a weight loss program involving subjects consuming either an 800-kcal mixed diet, an 800-kcal ketogenic diet, or undergoing starvation. Subjects on the mixed diet lost 1.3 kg of weight (59% fat loss, 3.4% protein loss, 37.6% water loss), subjects on the ketogenic diet lost 2.3 kg of weight (33.2% fat, 3.8% protein, 63.0% water), and subjects on starvation regimens lost 3.8 kg of weight (32.3% fat, 6.5% protein, 61.2% water). Grande (41) and Grande et al. (43) reported similar findings with a 1000-kcal carbohydrate diet. It was further reported that water restriction combined with 1000-kcal·d^{-1} of carbohydrate resulted in greater water loss and less fat loss.

Recently, there has been some renewed speculation about the efficacy of the very-low-calorie diet (VLCD). Krotkiewski and associates (51) studied the effects on body weight and body composition after 3 wk on the so-called Cambridge diet. Two groups of obese middle-aged women were studied. One group had a VLCD only, while the second group had a VLCD combined with a 55-min/d, 3-d/wk exercise program. The VLCD-only group lost 6.2 kg in 3 wk, of which only 2.6 kg was fat loss, while the VLCD-plus-exercise group lost 6.8 kg in 3 wk with only a 1.9-kg body fat loss. Thus it can be seen that VLCD results in undesirable losses of body fat, and the addition of the normally protective effect of chronic exercise to VLCD does not reduce the catabolism of fat-free tissue. Further, with VLCD, a large reduction (29%) in HDL-cholesterol is seen (94).

3. Even mild calorie restriction (reduction of 500-1000 kcal·d^{-1} from base-line caloric intake), when used alone as a tool for weight loss, results in the loss of moderate amounts of water and other fat-free tissue. In a study by Goldman et al. (39), 15 female subjects con-

sumed a low-calorie mixed diet for 7–8 wk. Weight loss during this period averaged 6.43 kg (0.85 kg·wk⁻¹), 88.6% of which was fat. The remaining 11.4% represented water and other fat-free tissue. Zuti and Golding (102) examined the effect of 500 kcal·d⁻¹ calorie restriction on body composition changes in adult females. Over a 16-wk period the women lost approximately 5.2 kg; however, 1.1 kg of the weight loss (21%) was due to a loss of water and other fat-free tissue. More recently, Weltman et al. (96) examined the effects of 500 kcal·d⁻¹ calorie restriction (from base-line levels) on body composition changes in sedentary middle-aged males. Over a 10-wk period subjects lost 5.95 kg, 4.03 kg (68%) of which was fat loss and 1.92 kg (32%) was loss of water and other fat-free tissue. Further, with calorie restriction only, these subjects exhibited a decrease in HDL-cholesterol. In the same study, the two other groups who exercised and/or dieted and exercised were able to maintain their HDL-cholesterol levels. Similar results for females have been presented by Thompson et al. (88). It should be noted that the decrease seen in HDL-cholesterol with weight loss may be an acute effect. There are data that indicate that stable weight loss has a beneficial effect on HDL-cholesterol (21,24,46,88).

Further, an additional problem associated with calorie restriction alone for effective weight loss is the fact that it is associated with a reduction in basal metabolic rate (5). Apparently exercise combined with calorie restriction can counter this response (14).

4. There are several studies that indicate that exercise helps maintain fat-free tissue while promoting fat loss. Total body weight and fat weight are generally reduced with endurance training programs (70) while fat-free weight remains constant (36,54,69,70,98) or increases slightly (62,96,102). Programs conducted at least 3 d/wk (66-69,98), of at least 20-min duration (58,69,98) and of sufficient intensity and duration to expend at least 300 kcal per exercise session have been suggested as a threshold level for total body weight and fat reduction (27,44,69,70). Increasing caloric expenditure above 300 kcal per exercise session and increasing the frequency of exercise sessions will enhance fat weight loss while sparing fat-free tissue (54,102). Leon et al. (54) had six obese male subjects walk vigorously for 90 min, 5 d/wk for 16 wk. Work output progressed weekly to an energy expenditure of 1000–1200 kcal/session. At the end of 16 wk, subjects averaged 5.7 kg of weight loss with a 5.9-kg loss of fat weight and a 0.2-kg gain in fat-free tissue. Similarly, Zuti and Golding (102) followed the progress of adult women who expended 500 kcal/exercise session 5 d/wk for 16 wk of exercise. At the end of 16 wk the women lost 5.8 kg of fat and gained 0.9 kg of fat-free tissue.

5. Review of the literature cited above strongly indicates that optimal body composition changes occur with a combination of calorie restriction (while on a well-balanced diet) plus exercise. This combination promotes loss of fat weight while sparing fat-free tissue. Data

of Zuti and Golding (102) and Weltman et al. (96) support this contention. Calorie restriction of 500 kcal·d^{-1} combined with 3–5 d of exercise requiring 300–500 kcal per exercise session results in favorable changes in body composition (96,102). Therefore, the optimal rate of weight loss should be between 0.45–1 kg (1–2 lb) per wk. This seems especially relevant in light of the data which indicates that rapid weight loss due to low caloric intake can be associated with sudden death (79). In order to institute a desirable pattern of calorie restriction plus exercise, behavior modification techniques should be incorporated to identify and eliminate habits contributing to obesity and/or overfatness (28,33,35,81,87,99,100).

6. The problem with losing weight is that, although many individuals succeed in doing so, they invariably put the weight on again (45). The goal of an effective weight loss regimen is not merely to lose weight. Weight control requires a lifelong commitment, an understanding of our eating habits and a willingness to change them. Frequent exercise is necessary, and accomplishment must be reinforced to sustain motivation. Crash dieting and other promised weight loss cures are ineffective (45).

REFERENCES

1 Alexander, J. K. and J. R. Pettigrove. Obesity and congestive heart failure. *Geriatrics* 22:101–108, 1967.

2 Alexander, J. K. and K. L. Peterson. Cardiovascular effects of weight reduction. *Circulation* 45:310–318, 1972.

3 Angel, A. Pathophysiologic changes in obesity. *Can. Med. Assoc. J.* 119:1401–1406, 1978.

4 Angel, A. and D.A.K. Roncari. Medical complications of obesity. *Can. Med. Assoc. J.* 119:1408–1411, 1978.

5 Appelbaum, M., J. Bostsarron, and D. Lacatis. Effect of caloric restriction and excessive caloric intake on energy expenditure. *Am. J. Clin. Nutr.* 24:1405–1409, 1971.

6 Bachman, L., V. Freschuss, D. Hallberg, and A. Melcher. Cardiovascular function in extreme obesity. *Acta Med. Scand.* 193:437–446, 1972.

7 Ball, M. F., J. J. Canary, and L. H. Kyle. Comparative effects of caloric restrictions and total starvation on body composition in obesity. *Ann. Intern. Med.* 67:60–67, 1967.

8 Barrett, P.V.D. Hyperbilirubinemia of fasting. *JAMA* 217:1349–1353, 1971.

9 Barrett. P.V.D. The effect of diet and fasting on the serum bilirubin concentration in the rat. *Gastroenterology* 60:572–576, 1971.

10 Beck, P., J.J.T. Koumans, C. A. Winterling, M. F. Stein, W. H. Daughaday, and D. M. Kipnis. Studies of insulin and growth hormone secretion in human obesity. *J. Lab. Clin. Med.* 64:654–667, 1964.

11 Benoit, F. L., R. L. Martin, and R. H. Watten. Changes in body composition during weight reduction in obesity. *Ann. Intern. Med.* 63:604–612, 1965.

12 Berger, H. Fatal lactic acidosis during "crash" reducing diet. *N.Y. State J. Med.* 67:2258–2263, 1967.

13 Billich, C., G. Bray, T. F. Gallagher, A. V. Hoffbrand, and R. Levitan. Absorptive capacity of the jejunum of obese and lean subjects; effect of fasting. *Arch. Intern. Med.* 130:377–387, 1972.

14 Bjorntorp, P. L. Sjostrom, and L. Sullivan. The role of physical exercise in the management of obesity. In: *The Treatment of Obesity*, J. F. Munro (Ed.). Lancaster, England: MTP Press, 1979.

15 Blitzer, P. H., E. C. Blitzer, and A. A. Rimm. Association between teenage obesity and cancer in 56,111 women. *Prev. Med.* 5:20–31, 1976.

16 Bloom, W. L. Fasting as an introduction to the treatment of obesity. *Metabolism* 8:214–220, 1959.

17 Bolinger, R. E., B. P. Lukert, R. W. Brown, L. Guevera, and R. Steinberg. Metabolic balances of obese subjects during fasting. *Arch. Intern. Med.* 118:3–8, 1966.

18 Bray, G. A., M. B. Davidson, and E. J. Drenick. Obesity: a serious symptom. *Ann. Intern. Med.* 77:779–805, 1972.

19 Burwell, C. S., E. D. Robin, R. D. Whaley, and A. G. Bickelmann. Extreme obesity associated with alveolar hypoventilation—a Pickwickian syndrome. *Am. J. Med.* 21:811–818, 1956.

20 Buskirk, E. R., R. H. Thompson, L. Lutwak, and G. D. Whedon. Energy balance of obese patients during weight reduction: influence of diet restriction and exercise. *Ann. NY Acad. Sci.* 110:918–940, 1963.

21 Caggiula, A. W., G. Christakis, M. Ferrand, et al. The multiple risk factors intervention trial. IV Intervention on blood lipids. *Prev. Med.* 10:443–475, 1981.

22 Chaing, B. M., L. V. Perlman, and F. H. Epstein. Overweight and hypertension: a review. *Circulation* 39:403–421, 1969.

23 Collison, D. R. Total fasting for up to 249 days. *Lancet* 1:112, 1967.

24 Contaldo, F., P. Strazullo, A. Postiglione, et al. Plasma high density lipoprotein in severe obesity after stable weight loss. *Atherosclerosis* 37:163–167, 1980.

25 Cruickshank, E. K. Protein malnutrition. In: Proceedings of a conference in Jamaica (1953), J. C. Waterlow (Ed.). Cambridge: University Press, 1955, p. 107.

26 Cubberley, P. T., S. A. Polster, and C. L. Shulman. Lactic acidosis and death after the treatment of obesity by fasting. *N. Engl. J. Med.* 272:628–633, 1965.

27 Cureton, T. K. *The Physiological Effects of Exercise Programs Upon Adults.* Springfield, IL: C. Thomas Company, 1969.

28 Dahlkoetter, J., E. J. Callahan, and J. Linton. Obesity and the unbalanced energy equation: exercise versus eating habit change. *J. Consult. Clin. Psychol.* 47:898–905, 1979.

29 Drenick, E. J. The relation of BSP retention during prolonged fasts to changes in plasma volume. *Metabolism* 17:522–527, 1968.

30 Drenick, E. J., I. F. Hunt, and M. E. Swendseid Magnesium depletion during prolonged fasting in obese males. *J. Clin. Endocrinol. Metab.* 29:1341–1348, 1969.

31 Drenick, E. J., F. Simmons, and J. F. Murphy. Effect on hepatic morphology of treatment of obesity by fasting, reducing diets and small-bowel bypass. *N. Engl. J. Med.* 282:829–834, 1970.

32 Drenick, E. J., M. E. Swendseid, W. H. Blahd, and S. G. Tuttle. Prolonged starvation as treatment for severe obesity. *JAMA* 187:100–105, 1964.

33 Epstein, L. H. and R. R. Wing. Aerobic exercise and weight. *Addict. Behav.* 5:371–388, 1980.

34 Felig, P., O. E. Owen, J. Wahren, and G. F. Cahill, Jr. Amino acid metabolism during prolonged starvation. *J. Clin. Invest.* 48:584–594, 1969.

35 Ferguson, J. *Learning to Eat: Behavior Modification for Weight Control.* Palo Alto, CA: Bull Publishing, 1975.

36 Franklin, B., E. Buskirk, J. Hodgson, H. Gahagan, J. Kollias, and J. Mendez. Effects of physical conditioning on cardiorespiratory function, body composition and serum lipids in relatively normal-weight and obese middle-aged women. *Int. J. Obesity* 3:97–109, 1979.

37 Garnett, E. S., J. Ford, D. L. Barnard, R. A. Goodbody, and M. A. Woodehouse. Gross fragmentation of cardiac myofibrils after therapeutic starvation for obesity. *Lancet* 1:914, 1969.

38 Garrow, J. S. *Energy Balance and Obesity in Man.* New York: American Elsevier, 1974.

39 Goldman, R. F., B. Bullen, and C. Seltzer. Changes in specific gravity and body fat in overweight female adolescents as a result of weight reduction. *Ann. NY Acad. Sci.* 110:913–917, 1963.

40 Gordon, T. and W. B. Kannel. The effects of overweight on cardiovascular diseases. *Geriatrics* 28:80–88, 1973.

41 Grande, F. Nutrition and energy balance in body composition studies In: *Techniques for Measuring Body Composition,* J. Brozek and A. Henschel (Eds.). Washington, DC: National Academy of Sciences—National Research Council, 1961. (Reprinted by the Office of Technical Services, U.S. Department of Commerce, Washington, DC as U.S. Government Research Report AD286, 1963, 560.)

42 Grande, F. Energy balance and body composition changes. *Ann. Intern. Med.* 68:467–480, 1968.

43 Grande, F., H. L. Taylor, J. T. Anderson, E. Buskirk, and A. Keys. Water exchange in men on a restricted water intake and a low calorie carbohydrate diet accompanied by physical work. *J. Appl. Physiol.* 12:202–210, 1958.

44 Gwinup, G. Effect of exercise alone on the weight of obese women. *Arch. Intern. Med.* 135:676–680, 1975.

45 Hafen, B. A. *Nutrition, Food and Weight Control.* Boston: Allyn and Bacon, 1981, pp. 271–289.

46 Hulley, S. B., R. Cohen, and G. Widdowson. Plasma high-density lipoprotein cholesterol level: influence of risk factor intervention. *JAMA* 238:2269–2271, 1977.

47 Jagenburg, R. and A. Svanborg. Self-induced protein-calorie malnutrition in a healthy adult male. *Acta Med. Scand.* 183:67–71, 1968.

48 Kahan, A. Death during therapeutic starvation. *Lancet* 1:1378–1379, 1968.

49 Katch, F. I. and W. B. McArdle. *Nutrition, Weight Control and Exercise.* Boston: Houghton Mifflin, 1977.

50 Keys, A., J. Brozek, A. Henshel, O. Mickelson, and H. L. Taylor. *The Biology of Human Starvation.* Minneapolis: University of Minnesota Press, 1950.

51 Krotkiewski, M., L. Toss, P. Bjorntorp, and G. Holm. The effect of a very-low-calorie diet with and without chronic exercise on thyroid and sex hormones, plasma proteins, oxygen uptake, insulin and c peptide concentrations in obese women. *Int. J. Obes.* 5:287–293, 1981.

52 Laszlo, J., R. F. Klein, and M. D. Bogdonoff. Prolonged starvation in obese patients, in vitro and in vivo effects. *Clin. Res.* 9:183, 1961. (Abstract)

53 Lawlor, T. and D. G. Wells. Metabolic hazards of fasting. *Am. J. Clin. Nutr.* 22:1142–1149, 1969.

54 Leon, A. S., J. Conrad, D. M. Hunninghake, and R. Serfass. Effects of a vigorous walking program on body composition, and carbohydrate and lipid metabolism of obese young men. *Am. J. Clin. Nutr.* 32:1776–1787, 1979.

55 Mabee, F. M., P. Meyer, L. DenBesten, and E. E. Mason. The mechanism of increased gallstone formation on obese human subjects. *Surgery* 79:460–468, 1978.

56 Matter, S., A. Weltman, and B. A. Stamford. Body fat content and serum lipid levels. *J. Am. Diet. Assoc.* 77:149–152, 1980.

57 McArdle, W. D., F. I. Katch, and V. L. Katch. *Exercise Physiology: Energy, Nutrition and Human Performance.* Philadelphia: Lea and Febiger, 1981.

58 Milesis, C. A., M. L. Pollock, M. D. Bah, J. J. Ayres, A. Ward, and A. C. Linerud. Effects of different durations of training on cardiorespiratory function, body composition and serum lipids. *Res. Q.* 47:716–725, 1976.

59 Murphy, R. and K. H. Shipman. Hyperuricemia during total fasting. *Arch. Intern. Med.* 112:954–959, 1963.

60 Nilsson, L. H. and E. Hultman. Total starvation or a carbohydrate-poor diet followed by carbohydrate refeeding. *Scand. J. Clin. Lab. Invest.* 32:325–330, 1973.

61 Norbury, F. B. Contraindication of long term fasting. *JAMA* 188:88, 1964.

62 O'Hara, W., C. Allen, and R. J. Shepard. Loss of body weight and fat during exercise in a cold chamber. *Eur. J. Appl. Physiol.* 37:205–218, 1977.

63 Oyama, J., J. A. Thomas, and R. L. Brant. Effect of starvation on glucose tolerance and serum insulin-like activity of Osborne-Mendel rats. *Diabetes* 12:332–334, 1963.

64 Passmore, R., J. A. Strong, and F. J. Ritchie. The chemical composition of the tissue lost by obese patients on a reducing regimen. *Br. J. Nutr.* 12:113–122, 1958.

65 Pittman, F. E. Primary malabsorption following extreme attempts to lose weight. *Gut* 7:154–158, 1966.

66 Pollock, M. L., T. K. Cureton, and L. Greninger. Effects of frequency of training on working capacity, cardiovascular function and body composition of adult men. *Med. Sci. Sports* 1:70–74, 1969.

67 Pollock, M. L., J. Tiffany, L. Gettman, R. Janeway, and H. Lofland. Effects of frequency of training on serum lipids, cardiovascular function and body composition. In: *Exercise and Fitness.* B.D. Franks (Ed.). Chicago: *Athletic Institute*, 1969, pp. 161–178.

68 Pollock, M. L., J. Broida, Z. Kendrick, H. S. Miller, Jr., R. Janeway, and A. C. Linnerud. Effects of training two days per week at different intensities on middle aged men. *Med. Sci. Sports* 4:192–197, 1972.

69 Pollock, M. L. The quantification of endurance training programs. *Exercise and Sports Sciences Reviews.* J. Wilmore (Ed.). New York: Academic Press, 1973, pp. 155–188.

70 Pollock, M. L. and A. Jackson. Body composition: measurement and changes resulting from physical training. In: *Proceedings National College Physical Education Association for Men and Women.* 1977, pp. 123–137.

71 Portnay, G. I., J. T. O'Brian, J. Bush, et al. The effect of starvation on the concentration and binding of thyroxine and triiodothyronine in serum and on the response to TRH. *J. Clin. Endocrinol. Metab.* 39:191–194, 1974.

72 Rimm, A. A., L. H. Werner, R. Bernstein, and B. VanYserloo. Disease and obesity in 73,532 women. *Obesity Bariatric Med.* 1:77–84, 1972.

73 Rooth, G. and S. Carlstrom. Therapeutic fasting. *Acta Med. Scand.* 187:455–463, 1970.

74 Rossner, S. and D. Hallberg. Serum lipoproteins in massive obesity. *Acta Med. Scand.* 204:103–110, 1978.

75 Rozental, P., C. Biara, H. Spencer, and H. J. Zimmerman. Liver morphology and function tests in obesity and during starvation. *Am J. Dig. Dis.* 12:198–208, 1967.

76 Runcie, J. Urinary sodium and potassium excretion in fasting obese subjects. *Br. Med. J.* 3:432–435, 1970.

77 Runcie, J. and T. J. Thomson. Total fasting, hyperuricemia and gout. *Postgrad. Med. J.* 45:251–254, 1969.

78 Runcie, J. and T. J. Thomson. Prolonged starvation—a dangerous procedure? *Br. Med. J.* 3:432–435, 1970.

79 Sours, H. E., V. P. Frattali, C. D. Brand, et al. Sudden death associated with very low calorie weight reduction regimens. *Am. J. Clin. Nutr.* 34:453–461, 1981.

80 Spencer, I.O.B. Death during therapeutic starvation for obesity. *Lancet* 2:679–680, 1968.

81 Stalonas, P. M., W. G. Johnson, and M. Christ. Behavior modification for obesity: the evaluation of exercise, contingency, management, and program behavior. *J. Consult. Clin. Psychol.* 46:463–467, 1978.

82 Stamler, R., J. Stamler, W. F. Riedlinger, G. Algera, and R. H. Roberts. Weight and blood pressure. Findings in hypertension screening of 1 million Americans. *JAMA* 240:1607–1610, 1978.

83 Stein, J. S. and J. Hirsch. Obesity and pancreatic function. In: *Handbook of Physiology, Section 1. Endocrinology,* Vol. 1, D. Steener and N. Frankel (Eds.). Washington, DC: American Physiological Society, 1972.

84 Stewart, W. K. and L. W. Fleming. Features of a successful therapeutic fast of 382 days duration. *Postgrad. Med. J.* 49:203–209, 1973.

85 Stewart, J. S., D. L. Pollock, A. V. Hoffbrand, D. L. Mollin, and C. C. Booth. A study of proximal and distal intestinal structure and absorptive function in idiopathic steatorrhea. *Q.J. Med.* 36:425–444, 1967.

86 Streja, D. A., E. B. Marliss, and G. Steiner. The effects of prolonged fasting on plasma triglyceride kinetics in man. *Metabolism* 26:505–516, 1977.

87 Stuart, R. B. and B. Davis. *Slim Chance in a Fat World. Behavioral Control of Obesity.* Champaign, IL: Research Press, 1972.

88 Thompson, P. D., R. W. Jeffrey, R. R. Wing, and P. D. Wood. Unexpected decrease in plasma high density lipoprotein cholesterol with weight loss. *Am. J. Clin. Nutr.* 32:2016–2021, 1979.

89 Thomson, T. J., J. Runcie, and V. Miller. Treatment of obesity by total fasting up to 249 days. *Lancet* 2:992–996, 1966.

90 Thorn, G. W., M. M. Wintrobe, R. D. Adams, E. Braunwald, K. J. Isselbacher, and R. G. Petersdorf. *Harrison's Principles of Internal Medicine,* 8th Edition. New York: McGraw-Hill, 1977.

91 Vegenakis, A. G., A. Burger, G. I. Portnay, et al. Diversion of peripheral thyroxine metabolism from activating to inactivating pathways during complete fasting. *J. Clin. Endocrinol. Metab.* 41:191–194, 1975.

92 Verdy, M. B.S.P. retention during total fasting. *Metabolism* 15:769, 1966.

93 Warner, W. A. and L. P. Garrett. The obese patient and anesthesia. *JAMA* 205:102–103, 1968.

94 Wechsler, J. G., V. Hutt, H. Wenzel, H. Klor, and H. Ditschuneit. Lipids and lipoproteins during a very-low-calorie diet. *Int. J. Obes.* 5:325–331, 1981.

95 Weisinger, J. R., A. Seeman, M. G. Herrera, J. P. Assal, J. S. Soeldner, and R. E. Gleason. The nephrotic syndrome: a complication of massive obesity. *Ann. Intern. Med.* 80:332–341, 1974.

96 Weltman, A., S. Matter, and B. A. Stamford. Caloric restriction and/or mild exercise: effects on serum lipids and body composition. *Am. J. Clin. Nutr.* 33:1002–1009, 1980.

97 West, K. *Epidemiology of Diabetes and its Vascular Lesions.* New York: Elsevier, 1978.

98 Wilmore, J. H., J. Royce, R. N. Girandola, F. I. Katch, and V. L. Katch. Body composition changes with a 10 week jogging program. *Med. Sci. Sports* 2:113–117, 1970.

99 Wilson, G. T. Behavior modification and the treatment of obesity. In: *Obesity,* A. J. Stunkard (Ed.). Philadelphia: W. B. Saunders, 1980.

100 Wooley, S. C., O. W. Wooley, and S. R. Dyrenforth. Theoretical, practical and social issues in behavioral treatments of obesity. *J. Appl. Behav. Anal.* 12:3–25, 1979.

101 Yang, M. and T. B. Van Itallie. Metabolic responses of obese subjects to starvation and low calorie ketogenic and nonketogenic diets. *J. Clin. Invest.* 58:722–730, 1976.

102 Zuti, W. B. and L. A. Golding. Comparing diet and exercise as weight reduction tools. *Phys. Sportsmed.* 4(1):49–53, 1976.

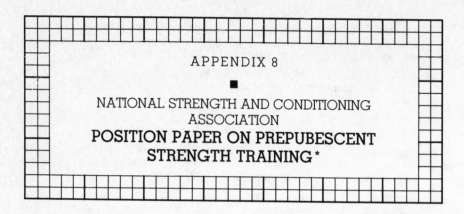

APPENDIX 8

■

NATIONAL STRENGTH AND CONDITIONING ASSOCIATION
POSITION PAPER ON PREPUBESCENT STRENGTH TRAINING*

Because of the increasing interest and use of strength training by the prepubescent athlete, and because of the recognition of reported injuries and potential long term harmful effects, the NSCA has developed a position paper on prepubescent strength training which addresses this issue and makes recommendations regarding appropriate guidelines for training.

DEFINITIONS

Evaluation of this topic has been hampered by the absence of the most fundamental ingredient for any discussion—an accepted definition of the subject. For the purpose of this position paper:

Resistance training is defined as any method or form used to resist, overcome or bear force.

Weight training is the use of barbells, dumbbells or machine type apparati as resistance.

Weight lifting and power lifting are the competitive sports which contest maximum lifting ability in the Olympic snatch and clean and jerk, or squat, bench press and dead lift, respectively.

Strength training is the use of resistance methods to increase one's ability to exert or resist force. The training may utilize free weights, the individual's own body weight, machines and/or other devices to attain this goal. In order to be measurably effective, the training sessions must include timely progressions in intensity, which impose sufficient demands to stimulate strength gains which are greater than those associated with normal growth and development.

The prepubescent athlete is defined as a child, male or female, up to the age of 15 or 16, who has not yet developed secondary sex characteristics according to Tanner's classification of childhood de-

---

*Reprinted with permission of the National Strength and Conditioning Association, P.O. Box 81410, Lincoln, NE 68501.

velopment (27). It should be noted that individuals vary considerably as to the onset of these characteristics. While 16 years of age is a reasonable upper age limit to be considered prepubescent, many children may mature before or after this age.

BENEFITS

Strength gains

Before proceeding with any recommendations, the committee carefully analyzed the relative risks and benefits of strength training for the prepubescent athlete. It is clear that the available literature does not provide a definitive position: few studies have specifically addressed the issue of strength training in prepubescents. What follows is the committee's analysis of those areas of controversy which have been defined.

At the center of the controversy regarding strength training for the prepubescent athlete is the question of whether or not this group is indeed capable of making strength gains. It has been stated that preadolescent children are unable to increase strength with resistance training. It has been theorized that boys lack adequate circulating androgens (male sex hormones) prior to puberty, while girls never have enough androgens unless exogenous anabolic steroids are used (2,3,18,28). Of particular note are the studies of Cahill, McGovern, (22) Michelli and Sewell (20, 26) which were specifically limited to the prepubescent group. All demonstrated gains with strength training.

Injury protection

It has been well-documented that appropriate strengthening of muscle and other tissue can decrease the rate and severity of certain common sports injuries in adults and adolescents (12). If strength gains can indeed be made by the prepubescent, it would seem logical that similar benefits would occur to them. In addition, literature indicates that well-conditioned athletes recover from an injury at an accelerated rate.

Self-image

Psychological benefits, such as improved self-esteem, body image and cosmesis are proven effects based upon clinical experience (4, 5, 12).

Improved motor performance

Evidence from those Eastern bloc countries which promote the commencement of strength training during prepubescence indicates performance records of the prepubescent athlete engaged in arduous sports can be improved with strength training. In the West, it has long been established that strength training enhances performance in the adolescent athlete (1, 8). It can therefore be conjectured that similar gains can be made in the prepubescent athlete.

Introduction of coaching techniques

The establishment of the prepubescent strength training program provides a forum through which the prepubescent athlete can be introduced to appropriate coaching techniques which will be used during the postpubescent period.

RISKS

Against the background of the reported benefits must be weighed the possible adverse effects of prepubescent strength training. If such reports should arise, they must be compared to the findings of similar injuries in any well-accepted athletic behavior, such as soccer, baseball, etc.

Acute musculoskeletal injuries

This type of trauma refers to a single episode-related injury. There have been several reports of epiphyseal fractures in young weight lifters (6, 7, 10, 23, 24, 25). In the child, the area of the bone surrounding the growth plate has not yet achieved its mature strength and is, therefore, predisposed to injury (29). Yet, the case reports cited above all describe fractures incurred during poorly performed overhead lifts (15). There have been no reports of these fractures secondary to a strength training program.

Chronic musculoskeletal injuries

This class of injury is thought to occur through repetition of small insults (microtrauma) to musculoskeletal structures (examples: stress fractures, musculotendinous strains, and osteochondritis dissecans of the knee and elbow) (13, 14, 16, 21). The majority of these problems are considered "overuse injuries" (17, 21). Such pathomechanics as inflexibility or weakness of a particular body part relative to the work required predispose the child to overuse injury (30). For example, runners who have tight hamstrings may be predisposed to muscle strains. Hence, this type of injury is not endemic to strength training per se. Moreover, these injuries may best be prevented by a directed program for increased strength and flexibility.

Similarly, osteochondritis dissecans is viewed by a number of practitioners as an overuse type insult (cumulative stress) to the subchondral bone of young athletes. This disorder is not unique to strength training, as it may be the result of too much load applied across the joint during any activity. The best prevention would be to decrease the total stress across the joint.

Hypertension and weight lifters' blackout

Several reports have described increased blood pressure with weight lifting. These have related loss of consciousness due to hypertension or associated cardiac arrythmias. Yet these episodes have been related to maximum efforts in pressing and similar exercises in which the breath is held while performing a valsalva maneuver (voluntary increase in abdominal pressure) (9, 19).

This phenomenon has not been described in properly executed strength training programs. Furthermore, while some studies have reported mild increases in blood pressure with strength training, others have noted decreases in blood pressure of patients with essential hypertension engaged in this type of exercise (11). Weight training may, in fact, maintain reductions in blood pressure similar to that seen in endurance training.

OTHER CONSIDERATIONS

Competition

Competitive weight lifting, as any athletic activity, may induce psychological damage to children (3). While this possibility does indeed exist, the program advocated by the NSCA is not designed for interathletic competition. Rather, it is suggested as a means by which the young athlete, under proper supervision, can improve beyond his or her own previous records.

Available equipment

It is clear the price of strength training equipment is steadily increasing. It is feared that acceptance of a strength training program for prepubescents would cause an undue burden on schools and clubs responsible for the physical education of its youngsters. Furthermore, a large part of the equipment already in use (particularly resistance machines) should not be used by prepubescent children. The recommended program can be implemented with relatively modest expenditure.

It is the firm belief of the NSCA that equipment manufacturers must be more responsible to the needs of the prepubescent athlete. To that end, the responsibility for developing, producing and marketing machines that are both reasonably priced and also adaptable to young children rests squarely on the shoulders of those manufacturers.

Intrusion on free time of children

The program suggested by the NSCA represents one more addition to the child's already busy schedule. Yet, part of that busy schedule is already being devoted to increasingly intensive participation in sports by children of lower ages. Strength training can help prevent injuries during sports: therefore, a strength training program may be advisable at the onset of sports participation. It is the opinion of the NSCA that time spent in a strength training program would help greatly in reversing declining scores on standard tests of physical fitness.

NSCA GUIDELINES FOR STRENGTH TRAINING IN THE PREPUBESCENT ATHLETE

The following guidelines outline a reasonable program for strength training in the prepubescent athlete.

Starting age

As there is evidence that strength can be enhanced through training in a very young child, strength training might begin at any age. Practical consideration as to where to begin is dependent upon a variety of factors, some of which are described below.

Appropriate health

Prior to beginning a strength training program, each child should have a preparticipatory medical examination by a physician knowledgeable in sports medicine.

Coachability and emotional maturity

Each child participating must have the emotional maturity to enable them to take direction from the coach.

Each child reaches this level of emotional maturity at their own rate.

WELL-TRAINED PERSONNEL, APPROPRIATE FACILITY AND QUALITY PROGRAM

The NSCA wishes to highlight the practical aspects of introducing and conducting a strength training program for prepubescent athletes. Each aspect requires close scrutiny, far beyond the scope of this position paper. Considerations presented here are to be used as basic guidelines and will need to be tailored to the specific needs of each individual program.

Proper techniques and weight room conduct must be introduced at the onset of training—good habits reduce the chance of injury.

Personnel

It is imperative that the supervisor of the strength training and conditioning program possess appropriate levels of strength training and conditioning knowledge. This knowledge is important to the development of a strong coach/young athlete relationship, one in which the athlete places his or her confidence in the supervisor as a primary source of information regarding physical development.

The supervisor must demonstrate the proper technique of each exercise in the program, including correct spotting. It should be emphasized that a young athlete should never train alone, without supervision and spotting. It is also the role of the supervisor to properly maintain the facility.

Facility

The weight training area should be well lit, clean and large enough to permit movement throughout the room without fear of coming in contact with other trainers or pieces of equipment. The floor should provide good support and traction.

Ideally, the young athlete should have several different types of training apparatus available (e.g., free weights, machines, pull-up bars, jump ropes).

Program

The coach must be concerned about all-around physical development, which entails a great deal more than just strength training. It is the NSCA's feeling that 50 to 80 percent of the prepubescent athlete's training must include a variety of different physical activities in addition to strength training. This will assure that these athletes will develop not only strength through their strength training, but also the other components of athletic performance (speed, power, flexibility, muscular endurance, cardiovascular endurance, agility, coordination, etc.).

It is imperative that the coach include in the young athlete's training the opportunity to acquire a rich and versatile repertoire of skills. This can be accomplished by having him/her participate in sports games requiring quick responses. Any sport with a great variety of possible movements in varying conditions provides ideal agility exercise (basketball, volleyball, table tennis, tennis, tumbling). Endurance training (distance runs, bicycling, swimming, rowing or cross country skiing) should be included with strength training in the total program. Training sessions should be preceded by a warm-up period of about 15 minutes. This warm-up period should include light calisthenics or jogging, along with appropriate flexibility exercise.

In order to introduce the athlete to specific strength training exercises, it is recommended that no load (resistance) be used initially. Once the athlete has the exercise skill mastered, gradual loads can be introduced in increments of two and a half to three pounds. The athlete is never allowed to move on to a more complex part of an exercise, or even to another exercise, until the previous part or exercise is mastered.

If the athlete's technique begins to break down, the load must be reduced to the point at which a proper technique is restored. The coach must stress the use of good form, body alignment and technique. All exercises must go through the complete range of motion.

A prepubescent athlete's training should be directed toward high repetitions and sets, and lower loads. The NSCA recommends that six to 15 repetitions be performed per set. One maximum repetition (1RM) should never be attempted at this age. After the session is completed, an additional 15 minutes should be devoted to cooling down with activities similar to the warm-up.

A model training session would be performed three times a week, with a day of active rest between training sessions. For the prepubescent, a 90-minute workout session could consist of: warm-up; 30 minutes of weight exercises; 20 to 30 minutes for a distance run; 20 to 30 minutes of soccer, gymnastics, basketball, etc., and cool down.

Priority selection of exercises would be based on the equipment available and its ability to develop major muscle groups (chest, back, legs, etc.). Exercises to develop secondary muscle groups (arms, shoulders, etc.) should be added as required to ensure a total body conditioning program.

In addition to strength training work with free weights or machines, the coach should remember to include exercises using the athlete's body weight as resistance (chins, dips, etc.). Sand bags, rubber tubing and other simple equipment may also be used.

CONCLUSION

This report represents the collective efforts of strength coaches, exercise physiologists and physicians. While perspectives vary, we are in agreement that strength training can be both safe and efficacious for the prepubescent. The program recommended by the NSCA will help meet that objective. During the preparation of this report, it has also become clear that there is a substantial need for ongoing research in the area of prepubescent strength training. It is hoped that such efforts will amend and refine our recommendations. The NSCA encourages and sponsors investigations into prepubescent strength training.

We hope that this report will serve as a basis for discussion with groups interested in strength training. The NSCA stands ready to enter dialogues with parents, educators, coaches, athletic trainers, physical therapists, pediatricians, orthopedists and others in order to achieve a comprehensive consensus in the best interest of our children.

SUMMARY

A review of the scientific literature does substantiate the risks of injury to the prepubescent athlete involved in strength training. Most of these injuries are not inherent to strengthening, and may be minimized by proper techniques and practices. In addition, data generated to date substantiates and infers that significant benefits may be obtained with strength training for the prepubescent athlete. Our analysis of the strength training literature, both pro and con, has established the clear need for ongoing research into the effects of this training on the prepubescent athlete.

The program prescribed by the NSCA in this position paper is based both on knowledge reported in scientific literature and also the practical experience of many coaches, instructors, physicians and athletes. This experience demonstrates that a well-organized strength training program, as prescribed by the NSCA, can be safe and beneficial to the prepubescent athlete.

In the Western world, there is no authoritative information available for the young athlete, parent or physical educator on the risk-benefit aspect of this program. The NSCA has accepted this educational responsibility by providing guidelines for reasonably safe and effective strength training in the prepubescent. Adherence to these guidelines will provide the safest environment for the prepubescent while making maximum use of the accruing benefits.

The opinion of the NSCA is that strength training for the prepubescent athlete is both efficacious and safe when performed according to the guidelines provided in this paper.

REFERENCES

1 Allingham, L. M. and Kirby, R. J. 1978. Relationships between explosive leg strength and physical characteristics in young swimmers. Australian Journal of Sports Medicine 10:4.

2 American Academy of Pediatrics Committee on Sports Medicine. 1982. Weight training and weight lifting: information for the pediatrician. News and Comments 33 (July):7–8.

3 American Academy of Pediatrics Committee on Sports Medicine. 1983. Weight training and weight lifting: information for the pediatrician. The Physician and Sports Medicine 11(3):157–61.

4 Bjornaraa, B. S. 1982. Flexibility and strength training considerations for young athletes. NSCA Journal 4(4):62–64.

5 Blanksby, B. and Gregor, J. 1981. Anthropometric, strength and physiological changes in male and female swimmers with progressive resistance training. Australian Journal of Sports Sciences 1:3–6.

6 Brady, T. A. 1982. Weight training-related injuries. American Journal of Sports Medicine 10(1):1–5.

7 Brown, E. W. and Kimball, R. G. 1983. Medical history associated with adolescent powerlifting. Pediatrics 72(5):636–44.

8 Cahill, B. R. 1978. Effects of pre-season conditioning on the incidence and severity of high school football knee injuries. American Journal of Sports Medicine 6(4):180–84.

9 Compton, D.; Hill, P. M.; and Sinclair, H. 1973. Weight lifters black out. Lancet 2(Dec. 1):1234–37.

10 Gumbs, V. L. 1982. Bilateral distal radius and ulnar fracture in weightlifters. American Journal of Sports Medicine 10(6):375–79.

11 Hasberg, J. M.: Bhsan, A. A.; Goldring, D. et al. 1984. Effect of weight training and hemodynamics in hypertensive adolescents. Journal of Pediatrics 104(1):147–51.

12 Hejna, W. F. 1982. Prevention of sports injuries in high school students through strength training. NSCA Journal 4(1):28–31.

13 Jackson, F. E. et al. 1971. J.A.C.H.A. 19:187–89.

14 Jackson, D. W. et al. 1982. Stress reactions involving the pars interarticularis in young athletes. American Journal of Sports Medicine 9:304–12.

15 Jesse, J. P. 1979. Misuse of strength development programs in athletic training. Physician and Sports Medicine 7(Oct.):46–52.

16 Kotani, P. T.; Ichikawa, N.; Wakabayashi, W., et al. 1971. Studies of lifters. Br. Journal of Sports Medicine 6:4.

17 Kosar, B. and Lord, R. M. 1983. Overuse injury in the young athlete. Physician and Sports Medicine 11(7):116–22.

18 Legworld, G. 1982. Does lifting weights harm a prepubescent athlete? Physician and Sports Medicine 10(7):141–44.

19 Lehman, M. 1984. Incidents of hypertension in 810 male sportsmen (English abstract). Z. Kardiol (Germany) 73(3):137–41.

20 Loffler, H. P. 1979. Young athletes and strength. Track and Field (Rose-Bay, N.S.W.) 1(1):3436. Translated from Leichtathlet. Reprinted from Modern Athlete and Coach.

21 Mason, T. A. 1977. Is weight lifting deleterious to the spines of young people? Br. Journal of Sports Medicine 5:61.

22 McGovern, M. 1983. Effects of circuit weight training on the physical fitness of prepubescent children. Ph.D. dissertation, Northern Illinois University, Dekalb, Illinois.

23 Miller, J.A. March 1983. Beginning weight training. Strength and Health 76:17.

24 Rowe, T. A. 1979. Cartilage fracture due to weight lifting. Br. Journal of Sports Medicine 13:130–31.

25 Ryan, J. R. and Salciccioli, G. G. 1976. Fxs. of the distal radial epiphysis in adolescent weight lifters. Sports Medicine 4(1):26–27.

26 Sewell, L. and Micheli, L. 1984. Strength development in children. Paper presented to the American College of Sports Medicine, San Diego. California.

27 Tanner, J. M. 1962. Growth at adolescence, ed. 2. Oxford, England: Blackwell Scientific Publications.

28 Vrijens, J. 1978. Muscle strength development in the pre and post pubescent age. Medicine and Sport (Basel, Switzerland) 11:152–58.

29 Wilkius, K. E. 1980. The uniqueness of the young athlete: musculoskeletal injuries. American Journal of Sports Medicine 8(8):377–82.

30 Wilkerson, J. 1982. Strength and endurance training for the youthful performer. The Olympic Ideal, 776 BC to the 21st century. Indiana University School of Health, Physical Education and Recreation Monograph, Series 2, pp. 589–609. Indiana University Press.

RELATED SUPPORTIVE LITERATURE

Alexander, J. and Molnar, G. E. 1973. Muscular strength in children. Arch Phys. Med. Rehab. 54:454–27.

Allen, D. Should kids lift weights? Family Safety. 9:1980–81, winter.

Anderson, T. and Kearney, J. T. 1982. Effects of three resistance training programs on muscular strength. Research Quarterly for Exercise and Sport. 53:1–7.

Asmussen, E. 1973. Growth in muscular strength and power. In Physical Activity: Human Growth and Development, ed. L. G. Rarick, pp. 60–79. New York: Academic Press.

Atha, John. 1981. Strengthening muscle. Exercise Spt. Sci. Review 9:1–73.

Bar-Or-O. 1982. Clinical implications of pediatric exercise physiology. Ann. Cloin. Res 14 (supple. 34):97–106.

Brown, E. W. 1982. Krinematics, krinetics and joint pain associated with teen-age powerlifting. J. Biomech 15:342.

Cahill, B. R. The young athlete and athletic advocacy. Peoria: Great Plains Sports Medicine Foundation.

Cahill, B. R. January 1985. Personal communication.

Chapman, B. 1978. East of the wall. Runner's World 13(3):60–63.

Cheek, T. 1971. A strength program for young athletes. Strength and Health 39(6):26.

Davies, C. T. and Young, K. 1984. Effects of external loading on short-term power output in children and young male adults. Journal European Applied Physiology 52(3):351–54.

DuRant, R. H. and Dover, E. V. 1983. Evaluation of five indices of physical working capacity in children. Medicine and Science in Sports and Exercise. 15:83–87.

Dvorkin, L. S. 1982. The young weightlifter. Moscow: Fizkultura i Sport. Trans. by Dr. Michael Yessis: Soviet Sports Review, 18(2, 3, 4) 1983; 19(1, 2, 3, 4) 1985.

Fleck, S. J. and Schutt, Jr., R. C. 1983. Types of strength training. Ortho. Clinics of N. Am. 14:449–57.

Frantagelo, F. 1981. Training youth and schoolboy Olympic weightlifters. Paper submitted to Tasmanian College of Advanced Education. Australia, November 1981.

Gillam, G. M. 1981. Effects of frequency of weight training on muscle strength enhancement. Journal of Sports Medicine. 21(4):432–35.

Goldberg, V. M. and Aadalen, R. 1978. Distal fibial epiphyseal injuries in athletics. American Journal of Sports Medicine 6:263–68.

Haring, V. M. 1981. Trauma to growth plate. Fortschr. Med. 99:1858–62.

Hatfield, F. C. and Krotee, M. L. 1980. Weight training for preadolescents. Arena Review (Sports. Med. Issue). 4:19–22.

Hatfield, F. C. 1980. Weight training for the young athlete. Vol. IX:118, New York: Atheneum.

Haywood, K. M. 1980. Strength and flexibility in gymnasts before and after menarche. Br. Journal of Sports Medicine 14(4):189–92.

Javorek, I. 1984. Biological selection of weight lifters. In American Weightlifting Coaches Association Yearbook. Warren, MI: AWCA.

Jesse, J. P. 1977. Olympic lifting movements endangering adolescents. Physician and Sports Medicine 5(9):60–67.

Jones, M. 1983. Strength training and the young athlete. Athletics Coach, 17(1):24–26.

Kath, W. O. 1983. Weight training for the young athlete. Mueller Spts Med. Guide. 2:13–15.

Knuttgen, H. G. 1978. Force, work, power and exercise. Medicine and Science in Sports:227–28.

Kuland, D. N. et al. 1978. Olympic weight lifting injuries. Physician and Sports Medicine. 6(11):111–19.

Kuland, D. N. and Tottossy, M. 1983. Warm-up, strength and power. Orthopedic Clinics of N. Am. 14(2):427–47.

Kummart, I. 1982. Georgia weight lifting club attracts juniors. Physician and Sports Medicine 10(7):143–44.

Kurowski, T. T. 1979. Anaerobic power of children from ages 9 through 15 years. Eugene: University of Oregon. Paper submitted as M.S. thesis. Florida State University, 1977. 1:43–45.

Larid, C. E. and Rozier, C. K. 1979. Toward understanding the terminology of exercise mechanics. Physical Therapy. 59:287–92.

Larson, L.; Grimby, G.; and Karlsson, J. 1979. Muscle strength and speed of movement in relation to age and muscle morphology. Journal of Applied Physiology, 46(3):451–56.

Legg, S. J. 1985. A physiological study of the repetitive lifting capabilities of healthy young males. Ergonomics. 27:259–72.

Micheli, L. 1983. Strength gains in pre-adolescents. Physician and Sports Medicine 11:25.

Micheli, L. 1983. Overuse injuries in children's sports: the growth factor. In Symposium on special considerations in sports medicine. Orth. Clinics of North America. 14(2):337–60.

Miller, C. 1975. The Bulgarian Coaching Clinic. Iron Man:38–56.

Moffroid, M. T. and Kusiak, E. T. 1975. The power struggle: definition and evaluation of power of muscular performance. Physical Therapy 55:1908–1104.

Nielson, B.; Nielsen, K.; Hansen, M. B.; and Asmussen, E. 1980. Training of "functional muscular strength" in girls 7–19 years old. In Children and Exercise IX, ed. K. Berg and B. O. Eriksson, pp. 69–78. Baltimore: Un.Pk. Press. Presented to the International Congress on Pediatric Work Physiology, 9th 1978, in Marstrand, Sweden.

Olson, J. R. and Hunter, G. R. Winter, 1980–1981. Weight training and safety guidelines: Athletic Purchasing and Facilities.

Priest, J. D. and Weise, D. J. 1981. Elbow injury in women's gymnastics. American Journal of Sports Medicine 9:288–95.

Rasrick, G. L. and Seefeldt, V. 1976. Characteristics of the young athlete. In Youth sports guide for coaches and parents, ed. J. R. Thomas, Washington, D.C.; AAHPERD.

Reilly, T. 1978. Some observations on weight training. Br. Journal of Sports Medicine 12:47.

Ryan, T. A. 1974. Need to know: weight lifting precautions. Physician and Sports Medicine 2(6):65.

Scott, C. Weight lifting and the junior lifter. International Olympic Lifter. VLL:7–9.

Shaffter, T. E. 1983. Letter to M. Yessis.

Singer, K. M. and Roy, S. P. 1984. Osteochondrosis of the humeral capitellum. American Journal of Sports Medicine 12(5):351–60.

Siwek, C. W. and Raw, J. P. 1981. Ruptures of the extensor mechanism of the knee joint. Journal of Bone and Joint Surgery 63A.

Smith, T. 1984. Preadolescent strength training: some considerations. JOPERD 55(1):43–44, 80, 14.

Stern, W. H. 1974. Weight training for children. Athletic Journal 55(1):80–81, 88–90, 92.

Stone, W. J. and Kross, W. A. 1978. Sports conditioning and weight training. Boston: Allyn and Bacon, Inc.

Stover, C. N. 1982. Physical conditioning of the immature athlete. Ortho. Clinics of N. Am. 13(3):525–39.

Todd, T. 1983. Behold Bulgaria's vest-pocket Hercules. Sports Illustrated 60(24):32–47.

Videman, T. 1981. Changes in compression and distances in knee during immobilization. Arch. of Ortho. and Traumatic Surg. 98:289–91.

Weight lifting gaining fans. Los Angeles Times Section V:1,4, July 12, 1983.

Weight training and sports injuries. Family Safety. Winter, 10:1980–81.

Weltman, A. et al. The results of a strength training program for prepubescents. Peoria: Center for Sports Medicine, St. Francis Hospital.

West, C. 1970. A beginning weight training program for teenagers. Strength and Health 38(6):18–20.

Woo, S. L. et al. 1981. Effect of prolonged physical training on long bone. Journal of Bone and Joint Surgery 63A(5):780–87.

Yessis, M. 1983. Are there "bad" exercises? Muscle and Fitness 44(12):13–14

Yessis, M. 1983. Weights and children: the Soviet head start. Muscle and Fitness 44(4):13–14.

■

APPENDIX 9

■

AMERICAN COLLEGE OF SPORTS MEDICINE
POSITION STAND ON
THE USE OF ALCOHOL IN SPORTS*

Based upon a comprehensive analysis of the available research relative to the effects of alcohol upon human physical performance, it is the position of the American College of Sports Medicine that:

1 The acute ingestion of alcohol can exert a deleterious effect upon a wide variety of psychomotor skills such as reaction time, hand-eye coordination, accuracy, balance, and complex coordination.

2 Acute ingestion of alcohol will not substantially influence metabolic or physiological functions essential to physical performance such as energy metabolism, maximal oxygen consumption (VO_2 max), heart rate, stroke volume, cardiac output, muscle blood flow, arteriovenous oxygen difference, or respiratory dynamics. Alcohol consumption may impair body temperature regulation during prolonged exercise in a cold environment.

3 Acute alcohol ingestion will not improve and may decrease strength, power, local muscular endurance, speed, and cardiovascular endurance.

4 Alcohol is the most abused drug in the United States and is a major contributing factor to accidents and their consequences. Also, it has been documented widely that prolonged excessive alcohol consumption can elicit pathological changes in the liver, heart, brain, and muscle, which can lead to disability and death.

5 Serious and continuing efforts should be made to educate athletes, coaches, health and physical educators, physicians, trainers, the sports media, and the general public regarding the effects of acute alcohol ingestion upon human physical performance and on the potential acute and chronic problems of excessive alcohol consumption.

RESEARCH BACKGROUND FOR THE POSITION STAND

This position stand is concerned primarily with the effects of acute alcohol ingestion upon physical performance and is based upon a comprehensive review of the pertinent international literature. When interpreting these results, several precautions should be kept in mind. First, there are varying reactions to alcohol ingestion, not only among individuals, but also within an individual depending upon the circumstances. Second, it is virtually impossible to conduct double-blind placebo research with alcohol because subjects can always tell when alcohol has been consumed. Nevertheless, the results cited below provide us with some valid general conclusions relative to the effects of alcohol on physical performance. In most of the research studies, a small dose consisted of 1.5-2.0 ounces (45-60 ml) of alcohol, equivalent to a blood alcohol level (BAL) of 0.04-0.05 in the average-size male. A moderate dose was equivalent to 3-4 ounces (90-120 ml), or a BAL of about 0.10. Few studies employed a large dose, with a BAL of 0.15.

1 Athletes may consume alcohol to improve psychological function, but it is psychomotor performance that deteriorates most. A consistent finding is the impairment of information processing. In sports involving rapid reactions to changing stimuli, performance will be affected most adversely. Research has shown that small to moderate amounts of alcohol will impair reaction time (8,25,26,34-36,42), hand-eye coordination (8,9,14,40), accuracy (36,39), balance (3), and complex coordination or gross motor skills (4,8,22,36,41). Thus, while Coopersmith (10) suggests that alcohol may improve self-confidence, the available research reveals a deterioration in psychomotor performance.

2 Many studies have been conducted relative to the effects of acute alcohol ingestion upon metabolic and physiological functions important to physical performance. Alcohol ingestion exerts no beneficial influence relative to energy sources for exercise. Muscle glycogen at rest was significantly lower after alcohol compared to control (30). However, in exercise at 50% maximal oxygen uptake (VO_2max), total glycogen depletion in the leg muscles was not affected by alcohol (30). Moreover, Juhlin-Dannfelt et al. (29) have shown that although alcohol does not impair lipolysis or free fatty acid (FFA) utilization during exercise, it may decrease splanchnic glucose output, decrease the potential contribution from liver gluconeogenesis, elicit a greater decline in blood glucose levels leading to hypoglycemia, and decrease the leg muscle uptake of glucose during the latter stages of a 3-h run. Other studies (17,19) have supported the theory concerning the hypoglycemic effect of alcohol during both moderate and prolonged exhaustive exercise in a cold environment. These studies also noted a significant loss of body heat and a resultant drop in body temperature and suggested alcohol may impair temperature regulation. These changes may impair endurance capacity.

In one study (5), alcohol has been shown to increase oxygen uptake significantly during submaximal work and simultaneously to decrease mechanical efficiency, but this finding has not been confirmed by others (6,15,33,44). Alcohol appears to have no effect on maximal or near-maximal VO_2 (5-7,44).

The effects of alcohol on cardiovascular-respiratory parameters associated with oxygen uptake are variable at submaximal exercise intensities and are negligible at maximal levels. Alcohol has been shown by some investigators to increase submaximal exercise heart rate (5,20,23) and cardiac output (5), but these heart rate findings have not been confirmed by others (6,15,33,36,44). Alcohol had no effect on stroke volume (5), pulmonary ventilation (5,15), or muscle blood flow (16,30) at submaximal levels of exercise, but did decrease peripheral vascular resistance (5). During maximal exercise, alcohol ingestion elicited no significant effect upon heart rate (5-7), stroke volume and cardiac output, arteriovenous oxygen difference, mean arterial pressure and peripheral vascular resistance, or peak lactate (5), but did significantly reduce tidal volume resulting in a lowered pulmonary ventilation (5).

In summary, alcohol appears to have little or no beneficial effect on the metabolic and physiological responses to exercise. Further, in those studies reporting significant effects, the change appears to be detrimental to performance.

3 The effects of alcohol on tests of fitness components are variable. It has been shown that alcohol ingestion may decrease dynamic muscular strength (24), isometric grip strength (36), dynamometer strength (37), power (20) and ergographic muscular output (28). Other studies (13,20,24,27,43) reported no effect of alcohol upon muscular strength. Local muscular endurance was also unaffected by alcohol ingestion (43). Small doses of alcohol exerted no effect upon bicycle ergometer exercise tasks simulating a 100-m dash or a 1500-m run, but larger doses had a deleterious effect (2). Other research has shown that alcohol has no significant effect upon physical performance capacity (15,16), exercise time at maximal levels (5), or exercise time to exhaustion (7).

Thus, alcohol ingestion will not improve muscular work capacity and may lead to decreased performance levels.

4 Alcohol is the most abused drug in the United States (11). There are an estimated 10 million adult problem drinkers and an additional 3.3 million in the 14–17 age range. Alcohol is significantly involved in all types of accidents—motor vehicle, home, industrial, and recreational. Most significantly, half of all traffic fatalities and one-third of all traffic injuries are alcohol related. Although alcohol abuse is associated with pathological conditions such as generalized skeletal myopathy, cardiomyopathy, pharyngeal and esophageal cancer, and brain damage, its most prominent effect is liver damage (11,31,32).

5 Because alcohol has not been shown to help improve physical performance capacity, but may lead to decreased ability in certain events, it is important for all those associated with the conduct of sports to educate athletes against its use in conjunction with athletic contests. Moreover, the other dangers inherent in alcohol abuse mandate that concomitantly we educate our youth to make intelligent choices regarding alcohol consumption. Anstie's rule, or limit (1), may be used as a reasonable guideline to moderate, safe drinking for adults (12). In essence, no more than 0.5 ounces of pure alcohol per 23 kg body weight should be consumed in any one day. This would be the equivalent of three bottles of 4.5% beer, three 4-ounce glasses of 14% wine, or three ounces of 50% whiskey for a 68-kg person.

REFERENCES

1 Anstie, F. E. *On the Uses of Wine in Health and Disease.* London: Macmillan, 1877, pp. 5–6.

APPENDICES

2 Asmussen, E. and O. Boje. The effects of alcohol and some drugs on the capacity for work. *Acta Physiol. Scand.* 15:109–118, 1948.

3 Begbie, G. The effects of alcohol and of varying amounts of visual information on a balancing test. *Ergonomics* 9:325–333, 1966.

4 Belgrave, B., K. Bird, G. Chesher, D. Jackson, K. Lubbe, G. Starmer, and R. Teo. The effect of cannabidiol, alone and in combination with ethanol, on human performance. *Psychopharmacology* 64:243–246, 1979.

5 Blomqvist, G., B. Saltin, and J. Mitchell. Acute effects of ethanol ingestion on the response to submaximal and maximal exercise in man. *Circulation* 42:463–470, 1970.

6 Bobo, W. Effects of alcohol upon maximum oxygen uptake, lung ventilation, and heart rate. *Res. Q.* 43:1–6, 1972.

7 Bond, V. Effect of alcohol on cardiorespiratory function. In: *Abstracts: Research Papers of 1979 AAHPER Convention.* Washington, DC: AAHPER, 1979, p. 24.

8 Carpenter, J. Effects of alcohol on some psychological processes. *Q.J. Stud. Alcohol* 23:274–314, 1962.

9 Collins, W., D. Schroeder, R. Gilson, and F. Guedry. Effects of alcohol ingestion on tracking performance during angular acceleration. *J. Appl. Psychol.* 55:559–563, 1971.

10 Coopersmith, S. The effects of alcohol on reaction to affective stimuli. *Q.J. Stud. Alcohol* 25:459–475, 1964.

11 Department of Health, Education, and Welfare. Third special report to the U.S. Congress on alcohol and health. *NIAAA Information and Feature Service.* DHEW Publication No. (ADM) 78–151, November 30, 1978, pp. 1–4.

12 *Dorland's Illustrated Medical Dictionary,* 24th Edition. Philadelphia: W.B. Saunders, 1974, p. 1370.

13 Enzer, N., E. Simonson, and G. Ballard. The effect of small doses of alcohol on the central nervous system. *Am J. Clin. Pathol.* 14:333–341, 1944.

14 Forney, R., F. Hughes, and W. Greatbatch. Measurement of attentive motor performance after alcohol. *Percept. Mot. Skills* 19:151–154, 1964.

15 Garlind, T., L. Goldberg, K. Graf, E. Perman, T. Strandell, and G. Strom. Effect of ethanol on circulatory, metabolic, and neurohumoral function during muscular work in man. *Acta Pharmacol. et Toxicol.* 17:106–114, 1960.

16 Graf, K. and G. Strom. Effect of ethanol ingestion on arm blood flow in healthy young men at rest and during work. *Acta Pharmacol. et Toxicol.* 17:115–120, 1960.

17 Graham, T. Thermal and glycemic responses during mild exercise in +5 to −15°C environments following alcohol ingestion. *Aviat. Space Environ. Med.* 52:517–522, 1981.

18 Graham, T. and J. Dalton. Effect of alcohol on man's response to mild physical activity in a cold environment. *Aviat. Space Environ. Med.* 51:793–796, 1980.

19 Haight, J. and W. Keatinge. Failure of thermoregulation in the cold during hypoglycemia induced by exercise and ethanol. *J. Physiol. (Lond.)* 229:87–97, 1973.

20 Hebbelinck, M. The effects of a moderate dose of alcohol on a series of functions of physical performance in man. *Arch. Int. Pharmacod.* 120:402–405, 1959.

21 Hebbelinck, M. The effect of a moderate dose of ethyl alcohol on human respiratory gas exchange during rest and muscular exercise. *Arch. Int. Pharmacod.* 126:214–218, 1960.

22 Hebbelinck, M. *Spierarbeid en Ethylalkohol.* Brussels: Arsica Uitgaven, N.V., 1961, pp. 81–84.

23 Hebbelinck, M. The effects of a small dose of ethyl alcohol on certain basic components of human physical performance. The effect on cardiac rate during muscular work. *Arch. Int. Pharmacod.* 140:61–67, 1962.

24 Hebbelinck, M. The effects of a small dose of ethyl alcohol on certain basic components of human physical performance. *Arch. Int. Pharmacod.* 143:247–257, 1963.

25 Huntley, M. Effects of alcohol, uncertainty and novelty upon response selection. *Psychopharmacologia* 39:259–266, 1974.

26 Huntley, M. Influences of alcohol and S-R uncertainty upon spatial localization time. *Psychopharmacologia* 27:131–140, 1972.

27 Ikai, M. and A. Steinhaus. Some factors modifying the expression of human strength. *J. Appl. Physiol.* 16:157–161, 1961.

28 Jellinek, E. Effect of small amounts of alcohol on psychological functions. In Yale University Center for Alcohol Studies. *Alcohol, Science and Society.* New Haven, CT: Yale University, 1954, pp. 83–94.

29 Juhlin-Dannfelt, A. G. Ahlborg, L. Hagenfeldt, L. Jorfeldt, and P. Felig. Influence of ethanol on splanchnic and skeletal muscle substrate turnover during prolonged exercise in man. *Am. J. Physiol.* 233:E195–E202, 1977.

30 Juhlin-Dannfelt, A. L. Jorfeldt, L. Hagenfeldt, and B. Hulten. Influence of ethanol on non-esterified fatty acid and carbohydrate metabolism during exercise in man. *Clin. Soc. Mol. Med.* 53:205–214, 1977.

31 Lieber, C. S. Liver injury and adaptation in alcoholism. *N. Engl. J. Med.* 288:356–362, 1973.

32 Lieber, C. S. The metabolism of alcohol. *Sci. Am.* 234(March): 25–33, 1976.

33 Mazess, R., E. Picon-Reategui, and R. Thomas. Effects of alcohol and altitude on man during rest and work. *Aerospace Med.* 39:403–406, 1968.

34 Moskowitz, H. and M. Burns. Effect of alcohol on the psychological refractory period. *Q.J. Stud. Alcohol* 32:782–790, 1971.

35 Moskowitz, H. and S. Roth. Effect of alcohol on response latency in object naming. *Q.J. Stud. Alcohol* 32:969–975, 1971.

36 Nelson, D. Effects of ethyl alcohol on the performance of selected gross motor tests. *Res. Q.* 30:312–320, 1959.

37 Pihkanen, T. Neurological and physiological studies on distilled and brewed beverages. *Ann. Med. Exp. Biol. Fenn.* 35:Suppl. 9, 1–152, 1957.

38 Riff, D., A. Jain, and J. Doyle. Acute hemodynamic effects of ethanol on normal human volunteers. *Am. Heart J.* 78:592–597, 1969.

39 Rundell, O. and H. Williams. Alcohol and speed-accuracy tradeoff. *Hum. Factors* 21:433–443, 1979.

40 Sidell, F. and J. Pless. Ethyl alcohol blood levels and performance decrements after oral administration to man. *Psychopharmacologia* 19:246–261, 1971.

41 Tang, P. and R. Rosenstein. Influence of alcohol and Dramamine, alone and in combination, on psychomotor performance. *Aerospace Med.* 39:818–821, 1967.

42 Tharp, V., O. Rundell, B. Lester and H. Williams. Alcohol and information processing. *Psychopharmacologia* 40:33–52, 1974.

43 Williams, M. H. Effect of selected doses of alcohol on fatigue parameters of the forearm flexor muscles. *Res. Q.* 40:832–840, 1969.

44 Williams, M. H. Effect of small and moderate doses of alcohol on exercise heart rate and oxygen consumption. *Res. Q.* 43:94–104, 1972.

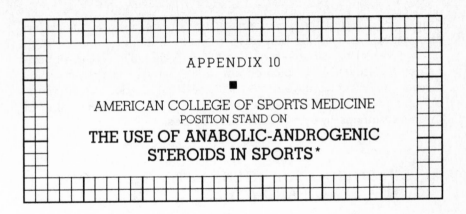

APPENDIX 10

■

AMERICAN COLLEGE OF SPORTS MEDICINE
POSITION STAND ON
THE USE OF ANABOLIC-ANDROGENIC STEROIDS IN SPORTS*

Based on a comprehensive literature survey and a careful analysis of the claims concerning the ergogenic effects and the adverse effects of anabolic-androgenic steroids, it is the position of the American College of Sports Medicine that:

1 Anabolic-androgenic steroids in the presence of an adequate diet can contribute to increases in body weight, often in the lean mass compartment.

2 The gains in muscular strength achieved through high-intensity exercise and proper diet can be increased by the use of anabolic-androgenic steroids in some individuals.

3 Anabolic-androgenic steroids do not increase aerobic power or capacity for muscular exercise.

4 Anabolic-androgenic steroids have been associated with adverse effects on the liver, cardiovascular system, reproductive system, and psychological status in therapeutic trials and in limited research on athletes. Until further research is completed, the potential hazards of the use of the anabolic-androgenic steroids in athletes must include those found in therapeutic trials.

5 The use of anabolic-androgenic steroids by athletes is contrary to the rules and ethical principles of athletic competition as set forth by many of the sports governing bodies. The American College of Sports Medicine supports these ethical principles and deplores the use of anabolic-androgenic steroids by athletes.

This document is a revision of the 1977 position stand of the American College of Sports Medicine concerning anabolic-androgenic steroids (4).

BACKGROUND

In 1935 the long-suspected positive effect of androgens on protein anabolism was documented (56). Subsequently, this effect was confirmed (53,77), and the development of 19-nortestosterone heralded the synthesis of steroids that have greater anabolic properties than natural testosterone but less of its virilizing effect (39). The use of androgenic steroids by athletes began in the early 1950s (106) and has increased through the years (60,62,83,98,104,106), despite warnings about potential adverse reactions (4,83,106,112) and the banning of these substances by sports governing bodies.

ANABOLIC-ANDROGENIC STEROIDS, BODY COMPOSITION AND ATHLETIC PERFORMANCE

Body composition

Animal studies investigating the effect of anabolic-androgenic steroids on body composition have shown increases in lean body mass, nitrogen retention and muscle growth in castrated males (37,57,58) and normal females (26,37,71). The effects of anabolic-androgenic steroids on the body weights of normal, untrained, male animals (37,40,71,105,114), treadmill-trained (43,97) or isometrically-trained rats (82), or strength-trained monkeys (80) have been minimal to absent; however, the effects of steroids on animals undergoing heavy resistance training have not been adequately studied. Human males who are deficient in natural androgens by castration or other causes have shown significant increases in nitrogen retention and muscular development with anabolic-androgenic steroid therapy (23,58,103). Human males and females involved in experimental (38) and therapeutic trials of anabolic steroids (15,16,93) have shown increases in body weight.

The majority of the strength-training studies in which body weight was reported showed greater increases in weight under steroid treatment than under placebo (17,41,42,50,61,74,94,96,107). Other training studies have reported no significant changes in body weight (21,27,31,34,100,108). The weight gained was determined to be lean body mass in three studies that made this determination with hydrostatic weighing techniques (41,42,107). Four other studies found no significant differences in lean body mass between steroid and placebo treatments (17,21,27,34), but in two of those the mean differences favored the steroid treatment (21,27). The extent to which increased water retention accounts for steroid-induced changes in body composition is controversial (17,42) and has yet to be resolved.

In summary, anabolic-androgenic steroids can contribute to an increase in body weight in the lean mass compartment of the body. The amount of weight gained in the training studies has been small but statistically significant.

Muscular strength

Strength is an important factor in many athletic events. The literature concerning the efficacy of anabolic steroids for promoting strength development is controversial. Many factors contribute to the development of strength, including heredity, intensity of training, diet, and the status of the psyche (112). It is very difficult to control all of these factors in an experimental design. The additional variable of dosage is included when drug research is undertaken. Some athletes claim that doses greater than therapeutic are necessary for strength gains (106) even though positive results have been reported using therapeutic (low-dose) regimens (50,74,94,107). Double-blind studies using anabolic-androgenic steroids are also difficult to conduct because of the physical and/or psychological effects of the drug that, for example, allowed 100% of the participants in one "double-blind" study to correctly identify the steroid phase of the experiment (32). The placebo effect has been shown to be a factor in studies of anabolic-androgenic steroids as in all drug studies (6).

In animal studies, the combination of anabolic-androgenic steroids and overload training has not produced larger gains in force production than training alone (80,97). However, steroid-induced gains in strength have been reported in experienced (42,74,94,107) and inexperienced weight trainers (50,51,96) with (50,51,74,94) and without dietary control or supplemental protein (42,96). In contrast, no positive effect of steroids on gains in strength over those produced by training alone were reported in other studies involving experienced (21,34,54) and inexperienced weight trainers (17,27,31,41,54, 61,100,108) with (21,34,61,100) and without dietary control or supplemental protein (17,27,31,41,54,108). The studies that reported no changes in strength with anabolic-androgenic steroids have been criticized (112) for the use of inexperienced weight trainers, lack of dietary control, low-intensity training (17,27,31,61), and nonspecific testing of strength (21). The studies that have shown strength gains with the use of anabolic-androgenic steroids have been criticized (83) for inadequate numbers of subjects (74,94,107), improper statistical designs, inadequate execution, and the unsatisfactory reporting of experimental results.

There have been no studies of the effects of the massive doses of steroids used by some athletes over periods of several years. Similarly, there have been no studies of the use of anabolic-androgenic steroids and training in women or children. Theoretically, anabolic and adrogenic effects would be greater in women and children because they have naturally lower levels of androgens than men.

Three proposed mechanisms for the actions of the anabolic-androgenic steroids for increases in muscle strength are:

1 Increase in protein synthesis in the muscle as a direct action of the anabolic-androgenic steroid (81,82,92).

2 Blocking of the catabolic effect of glucocorticoids after exercise by increasing the amount of anabolic-androgenic hormone available (1,92,112).

3 Steroid-induced enhancement of aggressive behavior that promotes a greater quantity and quality of weight training (14).

In spite of the controversial and sometimes contradictory results of the studies in this area, it can be concluded that the use of anabolic-androgenic steroids, especially by experienced weight trainers, can often increase strength gains beyond those seen with training and diet alone. This positive effect on strength is usually small and obviously is not exhibited by all individuals. The explanation for this variability in steroid effects is unclear. When small increments in strength occur, they can be important in athletic competition.

Aerobic capacity

The effect of anabolic-androgenic steroids on aerobic capacity has also been questioned. The potential of these drugs to increase total blood volume and hemoglobin (88) might suggest a positive effect of steroids on aerobic capacity. However, only three studies indicated positive effects (3,51,54), and there has been no substantiation of these results in subsequent studies (27,41,50,52). Thus, the majority of evidence shows no positive effect of anabolic-androgenic steroids on aerobic capacity over aerobic training alone.

ADVERSE EFFECTS

Anabolic-androgenic steroids have been associated with many undesirable or adverse effects in laboratory studies and therapeutic trials. The effects of major concern are those on the liver, cardiovascular, and reproductive systems, and on the psychological status of individuals who are using the anabolic-androgenic steroids.

Adverse effects on the liver

Impaired excretory function of the liver, resulting in jaundice, has been associated with anabolic-androgenic steroids in a number of therapeutic trials (76,84,90). The possible cause-and-effect nature of this association is strengthened by the observation of jaundice remission after discontinuance of the drug (76,84). In studies of athletes using anabolic-androgenic steroids (65 athletes tested) (89,98,104), no evidence of cholestasis has been found.

Structural changes in the liver following anabolic steroid treatment have been found in animals (95,101) and in humans (73,86). Conclusions concerning the clinical significance of these changes on a short- or long-term basis have not been drawn. Investigations in athletes for these changes have not been performed, but there is no reason to believe that the athlete using anabolic-androgenic steroids is immune from these effects of the drugs.

The most serious liver complications associated with anabolic-androgenic steroids are peliosis hepatis (blood-filled cysts in the liver of unknown etiology) and liver tumors. Cases of peliosis hepatis have been reported in individuals treated with anabolic-androgenic steroids for various conditions (7-10,13,35,65,66,70,88,102). Rupture of the cysts or liver failure resulting from the condition was fatal in some individuals (9,70,102). In other case reports the condition was an incidental finding at autopsy (8,10,66). The possible cause-and-effect nature of the association between peliosis hepatis and the use of anabolic-androgenic steroids is strengthened by the observation of improvement in the condition after discontinuance of drug therapy in some cases (7,35). There are no reported cases of this condition in athletes using anabolic-androgenic steroids, but investigations specific for this disorder have not been performed in athletes.

Liver tumors have been associated with the use of anabolic-androgenic steroids in individuals receiving these drugs as a part of their treatment regimen (28,29,49,67,69,99,115). These tumors are generally benign (29,67,69,115), but there have been malignant lesions associated with individuals using these drugs (28,99,115). The possible cause-and-effect nature of this association between the use of the drug and tumor development is strengthened by a report of tumor regression after cessation of drug treatment (49). The 17-alpha-alkylated compounds are the specific family of anabolic steroids indicated in the development of liver tumors (46,39). There is one reported case of a 26-year-old male body builder who died of liver cancer after having abused a variety of anabolic steroids for at least four years (75). The testing necessary for discovery of these tumors is not commonly performed, and it is possible that other tumors associated with steroid use by athletes have gone undetected.

Blood tests of liver function have been reported to be unchanged with steroid use in some training studies (31,41,54,94) and abnormal in other training studies (32,51) and in tests performed on athletes known to be using anabolic-androgenic steroids (54,89,104). However, the lesions of peliosis hepatis and liver tumors do not always result in blood test abnormalities (8,28,29,49,67,115), and some authors state that liver radioisotope scans, ultrasound, or computed tomography scans are needed for diagnosis (28,29,113).

In summary, liver function tests have been shown to be adversely affected by anabolic-androgenic steroids, especially the 17-alpha-alkylated compounds. The short- and long-term consequences of these changes, though potentially hazardous, have yet to be reported in athletes using these drugs.

Adverse effects on the cardiovascular system

The steroid-induced changes that may affect the development of cardiovascular disease include hyperinsulinism and altered glucose tolerance (111), decreased high-density lipoprotein cholesterol levels (72,98), and elevated blood pressure (68). These effects are variable for different individuals in various clinical situations. Triglycerides are lowered by anabolic-androgenic steroids in certain individuals (24,72) and are increased in others (18,78). Histological examinations of myofibrils and mitochondria from cardiac tissue obtained from laboratory animals have shown that administration of anabolic steroids leads to pathological alterations in these structures (5,11,12). The cardiovascular effects of the anabolic-androgenic steroids, though potentially hazardous, need further research before any conclusions can be made.

Adverse effects on the male reproductive system

The effects of the anabolic-androgenic steroids on the male reproductive system are oligospermia (small number of sperm) and azoospermia (lack of sperm in the semen), decreased testicular size, abnormal appearance of testicular biopsy material, and reductions in testosterone and gonadotropic hormones. These effects have been shown in training studies (19,41,100), studies of normal volunteers (38), therapeutic trials (44), and studies of athletes who were using anabolic-androgenic steroids (55,79,104). In view of the changes shown in the pituitary-gonadal axis, the dysfunction accounting for these abnormalities is believed to be steroid-induced suppression of gonadotrophin production (19,36,38,79). The changes in these hormones are ordinarily reversible after cessation of drug treatment, but the long-term effects of altering the hypothalamic-pituitary-gonadal axis remain unknown. However, there is a report of residual abnormalities in testicular morphology of healthy men 6 months after discontinuing steroid use (38). It has been reported that the metabolism of androgens to estrogenic compounds may lead to gynecomastia in males (23,58,98,112).

Adverse effects on the female reproductive system

The effects of androgenic steroids on the female reproductive system include reduction in circulating levels of luteinizing hormone, follicle-stimulating hormone, estrogens, and progesterone; inhibition of folliculogenesis and ovulation; and menstrual cycle changes including prolongation of the follicular phase, shortening of the luteal phase, and amenorrhea (20,63,91).

Adverse effects on psychological status

In both sexes, psychological effects of anabolic-androgenic steroids include increases or decreases in libido, mood swings, and aggressive behavior (38,98), which is related to plasma testosterone levels (25,85). Administration of steroids causes changes in the electroencephalogram similar to those seen with psycho-stimulant drugs (47,48). The possible ramifications of uncontrollably aggressive and possibly hostile behavior should be considered prior to the use of anabolic-androgenic steroids.

Other adverse effects

Other side effects associated with the anabolic-androgenic steroids include: ataxia (2); premature epiphysial closure in youths (23,58,64,109,110); virilization in youths and women, including hirsutism (45), clitoromegaly (63,112), and irreversible deepening of the voice (22,33); acne; temporal hair recession; and alopecia (45). These adverse reactions can occur with the use of anabolic-androgenic steroids and are believed to be dependent on the type of steroid, dosage and duration of drug use (58). There is no method for predicting which individuals are more likely to develop these adverse effects, some of which are potentially hazardous.

THE ETHICAL ISSUE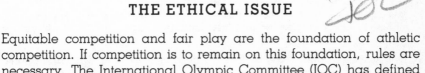

Equitable competition and fair play are the foundation of athletic competition. If competition is to remain on this foundation, rules are necessary. The International Olympic Committee (IOC) has defined "doping" as "the administration of or the use of a competing athlete of any substance foreign to the body or of any physiological substance taken in abnormal quantity or taken by an abnormal route of entry into the body, with the sole intention of increasing in an artificial and unfair manner his performance in competition." Accordingly, the medically unjustified use of anabolic steroids with the intention of gaining an athletic advantage is clearly unethical. Anabolic-androgenic steroids are listed as banned substances by the IOC in accordance with the rules against doping. The American College of Sports Medicine supports the position that the eradication of anabolic-androgenic steroid use by athletes is in the best interest of sport and endorses the development of effective procedures for drug detection and of policies that exclude from competition those athletes who refuse to abide by the rules.

The "win at all cost" attitude that has pervaded society places the athlete in a precarious situation. Testimonial evidence suggests that some athletes would risk serious harm and even death if they could obtain a drug that would ensure their winning an Olympic gold medal. However, the use of anabolic-androgenic steroids by athletes is contrary to the ethical principles of athletic competition and is deplored.

REFERENCES

1 Aakvaag, A., O. Bentdol, K. Quigstod, P. Walstod, H. Renningen, and F. Fonnum. Testosterone and testosterone binding globulin (TeBg) in young men during prolonged stress. *Int. J. Androl.* 1:22–31, 1978.

2 Agrawal, B. L. Ataxia caused by fluoxymesterone therapy in breast cancer. *Arch. Intern. Med.* 141:953–959, 1981.

3 Albrecht, H. and E. Albrecht. Ergometric, rheographic, reflexographic and electrographic tests at altitude and effects of drugs on human physical performance. *Fed. Proc.* 28:1262–1267, 1969.

4 American College of Sports Medicine. Position statement on the use and abuse of anabolic-androgenic steroids in sports. *Med. Sci. Sports* 9(4):xi–xiii, 1977.

5 Appell, H. J., B. Heller-Umpfenbach, M. Feraudi, and H. Weicker. Ultrastructural and morphometric investigations on the effects of training and administration of anabolic steroids on the myocardium of guinea pigs. *Int. J. Sports Med.* 4:268–274, 1983.

6 Ariel, G. and W. Saville. Anabolic steroids: the physiological effects of placebos. *Med. Sci. Sports* 4:124–126, 1972.

7 Arnold, G. L. and M. M. Kaplan. Peliosis hepatis due to oxymetholone—a clinically benign disorder. *Am. J. Gastroenterol.* 71:213–216, 1979.

8 Asano, A., H. Wakasa, S. Kaise, T. Nishimaki, and R. Kasukawa. Peliosis hepatis. Report on two autopsy cases with a review of literature. *Acta Pathol. Jpn.* 32:861–877, 1982.

9 Bagheri, S. and J. Boyer. Peliosis hepatis associated with androgenic-anabolic steroid therapy—a severe form of hepatic injury. *Ann. Intern. Med.* 81:610–618, 1974.

10 Bank, J. I., D. Lykkebo, and I. Hagerstrand. Peliosis hepatis in a child. *Acta Ped. Scand.* 67:105–107, 1978.

11 Behrendt, H. Effect of anabolic steroid on rat heart muscle cells. I. Intermediate filaments. *Cell Tissue Res.* 180:305–315, 1977.

12 Behrendt, H. and H. Boffin. Myocardial cell lesions caused by anabolic hormone. *Cell Tissue Res.* 181:423–426, 1977.

13 Benjamin, D. C. and B. Shunk. A fatal case of peliosis of the liver and spleen. *Am. J. Dis. Child.* 132:207–208, 1978.

14 Brooks, R. V. Anabolic steroids and athletes. *Phys. Sportsmed.* 8(3):161–163, 1980.

15 Buchwald, D., S. Argyres, R. E. Easterling, et al. Effects of Nandrolone Decanoate on the anemia of chronic hemodialysis patients. *Nephron* 18:232–238, 1977.

16 Carter, C. H. The anabolic steroid, Stanozolol, its evaluation in debilitated children. *Clin. Pediatr.* 4:671–680, 1965.

17 Casner, S. W., R. G. Early, and B. R. Carlson. Anabolic steroid effects on body composition in normal young men. *J. Sports Med. Phys. Fitness* 11:98–103, 1971.

18 Choi, E.S.K., T. Chung, R. S. Morrison, C. Myers, and M. S. Greenberg. Hypertriglyceridemia in hemodialysis patients during oral dromostanolone therapy for anemia. *Am. J. Clin. Nutr.* 27:901–904, 1974.

19 Clerico, A., M. Ferdeghini, C. Palombo, et al. Effects of anabolic treatment on the serum levels of gonadotropins, testosterone, prolactin, thyroid hormones and myoglobin of male athletes under physical training. *J. Nuclear Med. Allied Sci.* 25:79–88, 1981.

20 Cox, D. W., W. L. Heinrichs, C. A. Paulsen, et al. Perturbations of the human menstrual cycle by oxymetholone. *Am. J. Obstet. Gynecol.* 121:121–126, 1975.

21 Crist, D. M., P. J. Stackpole, and G. T. Peake. Effects of androgenic-anabolic steroids on neuromuscular power and body composition. *J. Appl. Physiol.* 54:366–370, 1983.

22 Damste, P. H. Voice change in adult women caused by virilizing agents. *J. Speech Hear. Disord.* 32:126–132, 1967.

23 Dorfman, R. I. and R. A. Shipley. *Androgens: Biochemistry, Physiology and Clinical Significance.* New York: J. Wiley and Sons, 1956.

24 Doyle, A. E., N. B. Pinkus, and J. Green. The use of oxandrolone in hyperlipidaemia. *Med. J. Australia* 1:127–129, 1974.

25 Ehrenkranz, J., E. Bliss, and M. H. Sheard. Plasma testosterone correlation with aggressive behavior and social dominance in man. *Psychosom. Med.* 36:469–475, 1974.

26 Exner, G. U., H. W. Staudte, and D. Pette. Isometric training of rats—effects upon fast and slow muscle and modification by an anabolic hormone (Nandrolone Decanoate) I. Female rats. *Pflügers Arch.* 345:1–14, 1973.

27 Fahey, T. D. and C. H. Brown. The effects of an anabolic steroid on the strength, body composition and endurance of college males when accompanied by a weight training program. *Med. Sci. Sports* 5:272–276, 1973.

28 Falk, H., L. Thomas, H. Popper, and H. G. Ishak. Hepatic angiosarcoma associated with androgenic-anabolic steroids. *Lancet* 2:1120–1123, 1979.

29 Farrell, G. C., D. E. Joshua, R. F. Uren, P. J. Baird, K. W. Perkins, and H. Kronenberg. Androgen-induced hepatoma. *Lancet* 1:430, 1975.

30 Forsyth, B. T. The effect of testosterone propianate at various protein calorie intakes in malnutrition after trauma. *J. Lab. Clin. Med.* 43:732–740, 1954.

31 Fowler, W. M., Jr., G. W. Gardner, and G. H. Egstrom. Effect of an

anabolic steroid on physical performance in young men. *J. Appl. Physiol.* 20:1038–1040, 1965.

32 Freed, D. L., A. J. Banks, D. Longson, and D. M. Burley. Anabolic steroids in athletics: crossover double-blind trial on weightlifters. *Br. Med. J.* 2:471–473, 1975.

33 Gelder, L. V. Psychosomatic aspects of endocrine disorders of the voice. *J. Commun. Disord.* 7:257–262, 1974.

34 Golding, L. A., J. E. Freydinger, and S. S. Fishel. The effect of an androgenic-anabolic steroid and a protein supplement on size, strength, weight and body composition in athletes. *Phys. Sportsmed.* 2(6):39–45, 1974.

35 Groos, G., O. H. Arnold, and G. Brittinger. Peliosis hepatis after long-term administration of oxymetholone. *Lancet* 1:874, 1974.

36 Harkness, R. A., B. H. Kilshaw, and B. M. Hobson. Effects of large doses of anabolic steroids. *Br. J. Sports Med.* 9:70–73, 1975.

37 Heitzman, R. J. The effectiveness of anabolic agents in increasing rate of growth in farm animals; report on experiments in cattle. In: *Anabolic Agents in Animal Production*, F. C. Lu and J. Rendell (Eds.). Stuttgart: Georg Thieme Publishers, 1976, pp. 89–98.

38 Heller, C. G., D. J. Moore, C. A. Paulsen, W. O. Nelson, and W. M. Laidlaw. Effects of progesterone and synthetic progestins on the reproductive physiology of normal men. *Fed. Proc.* 18:1057–1065, 1959.

39 Hershberger, J. G., E. G. Shipley, and R. K. Meyer. Myotrophic activity of 19-nortestosterone and other steroids determined by modified levator ani muscle method. *Proc. Soc. Exper. Biol. Med.* 83:175–180, 1953.

40 Hervey, G. R. and I. Hutchinson. The effects of testosterone on body weight and composition in the rat. *J. Endocrinol.* 57:xxiv–xxv, 1973.

41 Hervey, G. R., I. Hutchinson, A. V. Knibbs, et al. Anabolic effects of methandienone in men undergoing athletic training. *Lancet* 2:699–702, 1976.

42 Hervey, G. R., A. V. Knibbs, L. Burkinshaw, et al. Effects of methandienone on the performance and body composition of men undergoing athletic training. *Clin. Sci.* 60:457–461, 1981.

43 Hickson, R. C., W. W. Heusner, W. D. Van Huss, et al. Effects of Dianabol and high-intensity sprint training on body composition of rats. *Med. Sci. Sports* 8:191–195, 1976.

44 Holma, P. and H. Aldercreutz. Effect of an anabolic steroid (metandienon) on plasma LH, FSH, and testosterone and on the response to intravenous administration of LRH. *Acta Endocrinol.* 83:856–864, 1976.

45 Houssay, A. B. Effects of anabolic-androgenic steroids on the skin including hair and sebaceous glands. In: *Anabolic-Androgenic Steroids*, C. D. Kochakan (Ed.). New York: Springer-Verlag, 1976, pp. 155–190.

46 Ishak, K. G. Hepatic lesions caused by anabolic and contraceptive steroids. *Sem. Liver Dis.* 1:116–128, 1981.

47 Itil, T. M. Neurophysiological effects of hormones in humans: computer EEG profiles of sex and hypothalamic hormones. In: *Hormones, Behavior and Psychotherapy*, E. J. Sachar (Ed.). New York: Raven Press, 1976, pp. 31–40.

48 Itil, T. M., R. Cora, S. Akpinar, W. M. Herrmann, and C. J. Patterson. Psychotropic action of sex hormones: computerized EEG in establishing the immediate CNS effects of steroid hormones. *Curr. Ther. Res.* 16:1147–1170, 1974.

49 Johnson, F. L., K. G. Lerner, M. Siegel, et al. Association of androgenic-anabolic steroid therapy with development of hepatocellular carcinoma. *Lancet* 2:1273, 1972.

50 Johnson, L. C., G. Fisher, L. J. Silvester, and C. C. Hofheins. Anabolic steroid: effects of strength, body weight, oxygen uptake and spermatogenesis upon mature males. *Med. Sci. Sports* 4:43–45, 1972.

51 Johnson, L. C. and J. P. O'Shea. Anabolic steroid: effects on strength development. *Science* 164:957–959, 1969.

52 Johnson, L. C., E. S. Roundy, P. E. Allsen, A. G. Fisher, and L. J. Silvester. Effect of anabolic steroid treatment on endurance. *Med. Sci. Sports* 7:287–289, 1975.

53 Kenyon, A. T., K. Knowlton, and I. Sandiford. The anabolic effects of the androgens and somatic growth in man. *Ann. Intern. Med.* 20:632–654, 1944.

54 Keul, J., H. Deus, and W. Kinderman. Anabole hormone: Schadigung, Leistungsfahigkeit und Stoffwechses. *Med. Klin.* 71:497–503, 1976.

55 Kilshaw, B. H., R. A. Harkness, B. M. Hobson, and A.W.M. Smith. The effects of large doses of the anabolic steroid, methandrostenolone, on an athlete. *Clin. Endocrinol.* 4:537–541, 1975.

56 Kochakian, C. D. and J. R. Murlin. The effect of male hormones on the protein and energy metabolism of castrate dogs. *J. Nutr.* 10:437–458, 1935.

57 Kochakian, C. D. and B. R. Endahl. Changes in body weight of normal and castrated rats by different doses of testosterone propionate. *Proc. Soc. Exper. Biol. Med.* 100:520–522, 1959.

58 Kruskemper, H. L. *Anabolic Steroids*, New York: Academic Press, pp. 128–133, 162–164, 182.

59 Landau, R. L. The metabolic effects of anabolic steroids in man. In: *Anabolic-Androgenic Steroids*, C. D. Kochakian (Ed.). New York: Springer-Verlag, 1976, pp. 45–72.

60 Ljungqvist, A. The use of anabolic steroids in top Swedish athletes. *Br. J. Sports Med.* 9:82, 1975.

61 Loughton, S. J. and R. O. Ruhling. Human strength and endurance responses to anabolic steroid and training. *J. Sports Med.* 17:285–296, 1977.

62 MacDougall, J. D., D. G. Sale, G.C.B. Elder, and J. R. Sutton. Muscle ultrastructural characteristics of elite powerlifters and bodybuilders. *Eur. J. Applied Physiol.* 48:117–126, 1982.

63 Maher, J. M., E. L. Squires, J. L. Voss, and R. K. Shideler. Effect of anabolic steroids on reproductive function of young mares. *J. Am. Vet. Med. Assoc.* 183:519–524, 1983.

64 Mason, A. S. Male precocity: the clinician's view. In: *The Endocrine Function of the Human Testis*, V.H.T. James, M. Serra, and L. Martini (Eds.). New York: Academic Press, 1974, pp. 131–143.

65 McDonald, E. C. and C. E. Speicher. Peliosis hepatis associated with administration of oxymetholone. *JAMA* 240:243–244, 1978.

66 McGiven, A. R. Peliosis hepatis: case report and review of pathogenesis. *J. Pathol.* 101:283–285, 1970.

67 Meadows, A. T., J. L. Naiman, and M. Valdes-Dapena. Hepatoma associated with androgen therapy for aplastic anemia. *J. Pediatr.* 85:109–110, 1974.

68 Messerli, F. H. and E. D. Frohlich. High blood pressure: a side effect of drugs, poisons, and food. *Arch. Intern. Med.* 139:682–687, 1979.

69 Mulvihill, J. J., R. L. Ridolfi, F. R. Schultz, M. S. Brozy, and P.B.T. Haughton. Hepatic adenoma in Fanconi anemia treated with oxymetholone. *J. Pediatr.* 87:122–124, 1975.

70 Nadell, J. and J. Kosek. Peliosis hepatis. *Arch. Pathol. Lab. Med.* 101:405–410, 1977.

71 Nesheim, M. C. Some observations on the effectiveness of anabolic agents in increasing the growth rate of poultry. In: *Anabolic Agents in Animal Production*, F. C. Lu and J. Rendel (Eds.). Stuttgart: Georg Thieme Publishers, 1976, pp. 110–114.

72 Olsson, A. G., L. Oro, and S. Rossner. Effects of oxandrolone on plasma lipoproteins and the intravenous fat tolerance in man. *Atherosclerosis* 19:337–346, 1974.

73 Orlandi, F., A. Jezequel, and A. Melliti. The action of some anabolic steroids on the structure and the function of human liver cell. *Tijdschr. Gastro-Enterol.* 7:109–113, 1964.

74 O'Shea, J. P. The effects of an anabolic steroid on dynamic strength levels of weightlifters. *Nutr. Rep. Int.* 4:363–370, 1971.

75 Overly, W. L., J. A. Dankoff, B. K. Wang, and U. D. Singh. Androgens and hepatocellular carcinoma in an athlete. *Ann. Intern. Med.* 100:158–159, 1984.

76 Palva, I. P. and C. Wasastjerna. Treatment of aplastic anaemia with methenolone. *Acta Haematol.* 47:13–20, 1972.

77 Papanicolaou, G. N. and G. A. Falk. General muscular hypertrophy induced by androgenic hormone. *Science* 87:238–239, 1938.

78 Reeves, R. D., M. D. Morris, and G. L. Barbour. Hyperlipidemia due to oxymetholone therapy. *JAMA* 236:464–472, 1976.

79 Remes, K., P. Vuopio, M. Jarvinen, M. Harkonen, and H. Adlercreutz. Effect of short-term treatment with an anabolic steroid (methandienone) and dehydroepiandrosterone sulphate on plasma hormones, red cell volume and 2,3-diphosphoglycerate in athletes. *Scand. J. Clin. Lab. Invest.* 37:577–586, 1977.

80 Richardson, J. H. A comparison of two drugs on strength increase in monkeys. *J. Sports Med. Phys. Fitness* 17:251–254, 1977.

81 Rogozkin, V. A. The role of low molecular weight compounds in the regulation of skeletal muscle genome activity during exercise. *Med. Sci. Sports* 8:1–4, 1976.

82 Rogozkin, V. A. Anabolic steroid metabolism in skeletal muscle. *J. Steroid Biochem.* 11:923–926, 1979.

83 Ryan, A. J. Anabolic steroids are fool's gold. *Fed. Proc.* 40:2682–2688, 1981.

84 Sacks, P., D. Gale, T. H. Bothwell, K. Stevens. Oxymetholone therapy in

aplastic and other refractory anaemias. *S. Afr. Med. J.* 46:1607–1615, 1972.

85 Scaramella, T. J. and W. A. Brown. Serum testosterone and aggressiveness in hockey players. *Psychosom. Med.* 40:262–265, 1978.

86 Schaffner, F., H. Popper, and V. Perez. Changes in bile canaliculi produced by norethandrolone: electron microscopic study of human and rat liver. *J. Lab Clin. Med.* 56:623–628, 1960.

87 Shahidi, N. T. Androgens and erythropoeisis. *N. Engl. J. Med.* 289:72–80, 1973.

88 Shapiro, P., R. M. Ikedo, B. H. Ruebner, M. H. Conners, C. C. Halsted, and C. F. Abildgaard. Multiple hepatic tumors and peliosis hepatis in Fanconi's anemia treated with androgens. *Am. J. Dis. Child.* 131:1104–1106, 1977.

89 Shephard, R. J., D. Killinger, and T. Fried. Responses to sustained use of anabolic steroid. *Br. J. Sports Med.* 11:170–173, 1977.

90 Skarberg, K. O., L. Engstedt, S. Jameson, et al. Oxymetholone treatment in hypoproliferative anaemia. *Acta Haematol.* 49:321–330, 1973.

91 Smith, K. D., L. J. Rodriguez-Rigau, R. K. Tcholakian, and E. Steinberg. The relation between plasma testosterone levels and the lengths of phases of the menstrual cycle. *Fertil. Steril.* 32:403–407, 1979.

92 Snochowski, M., E. Dahlberg, E. Eriksson, and J. A. Gustafsson. Androgen and glucocorticoid receptors in human skeletal muscle cytosol. *J. Steroid Biochem.* 14:765–771, 1981.

93 Spiers, A.S.D., S. F. DeVita, M. J. Allar, S. Richards, and N. Sedransk. Beneficial effects of an anabolic steroid during cytotoxic chemotherapy for metastatic cancer. *J. Med.* 12:433–445, 1981.

94 Stamford, B. A. and R. Moffatt. Anabolic steroid: effectiveness as an ergogenic aid to experienced weight trainers. *J. Sports Med. Phys. Fitness* 14:191–197, 1974.

95 Stang-Voss, C. and H. J. Appel. Structural alterations of liver parenchyma induced by anabolic steroids. *Int. J. Sports Med.* 2:101–105, 1981.

96 Steinbach, M. Uber den Einfluss Anaboler wirkstoffe auf Korpergewicht, Muskelkraft und Muskeltraining. *Sportarzt Sportmed.* 11:485–492, 1968.

97 Stone, M. H., and M. E. Rush, and H. Lipner. Responses to intensive training and methandrostenelone administration: II. Hormonal, organ weights, muscle weights and body composition. *Pflugers Arch.* 375:147–151, 1978.

98 Strauss, R. H., H. E. Wright, G.A.M. Finerman, and D. H. Catlin. Side effects of anabolic steroids in weight-trained men. *Phys. Sportsmed.* 11(12):87–96, 1983.

99 Stromeyer, F. W., D. H. Smith, and K. G. Ishak. Anabolic steroid therapy and intrahepatic cholangiocarcinoma. *Cancer* 43:440–443, 1979.

100 Stromme, S. B., H. D. Meen, and A. Aakvaag. Effects of an androgenic-anabolic steroid on strength development and plasma testosterone levels in normal males. *Med. Sci. Sports* 6:203–208, 1974.

101 Taylor, W., S. Snowball, C. M. Dickson, and M. Lesna. Alterations of liver architecture in mice treated with anabolic androgens and di-

ethylnitrosamine. *NATO Adv. Study Inst. Series, Series A* 52:279–288, 1982.

102 Taxy, J. P. Peliosis: a morphologic curiosity becomes an iatrogenic problem. *Hum. Pathol.* 9:331–340, 1978.

103 Tepperman, J. *Metabolic and Endocrine Physiology.* Chicago: Yearbook Medical Publishers, 1973, p. 70.

104 Thomson, D. P., D. R. Pearson, and D. L. Costill. Use of anabolic steroids by national level athletes. *Med. Sci. Sports Exerc.* 13:111, 1981. (Abstract)

105 VanderWal, P. General aspects of the effectiveness of anabolic agents in increasing protein production in farm animals, in particular in bull calves. In: *Anabolic Agents in Animal Production*, F.C. Lu and J. Rendel (Eds.). Stuttgart: Georg Thieme Publishers, 1976, pp. 60–78.

106 Wade, N. Anabolic steroids: doctors denounce them, but athletes aren't listening. *Science* 176:1399–1403, 1972.

107 Ward, P. The effect of an anabolic steroid on strength and lean body mass. *Med. Sci. Sports* 5:277–282, 1973.

108 Weiss, V. and H. Muller. Aur Frage der Beeinflussung des Krafttrainings durch Anabole Hormone. *Schweiz. Z. Sportmed.* 16:79–89, 1968.

109 Whitelaw, M. J., T. N. Foster, and W. H. Graham. Methandrostenolone (Diabanol): a controlled study of its anabolic and androgenic effect in children. *Pediatric. Pharm. Ther.* 68:291–296, 1966.

110 Wilson, J. D. and J. E. Griffin. The use and misuse of androgens. *Metabolism* 29:1278–1295, 1980.

111 Woodard, T. L., G. A. Burghen, A. E. Kitabchi, and J. A. Wilimas. Glucose intolerance and insulin resistance in aplastic anemia treated with oxymetholone. *J. Clin. Endocrinol. Metab.* 53:905–908, 1981.

112 Wright, J. E. Anabolic steroids and athletes. *Exerc. Sport Sci. Rev.* 8:149–202, 1980.

113 Yamagishi, M., A. Hiraoka, and H. Uchino. Silent hepatic lesions detected with computed tomography in aplastic anemia patients administered androgens for a long period. *Acta Haematol. Jpn.* 45:703–710, 1982.

114 Young, M., H. R. Crookshank, and L. Ponder. Effects of an anabolic steroid on selected parameters in male albino rats. *Res. Q.* 48:653–656, 1977.

115 Zevin, D., H. Turani, A. Cohen, and J. Levi. Androgen-associated hepatoma in a hemodialysis patient. *Nephron* 29:274–276, 1981.

■

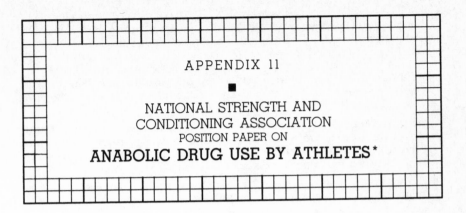

APPENDIX 11

■

NATIONAL STRENGTH AND
CONDITIONING ASSOCIATION
POSITION PAPER ON
ANABOLIC DRUG USE BY ATHLETES*

STATEMENT ON ANABOLIC DRUG USE BY ATHLETES

The NSCA has based this position stand on a comprehensive survey and analysis of the scientific literature dealing with the effects of anabolic steroids on physiology and physical capacities and performance. Additional concerns for safely improving performance, promoting fair play, protecting health and protecting the future of amateur sport were also important factors.

It is the position of the National Strength and Conditioning Association that:

1 The administration of therapeutic doses of anabolic steroids to healthy males has not been shown in itself to elicit significant improvement in maximum strength, maximum oxygen intake, aerobic performance, lean body mass, or weight.

2 When combined with resistance training, anabolic hormone administration generally results in an increased body weight gain as compared to training alone. Body composition may or may not change, although the majority of investigations suggest an increase in lean body mass with no change in fat, and thus a reduced percentage of body fat. The increases in weight and/or body mass and potential decreases in body fat may or may not be enhanced by higher drug dosages.

3 When combined with resistance training, anabolic steroid administration may increase maximum strength or power more than training alone. Facilitation of strength development occurs most often in experienced weight trainers and may be the result of physiological or psychological changes.

4 There is no conclusive scientific evidence regarding the effects of large doses or long term administration of anabolic steroids on the health or physical performance of athletes.

5 Anabolic steroid administration poses a threat, the extent of which over the long term remains undefined, to the liver, cardiovascular, immunological and endocrine systems, and thus to overall health and longevity.

*Reprinted with permission of the National Strength and Conditioning Association, P.O. Box 81410, Lincoln, NE 68501.

6 Serious and continuing efforts should be made to educate athletes, coaches, trainers, physicians, physical educators and the general public regarding the limited benefits and potential risks of steroid use as documented by the scientific method. An open dialogue between interested parties should be encouraged. Only by bridging the gap between all concerned can an environment of knowledge and understanding be created.

7 Based upon the limitations and deficiencies of our current data base and the universal and overwhelmingly positive empirical experiences of the athletic community, concurrent efforts by the above groups should be directed toward resolving the disputed and outstanding issues.

8 If drug testing is to be the deterrent to steroid usage, then testing should equitably encompass all levels of athletes.

9 All those concerned and supportive of athletic competition (coaches, fans, sports administrators, alumni, news media, etc.) should reevaluate their perspectives on sport. In this way, the accountability of anabolic steroid usage can more clearly be defined. A win-at-all-cost philosophy may create enormous pressure for the competitor. The competitor's response to this pressure may include anabolic steroid use, directly determining the type of role model projected to our youth—the athletes of tomorrow.

10 The NSCA should actively support research that will address questions concerning short- and long-term effects of steroids and take a responsible lead in research that may help cover methods of performance enhancement through proper conditioning and restoration technique.

11 The use of anabolic steroids in an attempt to improve physical capacity or performance is contrary to the ethical principles and regulations of competition as established and set down by all athletic federations and sports governing bodies. The National Strength and Conditioning Association supports these ethical principles and regulations.

In summary, because sports governing bodies have uniformly rejected the use of anabolic-androgenic steroids on the basis of ethics and the ideals of fair play of competition and because their use gives possible competitive advantage harmful to the user, the National Strength and Conditioning Association joins those sports governing bodies in condemning the use of anabolic-androgenic steroids by athletes.

ANABOLIC DRUG USE BY ATHLETES
LITERATURE REVIEW

by

James E. Wright Ph.D.
Health Fitness Center
Hawley Army Hospital
Fort Benjamin Harrison, Indiana

and

Michael H. Stone Ph.D.
National Strength Research Center
Department of Health, Physical Education, and Recreation
Auburn University, Alabama

Scientific and technological developments often promote changes in life style and occasionally in value systems. More specifically the growth of the pharmaceutical industry has increased the availability of both licit and illicit substances which affect the mind and body in various ways, a phenomenon which has been associated with concurrent changes in attitude of large segments of society toward the use of such substances. For example, the development of oral contraceptive steroids for women, the use of which remains controversial in some religious circles, is said to have contributed substantially to the altered birth rates, life style, and sexual "revolution" of the 1960s and 70s, and later made possible the legal manipulation of mental and physical states of female athletes in competition.

Coupled with this increased availability and use of drugs has been a growth in interest and participation in athletics and in the social and financial implications of success in sports. With the continued climb of athletic records and qualifying standards for competition and the empirical and anecdotal evidence on the ergogenic effects of drugs such as the anabolic steroids, the above factors have pushed the use of anabolic and other drugs among athletes to epidemic proportions.

The physiological, philosophical, and political ramifications of this phenomenon have prompted concerned reactions from all sports interest groups (Figures 1 and 2). The medical community, for one, has predominantly been involved with diseased or disabled persons with guiding principles such as *primum non nocere* ("first do not harm") and goals of protecting and restoring health and educating the population on how to promote health. Accordingly, physicians have a perspective which leads them to place a premium value on life and health and to condemn drug use for other than disease, deficiency, or injury states (Figure 1).

Sports federations and athletic federations tend to perceive drug use as unfair, dehumanizing, and as corrupting the physical, mental, emotional, social, and civic values of sport (Figure 1). Such organizations have attempted to legislatively eliminate drug use from sports. This perspective has resulted in the publication and adoption of regulations by the International Amateur Athletic Federation, International Olympic Committee, and others, which prohibit the administration of or use by competitors of not only any substance foreign to the body, but also of any physiological (i.e., endogenous or natural) substances taken in abnormal quantity or by an abnormal route of entry with the primary intention of artificially increasing performance capacity. Much time, effort, and money on the part of scientists (Figure 1), administrators, and the federations have been devoted to the development of methods to detect the presence of banned substances in urine samples of athletes in an effort to enforce these regulations. The resources invested in this enormous undertaking have, in fact, to

Perspectives of the Principal Interest Groups that have resulted in the Present Scientific and Emotional Controversy

1a Medical: Academic and Professional background and experience primarily directed to *clinical diagnosis* and *treatment* of patients—To restoration of *"normal"* health and function—rather than to the *scientific method* or to *enhancement* of performance. Increasing emphasis on preventive medicine and education of the patient.

Goal: To restore and protect health.

Guiding principles and philosophy: "Primum non nocere"

(first do not harm); drugs should only be used in disease, deficiency or injury states.

1b Sports federations and athletic governing bodies: with some exceptions (medical committees) not trained to interpret or apply the findings of basic research.

Goal: To promote friendship and brotherhood through sport; to promote equality and fair play; to protect the future of the sport.

1c Scientists: Trained to design, conduct, analyze, interpret and apply the results of research investigations using accepted scientific methods. Only recently, as the field of exercise science has developed, have they been interested or able to assist the other groups in achieving their goals in this area. Unfortunately, they have in the past and will likely continue to be legally, ethically, and financially constrained in addressing some of the critical aspects of this problem.

Goal: To ask and objectively answer the relevant basic and applied questions concerning sports and exercise training.

1d Athletes, Coaches, Trainers: Not typically trained in the scientific method, in physiology, pharmacology, or in the recognition and diagnosis of the signs and symptoms of medical disorders. Conduct experiments based on empirical data using trial and error approach resulting in exceptionally sophisticated and productive methods of enhancing performance.

> Goal: To improve performance to the maximal
> extent possible; to win in competition.
>
> le The above mentioned constraints coupled with the dif-
>   fering goals, perspectives and experiences of these
>   groups has resulted in:
>   A paucity of scientifically sound, athletically ap-
>   plicable research;
>   A controversy over the existence and extent of
>   both beneficial and adverse effects of the
>   drugs;
>   And an emotional polarization and counter-
>   productive alienation of groups.
>
> Figure 1

date far exceeded those utilized to address performance and health effects issues.

Athletes, along with many coaches and trainers, contend alternatively that more sophisticated athletes, with or without the support of physicians and scientists, will find methods to escape or obviate detection, thereby creating a situation conceivably more unfair than that which testing is intended to eliminate. Testing, they insist, is too impractical, expensive, and as yet insufficiently comprehensive to eliminate drug use. Rather than violating their moral code, many athletes consider the use of drugs (which are available to all and are thought to be used by virtually all) to be a personal decision and a practical necessity in the effort to become, or remain, competitive. Perhaps most importantly, the collective experiences of the athletic community suggest that the immediate performance rewards of steroid use outweigh the more distant and less defined health risks. The differing experiences, goals and attitudes of these groups combined with conflicting results of often inadequate or irrelevant research has led to a highly polarized and emotional situation and an escalating problem which has proven counterproductive for all factions but which impacts most seriously on the athletes themselves (Figure 2).

Androgenic-Anabolic Mechanisms

One of the principal physiological actions of anabolic steroids is the stimulation of a protein anabolic, or constructive, phase of metabolism in the body. Much of the theoretical basis for their application in both medicine and sports is derived from this fact, in that proteins make up the basic structural, contractile and enzymatic components of the body and can serve as precursors of various hormones and energy conveyors (ATP, CP). Problems and disagreements arise, despite several thousand research studies conducted, with regard to the organs, tissues and extent to which this anabolism is manifested under various conditions, particularly athletics, and in defining any consequent long and short term physical, physiological and psychological effects.

Following the isolation, chemical characterization (31) and initial studies establishing the nature of the protein anabolic response to androgenic steroids in dogs (89, 97), the rapid development of com-

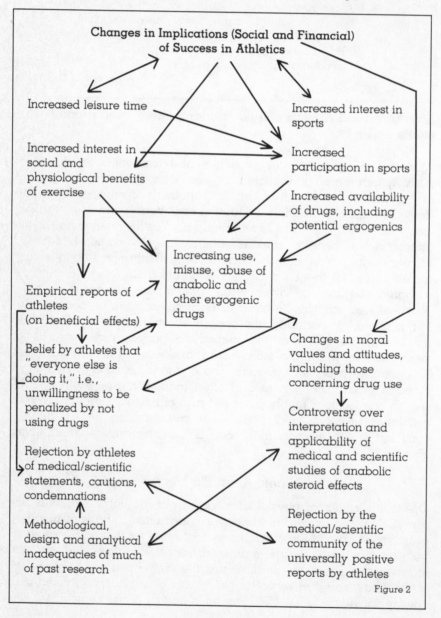

Figure 2

mercial preparations made possible the confirmation and extension of these findings to humans and other animals (91, 103). The growth of almost every tissue was shown to be influenced to some extent by anabolic hormone administration. The degree of effect, however, varied not only among different organs and tissues but also in accordance with the endocrine status, age, sex, species and strain of animal studied (91, 103).

In the human male, the characteristic responses to the increased androgen levels during puberty are:

1 Full development of the primary sexual characteristics, including growth of the penis and functional development of the testes and accessory sex glands, spermatogenesis, increased frequency of erections and awakening of sexual interest;

2 Changes in the skin and its derivatives, including an increased growth of hair on the body and face and in the genital region, an increase in liver, heart, and kidney size, an increase in the number of red blood cells, and a deepening of the voice due to enlargement of the larynx and lengthening of the vocal cords;

3 An acceleration of the growth rate of bone and muscle mass, resulting in a broadening of the shoulders and thorax, epiphyseal closure, an increase in bone density and an increase in the size, and possibly the number of muscle cells (26).

4 The period of puberty is also associated with marked changes in psychological perspective, particularly in relation to body image and personal identity (30). The above mentioned changes in skin, hair, voice, testes and accessory sex glands are considered to represent the "androgenic" effects of testosterone, whereas the changes in muscle, bone, and blood are labeled the "anabolic" effect. However, because virtually all cells in the body are potential targets for these steroids and because all steroids exert their effects in the same basic manner, "anabolic" effects differ from "androgenic" effects only in location and not in essence (103). A pure "anabolic" steroid has not yet been found (124, 1900).

The most important natural androgens are testosterone and adrostenedione which are produced by the testes, ovaries, and adrenal glands of both sexes. Daily production rates for these hormones, normally determined by the levels of circulating pituitary gonadotropins, range from 4–10 mg for testosterone and 1–2 mg for androstenedione in males, and from 0.04–0.12 mg and 2–4 mg, respectively in females (14). These levels fluctuate in a cyclical fashion (32) and may be negatively affected by physical or emotional stress or the consumption of various drugs such as alcohol and marijuana. Table 1 shows the chemical structures of the natural androgens and several of the more commonly used synthetic analogs. The structures of the synthetic compounds have been modified in an attempt to prolong and/or enhance the "anabolic" and minimize the "androgenic" effects they elicit.

The basic pattern of the protein anabolism involves a reduction in the excretion of urea in the urine without any change in the excretion of ammonia, uric acid, or nitrogen in the feces. The excretion of potassium, phosphate, calcium, and sometimes sodium and chloride is also reduced. The positive nitrogen balance does not continue indefinitely, but ordinarily returns to normal despite continued steroid administration. This reduction in anabolic effectiveness has been termed the "wearing-off" phase (90). Cessation of steroid administration generally produces a temporary "rebound" negative nitrogen balance and subsequent loss of body weight (90). The overall anabolic response pattern is qualitatively similar in both sexes of all animal species studies. However, the quantitative magnitude and duration of the response may be modified by the drug, dosage, route and duration of administration and by the physiological status of the animal studied (91).

CHEMICAL STRUCTURES, GENERAL AND TRADE NAMES OF THE FIVE MOST POPULAR ORAL AND INJECTABLE ANABOLIC-ANDROGENIC DRUGS AMONG U.S. ATHLETES

ORAL COMPOUNDS
Dianabol
(1-Dehydromethyl-testosterone,
Methandrostenolone,
Methandienone)
CIBA, Basel,
Switzerland

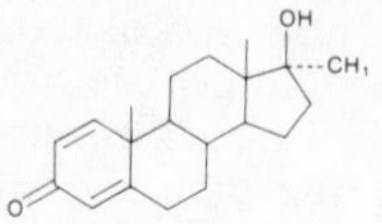

Anavar
(Oxandronone)
Searle, USA

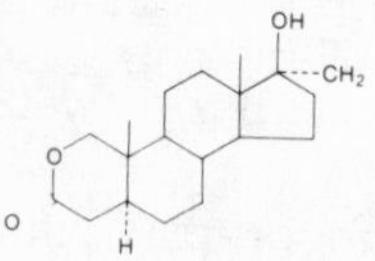

Androyd
Anadrol
(Oxymetholone)
Parke-Davis, USA
Syntex, Mexico

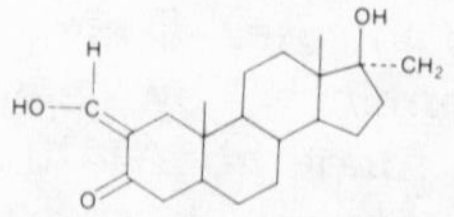

Winstrol
(Stanozolol)
Winthrop, USA

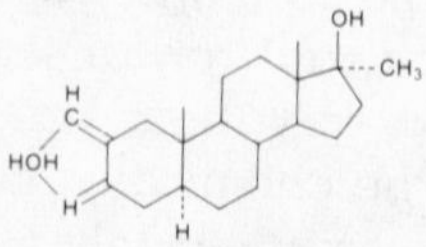

Maxibolin
(Ethylestrenol)
Organon, USA

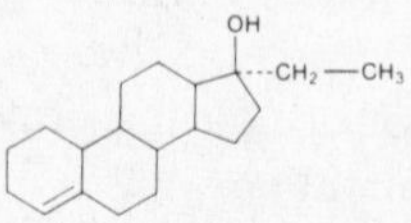

INJECTABLE COMPOUNDS

Deca-Durabolin
(Nandrolone
decanotate)
Organon, USA

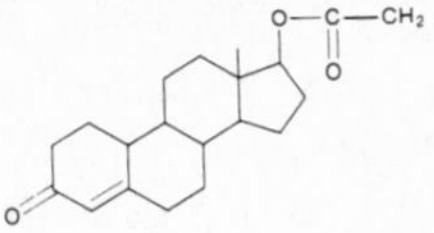

Delatestryl
(Testosterone
enanthate)
Squibb, USA

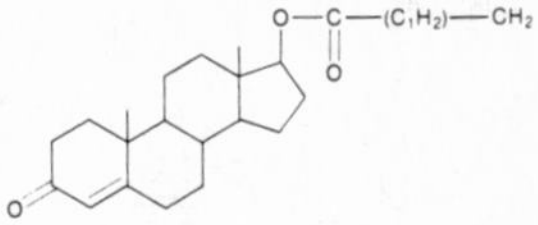

Depo-testosterone
(Testosterone
cypionate)
Upjohn, USA

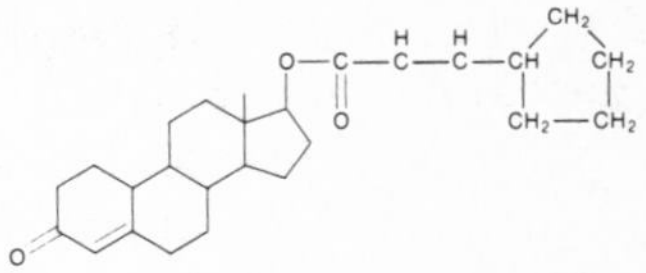

Druabolin
(Nandrolone
phenylpropionate)
Organon, USA

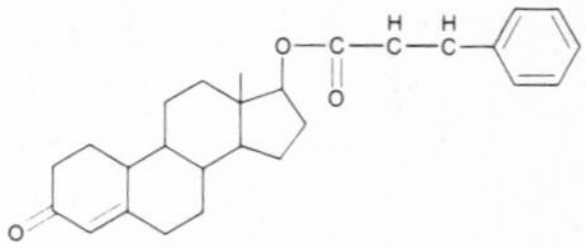

Primobolan-Depot
(Methenolone
enanthate)
Schering, Berlin,
Germany

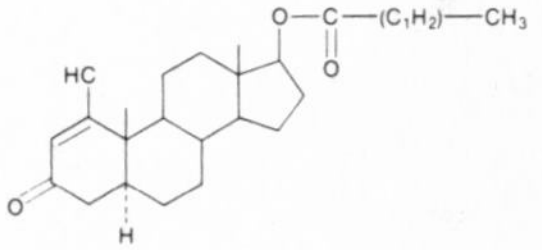

In attempts to compare the "anabolic effectiveness" of the synthetic steroids to one another, the manufacturers present results of both animal experiments and clinical human studies. Each drug by virtue of the fact that it is on the market has presumably been subjected to extensive animal testing. However, these studies have been done using different evaluation techniques, different strains of animals, routes of drug administration, dosage schedules, etc., and conclusions drawn from animal studies are not necessarily directly applicable even to the patients who need a drug, let alone to normal individuals or athletes. The clinical studies conducted by physicians on the other hand, have been performed on very different groups of patients, on different diets, and again using variable drug doses. Since there is such variation in the individual response to a given drug, it is impossible except in very specific cases to state objectively that one drug offers advantages not shared by several others. Personal experience with a variety of compounds and dosages seems to be the way in which most individuals determine what works best.

In regard to the physiologic status of the animal, and in particular the endocrine system and the state of body protein stores (based on numerous laboratory animal studies) the relationship of age and sex to anabolic steroid-induced nitrogen retention appears to be (in order of decreasing responsiveness): young castrated males, females, young males, adult males, old animals (103). Nitrogen retention in female rats begins and reaches a plateau later, wears off more gradually, and rebounds less than in males (93). The pattern in intact males is abbreviated; the muscles respond more weakly and the rebound results in the loss of a greater percentage of retained nitrogen than in castrated animals (96). With regard to body protein stores, while the anabolic effects are pronounced during protein repletion following a fast (94), low to moderate doses of steroids may elicit little or no response in healthy animals already in positive nitrogen balance due to normal linear growth or even due to simple ad lib feeding or other dietary manipulation (43).

Although significant qualitative differences are claimed by athletes for the various anabolic drugs, it is virtually impossible to demonstrate in animals that any one drug offers advantages for nitrogen retention not shown by at least several others. Desired therapeutic effects in patients are achieved with any given compound by dosage manipulations (103).

Both the dose and duration of steroid administration exert an influence on the anabolic response. In both castrated and intact rats, the response following a single injection is dose-related but only up to a point beyond which a suppression of myotrophic activity (21), nitrogen retention, body weight, food intake, and maximal growth occurs (95, 98, 99). Prolonging the period of steroid administration and increasing the dose appear to result in a reduction of the relative effects on nitrogen retention and body weight and an enhancement of the catabolic effects on fat (98). Increasing the dose with continued administration delays the wearing-off phase and may reduce the percentage of nitrogen lost in the rebound (96). Androgenic-anabolic agents alone appear to exert relatively minor effects on weight gain in normal male farm animals including cattle (60, 189), chickens, turkeys (126), or pigs (47).

Training and Anabolic Steroids: Animals

Several investigations have reported significant anticatabolic effects of anabolic hormones in animals. Evans and Ivy (39) observed in both castrated and immobilized intact rats, injected with 5 mg of testosterone propionate for 15 days, reductions in skeletal and cardiac atrophy, and a reduction in the decrease in metabolic capacity normally accompanying immobilization. Dahlmann et al (29) also found that the administration of 10 mg/kg body weight of testosterone propionate twice per week for eight weeks in normal male rats reduced the

dramatic increase in protein catabolic enzyme activity (alkaline pro-
teinase) that occurred following prolonged endurance training.
Rogozkin (151) found anabolic steroids to induce increases in amino
acid uptake, RNA polymerase activity, and RNA, myofibrillar (contractile) and scarcoplasmic (enzymes) protein synthesis in intact rat
skeletal muscle. He also determined that a single injection (0.5 mg/kg
body weight) prevented the exercise-induced decrement in RNA
polymerase activity and protein synthesis and enhanced the supercompensation of RNA synthesis following exercise (152). Wilkerson et
al (197) found that Durabolin (0.2 mg, six days/wk) for the last three
weeks of an eight week anaerobic (jumping) training program increased muscle water in male and female rats. Force production increased but not contractile time. The authors (197) suggested that the
increased water caused internal stretch resulting in a shortened elec-
tro-mechanical delay and increased force production. Nevertheless,
the majority of animal experiments with normal healthy males have
been unable to document consistent positive changes in performance
or underlying physiology exceeding those resulting from training
alone in muscle size or performance variables due to anabolic hormones (41, 67, 68, 84, 175, 176, 210). However, beneficial effects on
performance (and physiology) may occur in female rats as a result of
anaerobic training and androgen interaction (40, 84).

Training and Anabolic Steroids: Humans

More than two dozen studies and reviews have been published in the
past two decades dealing with the effects of anabolic steroids on
body mass and composition, strength, aerobic capacity, and performance in human subjects. These have been discussed in detail elsewhere (104, 177, 185, 199, 202).

Many of the original investigations were conducted utilizing college students who had little or no experience with weight training (24,
42, 48, 65, 81, 109, 123, 174, 178, 195, 200). Although limited in application from the perspective of the highly motivated experienced athlete, these investigations generally involved ample numbers of
subjects, a double-blind experimental design and adequate controls.
The results of these studies indicate that total or lean body weight,
strength, or aerobic power are not likely to be influenced by administration of therapeutic doses of anabolic hormones in the absence of
an exercise program which in itself promotes muscle anabolism and
meaningful performance enhancement. Even when the drugs are
applied in conjunction with strength training, six of nine studies reported no significant steroid effects on strength. Even when combining strength training, high drug dosages and protein supplementa-

tion, strength and body weight may increase no more than with training alone (178), although Hervey (64) did find a striking weight gain when using ten times the normal dosage as did Forbes (46). Furthermore it may be possible that increases in performance or beneficial alterations in body composition are more likely to occur in athletes already in (or beginning) hard training as has been suggested (59, 201, 202).

Seven of nine studies which utilized strength training did, however, find statistically significant increments in body weight due to steroid intake. No effect on aerobic power was demonstrated in these studies. Thus, inexperienced weight trainers, using therapeutic or even greater doses of anabolic hormones in conjunction with training over a three to six-week period, could expect a weight gain of questionable practical significance amounting to approximately 1.5 kg over what could be expected from training alone. The composition of the weight gain remains open to question, particularly since under these circumstances, strength may not be affected to the same extent as body weight.

Of those reports in which subjects accustomed to weight training were used (2,8*,9*,10,11,12,22,27*,35,49*,52*,56,66*,85,134*,135,136, 173,193) the majority suggested that therapeutic doses of steroids enabled the individuals to gain body weight and/or strength more rapidly than did training alone. However, deficiencies and inadequacies with respect to the generally accepted methods of scientific experimentation were evident in several of these studies.

The design, control, methodology and/or data analysis of many of these studies have made interpretation and application of the results difficult and controversial. Of 13 investigations concentrating on strength development only seven were conducted in a double-blind fashion (asterisked in the above list). Of these seven, one found no steroid effects on strength (52) while another suffered from loss (dropout) of subjects and from using data on strength and weight changes which were collected and reported by the subjects themselves (49). Of the five remaining double-blind studies, two could document a significant increment from steroids in only one of two (134) and three of ten (27) test exercises, although the latter study utilized weights for training and isokinetic devices for testing. It is of interest in this regard that Edgerton et al (35) likewise found no increments in isokinetic torque of knee extension muscles in their case studies of six Olympic style weight lifters despite marked improvements in squat, snatch and clean and jerk; nor did Fahey and Brown (42) observe improvement in isokinetic strength measures in weight-trained physical education students (emphasizing the importance of the specificity of training and testing modes). Of the last two studies (8, 9), only one showed unequivocably, using multiple statistical techniques, that steroids significantly aided strength development. Hervey et al (66) repeated an earlier study (64), but this time used seven experienced weight trainers. Significant improvements in maximal leg strength and arm and leg training loads were found during the drug period but not, as in their previous investigation, during the period of placebo administration. Peak arm and grip strengths measured isometrically, although favoring the steroid period, were not shown to change significantly. All four studies which used single-blind designs did find strength gains to be significantly enhanced due to anabolic steroid administration.

Several studies have researched the influence of these drugs on various measures of aerobic capacity and endurance performance. The stimulating effect of anabolic hormones on hemoglobin, hematocrit and total blood volume could theoretically increase aerobic power and performance (71, 51, 119, 168). Some investigations have shown improvements in estimated (1, 81) and measured (85) maximal aerobic capacity, while others have not (22, 42, 80, 82). Holma (71) reported pronounced increases in total blood volume, stroke volume of the heart both at rest and during exercise, and in blood flow to working muscles in well-trained athletes administered 15 mg of methandrostenolone per day for two months. These parameters tended to return to pre-treatment values following cessation of steroid administration.

The question of anabolic steroid effects on body composition is likewise unsettled and complicated by such factors as the lack of dietary control, the use of different drugs, dosage, training programs, study durations, methods of measurement, individual differences in body composition and metabolic rate. In studies employing skinfold measurements no significant changes in skinfold measures were observed due to drug use. Since body weight increased significantly in the majority of these studies, body composition may be at least temporarily altered by a reduction in the percentage of fat. Several studies used hydrostatic weighing to assess changes, the majority found no change in percent body fat. The investigations that used both methods found agreement between the methods, but some observed decreases in percent fat associated with drug use (65, 66) while others did not (27, 52).

It is well known that many athletes use steroids in much higher doses and for much longer periods than those which have currently been evaluated (44, 179, 185, 203). It is not uncommon for the dose level in a significant percentage of athletes to exceed 1 mg/kg of body weight per day with a substantial number of those individuals using two or more times that quantity. The minimal data collected suggest that the gains in highly trained athletes, like those in some patients (160) may well be greater at these higher dose levels. Forbes

(44, 45) suggests that training typically produces only modest changes in body composition unless accompanied by androgens. After studying body composition changes in exceptionally well-trained athletes, Forbes (44, 46) suggests that a dose-response effect may be evident; that is, the higher the dose the greater the gain in lean body mass and the greater the loss in total and percent body fat. However, these conclusions are largely based on two subjects, a body builder and a weight lifter (44, 46). Furthermore, they do not agree with other reports (49) or the majority of the authors' observations (unpublished data).

The cumulative effects of repetitive, high dose or long-term drug administration on physiology and performance have not yet been documented. The result of 3–12 week laboratory studies indicate that gains can be expected under certain conditions, but these studies may not accurately reflect the ultimate anabolic potential of these drugs. No study has investigated blood or tissue levels of the drug. "Normality" may be the ideal physiological status for health and even for long term performance, however, the evidence that it is indeed best for performance requiring high strength levels or body mass over the short term is open to question.

As previously pointed out, differences in methods and lack of adequate controls have made interpretation of data exceptionally difficult. Another problem concerns the possibility of side effects giving the drug away to the subject. Changes in energy levels, behavior, urine odor and color, insomnia, acne, etc., all make even double-blind studies difficult to carry out (177). In the studies of both Freed et al (49) and Hervey (66), all the subjects successfully broke the "code" early in the experimental periods. Thus any conclusions drawn from short term, low dose studies may not accurately reflect what occurs in athletes taking androgens at higher doses, repeatedly, and/or for longer durations.

Overtraining—Overstress

Overtraining manifests itself by a variety of changes in physiology. One of these changes may include a negative nitrogen balance due to overstress. Recent studies have suggested that beginning either intensive aerobic (53, 54) or anaerobic (weightlifting) training (25, 105) can produce a negative nitrogen balance. A negative nitrogen balance can (depending upon the severity and duration) produce losses of lean body mass. Furthermore, losses may include both structural and enzymatic proteins, antibodies, etc. This may increase the chances of some pathology developing (e.g., injury, disease, etc.)

Stress of sufficient intensity and duration may also produce dramatic and relatively long lasting decreases in resting testosterone levels in otherwise healthy males (55, 102, 121, 142). It is likely that this decrease in testosterone is related to the negative nitrogen balance sometimes observed during intensive training. Exogenous androgen administration has been shown to decrease or reverse a negative nitrogen balance (103). Furthermore, if decreased testosterone levels are produced by overstress, it is possible that the administered androgens act not simply to supplement, but perhaps foremost to replace, stress-induced losses, thereby reducing the potential adverse effects of overtraining-overstress. Such a mechanism, although speculative at this time, would assist in explaining and supporting the widely held belief of athletes that anabolic drugs increase their capacities to train with higher intensities and larger volumes and to recover faster. It should also be pointed out that a negative nitrogen balance may also be decreased or reversed by adding extra protein to the diet (54, 105, 157).

Effects on the Nervous System

Psychological Effects

Androgens and other steroid hormones have recently been shown to exert significant effects on the development and functioning of the nervous system. Arnold (7) suggests that androgens can alter neuron number and especially size. Furthermore androgens appear to influence specific neural systems involved in masculine and feminine behavior patterns (180).

Data from animal studies (180) suggest that both estrogens and androgens bind to receptors on neural structures that are identical or associated with sensory pathways and ventricular recess organs (periventricular organ). Androgens have been reported to selectively stimulate neurons of the somatomotor system and circuits associated with aggression (180). Furthermore, androgen receptors are located on alpha motor neurons (161). Such observations permit speculation as to effects of androgens on behavior or neuromuscular expression which might increase athletic capacities and performance.

Behavior

It has been postulated that androgens may increase aggressiveness and produce other psychological effects that may be related to "training drive" and "feeling of well being" (104, 175, 177, 179, 185, 201, 203).

Several studies have shown relationships between testosterone levels and dominance and aggressive behavior in many different species of animals (15, 141, 133) including non-human primates (83, 155). Although less clear, aggressive behavior and other "feelings of hostility" have been related to testosterone levels in humans (133, 147). Rozenek (156) has demonstrated increased anger and hostility as well as total mood disturbance among strength-power athletes taking large doses of androgens as compared to non-androgen taking strength-power athletes, runners or controls. The authors along with many other interested scientists, teachers, coaches and athletes (personal communications) have subjectively noted increased aggressiveness and mood lability among androgen users. It is possible that androgen use may create a "psychosomatic state" that when properly directed could increase training intensity or make it easier to become "aroused" both during training sessions and competition.

Neuromuscular Expression

It has been suggested that androgens have a trophic effect on the nervous system (7). Androgens have been implicated in facilitating acetylcholine release at the neuromuscular junction (levator ani) in castrated rats (192), and, as previously stated, there are androgen receptors located in both the brain and on alpha motor neurons (161, 180). In as much as improvements in muscle strength and power can in part be accounted for by neural factors (57, 120), these findings that androgens may in some manner modify neuromuscular function and expression underscore their role and potential significance in increased performance (2).

Anabolic Steroids and Health

The majority of investigations thus far discussed have focused their research efforts primarily on assessing potential "positive" changes (i.e., strength, body mass and anthropometry) (Figure 3) rather than "negative" effects of steroids on health. Concerned scientists, physicians, and sports administrators have attempted to extrapolate to athletes data which were obtained on patients with a diverse variety of debilitating diseases (Figure 4). The studies on athletes have generally been too short and/or the drug dosages used have been too low to more than hint at any possible pathological effects. Based on qualitative as well as quantitative physical and physiological differences (cardiovascular, metabolic, etc.) between athletes and nonathletic "normal" individuals, attempted extrapolations of findings on clinical patients to athletes have met with some degree of skepticism.

Suggested Physiological Bases for Application of Anabolic Steroids in Athletes
Body weight
Body composition (?)
Muscle size
Muscle strength
Blood volume
Red blood cells (number and volume)
Hemoglobin (Myoglobin?)
Anti-Catabolic effects
Recuperation (?)/enhances ability to accumulate backlog of quality training necessary to improve/win
Prophylaxis and therapy for hard and soft tissue injuries or disease
Behavioral effects including increased "aggressiveness," "competitiveness," "training drive," and feelings of "well being"

Figure 3

At present, the health/performance profession is restricted to making educated guesses as to the applicability of such data. From an objective standpoint, the issue will remain an open question until substantially more data are collected, particularly on athletes.

In general, it is known that anabolic hormones are metabolized by and are capable of exerting effects on virtually every cell in the body (92). Adverse effects are dependent upon the type (oral and/or injectable), specific biochemical characteristics of the drug and of the

---

Potential Medical Uses of Anabolic Steroids

The principal physiological basis for the medical use of anabolic steroids is their stimulation of *protein synthesis*.
Replacement therapy
Malnutrition
Skeletal disorders
Soft tissue injuries
Surgery
Anemias resulting from bone marrow failure
"Wasting" diseases (such as chronic bronchitis, pulmonary tuberculosis
To offset the catabolic effects of glucocorticoid therapy
To offset undesired effects of radiation therapy
Mammary gland carcinoma
Certain liver diseases
Certain pediatric growth deficiencies
Irretractable Raynaud's phenomenon

Figure 4

---

user, dosage of drugs used, and upon the duration of use (103). Beyond that, it is obvious that whenever any single organ, tissue or part of the body is negatively affected, the functional capacity of the entire body ultimately suffers accordingly, and the individual response to a specific therapeutic drug regimen is unique, based on one's biochemical individuality. Since so few data are available on athletes, consideration will also be given in this section to clinical findings in patients undergoing anabolic hormone therapy.

The major organs and systems whose functions may be altered as a result of steroid use include those which are involved in the transport, metabolism/detoxification, and excretion of drugs and hormones, nitrogen and energy metabolism, erythropoiesis, fluid and electrolyte balance, bone matrix integrity, and overall body hormone balance and reproduction. These consist principally of the liver, kidneys, skin, testes and accessory sex glands, neuroendocrine, cardiovascular and skeletal systems.

Liver

Since the liver serves a central function in the metabolism of drugs, it is not surprising that it is a frequent victim of drug-induced toxicity. A large number of drugs adversely affect liver function. Klatskin (87) listed nearly 1,000 references concerning liver pathology, the majority of which were reports of single cases involving one drug. Even pregnancy, it should be noted, can result in hepatic disorders.

Hepatic damage produced by drugs may result from either a direct toxic effect (as in the case of anabolic and contraceptive steroids) or from a hypersensitivity reaction. Direct hepatotoxicity is predictable and is characterized by: (1) a brief interval between exposure and the development of liver damage, (2) a toxicity which tends to be related to the dose, and (3) a generally similar and reproducible condition in animals. In fact, the accumulated clinical and laboratory observations concerning the hepatotoxic effects of anabolic steroids in humans have been corroborated in animal studies, indicating that the hepatic lesions caused by these drugs are due to interference with the (still unknown) mechanisms involved in the excretory functions of the liver. Elevations in serum bilirubin levels and BSP (bromsulphtalein) retention appear to be the major immediate consequences of steroid-induced disturbances of the excretory function of the liver. Some of the cases reported from clinical studies are presented below. BSP retention may be observed during the early stages of steroid use but it is not always accompanied by hyperbilirubinemia, which evidently results from a more severe obstruction of liver function. The reported clinical evidence suggests that this disorder is caused primarily by the 17-alphaaklylated (generally oral) steroids. Data from both animal and human studies further indicate not only that different steroids may elicit different responses but that there may be significant differences in the response of various individuals to a single drug and even to the same drug over time. In Wynn, Landon, and Kawerau's (207) study of the effects of methandrostenolone therapy on liver function in various patients, 11 of 14 patients receiving doses ranging from 12.5 to 100 mg per day (with an average of 25–50) continuously for nine months or more exhibited significant increases in BSP retention. Three patients (one on 50 mg per day and two on 25 mg per day) showed no significant increases. In six of the previous patients BSP retention returned to pre-treatment values while drug administration was continued. The time taken for this ranged from 70–126 days. In four of the remaining five patients with abnormal BSP retention the values fell toward normal with time but remained slightly elevated. In none of these 14, or 16 other patients, were clinically significant changes in serum or urinary bilirubin or alkaline phosphatase observed.

Serum transaminase levels (SGOT) were elevated in approximately one third of the patients in Wynn's study (207). Increases in SGOT levels tended to occur early in the course of treatment and were more pronounced when the drug dose exceeded 50 mg daily. Transaminase levels generally returned to normal rapidly upon cessation of drug administration and in many cases dropped to normal levels even when the drug and dosage were continued although more slowly. Although no obvious quantitative correlation was observed between increases in transaminase levels and BSP retention, the SGOT level generally was not elevated unless BSP retention was also raised. SGPT, an enzyme which may more closely signify hepatocellular damage has not been used extensively because it has only recently begun to be included in the typical liver enzyme profile.

Although Schaffner, Popper and Chesrow (162) have observed rare cases of jaundice in individuals without earlier significant increases in either serum bilirubin or alkaline phosphatase, elevations in these substances generally signify a more serious obstruction to bile excretion which in turn may secondarily lead to actual liver cell damage. In this study, in only four of 27 patients receiving 60 mg of norethandrolone (Nilevar) per day over three to five weeks was evidence of actual cholestasis found through liver biopsy. Sixty percent of the patients did exhibit increases in SGOT, and in those with evidence of cholestasis the levels were higher (180 units or higher) than in the rest. These authors indicated that when it occurred, jaundice could appear as early as two weeks after commencement of steroid administration and be quite severe or it could appear later and in a rather transient and mild form. Despite the absence of good correlations between the degree of cholestasis found by biopsy and any clinical or laboratory measures, 150 SGOT units was recommended as the level at which oral steroid administrations should cease.

Within the general guidelines as to the use of the fewest, simplest, most reliable and least expensive laboratory tests available for the protection of health, it is recommended that serum bilirubin, alkaline phosphatase and both transaminases (SGPT and SGOT) be evaluated periodically to assess the state of the liver exposed to anabolic steroids. It is difficult to specify critical (decision) levels for the entire population because of individual biochemical and physiological differences. It should be kept in mind that *no significantly abnormal value (for a given individual)* is okay. However, total bilirubin in excess of 2 mg/dl, transaminase or alkaline phosphatase evaluations above 150 units should result in cessation of oral drug use and a detailed clinical and laboratory follow-up. If only urine tests are to be done, the presence of bilirubin in the sample suggests the presence of conjugated hyperbilirubinemia which must be followed by a physical examination and complete blood workup.

No significant changes were found in most of the previously mentioned training studies which attempted to evaluate liver function changes in normal individual or trained athletes. Fowler, Gardner, and Egstrom (48), in a 16-week study with 20 mg methelone acetate/day, found no changes in transaminases, aldolase, or CPK in the 25 steroid-treated subjects during the last week of treatment. Stamford and Moffatt (173), although not reporting specific test results, indicated that 20 mg Dianabol/day for four weeks produced no significant changes in unspecified weekly tests of kidney and liver function in experienced weight trainers. Tahmindjis (182) also found no significant changes in transaminases or bilirubin in 20 athletes over an 18-month period during various portions of which time the athletes took steroids. Blood tests, however, were apparently conducted only at the end of the period of drug intake. Hervey and associates (65) found no changes in transaminases, alkaline phosphatase, plasma proteins, or bilirubin during the sixth week of administration of 100 mg Dianabol/day. Similarly, O'Shea (135) indicated that following five weeks of Winstrol administration at a dose of 8 mg/day, no effects on bilirubin, SGOT, alkaline phosphatase, total protein, or globulin were apparent in 18 college weightlifters. The results of Hagerman et al (56) indicated that no deleterious changes accompanied 12 weeks of Dianabol administration at a dose of 5 mg/day on a three-week-on, one-week-off schedule. Keul et al (85) found no deleterious effects of nandrolone deconoate (administered by injection) on 26 biochemical measurements, even in six weightlifters who had been using this drug for three years. However, they recorded elevations in transaminases, alkaline phosphatase, serum bilirubin and other tests for 31 athletes and three of their experimental group following the use of oral drugs, all of which reversed themselves after stopping the medication.

The trend of other reports suggests that changes were both mild

and infrequent. Freed et al (49) administering either 10 or 25 mg Di-
anabol/day for six weeks, found elevated transaminases in two of
their subjects. Levels in one other subject decreased spontaneously
with the result that normal enzyme levels were reattained within two
weeks. O'Shea and Winkler (136), giving 10 mg Anavar/day to three
weightlifters and eight swimmers, found a slight decrease in alkaline
phosphatase during the third week of drug administration which returned to baseline levels by the sixth and final week of drug use. No
changes were found in bilirubin, plasma proteins, or transaminases.
Johnson and O'Shea (81), however, in a three-week study of 12 untrained males using 5 mg Dianabol/day, found SGPT to be slightly
elevated although bilirubin and alkaline phosphatase decreased.
Ljungqvist (108), reporting on steroid use among top Swedish athletes, indicated that there had been elevations of the transaminases
in "some" of the athletes responding to a questionnaire. Shephard,
Killinger and Fried (170) collected blood chemistry data on six
bodybuilders who had been taking Dianabol at dosages from 10–20
mg/day for some weeks. Two of the six exhibited slight increases in
SGOT levels and one other (aged 52) had elevated alkaline phosphatase values.

Transaminase elevations seem to be the most commonly observed aberrations during the training studies. Where raw data have
been reported, the aberrant values usually range upwards of two to
three times normal. The significance of the steroid-induced changes
had been extensively discussed, but without agreement (137, 171).
While the levels of these enzymes may be increased ten to twenty
fold in cases of severe liver diseases, even deviations of lesser magnitude cannot be considered insignificant.

Transient changes in transaminase levels, ultrastructural changes
and fluctuation in alkaline phosphatases and bilirubin are seen after
the administration of many drugs, including oral contraceptives, anti-
inflammatories, anti-hypertensive medications, and high alcohol consumption. According to Orlandi and Jezequel (137), the occurrence of
these "silent" functional changes has been documented in 10 to 40
percent of patients, while in only 0.1 to 0.5 percent does the condition
degenerate to the point of jaundice. Any simplified extrapolation of the
minor changes to a level of toxicological significance is thus unjustified
(137). The fact that the changes in BSP retention and transaminase
levels usually disappear in spite of continued drug treatment suggest
that adaptive phenomena are occurring in the liver. Since fluctuations
in serum enzyme levels may be found even in untreated, apparently
normal persons, Sherlock (171) contends that it is extremely difficult to
assess the significance of these reactions in individuals taking various
drugs. It is interesting that in the study of Strauss et al (179) athletes
training intensively with weights had elevated transaminase levels
whether they were taking steroids or not. The effects of oral anabolic

drugs on the liver appear to resemble those accompanying the use of oral contraceptives (28, 38, 88, 138, 186). Oral activity of both androgens and estrogens is achieved by means of 17 alphaalkylation, and the structural similarity strongly suggests the possibility of some shared metabolic effects.

Oral steroids have also been increasingly implicated in two other extremely serious conditions, peliosis hepatis and liver tumors. Cases of peliosis hepatis associated with anabolic steroids have been reviewed extensively (23, 125) and continue to be reported (112, 169, 184). The pathogenesis of this disorder is not definitely established. Apparently, as intrahepatic cholestasis develops, and the liver cells become unable to excrete conjugated bilirubin and organic anions into the bile ducts, bilirubin accumulates within the liver cells, some of which ultimately is excreted into the liver sinusoids. This results in the so-called "feathery degeneration" of various areas of the liver cells including the endothelial lining of the sinusoids which in turn allows blood to escape into spaces created by the degeneration of liver cells (162).

Peliosis hepatis can develop in either sex and at any age as a result of oral steroid administration. At present, the relationship between the dose or duration of therapy and the occurrence of this disease is unclear. The liver is usually enlarged and tenderness may signal the onset of this complication which often terminates with liver failure. Most cases of peliosis hepatis have been fatal, although recovery has been reported following surgical intervention and cessation of steroid use. It should be noted that the spaces created by liver cell degeneration as a secondary result of cholestasis are ultimately filled with diffusely deposited collagen suggesting the early stages of and potential for the development of cirrhosis.

Because of the overall similarity in structure and mechanism of action between anabolic and contraceptive steroids, it is worthwhile to be aware of the data linking this latter group of drugs to liver growth disturbances. Basically, the evidence linking contraceptive steroids to hepatocellular adenoma has become increasingly convincing since the report of Baum and co-workers in 1973 (16). This tumor was reported very infrequently prior to the wide introduction and use of contraceptive steroids and is now found almost exclusively in women during the reproductive period of life. The tumor has been shown to regress following cessation of contraceptive steroid use. Furthermore, the risk of developing hepatocellular adenoma increases as the duration of use of these drugs increases. In one study (153), the risk ratio was found to increase steadily with the length of contraceptive steroid use up to approximately a 500-fold increase in women using these drugs for 85 or more months. Use by women over age 30 and use of drugs with a high hormonal potency were found to further increase the likelihood of developing this condition. At least five reports have been published linking anabolic steroids with tumors interpreted as hepatocellular adenomas in males (19, 20, 74, 63, 140).

With regard to hepatocellular carcinoma occurring in association with anabolic steroid use, the average age at the time of diagnosis has been approximately 18 years with 70 percent of the patients having been males. The majority of patients had been treated for various types of anemia. The average latent period from the initiation of steroid therapy to the diagnosis of hepatocellular carcinoma was 72 months. The cases have been reviewed recently by Paradinas et al (140), and Ishak (74). According to Ishak, metastases occurred in 20 percent of the patients although in many cases the tumors regressed following cessation of steroid therapy.

One case of liver cancer in a young bodybuilder (26 years) has been recently reported (139). This is the only case on record at present of an otherwise healthy individual developing liver carcinoma.

Although the final word is by no means in with regard to anabolic drug use and liver cancer it is significant that the conclusions from one critical survey of the literature (163) as well as from recent experimental investigations (183, 209) suggest that the synthetic sex steroids ((both extrogens and androgens) act to *promote* tumor growth rather than to *initiate* their formation.

With regard to other forms of cancer, a role for male sex hormones has been implicated in skin cancer, prostrate cancer, and a form of kidney cancer known as Wilm's tumor. The occurrence of Wilm's tumor in association with anabolic steroid use was first reported in the scientific literature in 1977 as a clinical case history and autopsy findings on a 38-year-old male who had devoted himself to competitive body-building for some years and who had first sought treatment after many months of increasing left flank pain (5, 146). This individual had, according to persons "closely associated" with him, taken self-prescribed anabolic steroids over a number of years. Strangely, this extremely rare cancer had also struck another weight trained athlete and former Mr. America winner several years previously. In this case, however, close friends and relatives of the individual adamantly denied that he had ever used any drugs, and certainly not anabolic steroids. Since the disease is not only rare but usually associated with congenital anomalies and chromosome defects, the drawing of definitive conclusions as to the role of steroids in the etiology and pathogenesis of Wilm's tumor is not possible. The occurrence of the tumor might simply have been coincidental with the individual's use of steroids, if indeed such use did occur. However, whether or not the drugs initiated the tumor, their role in promoting the growth and metastasis of this nephroblastoma must remain a worrisome possibility.

With respect to other malignancies in humans, although there is as yet no clear cut data linking them to anabolic hormones, circumstantial evidence suggests that they may play a role, however small or indirect. Certain tumors, such as those in sexual tissues, including skin, are known to be hormone sensitive. Preliminary epidemiological studies of differences between males and females in melanoma growth and dissemination and survival rates ominously suggest that these tumors may well be androgen sensitive (148).

Anabolic steroids are generally contraindicated in cases of prostate cancer. The work of Noble (128, 129, 130, 131, 132) and others on prostate cancer in laboratory rats is worthy of note in this regard. Noble (129) reported in 1977 an occurrence of prostate cancer in 20 percent of Nb rats treated with testosterone propionate for long periods with visible lesions detected as early as the 17th week following the onset of hormone administration (129, 130). Drago and colleagues (33, 34) confirmed this occurrence in the same strain of rats while Pollard (144) observed the effect in 40 percent of his Albany-Wistar strain. In his 1982 review of the literature, Noble (132) reported testosterone treatment to be the only currently known means of producing prostatic cancer in any species of animal. In studies of female rats, Noble (128) has reported finding a type of papillary carcinoma of the breast in animals treated with a combination of androgen and estrogen and more recently (131) observed severe bladder lesions with stones in testosterone-treated animals.

Cardiovascular System

The effects of male hormones on levels of high density (alpha) lipoproteins (50, 117) and their association with susceptibility to atherosclerosis and coronary heart disease (149) suggest that long-term or excessive use of anabolic drugs is likely to be detrimental to cardiovascular health. Wynn (204) observed (pre) diabetes type symptoms including reductions in resting blood glucose levels, oral and intravenous glucose tolerance, hyperinsulinemia, and elevation of cholesterol and triglycerides in various patients on anabolic steroid therapy. Wynn and Doar and colleagues (205, 206, 208) have documented comparable effects in women receiving oral contraceptives. If the effects of oral androgen use on cardiovascular health in males are comparable to the effects of oral contraceptive use in woman, then the threat may potentially be quite serious.

The effects of short-term use (especially cyclical use) of anabolic drugs on blood lipid levels and on energy metabolism remain unclear as few training studies have monitored these parameters. O'Shea and Winkler (136) found no changes in cholesterol levels in three weightlifters or eight swimmers over an eleven-week period, during six of which the subjects received 10 mg/day of Anavar. Nor did they observe changes in blood glucose levels in subjects on the drug (values were rather low throughout), but they did observe a significant increase the third week after the subjects stopped taking the steroid. Johnson and O'Shea (81) found a decrease in plasma cholesterol of their control subjects and presumably no change for the group which took 5 mg Dianabol/day for three weeks. O'Shea (135) reported no difference in cholesterol between the placebo and the steroid group who had taken 8 mg Winstrol/day for five weeks. Shephard, Killinger and Fried (170) observed slight elevations in total cholesterol in two of six subjects and elevations in triglycerides in one. More recent studies suggest that self-administered androgens (athletes) may produce large decreases in HDL-C and increases in LDL-C and total cholesterol (73). Similar reductions have been noted in HDL-C and increases in LDL in rats (106). Interestingly, anaerobic training reduced these effects (106). Elevated estrogen levels, it should be noted, have also been linked with adverse lipoprotein profiles (115). Changes in the concentration of several blood clotting factors induced by both male and female sex steroids agents may also have adverse implications for cardiovascular health.

Also possibly predisposing to atherosclerosis, according to Troxler et al (188), are increased levels of cortisol. Oral anabolic drugs may lead to higher levels of cortisol, possibly due to inhibition of cortisol, catabolism by the liver (78). Hervey et al (65) have reported dramatic elevations in both serum and urinary cortisol levels following their experiment. This phenomena could be related to the elevated blood pressures occasionally observed in steroid users (49), although Hervey et al (65) did not observe this.

Messerlli and Frohlich (116) suggest that in humans, as Wexler (196) has for rats, that anabolic drugs may increase blood pressure by means of a direct inhibition of 11-beta hydroxylation and consequent overproduction of deoxycorticosterone by the adrenal cortex. Elevations in blood pressure may also occur due to an increase in blood volume or fluid retention which may result from direct anabolic hormone effects on the kidney and/or hematopoietic system, or indirectly through their conversion to estrogen and their subsequent effects on the adrenal hormone levels. These data, coupled with reports implicating 17 alphaalkylated androgen in hypertensive disease, atherosclerosis, and nephrosclerosis in rats (118, 159, 172, 196), have further significant implications regarding the threat of anabolic hormones to cardiovascular and overall health.

Direct effects on myocardium may also occur. Cardiac muscle of rats (101) and primates (114) has recently been found to contain specific androgen receptors in concentrations that substantially exceed those found in skeletal muscle. It has been shown that anabolic steroids can produce myocardial hypertrophy (127) including increases of specific contractile proteins in dogs (191).

Ultrastructural changes suggesting pathologies have also been noted. These changes have included an increase in non-myofibrillar cytoplasmic filaments (17), cells with extended sarcoplasmic spaces containing many lysosomes, an increase in cells showing signs of mitochondriolysis, myofibrillolysis, destruction of intercalated discs, intracellular edema (6, 194) and fibrosis (7). While Behrendt and Boffin (7) could not find increased cellular lesions during the later stages of anabolic steroid treatment, they suggest that the disintegration of contractile proteins could represent loci of "low resistance" within the working heart, possibly leading to more severe lesions under additional stress. The progressive activation of myocardial cells by training (additional stress) and anabolic steroid administration may have led to the mitochondrial and myofibrillar destruction noted by Appell et al (6) in trained guinea pigs.

While androgen use implies increased cardiovascular disease (CVD) risk there is as yet no direct link between androgens and CVD. The authors are aware of cases of nonfatal myocardial infraction (MI) in athletes admittedly taking large doses of androgens for extended periods. It should be noted that there have been cases of nonfatal MI (58) and sudden death (110) among young male athletes who were not known to be using any drugs. This raises the possibility of overtraining/overstress, congenital defects or as yet unknown factors as being the precipitating cause. Regardless, the apparent effects of androgens on cardiovascular disease risk factors are ominous.

Reproductive System

Although anabolic-androgenic steroids can dramatically improve sexual function and reproductive capability in individuals deficient in natural hormone, these drugs can elicit opposite reactions in normal healthy males. The majority of these drugs may, depending upon the dose and duration of use, reduce total blood testosterone and gonadotrophin levels, testes size, sperm quality and production, and libido (42, 61, 65, 70, 77, 80, 150, 170, 178). The administration of androgens to animals (rats) has produced similar results including reduced gonadotrophin levels and testis weight (176) and reductions in testosterone in both male and females (197). Anaerobic training partially mutes the reduction in female, but not male, rats (197).

Too little evidence is currently available to make definitive statements as to exactly whether, to what extent and how these changes occur in athletes. Speculating on the basis of our personal observations, it seems that the more androgenic, the higher the dose and the longer a drug is used, the more likely is the occurrence of these physiological changes. In normal males, as an example, weekly injections of testosterone enanthate (200 mg)—a dose that produces moderately elevated integrated blood levels of testosterone—suppress both lutenizing and follicle stimulating hormone levels by approximately 50 percent. Spermatogenesis may be significantly (97%) but not completely suppressed at these dose levels (181). Administration of chorionic gonadotrophin, however, can apparently reverse the inhibitory effects of testosterone administration on spermatogenesis (61). Mauss et al. (111) using a dose of 250 mg testosterone enanthate per week for 22 weeks observed similar decreases in spermatogenesis within the initial nine week period. Recovery of spermatogenesis did not occur until 13 weeks after cessation of steroid administration, half the time required for recovery from eight to 17 weeks of norethandrolone administration (61). Changes in sperm motility and the percentage of normal sperm morphology generally paralleled those of concentration while the average semen volume, libido and potency remained unaffected. Sexual interest itself is quite variable and may increase, decrease and change during the period of drug administration. Initially, libido generally tends to increase although high doses and more potent androgens appear to elicit the most pronounced responses.

Miscellaneous Effects

The appearance and progressive development of male secondary sex characteristics is the most visibly obvious consequence of the use of anabolic steroids in young males and especially in females. These effects are manifested almost exclusively in the skin or its derivatives. The specific drug (strong androgenic drugs are more potent in this respect), dosage, and particularly the duration of use are predominant factors influencing the manifestation of such factors as: deepening of the voice; changes in hair growth patterns on the head, face, and genital area as well as over the chest, back, and arms and legs; acne; enlargement of the penis or clitoris and changes in fat distribution including a reduction in breast size in women. Women often experience disruption of menstrual cycle.

Steroids may stimulate precocious development of the whole body (macrogenitosomia precox). While short-term steroid therapy may be of value in specific cases in children, special care must be taken, since the steroids may diminish ultimate adult height by causing premature epiphyseal closure if used before the skeleton matures completely (30).

In mature males, steroid therapy can lead to increased facial and body hair, increased sebaceous secretions and thus indirectly to acne, priapism, deepening of the voice, alopecia, inhibition of the waves of hair growth, general thinning of scalp hair (72), and prostatic hypertrophy (103). Of these phenomena, only acne had been reported (in two subjects, 49) as a result of steroid use in any of the training studies.

In women, the first signs of virilization are usually oily skin, hoarsening and deepening of the voice, increased facial and body hair, and changes in libido (72, 207). The somatic changes appear to be greater in younger women. The changes most commonly observed are described as idiopathic hirsuitism (primary cutaneous virilism because the symptoms are localized in the skin, i.e., increased sebum production, increases in skin thickness, increased collagen content and increased sweat response to cholinergic stimulation) (72). The hirsuitism, male pattern baldness, voice changes and clitoral enlargement are usually not reversible even after prompt discontinuance of therapy; nor will the use of estrogen in combination with androgens prevent this virilization from occurring in females (103).

The following miscellaneous effects have also been reported, or observed in our laboratories, in studies of patients (103) and/or athletes (203): gastrointestinal disorders (restricted to the oral drugs); skin rash or local reaction at the site of infection; muscle cramps and spasms; headaches; nosebleeds during heavy exercises, particularly squat and dead lifts; dizziness, faintness, drowsiness or lethargy, sore nipples, gynecomastia, alterations in tests of thyroid and pituitary function test, insomnia, scrotal pain, increased incidence and severity of muscle and, particularly, connective tissue injuries; alterations in the immune system (103), and in the incidence of mild infectious disease (particularly following the cessation of steroid administration). Disturbance of the immune system, along with the possible disruption of normal rhythms of hormone secretion caused by steroid use, have potentially serious long-term implication for tumor development, overall health and the aging process (13, 36, 37, 100, 122, 154, 166, 167, 187).

The effects of anabolic steroids on personality, mood and behavior appear to be highly significant in many well-trained athletes, yet they have not been well-evaluated in a controlled experimental setting. Athletes of both sexes are said to report often dramatic changes, particularly in response to higher dosages and more androgenic drugs (185, 203; see also 179). The subjective reports describe increased feelings of "aggression and training drive" but included more frequent and unexplained mood swings (156). Such effects, although not yet scientifically confirmed, are not surprising given the relationship of sex hormones to brain electrical activity (95, 76), hormone and neurotransmitter release, (69, 145, 158), and to mood and behavior (113, 164). In a recent observation at Auburn University, weightlifters and powerlifters taking androgens showed increased anger and hostility and total mood disturbance (as measured by the Profile of Moods States Test) than lifters, long distance runners or controls not taking androgens (156).

Summary

Thus, just as the ultimate anabolic potential of these drugs is unknown, so, frighteningly, are the potential, and especially long-term, hazards. The oral drugs are known to be associated with a variety of aberrations in organ function and energy metabolism in patients and have been implicated in several potentially fatal complications. The liver and cardiovascular system particularly appear to be at risk. The different physiological status of young healthy individuals and athletes coupled with low doses and short durations used in the training studies preclude the drawing of definitive conclusions concerning health risks under these circumstances. However, elevations of blood pressure and disturbances of liver function were noted even in these studies. The injectable compounds appear to be safer than the oral drugs (59).

Both the available and unavailable data (concerning long-term effects) have led the American College of Sports Medicine to formulate (3) and update (4) a policy statement concerning the risk-benefit ratio of anabolic hormone use. The report concludes that, although benefits may be obtained in some cases or by some persons, for the majority of individuals any benefits are not likely to be worth the health risks involved. Despite such pronouncements and recommendations, the influx of money into sports converting them to the status of a business or an entertainment and the elevated social status of the athlete seem to be far more influential factors in shaping the athlete's perspective on ergogenic drug risk-benefit ratios. Value systems obviously cannot be dictated in a free society because, rather than eradicating use, the various educational and preventive measures instituted seem to have been effective only in curtailing drug use to a degree, if at all, and driving it further underground. Whether we like it or admit it, we live in an era of situational ethics in which the high personal and financial stakes involved and the winner-take-all pattern of compensation encourage the use of all available methods of "bio-engineering" irrespective of the ethics of cheating or of any threat to health.

These attitudes are not unique to the ranks of professionals. In fact the filtering of drug use habits down to amateur levels may be the most insidious and ominous aspect of this entire issue. Thus it is important to present the young athlete with an appropriate role model. Also alarming are our observations on the development of psychological dependencies on these drugs. The effects on mood, though relatively well known in patients, have been poorly studied. Many athletes, regardless of the presence or absence of competitive ambitions, increase the doses and durations of drug use in an ever escalating spiral of abuse.

Proposed Goals
Goal: Improve performance (safely)
    Protect health
    Protect future of "amateur" sports
    Promote equality and fair play to the maximum extent possible

Figure 5

Given the scope of the national and international problem of drug use and abuse, many question whether any realistic solution to the problem in athletics is possible. While sports federations and health professionals are doing their utmost to prevent the misuse of drugs in sports, there are others who suggest that expert-controlled conditioning by drugs in professional athletics would be less detrimental than the current pattern of unsupervised and clandestine self-administration. An editorial comment in the Medical Journal of Australia (1:984, 1976) addressing this issue suggested that anabolic drug use may ultimately be compared to cosmetic surgery, i.e., an unnecessary procedure, the risks of which the fully aware patient willingly accepts in return for any anticipated benefits.

Regardless of one's perspective, we are faced with a serious problem which demands more interest and attention, both philosophical and scientific. If the public and government are concerned with equality and fair play as well as with the health of athletes and the future of sports, then comprehensive research studies must be undertaken on national and, if possible, international levels to conclusively

Achieving the Goal:
Develop short and long term plans and policies.
Requires commitment, compromises and attitude changes on the part of all—athletes/coaches/trainers, scientists, and physicians.
Assist, conduct or cooperate on nationally (internationally?) coordinated interdisciplinary series of scientific investigations to resolve as expeditiously as possible outstanding/controversial issues.
Recognize and discourage misuse and abuse of drugs of any kind.
Provide education to athletes—a balanced, objective assessment of current medical/scientific and empirical findings regarding drug and effects.
Avoid drug use in our own teaching and performance framework.
All these steps are neccessary to bridge the gap in credibility and to build/restore the mutual respect and confidence among all elements of the sports community that are essential for the coordinated efforts required for reaching our objectives.

Figure 6

determine the efficacy and hazards of the multitude of physical and chemical treatments currently being used or considered by athletes (Figures 5 and 6).

References

1 Albrecht, H., & Albrecht, E. 1969. Ergometric, rhenographic, reflex-ographic, and electrocardiographic tests at altitude and effects of drugs on human physical performance. *Federation Proceedings* 28:1262–1267.

2 Alen, M., Hakkinen, H., & Komi, P.V. 1984. Changes in neuromuscular performance and muscle fiber characteristics of elite power athletes self-administering androgenic and anabolic steroids. *Acta Physiologica Scandinavica* 122:535–544.

3 American College of Sports Medicine. 1977. Position statement on the age and abuse of anabolic-androgenic steroids in sports. *Medicine and Science in Sports* 9:xi–xiii.

4 American College of Sports Medicine. 1984. Position stand on the use of anabolic-androgenic steroids in sports. *Sports Medicine Bulletin* 19: 13–18.

5 Antunes, C.M.F., & Stolley, P. D. 1977. Cancer induction by exogenous hormones: Possible androgen-induced cancer. *Cancer* 39:1896–1898.

6 Appell, H., Heller-Umpfenbach, B., Feraud, M., & Weicker, H. 1983. Ul-trastructural and morphometric investigations on the effects of training and administration of anabolic steroids on the myocardiam of guinea pigs. *International Journal of Sports Medicine* 4:268–274.

7 Arnold, A. P. 1984. Androgen regulation of motor neuron size and number. *Technology in Neural Sciences* 7:239–242.

8 Ariel, G. 1973. The effect of anabolic steroid upon skeletal muscle con-tractile force. *Journal of Sports Medicine and Physical Fitness* 13: 187–190.

9 Ariel, G. 1974. Residual effect of an anabolic steroid upon isotonic mus-cular force. *Journal of Sports Medicine and Physical Fitness* 14:103–111.

10 Ariel, G. 1974. Prolonged effects of anabolic steroid upon muscular con-tractile force. *Medicine and Science in Sports* 6:62–64.

11 Ariel, G., & Saville, W. 1972. Anabolic steroids: The physiological effects of placebos. *Medicine and Science in Sports* 4:124–126.

12 Ariel, G., & Saville, W. 1972. Effect of anabolic steroids on reflex compo-nents. *Journal of Applied Physiology* 32:795–797.

13 Bajusz, E. (Ed.). 1969. *Physiology and Pathology of Adaptation Mecha-nisms*. London: Pergamon Press.

14 Balieu, E. E., & Robel, P. 1970. Catabolism of testosterone and an-drostenedione. In K. B. Eik-Nes (Ed.). *The Androgens of the Testis*. New York: Marcel Dekker.

15 Barfield, R. J., & Chappelle, T. C. 1972. Gonadal influence on agonistic behavior in the male domestic rat. *Hormones and Behavior* 3:247–260.

16 Baum, J.K., Holtz, F., Bookstein, J.J., & Klein, F.W. 1973. Possible asso-ciation between benign hepatomas and oral contraceptives. *Lancet* 2:926–929.

17 Behrendt, H. 1977. Effect of anabolic steroids on rat heart muscle cells, I. Intermediate Filaments. *Cell Tissue Research* 180:303–315.

18 Behrendt, H. & Boffin, H. 1977. Myocardial cell lesions caused by an anabolic hormone. *Cell Tissue Research* 181:423–426.

19 Bird, D. R., & Vowles, K.D.J. 1977. Liver damage from long-term methyl-testosterone. *Lancet* 2:400–401.

20 Boyd, P. R., & Markes, G. J. 1977. Multiple hepatic adenomas and hepatocellular carcinoma in a man on methyltestosterone for eleven years. *Cancer* 40:1765–1770.

21 Boris, A. Stevenson, R. H., & Trmai, T. 1970. Comparative androgenic, myotrophic and antigonadotrophic properties of some anabolic steroids. *Steroids* 15:61–71.

22 Bowers, R. W., & Reardon, J. P. 1972. Effects of methandrostenolone (Dianabol) on strength development and aerobic capacity. *Medicine and Science in Sports* 4:54.

23 Boyer, J. L. 1978. Androgenic-anabolic steroid-associated peliosis hepatis in man: A review of 38 reported cases. *Advances in Pharmacy and Therapeutics* 8:175–184.

24 Casner, S. W., Jr., Early, R. G., & Carlson, B. B. 1971. Anabolic steroid effects on body composition in normal young men. *Journal of Sports Medicine and Physical Fitness* 11:98–103.

25 Celajowa, I. & Homa, M. 1970. Food intake, nitrogen and energy balance in Polish weightlifters during training camp. *Nutrition and Metabolism* 12:259–274.

26 Cheek, D. B., Brasel, J. A., & Graystone, J. E. 1968. Muscle cell growth in rodents. Sex differences and the role of hormones. In D.B. Cheek (Ed.). *Human Growth.* Philadelphia: Lea and Febiger.

27 Crist, D. M., Stackpole, P. J., & Peake, G. T. 1983. Effects of androgenic-anabolic steroids on neuromuscular power and body composition. *Journal of Applied Physiology* 54:366–370.

28 Contostavios, D. L. 1973. Benign hepatomas and oral contraceptives. *Lancet* 2:1200.

29 Dahlmann, B., Widjaja, A., & Reinauer, H. 1981. Antagonistic effects of endurance training and testosterone on alkaline proteolytic activity in rat skeletal muscle. *European Journal of Applied Physiology* 46:229–235.

30 Daniel, W. A., Jr., & Bennett, D. L. 1976. The use of anabolic-androgenic steroids in childhood and adolescence. In C.D. Kochakian (Ed.). *Anabolic-Androgenic Steroids.* New York: Springer-Verlag.

31 David, K., Dingemanse, E., Freud, J., & Lacqueur, E. 1935. Uber Krystallinsches mannliches Hormon aus Hoden (testosteron). Wirksamer als aus Harn oder aus Cholesterni bereitetes Androsteron. *Zeitschrift fur Physiologische Chemie* 233:281–282.

32 Doering, C. H., Kraemer, H. C., Brodie, H.K.H., & Hamburn, D. A. 1975. A cycle of plasma testosterone in the human male. *Journal of Clinical Endocrinology and Metabolism* 40:492–500.

33 Drago, J. R. Nb rat prostatic carcinoma model. 1983. *Prostate Cancer Newsletter* 10:4–5.

34 Drago, J. R., Goldman, L. B., & Gershwin, M. E. 1980. Chemotherapeutic and hormonal considerations of the Nb rat prostatic car-

cinoma model. In Murphy, C. P. (Ed.). *Models for Prostatic Cancer*, A. R. Liss, Inc., New York.

35 Edgerton, B. R., Garhammer, J. J., Simpson, D. R., & Compion, D. S. 1979. Case studies of competitive weightlifters taking anabolic steroids. Proceedings of the Soviet-American Symposium. Leningrad, September 18–22.

36 Eitinger, L. 1964. *Concentration Camp Survivors in Norway and Israel.* Second Edition, The Hague: Martinus Nijhoff.

37 Eitinger, L., & Strom, A. 1973 *Mortality and Morbidity after Excessive Stress: A Follow-up Investigation of Norwegian Concentration Camp Survivors.* New York: Humanities Press.

38 Emerson, Q. B., Nacntnebel, K. L., Penkava, R. R., & Rothenburg, J. 1980. Oral contraceptive-associated liver tumors. *Lancet* 1:1251.

39 Evans, W. J., & Ivy, J. L. 1982. Effects of testosterone propionate on hindlimb immobilized rats. *Journal of Applied Physiology* 52:1643–1647.

40 Exner, G. U., Staudte, H. W., & Pette, D. 1973. Isometric training rats—effects upon fast and slow muscle and modification by an anabolic hormone (nandrolone decanoate). I. Female rats. *Pflugers Archiv* 345:1–13.

41 Exner, G. U., Staudte, H. W., & Pette, D. 1973. Isometric training of rats—effects upon fast and slow muscle and modification by an anabolic hormone (nandrolone decanoate). II. Male rats. *Pflugers Archiv* 345:14–22.

42 Fahey, T. D., & Brown, C. H. 1973. The effects of an anabolic steroid on the strength, body composition and endurance of college males when accompanied by a weight training program. *Medicine and Science in Sports* 5:272–276.

43 Forbes, G. B. 1973. Another source of error in the metabolic balance method. *Nutrition Reviews* 31:297–300.

44 Forbes, G. B. 1983. Some influences on lean body mass: Exercise, androgens, pregnancy, and food. In P. L. White & T. Mondeika (Eds.). *Diet and Exercise Synergism in health maintenance.* Chicago: American Medical Association.

45 Forbes, G. B. 1985. Body composition as affected by physical activity and nutrition. *Federation Proceedings* 4:343–347.

46 Forbes, G. B. 1985. The effect of anabolic steroids on lean body mass: The dose response curve. *Metabolism* 34:571–573.

47 Fowler, V. R. 1976. Some aspects of the use of anabolic steroids in pigs. *Environmental Quality and Safety* 51:(Supplement), 109.

48 Fowler, W. M., Jr., Gardner, G. W., & Egstrom, G. H. 1965. Effect of an anabolic steroid on physical performance of young men. *Journal of Applied Physiology* 20:1038–40.

49 Freed, D.L.J., Banks, A. J., Longson, D., & Burley, D. M. 1975. Anabolic steroids in athletics: Crossover double-blind trial on weightlifters. *British Medical Journal* 2:471–473. (See also: Freed, D.L.J. & Banks, A. J. 1975. A double-blind crossover trial of methandienone [Dianabol, CIBA] in moderate dosage on highly trained experienced athletes. *British Journal of Sports Medicine* 9:78–81.)

50 Furman, R. H., Howard, P. R., Norcia, L. N., & Keaty, C. E. 1958. The influence of androgens, estrogens, and related steroids on serum lipids and lipoproteins. *American Journal of Medicine* 24:80–97.

51 Gardner, F. H., & Pringle, J. C. 1961. Androgens and erythropoiesis. *Archives of Internal Medicine* 107:112–128.

52 Golding, L. A., Freydinger, J. E., & Fishel, S. S. 1974. Weight, size and strength—unchanged with steroids. *Physician and Sports Medicine* 2:39–43.

53 Gontzea, I. 1974. The influence of muscular activity on nitrogen balance and on the need of man for proteins. *Nutrition Reports International* 10:35–43.

54 Gontzea, I. 1975. The influence of adaptation to physical effort on nitrogen balance in man. *Nutrition Reports International* 11:231–236.

55 Guezennec, C. Y., Ferre, P., Serrurier, B., Merino, D., Aymond, M., & Pesquies, P. C. 1984. Metabolic effects of testosterone during prolonged physical exercise and fasting. *European Journal of Applied Physiology* 52:300–304.

56 Hagerman, F. C., Jones-Witters, P., & Ransom, R. 1975. The effects of anabolic steroid ingestion on serum enzyme and urine 17-ketosteroid levels. *Journal of Sports Medicine and Physical Fitness* 15:287–295.

57 Hakkinen, K., & Komi, P. V. 1983. Electromyographic changes during strength training and detraining. *Medicine and Science in Sports and Exercise* 15:455–460.

58 Hanson, P. G., Vander Ark, C. R., Besozzi, M. C., & Rowe, G. G. 1982. Myocardial infarction in a national-class swimmer. *Journal of the American Medical Association* 248:2313–2314.

59 Haupt, H. A., & Rovere, G. D. 1984. Anabolic steroids—the facts. *Journal of Medical Technology* 1:553–557.

60 Heiztman, R. J. 1979. The efficacy and mechanism of action of anabolic agents as growth promoters in farm animals. *Journal of Steroid Biochemistry* 11:927–930.

61 Heller, C. G., Moore, D. J., Paulsen, C. A., Nelson, W. O., & Laidlaw, W. M. 1959. Effects of progesterone and synthetic progestins on the reproductive physiology of normal men. *Federation Proceedings* 18:1057–1065.

62 Heller, C. G., Morse, H. C., Sue, M., & Rowley, M. S. 1970. In E. Rosenbloom and C.A. Paulsen (Eds.). *Advances in Experimental Medicine and Biology, (The Human Testis)*, New York: Plenum.

63 Hernandes-Nieto, L., Bruguera, M., & Bombi, J. A. 1977. Benign liver cell adenoma associated with long-term administration of androgenic-anabolic steroid (methandienone). *Cancer* 40:1761–1764.

64 Hervey, G. R. 1975. Are athletes wrong about anabolic steroids? *British Journal of Sports Medicine* 9:74–77.

65 Hervey, G. R., Hutchinson, L., Knibbs, A. V., Burkinshaw, L., Jones, P.R.M., Noland, N. G., & Levell, M. J. 1976. "Anabolic" effects of methandienone in men undergoing athletic training. *Lanncet* 2:699–702.

66 Hervey, G. R., Knibbs, A. V., Burkinshaw, L., Morgan, D. B., Jones, P.R.M., Chettle, D. R., & Vartsky, D. 1981. Effects of methandienone on performance and body composition of men undergoing athletic training. *Clinical Science* 60:457–461.

67 Hickson, R. C., Hensner, W. D., Van Huss, D. E., Jackson, D. A., Jones, D. A., & Psaledas, A. T. 1976. Effects of dianabol and high-intensity

sprint training on body composition of rats. *Medicine and Science in Sports* 8:191–195.

68 Hickson, R. C., Hensner, W. D., Van Huss, D. E., Taylor, J. S., & Carow, R. E. 1976. Effects of an anabolic steroid and sprint training on selected histochemical and morphological observations in rat skeletal muscle types. *European Journal of Applied Physiology* 35:251–259.

69 Hollister, L. E., Davis, K. L., & Davis, B. M. 1975. Hormones in the treatment of psychiatric disorders. *Hospital Practice* 10:103–110.

70 Holma, P., & Adlercreutz, H. 1976. Effects of an anabolic steroid (Methandienone) on plasma LH-FSH and testosterone and on the response to intravenous administration of LHRH. *Acta Endocrinologica* 83:856–864.

71 Holma, P. 1977. Effect of an anabolic steroid (Methandienone) on central and peripheral blood flow in well trained male athletes. *Annals of Clinical Research* 9:215–221.

72 Houssay, A. B. 1976. Effects of anabolic-androgenic steroids on the skin, including hair and sebaceous glands. In C.D. Kochakian (Ed.), *Anabolic-Androgenic Steroids*. New York: Springer-Verlag.

73 Hurley, B. F., Seas, D. R., Hagberg, J. M., Goldberg, A. C., Ostrove, S. M., Holloszy, J. O., Wiest, W. G., & Goldberg, A. P. 1984. High density-lipoprotein cholesterol in bodybuilders and powerlifters (negative effects of androgens). *Journal of the American Medical Association* 252:507–513.

74 Ishak, K. G. 1979. Hepatic neoplasms associated with contraceptive and anabolic steroids. *Recent Results in Cancer Research* 66:73–128.

75 Itil, T. M., Cora, R., Akpinar, S., Herrmann, W. M., & Patterson, C. J. 1974. "Psychotropic" action of sex hormones: computerized EEG in establishing the immediate CNS effects of steroid hormones. *Current Therapeutic Research* 16:1147–1170.

76 Itil, T. M. 1976. Neurophysiological effects of hormones in humans: computer EEG profiles of sex and hypothalamic hormones. In E. J. Sachar (Ed.). *Hormones, Behavior and Psychotherapy* New York: Raven Press.

77 Jackson, H., & Jones, A. R. 1972. The effects of steroids and their antagonists on spermatogenesis. *Advances in Steroid Biochemistry and Pharmacology* 3:167–192.

78 James, V.H.T., Landon, J., & Wynn, V. 1962. Effect of an anabolic steroid (Methandienone) on the metabolism of cortisol in the human. *Endocrinology* 25:211–220.

79 Johnson, F. L. 1975. The association of oral androgenic-anabolic steroids and life threatening disease. *Medicine and Science in Sports* 7:284–286.

80 Johnson, L. C., Fisher, G., Silvester, L. J., & Hofheins, C. C. 1972. Anabolic steroid: Effects on strength, body weight, oxygen uptake and spermatogenesis. *Medicine and Science in Sports* 4:43–45.

81 Johnson, L. C. & O'Shea, J. P. 1969. Anabolic steroids: Effects on strength development. *Science* 164:957–959.

82 Johnson, L. C., Roundy, E. S., Allison, P. E., Fisher, A. B., & Silvester, L. J. 1975. Effect of anabolic steroid treatment on endurance. *Medicine and Science in Sports* 7:287–289.

83 Joslyn, W. D. 1973. Androgen-induced social dominance in infant female rhesus monkeys. *Journal of Child Psychology and Psychiatry* 14:137–145.

84 Kamen, G., Breedle, D., Brown, D., & Wilkerson, J. 1985. Muscle elec-

tromechanical properties following exercise training and anabolic steroid treatment in male and female rats. *Medicine and Science in Sports and Exercise* 17:195.

85 Keul, J., Deus, B., & Kindermann, W. 1976. Anabolic Hormone: Schadigung, Leistungsfahigkeit and Stoffwechsel. *Medizinische Klinik* 71:497–503.

86 Kilshaw, B. H., Harkness, R. A., Hobson, V. M., & Smith, A.W.M. 1975. The effects of large doses of the anabolic steroid, methandienone, on an athlete. *Clinical Endocrinology* 4:437–541. (See also: Harkness, R. A., Kilshaw, B. H., & Hobson, B. M. 1975. Effects of large doses of anabolic steroids. *British Journal of Sports Medicine* 9:70–73.)

87 Klatskin, G. 1977. Hepatic tumors: Possible relationship to use of oral contraceptives. *Gastroenterology* 73:386–394.

88 Knapp, W. A. & Ruebner, B. H. 1974. Hepatomas and oral contraceptives. *Lancet* 1:270–271.

89 Kochakian, C. D. 1935. The effect of male hormone on protein metabolism of castrate dogs. *Proceedings of the Society for Experimental Biology* 32:1064–1065.

90 Kochakian, C. D. 1950. Comparison of protein anabolic property of various androgens in the castrated rat. *American Journal of Physiology* 160:53–61.

91 Kochakian, C. D. 1976. (Ed.). *Anabolic-Androgenic Steroids*. New York: Springer-Verlag.

92 Kochakian, C. D. & Arimasa, N. 1976. The metabolism in vitro of anabolic-androgenic steroids by mammalian tissues. In C. D. Kochakian (Ed.). *Anabolic-Androgenic Steroids*. New York: Springer-Verlag.

93 Kochakian, C. D. & Beall, B. 1950. Comparison of protein anabolic property of testosterone propionate in the male and female rat. *American Journal of Physiology* 160:62–65.

94 Kochakian, C. D., Cohn, L., Quigley, E., & Trybalski, E. 1948. Effect of testosterone propionate on nitrogen and chloride excretion and body weight of castrated rats during recovery from fasting. *American Journal of Physiology* 155:272–277.

95 Kochakian, C. D. & Endahl, B. R. 1959. Changes in body weight of normal and castrated rats by different doses of testosterone propionate. *Proceedings of the Society for Experimental Biology and Medicine* 100: 520–523.

96 Kochakian, C. D., Moe, J. G., & Dolphin, J. 1950. Protein anabolic effect of testosterone propionate in adrenalectomized and normal rats. *American Journal of Physiology* 163:332–346.

97 Kochakian, C. D. & Murlin, J. R. 1935. The effect of male hormone on the protein and energy metabolism of castrate dogs. *Journal of Nutrition* 10:437–458.

98 Kochakian, C. D., Robertson, E., & Barlett, M. N. 1950. Sites and nature of protein anabolism stimulated by testosterone propionate in rats. *American Journal of Physiology* 163:322–346.

99 Kochakian, C. D. & Webster, J. A. 1958. Effect of testosterone propionate on the appetite, body weight and composition of the normal rat. *Endocrinology* 63:737–742.

100 Kositskiy, G. I. & Smirnov, V. S. 1972. The Nervous System and "Stress." (English translation of original 1970 Russian edition by Nauka.) Washington, D.C.: NASA.

101 Kreig, M., Smith, K., & Bartsch, W. 1978. Demonstration of a specific androgen receptor in rat heart muscle: Relationship between binding metabolism and tissue levels of androgens. *Endocrinology* 103: 1686–1694.

102 Kreuz, L. E., Rose, R. M., & Jennings, J. R. 1972. Suppression of plasma testosterone levels and psychological stress. A longitudinal study of young men in officer candidate school *Archives of General Psychiatry* 26:479–482.

103 Kruskemper, H. L. 1968. *Anabolic Steroids.* New York: Academic Press.

104 Lamb, D. R. 1984. Anabolic steroids in athletics: How well do they work and how dangerous are they? *The American Journal of Sports Medicine* 12:31–38.

105 Laritcheva, K. A., Valovarya, N. L., Shubin, V. L., & Smirnov, S. A. 1978. Study of energy expenditure and protein needs of top weightlifters. In J. Parizkova & V. A. Royozkin, (Eds.). *Nutrition, Physical Fitness, and Health. International Services on Sports Sciences.* Volume 7. Baltimore, University Park Press.

106 Leeds, E. M., Wilkerson, J. E., Kamen, G., Brown, G., & Bredle, D. 1985. The effect of anabolic steroids and anaerobic training on plasma lipoproteins and cholesterol in rats. *Federation Proceedings* 44:1372.

107 Levi, L. 1967. Emotional Stress. *Forvarsmedicin* 3:Supplement 2.

108 Ljungqvist, A. 1975. The use of anabolic steroids in top Swedish athletes. *British Journal of Sports Medicine* 9:82.

109 Loughton, S. J. & Ruhling, R. O. 1977. Human strength and endurance responses to anabolic steroid and training. *Journal of Sports Medicine and Physical Fitness* 17:285–296.

110 Maron, R. J., Roberts, W. C., McAllister, H. A., Rosing, D. R., & Epstein, S. E. 1980. Sudden death in young athletes. *Circulation* 62:218–229.

111 Mauss, J., Bovsch, G., Richter, E., & Bormacher, K. 1974. Investigations on the use of testosterone enanthate as a contraceptive agent. A preliminary report. *Contraception* 10:281–289.

112 McDonald, E. C. & Speicher, C. E. 1978. Peliosis hepatis associated with administration of oxymetholone. *Journal of the American Medical Association* 240:243–244.

113 McEwen, B. S. 1975. The brain as a target organ of endocrine hormones. *Hospital Practice* 10:95–104.

114 McGill, H. C., Jr., Anselmo, V. C., Buchanan, J. M., & Sheridan, P. J. 1980. The heart is a target organ for androgen. *Science* 207:775–777.

115 Mendoza, S. G., Osuna, A., Zerpa, A., Gartside, P. S., & Glueck, C. J. 1981. Hypertriglyceridemia and hypoalphalipo-proteinemia in azospermic and oligospermic young men: Relationships of endrogenous testosterone to triglyceride and high density lipoprotein cholesterol metabolism. *Metabolism* 30:481–486.

116 Messerli, F. H. & Frohlich, E. D. 1979. High blood pressure: A side effect of drugs, poisons, and food. *Archives of Internal Medicine* 139:682–687.

APPENDICES

117 Miller, G. J. & Miller, N. E. 1975. Plasma-high-density-lipoprotein concentration and development of ischaemic heart disease. *Lancet* 1:16–19.

118 Molteni, A., Brownie, A. C., & Skelton, F. R. 1969. Production of hypertensive vascular disease in the rat by methyltestosterone. *Laboratory Investigation* 21:129–137.

119 Moore, L. G., McMurtry, I. F., & Reeves, J. T. 1978. Effects of sex hormones on cardiovascular and hematologic responses to chronic hypoxia in rats. *Proceedings of the Society for Experimental Biology and Medicine* 158:658–662.

120 Moritani, T. & DeVries, H. 1979. Neural Factors versus hypertrophy in the time course of muscle strength gain. *American Journal of Physical Medicine* 58:115–130.

121 Morville, R., Pesquies, P. C., Guesennee, C. Y., Serrurier, B. D., & Guignard, M. 1979. Plasma variations in testicular and adrenal androgens during prolonged physical exercise in man. *Annals d'Endocrinologie* (Paris) 40:501–510.

122 Moss, G. E. 1973. *Illness, Immunity, and Social Interaction: The Dynamics of Biosocial Resonation.* New York: John Wiley & Sons.

123 Munson, A. R. 1970. Some effects of anabolic steroids during weight training. Unpublished Ed.D. Dissertation. University of Southern California.

124 Murad, F. & Haynes, R. C. 1980. Androgens and anabolic steroids. In A. Goodman, L. Goodman, & A. Gilman (Eds.). *The Pharmacological Basis of Therapeutics.* Sixth edition. New York, McMillan.

125 Nadell, J. & Kosek, J. 1977. Peliosis hepatis: Twelve cases associated with oral androgen therapy. *Archives of Pathology and Laboratory Medicine* 101:405–410.

126 Nesheim, M. C. 1976. Some observations on the effectiveness of anabolic agents in increasing the growth rate of poultry. (In F. C. Lu & J. Rendel Eds.). *Anabolic Agents in Animal Production* Stuttgart: Georg Thieme Publishing.

127 Neubauer, M. 1974. Hypertrophic desmyocards anaboler effekt auf hermuskel. *Sexualmedizin,* 11:599.

128 Noble, R. L. 1976. A new characteristic transplantable type of breast cancer in Nb rats following combined estrogen-androgen treatment. *Proceedings of the American Association for Cancer Research* 17:221.

129 Noble, R. L. 1977. The development of prostatic adenocarcinoma in Nb rats following prolonged sex hormone administration. *Cancer Research.* 37:1929–1933.

130 Noble, R. L. 1977. Sex steroids as a cause of adenocarcinoma of the dorsal prostate in Nb rats, and their influence on the growth of transplants. *Oncology* 34:138–141.

131 Noble, R. L. 1981. Progressive hyperplastic lesions of two bladder uroepithelium after hormone stimulation in Nb rats. *Investigations in Urology* 18:287–291.

132 Noble, R. L. 1982. Prostate carcinoma of the Nb rat in relation to hormones. *International Review of Experimental Pathology.* 23:113–159.

133 Olweus, D., Mattsson, Al, Schalling, D., and Lon, H. 1980. Testosterone, aggression, physical and personality dimensions in normal adolescent males. *Psychosomatic Medicine* 42:253–269.

134 O'Shea, J. P. 1971. The effects of anabolic steroids on dynamic strength levels of weightlifters. *Nutrition Reports International* 4:363–370.

135 O'Shea, J. P. 1974. Biochemical evaluation of the effects of stanozolol on adrenal, liver, and muscle function in man. *Nutrition Reports International* 10:381–388.

136 O'Shea, J. P. & Winkler, W. 1970. Biochemical and physical effects of an anabolic steroid in competitive swimmers and weightlifters. *Nutrition Reports International* 2:351–362.

137 Orlandl, F. & Jezequel, A. M. 1972. *Liver and Drugs.* New York: Academic Press.

138 O'Sullivan, J. P. & Wilding, R. P. 1974. Liver hematomas in patients on oral contraceptives. *British Medical Journal* 3:7–10.

139 Overly, W. L., Denkoff, J. A., Wong, B. K., & Singh, U. D. 1984. Androgens and hepatocellular carcinoma in an athlete (Letter to the Editor). *Annals of Internal Medicine* 100:158–159.

140 Paradinas, F. L., Bull, T. B., Westaby, D., & Murray-Lyon, L. M. 1977. Hyperplasia and prolapse of hepatocytes into hepatic veins during long-term methyl testosterone therapy: Possible relationship of these changes to the development of peliosis hepatis and liver tumors. *Histopathology* 1:225–246.

141 Payne, A. P. & Swanton, H. H. 1973. The effects of neonatal androgen administration on the aggression and related behavior of golden hamsters during interactions with females. *Journal of Endocrinology.* 58:627–636.

142 Pesquies, P. C., Morville, R., Guezennec, C. Y., & Serrarier, B. D. 1981. Effects of prolonged physical exercise on blood concentrations of adrenal and testicular androgens. In J. Poortmans and G. Niset (Eds.). *Biochemistry of Exercise IV-B.* Baltimore: University Park Press.

143 Phillips, G. B. 1977. Relationship between serum sex-hormones and glucose, insulin, and lipid abnormalities in men with myocardial infarction. *Proceedings of the National Academy of Sciences* 74:1729–1733.

144 Pollard, M. 1983. Investigations on prostate adenocarcinomas in rats. *Prostate Cancer Newsletter* 10:3–4.

145 Porter, J. C., Nansel, D. D., Gudelsky, G. A., Foreman, M. M., Pilotte, N. S., Parker, C. R., Burrows, G. H., Bates, G. W., & Madden, J. D. 1980. Neuroendocrine control of gonadotrophin secretion. *Federation Proceedings* 39:2896–2901.

146 Prat, J., Gray, G. F., Stolley, P. D., & Coleman, J. W. 1977. Wilms' tumor in an adult associated with androgen abuse. *Journal of the American Medical Association* 21:2322–2323.

147 Rada, R. T., Killner, R., & Winslow, W. W. 1976. Plasma testosterone and aggressive behavior. *Psychosomatics* 17:138–141.

148 Rampen, F.H.J., & Mulder, J. H. 1980. Malignant melanoma: An androgen-dependent tumor? *Lancet* 1:562–565.

149 Rhoads, G. G., Gulbrandsen, C. L., & Kagan, A. 1975. Serum Lipoproteins and coronary heart disease in a population study of Hawaiian Japanese men. *New England Journal of Medicine* 294:293–298.

150 Remes, K., Vuoplo, P., Jarvanen, M., Harkonen, M., & Aldercreutz, H. 1977. Effect of short-term treatment with an anabolic steroid (Methan-

dienone) and dehydrorepiandrosterone sulphate on plasma hormones, red cell volume, and 2, 3-diphosphoglycerate in athletes. *Scandinavian Journal of Clinical and Laboratory Investigation* 37:577–586.

151 Rogozkin, V. 1975. Anabolic and androgenic effects of methandrostenolone ("Nerobol") during systematic physical activity in rats. *British Journal of Sports Medicine* 9:65–69.

152 Rogozkin, V. & Feldkoren, B. 1979. The effect of Retabolil and training on activity of RNA polymerase in skeletal muscles. *Medicine and Science in Sports* 11:345–347.

153 Rooks, J. B., Ory, H. W., Ishak, K. G., Strauss, L. T., Greenspan, J. R., Hill, A. P., & Tyler, C. W. 1979. Epidemiology of hepatocellular adenoma. The role of oral contraceptive use. *Journal of the American Medical Association* 242:644–648.

154 Rose, R. M. 1969. Androgen responses to stress. 1. Psychoendocrine relationships and assessment of androgen activity. *Psychosomatic Medicine* 31:405–417.

155 Rose, R. M., Holady, J. W., & Bernstein, I. S. 1971. Plasma testosterone dominance rank and aggressive behavior in male rhesus monkeys. *Nature* 231:366–368.

156 Rozenek, E. 1985. Unpublished Ph.D. Dissertation. The Effects of an Acute Bout of Resistance Exercise and Self-Administered Anabolic Steroids on Plasma Levels of LH, Androgen, ACTH, Cortisol, Lactate, and Psychological Factors in Athletes, Auburn University.

157 Rozenek, K. & Stone, M. H. 1984. Protein metabolism related to athletes. *National Strength and Conditioning Association Journal* 6(2):42–62.

158 Sachar, E. J. 1975. Hormonal changes in stress and mental illness. *Hospital Practice* 10:49–55.

159 Salgado, E. & Selye, H. 1954. The production of hypertension, nephrosclerosis and cardiac lesions by methylandrostenediol treatment in the rat. *Endocrinology* 55:550–560.

160 Sanchez-Medal, L., Gomez-Leal, A., Duarte, L., & Rico, M. G. 1969. Anabolic androgenic steroids in the treatment of acquired aplastic anema. *Blood* 34:283–300.

161 Sar, M., & Stumpf, W. E. 1977. Androgen concentration in motor neurons of cranial nerves and spinal cord. *Science* 197:77–79.

162 Schaffner, F., Popper, H., & Chesrow, E. 1959. Cholestasis produced by the administration of norethandrolone. *American Journal of Medicine* 26:249–254.

163 Schappler, J. & Gunzel, P. 1979. Synthetic steroid sex hormones and liver tumors in experimental animals. *Advances in Pharmacology and Therapeutics* 8:159–168.

164 Schildkrautt, J. J. 1976. *Neuropharmacology and the Affective Disorders.* New York: Little, Brown & Co.

165 Seyle, H. 1956. *The Stress of Life.* New York: McGraw Hill.

166 Seyle, H. 1970. Stress and aging. *Journal of the American Geriatric Society.* 8:669–680.

167 Seyle, H. 1971. *Hormones and Resistance.* (2 volumes). New York: Springer-Verlag.

168 Shahidi, N. T. 1973. Androgens and erythropoiesis. *New England Journal of Medicine* 289:72–80.

169 Shapiro, P., Ikela, R. M., & Reubner, M. H. 1977. Multiple hepatic tumors and peloisis hepatis in Fanconi's anemia treated with androgens. *American Journal of Diseases of Children* 131:1105–1106.

170 Shephard, R. J., Killinger, D., & Fried, T. 1977. Responses to sustained use of anabolic steroid. *British Journal of Sports Medicine* 11:170–173.

171 Sherlock, S. 1972. Clinical techniques for the evaluation of therapeutic agents on the liver. In F. Orlandi and A. Jezequel (Eds.). *Liver and Drugs*. New York: Academic Press.

172 Skelton, F. R. 1953. The production of hypertension, nephrosclerosis and cardiac lesions by methylandrostenediol in the rat. *Endocrinology* 53:492–505.

173 Stamford, B. A. & Moffatt, T. 1974. Anabolic steroid: Effectiveness as an ergogenic aid to experienced weight trainers. *Journal of Sports Medicine and Physical Fitness* 14:191–197.

174 Steinbach, M. 1968. Uber den einfluss anoboler Wirkstoffe auf Korpergewicht, Mushelkraft and Muskeltraining. *Sportarzt und Sportmedizin* 19:485–592.

175 Stone, M. H. & Lipner, H. 1978. Responses to intensive training and methandrostenelone administration: I. Contractile and performance variables. *Pflugers Archiv* 375:141–146.

176 Stone, M. H., Rush, M. E., & Lipner, H. 1978. Responses to intensive training and methandrostenelone administration: II. Hormonal, organ weights, muscle weights and body composition. *Pflugers Archiv* 375:147–151.

177 Stone, N. H., & Lipner, H. 1980. Androgens and athletics. *Journal of Drug Issues* 10:351–359.

178 Stromme, S. B., Meen, H. D., & Aakvaag, A. 1974. Effects of an androgenic-anabolic steroid on strength development and plasma testosterone levels in normal males. *Medicine and Science in Sports* 6:203–208.

179 Strauss, R. H., Wright, J. E., Finermann, G.A.M., & Catlin, D. H. 1983. Side effects of anabolic steroids in weight trained men. *Physician and Sports Medicine* 11:86–98.

180 Stumpf, W. E., & Sar, M. 1976. Steroid hormone target sites in the brain: The differential distribution of estrogen, progestin, androgen and glucocorticosteroid. *Journal of Steroid Biochemistry* 7:1163–1170.

181 Swerdloff, R. S., Palacios, A., McClure, R. D., Compfield, L. A., & Bursman, S. A. 1978. In: *Proceedings of the Conference on Hormonal Control of Male Fertility*. Washington, D.C.: Department of HEW Publication, NIH 78–1097.

182 Tahmindjis, A. J. 1976. The use of anabolic steroids by athletes to increase body weight and strength. *Medical Journal of Australia.* 1:991–993.

183 Taper, H. S. 1978. The effect of estradiol-17-phenyl propionate and estradiol benzoate on n-nitrosomorpholine-induced carcinogenesis in ovariectomized female rats. *Cancer* 42:462–467.

184 Taxy, J. B. Peliosis: A morphologic curiosity becomes an iatrogenic problem. *Human Pathology* 9:331–340.

185 Taylor, W. N. 1982. *Anabolic Steroids and the Athlete.* Jefferson City, North Carolina: McFarland & Co.

186 Thalassinos, N. C., Lymberatos, C., Hadjioannou, J., & Gardikas, C. 1974. Liver cell carcinoma after long-term use of estrogen-like drugs. *Lancet* 1:270.

187 Timiras, P. S. 1972. *Development Physiology and Aging.* New York: MacMillan.

188 Troxler, R. G., Sprague, E. A., Albanese, R. A., Ruchs, R., & Thompson, A. J. 1977. The association of elevated plasma cortisol and early atherosclerosis as demonstrated by coronary

189 VanderWal, P. 1976. General aspects of the effectiveness of anabolic agents in increasing protein production in farm animals, in particular in bull calves. *Environmental Quality and Safety* (Suppl.)(5), 60–78.

190 Vida, J. A. 1969. *Androgens and Anabolic Agents. Chemistry and Pharmacology.* New York: Academic Press.

191 Voss, H. E. & Oertel, G. 1973. Androgene I. In A. Farah, H. Herken & A. D. Welch (Eds.). *Handbuch Experimental Pharmakologie* 35:359–580.

192 Vyskocil, F., Gutmann, E. 1977. Electrophysiological and contractile properties of the levator ani muscle after castration and testosterone administration. *Pflugers Archives* 368:104–109.

193 Ward, P. 1973. The effect of an anabolic steroid on strength and lean body mass. *Medicine and Science in Sports* 5:277–282.

194 Weicker, H., Hayle, H., Repp, B., & Kolb, J. 1982. Influence of training and anabolic steroids on the LDH isozyme pattern of skeletal and heart muscle fibers of guinea pigs. *International Journal of Sports Medicine* 3:90–96.

195 Weiss, V. & Muller, H. 1968. Zur frage der Beeinflussung des Krafttrainings durch anabole Hormone. *Schweizerische Zeitschrift fur Sportmedizin* 16:79–89.

196 Wexler, B. C. 1971. Pathophysiologic changes induced in arteriosclerotic and non-arteriosclerotic rats by methylandrostenediol. *Laboratory Investigation* 25:158–168.

197 Wilkerson, J. E., Leeds, E. M., Brown, G., Bredle, D., & Kamen, G. 1985. The effect of anabolic steroids and anaerobic training on plasma testosterone levels in male and female rats. *Medicine and Science in Sports and Exercise* 17:261.

198 Wilkerson, J. E., Leeds, E. M., Brown, G. D., Kamen, G., & Bredle, D. 1985. Anabolic steroid and exercise effects on muscle protein, water and contractile properties. *Aviation Space and Environmental Medicine* 56:500.

199 Williams, M. H. 1974. *Drugs and Athletic Performance.* Springfield, Illinois: Thomas.

200 Win-May, M. & Mya-Tu, M. 1975. The effects of anabolic steroids on physical fitness. *Journal of Sports Medicine and Physical Fitness* 15:266–271.

201 Wright, J. E. 1978. *Anabolic steroids and sports.* Natick, MA: Sports Science Consultants.

202 Wright, J. E. 1980. Anabolic steroids and athletic. In R. S. Hutton & D. I. Muller (Eds.). *Exercise and Sports Science Reviews* 8:149–202.

203 Wright, J. E. 1982. *Anabolic steroids and sports.* Volume II. Natick, MA: Sports Science Consultants.

204 Wynn, V. 1975. Metabolic effects of anabolic steroids. *British Journal of Sports Medicine* 9:60–64.

205 Wynn, V. & Doar, J.W.H. 1966. Some effects of oral contraceptives on carbohydrate metabolism. *Lancet* 2:715–719.

206 Wynn, V., Doar, J.W.H., & Mills, G. L. 1966. Some effects of oral contraceptives on serum-lipid and lipoprotein levels. *Lancet* 2:720–723.

207 Wynn, V., Landon, J., & Kawerau, E. 1961. Studies on hepatic function during methandienone therapy. *Lancet* 1:69–75.

208 Wynn, V., Mills, G. D., Doar, J. W., & Stokes, T. 1969. Fasting serum triglyceride, cholesterol and lipoprotein levels during oral contraceptive therapy. *Lancet* 2:756–760.

209 Yager, J. D. & Yager, R. 1980. Oral contraceptives steroids as promoters of hepatocarcinogenesis in female Sprague-Dauley rats. *Cancer Research* 40:3680–3685.

210 Young, M., Crookshank, H. R. & Ponder, L. 1977. Effects of an anabolic steroid on selected parameters in male albino rats. *Research Quarterly* 48:653–656.

■

A SELF-SCREENING EXAMINATION FOR THE MALE ATHLETE TAKING ANABOLIC STEROIDS,

by Anthony V. Maddalo, M.D.

The human body is a complex system of checks and balances, and drugs such as anabolic steroids can upset this balance and cause seemingly unrelated signs and symptoms. Athletes frequently experience discomforts while taking anabolic steroids, but because of a lack of medical knowledge, they may not attribute these signs and symptoms to the use of anabolic steroids. Furthermore, many athletes become confused when reading literature in this area because some articles regarding the use of steroids ignore their side effects while others dramatize their harmful effects. An alternative is to provide the athlete with enough information so that he may recognize for himself the effects steroids are having on his body. The purpose of this article is to present to the athlete the clinical signs and symptoms of some of the disorders caused by anabolic steroids.

If the athlete has one or more of the symptoms on the screening examination, he can refer to the appropriate paragraph indicated by Roman numerals for an explanation of how these symptoms relate to anabolic steroid use. However, the absence of these signs and symptoms does not preclude the possibility of an adverse effect which has no clinically noticeable signs.

A SCREENING EXAMINATION FOR THE MALE ATHLETE TAKING ANABOLIC STEROIDS

Part I. External Exam

A. Skin

1 Color ....
flushing (VIII), yellow tint (IV, VI)

2 Bruises ....
more frequent with minor injuries (III, VI)

3 Eruptions ....
usually on back (I)

4 Itching ....
in general (II, VI), after hot bath (VIII)

404

5 Sweating..
greatly increased with anabolics (IV)

6 Stretch marks.....................................
greater incidence than before anabolics (III)

B. Head

1 Face..
puffy or "moon" face (III)

2 Eyes ....
yellow (VI), red, irritated (II), blurred vision (IV)

3 Mouth..
bleeding from underside of tongue (VI)

4 Nose...
unprovoked bleeds (V), take longer to stop (VI)

C. Chest

1 Gynecomastia ....
female breast tissue over pectorals (VI)

2 Palpitations......................................
heart pounds heavily against chest (IV, V)

D. Abdomen

1 Mass...
left or right side (VI)

2 Flank pain ....
may radiate to back or groin (II)

3 Upper abd. pain ....
relieved by eating (II), after fatty meals (IV)

E. Genitals

1 Testes ....
decreased in size (X)

2 Pain ....
can be radiating from flank (II)

F. Extremities

1 Edema ....
swelling, usually at ankles (III, V, VI)

2 Joints..
swelling, pain, stiffness, usually in the hands (II)

3 Trembling ....
tremor or shaking, usually of hands (IV)

Part II. Internal Exam

A. General

1 Headaches ....
in morning at back of head (II, IV, V)

2 Fatigue ....
muscle weakness, tire easily (II, IV)

B. Cardiovascular

1 Blood Pressure ....
10 diastolic, 20 systolic at rest (II, III, V)

2 Heart rate...
7–10 beats/min. above normal (II, III, IV, V)

C. Nervous System

1 Hyperactivity ....
irritable, restless; insomnia (VII), psychotic (III)

2 Hypoactivity...
drowsy, apathetic (II), depressed (II, III, VII)

3 Lightheadedness ....
dizzy (IV, V)

D. Gastrointestinal

1 Vomiting ....
blood or coffee ground material (II, VI)

2 Stools...
bright red (II), black tarry (II), clay color (IV, VI)

3 Hemorrhoids ....
sometimes bleeding (VI)

E. Urogenital

1 Semen...
decrease in ejaculate volume (X)

2 Urination...
painful; small, frequent (IX)

3 Urine color...
brown (VI), red (II)

4 Urine "Bili-Labstix" Values*
       a. pH less than 5.......acid urine (II)

*"Bili-Labstix" are manufactured by Miles Laboratories and can be purchased without a pre-
scription.

b. ketones + ...(IV)
c. bilirubin + ...(IV, VI)
d. blood + + + ...(II) or normal after stress

I. ACNE

The androgenic effect of anabolic steroids can cause an increase in oil production by the sebaceous glands of the skin (1). As a result, large painful follicles may develop anywhere on the body, with a greater distribution on the back (2). As these follicles enlarge and subsequently burst, the skin will be perforated many times which will make it vulnerable to bacterial infection. Onset of infection will require appropriate medical treatment and cessation of anabolic steroids.

II. HYPERCALCEMIA

Anabolic steroids have been shown to inhibit calcium excretion and cause a subsequent increase in serum calcium (3). This increase can cause some of the common signs and symptoms of hypercalcemia. As calcium levels become elevated, the athlete may become weak and easily fatigued (3). Blood pressure will also rise and symptoms of hypertension may appear (4).

Severe hypercalcemia may lead to kidney stones (5), peptic ulcer (6), behavioral changes (7) and abnormal calcium deposits in the joints (8), eyes (9) and skin (10). Kidney stones are a serious problem because they can lead to permanent kidney damage (11). Symptoms may include severe flank pain radiating to the back or groin and blood in the urine. The danger period for kidney stone formation is not limited to the period of administration of anabolic steroids; in fact, the period just after anabolic drugs are stopped is when the highest concentration of calcium is passing through the kidneys. In addition, there is a greater incidence of kidney stone formation if the athlete is restricting his fluid intake, or is on a high protein diet. Both conditions promote kidney stone formation by creating acid urine.

A peptic ulcer may occur as a result of increased stomach acid secretion caused by high calcium levels. Peptic ulcers may be recognized by the passing of bloody or black, tarry stools, vomiting blood or coffee ground material or by a dull aching upper abdominal pain which is sometimes relieved by eating. As calcium levels increase, behavioral changes will be noticed either by the athlete or the people around him. He will become listless, drowsy, apathetic and depressed, and mental functions will be slow.

Although they are not very common, abnormal calcium deposits causing irritation and redness of the eyes, itching of the skin and swelling, numbness and pain around some joints have been attributed to hypercalcemia. The onset of any of the above symptoms requires increased fluid intake, cessation of anabolic drugs and prompt medical attention.

III. HYPERCORTISOLEMIA

Anabolic steroids have produced increased serum cortisol levels in men undergoing athletic training (12). This increase in cortisol is probably due to a decrease in the breakdown of cortisol by the liver. Because they have similar structures, anabolic steroids compete with cortisol for the pathway in the liver which deactivates both hormones (13). Moreover, 17α-alkylated anabolic steroids directly inhibit the main enzyme in this pathway, giving oral anabolics an added effect in the inhibition of cortisol metabolism.

Cortisol affects several systems of the human body. One of the effects is retention of salt and water by the kidneys, causing high blood pressure and edema. Cortisol also affects the central nervous system by creating behavior changes ranging from depression to psychotic behavior. In addition, metabolic changes in the subcutaneous fat and collagen tissues in the skin can result in abnormal fat deposits and a weakening or rupture of the dermis. These two conditions can cause a "moon" or puffy face and an increased incidence of stretch marks and bruises, respectively.

Although some of these individual signs and symptoms may be caused by conditions other than hypercortisolemia, as a group they are distinguishing characteristics of hypercortisolemia and should be brought to the attention of a physician.

IV. ALTERED CARBOHYDRATE METABOLISM

Anabolic steroids can have several effects on carbohydrate metabolism. In diabetic or pre-diabetic people, all anabolic steroids seem to decrease serum glucose levels, whereas only 17α-alkylated anabolic steroids have been shown to decrease serum glucose levels in the non-diabetic person (14, 15). The first effect is probably due to an increase in the body's sensitivity to insulin, making the initial amount of insulin more effective. If the initial glucose level is high, as in diabetes mellitus, the liver will not respond by deactivating insulin unless glucose levels approach normal. However, if glucose levels are normal, the liver will deactivate up to 40 percent of the circulating insulin in order to compensate for the increased sensitivity. This ability to deactivate insulin is altered by 17α-alkylated steroids, and abnormally low glucose levels may be unavoidable. Although this degree of hypoglycemia does not usually become symptomatic, symptoms of hypoglycemia should be recognized by the athlete. If the early signs such as sweating, trembling, palpitations, headaches, lightheadedness, or blurred vision should occur after periods of fasting, a physician should be consulted.

As a result of a decreased serum glucose, the body must mobilize fat as a source of energy (16). This increased fat mobilization may produce one of the following conditions. If an anabolic steroid is used, there will be a rise in serum-free fatty acids (FFA) due to an alteration of liver functions (17). However, if liver functions are not altered, as with the 19-nortestosterones, the liver will convert FFA into cholesterol and ketones. An increase in serum cholesterol levels increases the incidence of gall stones, which cause upper abdominal discomfort after fatty meals, cholestatic jaundice, and clay-colored stools. Ketones can cause abdominal cramps and will be present in the urine. In both cases, the increase in fat mobilization will lead to "fatty liver," which is the formation of fat globules in the liver, causing liver damage.

V. HYPERTENSION

Anabolic steroids can cause high blood pressure. The exact mechanism is not clearly understood; it may be that hypercalcemia and hypercortisolemia play a significant role in raising blood pressure. Although most cases result in little more than slightly elevated readings, several cases have been reported in which athletes have passed out due to hypertension (1).

Recording the actual blood pressure with a sphygmomanometer (blood pressure cuff) is the most accurate method the athlete has to detect hypertension. Recording blood pressures is not difficult for the properly instructed individual, and with the commercial availability of sphygmomanometers, it is quite convenient. This gives the athlete a reliable monitoring system for his blood pressure. However, if this is not possible, the athlete should be alerted to certain physical signs and symptoms of hypertension. Severe hypertension can result in morning headaches, palpitations, unprovoked nose bleeds, blurred vision, lightheadedness, and fainting. If any of these symptoms occur, a resting blood pressure should be recorded and compared to a pre-drug reading. If there is an increase of ten or more units in diastolic (bottom) number or an increase in twenty or more in the systolic (top) number, all anabolic drugs should be stopped and a physician should be consulted. A hypertensive crisis can lead to kidney damage or stroke.

VI. LIVER DYSFUNCTION

Nearly all oral anabolic steroids contain a 17α-alkyl group which increases their intestinal absorption and prevents their inactivation by the liver (18). Originally, this structural modification seemed to be an improvement in oral anabolic therapy. However, because of the abundance of reports citing the hepatotoxic effects of 17α-alkylated steroids (13, 19, 20, 21), they have virtually been abandoned as a mode of anabolic therapy. In the following section, hepatotoxic effects such as cholestatic jaundice, hepatoma, and peliosis hepatis will be discussed.

Cholestasis is the reduction of bile flow. Liver cells normally extract bile from the blood, concentrate it and send it to the gall bladder or intestine via small vessels in the liver. Oral anabolics have a toxic effect on these liver cells and inhibit their normal function (22). This causes an increase in bile in the blood and can cause yellow discoloration of the skin and eyes, itching, clay-colored stools, and a brown-colored urine that is positive for bilirubin. Continued toxic effects on these liver cells can lead to cell death and cirrhosis, which will impair normal liver functions.

One vital function of the liver is to produce some of the clotting factors of the blood. If they are not produced, prolonged nose bleeds, easy bruisability, and bleeding from the underside of the tongue may occur as signs of decreased clotting ability of the blood. Another vital function of the liver is the deactivation of estrogens from the adrenal gland. If this function is impaired, female breast development (gynecomastia) may occur (23). Furthermore, if liver functions are impaired for a long period of time, and cirrhosis becomes severe, congestion of the hepatic blood vessels will result. This obstruction of blood vessels can lead to an enlarged liver, enlarged spleen, edema, hemorrhoids, or vomiting of blood or coffee-ground material due to bleeding in the esophagus. This group of effects is known as portal hypertension.

Hepatoma, also known as hepatocellular carcinoma, may not be reflected in liver enzyme tests; however, the athlete will experience right abdominal pain and note a palpable mass in the same area. Most of the literature reports hepatoma in patients treated with oral anabolic steroids.

Peliosis hepatis is the formation of blood-filled cysts in the liver. These cysts result from dead liver cells blocking small veins in the liver, causing blood to pool behind the obstruction. These cysts may rupture and cause painful abdominal bleeding and possibly death; unfortunately, they usually cannot be detected by serum liver enzyme levels and must be diagnosed by a liver scan.

Bringing all these symptoms to the attention of a physician is critical. The symptoms described above are not early warning signs but rather signs of ongoing liver damage. Thus, cessation of anabolic steroids and immediate medical attention is necessary.

VII. BEHAVIORAL DISORDERS

Several types of behavioral changes have been attributed to anabolic steroid use. Anabolic steroids may cause an indirect increase in neurotransmitters in the central nervous system. This increase would have a stimulatory effect and could be responsible for the increased sexual drive, increased excitability, irritability, and insomnia seen during anabolic steroid therapy.

If there is an increased cortisol level, more drastic behavioral changes may be noticed. As mentioned in section III, the athlete may experience mood changes ranging from depression to psychotic behavior.

As mentioned in section II, hypercalcemia can also cause behavioral changes including listlessness, drowsiness, fatigue, and depression.

Of course, any combination of the above symptoms can occur and thus the underlying disease cannot be identified solely by the behavioral changes. Any severe changes should be brought to the attention of a physician so that further workup may be done.

VIII. POLYCYTHEMIA

Secondary polycythemia is the overproduction of red blood cells without any apparent demand for them (24). One of the primary therapeutic uses of anabolic steroids is the treatment of certain anemias (25). Anabolic steroids cause the secretion of a hormone that in turn stimulates the bone marrow to produce more red blood cells. In normal individuals, this may result in red blood cell counts well above normal (26). Polycythemia may result in flushing of the skin and an itching sensation after a hot bath or shower. Long-term elevation of red blood cell counts may increase the severity of the side effects and necessitate the discontinuation of anabolic therapy. If itching or flushing does occur, an occasional complete blood count (CBC) should be done by a physician to monitor the number of red blood cells.

IX. PROSTATIC ENLARGEMENT

There is strong evidence to suggest that the androgenic effect of anabolic steroids can cause benign hypertrophy of the prostate gland (27). Although the evidence regarding cancer of the prostate is not as convincing (28), this possibility must also be considered when evaluating the adverse effects of anabolic steroids. Although investigators vary in the reported incidence of steroid-induced prostatic hypertrophy, there is speculation that the hypertrophic effect is dose related.

Enlargement of the prostate may cause several distinct signs. The individual may experience painful urinations, inability to maintain a steady stream of urine and a frequent urge to urinate resulting only in frequent and small urinations. Benign prostatic hypertrophy has been shown to be reversible when caused by anabolic steroids; however, this may not be the case in carcinoma of the prostate. Any symptoms of prostatic enlargement require cessation of anabolic drugs and medical attention.

X. TESTICULAR ATROPHY

Anabolic steroids block the release of two hormones from the pituitary gland that normally stimulate the testes (2, 29). Anabolic steroids' interference with the release of these two hormones will cause the testes to atrophy and become dormant. Subsequently, the testes will shrink in size, sperm production will be markedly supressed, and the volume of semen per ejaculate may be decreased.

Although sperm counts may reach an infertile level, most athletes who take anabolic steroids either choose to ignore this fact or simply assume that sperm counts will return to normal. However, athletes should give serious consideration to the cases reported in which men on anabolic steroids did not return to pre-drug rates of sperm production (2, 29).

References

1 Freed, D. C., A. J. Banks, D. Longson, D. M. Burley. Anabolic steroids in athletics: Crossover double-blind trial on weightlifters. Brit. Med. J., 1975, ii, p. 471.

2 Mauss, J., K. Borsch, et al. Effect of long term testosterone Oenanthate administration on male reproductive function. Acta Endocrin., 78 (1975), 373–384.

3 Maxwell, M. H. and C. R. Kleeman. Clinical Disorders of Fluid and Electrolyte Metabolism. McGraw-Hill Book Company, 1972.

4 Earll, J. M. et al. Hypercalcemia and Hypertension. Ann. Int. Med., 64(2), Feb. 1966, 378–380.

5 Williams, H. E. Nephrolithiasis. New Eng. J. Med. 290:33, 1974.

6 Smallwood, R. A. Effect of intravenous calcium administration on gastric secretion of acid and pepsin in man. Gut, 1967, 8, 592.

7 Petersen, P. Psychiatric Disorders in Primary Hyperparathyroidism. J. Clin. Endocr. 28:1491, 1968.

8 Holman, C. B. Roentgenologic Manifestations of Vitamin D Intoxication. Radiology 59 (6):805, Dec. 1952.

9 Walsh, F. B. and J. E. Howard. Conjunctival & Corneal Lesions in Hypercalcemia.

10 McMillan, D. E. and R. B. Freeman. The Milk Alkali Syndrome. Medicine (Balt.) 44:486 (1965).

11 Epstein, F. H., Calcium and the Kidney. Am. J. Med. 45:700 (1968).

12 Hervey, G. R. and I. Hutchinson. Anabolic effects of Methandienone in men undergoing athletic training. Lancet Oct. 2, 1976;699.

13 Johnsen, S. G. Maintenance of spermatogenesis induced by HMG treatment by means of continuous HGC treatment in hypogonadotrophic men. Acta Endocrin, 89:763 1978.

14 Landon, J., V. Wynn and E. Samols. The effect of anabolic steroids on blood sugar and plasma insulin levels in man. Metab. 12 (10):924 Oct. 1963.

15 Tainter, M. L. et al. Anabolic steroids in the management of the diabetic patient. N.Y. State J. Med. April 15, 1964, p. 1001.

16 Keele, C. A. and E. Neil. Samson Wrights Applied Physiology (twelfth ed.) Oxford University Press, 1971.

17 Srikanta, S. G. et al. Effect of a C17-alkylated steroid Methandrostenolone on plasma lipids of normal subjects. Am. J. Med. Sci. Aug. 1967. p. 201.

18 Hirschhauser, C., et al. Testosterone Undecanoate: A new orally active androgen. Acta Endocrin. 80 (1975):179–187.

19 Farrell, G. C. and D. E. Joshua. Androgen-induced Hepatoma. Lancet, Feb. 22, 1975 p. 430.

20 Johnsen, S. G. Long-term oral testosterone and liver function. Lancet Jan. 7, 1978 p. 50.

21 Westaby, D., et al. Liver damage from long-term methyl testosterone. Lancet Aug. 6, 1977 p. 261.

22 Schiff, L. et al. Diseases of the Liver (fourth ed.) J. B. Lippincott Company 1977.

23 Van Thiel, D. H. et al. Plasma estrone and prolactin concentrations are elevated in men with gynecomastia and spider angiomata. Gastroenterology 68 (4) April 1975 p. 934.

24 Erslev, A. J. Secondary Polycythemia. In Hematology by W. J. Williams, McGraw-Hill Book Company 1972 p. 544.

25 Hendler, E. D. et al. Controlled study of androgen therapy in anemia of patients on maintenance hemodialysis. New Eng. J. Med 291 (20):1046 Nov. 14, 1974.

26 Galetti, F. et al. Erythropoietic action of an oral non-17-alkylated anabolic steroid. Clin. Ter. 1979, Nov. 15:91 (3) 267–78.

27 Feyel-Cabanes. Combined effect of testosterone and estrogen on rat ventral prostates. Cancer research 38: (11 Pt. 2) 4126–34 Nov. 1978.

28 Walsh, P. C. et al. The binding of a potent synthetic androgen Methyltrienolone (R1881) to cytosol preparations of human prostate cancer. Trans. Am. Assoc. Genitourin. Surg. 69:78, 1978.

29 Steinberger, E., and K. D. Smith. Effect of chronic administration of testosterone enanthate on sperm production and plasma testosterone, FSH and LH leves. Fertil Steril. 28, 1977 p. 1320.

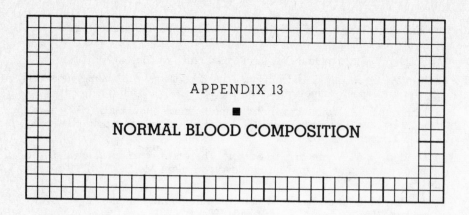

APPENDIX 13

■

NORMAL BLOOD COMPOSITION

The following are the normal values for different parameters found in human blood.

NORMAL HEMATOLOGIC VALUES

Fetal hemoglobin	<2% of total
Methemoglobin	<3% of total
Carboxyhemoglobin	<5% of total
Haptoglobins	Adults; 100–300 mg/100 ml
	Age 1–6 months: gradual increase to 30 mg/100 ml
	Newborn: absent in 90%; 10mg/100 ml in 10%
	Genetic absence in 1% of population
Osmotic fragility of RBC	Begins in 0.45–0.39% NaCl Complete in 0.33%–0.30% NaCl
Erythrocyte sedimentation rate	
Wintrobe	Males: 0–10 mm in 1 hour Females: 0–15 mm in 1 hour
Westergren	Males: 0–13 mm in 1 hour Females: 0-20 mm in 1 hour
Blood volume	Males: 75 ml/kg of body weight Females: 67 ml/kg of body weight (8.5–9.5% of body weight in kg)

Plasma volume   Males: 44 ml/kg of body weight
                            Females: 43 ml/kg of body weight

Red blood cell volume   Males: 30 ml/kg of body weight
                            Females: 24 ml/kg of body weight

RBC survival time (^{51}Cr)   Half-life: 25–35 days

Reticulocyte count   0.5–1.5% of erythrocytes

Plasma iron turnover rate   38 mg/24 hours (0.47 mg/kg)

Hemoglobin   Males 15 (± 2)
                            Females 13 (± 2)

Hematocrit   Males 45 (± 5)
                            Females 42 (± 5)

■

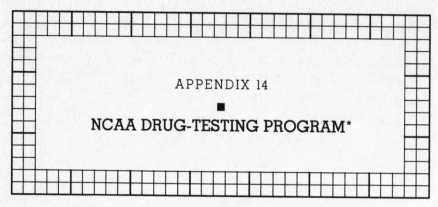

APPENDIX 14

■

NCAA DRUG-TESTING PROGRAM*

STUDENT-ATHLETE CONSENT FORM

Each year, student-athletes will sign a consent form demonstrating their understanding of the NCAA drug-testing program and their willingness to participate. This consent statement is part of a total Student-Athlete Statement required of all student-athletes prior to participation in intercollegiate competition during the year in question. Failure to complete and sign the statement annually shall result in the student-athlete's ineligibility for participation in all intercollegiate competition.

The text of the Student-Athlete Statement follows:

National Collegiate Athletic Association Student-Athlete Statement
1986–87 Academic Year

_____

Name of Institution

I,_____, *certify the following:*

1 This statement has been administered to me by my institution's director of athletics;

2 I reviewed in detail the NCAA Rules and Regulations Information Sheet, which I understand is a summary of NCAA Constitution 3-1, 3-3, 3-4, 3-6 and 3-9, and Bylaws 1-1, 1-2, 1-4, 1-5, 1-6, 1-7, 1-9, 1-10, 4-1, 5-1, 5-2 and 5-6, and Executive Regulation 1-7;

3 I was given the opportunity by my director of athletics to ask any questions with regard to these regulations and to review the actual regulations and the official interpretations thereof in the NCAA Manual;

*Reprinted by permission of the National Collegiate Athletic Association from the NCAA Drug-Testing Program (1986). This material is subject to annual review and change.

416

4 To the best of my knowledge, I am eligible for athletics participation under these regulations and I was not recruited contrary to NCAA regulations by my institution or any representative of its athletics interests;

5 I am not aware of any violations of NCAA regulations involving me and my institution;

6 I have revealed any involvement on my part in organized gambling activities, both past and current, concerning intercollegiate athletics competition, including any solicitations made to me in this regard, and

7 I understand that under the provisions of Constitution 3-6-(a) and 3-9-(d), I may jeopardize my eligibility to participate in intercollegiate athletics competition by falsely or erroneously signing this certification statement.

_____   _____

Signature of Student-Athlete   Date

Home Address

Buckley Amendment Consent

I understand that this Student-Athlete Statement, including the consents attached, and the results of any NCAA drug test I may undergo, are part of my education records under the Family Educational Rights and Privacy Act of 1974 and may not be disclosed without my consent. I hereby consent to the release of said statement, NCAA drug-test results, and any other papers, documents or information obtained by my institution pertaining to the matters referred to therein, including any transcript of my high school or junior college grades and my academic record at this or other four-year institutions and any records concerning my financial aid, only to authorized representatives of this institution, its athletics conference (if any) and the NCAA, and only for the purposes of determining my eligibility for intercollegiate athletics, my recruitment by this institution and my eligibility for athletically related financial aid.

_____   _____

Signature of Student-Athlete   Date

I have administered this statement after providing the student-athlete: (1) a copy of the NCAA Rules and Regulations Information Sheet; (2) an opportunity to ask any questions and receive answers thereto with regard to NCAA regulations, and (3) an opportunity to review NCAA regulations and the official interpretations thereof in the NCAA Manual; further, to the best of my knowledge, the student-athlete's certification on this form is true and correct, and the student is_____(insert "eligible" or "ineligible" in blank) to participate in the sport or sports of intercollegiate_____; finally, I am not aware of any additional information concerning the student-athlete that would result in ineligibility under NCAA legislation or constitute a violation of NCAA regulations on the part of the student or this institution.

_____   _____

Signature of Director of Athletics   Date

I have reviewed the student-athlete on this form and to the best of my knowledge the student's certification is true and correct; further, I am not aware of any additional information concerning the student-athlete that would result in ineligibility under NCAA legislation or constitute a violation of NCAA regulations on the part of the student or this institution.

_____   _____

Signature of Head Coach   Date

[NOTE: The institution should retain this completed form in its files until one calendar year after the date on which the student-athlete's eligibility for intercollegiate athletics under NCAA legislation is exhausted.]

Drug-Testing Consent

In the event I participate in any NCAA championship event or in any NCAA-certified postseason football contest in behalf of an NCAA member institution during the current academic year, I hereby consent to be tested in accordance with procedures adopted by the NCAA to determine if I have utilized, in preparation for or participation in such event or contest, a substance on the list of banned drugs set forth in Executive Regulation 1-7-(b). I have reviewed the rules and procedures for NCAA drug testing and I understand that if I test "positive" I shall be ineligible for postseason competition for a minimum period of 90 days and may be charged thereafter upon further testing with the loss of postseason eligibility in all sports for the current and succeeding academic year. I further understand that this consent and my test results will become a part of my educational records subject to disclosure only in accordance with my written Buckley Amendment consent and the Family Education Rights and Privacy Act of 1974.

_____   _____

Signature of Student-Athlete   Date

Signature of Parent or Guardian   Date
(required only if student-athlete
is a minor)

NCAA BANNED DRUGS LIST 1986 (WITH EXAMPLES)

A. Psychomotor stimulants:

amphetamine
benzphetamine
chlorphentermine
cocaine
diethylproplon
dimethylamphetamme
ethylamphetamine
fencamfamine
meclofenoxate
methylamphetamine

methylphenidate
norpseudoephedrine
pemoline
phendimetrazine
phenmetrazine
phentermine
pipradol
prolintane
AND RELATED COMPOUNDS

B. Sympathomimetic amines:

chlorprenaline
ephedrine
etafedreine
isoetharine
isoprenaline

methoxyphenamine
methylephedrine
phenylpropanolamine
AND RELATED COMPOUNDS

C. Miscellaneous central nervous system stimulants:

amiphenazole
bemigride
caffeine[1]
cropropamide
crolethamide
doxapram

ethamivan
leptazol
nikethamide
picrotoxine
strychnine
AND RELATED COMPOUNDS

D. Anabolic Steroids:

clostebol
dehydrochlormethyl-
  testosterone
fluoxymesterone
mesterolone
methenolone
methandienone
nandrolone

norethandrolone
oxandrolone
oxymesterone
oxymetholone
stanozolol
testosterone[2]
AND RELATED COMPOUNDS

E. Substances banned for specific sports:

Rifle:
alcohol
atenolol
metoprolol
nadolol

pindolol
propranolol
timolol
AND RELATED COMPOUNDS

F. Diuretics:

bendroflumethiazide
benzthiazide
bumetanide
chlorothiazide
chlorthalidone
cyclothiazide
ethacrynic acid
flumethiazide
flurosemide
hydrochlorothiazide

hydroflumethiazide
methyclothiazide
metolazone
polythiazide
quinethazone
spironolactone
triamterene
trichlormethiazide
AND RELATED COMPOUNDS

G. Street Drugs:

amphetamine
cocaine
heroin
marijuana[3]

methamphetamine
THC (tetrahydrocannabinol)[3]
OTHERS

Definition of positive depends on the following:

[1] for caffeine—if the concentration in urine exceeds 15 micrograms/ml.

[2] for testosterone—if the ratio of the total concentration of testosterone to that of epitestosterone in the urine exceeds 6.

[3] for marijuana and THC—based on a repeat testing.

H. Substances Given Special Consideration.

[Note: Usage of these substances may or may not be permissible, depending on limitations expressed in the following guidelines and/or quantities used of these substances.]

1 **Blood Doping.** The practice of blood doping (the intravenous injection of whole blood, packed red blood cells or blood substitutes), as well as the use of growth hormone (human, animal or synthetic), is prohibited and any evidence confirming use may be cause for punitive action.

2 **Local Anesthetics.** The NCAA Executive Committee will not be opposed to the limited use of local anesthetics under the following conditions:
   (a) That procaine, xylocaine, carbocaine without epinephrine, or any other vaso-constrictor may be used, but not cocaine;
   (b) That only local or topical injections can be used (i.e., intravenous injections are not permitted);
   (c) That use is medically justified only when permitting the athlete to continue the competition without potential risk to his health.

   The NCAA crew chief in charge of testing must be advised in writing by the team physician if the anesthetic has been administered within 24 hours of the competition. He must also be advised of time, route and dose of administration.

3 **Asthma or Exercise-Induced Bronchospasm.** The use of three beta-agonists, Terbutaline, Salbutamol and Biltolterol, for the treatment of asthma are approved under the following condition: The team doctor must notify the crew chief beforehand of which athletes in his team are asthmatics and are using, or may require the use of, either one or all of these drugs. Requests must be in writing identifying the drugs, dose and frequency of administration. All other sympathomimetic amines are banned. Drugs such as Cromolyn Sodium, Aminophylline and Theophyllines, Beclomethasone and Altropine Sulfate may be used.

4 **Corticosteroids.** The NCAA has become increasingly concerned by the misuse of corticosteroids in some sports. The Executive Committee therefore has decided that the use of these drugs at NCAA championships or certified football bowl games must be declared. A doctor using them must state in writing to the crew chief the name of the competitor being treated; the name, dose and route of administration of the drug; the reason for this use; the date of administration; the time of administration, and the name and signature of the doctor.

PROCEDURAL GUIDELINES

These guidelines are taken from the NCAA Drug-Testing Program Protocol.
   1.0. Medical Code.
   1.1. Any use of a substance currently listed by the NCAA as banned will be considered "doping" and cause for disciplinary action.
   1.2. Evidence of use of a banned substance will be from analysis of

the student-athlete's urine by gas chromatography/mass spectrometry by an NCAA-certified laboratory.

1.3. The current NCAA list of banned substances is in Part IV of this brochure. In addition, other compounds may be included in the screening process for nonpunitive research purposes, in order to gather data for making decisions as to whether other drugs should be added to the list of banned substances. The NCAA Executive Committee will be responsible for reviewing and revising the list of banned substances on a periodic basis.

2.0. Organization.

2.1. The NCAA Executive Committee will oversee the procedures and implementation of the NCAA drug-testing program.

2.1.1. The NCAA drug-testing program will consist of testing at NCAA championships events and designated NCAA-certified post-season football bowl games.

2.1.2. An NCAA drug-testing committee will recommend particular individuals to the NCAA Executive Committee for appointment as "crew chiefs" in the implementation of the NCAA drug-testing program.

2.1.3. An NCAA staff member will be responsible for general administration of the testing program under the supervision of the director of research and sports sciences.

2.2. The NCAA drug-testing committee will be responsible for supervision of the training of the crew chiefs, who will take responsibility for respective drug-testing occasions and who will be responsible for appointing their crew members.

2.2.1. No member of a drug-testing crew may concurrently be serving at an NCAA championship in any other capacity.

2.3. The drug-testing committee will assign each crew chief to one or more NCAA championships and/or football bowl games. If a subsequent schedule conflict precludes use of the principal crew chief at a particular testing occasion, the drug-testing committee will assign another crew chief or crew for that occasion.

2.4. The Games Committee for an NCAA championship or certified football bowl game will recommend an individual to serve as liaison with the NCAA and the crew chief assigned to that testing site.

2.4.1. The Games Committee will recommend a local site coordinator to assist the drug-testing crew.

2.5. Members of a laboratory advisory board, when requested by the laboratory director, will review test results.

2.5.1. The members of the laboratory advisory board will be selected by the laboratory director in consultation with the NCAA drug-testing committee, which will have final approval of the board members. The advisory board will be comprised of a maximum of four individuals from the disciplines of analytical chemistry, clinical pharmacology and medicine. The director of the analytical laboratory will be a member of this board.

2.6. The NCAA national administration will support, coordinate and supply the drug-testing program operations within established policies and procedures.

2.6.1. The NCAA executive director will approve the contractual arrangements necessary for an effective specimen forwarder service and laboratory analysis service.

2.6.2. The drug-testing program laboratory(ies) will be required to demonstrate, to the satisfaction of the NCAA drug-testing committee, proficiency in detection and confirmation of the banned substance categories on the NCAA list of banned drugs. A periodic quality control check of the laboratory(ies) will be maintained.

2.6.3. The specimen forwarder system will have the capability of expeditious and efficient service with complete signature confirmation from testing site to laboratory.

3.0. Penalties.

3.1. All student-athletes found to be positive for a banned substance are subject to disciplinary action(s) consistent with existing policies, as designated in NCAA Bylaw 5-2-(b).

3.2. Staff members of the athletics department of a member institution or others employed by the intercollegiate athletics program who have knowledge of the use contrary to Bylaw 5-2 by a student-athlete of a substance on the list of banned drugs set forth in.Executive Regulation 1-7-(b), and who fail to follow institutional procedures dealing with drug abuse, will be subject to action as set forth in Section 7-(b)-(12) of the NCAA enforcement procedure.

3.3. Penalties may be found in other parts of the protocol (e.g., 5.4.1. and 5.4.3.).

4.0. Athlete Selection.

4.1. The method for selecting student-athletes will be recommended by the NCAA drug-testing committee, approved by the Executive Committee, and implemented by the NCAA staff and assigned principal crew chiefs, in advance of the testing occasion. All student-athletes entered in the event are subject to testing.

4.2. At NCAA individual/team championships events, selection of athletes may be based on random draw, position or suspicion. Whenever random selection occurs, the method will be determined under the authority of Section No. 4.1. Crew chiefs will be notified by the Executive Committee or its designate which method or combination of methods should be used. An approved random sample of student-athletes will be employed. All student-athletes participating in the event are subject to testing.

4.3. In team championships and certified football bowl games, student-athletes may be selected on the basis of playing time, positions and/or an NCAA-approved random selection. The selection will be determined prior to or during the competition. During the competition includes up to one hour following the conclusion of an individual's last participation on any particular day.

4.4. If "doping" is suspected, the crew chief will have the authority to select specific additional student-athletes to be tested.

4.5. Any person who tests positive at one championship will automatically be tested at the next championship at which he or she appears.

4.6. Student-athletes may be tested on more than one occasion.

5.0. Specimen-Collection Procedures.

5.1. At NCAA championships events, immediately following the final participation of the student-athlete selected for drug testing, the student-athlete will be handed a completed Student-Athlete Notification Card by the official courier that informs the student-athlete to accompany the courier to the collection station within one hour, unless otherwise directed by the crew chief or his designate.

5.1.1. The time of notification will be recorded by the courier. The student-athlete will sign the form and will be given a copy of the form.

5.1.2. The courier will give the crew chief the original of the form upon return to the testing station.

5.1.3. During an NCAA competition, if the student-athlete must compete in another event that day, the student-athlete may be excused from reporting to the collection station within the one-hour time limit; however, the student-athlete must report to the collection station within one hour following completion of his or her last event of the day.

5.1.4. The student-athlete may have a witness accompany him or her to the station to certify identification of the student-athlete and to monitor the ensuing procedures.

5.2. Only those persons authorized by the crew chief will be in the testing station.

5.2.1. Upon entering the collection station, the student-athlete will provide adequate identification to the crew chief or a designate. The time of arrival is recorded on the Student-Athlete Signature Form and a crew member (Urine Donor Validator) will be assigned to the student-athlete for continuous observation within the station.

5.2.2. The student-athlete will select a new beaker that is sealed in a plastic bag from a supply of such and will be accompanied by the crew member until a specimen of at least 100ml, preferably 200ml, is provided.

5.2.3. Fluids given student-athletes who have difficulty voiding must be in unopened containers (certified by the crew chief) that are opened and consumed in the station. These fluids must be caffeine- and alcohol-free.

5.2.4. If the specimen is incomplete or inadequate, the student-athlete must remain in the collection area under observation of the validator until the sample is completed. During this period, the collection beaker must be kept covered and controlled by the student-athlete being tested. "Inadequate" includes measures of the specific gravity and alkalinity of the urine.

5.2.5. The student-athlete will select a pair of new specimen bottles that are sealed in a plastic bag from a supply of such and will pour approximately two-thirds of the specimen into the bottle marked "A" and the remaining one-third into bottle "B," leaving a small amount (approximately 5ml) of the sample remaining in the beaker.

5.2.6. The crew member will then stopper, cap, crimp and seal each bottle in the required manner under the observation of the student-athlete and the witness.

5.2.7. The student-athlete will select a personal code number from a list provided. This is recorded on the Student-Athlete Signature Form and on the bottles.

5.2.7.1. A crew member will check the specific gravity of the specimen and the pH of the urine remaining in the beaker. If the urine has a specific gravity below 1.004 or is alkaline, the student-athlete will be detained until an appropriate specimen is provided. This finding is recorded on the Manifest and Student-Athlete Signature Form.

5.2.7.2. A new student-athlete code number, selected by the student-athlete, will be applied to the new set of bottles. Both sets of specimens provided by the student-athlete will be sent to the laboratory appropriately identified.

5.3. The crew member will apply the student-athlete's code number in a secure manner to each bottle under the observation of the student-athlete and witness.

5.4. The student-athlete and witness will sign the Student-Athlete Signature Form, certifying that there were no irregularities in the entire process. Any perceived irregularity must be characterized and recorded on the Student-Athlete Signature Form at that time.

5.4.1. Failure to sign without justification is cause for the same action(s) as evidence of use of a banned substance. The crew chief will inform the student-athlete of these implications in the presence of witnesses and record such on the Student-Athlete Signature Form if the student-athlete still will not sign.

5.4.2. The crew member will sign the Student-Athlete Signature Form, give the student-athlete a copy and secure all remaining copies. The compiled Student-Athlete Signature Forms constitute the "Master Code" for that testing occasion.

5.4.3. If the student-athlete refuses to provide urine or fails to appear, the crew chief will inform the student-athlete, if he or she is available, of the implications in the presence of witnesses and record such on the Student-Athlete Signature Form if the student-athlete still will not cooperate. The student-athlete will be considered to have withdrawn his or her consent, thereby rendering himself or herself ineligible.

5.5. All sealed bottles will be secured in an NCAA shipping case. When the case is full or completed, the crew chief will sign the manifest, put the original and one copy in the case, prepare the case for forwarding and apply the official seal, having recorded its number on the manifest.

5.6. After the last student-athlete has been processed, the cases will be forwarded to the laboratory in the required manner, the remaining supplies kept or returned, and all copies of all forms mailed to the designated persons.

6.0. Chain of Custody.

6.1. An NCAA forwarder's agent will sign for the shipping cases at the testing station and deliver them to the air carrier.

6.1.1. A carrier's agent will sign for the cases and forward them to the destination.

6.1.2. A forwarder's agent will sign for the shipping cases at the destination and deliver them to the laboratory.

6.1.3. A laboratory employee will sign that the shipping cases have been received.

6.2. All signatures will attest that the official seal on the shipping cases remains intact.

6.3. The laboratory will register on the manifest whether the seals on each bottle arrived intact.

7.0. Notification of Results.

7.1. The laboratory will use specimen A for its initial analysis.

7.1.1. Positives for a banned substance will be reconfirmed with another sample from specimen A before it is determined to be a positive.

7.1.2. The laboratory director will review any positive results from specimen A and determine if the results should be presented to the laboratory advisory board.

7.1.2.1. If the results are to be reviewed by the laboratory advisory board, the laboratory director will make appropriate arrangements for review of all information pertaining to the sample by the members of the board.

7.1.2.2. The deliberations and findings of the laboratory advisory board will be summarized in a confidential report by the laboratory director.

7.1.3. By telephone, the laboratory will inform the NCAA of the results by each respective code number. Subsequently, the laboratory will mail to the NCAA director of research and sports sciences the original manifest with the respective finding recorded for each code number.

7.2. Upon receipt of the original manifest and the laboratory findings, the NCAA director of research and sports sciences or her designate will break the number code to identify any individuals with positive findings.

7.2.1. If a member institution has not heard from the NCAA within 30 days after the specimen was provided, the test results will be assumed to be negative.

7.2.2. For student-athletes who have a positive finding, that information will be sent by the NCAA to the chief executive officer and the director of athletics immediately by "overnight/signature-required" letter. Concurrently, the student-athlete's director of athletics will be contacted by telephone if possible.

7.2.2.1. A positive drug test may be appealed to the NCAA Eligibility Committee; such an appeal will be available only on non-collection-related matters. A technical expert will serve as consultant to the Eligibility Committee in those cases involving drug-testing appeals.

7.2.2.2. Accompanying the notice of the positive finding will be the option to have specimen B tested. Whether or not the institution chooses to have specimen B tested, written notice of the decision must be received by the NCAA within 24 hours of receipt of the notice described in 7.2.2. The institution will be given the option to be represented at the laboratory for the testing of specimen B.

7.2.2.3. If the institution does not choose to have specimen B analyzed, the specimen becomes the property of the laboratory. The NCAA will compile all written laboratory and any laboratory advisory board reports for confidential distribution to the enforcement department for consideration.

7.2.2.4. If the institution cannot arrange for representation or cannot be reached in 24 hours, the NCAA will arrange for a surrogate to represent the institution at the analysis of specimen B. For this purpose, the NCAA Postseason Drug-Testing Committee will develop a list of surrogate witnesses residing in the city where the laboratory is located.

7.2.2.5. The institution's representative or the surrogate will attest by signature as to the code number on the bottle of specimen B, that the bottle's seal has not been broken and that there is no evidence of tampering or contamination.

7.3. Specimen B will be analyzed by a technician other than the technician who analyzed that student-athlete's specimen A.

7.3.1. Specimen B findings will be final. By telephone, the laboratory will inform the NCAA of the findings. The laboratory will send the completed Specimen B Result Form to the NCAA, which will be responsible for confidential distribution of this material along with laboratory reports for specimen A and any written findings of the laboratory advisory board.

7.4. The NCAA will notify the institution's chief executive officer and director of athletics of the findings. It is the institution's responsibility to inform the student-athlete. At this point, normal NCAA eligibility procedures will apply. This notification will be initiated by telephone to the athletics director. This will be followed by another "overnight/signature-required" letter to the chief executive officer and the director of athletics.

7.5. The NCAA director of research and sports sciences will send a confidential report of the aggregate findings for that drug-testing occasion to the NCAA executive director for reporting to the Executive Committee. No report of aggregate data will be otherwise released without the approval of the NCAA Executive Committee.

7.6. The following is a recommended statement concerning a positive testing that results in a student-athlete's declaration of ineligibility (following the conclusion of the appeals process) both before and following an NCAA championship event.

If inquiries are received, this statement could be released:
"That the student-athlete in question was found in violation of the NCAA eligibility rules and has been declared ineligible for postseason competition."

SUGGESTED GUIDELINES

(For consideration by NCAA member institutions contemplating a drug-screening program)

These Suggested Guidelines extend and replace the guidelines from the NCAA Drug Education Committee as published in the February 1, 1984, edition of The NCAA News.

1 A member institution considering drug testing of student-athletes should involve the institution's legal counsel at an early stage, particularly in regard to right-to-privacy statutes, which may vary from one state and locale to another. With the use of proper safeguards such as those listed below, drug testing is considered legally acceptable; however, the legal aspects involved at each individual institution should be clarified.

2 Before initiating drug-testing activity, a specific written policy on drug testing should be developed, distributed and publicized. The policy should include such information as: (a) a clear explanation of the purposes of the drug-testing program; (b) who will be tested and by what methods; (c) the drugs to be tested, how often and under what conditions (i.e., announced, unannounced or both), and (d) the actions, if any, to be taken against those who test positive. (It is advisable that a copy of such a policy statement be given to all student-athletes entering the institution's intercollegiate athletics program and that they confirm in writing that they have received and read the policy. This written confirmation should be kept on file by the athletics department.)

3 At many institutions, student-athletes sign waiver forms regarding athletics department access to academic and medical records. It is recommended that specific language be added to such waiver forms wherein

the student-athlete agrees to submit to drug testing at the request of the institution in accordance with the published guidelines. The NCAA student-athlete statement covers postseason drug testing.

4 An institution considering drug testing should develop a list of drugs for which the student-athlete will be tested. The NCAA list of banned drugs may be used if the institution wishes.

5 Any institution considering drug testing of student-athletes confronts several logistical, technical and economic questions. Among them are:
   a. When and how samples will be collected, secured and transported.
   b. Laboratory(ies) to be used.
   c. How samples will be stored and for how long before analysis.
   d. Analytical procedures to be utilized in the laboratory.
   e. Cost.
   f. Accuracy of tests. What are the false-positive and false-negative rates. (These will vary from one type of test to another and from one laboratory to another.)
   g. How will false-positives be identified and handled.
   h. Who will get the results and how will the results be used.

The Special NCAA Postseason Drug-Testing Committee recommends that each institution considering drug testing of student-athletes appoint a committee of representatives from various relevant academic departments and disciplines (e.g., pharmacy, pharmacology, chemistry, medicine) to deal with the issues.

The question of where the samples will be analyzed is critical. No matter where the analyses are done, data on false-positive and false-negative rates for the specific tests to be used should be provided. If the laboratory cannot provide such information, another laboratory should be considered.

There is one important consideration that must be dealt with by institutions that are planning to utilize the results of drug testing as a basis for action involving the student-athlete who tests positive. No matter what screening methods may be used, including thin layer chromotography and radioimmunoassay, there is a finite probability of a false-positive result (i.e., the test is positive even though the student-athlete is actually "clean"). The Special NCAA Drug-Testing Committee urges that before any action is taken on the basis of a positive result from such tests, the results should be confirmed by gas chromatography/mass spectrometry, with the latter test providing the definitive result.

The Special NCAA Postseason Drug-Testing Committee will continue to monitor guidelines and protocol in an effort to share new developments with the membership through The NCAA News.

For additional copies, contact:
NCAA Publishing
P.O. Box 1906
Mission, Kansas 66201
913-384-3220

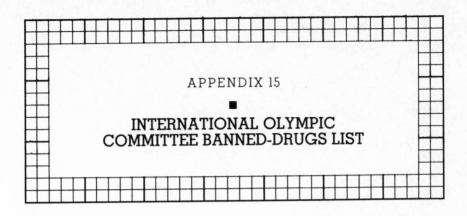

APPENDIX 15

■

INTERNATIONAL OLYMPIC COMMITTEE BANNED-DRUGS LIST

The following is the most complete list of drugs banned by IOC and USOC for athletic competition known at present. If use of any of these is detected by drug-testing, you stand to lose your eligibility in amateur sport as well as any honors earned at that event. Further, any person who helped a disqualified athlete take a banned substance will be subject to equivalent penalties to the extent USOC has prerogative.

The first name listed is the *generic* (pharmacological) name of the drug, while subsequent names listed (in full capital letters) are the various *brand names* by which it is sold. We have listed most of the commonly known drugs that are banned, but new brand names may come on the market that also contain a banned substance.

Be especially alert to the exact name of your medication because many sound alike. For example, Tylenol and Afrin are safe while Co-Tylenol and Afrinol are banned (contain pseudoephedrine).

Although the following list of banned drugs may seem to be extensive, it represents only a small percentage of the currently available medications and does not hinder the proper treatment of athletes for justifiable therapeutic reasons.

. A complete list of drugs considered "safe" to use would be impossible since new products are introduced on the market constantly. Periodically the list of banned drugs is revised, therefore all medicines should be reviewed by a knowledgeable U.S. Medical staff member. This list will be revised every six months.

To answer any questions regarding drugs the USOC provides a Drug Control hotline: 1-800-233-0393.

IOC DOPING SUBSTANCES

Psychomotor Stimulant Drug: e.g.,

amphetamine - DELCOBESE, OBETROL, BENZEDRINE, DEXEDRINE

429

benzphetamine - DIDREX

chlorphentermine - PRE SATE, LUCOFEN

cocaine - "COKE"

diethylpropion - TENUATE, TEPANIL

dimethylamphetamine - PHENOPANE

ethylamphetamine - APETINIL

fencamfamine - ENVITROL, ALTIMINE, PHENCAMINE

meclofenoxate - LUCIDRIL, BRENAL

methylamphetamine - DESOXYN, MET-AMPI

methylphenidate - RITALIN

norpseudoephedrine - NABESE, CATHINE, AMORPHAN, REDUFORM

pemoline - CYLERT, DELTAMIN, STIMUL

phendimetrazine - PHENAZINE, BONTRIL, PLEGINE

phenmetrazine - PRELUDIN

phentermine - ADIPEX, FASTIN, IONAMIN

pipradol - MERATRAN, CONSTITUENT OF ALERTONIC

prolintane - VILLESCON, PROMOTIL, KATOVIT

  and related compounds . . .

Miscellaneous Central Nervous System Stimulants: e.g.,

amiphenazole - DAPTIZOLE, AMPHISOL

bemigride - MEGIMIDE

doxapram - DOPRAM

ethamivan - EMIVAN, VANDID

leptazol - PENTYLENTENTRAZAL, CARDIAZOL, METRAZOL, VENTRASOL

nikethamide - CORAMINE

picrotoxine - COCCULIN

strychnine
  and related compounds . . . e.g.,
    caffeine: greater than 15 mcg/ml in the urine
      2 cups coffee = 3–6 mcg/ml (½ life = 2–3 hrs.)
      2 colas = 1.5–3 mcg/ml
      1 Nō-Dōz = 3–6 mcg/ml
      1 APC, EMPIRIN, ANACIN = 2–3 mcg/ml

Sympathomimetic Amines:

(these drugs act as central nervous system stimulants and are used for asthma, allergy, colds, sinus infections, etc.) e.g.,

chlorprenaline - VORTEL, ASTHONE (JAPANESE)

ephedrine - AMESEC, QUIBRON, LUFYLLIN, QUADRINAL, TEDRAL, VEREGUAD, BRONKOTABS, RYNATUSS, MARAX, PRIMATENE

etafedrine - MERCODAL, DECAPRYN, NETAMINE

isoetharine - BRONKOSOL, BRONKOMETER, NUMOTAC, DILABRON

methoxyphenamine - RITALIN, ORTHOXICOL COUGH SYRUP

methylephedrine - TZBRAINE, METHEP (GERMAN, GB)

metaproterenol - ALUPENT, METAPREL

isoproterenol - ISUPREL, NORISODRINE, METIHALER-ISO

   and related compounds . . . epinephrine - PRIMATENE PRODUCTS, VAPONEPHRIN

Over-the Counter Drugs for Colds and Sinus (Containing Sympathomimetic Amines)

pseudoephedrine - ACTIFED, AMBENYL, ANAMINE, AFRINOL, CO-TYLENOL DECONAMINE, DIMACOL, EMPRAZIL, FEDAHIST, FEDRAZIL, HISTALET, HISTORAL, ISOCLOR, LO-TUSSIN, NASAL-SPAN, NOVAFED, NUCOFED, POLY-HISINE PSEUDO-BID PSEUDO-HIST, RHYMOSYN, RYNA, SUDAFED, TRIPROLIDINE, TUSSEND, CHLORAFED, CHLORTRIMETON-DC, DISOPHORAL, DRIXORAL, POLARAMINE, RONDEC

phenylephrine - CORICIDIN, DRISTAN, NTZ, NEO-SYNEPHRINE, SINEX

Phenylpropanolamine - ARM, ALLEREST, CONTAC, DEXATRIM, DIETAC, 4-WAY FORMULA 44, NALDECON, NOVAHISTINE, ARNEX, SINE-AID, SINE-OFF, SINUTAB, TRIAMINIC, TRI-AMINICIN, SUCRETS COLD DECONGESTANT, AND RELATED "COLD" PRODUCTS

propylhexedrine - BENZEDREX INHALER

ephedrine - BRONKAID, COLLYRIUM WITH EPHEDRINE, PAZO SUPPOSITORY, WYANOID SUPPOSITORY, VITRONOL NOSE DROPS, NYQUIL NIGHTTIME COLD MEDICINE, VICKS NIGHT-

TIME COLD MEDICINE, Herbal Teas and Medicines containing Ma Huang (Chinese Ephedra).

CAUTION: There are new products on the market almost monthly and all products carrying the name "decongestant" generally contain banned substances.

Narcotic Analgesics: e.g.,

anileridine - LERITINE, APODOL

codeine - Present in many cough and cold syrups

Dextromoramide - PALFIUM, JETRIUM, D-MORAMID, DIMORLIN

dihydrocodeine - SYNALGOS DC, PARACODIN

dipipanone - PIPADONE

ethylmorphine - DIONIN

heroin

hydrocodone - ADATUSS, CITRA FORTE, DICODID, ENTURSS, HYCODAN, HYCOMINE, ROBIDANE, TUSSIONEX, TUSSEND, VICODIN (commonly found in cough medicines)

hydromorphone - DILAUDID

levorphanol - LEVO-DROMORAN

methadone - DOLOPHINE, AMIDON

morphine

oxocodone - PERCOCET, PERCODAN, TYLEX, SUPEUDOL

oxomorphine - NARCAN, NUMORPHAN

pentazocine - TALWIN

pethidine - CENTRALGIN, DOLANTIN, DOLOSOL, PETHOLD

phenazocine - NARPHEN, PRINADOL

piminodine - ALVODINE, CIMADON

thebacon - ADEDICON, THEBACETYL

trimerperidine - DEMEROL, MEPERGAN

 and related compounds: propoxyphene - DARVON

dextromethorphan - DM

diphenoxylate - LOMOTIL without atropine sulfate*

camphorated tincture of opium - PAREGORIC

---

*LOMOTIL (trademark Searle) with atrophine sulfate is permissible

APPENDICES
Anabolic Steroids: e.g.,

clostebol - STERANOBOL

dehydrochlormethyltestosterone - TURINABOL

danazol - DANOCRINE

fluoxymesterone - ANDROID F, HALOTESTIN, ORA-TESTRYL, ULTANDREN

mesterolone - ANDROVIRON, PROVIRON

methenolone - PRIMOBOLAN, PRIMONABOL - DEPOT

methandienone - DIANABOL, DANABOL

methyltestosterone - ANDROID, ESTRATEST, METHANDREN, ORETON, TESTRED, VIGOREX, VIRILON

norethandrolone - NILEVAR

nandrolone - (19-nortestosterone) - DURABOLIN, DECA-DURABOLIN, KABOLIN, NANDROBOLIC, ANABOL

oxandrolone - ANAVAR

oxymesterone - ORANABOL, THERANABOL

oxymetholone - ANADROL, NILEVAR, ANAPOLON 50, ADROYD

stanozolol - WINSTROL, STROMBA

*Testosterone** MALOGEN, MALOGEX, DELATESTRYL, ORETON *and related compounds*

*For testosterone - if the ratio of the total concentration of testosterone to that of epi-testosterone in the urine exceeds 6.

■

APPENDIX 16
■
UNITED STATES OLYMPIC
COMMITTEE BANNED DRUGS

COMMITTEE ON SUBSTANCE ABUSE, RESEARCH AND EDUCATION
USOC/IOC BANNED DRUGS
March 10, 1986

Essentially USOC observes the IOC list of banned drugs for its drug control program. Before taking any medication prior to competition, have it verified by the head physician for the event or a knowledgeable USOC medical staff member, or call the USOC Hot line **1-800-233-0393!** In addition, always declare every drug or substance that you are taking to the officials at drug testing.

The following is a brief explanation of each of the banned drug categories:

IOC/USOC BANNED SUBSTANCES

THREE CLASSES OF CENTRAL NERVOUS SYSTEM STIMULANTS

PSYCHOMOTOR STIMULANTS
MISCELLANEOUS CENTRAL NERVOUS STIMULANTS
SYMPATHOMIMETIC AMINES

Although these drugs produce a psychological as well as physical stimulant to athletic performance, they bring about physiological side effects that can be detrimental. They produce an aggressiveness, anxiety, and tremor which can lead to poor judgment, placing the individual at risk of injury. Heart rate and blood pressure can be increased causing dehydration and decreased circulation. Complications from these side effects include the risk of cerebral hemorrhage (stroke), cardiac (heart) arrhythmias (heart-beat irregularities), that can result in cardiac arrest and death.

Narcotic Analgesics or Pain Killers

Narcotic analgesics or pain killers produce a sensation of euphoria or psychological stimulation, a false feeling of invincibility, and illusions of athletic prowess beyond the athlete's inherent ability. They also increase the pain threshold so that the athlete may fail to recognize injury thus leading to more serious injury. The athlete may also perceive dangerous situations as safe, thus placing himself and others at risk for injury. These drugs also produce physical dependence, leading to the many problems associated with addiction and withdrawal.

Anabolic Steroids

These drugs are derivatives of the male hormone testosterone. They increase protein synthesis which can, with training, create an increase in lean muscle mass. This is perceived by athletes to increase strength and endurance. These drugs being hormones greatly interfere with the normal hypothalamic-pituitary-gonadal thermostat of hormonal balance. This interference in normal hormone function produces detrimental side effects such as: in the adolescent, premature closure of the growth centers; in the adult male, increase in aggressiveness and sexual appetite, sometimes resulting in aberrant sexual and criminal behavior; testicular atrophy and cessation of spermatogenesis; enlargement of breasts, premature baldness; enlargement of the prostate gland and prostatitis; and long-term effects of liver dysfunction, cystic degeneration of the liver and cancer of the liver; premature hardening of the arteries and high blood pressure which can lead to early stroke and heart attack. In the female, these drugs can cause irreversible masculinization, abnormal menstrual cycles, excessive permanent hair growth on the face and body, enlargement of the clitoris and deepening of the voice.

Alcohol and Beta-Blockers

Alcohol is used to calm the nerves. Beta-blockers are drugs commonly used for heart disease to lower blood pressure, decrease the heart rate and block stimulatory responses. They are used in sports such as shooting to steady the trigger finger. This is considered doping and they are therefore banned.

Blood Doping

The practice of blood doping (the intravenous injection of whole blood, packed red blood cells or blood substitutes), as well as the use of Growth Hormone (human, animal or synthetic) is prohibited and any evidence confirming use will be cause for punitive action comparable to that for using a banned substance.

The IOC Medical Commission has **provided** the following rules for special consideration *in addition* to the attached banned list.

Special Additions

I Local Anesthetics:
   The IOC Medical Commission will not be opposed to the limited use of local anaesthetics under the following conditions:

(a) That procaine, xylocaine, carbocaine without epinephrine, etc. may be used, but not cocaine;

(b) That only local injections can be used (i.e., intravenous injections are not permitted);

(c) That use is medically justified only when permitting the athlete to continue the competition without potential risk to his health.

The IOC Medical Commission must be advised in writing by the head physician if the anaesthetic has been administered within 24 hours of the competition.

2 Asthma or exercise-induced bronchospasm:

The use of three beta-agonists, **Terbutaline, Salbuterol,** and **Biltolterol,** for the treatment of asthma are approved under the following condition: The team doctor must notify the head physician for the games beforehand of which athletes in his team are asthmatics and are using, or may require the use of, either one or both of these drugs. Permission must be in writing identifying the drug, dose and frequency of administration. All other sympathomimetic amines are banned. Drugs such as Cromolyn Sodium, Aminophylline and Theophylines, Beclomethasone and Atropine Sulfate are safe to use.

3 Corticosteroids:

The IOC Medical Commission has become increasingly concerned by the misuse of corticosteroids in some sports.

The Medical Commission has therefore decided that the use of these drugs at the Olympic Games must be declared on the occasion of the Olympic Games. Any doctor using them must state the country and the name of the competitor being treated, the name, dose and route of administration of the drug, the reason for this use, the date of administration and the name, country and signature of the doctor.

4 Diuretics:

The IOC Medical Commission points out that the misuse of these drugs in sport in certain circumstances, such as "making weight" in boxing or wrestling, is potentially dangerous.

5 Caffeine:

Greater than 12 mcg/ml in the urine is doping. To reach this limit one would have to consume approximately 6 cups of coffee in one sitting. However, there are other sources of caffeine and the following examples are listed to indicate how excessive levels might be inadvertently accumulated.

2 cups coffee = 3–6 mcg/ml
2 colas = 1½–3 mcg/ml
1 Nō-Dōz = 3–6 mcg/ml
1 APC, Empirin or Anacin = 2–3 mcg/ml

Summary

In summary, if use of any of these banned drugs is detected by drug testing, loss of eligibility will result for at least six months if the first offense, and at least four years if a repeated offense, as the existing policies of the National Governing Body shall determine. Further, any person who helped a disqualified athlete take a banned substance will be subject to equivalent penalties to the extent the USOC has prerogative.

Hotline

If you have any further questions regarding drugs, the USOC provides a **Drug Control Hotline 1-800-233-0393.**

Warning

Attached is a list of drugs banned by the IOC and the USOC for athletic competition. The drugs are listed in alphabetical order with the first designation that of the trade (brand) name; second, the generic or IOC banned substance name; third, the therapeutic pharmacological classification; and lastly, categorized as to prescription or over-the-counter medication. Although the list may seem to be extensive and does represent the majority of the drugs found in the United States, no list can ever be complete. *Therefore this list should not be considered complete.* One should not consider a medication that is missing from this list to be safe to take without checking with the team physician.

A new category of banned drugs

Aside from the two major categorical reasons for banning drugs (those that enhance performance, and those that are dangerous to the health of the athlete), a third and new category seems to be emerging.

This new catagory may be those drugs used to beat the test, or foul up the results of the urine tests. They will then contribute to the athlete's taking harmful drugs or cheating. It is expected such a new category will be proposed in the near future.

■

USOC BANNED DRUG LIST

PS = PSYCHOMOTOR STIMULANT

SA = SYMPATHOMIMETIC AMINE
AS = ANABOLIC STEROID

CN = CENTRAL NERVOUS SYSTEM
STIMULANT
NA = NARCOTIC ANALGESIC
BB = BETA-BLOCKER

Brand Name	Generic Name	Class	SRC
A 21	ISOPROTERENOL	SA	RX
A 4624	METHADONE	NA	RX
A 66	PHENMETRAZINE	PS	RX
A.P.C. WITH CODEINE #3 AND #4 TABLOID BRAND	CODEINE PHOSPHATE	NA	RX
A.R.M. ALLERGY RELIEF MEDICINE TABLETS	PHENYLPROPANOLAMINE HCL	SA	OTC
AB 01	BEMIGRIDE	CN	RX
ABALGIN	PROPOXYPHENE	NA	RX
ABIC	METHADONE	NA	RX
ABIROL	METHANDROSTENOLONE & OXABOLONE CYPIONA	AS	RX
ABIROL	OXABOLONE CYPIONATE	AS	RX
ABOLEN	NANDROLONE DECANOATE	AS	RX
ACEDICON	THEBACON	NA	RX
ACEPHEN	MECLOFENOXATE	PS	RX
ACETA WITH CODEINE	CODEINE	NA	RX
ACETACO TABLETS	CODEINE PHOSPHATE	NA	RX
ACETAMINOPHEN WITH CODEINE TABLETS AND CAPSULES	CODEINE PHOSPHATE	NA	RX
ACETHYDROCODONE	THEBACON	NA	RX
ACETOMORFIN	HEROIN	NA	RX
ACETOMORPHIN	HEROIN	NA	RX
ACORDIN	PHENYLEPHRINE	SA	OTC
ACTIFED TABLETS & SYRUP	PSEUDOEPHEDRINE HCL	SA	OTC
ACTIFED WITH CODEINE COUGH SYRUP	CODEINE PHOSPHATE	NA	RX
ACTIVAMINA	AMPHETAMINE	PS	RX
ACTIVIN	NANDROLONE PHENYLPROPIONATE	AS	RX
ACUTRIM II, & MAXIMUM STRENGTH, & PRECISION RELEASE TABS.	PHENYLPROPANOLAMINE HCL	SA	OTC
ADANON	METHADONE	NA	RX
ADATUSS	HYDROCODONE	NA	RX
ADEDICON	THEBACON	NA	RX
ADERAN	CHLORPHENTERMINE	PS	RX
ADILOSS TY-MED	METHYLAMPHETAMINE	PS	RX
ADIOL	ANDROSTANDIOL	AS	RX
ADIPARTHROL-WIRKSTOFF	ETHYLAMPHETAMINE	PS	RX
ADIPEX, & ADIPEX-P TABLETS	PHENTERMINE	PS	RX
ADIPO II	PHENDIMETRAZINE	PS	RX
ADIPOSETTEN N	NORPSEUDOEPHEDRINE	PS	RX
ADIPOSID	PHENMETRAZINE	PS	RX
ADIPOST	PHENDIMETRAZINE TARTRATE	PS	RX
ADNEPHRINE	EPINEPHRINE	SA	RX
ADOLAN	METHADONE	NA	RX

ADOLENS	DEMEROL	NA	RX
ADOPOL	ANILERIDINE	NA	RX
ADPHEN	PHENDIMETRAZINE TARTRATE	PS	RX
ADREMAD	EPINEPHRINE	SA	RX
ADRENAL	EPINEPHRINE	SA	RX
ADRENALIN CHLORIDE SOLUTION INJECTABLE	EPINEPHRINE	SA	RX
ADRENAMINE	EPINEPHRINE	SA	RX
ADRENAN	EPINEPHRINE	SA	RX
ADRENAPAX	EPINEPHRINE	SA	RX
ADRENASOL	EPINEPHRINE	SA	RX
ADRENATE	EPINEPHRINE	SA	RX
ADRENATRATE	EPINEPHRINE	SA	RX
ADRENEFRINE	EPINEPHRINE	SA	RX
ADRENHORMON	EPINEPHRINE	SA	RX
ADRENINE	EPINEPHRINE	SA	RX
ADRENO-MIST	EPINEPHRINE	SA	RX
ADRENODIS	EPINEPHRINE	SA	RX
ADRENOHORMA	EPINEPHRINE	SA	RX
ADRENOL	EPINEPHRINE	SA	RX
ADRENORITARD	EPINEPHRINE	SA	RX
ADRENOSAN	EPINEPHRINE	SA	RX
ADRENUTOL	EPINEPHRINE	SA	RX
ADRIANOL	PHENYLEPHRINE	SA	OTC
ADRINE	EPINEPHRINE	SA	RX
ADROIDIN	OXYMETHOLONE	AS	RX
ADROYD	OXYMETHOLONE	AS	RX
ADROYED	OXYMETHOLONE	AS	RX
AEROFED	PSEUDOEPHEDRINE	SA	OTC
AEROLONE SOLUTION	ISOPROTERENOL	SA	RX
AEROTROL	ISOPROTERENOL	SA	RX
AETHAPHEN	PHENYLEPHRINE	SA	OTC
AETHOMORPHINUM	ETHYLMORPHINE	NA	RX
AFAGIL	PHENMETRAZINE	PS	RX
AFLUTESTON	FLUOXYMESTERONE	AS	RX
AFRINOL & AFRINOL REPETABS	PSEUDOEPHEDRINE	SA	OTC
AGOVIRIN-DRAGEES	METHYLTESTOSTERONE	AS	RX
AHR-619	DOXAPRAM	CN	RX
AHYPNON	BEMIGRIDE	CN	RX
AKTEDRIN	AMPHETAMINE	PS	RX
AKTILIN	METHYLPHENIDATE	PS	RX
AL 842	ISOPROTERENOL	SA	RX
ALADRINE SUSPENSION & TABLETS	EPHEDRINE SULFATE	SA	RX
ALBATUSSIN	PHENYLEPHRINE HYDROBROMIDE	SA	RX
ALBATUSSIN	DEXTROMETHORPHAN HYDROBROMIDE	NA	RX
ALBUTEROL (SPECIAL CONSIDERATION DRUG)	ALBUTEROL	SA	RX
ALCLEAR ANTI-ALLERGY TABLET	PHENYLPROPANOLAMINE HCL	SA	RX
ALCOID	DEXTOMORAMIDE	NA	RX
ALCON DECONGESTANT TABLETS—LIQUID	PHENYLPROPANOLAMINE HCL	SA	RX
ALCON-EFRIN	PHENYLEPHRINE	SA	RX
ALCONEFRIN 12, 25, 50	PHENYLEPHRINE	SA	OTC
ALENTOL	AMPHETAMINE	PS	RX
ALERTOL	PIPRADOL	PS	RX
ALERTONIC	PIPRADOL	PS	RX
ALEUDRIN "INGELHEIM"	ISOPROTERENOL	SA	RX
ALGAFAN	PROPOXYPHENE	NA	RX

Brand Name	Generic Name	Class	SRC
ALGANTINE	DEMEROL	NA	RX
ALGAPHAN	PROPOXYPHENE	NA	RX
ALGECOL TABLETS	PHENYLPROPANOLAMINE HCL	SA	RX
ALGELUSS LIQUID	PHENYLPROPANOLAMINE HCL	SA	RX
ALGIDON	METHADONE	NA	RX
ALGIL	DEMEROL	NA	RX
ALGITON	METHADONE	NA	RX
ALGODIN	PROPOXYPHENE	NA	RX
ALGOLYSIN	METHADONE	NA	RX
ALGOVETAN	METHADONE	NA	RX
ALGOXALE	METHADONE	NA	RX
ALIDINE	ANILERIDINE	NA	RX
ALIDRIL	ISOPROTERENOL	SA	RX
ALKA-SELTZER PLUS COLD MEDICINE	PHEYLPROPANOLAMINE	SA	OTC
ALLEN & HANBURY (EUVITOL)	FENCAMFAMINE	PS	RX
ALLEREST HEADACHE STRENGTH TABLETS	PHENYLPROPANOLAMINE HCL	SA	OTC
ALLEREST NASAL	PHENYLEPHRINE	SA	OTC
ALLEREST SINUS PAIN FORMULA	PHENYLPROPANOLAMINE HCL	SA	OTC
ALLEREST TABLETS CHILDREN'S CHEWABLE	PHENYLPROPANOLAMINE HCL	SA	OTC
ALLERGESIC TABLETS	PHENYLPROPANOLAMINE HCL	SA	RX
ALLERSTAT CAPSULES	PHENYLPROPANOLAMINE HCL	SA	RX
ALLODENE	AMPHETAMINE	PS	RX
ALMEFRIN	PHENYLEPHRINE	SA	OTC
ALODAN	DEMEROL	NA	RX
ALOTEC	METAPROTERENOL	SA	RX
ALPRENOLOL	ALPRENOLOL	BB	RX
ALTHOSE	METHADONE	NA	RX
ALTIMINE	FENCAMFAMINE	PS	RX
ALUDRASMA	ISOPROTERENOL	SA	RX
ALUDRIN	ISOPROTERENOL	SA	RX
ALUPENT INHALANT, SYRUP & TABLETS	METAPROTERENOL SULFATE	SA	RX
ALVODINE	PIMINODINE	NA	RX
AMACODONE TABLETS	HYDROCODONE	NA	RX
AMAPHEN WITH CODEINE #3	CODEINE PHOSPHATE	NA	RX
AMARIL 'D' SPANCAP	PHENYLPROPANOLAMINE HCL	SA	RX
AMBAR	METHYLAMPHETAMINE	PS	RX
AMBENYL	PSEUDOEPHEDRINE	SA	OTC
AMBENYL COUGH SYRUP	CODEINE SULFATE	NA	RX
AMBENYL-D DECONGESTANT COUGH FORMULA	PSEUDOEPHEDRINE HCL	SA	OTC
AMBENYL-D DECONGESTANT COUGH FORMULA	DEXTROMETHORPHAN HYDROBROMIDE	NA	RX
AMDRAM	METHYLAMPHETAMINE	PS	RX
AMEDRINE	METHYLAMPHETAMINE	PS	RX
AMESEC	EPHEDRINE	SA	RX
AMFETAMINE	AMPHETAMINE	PS	RX
AMFETAMMINA	AMPHETAMINE	PS	RX
AMFETASUL	AMPHETAMINE	PS	RX
AMIDON	METHADONE HCL	NA	RX
AMIDOSAN	METHADONE	NA	RX
AMILONE	METHADONE	NA	RX
AMINOCARDIN(A)	NIKETHAMIDE	CN	RX

AMINOCORDIN	NIKETHAMIDE	CN	RX
AMIPHENAZOL (E)	AMIPHENAZOLE	CN	RX
AMIPOLEN	MECLOFENOXATE	PS	RX
AMITRENE	AMPHETAMINE	PS	RX
AMORPHAN	NORPSEUDOEPHEDRINE	PS	RX
AMPHAETAMIN	AMPHETAMINE	PS	RX
AMPHAMED	AMPHETAMINE	PS	RX
AMPHAMINE	AMPHETAMINE	PS	RX
AMPHASUB	PHENDIMETRAZINE	PS	RX
AMPHEDRINE	AMPHETAMINE	PS	RX
AMPHEDROXYN	METHYLAMPHETAMINE	PS	RX
AMPHETAMIN	AMPHETAMINE	PS	RX
AMPHETAMINE	DEXTROAMPHETAMINE SULFATE	PS	RX
AMPHEZAMIN	AMPHETAMINE	PS	RX
AMPHISOL	AMIPHENAZOLE	CN	RX
AMPHOBESE "DOUGLAS"	PHENDIMETRAZINE	PS	RX
AMPHOIDS-S	AMPHETAMINE	PS	RX
AMPHOSEDAL	DEMEROL	NA	RX
AN 148	METHADONE	NA	RX
ANABIOL	BOLANDIOL DI PROPIONATE	AS	RX
ANABO	NANDROLONE CYCLOPENTYLPROPIONATE	AS	RX
ANABOL	NANDROLONE	AS	RX
ANABOL	METHANDRIOLDIPROPIONATE	AS	RX
ANABOL	STANOZOLOL	AS	RX
ANABOL	NORDOSTEBOL	AS	RX
ANABOL	STANOZOLOL	AS	RX
ANABOL "PIEM"	METHANDROSTENOLONE	AS	RX
ANABOLEEN	ANDROSTANOLONE	AS	RX
ANABOLEX	METHANDROSTENOLONE	AS	RX
ANABOLICO	NANDROLONE HYDROGEN SUCCINATE	AS	RX
ANABOLICUM	NANDROLONE CYCLOHEXYLPROPIONATE	AS	RX
ANABOLICUM	QUINBOLONE	AS	RX
ANABOLICUS	NANDROLONE PROPIONATE	AS	RX
ANABOLIN	METHANDRIOL DIPROPIONATE	AS	RX
ANABOLIN "GEA; MEDICA"	METHANDROSTENOLONE	AS	RX
ANABOLIN I.M.	NANDROLONE PHENPROPIONATE	AS	RX
ANABOLIN LA 100	NANDROLONE DECANOATE	AS	RX
ANABOLIN-DEPO	NANDROLONE CAPRIONATE	AS	RX
ANABOLINE	NANDROLONE PHENYLPROPIONATE	AS	RX
ANABOLIT	CLOSTEBOL ACETATE	AS	RX
ANABOLVIS	QUINBOLONE	AS	RX
ANABORAL	METHANDROSTENOLONE	AS	RX
ANABOSAN	NANDROLONE PHENYLPROPIONATE	AS	RX
ANABOSAN	NANDROLONE DECANOATE	AS	RX
ANACARDONE	NIKETHAMIDE	CN	RX
ANACIN-3 WITH CODEINE TABLETS	CODEINE PHOSPHATE	NA	RX
ANADIOL	METHANDRIOL	AS	RX
ANADOR	NANDROLONE HEXYLOXYPHENYL PROPIONATE	AS	RX
ANADROL AND 50	OXYMETHOLONE	AS	RX
ANADROYD	OXYMETHOLONE	AS	RX
ANADROYOL	OXYMETHOLONE	AS	RX
ANADUR	NANDROLONE HEXYLOXYPHENYL PROPIONATE	AS	RX
ANADURINE	NANDROLONE HEXYLOXYPHENYL PROPIONATE	AS	RX

Brand Name	Generic Name	Class	SRC
ANALEPTICON	ETHAMIVAN	CN	RX
ANALEPTIN "RIVOPHARM"	NIKETHAMIDE	CN	RX
ANALEPTIN "SPOFA"	PHENYLEPHRINE	SA	OTC
ANALONE-100, & -50	NANDROLONE DECANOATE	AS	RX
ANALUCIN	LEPTAZOL	CN	RX
ANALUX	MECLOFENOXATE	PS	RX
ANAMIDOL	OXYMESTERONE	AS	RX
ANAMINE	PSEUDOEPHEDRINE	SA	OTC
ANAPETOL	PHENMETRAZINE	PS	RX
ANAPOLIN	OXYMESTHOLONE	AS	RX
ANAPOLON 50	OXYMETHOLONE	AS	RX
ANARA (ALTE FORM)	AMPHETAMINE	PS	RX
ANASTERON	NANDROLONE PHENYLPROPIONATE	AS	RX
ANASTERON	OXYMESTHOLONE	AS	RX
ANASTERONAL	OXYMESTHOLONE	AS	RX
ANASYTH	STANOZOLOL	AS	RX
ANATROPHIN STENOBOLONE	STENBOLONE	AS	RX
ANAVAR	OXANDROLONE	AS	RX
ANAVORMOL	MESTANOLONE	AS	RX
ANDORON	MESTANOLON	AS	RX
ANDREST-TABL.	METHYLTESTOSTERONE	AS	RX
ANDRHORMONE-TABL.	METHYLTESTOSTERONE	AS	RX
ANDRIFAR-COMPR.	METHYLTESTOSTERONE	AS	RX
ANDRIS	METHANDRIOL	AS	RX
ANDRO L.A. 200	TESTOSTERONE ENANTHATE	AS	RX
ANDRO 100	TESTOSTERONE	AS	RX
ANDRO-CYP 100 AND 200	TESTOSTERONE CYPIONATE	AS	RX
ANDROFLUORONE	FLUOXYMESTERONE	AS	RX
ANDROFURAZANOL	FURAZEBOL	AS	RX
ANDROGEN	TESTOSTERONE	AS	RX
ANDROGENOL	HEXOXYMESTROL	AS	RX
ANDROGONYL	METHANDRIOL	AS	RX
ANDROID-F	FLUOXYMESTERONE	AS	RX
ANDROID-T	TESTOSTERONE-ENANTHATE	AS	RX
ANDROID-5 (-10, -25)	METHYLTESTOSTERONE	AS	RX
ANDROISOXAZOL	ANDROISOXAZOL	AS	RX
ANDROKININE	ANDROSTERON	AS	RX
ANDROL	NANDROLONE CYCLOHEXYLPROPIONATE	AS	RX
ANDROLAN AQUEOUS	TESTOSTERONE	AS	RX
ANDROLIN	TESTOSTERONE	AS	RX
ANDROLONE	NANDROLONE PHENPROPIONATE	AS	RX
ANDROLONE	ANDROSTANOLONE PROPIONATE	AS	RX
ANDROLONE 50	NANDROLONE PHENPROPIONATE	AS	RX
ANDROLONE-D 100, & D 50	NANDROLONE DECANOATE	AS	RX
ANDROLONE-D 50	NANDROLONE DECANOATE	AS	RX
ANDROMACO (OBESIN)	AMPHETAMINE	PS	RX
ANDROMETH	METHYLTESTOSTERONE	AS	RX
ANDRONAQ	TESTOSTERONE	AS	RX
ANDRONATE 100 AND 200	TESTOSTERONE CYPIONATE	AS	RX
ANDRONE	MESTANOLONE	AS	RX
ANDRONEX-TABL.	METHYLTESTOSTERONE	AS	RX
ANDRORAL	METHYLTESTOSTERONE	AS	RX
ANDROSAN-TABL.	METHYL TESTOSTERONE	AS	RX
ANDROSTALONE	MESTANOLON	AS	RX
ANDROSTANAZOL	STANOZOLOL	AS	RX

ANDROSTANDIOL	ANDROSTANDIOL	AS	RX
ANDROSTANOLONE	ANDROSTANOLONE	AS	RX
ANDROSTANOLONE BENZOATE	ANDROSTANOLONE BENZOATE	AS	RX
ANDROSTANOLONE ENANTHATE	ANDROSTANOLONE ENANTHATE	AS	RX
ANDROSTANOLONE PROPIONATE	ANDROSTANOLONE PROPIONATE	AS	RX
ANDROSTANOLONE VALERATE	ANDROSTANOLONE VALERATE	AS	RX
ANDROSTEN	METHYLTESTOSTERONE	AS	RX
ANDROSTENDIOL DIPROPIONATE	ANDROSTENDIOL DIPROPIONATE	AS	RX
ANDROSTEROLO	FLUOXYMESTERONE	AS	RX
ANDROSTERONE	ANDROSTERONE	AS	RX
ANDROTEST	TESTOSTERONE	AS	RX
ANDROTESTON	METHANDRIOL	AS	RX
ANDROTESTON-TABL.	METHYLTESTOSTERONE	AS	RX
ANDROTINE	ANDROSTERONE	AS	RX
ANDROVIRON	MESTEROLONE	AS	RX
ANDROXAN	ANDROISOXAZOL	AS	RX
ANDROXIL-ORAL	METHYLTESTOSTERONE	AS	RX
ANDRUSOL	TESTOSTERONE	AS	RX
ANDRYL 200	TESTOSTERONE ENANTHATE	AS	RX
ANEBOX	OXYMETHOLONE	AS	RX
ANERTAN PERLINGUAL	METHYLTESTOSTERONE	AS	RX
ANFORM	PEMOLINE	PS	RX
ANGIAZOL	LEPTAZOL	CN	RX
ANGIOTON "CHROPI"	PHENYLEPHRINE	SA	OTC
ANGIOTON "LEO"	LEPTAZOL	CN	RX
ANGIOTONIN	LEPTAZOL	CN	RX
ANILERIDINE	ANILERIDINE	NA	RX
ANOPRIDINE	PIMINODINE	NA	RX
ANOREX	PHENMETRAZINE	PS	RX
ANOREX "ATRAL"	CHLORPHENTERMINE	PS	RX
ANOREX "DUNHALL"	PHENDIMETRAZINE TARTRATE	PS	RX
ANOREXIL	PHENMETRAZINE	PS	RX
ANOREXINE	AMPHETAMINE	PS	RX
ANORMON	METHANDRIOL	AS	RX
ANOXINE	PHENDIMETRAZINE	PS	RX
ANOXINE-T	PHENDIMETRAZINE	PS	RX
ANP 235	MECLOFENOXATE	PS	RX
ANTALON	MESTANOLON	AS	RX
ANTALVIC	PROPOXYPHENE	NA	RX
ANTAPENTAN	PHENDIMETRAZINE	PS	RX
ANTASTHMIN "KWIZDA"	ISOPROTERENOL	SA	RX
ANTHATEST	TESTOSTERONE ENANTHATE	AS	RX
ANTI-B	PHENYLEPHRINE	SA	RX
ANTIASMATICO "SERPERO"	ISOPROTERENOL	SA	RX
ANTIBARBI	BEMIGRIDE	CN	RX
ANTICATABOLIN	NANDROLONE PHENYLPROPIONATE	AS	RX
ANTIDOL	DEMEROL	NA	RX
ANTIDUOL	DEMEROL	NA	RX
ANTIMERAN	PEMOLINE	PS	RX
ANTISEP	DEXTROMETHORPHAN	NA	RX
ANTITRIOL	OXANDROLONE	AS	RX
APAMINE	METHYLAMPHETAMINE	PS	RX
APAP W/CODEINE TABLETS AND #3 AND #4	ANILERIDINE	NA	RX
APAP WITH CODEINE ELIXIR	ANILERIDINE	NA	RX

Brand Name	Generic Name	Class	SRC
APAP 300MG WITH CODEINE TABLETS AND CAPSULES	ANILERIDINE	NA	RX
APETINIL	ETHYLAMPHETAMINE	PS	RX
APETINIL-WIRKSTOFF	ETHYLAMPHETAMINE	PS	RX
APETON DEPOT	ANDROSTANOLONE VALERATE	AS	RX
APODOL	ANILERIDINE	NA	RX
APPEDRINE MAXIMUM STRENGTH TABLETS	PHENYLPROPANOLAMINE HCL	SA	OTC
APSEDON	CHLORPHENTERMINE	PS	RX
AQUA-TESTERONE	TESTOSTERONE	AS	RX
AQUAVIRON	TESTOSTERONE	AS	RX
ARCOSTERONE	METHYLTESTOSTERONE	AS	RX
ARCOTROL	PHENDIMETRAZINE	PS	RX
ARCUM (REDUCTO)	PHENDIMETRAZINE	PS	RX
ARM-A-MED	ISOETHARINE HCL	SA	RX
ARNEX	PHENYLPROPANOLAMINE HCL	SA	OTC
AROMARONE	LEVORPHANOL	NA	RX
ARRESTOL	DEXTROMETHORPHAN	NA	RX
ASCRIPTIN WITH CODEINE	CODEINE PHOSPHATE	NA	RX
ASDRIN	ISOPROTERENOL	SA	RX
ASMA-JET	ISOPROTERENOL	SA	RX
ASMADREN	ISOPROTERENOL	SA	RX
ASMALAR	ISOPROTERENOL	SA	RX
ASMALIDRINA	ISOPROTERENOL	SA	RX
ASMANOR	ISOPROTERENOL	SA	RX
ASMATANE-MIST	EPINEPHRINE	SA	RX
ASMI	METHOXYPHENAMINE	SA	RX
ASMOLIN	EPINEPHRINE	SA	RX
ASPIRIN WITH CODEINE TABLETS	CODEINE SULFATE	NA	RX
ASPIRIN 325MG WITH CODEINE TABLETS	ANILERIDINE	NA	RX
ASPRON	HEROIN	NA	RX
ASSICODID	HYDROCODONE	NA	RX
ASSILAUDID	HYDROMORPHONE	NA	RX
ASSIMIL	MESTANOLONE	AS	RX
ASSIPRENOL	ISOPROTERENOL	SA	RX
ASTEDIN	AMPHETAMINE	PS	RX
ASTHMA HALER ORAL INHALATION FOR BRONCHIAL ASTHMA	EPINEPHRINE BITARTRATE	SA	OTC
ASTHMA NEFRIN	EPINEPHRINE	SA	OTC
ASTHMA-METER-MIST	EPINEPHRINE	SA	RX
ASTHMALITAN	ISOETHARINE	SA	RX
ASTHMATERMINE	ISOPROTERENOL	SA	RX
ASTHONE (JAPANESE)	CHLOROPRENALINE	SA	RX
ASTMAHALIN	EPINEPHRINE	SA	RX
ASTMEDRIN	EPHEDRINE	SA	RX
ASTMINHAL	EPINEPHRINE	SA	RX
ASTMO	ISOPROTERENOL	SA	RX
ASTMOPENT	METAPROTERENOL	SA	RX
ASTOP	METAPROTERENOL	SA	RX
ASTROCAR	NIKETHAMIDE	CN	RX
ATHOS	DEXTROMETHORPHAN	NA	RX
ATHYLAMPHETAMIN	ETHYLAMPHETAMINE	PS	RX
ATHYLEPHEDRIN	ETAFEDRINE	SA	RX
ATHYLMORPHINHYDRO-CHLORID	ETHLMORPHINE	NA	RX

ATHYLNORTESTOSTERON	NORETHANDROLONE	AS	RX
ATHYLOESTRENOL	ETHYLESTRENOL	AS	RX
ATHYLOESTRENOLON	NORETHANDROLONE	AS	RX
ATRAL (ANOREX)	CHLORPHENTERMINE	PS	RX
ATSEFEN	MECLOFENOXATE	PS	RX
AVICOL	CHLORPHENTERMINE	PS	RX
AVIPRON	CHLORPHENTERMINE	PS	RX
AXEDAMINE	NANDROLONE DECANOATE	AS	RX
AYERST EPITRATE	EPINEPHRINE BITARTRATE	SA	RX
AZODRINE	EPINEPHRINE	SA	RX
AZOXODON	PEMOLINE	PS	RX
B-PETHIDIN	DEMEROL	NA	RX
BACARATE	PHENDIMETRAZINE TARTRATE	PS	RX
BADRIN	AMPHETAMINE	PS	RX
BALMADREN	EPINEPHRINE	SA	RX
BALMINIL-SYR.	DEXTROMETHORPHAN	NA	RX
BALNIMAX	OXYMESTERONE	AS	RX
BANCAP HC CAPSULES	HYDROCODONE	NA	RX
BANCAP WITH CODEINE CAPSULES	CODEINE PHOSPHATE	NA	RX
BASTA	PENTAZOCINE	NA	RX
BAY TESTONE-50 AND 100	TESTOSTERONE	AS	RX
BAYAPAP WITH CODEINE ELIXIR	CODEINE	NA	RX
BAYER CHILDREN'S COLD TABLETS	PHENYLPROPANOLAMINE HCL	SA	OTC
BAYER COUGH SYRUP FOR CHILDREN	PHENYLPROPANOLAMINE HCL	SA	OTC
BAYER COUGH SYRUP FOR CHILDREN	DEXTROMETHORPHAN HYDROBROMIDE	SA	RX
BAYTUSSIN	DEXTROMETHORPHAN HYDROBROMIDE	SA	OTC
BECOREL	OXYMETHOLONE	AS	RX
BEIERSDORF (TRADON)	PEMOLINE	PS	RX
BEKADID	HYDROCODONE	NA	RX
BELLASTHMAN-MEDIHALER	ISOPROTERENOL	SA	RX
BEMIGRID(E)	BEMIGRIDE	CN	RX
BENHALER	PROPYLHEXEDRINE	SA	OTC
BENZAFINYL	AMPHETAMINE	PS	RX
BENZEBAR	AMPHETAMINE	PS	RX
BENZEDREX INHALER	PROPYLHEXEDRINE	SA	OTC
BENZEDRIN(E)	DEXTROAMPHETAMINE SULFATE	PS	RX
BENZFETAMINHYDRO-CHLORID	BENZPHETAMINE	PS	RX
BENZOLONE	AMPHETAMINE	PS	RX
BENZOYLMETHYLECGONIN	COCAINE	PS	RX
BENZPHETAMINE	BENZPHETAMINE	PS	RX
BENZPROPAMIN	AMPHETAMINE	PS	RX
BERNARENIN	EPINEPHRINE	SA	RX
BESAN	PSEUDOEPHEDRINE	SA	OTC
BETA-2	ISOETHARINE HCL	SA	RX
BETAFEN	AMPHETAMINE	PS	RX
BETAPYRIMIDUM	NIKETHAMIDE	CN	RX
BETHADONE	METHADONE	NA	RX
BI-CO-TUSSIN	HYDROCODONE	NA	RX
BI-EPINEPHRIN	EPINEPHRINE	SA	RX
BICODEIN	DEXTROMORAMIDE	NA	RX
BICODONE	HYDROCODONE	NA	RX
BIFED CAPSULES	PHENYLPROPANOLAMINE HCL	SA	RX
BIOFARMACOTERAPICO	PHENYLEPHRINE	SA	OTC
BIOLMON-CAP.	METHYLTESTOSTERONE	AS	RX

Brand Name	Generic Name	Class	SRC
BIOMORPHYL	HYDROMORPHONE	NA	RX
BIONABOL	METHANDROSTENOLONE	AS	RX
BIONONE	OXOCODONE	NA	RX
BIOPHEDRIN	EPHEDRINE	SA	RX
BIORENINE	EPINEPHRINE	SA	RX
BIPHENAL	DEMEROL	NA	RX
BIPHETAMINE 12½, & 20	DEXTROAMPHETAMINE SULFATE	PS	RX
BISHOP'S TEA	EPHEDRA	SA	OTC
BITOLTEROL MESYLATE (SPECIAL CONSIDERATION)	BITOLTEROL MESYLATE	SA	RX
BLOCADREN TABLETS	TIMOLOL MALEATE	BB	RX
BLOMBERG (CARDIOTONICUM)	LEPTAZOL	CN	RX
BLU-HIST CAPSULES	PHENYLPROPANOLAMINE HCL	SA	RX
BLUZEDRIN	AMPHETAMINE	PS	RX
BO COLD TABLETS	PHENYLPROPANOLAMINE HCL	SA	RX
BOLANDIOL DIPROPIONATE	BOLANDIOL DIPROPIONATE	AS	RX
BOLASTERONE	BOLASTERONE	AS	RX
BOLAZIN	BOLAZIN	AS	RX
BOLAZIN-CAPRONATE	BOLAZIN-CAPRONATE	AS	RX
BOLDANE	BOLDENONE UNDECYLATE	AS	RX
BOLDENONE	BOLDENONE	AS	RX
BOLDENONE UNDECYLATE	BOLDENONE UNDECYLATE	AS	RX
BOLENOL	BOLENOL	AS	RX
BOLMANTALAT	BOLMANTALAT	AS	RX
BONCODAL	OXOCODONE	NA	RX
BONTRIL PDM, & SLOW RELEASE	PHENDIMETRAZINE TARTRATE	PS	RX
BOSMIN	EPINEPHRINE	SA	RX
BOWMAN DECONGESTANT COMPOUND INJECTION	PHENYLPROPANOLAMINE HCL	SA	RX
BP 81	METHYLAMPHETAMINE	PS	RX
BREACOL COUGH MEDICATION LIQUID	PHENYLPROPANOLAMINE HCL	SA	RX
BRENAL	MECLOFENOXATE	PS	RX
BRETHAIRE	TERBUTALINE SULFATE	SA	RX
BRETHINE (SPECIAL CONSIDERATION DRUG)	TERBUTALINE SULFATE	SA	RX
BREVEDRIN	EPHEDRINE	SA	RX
BREVIRENIN	EPINEPHRINE	SA	RX
BRICANYL SUBCUTANEOUS INJECTION	TERBUTALINE SULFATE	SA	RX
BROMANYL EXPECTORANT	CODEINE PHOSPHATE	NA	RX
BROMPHEN COMPOUND ELIXIR—SUGAR FREE, & TABLETS	PHENYLEPHRINE HCL	SA	RX
BROMPHEN DC EXPECTORANT	PHENYLEPHRINE HCL	SA	RX
BROMPHEN DC EXPECTORANT	CODEINE PHOSPHATE	NA	RX
BROMPHEN EXPECTORANT	PHENYLEPHRINE HCL	SA	RX
BRONCHOMISTER	ISOPROTERENOL	SA	RX
BRONCODID	HYDROCODONE	NA	RX
BRONHODILATIN	ISOPROTERENOL	SA	RX
BRONITIN MIST	EPINEPHRINE	SA	OTC
BRONKAID MIST	EPINEPHRINE	SA	OTC
BRONKAID TABLETS	EPHEDRINE	SA	OTC
BRONKEPHRINE (INJECTION)	ETHYLNOREPINEPHRINE HCL	SA	RX

BRONKOLIXIR	EPHEDRINE	SA	RX
BRONKOMETER	ISOETHARINE HCL	SA	RX
BRONKOSOL	ISOETHARINE HCL	SA	RX
BRONKOTABS	EPHEDRINE	SA	OTC
BRONKOTUSS	EPHEDRINE	SA	RX
BROWN MIXTURE	OPIUM	NA	RX
BUFF-A COMP #3 TABLETS	CODEINE PHOSPHATE	NA	RX
BUR-TUSS EXPECTORANT	PHENYLPROPANOLAMINE HCL	SA	RX
BUTALGIN	METHADONE	NA	RX
C 4311	METHYLPHENIDATE	PS	RX
C.F. (CARDIOTONICO)	LEPTAZOL	CN	RX
CAFFEINE (GREATER THAN 12 MCG/ML IN THE URINE)	CAFFEINE	CN	OTC
CALCIDRINE SYRUP	CODEINE PHOSPHATE	NA	RX
CALMODID	HYDROCODONE	NA	RX
CAMPHORATED TINCTURE OF OPIUM	OPIUM	NA	RX
CAMPHOZONE	NIKETHAMIDE	CN	RX
CANFODIAMINA	NIKETHAMIDE	CN	RX
CAPITAL WITH CODEINE SUSPENSION AND TABLETS	CODEINE PHOSPHATE	NA	RX
CAPROSEM	CLOXOTESTOSTERONE ACETATE	AS	RX
CARBMIDAL	NIKETHAMIDE	CN	RX
CARDAMIN	NIKETHAMIDE	CN	RX
CARDANON	OXOCODONE	NA	RX
CARDEC DM DROPS & SYRUP	DEXTROMETHORPHAN HYDROBROMIDE	NA	RX
CARDIA-NOXI	LEPTAZOL	CN	RX
CARDIAGEN	NIKETHAMIDE	CN	RX
CARDIAMID	NIKETHAMIDE	CN	RX
CARIAMIN(E)	NIKETHAMIDE	CN	RX
CARDIAMINE "CHROPI"	LEPTAZOL	CN	RX
CARDIARINOL	LEPTAZOL	CN	RX
CARDIAZOL	LEPTAZOL	CN	RX
CARDIBIOM	LEPTAZOL	CN	RX
CARDIFORTAN	LEPTAZOL	CN	RX
CARDIMON	NIKETHAMIDE	CN	RX
CARDIO-ALPIN	LEPTAZOL	CN	RX
CARDIO-ASEY	LEPTAZOL	CN	RX
CARDIODINAMIN	PHENYLEPHRINE	SA	OTC
CARDIODYNAMIN	PHENYLEPHRINE	SA	OTC
CARDIOFOR	LEPTAZOL	CN	RX
CARDIOKALAN	LEPTAZOL	CN	RX
CARDIOL	LEPTAZOL	CN	RX
CARDIOLADBI	LEPTAZOL	CN	RX
CARDIOLEIC	NIKETHAMIDE	CN	RX
CARDIOLIFSA	LEPTAZOL	CN	RX
CARDIOPIRIDINA	NIKETHAMIDE	CN	RX
CARDIORAPIDE	LEPTAZOL	CN	RX
CARDIOSAN	LEPTAZOL	CN	RX
CARDIOSIMPA-BIS	PHENYLEPHRINE	SA	OTC
CARDIOTETRAZOL	LEPTAZOL	CN	RX
CARDIOTON	LEPTAZOL	CN	RX
CARDIOTONICO "C. F."	LEPTAZOL	CN	RX
CARDIOTONICUM "BLOMBERG"	LEPTAZOL	CN	RX
CARDIOTRAVA	LEPTAZOL	CN	RX
CARDIOVANIL	ETHAMIVAN	CN	RX
CARDIOVISA	LEPTAZOL	CN	RX
CARDIRENE P.	LEPTAZOL	CN	RX
CARDOSAL	LEPTAZOL	CN	RX

Brand Name	Generic Name	Class	SRC
CARDOSAN	LEPTAZOL	CN	RX
CAROPAN	PIPRADOL	PS	RX
CATHIN(E)	NORPSEUDOEPHEDRINE	PS	RX
CATOVIT-WIRKSTOFF	PROLINTANE	PS	RX
CATOVITAN-WIRKSTOFF	PROLINTANE	PS	RX
CB 8022	NORETHANDROLONE	AS	RX
CB 8075	OXANDROLONE	AS	RX
CELLATIVE	MECLOFENOXATE	PS	RX
CENABOLIC	METHANDRIOL	AS	RX
CENAFED	PSEUDOEPHEDRINE HCL	SA	RX
CENAFED SYRUP	PSEUDOEPHEDRINE HCL	SA	RX
CENALENE-M	LEPTAZOL	CN	RX
CENAZOL	LEPTAZOL	CN	RX
CENTALEX	LEPTAZOL	CN	RX
CENTEDRIN	METHYLPHENIDATE	PS	RX
CENTRALGIN (FROM SWITZERLAND)	DEMEROL	NA	RX
CENTRAMIN "YOSHITOMI"	PEMOLINE	PS	RX
CENTRAMINE	AMPHETAMINE	PS	RX
CENTRAZOLE	LEPTAZOL	CN	RX
CENTROPHENOXINE	MECLOFENOXATE	PS	RX
CERUTIL	MECLOFENOXATE	PS	RX
CETREXIN	MECLOFENOXATE	PS	RX
CHELAFRIN	EPINEPHRINE	SA	RX
CHEMETRAZINE	PHENMETRAZINE	PS	RX
CHERACOL PLUS HEAD COLD/COUGH FORMULA	PHENYLPROPANOLAMINE HCL	SA	OTC
CHESTOX	METHYLAMPHETAMINE	PS	RX
CHEXIT TABLETS	PHENYLPROPANOLAMINE HCL	SA	RX
CHILDREN'S HOLD	PHENYLPROPANOLAMINE HCL	SA	OTC
CHILDRENS CO-TYLENOL CHEWABLE COLD TABLETS & LIQUID COLD FORMULA	PHENYLPROPANOLAMINE HCL	SA	OTC
CHLOR-TRIMETON DECONGESTANT TABLETS	PSEUDOEPHEDRINE SULFATE	SA	OTC
CHLORAFED	PSEUDOEPHEDRINE	SA	OTC
CHLORDROLONE	CHLORDROLONE	AS	RX
CHLOROHIST-LA	XYLOMETAZOLINE HCL	SA	OTC
CHLOROMYL	ETHYLMORPHINE	NA	RX
CHLOROXYDIENONE	CHLOROXYDIENONE	AS	RX
CHLOROXYMESTERONE	CHLOROXYMESTERONE	AS	RX
CHLORPHENTERMINE	CHLORPHENTERMINE	PS	RX
CHLORPHENTERMINHYDRO-CHLORID	CHLORPHENTERMINE	PS	RX
CHLORTESTOSTERONE	CLOSTEBOL	AS	RX
CHLORTRIMETON-DC	PSEUDOEPHEDRINE	SA	OTC
CHOLR-TRIMETON LONG ACTING DECONGESTANT REPETABS TABLETS	PSEUDOEPHEDRINE SULFATE	SA	OTC
CHP	PROPYLHEXEDRINE	SA	OTC
CHROPI (ANGIOTON)	PHENYLEPHRINE	SA	OTC
CHROPI (CARDIAMINE)	LEPTAZOL	CN	RX
CI-406	OXYMETHOLONE	AS	RX
CIBA 17309-BA	METHANDROSTENOLONE	AS	RX
CIMADON	PIMINODINE	NA	RX
CITOCOR	NIKETHAMIDE	CN	RX
CITRA FORTE CAPS AND SYRUP	HYDROCODONE	NA	RX

CLARETIL	MECLOFENOXATE	PS	RX
CLINIBOLIN	NANDROLONE LAURATE	AS	RX
CLOCETE	MECLOFENOXATE	PS	RX
CLOFENOXINE	MECLOFENOXATE	PS	RX
CLOMINA	CHLORPHENTERMINE	PS	RX
CLORO-NONA	METHADONE	NA	RX
CLORPRENALINHYDRO- CHLORID	CHLORPRENALINE	SA	RX
CLOSETE	MECLOFENOXATE	PS	RX
CLOSTEBOL	CLOSTEBOL	AS	RX
CLOSTEBOL ACETATE	CLOSTEBOL ACETATE	AS	RX
CLOSTEBOL CAPRONATE	CLOSTEBOL CAPRONATE	AS	RX
CLOXOTESTOSTERONE ACETATE	CLOXOTESTOSTERONE ACETATE	AS	RX
CO-TYLENOL MEDICATION TABLETS & CAPSULES & LIQUID	PSEUDOEPHEDRINE HCL	SA	OTC
CO-TYLENOL COLD MEDICATION TABLETS AND CAPSULES	DEXTROMETHORPHAN HYDROBROMIDE	NA	RX
CO-GESIC TABLETS	HYDROCODONE	NA	RX
CO-TYLENOL	PSEUDOEPHEDRINE	SA	OTC
COCAIN	COCAINE	PS	RX
COCAINE—"COKE"	COCAINE	PS	RX
COCCULIN	PICROTOXINE	CN	RX
CODALAN	CODEINE PHOSPHATE	NA	RX
CODEINE	CODEINE	NA	RX
CODEINE PHOSPHATE IN TUBES, INJECTION & ORAL SOLUTION	CODEINE PHOSPHATE	NA	RX
CODEINE SULFATE TABLETS	CODEINE SULFATE	NA	RX
CODEINONA	OXOCODONE	NA	RX
CODENON	OXOCODONE	NA	RX
CODETHYLINE	ETHYLMORPHINE	NA	RX
CODETILINA	ETHYLMORPHINE	NA	RX
CODHYDRINE	DEXTROMORAMIDE	NA	RX
CODICLEAR DH SYRUP	HYDROCODONE	NA	RX
CODIMAL DH	PHENYLEPHRINE HCL	SA	RX
CODIMAL DH	HYDROCODONE	NA	RX
CODIMAL DM	DEXTROMETHORPHAN HYDROBROMIDE	NA	RX
CODIMAL PH	PHENYLEPHRINE HCL	SA	RX
CODIMAL PH	CODEINE PHOSPHATE	NA	RX
CODINAN	HYDROCODONE	NA	RX
CODINON	HYDROCODONE	NA	RX
CODINOVO	HYDROCODONE	NA	RX
CODONE	HYDROCODONE	NA	RX
CODUCEPT	CODEIN	NA	RX
COFACODAL	OXOCODONE	NA	RX
COFACODIDE	HYDROCODONE	NA	RX
COFADICON	THEBACON	NA	RX
COFALAUDIDE	HYDROMORPHONE	NA	RX
COKE	COCAINE	PS	RX
COLD FACTOR 12 LIQUID AND CAPSULES	PHENYLPROPANOLAMINE HCL	SA	OTC
COLDRINE TABLETS	PSEUDOEPHEDRINE HCL	SA	RX
COLI	PENTAZOCINE	NA	RX
COLLYRIUM WITH EPHEDRINE	EPHEDRINE	SA	OTC
COMHIST LA CAPSULES	PHENYLEPHRINE HCL	SA	RX
COMHIST TABLETS	PHENYLEPHRINE HCL	SA	RX
COMPOL CAPSULES	DIHYDROCODEINE BITARTRATE	NA	RX

Brand Name	Generic Name	Class	SRC
COMPOUND 20 025	CHLORPRENALINE	SA	RX
COMTREX	PHENYLPROPANOLAMINE HCL	SA	OTC
COMTREX	DEXTROMETHORPHAN HYDROBROMIDE	NA	RX
CONEX WITH CODEINE	CODEINE PHOSPHATE	NA	RX
CONGESPIRIN ASPIRIN-FREE CHEWABLE COLD TABLETS FOR CHILDREN	PHENYLEPHRINE	SA	OTC
CONGESPIRIN CHEWABLE COLD TABS FOR CHILDREN	PHENYLEPHRINE	SA	OTC
CONGESPIRIN COUGH SYRUP	DEXTROMETHORPHAN HYDROBROMIDE	NA	RX
CONGESPIRIN LIQUID COLD MEDICINE	PHENYLPROPANOLAMINE HCL	SA	OTC
CONGESTAC TABLETS	PSEUDOEPHEDRINE HCL	SA	OTC
CONSDRIN	PHENYLEPHRINE	SA	OTC
CONTIMOL	PEMOLINE	PS	RX
CONSTITUENT OF ALERTONIC	PIPRADOL	PS	RX
CONTAC CAPSULES	PHENYLPROPANOLAMINE HCL	SA	OTC
CONTAC COUGH CAPSULES	PSEUDOEPHEDRINE HCL	SA	OTC
CONTAC JR. CHILDRENS' COLD MEDICINE	PHENYLPROPANOLAMINE HCL	SA	OTC
CONTAC SEVERE COLD FORMULA CAPSULES & NIGHT STRENGTH	PSEUDOEPHEDRINE HCL	SA	OTC
CONTRADOL	DEMEROL	NA	RX
CONTRASMA-COMPR.	ISOPROTERENOL	SA	RX
CONTRATUSS	DEXTROMETHORPHAN	NA	RX
CONTROL CAPSULES	PHENYLPROPANOLAMINE HCL	SA	OTC
CONTROLGRAS	PHENMETRAZINE	PS	RX
COPHEDRINE	EPHEDRINE	SA	RX
COPHENE NO. 2 CAPSULES	PHENYLPROPANOLAMINE HCL	SA	RX
COR-SEMAR	LEPTAZOL	CN	RX
CORA-LEFA	NIKETHAMIDE	CN	RX
CORA-RAPIDE	NIKETHAMIDE	CN	RX
CORACANFOR	NIKETHAMIDE	CN	RX
CORACID	NIKETHAMIDE	CN	RX
CORACON	NIKETHAMIDE	CN	RX
CORAETHAMIDUM	NIKETHAMIDE	CN	RX
CORAFASA	NIKETHAMIDE	CN	RX
CORAFORSAN	NIKETHAMIDE	CN	RX
CORAL	NIKETHAMIDE	CN	RX
CORALEPT	NIKETHAMIDE	CN	RX
CORAMIDE	NIKETHAMIDE	CN	RX
CORAMIN(E)	NIKETHAMIDE	CN	RX
CORANORMAL	LEPTAZOL	CN	RX
CORAPHENE	PHENYLEPHRINE	SA	OTC
CORASID	LEPTAZOL	CN	RX
CORASOL	LEPTAZOL	CN	RX
CORATOL-INE	LEPTAZOL	CN	RX
CORAVERK	NIKETHAMIDE	CN	RX
CORAZOL "BIOFARMACOTERAPICO"	PHENYLEPHRINE	SA	OTC
CORAZOL(UM)	LEPTAZOL	CN	RX
CORAZON(E)	NIKETHAMIDE	CN	RX
CORDIA-MED	NIKETHAMIDE	CN	RX
CORDIAMIN(UM)	NIKETHAMIDE	CN	RX

CORDIN	NIKETHAMIDE	CN	RX
CORDINA	NIKETHAMIDE	CN	RX
CORDITON	NIKETHAMIDE	CN	RX
CORDYNIL	NIKETHAMIDE	CN	RX
COREDIOL	NIKETHAMIDE	CN	RX
CORERTAN	LEPTAZOL	CN	RX
CORESPIN	NIKETHAMIDE	CN	RX
CORETHAMIDUM	NIKETHAMIDE	CN	RX
CORETONE	NIKETHAMIDE	CN	RX
CORGARD (BANNED FOR SHOOTERS)	NADOLOL	BB	RX
CORICIDIN "D" DECONGESTANT TABLETS	PHENYLPROPANOLAMINE HCL	SA	OTC
CORICIDIN COUGH SYRUP	PHENYLPROPANOLAMINE HCL	SA	OTC
CORICIDIN DEMILETS TABLETS FOR CHILDREN	PHENYLPROPANOLAMINE HCL	SA	OTC
CORICIDIN EXTRA STRENGTH SINUS HEADACHE TABLETS	PHENYLPROPANOLAMINE HCL	SA	OTC
CORICIDIN MEDILETS TABLETS FOR CHILDREN	PHENYLPROPANOLAMINE HCL	SA	OTC
CORICIDIN NASAL MIST	PHENYLEPHRINE	SA	OTC
CORILENO F	NIKETHAMIDE	CN	RX
CORISAN	LEPTAZOL	CN	RX
CORISOL	EPINEPHRINE	SA	RX
CORIVANIL	ETHAMIVAN	CN	RX
CORIVO	NIKETHAMIDE	CN	RX
CORMED "REISS"	NIKETHAMIDE	CN	RX
CORMORPHIN	HYDROMORPHONE	NA	RX
CORMOTYL	NIKETHAMIDE	CN	RX
COROLIQ	NIKETHAMIDE	CN	RX
COROTONIN	NIKETHAMIDE	CN	RX
COROVASOL	PHENYLEPHRINE	SA	OTC
COROVIT	NIKETHAMIDE	CN	RX
CORSEDROL	LEPTAZOL	CN	RX
CORSYMPAL	PHENYLEPHRINE	SA	OTC
CORTALIT	PHENYLEPHRINE	SA	OTC
CORTON	NIKETHAMIDE	CN	RX
CORTRAZOL	LEPTAZOL	CN	RX
CORUTOL DH	HYDROCODONE	NA	RX
CORVASOL	LEPTAZOL	CN	RX
CORVASYMTON	PHENYLEPHRINE	SA	OTC
CORVIN	NIKETHAMIDE	CN	RX
CORVIS	LEPTAZOL	CN	RX
COVITAN	NIKETHAMIDE	CN	RX
CORVITIN	METHYLAMPHETAMINE	PS	RX
CORVITOL	NIKETHAMIDE	CN	RX
CORVOTONE	NIKETHAMIDE	CN	RX
CORYBAN-D CAPSULES	PHENYLPROPANOLAMINE HCL	SA	OTC
CORYBAN-D COUGH SYRUP	PHENYLEPHRINE	SA	OTC
CORYBAN-D COUGH SYRUP	DEXTROMETHORPHAN HYDROBROMIDE	NA	RX
CORYVET	LEPTAZOL	CN	RX
CORYWAS	NIKETHAMIDE	CN	RX
CORYZA BRENGLE CAPSULETS (TABLETS)	PSEUDOEPHEDRINE HCL	SA	RX
CORZIDE	NADOLOL	BB	RX
CORZONE SYRUP	PHENYLPROPANOLAMINE HCL	SA	RX
COSYLAN (ALTE FORM)	ETHYLMORPHINE	NA	RX
COTUSSATE	HYDROCODONE	NA	RX
CO-TYLENOL LIQUID COLD MEDICATION	DEXTROMETHORPHAN HYDROBROMIDE	NA	RX
COUGHCON	DEXTROMETHORPHAN	NA	RX

Brand Name	Generic Name	Class	SRC
COVANAMINE TABLETS	PHENYLPROPANOLAMINE HCL	SA	RX
COVITINE	METHYLAMPHETAMINE	PS	RX
CREIN	METHANDROSTENOLONE	AS	RX
CREMACOAT 1 & 3 & 4	DEXTROMETHORPHAN HYDROBROMIDE	NA	RX
CREMACOAT 3 & 4	PHENYLPROPANOLAMINE HCL	SA	OTC
CRESTABOLIC	METHANDRIOLDIPROPIONATE	AS	RX
CRISTAVIRON	TESTOSTERONE	AS	RX
CROPROPAMIDE	CROPROPAMIDE	CN	RX
CROTETHAMIDE	CROTETHAMIDE	CN	RX
CS 350	PENTAZOCINE	NA	RX
CURADOL	HYDROCODONE	NA	RX
CYLERT TABLETS	PEMOLINE	PS	RX
D.O.E.	METHYLAMPHETAMINE	PS	RX
D-DESYNE	METHYLAMPHETAMINE	PS	RX
D-FEDA	PSEUDOEPHEDRINE	SA	OTC
D-METHORPHAN	DEXTROMETHORPHAN	NA	RX
D-MORAMID	DEXTROMORAMIDE	NA	RX
D-140	DEMEROL	NA	RX
D-3-METHYLDROMORAN	DEXTROMETHORPHAN	NA	RX
DAEFE	PHENDIMETRAZINE	PS	RX
DAFTAZOL	AMIPHENAZOLE	CN	RX
DALCA TABLETS	PHENYLPROPANOLAMINE HCL	SA	OTC
DALLERGY CAPSULES	PHENYLEPHRINE HCL	SA	RX
DALOXEN	PROPOXYPHENE	NA	RX
DAMACET-P	HYDROCODONE	NA	RX
DAMASON-P	HYDROCODONE	NA	RX
DANABOL	METHANDROSTENOLONE	AS	RX
DANATROL	DANAZOL	AS	RX
DANAZOL	XYLOMETAZOLINE	SA	OTC
DANAZOL	DANAZOL	AS	RX
DANEPHRINE	PHENYLEPHRINE	SA	OTC
DANIELS (PEDIATRIC NASAL DROPS)	PHENYLEPHRINE	SA	OTC
DANOCRINE	DANAZOL	AS	RX
DANOL	DANAZOL	AS	RX
DANTROMIN	PEMOLINE	PS	RX
DAPEX-37-5	PHENTERMINE HYDROCHLORIDE	PS	RX
DAPT	AMIPHENAZOLE	CN	RX
DAPTA 12	AMIPHENAZOLE	CN	RX
DAPTAZILE	AMIPHENAZOLE	CN	RX
DAPTAZOLE	AMIPHENAZOLE	CN	RX
DAPTIZOLE	AMIPHENAZOLE	CN	RX
DARO-ASTHMA TABL.	EPHEDRINE	SA	RX
DAROPERVAMIN	METHYLAMPHETAMINE	PS	RX
DAROPHEDRIN	EPHEDRINE	SA	RX
DARVOCET-N 50 & 100	PROPOXYPHENE NAPSYLATE	NA	RX
DARVON N WITH A.S.A.	PROPOXYPHENE NAPSYLATE	NA	RX
DARVON, COMPOUND (65), PULVULES, WITH A.S.A.	PROPOXYPHENE HCL	NA	RX
DAURAN	DEXTOMORAMIDE	NA	RX
DAYCARE LIQUID	PHENYLPROPANOLAMINE HCL	SA	OTC
DAYCARE MULTI-SYMPTOM COLDS MEDICINE CAPSULES & LIQUID	PSEUDOEPHEDRINE HCL	SA	OTC
DEAMIN	METHADONE	NA	RX
DECA-DURABOL	NANDROLONE DECANOATE	AS	RX
DECA-DURABOLIN	NANDROLONE DECANOATE	AS	RX

DECA-NEPHRINE	PHENYLEPHRINE	SA	OTC
DECANANDROLINE	NANDROLONE DECANOATE	AS	RX
DECANOLONA	NANDROLONE DECANOATE	AS	RX
DECAPRYN	ETAFEDRINE	SA	RX
DECOBEL CAPSULES	PHENYLPROPANOLAMINE HCL	SA	RX
DECOFAN	DEXTROMETHORPHAN	NA	RX
DECOFED SYRUP	PSEUDOEPHEDRINE HCL	SA	RX
DECONAMINE	PSEUDOEPHEDRINE	SA	OTC
DECONGESTANT EXPECTORANT	CODEINE PHOSPHATE	NA	RX
DECONGESTANT INJECTION	PHENYLPROPANOLAMINE HCL	SA	RX
DECONGESTANT-AT (ANTITUSSIVE) LIQUID	CODEINE PHOSPHATE	NA	RX
DECONGESTCAPS TDC CAPSULES	PHENYLPROPANOLAMINE HCL	SA	RX
DEE DEX 10	METHYLAMPHETAMINE	PS	RX
DEE-10	METHYLAMPHETAMINE	PS	RX
DEGEST	PHENYLEPHRINE	SA	OTC
DEHACODIN	DEXTROMORAMIDE	NA	RX
DEHYDROANDROSTERONE	DEHYDROEPIANDROSTERONE	AS	RX
DEHYDROCHLORMETHYL TESTOSTERONE	DEHYDROCHLORMETHYL TESTOSTERONE	AS	RX
DEHYDROEPIANDROS-TERONE	DEHYDROEPIANDROSTERONE	AS	RX
DEHYDROMETHYLTESTOS-TERON	METHANDROSTENOLONE	AS	RX
DEKANABOL	NANDROLONE DECANOATE	AS	RX
DEKZOFEN	PROPOXYPHENE	NA	RX
DELATESTRYL	TESTOSTERONE ENANTHATE	AS	RX
DELCOBESE	DEXTROAMPHETAMINE SULFATE	PS	RX
DELFETAMINE	METHYLAMPHETAMINE	PS	RX
DELGACEROL	PHENMETRAZINE	PS	RX
DELMATIN	PEMOLINE	PS	RX
DELSYM	DEXTROMETHORPHAN POLISTIREX	NA	RX
DELTA-LUCIDRIL	MECLOFENOXATE	PS	RX
DELTAMINE	PEMOLINE	PS	RX
DELTRAX	PHENMETRAZINE	PS	RX
DELZOL-W	LEPTAZOL	CN	RX
DEMALON	DIMETHYLANDROSTANOLONE	AS	RX
DEMAZIN DECONGESTANT-ANTIHISTAMINE REPETABS TABS/ & SYRUP	PHENYLEPHRINE	SA	OTC
DEMELON	NANDROLONE FURYLPROPIONATE	AS	RX
DEMER-IDINE (FROM CANADA)	DEMEROL	NA	RX
DEMEROL	MEPERIDINE HCL	NA	RX
DEMORPHAN	DEXTROMETHORPHAN	NA	RX
DEOFED	METHYLAMPHETAMINE	PS	RX
DEP-ANDROLE	TESTOSTERONE	AS	RX
DEPANDRO 100 AND 200	TESTOSTERONE CYPIONATE	AS	RX
DEPLETITE 25	DIETHYLPROPION HYDROCHLORIDE	PS	RX
DEPO-TESTOSTERONE	TESTOSTERONE CYPIONATE	AS	RX
DEPOTEST "HYREX"	TESTOSTERONE	AS	RX
DEPRANCOL	PROPOXYPHENE	NA	RX
DEPRIDOL	METHADONE	NA	RX
DEPROIST EXPECTORANT WITH CODEINE	CODEINE PHOSPHATE	NA	RX
DEPROMIC	PROPOXYPHENE	NA	RX

Brand Name	Generic Name	Class	SRC
DEPRONAL	PROPOXYPHENE	NA	RX
DEPTADOL	METHADONE	NA	RX
DERIZENE	PHENYLEPHRINE	SA	OTC
DERMA MEDICONE HC OINTMENT	EPHEDRINE	SA	RX
DES-O-E	METHYLAMPHETAMINE	PS	RX
DES-OXA-D	METHYLAMPHETAMINE	PS	RX
DES-OXO-5	METHYLAMPHETAMINE	PS	RX
DESA-HIST-ANTITUSSIVE SYRUP, & AT TABLETS, & PF CAPSULES	PHENYLPROPANOLAMINE HCL	SA	RX
DESAMINE	METHYLAMPHETAMINE	PS	RX
DESANCA	METHYLAMPHETAMINE	PS	RX
DESEPHRINE	METHYLAMPHETAMINE	PS	RX
DESEPIN	METHYLAMPHETAMINE	PS	RX
DESODEX	METHYLAMPHETAMINE	PS	RX
DESOPIMON	CHLORPHENTERMINE	PS	RX
DESOXEDRINE	METHYLAMPHETAMINE	PS	RX
DESOXIN	METHYLAMPHETAMINE	PS	RX
DESOXYADRENALIN	PHENYLEPHRINE	SA	OTC
DESOXYEPHEDRIN	METHYLAMPHETAMINE	PS	RX
DESOXYEPHEDRINE	DESOXYEPHEDRINE	SA	OTC
DESOXYEPINEPHRIN	PHENYLEPHRINE	SA	OTC
DESOXYFED	METHYLAMPHETAMINE	PS	RX
DESOXYN GRADUMET TABLETS	METHAMPHETAMINE HYDROCHLORIDE	PS	RX
DESOXYN(E)	METHYLAMPHETAMINE	PS	RX
DESOXYNOREPHEDRIN	AMPHETAMINE	PS	RX
DESTAFRINA	PHENYLEPHRINE	SA	OTC
DESTIM	METHYLAMPHETAMINE	PS	RX
DESTROMETORFANO	DEXTROMETHORPHAN	NA	RX
DESTROMORAMIDE	DEXTOMORAMIDE	NA	RX
DESYPHED	METHYLAMPHETAMINE	PS	RX
DETARIL	PIPRADOL	PS	RX
DETERENOLHYDROCHLORID	ISOPROTERENOL	SA	RX
DETREX	METHYLAMPHETAMINE	PS	RX
DETUSSIN EXPECTORANT AND LIQUID	HYDROCODONE	NA	RX
DEUMACARD	LEPTAZOL	CN	RX
DEVELIN RETARD	PROPOXYPHENE	NA	RX
DEX-A-DIET	PHENYLPROPANOLAMINE HCL	SA	OTC
DEXAMPEX	DEXTROAMPHETAMINE SULFATE	PS	RX
DEXATRIM	PHENYLPROPANOLAMINE HCL	SA	OTC
DEXEDRINE	DEXTROAMPHETAMINE SULFATE	PS	RX
DEXEDRINE SPANSULES	DEXTROAMPHETAMINE SULFATE	PS	RX
DEXFENMETRAZIN	PHENMETRAZINE	PS	RX
DEXOPHRINE	METHYLAMPHETAMINE	PS	RX
DEXOSYN	METHYLAMPHETAMINE	PS	RX
DEXOVAL	METHYLAMPHETAMINE	PS	RX
DEXSTIM	METHYLAMPHETAMINE	PS	RX
DEXTRODIPHENOPYRINE	DEXTOMORAMIDE	NA	RX
DEXTROMETHORPHAN	DEXTROMETHORPHAN	NA	RX
DEXTROMORAMIDE	DEXTROMORAMIDE	NA	RX
DEXTROPROPOXIPHENI CHLORIDUM	PROPOXYPHENE	NA	RX
DEXTROPROPOXYPHEN- HYDROCHLORID	PROPOXYPHENE	NA	RX
DEY-DOSE	ISOPROTERENOL	SA	RX

DEY-DOSE ISOETHARINE HCL	ISOETHARINE HCL	SA	RX
DEY-LUTE ISOETHARINE	ISOETHARINE HCL	SA	RX
DEZEST CAPSULES	PHENYLPROPANOLAMINE HCL	SA	RX
DF 118	DEXTROMORAMIDE	NA	RX
DH 245	FURAZEBOL	AS	RX
DH-CODEINE	DEXTROMORAMIDE	NA	RX
DHA-245	AMIPHENAZOLE	CN	RX
DI-AP-TROL	PHENDIMETRAZINE TARTRATE	PS	OTC
DIA-GESIC	HYDROCODONE	NA	RX
DIACEPHIN	HEROIN	NA	RX
DIACETYLMORPHIN	HEROIN	NA	RX
DIACODON	THEBACON	NA	RX
DIADEX	PHENYLPROPANOLAMINE HCL	SA	OTC
DIADONE	METHADONE	NA	RX
DIAETHYLNICOTINAMIDUM	NIKETHAMIDE	CN	RX
DIAMINON	METHADONE	NA	RX
DIANABOL	METHANDROSTENOLONE	AS	RX
DIANDRIN	METHANDRIOL	AS	RX
DIANDRON	DEHYDROEPIANDROSTERONE	AS	RX
DIANONE	METHADONE	NA	RX
DIAPHORM	HEROIN	NA	RX
DIARSED	DIPHENOXYLATE	NA	RX
DICO	DEXTROMORAMIDE	NA	RX
DICODAL	HYDROCODONE	NA	RX
DICODETHAL	HYDROCODONE	NA	RX
DICODID	HYDROCODONE	NA	RX
DICODINON	HYDROCODONE	NA	RX
DICODRINE	HYDROCODONE	NA	RX
DICONON	HYDROCODONE	NA	RX
DICOSED	HYDROCODONE	NA	RX
DIDRATE	DEXTROMORAMIDE	NA	RX
DIDREX	BENZPHETAMINE HYCLROCHLORIDE	PS	RX
DIETAC	PHENYLPROPANOLAMINE HCL	SA	OTC
DIETAMINE	AMPHETAMINE	PS	RX
DIETHYLPROPION HCL TABLETS & TIMED TABLETS	DIETHYLPROPION HYDROCHLORIDE	PS	RX
DIETROL	PHENDIMETRAZINE	PS	RX
DIHIDROMORFON	HYDROMORPHONE	NA	RX
DIHYDRIN	DEXTROMORAMIDE	NA	RX
DIHYDROANDROSTERONE	ANDROSTANDIOL	AS	RX
DIHYDROCODEINE COMPOUND TABLETS	DIHYDROCODEINONE BITARTRATE	NA	RX
DIHYDROCODEINON(E)	HYDROCODONE	NA	RX
DIHYDROHYDROXYCO- DEINONHYDROCHLORID	OXOCODONE	NA	RX
DIHYDROKON	HYDROCODONE	NA	RX
DIHYDROMORPHINON(E)	HYDROMORPHONE	NA	RX
DIHYDRONE	OXOCODONE	NA	RX
DIHYDRONEOPINE	DEXTROMORAMIDE	NA	RX
DIHYDROTESTOSTERONE	ANDROSTANOLONE	AS	RX
DIKODID	HYDROCODONE	NA	RX
DILABRON	ISOETHARINE HCL	SA	RX
DILAFRIN	PHENYLEPHRINE	SA	OTC
DILAUDEN	HYDROMORPHONE	NA	RX
DILAUDID COUGH SYRUP	HYDROMORPHONE HCL	NA	RX
DILAUDID COUGH SYRUP	DIHYDROMORPHINONE HYDROCHLORIDE	NA	RX
DILAUDID HCL, & HP INJECTION	HYDROMORPHONE HCL	NA	RX
DILAUDID-HP INJECTION	HYDROMORPHONE HCL	NA	RX
DIMACOL CAPSULES	PSEUDOEPHEDRINE HCL	SA	OTC

Brand Name	Generic Name	Class	SRC
DIMATINA	MEBOLAZINE	AS	RX
DIMEFENOPAN	DIMETHYLAMPHETAMINE	PS	RX
DIMEPHENOPANE	DIMETHYLAMPHETAMINE	PS	RX
DIMETAMFETAMIN	DIMETHYLAMPHETAMINE	PS	RX
DIMETANE DECONGESTANT TABLETS	PHENYLEPHRINE	SA	OTC
DIMETANE EXPECTORANT LIQUID, & DC LIQUID	PHENYLPROPANOLAMINE HCL	SA	OTC
DIMETANE EXPECTORANT-DC LIQUID	PHENYLPROPANOLAMINE HCL	SA	OTC
DIMETANE-DC COUGH SYRUP	CODEINE PHOSPHATE	NA	RX
DIMETAPP ELIXIR	PHENYLEPHRINE HCL	SA	RX
DIMETAPP ELIXIR EXTENTABS	PHENYLPROPANOLAMINE HCL	SA	RX
DIMETAPP EXTENTABS	PHENYLEPHRINE HCL	SA	RX
DIMETAZIN	MEBOLAZINE	AS	RX
DIMETHAMPHETAMIN	DIMETHYLAMPHETAMINE	PS	RX
DIMETHAZINE	MEBOLAZINE	AS	RX
DIMETHYLAMPHETAMIN(E)	DIMETHYLAMPHETAMINE	PS	RX
DIMETHYLANDROSTANO-LONE	DIMETHYLANDROSTANOLONE	AS	RX
DIMETHYLTESTOSTERONE	BOLASTERONE	AS	RX
DIMORLIN	DEXTROMORAMIDE	NA	RX
DIMORPHID	HYDROMORPHONE	NA	RX
DIMORPHINON	HYDROMORPHONE	NA	RX
DIMORPHISID	HYDROMORPHONE	NA	RX
DIMORPHONE	HYDROMORPHONE	NA	RX
DINARKON	OXOCODONE	NA	RX
DINERGIL	PEMOLINE	PS	RX
DIOCIL	ETHYLMORPHINE	NA	RX
DIOLAN	ETHYLMORPHINE	NA	RX
DIOLANDRONE	METHANDRIOL	AS	RX
DIOLOSTENE	METHANDRIOL	AS	RX
DIONIN	ETHYLMORPHINE	NA	RX
DIONJUSTE	ETHYLMORPHINE	NA	RX
DIOSAN	ETHLMORPHINE	NA	RX
DIOVASCOL	LEPTAZOL	CN	RX
DIPHENOXYLATE HCL & ATROPINE SULFATE TABLETS	DIPHENOXYLATE HCL	NA	RX
DIPIPANONE	DIPIPANONE	NA	RX
DISEFONIN	METHADONE	NA	RX
DISIPAN	METHADONE	NA	RX
DISKET	METHADONE	NA	RX
DISOPHORAL	PSEUDOEPHEDRINE	SA	OTC
DISOPHROL CHRONOTAB SUSTAINED-ACTION TABLETS	PSEUDOEPHEDRINE SULFATE	SA	OTC
DISPADOL	DEMEROL	NA	RX
DISPNOESAN	ISOPROTERENOL	SA	RX
DISPOS-A-MED	ISOETHARINE HCL—ISOPROTERENOL	SA	RX
DISTRANORM	METHANDROSTENOLONE	AS	RX
DITATE-DS	TESTOSTERONE ENANTHATE	AS	RX
DIVANAL	ETHAMIVAN	CN	RX
DIZOL	AMIPHENAZOLE	CN	RX
DL-EPHEDRIN	EPHEDRINE	SA	RX
DM	DEXTROMETHORPHAN	NA	RX

DMA	DIMETHYLANDROSTANOLONE	AS	RX
DODIMAL DM	PHENYLEPHRINE HCL	SA	RX
DOFEDRIN	PSEUDOEPHEDRINE	SA	OTC
DOKTORS NOSE DROPS	PHENYLEPHRINE	SA	OTC
DOL	DEMEROL	NA	RX
DOLACET CAPSULES	HYDROCODONE	NA	RX
DOLAFIN	METHADONE	NA	RX
DOLAMID	METHADONE	NA	RX
DOLAMINA	METHADONE	NA	RX
DOLAN	PROPOXYPHENE	NA	RX
DOLANQUIFA	DEMEROL	NA	RX
DOLANTIN (GERMANY & SWITZERLAND)	DEMEROL	NA	RX
DOLAPENT	PENTAZOCINE	NA	RX
DOLAREN	DEMEROL	NA	RX
DOLARENIL	DEMEROL	NA	RX
DOLARGAN	DEMEROL	NA	RX
DOLARIN	DEMEROL	NA	RX
DOLATOL	DEMEROL	NA	RX
DOLCONTRAL	DEMEROL	NA	RX
DOLENAL	DEMEROL	NA	RX
DOLENE, & DOLENE 65	PROPOXYPHENE HCL	NA	RX
DOLENTAL	DEMEROL	NA	RX
DOLESONA	METHADONE	NA	RX
DOLESTINE	DEMEROL	NA	RX
DOLEVAL	DEMEROL	NA	RX
DOLFIN	DEMEROL	NA	RX
DOLIN	DEMEROL	NA	RX
DOLINAL	DEMEROL	NA	RX
DOLISAN	DEMEROL	NA	RX
DOLISINA	DEMEROL	NA	RX
DOLOCAP	PROPOXYPHENE	NA	RX
DOLODORM	OXOCODONE	NA	RX
DOLOFIN	METHADONE	NA	RX
DOLOFORTIN	PENTAZOCINE	NA	RX
DOLOHEPTAN	METHADONE	NA	RX
DOLOMIT	ISOPROTERENOL	SA	RX
DOLONEURIN (FROM NETHERLANDS)	DEMEROL	NA	RX
DOLOPETHIN	DEMEROL	NA	RX
DOLOPETIN	DEMEROL	NA	RX
DOLOPHINE HCL AMPULES AND VIALS AND TABLETS	METHADONE HCL	NA	RX
DOLOR	DEMEROL	NA	RX
DOLOREX	METHADONE	NA	RX
DOLORIDINE	DEMEROL	NA	RX
DOLORMIN	DEMEROL	NA	RX
DOLORPHEN	PROPOXYPHENE	NA	RX
DOLOSAN	DEMEROL	NA	RX
DOLOSIL	DEMEROL	NA	RX
DOLOSOL (FROM BELGIUM & FRANCE)	DEMEROL	NA	RX
DOLOTARD	PROPOXYPHENE	NA	RX
DOLOXENE	PROPOXYPHENE	NA	RX
DOLPRN #3 TABLETS	CODEINE PHOSPHATE	NA	RX
DOLSIN	DEMEROL	NA	RX
DOLVANAL	DEMEROL	NA	RX
DOLVANOL	DEMEROL	NA	RX
DONATUSSIN DC SYRUP	HYDROCODONE	NA	RX
DONATUSSIN DC SYRUP & DROPS	PHENYLEPHRINE HCL	SA	RX

Brand Name	Generic Name	Class	SRC
DOPIDRIN	METHYLAMPHETAMINE	PS	RX
DOPRAM INJECTABLE	DOXAPRAM HCL	CN	RX
DORCOL CHILDREN'S COUGH SYRUP	DEXTROMETHORPHAN HYDROBROMIDE	NA	RX
DORCOL CHILDREN'S COUGH SYRUP, & DECONGESTANT LIQUID, & COLD FORMULA	PSEUDOEPHEDRINE HCL	SA	OTC
DORCOL CHILDREN'S DECONGESTANT LIQUID	PSEUDOEPHEDRINE HCL	SA	OTC
DORCOL CHILDREN'S LIQUID COLD FORMULA	PSEUDOEPHEDRINE HCL	SA	OTC
DORCOL PEDIATRIC COUGH SYRUP	PHENYLPROPANOLAMINE HCL	SA	OTC
DORCOL PEDIATRIC FORMULA	PSEUDOEPHEDRINE HCL	SA	OTC
DOREXOL	METHADONE	NA	RX
DORMETHAN	DEXTROMETHORPHAN	NA	RX
DOSALUPENT	METAPROTERENOL	SA	RX
DOSICODID	HYDROCODONE	NA	RX
DOSOXY	METHYLAMPHETAMINE	PS	RX
DOUGLAS (AMPHOBESE)	PHENDIMETRAZINE	PS	RX
DOXAPHENE	PROPOXYPHENE HCL	NA	RX
DOXAPRAM	DOXAPRAM HCL	CN	RX
DOXAPRIL	DOXAPRAM	CN	RX
DOXEPHRIN	METHYLAMPHETAMINE	PS	RX
DOXYFED	METHYLAMPHETAMINE	PS	RX
DRENAMIST	EPINEPHRINE	SA	RX
DRI-DRIP CAPSULES—LIQUID	PHENYLPROPANOLAMINE HCL	SA	RX
DRINALFA	METHYLAMPHETAMINE	PS	RX
DRINOPHEN CAPSULES	PHENYLPROPANOLAMINE HCL	SA	RX
DRISTAN	PHENYLEPHRINE	SA	OTC
DRISTAN ADVANCED FORMULA DECONGESTANT/ ANTIHISTAMINE/ ANALGESIC TABLETS	PHENYLEPHRINE	SA	OTC
DRISTAN ADVANCED FORMULA DECONGESTANT/ ANTIHISTIMINE/ ANALGESIC CAPSULES	PHENYLPROPANOLAMINE HCL	SA	OTC
DRISTAN ADVANCED FORMULA DECONGESTANT/ ANTIHISTIMINE/ ANALGESIC TABLETS	PHENYLPROPANOLAMINE HCL	SA	OTC
DRISTAN NASAL SPRAY	PHENYLEPHRINE	SA	OTC
DRIXORAL	PSEUDOEPHEDRINE	SA	OTC
DROCODE	DIHYDROCODEINE	NA	RX
DROLBAN	DROSTANOLONE PROPIONATE	AS	RX
DROMORAN	LEVORPHANOL	NA	RX
DROMOSTANOLON PROPIONAT	DROSTANOLONE PROPIONATE	AS	RX
DROSTALON	MEBOLAZINE	AS	RX
DROSTANOLONE	DROSTANOLONE	AS	RX
DROSTANOLONE PROPIONATE	DROSTANOLONE PROPIONATE	AS	RX

DROSTENE	METHANDRIOL	AS	RX
DROSYN	PHENYLEPHRINE	SA	OTC
DUCODAL	OXOCODONE	NA	RX
DUNHALL (ANOREX)	PHENDIMETRAZINE	PS	RX
DUO-MEDIHALER	ISOPROTERENOL & PHENYLEPHRINE	SA	RX
DUODIN	HYDROCODONE	NA	RX
DURA TAP-PD	PHENYLEPHRINE HCL	SA	RX
DURA VENT/DA	PHENYLEPHRINE HCL	SA	RX
DURABOL	NANDROLONE PHENYLPROPIONATE	AS	RX
DURABOLIN	NANDROLONE PHENYLPROPIONATE	AS	RX
DURABOLIN-O	ETHYLESTRENOL	AS	RX
DURABOLIN-ORAL	ETHYLESTRENOL	AS	RX
DURABORAL	ETHYLESTRENOL	AS	RX
DURADYNE DHC TABLETS	HYDROCODONE	NA	RX
DURALIN	NANDROLONE PHENYLPROPIONATE	AS	RX
DURALUDRIN	ISOPROTERENOL	SA	RX
DURAMORPH PF	MORPHINE	NA	RX
DURAPLON	NANDROLONE PHENYLPROPIONATE	AS	RX
DURATEST 100 AND 200	TESTOSTERONE CYPIONATE	AS	RX
DURATION MILD, & 4 HOUR NASAL SPRAY	PHENYLEPHRINE	SA	OTC
DUROMORPH	MORPHINE	NA	RX
DYLEPHRIN	EPINEPHRINE	SA	RX
DYMOPOXYPHENE	PROPOXYPHENE	NA	RX
DYNABOLIN	NANDROLONE UNDECYLATE	AS	RX
DYNACORYL	NIKETHAMIDE	CN	RX
DYNAMICARDE	NIKETHAMIDE	CN	RX
DYNASTEN	OXYMETHOLONE	AS	RX
DYREXAN-OD CAPSULES	PHENDIMETRAZINE TARTRATE	PS	RX
DYSNE-INHAL	EPINEPHRINE	SA	RX
DYSPNOESAN	ISOPROTERENOL	SA	RX
E 1	EPINEPHRINE	SA	RX
E 50	NORPSEUDOEPHEDRINE	PS	RX
E.N.T. SYRUP & TABLETS	PHENYLEPHRINE HCL	SA	RX
ECIPHIN	EPHEDRINE	SA	RX
ECLORION	HEROIN	NA	RX
ECTASULE MINUS	EPHEDRINE	SA	RX
EDUSAN COMPR.	OXOCODONE	NA	RX
EFED II CAPSULES	EPHEDRINE—EPHEDRINE SULFATE	SA	RX
EFED TABLETS	EPHEDRINE SULFATE	SA	RX
EFEDRIL	EPHEDRINE	SA	RX
EFEDRIN	EPHEDRINE	SA	RX
EFEDRINETTER	EPHEDRINE	SA	RX
EFEDRON NASAL JELLY	EPHEDRINE	SA	RX
EFETONINA	EPHEDRINE	SA	RX
EFRICEL	PHENYLEPHRINE	SA	OTC
EFROXINE	METHYLAMPHETAMINE	PS	RX
EGGOBESIN	PROPYLHEXEDRINE	SA	OTC
EGGOPHEDRIN	EPHEDRINE	SA	RX
EGHERIT	METHYLAMPHETAMINE	PS	RX
ELASTONON	AMPHETAMINE	PS	RX
ELDATAPP TABLETS—LIQUID	PHENYLPROPANOLAMINE HCL	SA	RX
ELEVATON	LEPTAZOL	CN	RX
ELITONE	NIKETHAMIDE	CN	RX
ELPHEMET	PHENDIMETRAZINE	PS	RX

Brand Name	Generic Name	Class	SRC
ELTOR	PSEUDOEPHEDRINE	SA	OTC
EMBADOL	TIOMESTERONE	AS	RX
EMDABOLIN	TIOMESTERONE	AS	RX
EMDISTERONE	DROSTANOLONE PROPIONATE	AS	RX
EMEDIA EXPORT (NORCAMPHANE)	FENCAMFAMINE	PS	RX
EMIVAN	ETHAMIVAN	CN	RX
EMPIRIN WITH CODEINE	CODEINE PHOSPHATE	NA	RX
EMPRACET WITH CODEINE PHOSPHATE #3 AND #4	ANILERIDINE	NA	RX
EMPRAZIL	PSEUDOEPHEDRINE	SA	OTC
EN-1530	OXOMORPHINE	NA	RX
EN-15304	OXOMORPHINE	NA	RX
EN-1627	MECLOFENOXATE	PS	RX
ENARMON	TESTOSTERONE	AS	RX
ENARMON-TABL.	METHYLTESTOSTERONE	AS	RX
ENDO (SISTRAL)	PEMOLINE	PS	RX
ENDOLAT	DEMEROL	NA	RX
ENDOLIN	PEMOLINE	PS	RX
ENESTEBOL	ENESTEBOL	AS	RX
ENOLTESTOVIS	HEXOXYMESTROL	AS	RX
ENTESTIL-M	METHYLTESTOSTERONE	AS	RX
ENTEX CAPSULES	PHENYLPROPANOLAMINE HCL	SA	RX
ENTEX CAPSULES & LIQUID	PHENYLEPHRINE HCL	SA	RX
ENTEX LA TABLETS	PHENYLPROPANOLAMINE HCL	SA	RX
ENTEX LIQUID	PHENYLPROPANOLAMINE HCL	SA	RX
ENTUS-D LIQUID & TABLETS	HYDROCODONE	NA	RX
ENTUSS EXPECTORANT TABLETS & LIQUID	HYDROCODONE	NA	RX
ENVITROL	FENCAMFAMINE	PS	RX
EPHALONE	EPHEDRINE	SA	RX
EPHECARDOL	EPHEDRINE	SA	RX
EPHEDRA	EPHEDRINE	SA	OTC
EPHEDRA "ORION"	EPHEDRINE	SA	RX
EPHEDRAL	EPHEDRINE	SA	RX
EPHEDRATE	EPHEDRINE	SA	RX
EPHEDREMAL	EPHEDRINE	SA	RX
EPHEDRENAN	EPHEDRINE	SA	RX
EPHEDRINE	EPHEDRINE	SA	OTC
EPHEDRINE AND AMYTAL PULVULES	EPHEDRINE SULFATE	SA	RX
EPHEDRINE INJECTION	EPHEDRINE	SA	RX
EPHEDRINE SULFATE	EPHEDRINE	SA	OTC
EPHEDRINEALINE	CHLORPRENALINE	SA	RX
EPHEDRINHYDROCHLORID	PSEUDOEPHEDRINE	SA	OTC
EPHEDRITAL	EPHEDRINE	SA	RX
EPHEDROIDES	EPHEDRINE	SA	RX
EPHEDROL	EPHEDRINE	SA	RX
EPHEDRONAL	EPHEDRINE	SA	RX
EPHEDROPRISES	EPHEDRINE	SA	RX
EPHEDROSAN	EPHEDRINE	SA	RX
EPHEDROSST	EPHEDRINE	SA	RX
EPHEDROTAL	EPHEDRINE	SA	RX
EPHEDSOL	EPHEDRINE	SA	RX
EPHERIT	EPHEDRINE	SA	RX
EPHETONIN	EPHEDRINE	SA	RX
EPHINE	EPHEDRINE	SA	RX
EPI 6	EPINEPHRINE	SA	RX

EPI-PEN JR.	EPINEPHRINE	SA	RX
EPI-PEN-EPINEPHRINE AUTO INJECTOR	EPINEPHRINE	SA	RX
EPIFRIN	EPINEPHRINE	SA	RX
EPIGLAUFRIN	EPINEPHRINE	SA	RX
EPINEPHRAN	EPINEPHRINE	SA	RX
EPINEPHRIN(E)	EPINEPHRINE	SA	RX
EPINEPHRINE IN TUBEX	EPINEPHRINE	SA	RX
EPINEPHRINE INJECTION	EPINEPHRINE	SA	RX
EPININ(E)	PHENYLEPHRINE	SA	OTC
EPIRENAMINE	EPINEPHRINE	SA	RX
EPIRENAN	EPINEPHRINE	SA	RX
EPIRENIN	EPINEPHRINE	SA	RX
EPITOIN	PEMOLINE	PS	RX
EPITRATE	EPINEPHRINE	SA	RX
EPJ	DEMEROL	NA	RX
EPRINAL	EPINEPHRINE	SA	RX
EPTADONE	METHADONE	NA	RX
EQUIPOSE	BOLDENONE UNDECYLATE	AS	RX
ERANTIN	PROPOXYPHENE	NA	RX
ERBA (PROPAMIN)	METHYLAMPHETAMINE	PS	RX
ERI	DEXTROMETHORPHAN	NA	RX
ERMALONE	MESTANOLON	AS	RX
ERMALONE	ANDROSTANOLONE BENZOATE	AS	RX
EROIN	HEROIN	NA	RX
ERRECALMA	DEXTOMORAMIDE	NA	RX
ERYDIN	ISOPROTERENOL	SA	RX
ERYTHROXYLIN	COCAINE	PS	RX
ESICLENE	FORMEBOLONE	AS	RX
ESJAYDIOL	METHANDRIOL	AS	RX
ESPHYGMOGENINA	EPINEPHRINE	SA	RX
ESTAZOL	STANOZOLOL	AS	RX
ESTIMULEX	METHYLAMPHETAMINE	PS	RX
ESTIMULO-POWEL	PEMOLINE	PS	RX
ESTRATEST H.S. TABLETS	METHYLTESTOSTERONE	AS	RX
ESTRATEST TABLETS	METHYLTESTOSTERONE	AS	RX
ESTRENOLONE	NANDROLONE	AS	RX
ETAFEDRINE	EETAFEDRINE	SA	RX
ETAFEDRINHYDROCHLORID	ETAFEDRINE	SA	RX
ETAMIVAN	ETHAMIVAN	CN	RX
ETHAMIVAN	ETHAMIVAN	CN	RX
ETHAMPHETAMINE	ETHYLAMPHETAMINE	PS	RX
ETHAPHENE	PHENYLEPHRINE	SA	OTC
ETHYLMORPHINE	ETHYLMORPHINE	NA	RX
ETHYLAMPHETAMINE	ETHYLAMPHETAMINE	PS	RX
ETHYLESTRENOL	ETHYLESTRENOL	AS	RX
ETHYLMORPHINE	ETHYLMORPHINE	NA	RX
ETHYLNOREPINEPHRINE HCL	ETHYLNOREPINEPHRINE HCL	SA	RX
ETHYLNORTESTOSTERONE	NORETHANDROLONE	AS	RX
ETHYLOESTRENOL (UM)	ETHYLESTRENOL	AS	RX
ETILESTRENOLO	ETHYLESTRENOL	AS	RX
ETIMID	BEMIGRIDE	CN	RX
ETNABOLATE	MESTANOLON	AS	RX
ETYFIN	ETHYLMORPHINE	NA	RX
ETYPRENALINUM	ISOETHARINE	SA	RX
EUBINE	OXOCODONE	NA	RX
EUBOLIN	NANDROLONE DECANOATE	AS	RX
EUCODALE	OXOCODONE	NA	RX
EUCODAMINE	OXOCODONE	NA	RX
EUCORAN	NIKETHAMIDE	CN	RX
EUCOSAN	OXOCODONE	NA	RX

Brand Name	Generic Name	Class	SRC
EUDIN	OXOCODONE	NA	RX
EUDOL	OXOCODONE	NA	RX
EUFODRIN	METHYLAMPHETAMINE	PS	RX
EUFODRINAL	METHYLAMPHETAMINE	PS	RX
EUKDIN	OXOCODONE	NA	RX
EUKODAL	OXOCODONE	NA	RX
EUKODAN	OXOCODONE	NA	RX
EUKRATON	BEMIGRIDE	CN	RX
EUMORPHAL	OXOCODONE	NA	RX
EUPHODRIN	METHYLAMPHETAMINE	PS	RX
EUPHODYN	AMPHETAMINE	PS	RX
EUSPIRAN	ISOPROTERENOL	SA	RX
EUSPIROL	METHOXYPHENAMINE	SA	RX
EUTAGEN	OXOCODONE	NA	RX
EUVASOL	PHENYLEPHRINE	SA	OTC
EUVITOL "ALLEN & HANBURY"	FENCAMFAMINE	PS	RX
EVENTIN	PROPYLHEXEDRINE	SA	OTC
EVERONE	TESTOSTERONE ENANTHATE	AS	RX
EXADRIN	EPINEPHRINE	SA	RX
EXPONCIT	NORPSEUDOEPHEDRINE	PS	RX
EXTENDRYL CHEWABLE TABLETS	PHENYLEPHRINE HCL	SA	RX
EXTENDRYL SR & JR T.D. CAPSULES	PHENYLEPHRINE HCL	SA	RX
EXTRA STRENGTH GRAPEFRUIT DIET PLAN W/DIADAX	PHENYLPROPANOLAMINE HCL	SA	OTC
EYELO	PHENYLEPHRINE	SA	OTC
F.I.5852	OXABOLONE CYPIONATE	AS	RX
F.T.19	NANDROLONE PHENYLPROPIONATE	AS	RX
FABEDRINE	AMPHETAMINE	PS	RX
FARMIT	FLUOXYMESTERONE	AS	RX
FARMIT	TERBUTALINE SULFATE	SA	RX
FASTIN CAPSULES	PHENTERMINE HYDROCHLORIDE	PS	RX
FEDAHIST	PSEUDOEPHEDRINE	SA	OTC
FEDRAZIL TABLETS	PSEUDOEPHEDRINE HCL	SA	OTC
FEDRIN	EPHEDRINE	SA	RX
FELIDIN	DEMEROL	NA	RX
FELLOWS (FORDEX)	AMPHETAMINE	PS	RX
FEMADOL	PROPOXYPHENE	NA	RX
FENADONE	METHADONE	NA	RX
FENAMIN	AMPHETAMINE	PS	RX
FENAMIZOL	AMIPHENAZOLE	CN	RX
FENARA	AMPHETAMINE	PS	RX
FENATSOKIN	PHENAZOCINE	NA	RX
FENCAMFAMIN(E)	FENCAMFAMINE	PS	RX
FENDIMETRAZIN(A)	PHENDIMETRAZINE	PS	RX
FENEDRIN	AMPHETAMINE	PS	RX
FENILEFRINA	PHENYLEPHRINE	SA	OTC
FENILFAR	PHENYLEPHRINE	SA	OTC
FENMETRALIN	PHENMETRAZINE	PS	RX
FENMETRAZINA CLORIDRATO	PHENMETRAZINE	PS	RX
FENOBOLIN	NANDROLONE DECANOATE	AS	RX
FENOPROMIN	AMPHETAMINE	PS	RX
FENOX	PHENYLEPHRINE	SA	OTC

FENOXAZOLUM	PEMOLINE	PS	RX
FENPIDON	DIPIPANONE	NA	RX
FENTANYL	FENTANYL	NA	RX
FENTANYL CITRATE & DROPERIDOL	FENTANYL	NA	RX
FENYLEFRINE	PHENYLEPHRINE	SA	OTC
FENYPRIN	METHYLAMPHETAMINE	PS	RX
FERNDEX	DEXTROAMPHETAMINE SULFATE	PS	RX
FERONA "SIDUS"	FLUOXYMESTERONE	AS	RX
FETAMIN	METHYLAMPHETAMINE	PS	RX
FINAJECT	TRENBOLON ACETATE	AS	RX
FINAPLEX	TRENBOLON ACETATE	AS	RX
FIOGESIC TABLETS	PHENYLPROPANOLAMINE HCL	SA	RX
FIORINAL WITH CODEINE	CODEINE PHOSPHATE	NA	RX
FISEPTONA	METHADONE	NA	RX
FLUDESTRIN	TESTOLACTONE	AS	RX
FLUOSSIMESTERONE	FLUOXYMESTERONE	AS	RX
FLUOTESTIN	FLUOXYMESTERONE	AS	RX
FLUOXIMESTERONUM	FLUOXYMESTERONE	AS	RX
FLUOXYMESTERON(E)	FLUOXYMESTERONE	AS	RX
FLUSTERON	FLUOXYMESTERONE	AS	RX
FLUTESTOS	FLUOXYMESTERONE	AS	RX
FORDEX	AMPHETAMINE	PS	RX
FORMEBOLONE	FORMEBOLONE	AS	RX
FORMULA 44D DECONGESTANT COUGH MIXTURE	PHENYLPROPANOLAMINE HCL	SA	OTC
FORMULA 44M MULTISYMPTOM COUGH MIXTURE	PSEUDOEPHEDRINE HCL	SA	OTC
FORMYLDIENOLONE	FORMEBOLONE	AS	RX
FORTABOLIN	NANDROLONE DECANOATE	AS	RX
FORTAL	PENTAZOCINE	NA	RX
FORTALGESIC	PENTAZOCINE	NA	RX
FORTRAL	PENTAZOCINE	NA	RX
FORTRALIN	PENTAZOCINE	NA	RX
FORTUSS	DIHYDROCODEINE	NA	RX
FOUR-WAY COLD TABLETS	PHENYLPROPANOLAMINE HCL	SA	OTC
FOUR-WAY NASAL SPRAY	PHENYLEPHRINE, PHENYLPROPANOLAMINE	SA	OTC
FRAZALON	FURAZEBOL	AS	RX
FRAZOBOL	FURAZEBOL	AS	RX
FTS	NANDROLONE PHENYLPROPIONATE	AS	RX
FYSEPTON	METHADONE	NA	RX
G-2 CAPSULES	CODEINE PHOSPHATE	NA	RX
G-3 CAPSULES	CODEINE PHOSPHATE	NA	RX
GADEXYL (ALTE FORM)	PIPRADOL	PS	RX
GASTASTERONE	METHYLTESTOSTERONE	AS	RX
GAVROL	MESTEROLONE	AS	RX
GEA	METHADONE	NA	RX
GEABOL	METHANDROSTENOLONE	AS	RX
GENABOL	NORBOLETONE	AS	RX
GEROBIT	METHYLAMPHETAMINE	PS	RX
GEROBIT-NEU	PHENDIMETRAZINE	PS	RX
GERODYL	PIPRADOL	PS	RX
GEROT	DEMEROL	NA	RX
GEWAZOL	LEPTAZOL	CN	RX
GINANDRIN	ANDROSTENDIOL DIPROPIONATE	AS	RX
GINSOPAN TABLETS— CAPSULES	PHENYLPROPANOLAMINE HCL	SA	RX

Brand Name	Generic Name	Class	SRC
GLAUCON	EPINEPHRINE	SA	RX
GLAUCONIN	EPINEPHRINE	SA	RX
GLAUFRIN	EPINEPHRINE	SA	RX
GLAUKOSAN	EPINEPHRINE	SA	RX
GLIN-EPIN	EPINEPHRINE	SA	RX
GLOSSO-STERANDRYL	METHYLTESTOSTERONE	AS	RX
GLUCOENERGAN	FENCAMFAMINE	PS	RX
GLUTAMISOL	BEMIGRIDE	CN	RX
GLYCIRENAN	EPINEPHRINE	SA	RX
GRACIDIN	PHENMETRAZINE	PS	RX
GRAPEFRUIT DIET PLAN W/DIADAX VITAMIN FORTIFIED	PHENYLPROPANOLAMINE HCL	SA	OTC
GRATIDINE	DEMEROL	NA	RX
GROSSAGENUS	NANDROLONE DECANOATE	AS	RX
GROTHIC	NANDROLONE PHENYLPROPIONATE	AS	RX
GUIATUSS A-C SYRUP	CODEINE PHOSPHATE	NA	RX
GUIATUSS D-M SYRUP	DEXTROMETHORPHAN	NA	RX
GUTTALETTEN	PHENYLEPHRINE	SA	OTC
GYNEDIOLO	METHANDRIOL	AS	RX
H 610	FENCAMFAMINE	PS	RX
H.E.S.	METHADONE	NA	RX
HAEMOSTASIN	EPINEPHRINE	SA	RX
HALLS MENTHO-LYPTUS COUGH FORMULA LIQUID	PHENYLPROPANOLAMINE HCL	SA	OTC
HALOFED	PSEUDOEPHEDRINE HCL	SA	RX
HALOTESTIN	FLUOXYMESTERONE	AS	RX
HANSACOR	NIKETHAMIDE	CN	RX
HARMAR	PROPOXYPHENE	NA	RX
HARVOGEN	TESTOSTERONE	AS	RX
HEADWAY CAPSULES & TABLETS	PHENYLPROPANOLAMINE HCL	SA	OTC
HEALTH INCA TEA	COCAINE	PS	OTC
HEKTALIN	EPINEPHRINE	SA	RX
HELFERGIN	MECLOFENOXATE	PS	RX
HEMISINE	EPINEPHRINE	SA	RX
HEMOGENIN	OXYMETHOLONE	AS	RX
HEMOREX	PHENYLEPHRINE	SA	OTC
HEMOSTATIN	EPINEPHRINE	SA	RX
HEPA-DURABOLIN	NANDROLONE PHENYLPROPIONATE	AS	RX
HEPTADOL	METHADONE	NA	RX
HEPTADON	METHADONE	NA	RX
HEPTANAL	METHADONE	NA	RX
HEPTANON	METHADONE	NA	RX
HERMALONE-GLOSSET	MESTANOLON	AS	RX
HEROIN	HEROIN	NA	RX
HEROLAN	HEROIN	NA	RX
HEXABOLIN	TRENBOLONE	AS	RX
HEXOXYMESTEROL	HEXOXYMESTEROL	AS	RX
HIBOL	METHANDRIOL	AS	RX
HIDROMORFON	HYDROMORPHONE	NA	RX
HIGIENE	OXOCODONE	NA	RX
HIHUSTAN-M	DEXTROMETHORPHAN	NA	RX
HIROPON	METHYLAMPHETAMINE	PS	RX
HISPANOFEDRINA	EPHEDRINE	SA	RX
HISTA-VADRIN SYRUP AND TABLETS AND CAPSULES	PHENYLPROPANOLAMINE HCL	SA	RX

HISTABID CAPSULES	PHENYLPROPANOLAMINE HCL	SA	RX
HISTALET	PSEUDOEPHEDRINE	SA	OTC
HISTALET DM SYRUP	DEXTROMETHORPHAN HYDROBROMIDE	NA	RX
HISTALET FORTE T.D. TABLETS	PHENYLPROPANOLAMINE HCL	SA	RX
HISTALET FORTE TABLETS	PHENYLEPHRINE HCL	SA	RX
HISTAPP PRODUCTS	PHENYLPROPANOLAMINE HCL	SA	RX
HISTASPAN-D CAPSULES	PHENYLEPHRINE HCL	SA	RX
HISTASPAN-PLUS CAPSULES	PHENYLEPHRINE HCL	SA	RX
HISTERONE 50 AND 100	TESTOSTERONE	AS	RX
HISTOR-D TIMECELLES	PHENYLEPHRINE HCL	SA	RX
HISTORAL	PSEUDOEPHEDRINE	SA	OTC
HIT (HEALTH INCA TEA)	COCAINE	PS	OTC
HMD	OXYMETHOLONE	SA	RX
HOECHST 10805	DIPIPANONE	NA	RX
HOECHST 10820	METHADONE	NA	RX
HOECHST 8909	DEMEROL	NA	RX
HOMAN	METHYLTESTOSTERONE	AS	RX
HOMANDREN-TABL.	METHYLTESTOSTERONE	AS	RX
HOMOGENE-S	TESTOSTERONE	AS	RX
HOMOSTERON	TESTOSTERONE	AS	RX
HORMALE	METHYLTESTOSTERONE	AS	RX
HORMO-RETARD	NANDROLONE DECANOATE	AS	RX
HORMOBOLIN	NANDROLONE PHENYLPROPIONATE	AS	RX
HORMONABOL	NANDROLONE PHENYLPROPIONATE	AS	RX
HORMONDRINE-TABL.	METHYLTESTOSTERONE	AS	RX
HORMONETA	METHYLTESTOSTERONE	AS	RX
HUBERNOL	FORMEBOLONE	AS	RX
HUNGREX	PHENYLPROPANOLAMINE	SA	OTC
HUSMEDIN	DEXTROMETHORPHAN	NA	RX
HUSTEP	DEXTROMETHORPHAN	NA	RX
HYBOLIN	METHANDRIOL	AS	RX
HYBOLIN DECANOATE	NANDROLONE DECANOATE	AS	RX
HYBOLIN IMPROVED	NANDROLONE PHENPROPIONATE	AS	RX
HYCO-PAP	HYDROCODONE	NA	RX
HYCODAN	HYDROCODONE	NA	RX
HYCOMINE COMPOUND	PHENYLEPHRINE HCL	SA	RX
HYCOMINE COMPOUND	HYDROCODONE	NA	RX
HYCOMINE PEDIATRIC SYR.	HYDROCODONE	NA	RX
HYCOMINE SYRUP	HYDROCODONE	NA	RX
HYCOMINE-WIRKSTOFF	HYDROCODONE	NA	RX
HYCORPHAN	DEXTROMETHORPHAN	NA	RX
HYCOTUSS EXPECTORANT	HYDROCODONE	NA	RX
HYDEX	METHYLAMPHETAMINE	PS	RX
HYDROCODAL	OXOCODONE	NA	RX
HYDROCODAN	HYDROCODONE	NA	RX
HYDROCODEIN(A)	DIHYDROCODEINE	NA	RX
HYDROCODEINONBITARTRAT	HYDROCODONE	NA	RX
HYDROCODIN	DIHYDROCODEINE	NA	RX
HYDROCODONE SYRUP	HYDROCODONE	NA	RX
HYDROCON	HYDROCODONE	NA	RX
HYDROKODIN	HYDROCODONE	NA	RX
HYDROKON	HYDROCODONE	NA	RX
HYDROMORPHONE HCL IN TUBEX	HYDROMORPHONE HCL	NA	RX
HYDROMORPHONE HCL INJECTION	DIHYDROMORPHINONE HYDROCHLORIDE	NA	RX
HYDROMORPHONHYDRO-CHLORID	HYDROMORPHONE	NA	RX

Brand Name	Generic Name	Class	SRC
HYDROOXAZIN	PHENMETRAZINE	PS	RX
HYDROOXYCODEINONA	OXOCODONE	NA	RX
HYDROTEST	TESTOSTERONE	AS	RX
HYDROXYMETHOLONE	OXYMETHOLONE	AS	RX
HYDROXYMETHYLTESTERON	OXYMESTERONE	AS	RX
HYDROXYMETHYLTES- TOSTERON	OXYMESTERONE	AS	RX
HYDROXYSTENOZOL	HYDROXYSTENOZOL	AS	RX
HYMORPHAN	HYDROMORPHONE	NA	RX
HYPERNEPHRIN	EPINEPHRINE	SA	RX
HYPHET	METHYLAMPHETAMINE	PS	RX
HYPORENIN	EPINEPHRINE	SA	RX
HYREX (DEPOTEST)	TESTOSTERONE	AS	RX
HYREX-105	PHENDIMETRAZINE TARTRATE	PS	RX
HYTON	PEMOLINE	PS	RX
I.P.A.	ISOPROTERENOL	SA	RX
I-CARE	PHENYLEPHRINE	SA	OTC
IBADEX	METHYLAMPHETAMINE	PS	RX
IBIOZEDRINE	AMPHETAMINE	PS	RX
IDRIANOL	PHENYLEPHRINE	SA	OTC
IDROCODONE	HYDROCODONE	NA	RX
IDROMORFONE CLORIDRATO	HYDROMORPHONE	NA	RX
IEROIN	HEROIN	NA	RX
ILUDRIN(A)	ISOPROTERENOL	SA	RX
INAPETYL	BENZPHETAMINE	PS	RX
INDERAL LA LONG ACTING CAPSULES	PROPRANOLOL HCL	BB	RX
INDERAL TABLETS AND INJECTABLE	PROPRANOLOL HCL	BB	RX
INDERIDE	PROPRANOLOL HCL	BB	RX
INGELAN	ISOPROTERENOL	SA	RX
INGELHEIM (ALEUDRIN)	ISOPROTERENOL	SA	RX
INNOVAR	FENTANYL	NA	RX
INOCOR	LEPTAZOL	CN	RX
INTRANEFRIN	EPINEPHRINE	SA	RX
IONAMIN	PHENTERMINE HCL— PHENTERMINE	PS	RX
IOP	EPINEPHRINE	SA	RX
IOPHEN-C LIQUID	CODEINE PHOSPHATE	NA	RX
IPRADOL "ISIS-PORTUGAL"	METAPROTERENOL	SA	RX
IPRENOL	ISOPROTERENOL	SA	RX
IROINI	HEROIN	NA	RX
ISADREN	ISOPROTERENOL	SA	RX
ISADRIN	ISOPROTERENOL	SA	RX
ISIS-PORTUGAL (IPRADOL)	METAPROTERENOL	SA	RX
ISO-AUTOHALER	ISOPROTERENOL	SA	RX
ISO-BROVON	ISOPROTERENOL	SA	RX
ISO-INTRANEFRIN	ISOPROTERENOL	SA	RX
ISO-PHEDRIZEM	EPHEDRINE	SA	RX
ISOAMIN	AMPHETAMINE	PS	RX
ISOAMYN	AMPHETAMINE	PS	RX
ISOBRONCHISAN	ISOPROTERENOL	SA	RX
ISOCLOR	PSEUDOEPHEDRINE	SA	OTC
ISODRENAL	ISOPROTERENOL	SA	RX
ISOEPHEDRINHYDRO- CHLORID	PSEUDOEPHEDRINE	SA	OTC
ISOETARIN	ISOETHARINE	SA	RX

ISOETHARIN(E) HCL	ISOETHARINE HCL	SA	RX
ISOFEDRIN	PSEUDOEPHEDRINE	SA	OTC
ISOFEDROL	EPHEDRINE	SA	RX
ISOFORTE-MEDIHALER	ISOPROTERENOL	SA	RX
ISOGLYCIRENAN	ISOPROTERENOL	SA	RX
ISOLEVIN	ISOPROTERENOL	SA	RX
ISOLIN	ISOPROTERENOL	SA	RX
ISOMIST	ISOPROTERENOL	SA	RX
ISOMYN	AMPHETAMINE	PS	RX
ISONEFRINE	PHENYLEPHRINE	SA	OTC
ISONIPECAINHYDRO- CHLORID	DEMEROL	NA	RX
ISONORIN	ISOPROTERENOL	SA	RX
ISOPETHIDIN	DEMEROL	NA	RX
ISOPHEN	METHYLAMPHETAMINE	PS	RX
ISOPHRIN	PHENYLEPHRINE	SA	OTC
ISOPRENALIN(E)	ISOPROTERENOL	SA	RX
ISOPRO	ISOPROTERENOL	SA	RX
ISOPROFENAMIN	CHLORPRENALINE	SA	RX
ISOPROPHENAMIN	CHLORPRENALINE	SA	RX
ISOPROPYLARTERENOL	ISOPROTERENOL	SA	RX
ISOPROPYLNORADRENALIN	ISOPROTERENOL	SA	RX
ISOPROPYLNOREPINEPHRIN	ISOPROTERENOL	SA	RX
ISOPROTERENOL HCL	ISOPROTERENOL	SA	RX
ISOPROTERENOL HCL INJECTION	ISOPROTERENOL HCL	SA	RX
ISOPTO-FRIN	PHENYLEPHRINE	SA	OTC
ISOPTOEPINAL	EPINEPHRINE	SA	RX
ISORENIN	ISOPROTERENOL	SA	RX
ISORMON	METHANDRIOL	AS	RX
ISOTROPINA	PHENYLEPHRINE	SA	OTC
ISOVON	ISOPROTERENOL	SA	RX
ISPRANIL	ISOPROTERENOL	SA	RX
ISTIMIL	METHYLPHENIDATE	PS	RX
ISUPREL	ISOPROTERENOL	SA	RX
ISUPREL HCL COMPOUND ELIXIR	EPHEDRINE—ISOPROTERENOL	SA	RX
ISUPREL HCL GLOSSETS & INJECTION & MISTOMETER & SOLUTION	ISOPROTERENOL	SA	RX
ISUPREN	ISOPROTERENOL	SA	RX
JENAPHARM (TESTOSTERON- TABL.)	METHYLTESTOSTERONE	AS	RX
JENKINS (PHENAZINE)	PHENDIMETRAZINE	PS	RX
JETRIUM	DEXTROMORAMIDE	NA	RX
JUVACOR	NIKETHAMIDE	CN	RX
KABOLIN	NANDROLONE DECANOATE	AS	RX
KARDONYL	NIKETHAMIDE	CN	RX
KATEVAN	DIPHENOXYLATE	NA	RX
KATINE	NORPSEUDOEPHEDRINE	PS	RX
KATOVIT-WIRKSTOFF	PROLINTANE	PS	RX
KEMODRIN	METHYLAMPHETAMINE	PS	RX
KENTY	NANDROLONE PHENYLPROPIONATE	AS	RX
KESSO-GESIC	PROPOXYPHENE	NA	RX
KETALGIN	METHADONE	NA	RX
KETHAMED	PEMOLINE	PS	RX
KIBON S	DEXTROMETHORPHAN	NA	RX
KIDOLINE	EPINEPHRINE	SA	RX
KLARICORA	LEPTAZOL	CN	RX
KLEER COMPOUND TABLETS	PHENYLPROPANOLAMINE HCL	SA	RX

Brand Name	Generic Name	Class	SRC
KLIX KERNEL CAPSULES	PHENYLPROPANOLAMINE HCL	SA	RX
KODEIN	CODEINE	NA	RX
KOKAIN	COCAINE	PS	RX
KOKAYEEN	COCAINE	PS	RX
KOLIKODAL	HYDROCODONE	NA	RX
KORAZOL	LEPTAZOL	CN	RX
KORDIAMIN	NIKETHAMIDE	CN	RX
KORIGESIC TABLETS	PHENYLEPHRINE HCL	SA	RX
KORYZA TABLETS	PHENYLPROPANOLAMINE HCL	SA	RX
KRATEDYN	EPHEDRINE	SA	RX
KROHEKIS	MECLOFENOXATE	PS	RX
KWIZDA (VASAZOL)	NIKETHAMIDE	CN	RX
L-16298	PROPOXYPHENE	NA	RX
L-ISOPRENALIN	ISOPROTERENOL	SA	RX
L-ISOPROTERENOL	ISOPROTERENOL	SA	RX
LA 956	PEMOLINE	PS	RX
LAEMORANUM	LEVORPHANOL	NA	RX
LANABOLIN	METHANDROSTENOLONE	AS	RX
LANAZINE	METHYLAMPHETAMINE	PS	RX
LAUDACON	HYDROMORPHONE	NA	RX
LAUDADIN	HYDROMORPHONE	NA	RX
LAUDAKON	HYDROMORPHONE	NA	RX
LAUDEMED	HYDROMORPHONE	NA	RX
LAURABOLIN	NANDROLONE LAURATE	AS	RX
LAVISIN	PHENYLEPHRINE	SA	OTC
LAVOEPHAN	LEVORPHANOL	NA	RX
LEDER PRODUCTS	PHENYLPROPANOLAMINE HCL	SA	RX
LEMORAN	LEVORPHANOL	NA	RX
LENASMA	METAPROTERENOL	SA	RX
LENIDOL	DEMEROL	NA	RX
LENTABOL	NORDOSTEBOL	AS	RX
LENTADOL	PROPOXYPHENE	NA	RX
LENTADREN	EPINEPHRINE	SA	RX
LEO (ANGIOTON)	LEPTAZOL	CN	RX
LEO (TESTORAL)	METHYLTESTOSTERONE	AS	RX
LEODRIN	AMPHETAMINE	PS	RX
LEPTAMIN	NIKETHAMIDE	CN	RX
LEPTAZOL	LEPTAZOL	CN	RX
LEPTIDROL	PIPRADOL	PS	RX
LERINOL	ANILERIDINE	NA	RX
LERITINE	ANILERIDINE	NA	RX
LETOVISTE	DEHYDROEPIANDROSTERONE	AS	RX
LEVADOL	PROPOXYPHENE	NA	RX
LEVISOL	ISOPROTERENOL	SA	RX
LEVISOPRENALIN	ISOPROTERENOL	SA	RX
LEVITAN	PROPOXYPHENE	NA	RX
LEVO-DROMORAN	LEVORPHANOL	NA	RX
LEVOCON	EPINEPHRINE	SA	RX
LEVOPROPYLHEXEDRIN	PROPYLHEXEDRINE	SA	OTC
LEVORENE	EPINEPHRINE	SA	RX
LEVORENINE	EPINEPHRINE	SA	RX
LEVORPHAN	LEVORPHANOL	NA	RX
LEVORPHANOL	LEVORPHANOL	NA	RX
LEXATOL	PHENYLEPHRINE	SA	OTC
LEXOFEDRIN	EPHEDRINE	SA	RX
LIADREN	EPINEPHRINE	SA	RX
LIBEREN	PROPOXYPHENE	NA	RX
LICIDRIL	MECLOFENOXATE	PS	RX

LIDOL	DEMEROL	NA	RX
LILLY 38851	BOLMANTALAT	AS	RX
LIMIT	PHENDIMETRAZINE	PS	RX
LINAMPHETA	AMPHETAMINE	PS	RX
LINFADOL	DEXTOMORAMIDE	NA	RX
LIPIDEX	OXANDROLONE	AS	RX
LIPOMIN "WELLS"	PHENMETRAZINE	PS	RX
LITICON	PENTAZOCINE	NA	RX
LIVISOL	ISOPROTERENOL	SA	RX
LO-TUSSIN	PSEUDOEPHEDRINE	SA	OTC
LOCATELLI	DEMEROL	NA	RX
LOCOFEN	CHLORPHENTERMINE	PS	RX
LOMOTIL (WITH ATROPINE SULFATE IS PERMISSIBLE)	DIPHENOXYLATE HCL	NA	RX
LOMOTIL LIQUID AND TABLETS	DIPHENOXYLATE HCL	NA	RX
LOMUPREN (ALTE FORM)	ISOPROTERENOL	SA	RX
LONAVAR	OXANDROLONE	AS	RX
LONOX TABLETS	DIPHENOXYLATE HCL	NA	RX
LOPRESSOR AMPULS & TABLETS	METOPROLOL TARTRATE	BB	RX
LORCET	PROPOXYPHENE HCL	NA	RX
LORCET-HD	HYDROCODONE	NA	RX
LOREMID	DEMEROL	NA	RX
LUCIDRIL	MECLOFENOXATE	PS	RX
LUCODAN	HYDROMORPHONE	NA	RX
LUCOFEN	CHLORPHENTERMINE	PS	RX
LUCOFENE	CHLORPHENTERMINE	PS	RX
LUDONAL	OXOCODONE	NA	RX
LUF-ISO	ISOPROTERENOL	SA	RX
LUFYLLIN	EPHEDRINE	SA	RX
LUNCIDRIL	MECLOFENOXATE	PS	RX
LUTENIN	METHYLNORTESTOSTERONE	AS	RX
LUTIARON	MECLOFENOXATE	PS	RX
LUXIDIN	PIPRADOL	PS	RX
LUYCARDIOL	LEPTAZOL	CN	RX
LYDOL	DEMEROL	NA	RX
LYOPHRIN	EPINEPHRINE	SA	RX
L20 025	CHLORPRENALINE	SA	RX
M.C.P. 875	DEXTOMORAMIDE	NA	RX
M-SYMPATOL	PHENYLEPHRINE	SA	OTC
MA HUANG (CHINESE EPHEDRA)	EPHEDRINE	SA	OTC
MA HUANG (HERB)	EPHEDRA	SA	OTC
MACROBIN	CLOSTEBOL ACETATE	AS	RX
MACROBIN (TAB. & SYRUP)	MESTANOLON	AS	RX
MAD	METHANDRIOL	AS	RX
MADIOL	METHANDRIOL	AS	RX
MADRINE	METHYLAMPHETAMINE	PS	RX
MALERONE	TESTOSTERONE	AS	RX
MALESTRONE-TAB.	METHYLTESTOSTERONE	AS	RX
MALOGEN	METHYLTESTOSTERONE	AS	RX
MALOGEN AQUEOUS INJ.	TESTOSTERONE	AS	RX
MALOGEX	TESTOSTERONE	AS	RX
MALOTRONE	TESTOSTERONE	AS	RX
MALYSOL	BEMIGRIDE	CN	RX
MANADRIN	EPHEDRINE	SA	RX
MAPERIDINA	DEMEROL	NA	RX
MARAX TABLETS & DF SYRUP	EPHEDRINE	SA	RX
MARCAINE HCL WITH EPINEPHRINE	EPINEPHRINE	SA	RX
MARDON	PROPOXYPHENE	NA	RX

Brand Name	Generic Name	Class	SRC
MARSIN	PHENMETRAZINE	PS	RX
MARUCOTOL	MECLOFENOXATE	PS	RX
MASDIOL	METHANDRIOL	AS	RX
MASENONE	METHYLTESTOSTERONE	AS	RX
MASTER	NANDROLONE HYDROGEN SUCCINATE	AS	RX
MASTERID	DROSTANOLONE PROPIONATE	AS	RX
MASTERIL	DROSTANOLONE PROPIONATE	AS	RX
MASTERON	DROSTANOLONE PROPIONATE	AS	RX
MASTESTONA	METHYLTESTOSTERONE	AS	RX
MASTISOL	DROSTANOLONE PROPIONATE	AS	RX
MATE DE COCA (TEA)	COCAINE	PS	OTC
MATRONAL	METHYLNORTESTOSTERONE	AS	RX
MAXEFED	METHYLAMPHETAMINE	PS	RX
MAXIBOLIN	ETHYLESTRENOL	AS	RX
MAXIMUM STRENGTH SINUTAB 11	PSEUDOEPHEDRINE HCL	SA	OTC
MAZANOR	MAZINDOL	PS	RX
MC N -R-747-11	PHENDIMETRAZINE	PS	RX
MEBOLAZINE	MEBOLAZINE	AS	RX
MECHLORPHENOXATUM HYDROCHLORICUM	MECLOFENOXATE	PS	RX
MECLIROL	MECLOFENOXATE	PS	RX
MECLOFENOXANE	MECLOFENOXATE	PS	RX
MECLOFENOXATE	MECLOFENOXATE	PS	RX
MECLOFENOXATHYDRO-CHLORID	MECLOFENOXATE	PS	RX
MECLON	MECLOFENOXATE	PS	RX
MECLOSATE	MECLOFENOXATE	PS	RX
MECLOSERT	MECLOFENOXATE	PS	RX
MECLOXATE	MECLOFENOXATE	PS	RX
MECODIN	METHADONE	NA	RX
MECODRIN	AMPHETAMINE	PS	RX
MECONIUM	MORPHINE	NA	RX
MECROEAT	MECLOFENOXATE	PS	RX
MEDEPERIN	DEMEROL	NA	RX
MEDEPROPIL	ISOPROTERNOL	SA	RX
MEDIAMID	NIKETHAMIDE	CN	RX
MEDIASTMAN	EPINEPHRINE	SA	RX
MEDICODAL	OXOCODONE	NA	RX
MEDICON	DEXTROMETHORPHAN	NA	RX
MEDIHALER-EPI	EPINEPHRINE BITARTRATE	SA	OTC
MEDIHALER-ISO	ISOPROTERNOL	SA	RX
MEDIMPEX (PONDEX)	PEMOLINE	PS	RX
MEDITUSS	DEXTROMETHORPHAN	NA	RX
MEDITUSSIN SYRUP	PHENYLPROPANOLAMINE HCL	SA	RX
MEDITUSSIN-X LIQUID	PHENYLPROPANOLAMINE HCL	SA	RX
MEDROTESTRONPROPIONAT	DROSTANOLONE PROPIONATE	AS	RX
MEDTHYLPHENIDATE	METHYLPHENIDATE	PS	RX
MEFEDINA	DEMEROL	NA	RX
MEFOLIN	PHENMETRAZINE	PS	RX
MEGABION	METHANDRIOL	AS	RX
MEGIBAL	BEMIGRIDE	CN	RX
MEGIMIDE	BEMIGRIDE	CN	RX
MEKODIN	METHADONE	NA	RX
MELFIAT TABLETS & 105 UNICELLES	PHENDIMETRAZINE TARTRATE	PS	RX
MELFIAT 105 UNICELLES	PHENDIMETRAZINE TARTRATE	PS	RX

MENDELGINA	DEMEROL	NA	RX
MENETYL	ETAFEDRINE	SA	RX
MENIDRABOL	NANDROLONE HYDROGEN SUCCINATE	AS	RX
MEPADIN	DEMEROL	NA	RX
MEPECTON	METHADONE	NA	RX
MEPERGAN INJECTION & TUBEX	MEPERIDINE HCL	NA	RX
MEPERIDINE HYDROCHLORIDE	DEMEROL	NA	RX
MEPERIDINE INJECTION & TUBEX	MEPERIDINE HCL	NA	RX
MEPERIDOL	DEMEROL	NA	RX
MEPHEDINE	DEMEROL	NA	RX
MEPHENON	METHADONE	NA	RX
MEPHOLIN	PHENMETRAZINE	PS	RX
MERADONE	METHADONE	NA	RX
MERATONIC	PIPRADOL	PS	RX
MERATRAN	PIPRADOL	PS	RX
MERCODAL	ETAAFEDRINE	SA	RX
MERCODINONE	HYDROCODONE	NA	RX
MERETRAN	PIPRADOL	PS	RX
MERIIDIL	METHYLPHENIDATE	PS	RX
MERTESTATE	TESTOSTERONE	AS	RX
MESABOLONE	MESABOLONE	AS	RX
MESANOLON	MESTANOLON	AS	RX
MESATON(UM)	PHENYLEPHRINE	SA	OTC
MESTALONE	MESTANOLON	AS	RX
MESTANOLONE	MESTANOLONE	AS	RX
MESTENEDIOL	METHANDRIOL	AS	RX
MESTERANUM	MESTEROLONE	AS	RX
MESTEROLON(E)	MESTEROLONE	AS	RX
MESTERON	METHYLTESTOSTERONE	AS	RX
MET-AMPI	METHAMPHETAMINE HYDROCHLORIDE	PS	RX
META-SYNEPHRINE	PHENYLEPHRINE	SA	OTC
METABOL	NANDROLONE PHENYLPROPIONATE	AS	RX
METABOLINA	METHANDROSTENOLONE	AS	RX
METADIN	PIPRADOL	PS	RX
METALAR	OXYMETHOLONE	AS	RX
METALEX-P	LEPTAZOL	CN	RX
METALONA PROPIONATO	DROSTANOLONE PROPIONATE	AS	RX
METALUTIN	METHYLNORTESTOSTERONE	AS	RX
METAMINA	METHYLAMPHETAMINE	PS	RX
METAMINE "ZORI"	METHYLAMPHETAMINE	PS	RX
METAMPHETAMINE	METHYLAMPHETAMINE	PS	RX
METAMSUSTAC	METHYLAMPHETAMINE	PS	RX
METANABOL	METHANDROSTENOLONE	AS	RX
METANDIENON	METHANDROSTENOLONE	AS	RX
METANDIOL	METHANDRIOL	AS	RX
METANDREN	METHYLTESTOSTERONE	AS	RX
METANNDREN LINGUETS	METHYLTESTOSTERONE	AS	RX
METANDROSTENOLON	METHANDROSTENOLONE	AS	RX
METAOXEDRIN	PHENYLEPHRINE	SA	OTC
METAPHET	METHYLAMPHETAMIINE	PS	RX
METAPREL INHALANT SOLUTION INHALER SYRUP & TABS	METAPROTERENOL SULFATE	SA	RX
METAPROTERENOL	METAPROTERENOL	SA	RX
METAPROTERENOLSULFAT	METAPROTERENOL	SA	RX

Brand Name	Generic Name	Class	SRC
METASEDIN	METHADONE	NA	RX
METASMA	METHOXYPHENAMINE	SA	RX
METASTENOL	METHANDROSTENOLONE	AS	RX
METASTERON	METHANDRIOL	AS	RX
METATONE	METHADONE	NA	RX
METAZINA	BOLAZIN-CAPRONATE	AS	RX
METENDIOL	METHANDRIOL	AS	RX
METENOLONE	METENOLONE	AS	RX
METENOLONE ACETATE	METENOLONE ACETATE	AS	RX
METERDOS-ISO	ISOPROTERENOL	SA	RX
METESTINE	METHYLTESTOSTERONE	AS	RX
METESTONE	METHYLTESTOSTERONE	AS	RX
METEXTERONA	METHYLTESTOSTERONE	AS	RX
METHABOL	OXYMETHOLONE	AS	RX
METHADIN	DEMEROL	NA	RX
METHADONE HCL DISKETS & ORAL SOLUTION & TABLETS	METHADONE HCL	NA	RX
METHAJADE	METHADONE	NA	RX
METHALONE	DROSTANOLONE	AS	RX
METHALUTIN	METHYLNORTESTOSTERONE	AS	RX
METHAMINE	METHYLAMPHETAMINE	PS	RX
METHAMPEX	METHAMPHETAMINE HYDROCHLORIDE	PS	RX
METHAMPHETAMINHYDRO-CHLORID	METHYLAMPHETAMINE	PS	RX
METHAMPHIN	METHYLAMPHETAMINE	PS	RX
METHANABOL	METHANDRIOL	AS	RX
METHANDIENONE	METHANDROSTENOLONE	AS	RX
METHANDIOL	METHANDRIOL	AS	RX
METHANDRIOL	METHANDRIOL	AS	RX
METHANDRIOL BIS-EUANTHOYLACETATE	METHANDRIOL BIS-EUANTHOYLACETATE	AS	RX
METHANDRIOL DIPROPIONATE	METHANDRIOL DIPROPIONATE	AS	RX
METHANDRIOL PROPIONATE	METHANDRIOL PROPIONATE	AS	RX
METHANDROL	METHANDRIOL	AS	RX
METHANDROSTENEDIOLONE	OXYMESTERONE	AS	RX
METHANDROSTENOLONE	METHANDROSTEROLONE	AS	RX
METHANEDIONE	METHANEDIONE	AS	RX
METHASTENON	METHANDROSTENOLONE	AS	RX
METHBOLIN	METHANDROSTENOLONE	AS	RX
METHEDRINAL	METHYLAMPHETAMINE	PS	RX
METHEDRINE	METHYLAMPHETAMINE	PS	RX
METHENOLONE	METENOLONE ENANTHATE	AS	RX
METHEP (GERMAN - GB)	METHYLEPHEDRINE	SA	RX
METHETHARIMIDE	BEMIGRIDE	CN	RX
METHIDATE	METHYLPHENIDATE	PS	RX
METHIDINE	DEMEROL	NA	RX
METHIDON	METHADONE	NA	RX
METHONAMIN	METHOXYPHENAMINE	SA	RX
METHORATE	DEXTROMETHORPHAN	NA	RX
METHORCON	DEXTROMETHORPHAN	NA	RX
METHOSTAN	METHANDRIOL	AS	RX
METHOXIPHENADRINUM	METHOXYPHENAMINE	SA	RX
METHOXYN	METHYLAMPHETAMINE	PS	RX
METHOXYNAL	MECLOFENOXATE	PS	RX
METHOXYPHENAMINE HCL	METHOXYPHENAMINE	SA	RX

METHY-F	METHYLEPHEDRINE	SA	RX
METHYANTALON	MESTANOLON	AS	RX
METHYBOL	MESTANOLON	AS	RX
METHYLAMPHETAMIN	METHYLAMPHETAMINE	PS	RX
METHYLAMPHETAMINE	METTHYLAMPHETAMINE	PS	RX
METHYLANDROSTANDIOL	METHYLANDROSTANDIOL	AS	RX
METHYLANDROSTANOLON (1A)	MESTEROLONE	AS	RX
METHYLANDROSTENDIOL	METHANDRIOL	AS	RX
METHYLANDROSTENE DIOLPROPIONATE	METHANDRIOLPROPIONATE	AS	RX
METHYLARTERENOL	EPINEPHRINE	SA	RX
METHYLBENZEDRIN	METHYLAMPHETAMINE	PS	RX
METHYLEPHEDRIN(E)	METHYLEPHEDRINE	SA	RX
METHYLETS	METHYLTESTOSTERONE	AS	RX
METHYLISOMYN	METHYLAMPHETAMINE	PS	RX
METHYLMORPHIN	CODEINE	NA	RX
METHYLMYDRIATIN	EPHEDRINE	SA	RX
METHYLNORTESTERONE	METHYLNORTESTOSTERONE	AS	RX
METHYLOESTRENOLON	METHYLNORTESTOSTERONE	AS	RX
METHYLPHENIDATE	METHYLPHENIDATE HCL	PS	RX
METHYLPHENIDATHYDRO- CHLORID	METHYLPHENIDATE	PS	RX
METHYLPHENIDYLAT	METHYLPHENIDATE	PS	RX
METHYLPROPAMINE	METHYLAMPHETAMINE	PS	RX
METHYLSTANAZOLUM	STANOZOLOL	AS	RX
METHYLTESTEDIOL	METHANDRIOL	AS	RX
METHYLTESTOSTERONE TABLETS	METHYLTESTOSTERONE	AS	RX
METHYLTRIENOLONE	METRIBOLONE	AS	RX
METHYTESTOSTERONE SUBLINGUAL	METHYTESTOSTERONE	AS	RX
METIDIONE	METHANDRIOL	AS	RX
METILANDROSTENDIOLO	METHANDRIOL	AS	RX
METIBISEXOVIS-COMPR.	METHANDRIOL	AS	RX
METILDIOLO	METHANDRIOL	AS	RX
METILFENIDATO CLORURO	METHYLPHENIDATE	PS	RX
METILTESTOSTERONE	METHYLTESTOSTERONE	AS	RX
METOCRYST	METHANDRIOL	AS	RX
METORMON	DROSTANOLONE PROPIONATE	AS	RX
METRA	PHENDIMETRAZINE TARTRATE	PS	RX
METRAZINE	PHENMETRAZINE	PS	RX
METRAZOL	LEPTAZOL	CN	RX
METRIBOLONE	METRIBOLONE	AS	RX
METRONE	METHYLTESTOSTERONE	AS	RX
METYLAN	METHADONE	NA	RX
METYLOFENIDAN	METHYLPHENIDATE	PS	RX
MEXAZINE	MECLOFENOXATE	PS	RX
MEXYPHAMINHYDRO- CHLORID	METHOXYPHENAMINE	SA	RX
MEZATON	PHENYLEPHRINE	SA	OTC
MI 35	PHENYLEPHRINE	SA	OTC
MIADON(E)	METHADONE	NA	RX
MIALGIN	DEMEROL	NA	RX
MIBOLERONE	MIBOLERONE	AS	RX
MICONEFRIN	EPINEPHRINE	SA	RX
MICOREN	CROPROPAMIDE, CROTETHAMIDE	CN	RX
MICRO NEFRIN	EPINEPHRINE	SA	RX
MICTOBEN	OXOCODONE	NA	RX
MIDADONE	METHADONE	NA	RX
MIKEDIMIDE	BEMIGRIDE	CN	RX

Brand Name	Generic Name	Class	SRC
MILLER-DRINE	METHYLAMPHETAMINE	PS	RX
MIMETINA	AMPHETAMINE	PS	RX
MIMEXINA	METHOXYPHENAMINE	SA	RX
MINADIT	PHENMETRAZINE	PS	RX
MINISCAP M.D.	NORPSEUDOEPHEDRINE	PS	RX
MINUS	PHENDIMETRAZINE	PS	RX
MINUSIN	NORPSEUDOEPHEDRINE	PS	RX
MIOCARDINA	NIKETHAMIDE	CN	RX
MISTAPREL	ISOPROTERENOL	SA	RX
MISTURA D	PHENYLEPHRINE	SA	OTC
MISTURA E	EPINEPHRINE	SA	RX
MITIZAN	DEMEROL	NA	RX
MITOLON	FURAZEBOL	AS	RX
MK-89	ANILERIDINE	NA	RX
MOHEPTAN	METHADONE	NA	RX
MONETAMIN	AMPHETAMINE	PS	RX
MORFELEN	DEMEROL	NA	RX
MORFIKON	HYDROMORPHONE	NA	RX
MORFIN	MORPHINE	NA	RX
MORMON'S TEA	NORPSEUDOEPHEDRINE	CN	OTC
MORPHACETIN	HEROIN	NA	RX
MORPHICON	HYDROMORPHONE	NA	RX
MORPHINDIACETAT	HEROIN	NA	RX
MORPHINE	MORPHINE	NA	RX
MORPHINE SULFATE	MORPHINE	NA	RX
MORPHIUM	MORPHINE	NA	RX
MORPHODID	HYDROMORPHONE	NA	RX
MRD-108	PIPRADOL	PS	RX
MS CONTIN	MORPHINE	NA	RX
MUCIDRINA	EPINEPHRINE	SA	RX
MUCORAMA	PHENYLPROPANOLAMINE	SA	OTC
MUDRANE GG ELIXIR - GG TABLETS - TABLETS	EPHEDRINE	SA	RX
MULTACODIN	HYDROCODONE	NA	RX
MYAGEN	BOLASTERONE	AS	RX
MYAMIN	PEMOLINE	PS	RX
MYCI-SPRAY	PHENYLEPHRINE	SA	OTC
MYDRIATIN	PHENYLPROPANOLAMINE	SA	OTC
MYOSTHENINE	EPINEPHRINE	SA	RX
MYTRATE	EPINEPHRINE	SA	RX
NA-CO-AL TABLETS	PHENYLPROPANOLAMINE HCL	SA	RX
NABADIAL	METHANDRIOL	AS	RX
NABESE	NORPSEUDOEPHEDRINE	PS	RX
NABOLIN	METHANDROSTENOLONE	AS	RX
NADEINE	DIHYDROCODEINE	NA	RX
NADOSTERONE	METHYLTESTOSTERONE	AS	RX
NAGA-HORMO-M	TESTOSTERONE	AS	RX
NALDECON	PHENYLEPHRINE HCL	SA	RX
NALDECON-CX SUSPENSION	PHENYLPROPANOLAMINE HCL	SA	OTC
NALDECON-CX SUSPENSION	CODEINE PHOSPHATE	NA	RX
NALDECON-DX PEDIATRIC SYRUP	PHENYLPROPANOLAMINE HCL	SA	OTC
NALDECON-EX PEDIATRIC DROPS	PHENYLPROPANOLAMINE HCL	SA	OTC
NALDEGESIC TABLETS	PSEUDOEPHEDRINE HCL	SA	RX
NALONE	OXOMORPHINE	NA	RX
NALOXONHYDOCHLORIDE	OXOMORPHINE	NA	RX
NANBOLIN	NANDROLONE	AS	RX

	PHENYLPROPIONATE		
NANDRABOLIN	NANDROLONE	AS	RX
	PHENYLPROPIONATE		
NANDROBOLIC	NANDROLONE	AS	RX
	PHENYLPROPIONATE		
NANDROBOLIC L.A.	NANDROLONE DECANOATE	AS	RX
NANDROLIN	NANDROLONE PHENPROPIONATE	AS	RX
NANDROLON-DECANOAT	NANDROLONE DECANOATE	AS	RX
NANDROLONE	NANDROLONE	AS	RX
	CYCLOPENTYLPROPIONATE		
NANDROLONE CAPRONATE	NANDROLONE CAPRONATE	AS	RX
NANDROLONE	NANDROLONE	AS	RX
CYCLOHEXYLPROPIONATE	CYCLOHEXYLPROPIONATE		
NANDROLONE CYCLOTATE	NANDROLONE CYCLOTATE	AS	RX
NANDROLONE DECANOATE	NANDROLONE DECANOATE	AS	RX
NANDROLONE	NANDROLONE	AS	RX
FURYLPROPIONATE	FURYLPROPIONATE		
NANDROLONE	NANDROLONE	AS	RX
HEXAHYDROBENZOATE	HEXAHYDROBENZOATE		
NANDROLONE	NANDROLONE	AS	RX
HEXYLOXYPHENYL-	HEXYLOXYPHENYLPROPIONATE		
PROPIONATE			
NANDROLONE HYDROGEN	NANDROLONE HYDROGEN	AS	RX
SUCCINATE	SUCCINATE		
NANDROLONE LAURATE	NANDROLONE LAURATE	AS	RX
NANDROLONE	NANDROLONE PHENPROPIONATE	AS	RX
PHENPROPIONATE			
NANDROLONE	NANDROLONE	AS	RX
PHENYLPROPIONAT	PHENYLPROPIONATE		
NANDROLONE	NANDROLONE	AS	RX
PHENYLPROPIONATE	PHENYLPROPIONATE		
NANDROLONE PROPIONATE	NANDROLONE PROPIONATE	AS	RX
NANDROLONE UNDECYLATE	NANDROLONE UNDECYLATE	AS	RX
NAP	NANDROLONE	AS	RX
	PHENYLPROPIONATE		
NAPHAZOLINE	NAPHAZOLINE HCL	SA	OTC
NAPOSIM	METHANDROSTENOLONE	AS	RX
NARCAN	OXOMORPHINE	NA	RX
NARCANTI	OXOMORPHINE	NA	RX
NARCIDINE	PHENAZOCINE	NA	RX
NARCOBASINA	OXOCODONE	NA	RX
NARCODAL	OXOCODONE	NA	RX
NARCOFOR	DEMEROL	NA	RX
NARCOLO	DEXTOMORAMIDE	NA	RX
NARCOSIN	OXOCODONE	NA	RX
NARFEN	PHENAZOCINE	NA	RX
NARGENOL	OXOCODONE	NA	RX
NARISYN	PHENYLEPHRINE	SA	OTC
NARPHEN	PHENAZOCINE	NA	RX
NARZOCINA	PHENAZOCINE	NA	RX
NASAHIST CAPSULES—	PHENYLPROPANOLAMINE HCL	SA	RX
INJECTION			
NASALSPAN	PSEUDOEPHEDRINE	SA	OTC
NASOFEDRIN	PHENYLEPHRINE	SA	OTC
NASOLIN "PEDIATRICA"	EPHEDRINE	SA	RX
NASOPHEN	PHENYLEPHRINE	SA	OTC
NASTENEN	OXYMETHOLONE	AS	RX
NASTENON	OXYMETHOLONE	AS	RX
NECTABULIN	NANDROLONE	AS	RX
	PHENYLPROPIONATE		
NEFERTAL	PROPOXYPHENE	NA	RX

Brand Name	Generic Name	Class	SRC
NEGADOL	THEBACON	NA	RX
NENDRABOL	NANDROLONE PHENYLPROPIONATE	AS	RX
NENDRON	TESTOSTERONE	AS	RX
NEO-BUFFERIN	PHENYLEPHRINE	SA	OTC
NEO-DURABOLIC	NANDROLONE DECANOATE	AS	RX
NEO-EPININE	ISOPROTERENOL	SA	RX
NEO-FEDRIN	EPHEDRINE	SA	RX
NEO-HOMBREOL F	TESTOSTERONE	AS	RX
NEO-HOMBREOL-M	METHYLTESTOSTERONE	AS	RX
NEO-MAL	PROPOXYPHENE	NA	RX
NEO-NILOREX	PHENDIMETRAZINE	PS	RX
NEO-ORMONAL	FLUOXYMESTERONE	AS	RX
NEO-PONDEN	ANDROISOXAZOL	AS	RX
NEO-RINOSAN	EPHEDRINE	SA	RX
NEO-SINEFRINA	PHENYLEPHRINE	SA	OTC
NEO-SPRAY LONG ACTING	XYLOMETAZOLINE HCL	SA	OTC
NEO-SYNEPHRINE	PHENYLEPHRINE	SA	OTC
NEO-SYNEPHRINE HCL (OPTHALMIC)	PHENYLEPHRINE HCL	SA	RX
NEO-SYNEPHRINE HCL 1% INJECTION	PHENYLEPHRINE HCL	SA	RX
NEO-SYNEPHRINE II LONG ACTING CHILDREN'S NOSE DROPS	XYLOMETAZOLINE HCL	SA	OTC
NEO-SYNEPHRINOL DAY RELIEF	PSEUDOEPHEDRINE HCL	SA	RX
NEO-ULCOID	DEXTROMETHORPHAN	NA	RX
NEO-ZINE	PHENMETRAZINE	PS	RX
NEOASMAN	ISOPROTERENOL	SA	RX
NEOCARDOL	LEPTAZOL	CN	RX
NEOCODE	HYDROCODONE	NA	RX
NEOCORDIAL	NIKETHAMIDE	CN	RX
NEODRENAL	ISOPROTERENOL	SA	RX
NEODRINE	METHYLAMPHETAMINE	PS	RX
NEOEPINEPHRIN	ISOPROTERENOL	SA	RX
NEOFED	PSEUDOEPHEDRINE HCL	SA	RX
NEOISUPREL	ISOETHARINE	SA	RX
NEOMOCHIN	DEMEROL	NA	RX
NEOMOHIN	DEMEROL	NA	RX
NEOOXEDRINE	PHENYLEPHRINE	SA	OTC
NEOPHARMEDRINE	METHYLAMPHETAMINE	PS	RX
NEOPHRYN	PHENYLEPHRINE	SA	OTC
NEOSTENE	METHANDRIOL	AS	RX
NEOSTERON	METHANDRIOL	AS	RX
NEOSYMPATOL	PHENYLEPHRINE	SA	OTC
NEOSYNEPHRINE	PHENYLEPHRINE	SA	OTC
NEOSYNESIN	PHENYLEPHRINE	SA	OTC
NEOTESTIS	TESTOSTERONE	AS	RX
NEOVIRON-TABL.	METHYLTESTOSTERONE	AS	RX
NEPHENAL	ISOPROTERENOL	SA	RX
NEPHENALIN	ISOPROTERENOL	SA	RX
NEPHRIDINE	EPINEPHRINE	SA	RX
NEPHRONE	PHENYLEPHRINE	SA	OTC
NEROBOL(ETTES)	METHANDROSTENOLONE	AS	RX
NEROBOLIL	NANDROLONE PHENYLPROPIONATE	AS	RX
NETAMINE	ETAFEDRINE	SA	RX
NETHAMINE	ETAFEDRINE	SA	RX

NEURAZOL	LEPTAZOL	CN	RX
NEUROCAINE	COCAINE	PS	RX
NEUSTERON	METHANDRIOL	AS	RX
NEUTRORMONE	METHANDRIOL	AS	RX
NEUTROSTERON	METHANDRIOL	AS	RX
NEVIRON	METHANDRIOL	AS	RX
NEWPHRINE	PHENYLEPHRINE	SA	OTC
NI-COR	NIKETHAMIDE	CN	RX
NIAMINE	NIKETHAMIDE	CN	RX
NIBAL	METENOLONE ACETATE	AS	RX
NICAETHACOR	NIKETHAMIDE	CN	RX
NICAETHAMIDUM	NIKETHAMIDE	CN	RX
NICALGENE	DEMEROL	NA	RX
NICAMIDE	NIKETHAMIDE	CN	RX
NICARDIN	NIKETHAMIDE	CN	RX
NICETAMID	NIKETHAMIDE	CN	RX
NICETHAMID	NIKETHAMIDE	CN	RX
NICORDAMIN	NIKETHAMIDE	CN	RX
NICORINE LATEMA	NIKETHAMIDE	CN	RX
NICORYL	NIKETHAMIDE	CN	RX
NICOTINOYLDIAETHYLAM- IDUM	NIKETHAMIDE	CN	RX
NIERALINE	EPINEPHRINE	SA	RX
NIH 7519	PHENAZOCINE	NA	RX
NIH 7590	PIMINODINE	NA	RX
NIH 7958	PENTAZOCINE	NA	RX
NIKARDIN	NIKETHAMIDE	CN	RX
NIKAVITE	NIKETHAMIDE	CN	RX
NIKECOR	NIKETHAMIDE	CN	RX
NIKETAMIN	NIKETHAMIDE	CN	RX
NIKETHAMIDE	NIKETHAMIDE	CN	RX
NIKETHAROL	NIKETHAMIDE	CN	RX
NIKKETHYL	NIKETHAMIDE	CN	RX
NIKORIN	NIKETHAMIDE	CN	RX
NILEVAR	NORETHANDROLONE	AS	RX
NILEVAR	OXYMETHOLONE	AS	RX
NILGANA	CHLORPHENTERMINE	PS	RX
NIORIC MODIFIED	LEPTAZOL	CN	RX
NIPECOTAN	ANILERIDINE	NA	RX
NIQUETAMIDA	NIKETHAMIDE	CN	RX
NISANTOL	MECLOFENOXATE	PS	RX
NISINE M	LEPTAZOL	CN	RX
NIVELINA	PHENYLEPHRINE	SA	OTC
NIZETHAMID	NIKETHAMIDE	CN	RX
NOCLON	AMPHETAMINE	PS	RX
NOLAMINE TABLETS	PHENYLPROPANOLAMINE HCL	SA	RX
NOPHRINE	PHENYLEPHRINE	SA	OTC
NOR TPP	NANDROLONE PHENYLPROPIONATE	AS	RX
NOR-ANABOL	NANDROLONE PROPIONATE	AS	RX
NOR-DURANDRON	NANDROLONE HEXAHYDROBENZOATE	AS	RX
NORABOL	NANDROLONE PHENYLPROPIONATE	AS	RX
NORADREN	ISOPROTERENOL	SA	RX
NORANDROL	NANDROLONE PHENYLPROPIONATE	AS	RX
NORANDROS	NANDROLONE PHENYLPROPIONATE	AS	RX
NORANDROSTENOLONE	NANDROLONE	AS	RX
NORATHANDROLON	NORETHANDROLONE	AS	RX
NORBALIN	NANDROLONE	AS	RX

Brand Name	Generic Name	Class	SRC
	PHENYLPROPIONATE		
NORBOLETHONE	NORBOLETONE	AS	RX
NORBOLETONE	NORBOLETONE	AS	RX
NORCAMPHANE "EMEDIA EXPORT"	FENCAMFAMINE	PS	RX
NORDECON	NANDROLONE DECANOATE	AS	RX
NORDEMEROL	DEMEROL	NA	RX
NORDOSTEBOL	NORDOSTEBOL	AS	RX
NORDOSTEBOL ACETATE	NORDOSTEBOL ACETATE	AS	RX
NOREPHEDRANE	AMPHETAMINE	PS	RX
NOREPHEDRIN	PHENYLPROPANOLAMINE	SA	OTC
NORETANDROLONE	NORETHANDROLONE	AS	RX
NORETHANDROLON(E)	NORETHANDROLONE	AS	RX
NORGAN	HYDROCODONE	NA	RX
NORISEDRIN	ISOPROTERENOL	SA	RX
NORISODRINE AEROTROL	ISOPROTERENOL	SA	RX
NORISODRINE SULFATE	ISOPROTERENOL	SA	RX
NORISODRINE WITH CALCIUM IODIDE SYRUP	ISOPROTERENOL	SA	RX
NORISOEPHEDRIN	NORPSEUDOEPHEDRINE	PS	RX
NORLONGANDRON	NANDROLONE HEXAHYDROBENZOATE	AS	RX
NORMEPERIDINE	DEMEROL	NA	RX
NORMETHANDROLONE	METHYLNORTESTOSTERONE	AS	RX
NORMETHANDRONE	METHYLNORTESTOSTERONE	AS	RX
NORMETHISTERONE	METHYLNORTESTOSTERONE	AS	RX
NORMODYNE INJECTION	LEBETALOL HCL	BB	RX
NORMODYNE TABLETS	LEBETALOL HCL	BB	RX
NORODIN	METHYLAMPHETAMINE	PS	RX
NOROMON	NANDROLONE PHENYLPROPIONATE	AS	RX
NORPETHIDIN	DEMEROL	NA	RX
NORPHEDRINUM	PHENYLPROPANOLAMINE	SA	OTC
NORPROPANDROLATE	BOLANDIOL DIPROPIONATE	AS	RX
NORPSEUDOEPHEDRINE	NORPSEUDOEPHEDRINE	PS	RX
NORSTENOL	NANDROLONE PHENYLPROPIONATE	AS	RX
NORTANDROLONE	NORETHANDROLONE	AS	RX
NORTESTO	NANDROLONE PROPIONATE	AS	RX
NORTESTONATE	NANDROLONE	AS	RX
NORTESTOSTERONADAM- ANTANCARBOXYLATE	BOLMANTALAT	AS	RX
NORTESTOSTERON- DECANOAT	NANDROLONE DECANOATE	AS	RX
NORTESTOSTERONE	NANDROLONE	AS	RX
NORTESTOSTERONE UNDECANOATE	NANDROLONE UNDECYLATE	AS	RX
NORTESTOSTERONPHENYL- PROPIONAT	NANDROLONE PHENYLPROPIONATE	AS	RX
NOSTRIL	PHENYLEPHRINE	SA	OTC
NOTAIR	PEMOLINE	PS	RX
NOTANDRON	METHANDRIOL	AS	RX
NOTANDRON-DEPOT	METHANDRIOL-BIS- ONANTHOYLACTATE	AS	RX
NOVABOL	METHANDROSTENOLONE	AS	RX
NOVADREN	ISOPROTERENOL	SA	RX
NOVAFED	PSEUDOEPHEDRINE	SA	OTC
NOVAHISTINE	PHENYLPROPANOLAMINE HCL	SA	OTC

NOVAHISTINE COUGH & COLD FORMULA	PSEUDOEPHEDRINE HCL	SA	OTC
NOVAHISTINE DH AND EXPECTORANT	CODEINE PHOSPHATE	NA	RX
NOVAHISTINE DMX	PSEUDOEPHEDRINE HCL	SA	OTC
NOVAHISTINE ELIXIR	PHENYLEPHRINE	SA	OTC
NOVANDROL	METHANDRIOL	AS	RX
NOVASMASOL	METAPROTERENOL	SA	RX
NOVEDRIN	ETAFEDRINE	SA	RX
NOVICODIN	DIHYDROCODEINE	NA	RX
NOVICODINA	HYDROCODONE	NA	RX
NOVIRIL	METHANDRIOL	AS	RX
NOVO CORA-VINCO	LEPTAZOL	CN	RX
NOVO-BIOSCARDIOL	LEPTAZOL	CN	RX
NOVOCODON	THEBACON	NA	RX
NOVODRIN	ISOPROTERENOL	SA	RX
NOVOLAUDON	HYDROMORPHONE	NA	RX
NOVOPHENMETRAZINE	PHENMETRAZINE	PS	RX
NOVYDRINE	AMPHETAMINE	PS	RX
NP 13	BEMIGRIDE	CN	RX
NSC-12165	FLUOXYMESTERONE	AS	RX
NSC-12198	DROSTANOLONE PROPIONATE	AS	RX
NSC-19043	OXOCODONE	NA	RX
NSC-23759	TESTOLACTONE	AS	RX
NSC-25159	PEMOLINE	PS	RX
NSC-26198	OXYMETHOLONE	AS	RX
NSC-42722	METHANDROSTENOLONE	AS	RX
NSC-64967	METENOLONE ENANTHATE	AS	RX
NSC-9700	TESTOSTERONE	AS	RX
NSC-9701	METHYLTESTOSTERONE	AS	RX
NTZ	PHENYLEPHRINE	SA	OTC
NU-MAN	METHYLTESTOSTERONE	AS	RX
NUCODAN	OXOCODONE	NA	RX
NUCOFED	PSEUDOEPHEDRINE	SA	OTC
NUCOFED CAPSULES	CODEINE PHOSPHATE	NA	RX
NOCOFED EXPECTORANT AND PEDIATRIC EXPECTORANT AND SYRUP	CODEINE PHOSPHATE	NA	RX
NUMORPHAN	OXYMORPHONE HCL	NA	RX
NUMOTAC	ISOETHARINE HCL	SA	RX
NYODID	HYDROCODONE	NA	RX
NYQUIL NIGHTTIME COLD MEDICINE	PSEUDOEPHEDRINE HCL	SA	OTC
NYQUIL NIGHTTIME COLD MEDICINE	EPHEDRINE	SA	OTC
OBALAN	PHENDIMETRAZINE TARTRATE	PS	RX
OBE-DEL	PHENDIMETRAZINE	PS	RX
OBE-NIX	PHENTERMINE HYDROCHLORIDE	PS	RX
OBEPAR	PHENDIMETRAZINE	PS	RX
OBEPHEN	PHENTERMINE HYDROCHLORIDE	PS	RX
OBERMINE	PHENTERMINE HYDROCHLORIDE	PS	RX
OBESAN	PHENDIMETRAZINE	PS	RX
OBESIN "ANDROMACO"	AMPHETAMINE	PS	RX
OBESIN "VEB FAHLBERG-LIST"	PROPYLHEXEDRINE	SA	OTC
OBESIN "ZORI"	PHENTERMINE	PS	RX
OBESTAT CAPSULES	PHENYLPROPANOLAMINE HCL	SA	RX
OBLSTAT 150 CAPSULES	PHENYLPROPANOLAMINE HCL	SA	RX
OBESTIN-30	PHENTERMINE HYDROCHLORIDE	PS	RX
OBETROL 10, & 20	DEXTROAMPHETAMINE SULFATE	PS	RX
OBEVAL	PHENDIMETRAZINE TARTRATE	PS	RX
OBEX	PHENDIMETRAZINE	PS	RX

Brand Name	Generic Name	Class	SRC
OBEX "RIO ETH"	PHENMETRAZINE	PS	RX
OBY-TRIM 30 CAPSULES & TABLETS	PHENTERMINE HYDROCHLORIDE	PS	RX
OESTRENOLON	NANDROLONE	AS	RX
OFTAFRIN	PHENYLEPHRINE	SA	OTC
OFTALFRINE	PHENYLEPHRINE	SA	OTC
OKODON	PEMOLINE	PS	RX
OKTEDRIN	AMPHETAMINE	PS	RX
OP-ISOPHRIN	PHENYLEPHRINE	SA	OTC
OPASAL CAPSULES	PHENYLPROPANOLAMINE HCL	SA	RX
OPERIDINE	DEMEROL	NA	RX
OPIUM TINCTURE DEODORIZED	OPIUM	NA	RX
OPOTESTAN-PERLINGUAL	METHYLTESTOSTERONE	AS	RX
OPTALGIN	METHADONE	NA	RX
OPTICOR	LEPTAZOL	CN	RX
OPTON	OXOCODONE	NA	RX
OPYSTAN	DEMEROL	NA	RX
ORA-TESTRYL	FLUOXYMESTERONE	AS	RX
ORABOLIN	ETHYLESTRENOL	AS	RX
ORAL-TURINABOL	DEHYDROCHLORMETHYL TESTOSTERONE	AS	RX
ORALSTERONE	FLUOXYMESTERONE	AS	RX
ORAMINIC PRODUCTS	PHENYLPROPANOLAMINE HCL	SA	RX
ORANABOL	OXYMESTERONE	AS	RX
ORATESTIN	FLUOXYMESTERONE	AS	RX
ORAVIRON	METHYLTESTOSTERONE	AS	RX
ORCHISTERON-LINGULTABL.	METHYLTESTOSTERONE	AS	RX
ORCHISTERONE-M	METHYLTESTOSTERONE	AS	RX
ORCIPRENALINSULFAT	METAPROTERENOL	SA	RX
ORETON	TESTOSTERONE	AS	RX
ORETON F	TESTOSTERONE	AS	RX
ORETON METHYL	METHYLTESTOSTERONE	AS	RX
ORETON-M	METHYLTESTOSTERONE	AS	RX
ORG-OD-14	TIBOLONE	AS	RX
ORG-483	ETHYLESTRENOL	AS	RX
ORGABOLIN	ETHYLESTRENOL	AS	RX
ORGABORAL	ETHYLESTRENOL	AS	RX
ORGASTERON	METHYNORTESTOSTERONE	AS	RX
ORION (EPHEDRA)	EPHEDRINE	SA	RX
ORION (TESTOSTERON RESORIBL.)	METHYLTESTOSTERONE	AS	RX
ORNACOL CAPSULES	PHENYLPROPANOLAMINE HCL	SA	OTC
ORNADE CAPSULES	PHENYLPROPANOLAMINE HCL	SA	RX
ORNEX CAPSULES	PHENYLPROPANOLAMINE HCL	SA	OTC
OROSTERON	METHYNORTESTOSTERONE	AS	RX
ORQUISTERON	TESTOSTERONE	AS	RX
ORTEDRINE	AMPHETAMINE	PS	RX
ORTHOXICOL COUGH SYRUP	METHOXYPHENAMINE	SA	OTC
ORTHOXIN(E)	METHOXYPHENAMINE	SA	RX
ORTHOXYCOL	HYDROCODONE	NA	RX
ORTODRINEX	METHOXYPHENAMINE	SA	RX
ORTOXIN	METHOXYPHENAMINE	SA	RX
OSPALIVINA	MORPHINE	NA	RX
OSSIMESTERONE	OXYMESTERONE	AS	RX
OSSIMETOLONE	OXYMETHOLONE	AS	RX
OTRIVIN PEDIATRIC NASAL DROPS	XYLOMETAZOLINE HCL	SA	OTC

OXABOLINI	OXABOLONE CYPIONATE	AS	RX
OXABOLONE CYPIONATE	OXABOLONE CYPIONATE	AS	RX
OXADRON	METHYLAMPHETAMINE	PS	RX
OXANDROLONE	OXANDROLONE	AS	RX
OXANEST	OXOCODONE	NA	RX
OXAZIMEDRINE	PHENMETRAZINE	PS	RX
OXEDRIN	PHENYLEPHRINE	SA	OTC
OXICONUM	OXOCODONE	NA	RX
OXIKON	OXOCODONE	NA	RX
OXIMESTERONUM	OXYMESTERONE	AS	RX
OXIMETHOLONUM	OXYMETHOLONE	AS	RX
OXIMETOLONA	OXYMETHOLONE	AS	RX
OXITOSONA-50	OXYMETHOLONE	AS	RX
OXOCODONE	OXOCODONE	NA	RX
OXOMORPHINE	OXOMORPHINE	NA	RX
OXOMORPHONE	OXOMORPHONE	NA	RX
OXPRENOLOL	OXPRENOLOL	BB	RX
OXYCODEINONHYDRO- CHLORID	OXOCODONE	NA	RX
OXYCODONE HCL & ACETAMINOPHEN TABLETS	OXYCODONE	NA	RX
OXYCODONE HCL OXYCODONE TEREPHTHALATE & ASPIRIN TABLETS	OXYCODONE TEREPHTHALATE	NA	RX
OXYCODONE HCLUSP SINGLE ENTITY TABLETS & LIQUID	OXYCODONE	NA	RX
OXYCODONE HYDROCHLORIDE ORAL SOLUTION & TABLETS	OXYCODONE	NA	RX
OXYCODYL	OXOCODONE	NA	RX
OXYDESS	METHYLAMPHETAMINE	PS	RX
OXYDESS II	DEXTROAMPHETAMINE SULFATE	PS	RX
OXYDRIN	METHYLAMPHETAMINE	PS	RX
OXYFED	METHYLAMPHETAMINE	PS	RX
OXYKODAL	OXOCODONE	NA	RX
OXYKON	OXOCODONE	NA	RX
OXYMESTERON(E)	OXYMESTERONE	AS	RX
OXYMESTRONE	OXYMESTERONE	AS	RX
OXYMETHOLON(E)	OXYMETHOLONE	AS	RX
P-V-TUSSIN SYRUP	PHENYLEPHRINE HCL	SA	RX
P-V-TUSSIN SYRUP AND TABLETS	HYDROCODONE	NA	RX
PADRINA	HYDROCODONE	NA	RX
PAFADRIN	ISOPROTERENOL	SA	RX
PALACTIN	NANDROLONE DECANOATE	AS	RX
PALFADONNA	DEXTOMORAMIDE	NA	RX
PALFIUM	DEXTROMORAMIDE	NA	RX
PALPHIUM	DEXTROMORAMIDE	NA	RX
PAMEDONE	DIPIPANONE	NA	RX
PAN-TEST	TESTOSTERONE	AS	RX
PANADOL WITH CODEINE	CODEINE	NA	RX
PANADYL TABLETS & CAPSULES	PHENYLPROPANOLAMINE HCL	SA	RX
PANALGEN	METHADONE	NA	RX
PANAMINE	PHENYLPROPANOLAMINE	SA	OTC
PANCODINE	OXOCODONE	NA	RX
PANDOCRINE	PENMESTEROL	AS	RX
PANDRENIL	PHENYLEPHRINE	SA	OTC
PANREXIN-M	PHENDIMETRAZINE	PS	RX
PANTALGIN	DEMEROL	NA	RX

Brand Name	Generic Name	Class	SRC
PANTESTIN-ORAL	METHYLTESTOSTERONE	AS	RX
PANTOPON	OPIUM	NA	RX
PANZOL	LEPTAZOL	CN	RX
PARACODEIN	DIHYDROCODEINE	NA	RX
PARACODIN	DIHYDROCODEINE	NA	RX
PARANEPHRIN	EPINEPHRINE	SA	RX
PARASMINA	EPINEPHRINE	SA	RX
PARASYMPATOL	PHENYLEPHRINE	SA	OTC
PAREGORIC	OPIUM	NA	RX
PARENABOL	BOLDENONE UNDECYLATE	AS	RX
PAREPECTOLIN	OPIUM	NA	RX
PARIPHER	PHENYLEPHRINE	SA	OTC
PARKEVRINE	EPHEDRINE	SA	RX
PARLAM	BEMIGRIDE	CN	RX
PARMINE	PHENTERMINE HYDROCHLORIDE	PS	OTC
PARTUSS T.D. TABLETS	PHENYLPROPANOLAMINE HCL	SA	RX
PARTUSS-A TABLETS	PHENYLPROPANOLAMINE HCL	SA	RX
PARVON	PROPOXYPHENE	NA	RX
PARZONE	DIHYDROCODEINE	NA	RX
PATHEDINE	DEMEROL	NA	RX
PAVINAL	OXOCODONE	NA	RX
PAVISOID	OXYMETHOLONE	AS	RX
PAZO (HEMORRHOID OINTMENT/ SUPPOSITORIES)	EPHEDRINE	SA	OTC
PECTOBRON-GOTAS	DEXTROMETHORPHAN	NA	RX
PEDIACARE 2 CHILDREN'S COUGH RELIEF, & 3	PSEUDOEPHEDRINE HCL	SA	OTC
PEDIACOF	PHENYLEPHRINE HCL	SA	RX
PEDIACOF	CODEINE PHOSPHATE	NA	RX
PEDIATRIC NASAL DROPS "DANIELS"	PHENYLEPHRINE	SA	OTC
PEDIATRICA (NASOLIN)	EPHEDRINE	SA	RX
PEEDEE DOSE DECONGESTANT	PSEUDOEPHEDRINE HCL	SA	RX
PELTAZON	PENTAZOCINE	NA	RX
PEMETESAN	LEPTAZOL	CN	RX
PEMOLIN(E)	PEMOLINE	PS	RX
PENMESTEROL	PENMESTEROL	AS	RX
PENTACARD	LEPTAZOL	CN	RX
PENTACINA	PENTAZOCINE	NA	RX
PENTACOR	LEPTAZOL	CN	RX
PENTACORINA	LEPTAZOL	CN	RX
PENTAFEN	PENTAZOCINE	NA	RX
PENTAFORT	PENTAZOCINE	NA	RX
PENTAGIN	PENTAZOCINE	NA	RX
PENTALGINA	PENTAZOCINE	NA	RX
PENTAMETHAZOL	LEPTAZOL	CN	RX
PENTAMETHYLENTETRAZOL	LEPTAZOL	CN	RX
PENTASOL	LEPTAZOL	CN	RX
PENTAZOCINE	PENTAZOCINE	NA	RX
PENTAZOLUM	LEPTAZOL	CN	RX
PENTEDRIN	PHENYLEPHRINE	SA	OTC
PENTEMESAN	LEPTAZOL	CN	RX
PENTETRAZOL	LEPTAZOL	CN	RX
PENTRAZOL	LEPTAZOL	CN	RX
PENTYLENETETRAZOL	LEPTAZOL	CN	RX
PENTYLENTENTRAZAL	LEPTAZOL	CN	RX

PENZIN	PENTAZOCINE	NA	RX
PERABOL	METHANDROSTENOLONE	AS	RX
PERANDREN	TESTOSTERONE	AS	RX
PERANDREN-LINGUETTEN	METHYLTESTOSTERONE	AS	RX
PERANDRONE-LINGUETTES	METHYLTESTOSTERONE	AS	RX
PERBOLIN	METHANDROSTENOLONE	AS	RX
PERCOCET	OXYCODONE	NA	RX
PERCODAL	OXYCODONE	NA	RX
PERCODAN & PERCODAN-DEMI TABLETS	OXYCODONE	NA	RX
PERCOMON	AMPHETAMINE	PS	RX
PERCORAL	NIKETHAMIDE	CN	RX
PERKULEN	METHYLAMPHETAMINE	PS	RX
PERMASTRIL	DROSTANOLONE PROPIONATE	AS	RX
PERNASATOR-WIRKSTOFF	PROPYLHEXEDRINE	SA	OTC
PERVITIN	METHYLAMPHETAMINE	PS	RX
PETALGIN	METHADONE	NA	RX
PETANTIN	DEMEROL	NA	RX
PETEZOL	LEPTAZOL	CN	RX
PETHADOL	MEPERIDINE HCL	NA	RX
PETHANAL	DEMEROL	NA	RX
PETHANOL	DEMEROL	NA	RX
PETHEDINE	DEMEROL	NA	RX
PETHENAL	DEMEROL	NA	RX
PETHIDIN-ZWISCHENPRODUKT B	DEMEROL	NA	RX
PETHIDINE	DEMEROL (EUROPEAN NAME FOR)	NA	RX
PETHIDINE INTERMEDIATE B	DEMEROL	NA	RX
PETHIDINHYDROCHLORID	DEMEROL	NA	RX
PETHIIDONE	DEMEROL	NA	RX
PETHOID (FROM AUSTRALIA)	DEMEROL	NA	RX
PETHOLD	PETHIDINE	NA	RX
PETIDINA CLORIDRATO	DEMEROL	NA	RX
PETISEDOL	DEMEROL	NA	RX
PETROLONE	LEPTAZOL	CN	RX
PHARGEDRINE "F"	AMPHETAMINE	PS	RX
PHARMAMEDRINE	AMPHETAMINE	PS	RX
PHEDASU	PSEUDOEPHEDRINE	SA	OTC
PHEDOXE	METHYLAMPHETAMINE	PS	RX
PHEDRISOX	METHYLAMPHETAMINE	PS	RX
PHENADON(UM)	METHADONE	NA	RX
PHENAMIN(UM)	AMPHETAMINE	PS	RX
PHENAMIZOL	AMIPHENAZOLE	CN	RX
PHENAPHEN WITH CODEINE CAPSULES	CODEINE PHOSPHATE	NA	RX
PHENAPHEN-650 WITH CODEINE TABLETS	CODEINE PHOSPHATE	NA	RX
PHENAZINE "JENKINS"	PHENDIMETRAZINE	PS	RX
PHENAZINE TABLETS & CAPSULES	PHENDIMETRAZINE	PS	RX
PHENAZOCINE	PHENAZOCINE	NA	RX
PHENCAMINE	FENCAMFAMINE	PS	RX
PHENDIMETRAZIN(E)	PHENDIMETRAZINE	PS	RX
PHENEDRINE	AMPHETAMINE	PS	RX
PHENEPHRIN	PHENYLEPHRINE	SA	OTC
PHENERGAN VC WITH CODEINE	CODEINE PHOSPHATE	NA	RX
PHENERGAN WITH CODEINE	CODEINE PHOSPHATE	NA	RX
PHENERGAN WITH DEXTROMETHORPHAN	DEXTROMETHORPHAN HYDROBROMIDE	NA	RX
PHENERGRAN VC	PHENYLEPHRINE HCL	SA	RX

Brand Name	Generic Name	Class	SRC
PHENERGRAN VC WITH CODEINE	PHENYLEPHRINE HCL	SA	RX
PHENETHYLAZOCINUM	PHENAZOCINE	NA	RX
PHENIDYLATE	METHYLPHENIDATE	PS	RX
PHENIMETHOXAZINE	PHENDIMETRAZINE	PS	RX
PHENMETRALINI CHLORIDUM	PHENMETRAZINE	PS	RX
PHENMETRAZINAL	PHENMETRAZINE	PS	RX
PHENMETRAZINE	PHENMETRAZINE	PS	RX
PHENMETRAZINHYDRO-CHLORID	PHENMETRAZINE	PS	RX
PHENOBOLIN	NANDROLONE PHENYLPROPIONATE	AS	RX
PHENOPANE	DIMETHYLAMPHETAMINE	PS	RX
PHENOPROMIN	AMPHETAMINE	PS	RX
PHENOXAZOL	PEMOLINE	PS	RX
PHENOXINE	PEMOLINE	PS	RX
PHENTERMINE HCL CAPSULES & TABLETS	PHENTERMINE HYDROCHLORIDE	PS	RX
PHENTROL	PHENTERMINE HYDROCHLORIDE	PS	RX
PHENTROL	PHENMETRAZINE	PS	RX
PHENTROL 2, 4, 5	PHENTERMINE HYDROCHLORIDE	PS	RX
PHENYL-DRANE	PHENYLEPHRINE	SA	OTC
PHENYLENE	PHENYLEPHRINE	SA	OTC
PHENYLEPHRIN(E)	PHENYLEPHRINE	SA	OTC
PHENYLISOHYDANTOIN	PEMOLINE	PS	RX
PHENYMETHYLAMINO-PROPANHYDROCHLORID	METHYLAMPHETAMINE	PS	RX
PHENYLPIPERONE	DIPIPANONE	NA	RX
PHENYLPROPANOLAMINE HCL	PHENYLPROPANOLAMINE	SA	OTC
PHENZINE	PHENDIMETRAZINE TARTRATE	PS	RX
PHILOPON	METHYLAMPHETAMINE	PS	RX
PHRENAZOL	LEPTAZOL	CN	RX
PHRENILIN WITH CODEINE #3	CODEINE PHOSPHATE	NA	RX
PHYSEPTON(E)	METHADONE	NA	RX
PHYTADON	DEMEROL	NA	RX
PIAM	METHANDIENONE	AS	RX
PICROTOXIMUN	PICROTOXINE	CN	RX
PICROTOXINE	PICROTOXINE	CN	RX
PIKROTOXIN	PICROTOXINE	CN	RX
PIMADIN	PIMINODINE	NA	RX
PIMINODINE	PIMINODINE	NA	RX
PIOXOL	PEMOLINE	PS	RX
PIPADONE	DIPIPANONE	NA	RX
PIPERIDYL-AMIDON	DIPIPANONE	NA	RX
PIPERIDYL-METHADON	DIPIPANONE	NA	RX
PIPEROSAL	DEMEROL	NA	RX
PIPRADOL	PIPRADOL	PS	RX
PIPRADROLHYDROCHLORID	PIPRADOL	PS	RX
PIPRAL	PIPRADOL	PS	RX
PIPRALON	PIPRADOL	PS	RX
PIPRDOL	PIPRADOL	PS	RX
PIRIDOSAL	DEMEROL	NA	RX
PIRIDROL	PIPRADOL	PS	RX
PIRIL	PROPOXYPHENE	NA	RX
PL 35	PHENYLEPHRINE	SA	OTC
PLEGINE	PHENDIMETRAZINE TARTRATE	PS	RX
PLENASTRIL	OXYMETHOLONE	AS	RX

PLENIUM	PEMOLINE	PS	RX
PLEUROPON	NANDROLONE CYCLOHEXYLPROPIONATE	AS	RX
PLUROCRIN 13	AMPHETAMINE	PS	RX
POLAMIDON	METHADONE	NA	RX
POLAMIVET	METHADONE	NA	RX
POLARAMINE	PSEUDOEPHEDRINE	SA	OTC
POLY-HISINE	PSEUDOEPHEDRINE	SA	OTC
POLY-HISTINE EXPECTORANT WITH CODEINE	CODEINE PHOSPHATE	NA	RX
PONDEX "MEDIMPEX"	PEMOLINE	PS	RX
PONDIMIN	FENFLURAMINE HCL	PS	RX
PONDUS	NANDROLONE PROPIONATE	AS	RX
POPMA-AETHANOL	PHENYLEPHRINE	SA	OTC
PORFOLAN	METHADONE	NA	RX
PORPOX 65 WITH APAP TABLETS	PROPOXYPHENE HCL	NA	RX
POSOGLAUKOM	EPINEPHRINE	SA	RX
PRAEDIL	ISOPROTERENOL	SA	RX
PRAIA	PROPOXYPHENE	NA	RX
PRASTERONE	DEHYDROEPIANDROSTERONE	AS	RX
PRE SATE	CHLORPHENTERMINE	PS	RX
PRECEDYL	DEMEROL	NA	RX
PREFIN	PHENYLEPHRINE	SA	OTC
PREFRIN LIQUIFILM	PHENYLEPHRINE	SA	OTC
PRELAZINE	PHENMETRAZINE	PS	RX
PRELU-2 TIMED RELEASE CAPSULES	PHENDIMETRAZINE TARTRATE	PS	RX
PRELUDIN ENDURETS	PHENMETRAZINE HYDROCHLORIDE	PS	RX
PRELUDIN TABLETS	PHENMETRAZINE HYDROCHLORIDE	PS	RX
PREMARIN WITH METHYLTES- TOSTERONE TESTRED	METHYLTESTOSTERONE	AS	RX
PREMODRIN	METHYLAMPHETAMINE	PS	RX
PRENOMISER FORTE	ISOPROTERENOL	SA	RX
PREPARTEN	PROPOXYPHENE	NA	RX
PREROIDE	MESTANOLON	AS	RX
PRESSEDRIN	PHENYLPROPANOLAMINE	SA	OTC
PREXCIDE	PEMOLINE	PS	RX
PREZA	HEROIN	NA	RX
PRIMATENE MIST	EPINEPHRINE	SA	OTC
PRIMATENE MIST SUSPENSION	EPINEPHRINE BITARTRATE	SA	OTC
PRIMATENE TABLETS M FORMULA & P FORMULA	EPHEDRINE	SA	OTC
PRIMOBOLAN	METHENOLONE ACETATE	AS	RX
PRIMOBOLAN-DEPOT	METENOLONE ENANTHATE	AS	RX
PRIMONABOL—DEPOT	METHENOLONE	AS	RX
PRIMONIAT T	TESTOSTERONE	AS	RX
PRIMOTEST T	TESTOSTERONE	AS	RX
PRIMOTESTON T	TESTOSTERONE	AS	RX
PRIMOTESTON-TABL.	METHYLTESTOSTERONE	AS	RX
PRINADOL	PHENAZOCINE	NA	RX
PRIVINE	NAPHAZOLINE	SA	OTC
PRO 65	PROPOXYPHENE	NA	RX
PRO-MEPERDAN	DEMEROL	NA	RX
PROASMA	METHOXYPHENAMINE	SA	RX
PROBESE-P	PHENMETRAZINE	PS	RX
PROBOLIN	METHANDRIOLDIPROPIONATE	AS	RX
PROCAPS-65	PROPOXYPHENE	NA	RX
PROCARDIN(E)	NIKETHAMIDE	CN	RX

Brand Name	Generic Name	Class	SRC
PROCODAL	HYDROCODONE	NA	RX
PROCORMAN	NIKETHAMIDE	CN	RX
PROFAMINA	AMPHETAMINE	PS	RX
PROFENE 65	PROPOXYPHENE HCL	NA	RX
PROGESIC	PROPOXYPHENE	NA	RX
PROHORMO	MESTANOLON	AS	RX
PROLAMINE CAPSULES MAXIMUM STRENGTH CAPSULES	PHENYLPROPANOLAMINE HCL	SA	OTC
PROLINTANE	PROLINTANE	PS	RX
PROLINTANHYDROCHLORID	PROLINTANE	PS	RX
PROMETHOLONE	DROSTANOLONE PROPIONATE	AS	RX
PROMOTIL	PROLINTANE	PS	RX
PRONABOL	NORETHANDROLONE	AS	RX
PRONALGIC	PROPOXYPHENE	NA	RX
PRONARCIN	OXOCODONE	NA	RX
PRONARE	PHENYLEPHRINE	SA	OTC
PRONEPHRINE	PHENYLEPHRINE	SA	OTC
PROPADRIN(E)	PHENYLPROPANOLAMINE	SA	OTC
PROPADRINE HYDROCHLONDE PREPS.	PHENYLPROPANOLAMINE HCL	SA	RX
PROPAGEST TABLETS & SYRUP	PHENYLPROPANOLAMINE HCL	SA	OTC
PROPAHIST TABLETS & SYRUP & CAPSULES & INJECTION	PHENYLPROPANOLAMINE HCL	SA	RX
PROPAL	ISOPROTERENOL	SA	RX
PROPAMIN "ERBA"	METHYLAMPHETAMINE	PS	RX
PROPANOVITAN	METHYLAMPHETAMINE	PS	RX
PROPENYL	AMPHETAMINE	PS	RX
PROPETANDROL	PROPETANDROL	AS	RX
PROPETHANDROL	PROPETANDROL	AS	RX
PROPISAMINE	AMPHETAMINE	PS	RX
PROPOX	PROPOXYPHENE	NA	RX
PROPOXYCHEL	PROPOXYPHENE	NA	RX
PROPOXYPHEN	PROPOXYPHENE	NA	RX
PROPOXYPHENE & APAP TABLETS 65/650	PROPOXYPHENE HCL	NA	RX
PROPOXYPHENE AC CAPSULES	PROPOXYPHENE HCL	NA	RX
PROPOXYPHENE COMPOUND 65	PROPOXYPHENE HCL	NA	RX
PROPOXYPHENE HCL CAPSULES	PROPOXYPHENE HCL	NA	RX
PROPYLHEXEDRINE	PROPYLHEXEDRINE	SA	OTC
PROPYLON	ISOPROTERENOL	SA	RX
PROPYNALIN	ISOPROTERENOL	SA	RX
PROSEROUT	MECLOFENOXATE	PS	RX
PROTABOL	TIOMESTERONE	AS	RX
PROTAN	DEXTROMETHORPHAN	NA	RX
PROTANABOL	OXYMETHOLONE	AS	RX
PROTANDREN	METHANDRIOL	AS	RX
PROTECTOR	DIPHENOXYLATE	NA	RX
PROTENDIOL	METHANDRIOL	AS	RX
PROTENOLON	MESTANOLON	AS	RX
PROTERENAL	ISOPROTERENOL	SA	RX
PROTERGINE	MESTANOLON	AS	RX
PROTERENOL	CISOPROTERENOL	SA	RX

PROTERNOL-L	ISOPROTERENOL	SA	RX
PROTERON	MESTANOLON	AS	RX
PROTID—IMPROVED FORMULA	PHENYLEPHRINE HCL	SA	RX
PROTIVAR	OXANDROLONE	AS	RX
PROTOBOLIN	METHANDROSTENOLONE	AS	RX
PROVENTIL (SPECIAL CONSIDERATION DRUG)	ALBUTEROL	SA	RX
PROVIRON (NEUE FORM)	MESTEROLONE	AS	RX
PROVIRON T	TESTOSTERONE	AS	RX
PROXAGESIC	PROPOXYPHRENE	NA	RX
PROXYDRIN	PHENYLEPHRINE	SA	OTC
PROXYPHENE	PROPOXYPHENE	NA	RX
PSEUDO-BID	PSEUDOEPHEDRINE	SA	OTC
PSEUDO-HIST	PSEUDOEPHEDRINE	SA	OTC
PSEUDOEPHEDRINE HCL	PSEUDOEPHEDRINE HCL	SA	OTC
PSEUDONOREPHEDRIN	NORPSEUDOEPHEDRINE	PS	RX
PSICHERGINA	METHYLAMPHETAMINE	PS	RX
PSICO-SARTO	PEMOLINE	PS	RX
PSICOPAN	METHYLAMPHETAMINE	PS	RX
PSIQUERGINA	METHYLAMPHETAMINE	PS	RX
PSYCHAMINE A 66	PHENMETRAZINE	PS	RX
PSYCHEDRIN	AMPHETAMINE	PS	RX
PSYCHERGINE	METHYLAMPHETAMINE	PS	RX
PSYCHOTON	AMPHETAMINE	PS	RX
PSYKOTON	METHYLAMPHETAMINE	PS	RX
PT 105 CAPSULES	PHENDIMETRAZINE	PS	RX
PTZ	LEPTAZOL	CN	RX
PULMOLUY-S	OXOCODONE	NA	RX
PUPILETTO	PHENYLEPHRINE	SA	OTC
PYCARDINE	NIKETHAMIDE	CN	RX
PYRACORT-D	PHENYLEPHRINE	SA	OTC
PYRICARDYL	NIKETHAMIDE	CN	RX
PYRIDROL	PIPRADOL	PS	RX
PYRISTAN CAPSULES & ELIXIR	PHENYLPROPANOLAMINE HCL	SA	RX
PYRROLAMIDOL	DEXTOMORAMIDE	NA	RX
PYRROXATE CAPSULES	PHENYLPROPANOLAMINE HCL	SA	OTC
QUADRAHIST PEDIATRIC SYRUP - SYRUP & TIMED RELEASE TABLETS	PHENYLEPHRINE	SA	RX
QUADRINAL TABLETS & SUSPENSION	EPHEDRINE	SA	RX
QUELIDRINE SYRUP	EPHEDRINE	SA	RX
QUELIDRINE SYRUP	PHENYLEPHRINE HCL	SA	RX
QUELIDRINE SYRUP	DEXTROMETHORPHAN HYDROBROMIDE	NA	RX
QUIBRON PLUS	EPHEDRINE	SA	RX
QUINBOLONE	QUINBOLONE	AS	RX
QUOTIDINE	METHADONE	NA	RX
QUOTIDON-WIRKSTOFF	METHADONE	NA	RX
R. 875	DEXTOMORAMIDE	NA	RX
R.A.S.	AMPHETAMINE	PS	RX
R-2580	TRENBOLONE	AS	RX
RACEDRIN	EPHEDRINE	SA	RX
RACEPHEDRIN	EPHEDRINE	SA	RX
RACEPIN	EPINEPHRINE	SA	RX
RAPACODIN	DIHYDROCODEINE	NA	RX
REACTIMERCK-WIRKSTOFF	FENCAMFAMINE	PS	RX
REACTIVAN-WIRKSTOFF	FENCAMFAMINE	PS	RX
REASEC	DIPHENOXYLATE	NA	RX
REBAL	CHLORPHENTERMINE	PS	RX

Brand Name	Generic Name	Class	SRC
REDUCTO "ARCUM"	PHENDIMETRAZINE	PS	RX
REDUFORM	NORPSEUDOEPHEDRINE	PS	RX
REFORMIN	NIKETHAMIDE	CN	RX
REGREDOL	PROPOXYPHENE	NA	RX
REISS (CORMED)	NIKETHAMIDE	CN	RX
REKTANDRON	TESTOSTERONE	AS	RX
RENAGLANDIN	EPINEPHRINE	SA	RX
RENALEPTINE	EPINEPHRINE	SA	RX
RENALINA	EPINEPHRINE	SA	RX
RENOFORM	EPINEPHRINE	SA	RX
RENOSTYPTICIN	EPINEPHRINE	SA	RX
RENOSTYPTIN	EPINEPHRINE	SA	RX
RESO-BRONKOTAL	ISOPROTERENOL	SA	RX
RESOLUTION I MAXIMUM STRENGTH, & II HALF STRENGTH	PHENYLPROPANOLAMINE HCL	SA	OTC
RESPIFRAL	ISOPROTERENOL	SA	RX
RESTORE	MESTANOLON	AS	RX
RETABOLIL	NANDROLONE DECANOATE	AS	RX
RETARDIN	DIPHENOXYLATE	NA	RX
REVIBOL	PEMOLINE	PS	RX
RHINALATOR	AMPHETAMINE	PS	RX
RHINALL	PHENYLEPHRINE	SA	OTC
RHINALL-10	PHENYLEPHRINE	SA	OTC
RHINASCO	PHENYLEPHRINE	SA	OTC
RHINDECON	PHENYLPROPANOLAMINE	SA	RX
RHINEX DM LIQUID	PHENYLPROPANOLAMINE HCL	SA	RX
RHYMOSYN	PSEUDOEPHEDRINE	SA	OTC
RIKODEINE	DIHYDROCODEINE	NA	RX
RILATIN	METHYLPHENIDATE	PS	RX
RINEX	PHENYLEPHRINE	SA	OTC
RINISOL	PHENYLEPHRINE	SA	OTC
RIO ETH (OBEX)	PHENMETRAZINE	PS	RX
RITABOLIN	NANDROLONE PHENYLPROPIONATE	AS	RX
RITALIN HYDROCHLORIDE AND SR TABLETS	METHYLPHENIDATE HYDROCHLORIDE	PS	RX
RITALIN SR TABLETS (METHYLPHENIDATE HYDROCHLORIDE)	METHOXYPHENAMINE	SA	RX
RIVOPHARM (ANALEPTIN)	NIKETHAMIDE	CN	RX
RMS SUPPOSITORIES	MORPHINE	NA	RX
RMS UNISERTS	MORPHINE	NA	RX
RO 1-5431	LEVORPHANOL	NA	RX
RO 1-5470/5	DEXTROMETHORPHAN	NA	RX
RO-FEDRIN	PSEUDOEPHEDRINE	SA	OTC
ROBIDANE	HYDROCODONE	NA	RX
ROBIDONE	HYDROCODONE	NA	RX
ROBITUSSIN A-C AND DAC	CODEINE PHOSPHATE	NA	RX
ROBITUSSIN NIGHT RELIEF	PHENYLEPHRINE	SA	OTC
ROBITUSSIN-CF	PHENYLPROPANOLAMINE HCL	SA	OTC
ROBITUSSIN-PE	PSEUDOEPHEDRINE HCL	SA	OTC
ROBORAL	OXYMETHOLONE	AS	RX
ROHIST-D CAPSULES - VIAL	PHENYLPROPANOLAMINE HCL	SA	RX
ROLANADE CAPSULES	PHENYLPROPANOLAMINE HCL	SA	RX
ROMECOR	ETHAMIVAN	CN	RX
ROMIDON	PROPOXYPHENE	NA	RX
ROMILAR	DEXTROMETHORPHAN	NA	RX

RONDEC	PSEUDOEPHEDRINE	SA	OTC
RONDEC-ORAL DROPS AND SYRUP	DEXTROMETHORPHAN HYDROBROMIDE	NA	RX
RONYL	PEMOLINE	PS	RX
ROPOXYL	MECLOFENOXATE	PS	RX
ROXANOL	MORPHINE	NA	RX
ROXILIN	BOLAZIN-CAPRONATE	AS	RX
R OXILON	MEBOLAZINE	AS	RX
ROXYN	METHYLAMPHETAMINE	PS	RX
RP-12222	PENMESTEROL	AS	RX
RS-2106	STENBOLONE ACETATE	AS	RX
RS-3268R	NANDROLONE CYCLOTATE	AS	RX
RU-TUSS EXPECTORANT	CODEINE PHOSPHATE	NA	RX
RU-TUSS EXPECTORANT AND PLAIN AND TABLETS	PHENYLEPHRINE HCL	SA	RX
RU-TUSS WITH HYDROCODONE	PHENYLEPHRINE HCL	SA	RX
RU-TUSS WITH HYDROCODONE	HYDROCODONE	NA	RX
RU-1881	METRIBOLON E	AS	RX
RYMED PRODUCTS	PHENYLPROPANOLAMINE HCL	SA	RX
RYNA	PSEUDOEPHEDRINE	SA	OTC
RYNA LIQUID, C LIQUID & CX LIQUID	PSEUDOEPHEDRINE HCL	SA	OTC
RYNA-TUSSADINE TABLETS - LIQUID	PHENYLPROPANOLAMINE HCL	SA	RX
RYNATAN TABLETS & PEDIATRIC SOLUTION	PHENYLEPHRINE TANNATE	SA	RX
RYNATUSS TABLETS & PEDIATRIC SOLUTION	PHENYLEPHRINE TANNATE	SA	RX
RYNATUSS TABLETS & PEDIATRIC SUSPENSION	EPHEDRINE	SA	RX
S 3790	STENBOLONE ACETATE	AS	RX
S 62	CHLORPHENTERMINE	PS	RX
S-T DECONGESTANT SUGAR FREE AND DYE FREE	PHENYLEPHRINE HCL	SA	RX
S-T FORTE SYRUP & SUGAR FREE	PHENYLEPHRINE HCL	SA	RX
S-T FORTE SYRUP & SUGAR FREE	HYDROCODONE	NA	RX
S-140	DEMEROL	NA	RX
SACIETYL-FINADIET	PHENMETRAZINE	PS	RX
SACOPHAN	DEXTROMETHORPHAN	NA	RX
SAL-PHEDRINE	EPHEDRINE	SA	RX
SALVACARD	NIKETHAMIDE	CN	RX
SALVACORIN	NIKETHAMIDE	CN	RX
SANABO	NANDROLONE CYCLOHEXYLPROPIONATE	AS	RX
SANABORAL	OXYMESTERONE	AS	RX
SANASMA	ISOPROTERENOL	SA	RX
SANCORA	NIKETHAMIDE	CN	RX
SANCOTON	LEPTAZOL	CN	RX
SANEDRINE	EPHEDRINE	SA	RX
SANEPI	EPINEPHRINE	SA	RX
SANHIST TD TABLETS & VIAL	PHENYLPROPANOLAMINE HCL	SA	RX
SANOREX	MAZINDOL	PS	RX
SANTUSSIN CAPSULES & SUSP.	PHENYLPROPANOLAMINE HCL	SA	RX
SARCOSAN	ANDROSTANOLONE BENZOATE	AS	RX
SAUTERALGYL	DEMEROL	NA	RX
SAVENTRINE	ISOPROTERENOL	SA	RX
SC 7294	PROPETANDROL	AS	RX

Brand Name	Generic Name	Class	SRC
SC-11585	OXANDROLONE	AS	RX
SC-16148	SILANDROL	AS	RX
SCHLANK-SCHLANK EB 2000	NORPSEUDOEPHEDRINE	PS	RX
SCOT-TUSSIN SUGAR FREE 5-ACTION COLD FORMULA	DEXTROMETHORPHAN HYDROBROMIDE	NA	RX
SCURENALINE	EPINEPHRINE	SA	RX
SECTRAL	ACEBUTOLOL HCL	BB	RX
SEDAFAMEM	PHENDIMETRAZINE	PS	RX
SEDANSOL-ISO	ISOPROTERENOL	SA	RX
SEDASMA	METAPROTERENOL	SA	RX
SEDATUSS	DEXTROMETHORPHAN	NA	RX
SEDIONAL-DM	DEXTROMETHORPHAN	NA	RX
SEDISTAL	DIPHENOXYLATE	NA	RX
SEDO-RAPIDE	METHADONE	NA	RX
SEDOLIN	AMPHETAMINE	PS	RX
SEDOPATOL	PHENYLEPHRINE	SA	OTC
SEDOTUS	DEXTROMETHORPHAN	NA	RX
SEMCOX	HYDROMORPHONE	NA	RX
SEMOXYDRINE	METHYLAMPHETAMINE	PS	RX
SEPTA-OM	METHADONE	NA	RX
SERPERO (ANTIASMATICO)	ISOPROTERENOL	SA	RX
SEVANIL	ETHAMIVAN	CN	RX
SH 723	MESTEROLONE	AS	RX
SH-60723	MESTEROLONE	AS	RX
SIDUS (FERONA)	FLUOXYMESTERONE	AS	RX
SIGMADYN	PEMOLINE	PS	RX
SILANDROL	SILANDROL	AS	RX
SILENTIUM	DEXTROMETHORPHAN	NA	RX
SIMARON	ETHAMIVAN	CN	RX
SIMCOR	PHENYLEPHRINE	SA	OTC
SIMESALGINA	DEMEROL	NA	RX
SIMPADREN	PHENYLEPHRINE	SA	OTC
SIMPALON	PHENYLEPHRINE	SA	OTC
SIMPAMINA	AMPHETAMINE	PS	RX
SIMPATEDRIN	AMPHETAMINE	PS	RX
SIMPATINA	AMPHETAMINE	PS	RX
SIMPLENE	EPINEPHRINE	SA	RX
SIN-ALGIN	METHADONE	NA	RX
SINAREST NASAL	PHENYLEPHRINE	SA	OTC
SINAREST REGULAR & EXTRA STRENGTH TABLETS	PHENYLPROPANOLAMINE HCL	SA	OTC
SINDRENINA	EPINEPHRINE	SA	RX
SINDROMIDA	PEMOLINE	PS	RX
SINE-AID	PHENYLPROPANOLAMINE HCL	SA	OTC
SINE-AID EXTRA STRENGTH SINUS HEADACHE CAPSULES	PSUEDOEPHEDRINE HCL	SA	OTC
SINE-AID SINUS HEADACHE TABLETS	PSEUDOEPHEDRINE HCL	SA	OTC
SINE-OFF EXTRA STRENGTH NO DROWSINESS CAPSULES	PHENYLPROPANOLAMINE HCL	SA	OTC
SINE-OFF EXTRA STRENGTH SINUS MEDICINE ASPIRIN FREE	PHENYLPROPANOLAMINE HCL	SA	OTC
SINE-OFF SINUS MEDICINE TABLETS-ASPIRIN FORMULA	PHENYLPROPANOLAMINE HCL	SA	OTC

SINESEX	METHANDRIOL	AS	RX
SINEX DECONGESTANT NASAL SPRAY	PHENYLEPHRINE	SA	OTC
SINGLET	PHENYLEPHRINE HCL	SA	RX
SINOPHEN	PHENYLEPHRINE	SA	OTC
SINOVAN TIMED	PHENYLEPHRINE	SA	RX
SINTABOLIN	NANDROLONE PHENYLPROPIONATE	AS	RX
SINTALGON	METHADONE	NA	RX
SINTIODAL	OXOCODONE	NA	RX
SINUBID TABLETS	PHENYLPROPANOLAMINE HCL	SA	RX
SINULIN TABLETS	PHENYLPROPANOLAMINE HCL	SA	RX
SINUTAB	PHENYLPROPANOLAMINE HCL	SA	OTC
SINUTABL II MAXIMUM STRENGTH NO DROWSINESS FORMULA CAPSULES AND TABLETS	PSEUDOEPHEDRINE HCL	SA	OTC
SINUTAB MAXIMUM STRENGTH CAPSULES & TABLETS	PSEUDOEPHEDRINE HCL	SA	OTC
SISAAL	DEXTROMETHORPHAN	NA	RX
SISTOCARDIL	LEPTAZOL	CN	RX
SISTRAL "ENDO"	PEMOLINE	PS	RX
SK-OXYCODONE WITH ASPIRIN TABLETS	OXYCODONE TEREPHTHALATE	NA	RX
SK-APAP WITH CODEINE TABLETS	CODEINE PHOSPHATE	NA	RX
SK-DIPHENOXYLATE TABLETS	DIPHENOXYLATE	NA	RX
SK-OXYCODONE WITH ACETAMINOPHEN TABLETS	OXYCODONE	NA	RX
SK-OXYCODONE WITH ASPIRIN TABLETS	OXYCODONE	NA	RX
SK-65	PROPOXYPHENE HCL	NA	RX
SK-65 APAP TABLETS & CAPSULES	PROPOXYPHENE HCL	NA	RX
SK-65 COMPOUND CAPSULES	PROPOXYPHENE HCL	NA	RX
SKF 5137	DEXTOMORAMIDE	NA	RX
SKF 6574	PHENAZOCINE	NA	RX
SKF-6612	CHLORDROLONE	AS	RX
SLYN-LL	PHENDIMETRAZINE TARTRATE	PS	RX
SOFRO	PEMOLINE	PS	RX
SOLADRENE	EPINEPHRINE	SA	RX
SOLEVAR	PROPETANDROL	AS	RX
SOLVASMA	ISOPROTERENOL	SA	RX
SOMA COMPOUND WITH CODEINE	CODEINE PHOSPHATE	NA	RX
SOMAGUM	AMPHETAMINE	PS	RX
SONATMIN	ISOPROTERENOL	SA	RX
SOONER	ISOPROTERENOL	SA	RX
SORBUTUSS	DEXTROMETHORPHAN HYDROBROMIDE	NA	RX
SOSEGON	PENTAZOCINE	NA	RX
SOSENYL	PENTAZOCINE	NA	RX
SOSIGON	PENTAZOCINE	NA	RX
SOSSEGON	PENTAZOCINE	NA	RX
SOXYFED	METHYLAMPHETAMINE	PS	RX
SOXYSYMPAMINE	METHYLAMPHETAMINE	PS	RX
SP 732	PROLINTANE	PS	RX
SPANCAP NO. 1	DEXTROAMPHETAMINE SULFATE	PS	RX
SPANEPH	EPHEDRINE	SA	RX
SPASMEDAL	DEMEROL	NA	RX
SPASMODOLIN	DEMEROL	NA	RX

Brand Name	Generic Name	Class	SRC
SPEC-T SORE THROAT- DECONGESTANT LOZ.	PHENYLPROPANOLAMINE HCL	SA	OTC
SPENBOLIC	METHANDRIOL	AS	RX
SPHYGMOGENIN	EPINEPHRINE	SA	RX
SPOFA (ANALEPTIN)	PHENYLEPHRINE	SA	OTC
SPRAYNAL	EPINEPHRINE	SA	RX
SPRX-1	PHENDIMETRAZINE TARTRATE	PS	RX
SPRX-105	PHENDIMETRAZINE TARTRATE	PS	RX
SPRX-3	PHENDIMETRAZINE TARTRATE	PS	RX
SQ 16374	METENOLONE ENANTHATE	AS	RX
SQ 16469	METENOLONE ACETATE	AS	RX
SQ 9538	TESTOLACTONE	AS	RX
ST. JOSEPH COLD TABLETS FOR CHILDREN	PHENYLPROPANOLAMINE HCL	SA	OTC
STANAPROL	ANDROSTANOLONE	AS	RX
STANAZOLOL	STANOZOLOL	AS	RX
STANEPHRIN	PHENYLEPHRINE	SA	OTC
STANOLONE	ANDROSTANOLONE	AS	RX
STANOZOLOL	STANOZOLOL	AS	RX
STAR (VASOTON)	NIKETHAMIDE	CN	RX
STATOBEX & STATOBEX-G	PHENDIMETRAZINE TARTRATE	PS	RX
STCHININ	STRYCHNINE	CN	RX
STELLACARDIOL	LEPTAZOL	CN	RX
STELLAMINE	NIKETHAMIDE	CN	RX
STEN-OR	MESTEROLONE	AS	RX
STENANDIOL	ANDROSTENDIOL DIPROPIONATE	AS	RX
STENBOLONE	STENBOLONE	AS	RX
STENBOLONE ACETATE	STENBOLONE ACETATE	AS	RX
STENEDIOL	METHANDRIOL	AS	RX
STENESIUM	METHANDRIOL	AS	RX
STENIBELL	METHANDRIOL	AS	RX
STENIFORM	METHANDRIOL	AS	RX
STENOLON	MERTHANDROSTENOLONE	AS	RX
STENOSTERONE	METHANDRIOLPROPIONATE	AS	RX
STERABOL	CLOSTEBOL ACETATE	AS	RX
STERANABOL-RITARDO	OXABOLONE CYPIONATE	AS	RX
STERANDRYL	TESTOSTERONE	AS	RX
STERANOBOL	CLOSTEBOL ACETATE	AS	RX
STEROBOLIN	NANDROLONE PHENYLPROPIONATE	AS	RX
STEROCRINOLOL	NANDROLONE CYCLOPENTYLPROPIONATE	AS	RX
STERONYL	METHYLTESTOSTERONE	AS	RX
STEROTATE	TESTOSTERONE	AS	RX
STIMDEX	METHYLAMPHETAMINE	PS	RX
STIMINOL	NIKETHAMIDE	CN	RX
STIMOLAG	PIPRADOL	PS	RX
STIMUL (WIRKSTOFF)	PEMOLINE	PS	RX
STIMULAN	AMPHETAMINE	PS	RX
STIMULEXIN	DOXAPRAM	CN	RX
STIMULIN	NIKETHAMIDE	CN	RX
STIMULOL	PEMOLINE	PS	RX
STO-CAPS	PHENYLPROPANOLAMINE HCL	SA	RX
STODCODON	HYDROCODONE	NA	RX
STODEX	PHENDIMETRAZINE	PS	RX
STOPAYNE CAPSULES	HYDROCODONE	NA	RX
STOPAYNE SYRUP	CODEINE PHOSPHATE	NA	RX
STORINAL	BOLANDIOL DIPROPIONATE	AS	RX

APPENDICES 493

STRABOLENE	NANDROLONE PHENYLPROPIONATE	AS	RX
STROMBA	STANOZOLOL	AS	RX
STROMBAJECT	STANOZOLOL	AS	RX
STRONG-LAR	TESTOSTERONE	AS	RX
STRYCHINTRAN	STRYCHNINE	CN	RX
STRYCHNINE	STRYCHNINE	CN	RX
STRYCHNOVET	STRYCHNINE	CN	RX
STUPENAL	OXOCODONE	NA	RX
STUPENONE	OXOCODONE	NA	RX
STYPIRENAL	EPINEPHRINE	SA	RX
SU-FRIN	PSEUDOEPHEDRINE	SA	OTC
SUBLIMAZE	FENTANYL	NA	RX
SUBLINGS	METHYLTESTOSTERONE	AS	RX
SUCRAPHEN	PHENYLEPHRINE	SA	OTC
SUCRETS-COLD DECONGESTANT FORMULA	PHENYLPROPANOLAMINE HCL	SA	OTC
SUDAFED	PSEUDOEPHEDRINE HCL	SA	OTC
SUDAFED COUGH SYRUP	PSEUDOEPHEDRINE HCL	SA	OTC
SUDAFED PLUS TABLETS AND SYRUP	PSEUDOEPHEDRINE HCL	SA	OTC
SUDAFED S.A.	PSEUDOEPHEDRINE HCL	SA	OTC
SUDAFED SYRUP	PSEUDOEPHEDRINE HCL	SA	OTC
SUDAFED TABLETS ADULT STRENGTH	PSEUDOEPHEDRINE HCL	SA	OTC
SUDAFED TABLETS AND SYRUP	PSEUDOEPHEDRINE HCL	SA	OTC
SUDAGEST DECONGESTANT	PSEUDOEPHEDRINE HCL	SA	OTC
SUDHINOL	PROPOXYPHENE	NA	RX
SUDOMYL	PSEUDOEPHEDRINE	SA	OTC
SUDRIN	PSEUDOEPHEDRINE HCL	SA	OTC
SUFENTA	SUFENTANIL	NA	RX
SUFENTANIL	SUFENTANIL	NA	RX
SUFENTANIL CITRATE	SUFENTANIL	NA	RX
SUNEPHRINE	PHENYLEPHRINE	SA	OTC
SUPER ANAHIST TABLETS	PSEUDOEPHEDRINE HCL	SA	RX
SUPER ODRINEX	PHENYLPROPANOLAMINE HCL	SA	OTC
SUPER-ANAHIST TABLETS	PHENYLPROPANOLAMINE HCL	SA	RX
SUPERANABOLON	NANDROLONE PHENYLPROPIONATE	AS	RX
SUPERBOLAN	NANDROLONE DECANOATE	AS	RX
SUPERBOLIN	NANDROLONE PHENYLPROPIONATE	AS	RX
SUPERGOTAL-CARDIACO	LEPTAZOL	CN	RX
SUPERORABOLON	DIMETHYLANDROSTANOLONE	AS	RX
SUPEUDOL	OXYCODONE	NA	RX
SUPLIN	PHENMETRAZINE	PS	RX
SUPOPRENALIN	ISOPROTERENOL	SA	RX
SUPOTUSIL INFANTIL	DEXTROMETHORPHAN	NA	RX
SUPPOLOSAL	DEMEROL	NA	RX
SUPRACAPSULIN	EPINEPHRINE	SA	RX
SUPRACODIN	HYDROCODONE	NA	RX
SUPRADOL	DEMEROL	NA	RX
SUPRANEFRAN	EPINEPHRINE	SA	RX
SUPRANEPHRIN	EPINEPHRINE	SA	RX
SUPRANOL	EPINEPHRINE	SA	RX
SUPRARENALIN	EPINEPHRINE	SA	RX
SUPRARENIN	EPINEPHRINE	SA	RX
SUPRASTERON-TABL.	METHYLTESTOSTERONE	AS	RX
SUPREL	EPINEPHRINE	SA	RX
SUPRESSIN	DEXTROMETHORPHAN	NA	RX

Brand Name	Generic Name	Class	SRC
SURENINE	EPINEPHRINE	SA	RX
SURRENINE	EPINEPHRINE	SA	RX
SUS-PHRINE	EPINEPHRINE	SA	RX
SUSCARDIA	ISOPROTERENOL	SA	RX
SYMCORAL	PHENYLEPHRINE	SA	OTC
SYMCORTHAL	PHENYLEPHRINE	SA	OTC
SYMCORTOL	PHENYLEPHRINE	SA	OTC
SYMETRA	PHENDIMETRAZINE	PS	RX
SYMORON	METHADONE	NA	RX
SYMPADRIN	PHENYLEPHRINE	SA	OTC
SYMPAETHAMIN	PHENYLEPHRINE	SA	OTC
SYMPALEPT	PHENYLEPHRINE	SA	OTC
SYMPAMETIN	AMPHETAMINE	PS	RX
SYMPAMIN	AMPHETAMINE	PS	RX
SYMPATEDRINE	AMPHETAMINE	PS	RX
SYMPATHICUS-WIEDENMANN	PHENYLEPHRINE	SA	OTC
SYMPATHIN I	EPINEPHRINE	SA	RX
SYMPATHOMIM	PHENYLEPHRINE	SA	OTC
SYMPATIZIN	PHENYLEPHRINE	SA	OTC
SYMPATOL	PHENYLEPHRINE	SA	OTC
SYMPTOL	PHENYLEPHRINE	SA	OTC
SYMPTOMAX LIQUID	PHENYLPROPANOLAMINE HCL	SA	RX
SYMPTOVAS	PHENYLEPHRINE	SA	OTC
SYMPTROL SYRUP & CAPSULES & INJECTION	PHENYLPROPANOLAMINE HCL	SA	RX
SYNADREN	PHENYLEPHRINE	SA	OTC
SYNADROL F	TESTOSTERONE	AS	RX
SYNALGOS-DC CAPSULES	DIHYDROCODEINE BITARTRATE	NA	RX
SYNANDRETS	TESTOSTERONE	AS	RX
SYNANDROTABS	METHYLTESTOSTERONE	AS	RX
SYNANDRULIN	TESTOSTERONE	AS	RX
SYNARIN PEDIATRIC	PHENYLEPHRINE	SA	OTC
SYNASAL	PHENYLEPHRINE	SA	OTC
SYNASTERON	OXYMETHOLONE	AS	RX
SYNCALTON	PHENYLEPHRINE	SA	OTC
SYNDREN-TABL.	METHYLTESTOSTERONE	AS	RX
SYNDROX	METHYLAMPHETAMINE	PS	RX
SYNEPHRINE	PHENYLEPHRINE	SA	OTC
SYNERGOL	PHENYLEPHRINE	SA	OTC
SYNKONIN	HYDROCODONE	NA	RX
SYNLAUDINE	DEMEROL	NA	RX
SYNTHANAL	METHADONE	NA	RX
SYNTHENATE	PHENYLEPHRINE	SA	OTC
SYRCO	METHADONE	NA	RX
SYROPON	ETHYLMORPHINE	NA	RX
T.E.H. TABLETS	EPHEDRINE	SA	RX
T.E.P. TABLETS	EPHEDRINE	SA	RX
T-CYPIONATE	TESTOSTERONE CYPIONATE	AS	RX
T-IONATE P.A.	TESTOSTERONE CYPIONATE	AS	RX
TAKAMINA	EPINEPHRINE	SA	RX
TALACEN	PENTAZOCINE	NA	RX
TALWIN COMPOUND, & NX	PENTAZOCINE	NA	RX
TALWIN INJECTION	PENTAZOCINE LACTATE	NA	RX
TALWINSUP	PENTAZOCINE	NA	RX
TALWINTAB	PENTAZOCINE	NA	RX
TAMINE S.R. TABLETS	PHENYLEPHRINE HCL	SA	RX
TANCOLIN	DEXTROMETHORPHAN	NA	RX

TANOGEN	EPINEPHRINE	SA	RX
TANTARONE	MESTANOLON	AS	RX
TARTRINA	DEXTROMETHORPHAN	NA	RX
TAWASAN	PROPOXYPHENE	NA	RX
TEAS - HERBAL CONTAINING MA HUANG	EPHEDRINE	SA	OTC
TEBACONE	THEBACON	NA	RX
TEBAKON	THEBACON	NA	RX
TEBODAL	OXOCODONE	NA	RX
TEDRAL ELIXIR & SUSPENSION - TEDRAL SA TABLETS	EPHEDRINE	SA	RX
TEKODIN	OXOCODONE	NA	RX
TELDRIN MULTI-SYMPTOM ALLERGY RELIEVER	PSEUDOEPHEDRINE HCL	SA	OTC
TELIPEX TABL.	METHYLTESTOSTERONE	AS	RX
TELIPEX-LOSUNG	TESTOSTERONE	AS	RX
TELUCIDON	MECLOFENOXATE	PS	RX
TENORETIC TABLETS	ATENOLOL	BB	RX
TENORMIN TABLETS	ATENOLOL	BB	RX
TENSAMIN	PHENYLEPHRINE	SA	OTC
TENUATE DOSPAN	DIETHYLPROPION HYDROCHLORIDE	PS	RX
TENUATE 25 MG	DIETHYLPROPION HYDROCHLORIDE	PS	RX
TEOLIT	TESTOLACTONE	AS	RX
TEPANIL, & TEN-TAB	DIETHYLPROPION HYDROCHLORIDE	PS	RX
TERAGEN TABLETS	PHENYLPROPANOLAMINE HCL	SA	RX
TERAMINE	CHLORPHENTERMINE	PS	RX
TERAMINE CAPSULES	PHENTERMINE HYDROCHLORIDE	PS	RX
TERBUTALINE (SPECIAL CONSIDERATION DRUG)	TERBUTALINE SULFATE	SA	RX
TERE-CARDIOL	LEPTAZOL	CN	RX
TERPIN HYDRATE & CODEINE ELIXIR	ANILERIDINE	NA	RX
TES-HOL "Z"	TESTOSTERONE	AS	RX
TESAMONE	TESTOSTERONE	AS	RX
TESLAC	TESTOLACTONE	AS	RX
TESLEN	TESTOSTERONE	AS	RX
TESONE	TESTOSTERONE	AS	RX
TESTA-C	TESTOSTERONE CYPIONATE	AS	RX
TESTADENOS	TESTOSTERONE	AS	RX
TESTAFORM-TABL.	METHYLTESTOSTERONE	AS	RX
TESTAHOMEN T	TESTOSTERONE	AS	RX
TESTAHOMEN-TABL.	METHYLTESTOSTERONE	AS	RX
TESTAMIN	DEXTROMETHORPHAN	NA	RX
TESTANDRONE	TESTOSTERONE	AS	RX
TESTAQUA	TESTOSTERONE	AS	RX
TESTATE	TESTOSTERONE ENANTHATE	AS	RX
TESTAVAL 90/4	TESTOSTERONE ENANTHATE	AS	RX
TESTEPLEX AQ. INJ.	TESTOSTERONE	AS	RX
TESTEPLEX-TABL.	METHYLTESTOSTERONE	AS	RX
TESTERONE PROPIONATE	TESTOSTERONE PROPIONATE	AS	RX
TESTEX	TESTOSTERONE PROPIONATE	AS	RX
TESTHORMONA	METHYLTESTOSTERONE	AS	RX
TESTIKELHORMON	TESTOSTERONE	AS	RX
TESTIN-TABL.	METHYLTESTOSTERONE	AS	RX
TESTIPRON	METHYLTESTOSTERONE	AS	RX
TESTIWOP	MESTEROLONE	AS	RX
TESTOBAN	TESTOSTERONE	AS	RX
TESTOBASE	METHYLTESTOSTERONE	AS	RX

Brand Name	Generic Name	Class	SRC
TESTOBASE AQUEOUS	TESTOSTERONE	AS	RX
TESTOBOLIN	NANDROLONE PROPIONATE	AS	RX
TESTODIOL	METHANDRIOL	AS	RX
TESTODRIN-LOSNING	TESTOSTERONE	AS	RX
TESTOGENINA	METHYLTESTOSTERONE	AS	RX
TESTOJECT-E.P.	TESTOSTERONE ENANTHATE	AS	RX
TESTOJECT-LA	TESTOSTERONE CYPIONATE	AS	RX
TESTOJECT-50	TESTOSTERONE	AS	RX
TESTOLACTONE	TESTOLACTONE	AS	RX
TESTOMED	CLOSTEBOL ACETATE	AS	RX
TESTOMET	METHYLTESTOSTERONE	AS	RX
TESTON-TABL.	METHYLTESTOSTERONE	AS	RX
TESTONE LA 100 AND 200	TESTOSTERONE ENANTHATE	AS	RX
TESTONORPON-TABL.	METHYLTESTOSTERONE	AS	RX
TESTOPAN	PENMESTEROL	AS	RX
TESTOPROPON	TESTOSTERONE	AS	RX
TESTORA	METHYLTESTOSTERONE	AS	RX
TESTORAL "FARMIT"	FLUOXYMESTERONE	AS	RX
TESTORAL "LEO"	METHYLTESTOSTERONE	AS	RX
TESTORAL "ORGANON"	TESTOSTERONE	AS	RX
TESTOREX	METHYLTESTOSTERONE	AS	RX
TESTORMON-TABL.	METHYLTESTOSTERONE	AS	RX
TESTORONA-TROPFEN	TESTOSTERONE	AS	RX
TESTOSID-TABL.	METHYLTESTOSTERONE	AS	RX
TESTOSIR	TESTOSTERONE	AS	RX
TESTOSTELETS	METHYLTESTOSTERONE	AS	RX
TESTOSTEROID	TESTOSTERONE	AS	RX
TESTOSTERON GRO B MANN-TABL.	METHYLTESTOSTERONE	AS	RX
TESTOSTERON LINGVALETE	METHYLTESTOSTERONE	AS	RX
TESTOSTERON RESORIBL. "ORION"	METHYLTESTOSTERONE	AS	RX
TESTOSTERON-LINGUALTABL.	METHYLTESTOSTERONE	AS	RX
TESTOSTERON-TABL. "JENAPHARM"	METHYLTESTOSTERONE	AS	RX
TESTOSTERONA DEXTER COMPR.	METHYLTESTOSTERONE	AS	RX
TESTOSTERONE (IF RATIO TO EPI-TESTOSTERONE IN URINE EXCEEDS 6)	TESTOSTERONE	AS	RX
TESTOSTERONE AQUEOUS	TESTOSTERONE	AS	RX
TESTOSTERONE CYPIONATE	TESTOSTERONE CYPIONATE	AS	RX
TESTOSTERONE ENANTHATE	TESTOSTERONE ENANTHATE	AS	RX
TESTOSTERONE PROPIONATE	TESTOSTERONE PROPIONATE	AS	RX
TESTOSTERONE-VIFOR	METHYLTESTOSTERONE	AS	RX
TESTOSTROVAL-P.A.	TESTOSTERONE ENANTHATE	AS	RX
TESTOVENA	TESTOSTERONE	AS	RX
TESTOVIRON T	TESTOSTERONE	AS	RX
TESTOVIRON-TABL.	METHYLTESTOSTERONE	AS	RX
TESTOVIS COMPR.	METHYLTESTOSTERONE	AS	RX
TESTOXYL PERLINGUALE	METHYLTESTOSTERONE	AS	RX
TESTRAL	METHYLTESTOSTERONE	AS	RX
TESTRAQ	TESTOSTERONE	AS	RX
TESTRED	METHYLTESTOSTERONE	AS	RX
TESTRIN PA	TESTOSTERONE ENANTHATE	AS	RX
TESTRO-MED	TESTOSTERONE	AS	RX
TESTRONE	TESTOSTERONE	AS	RX

TESTRYL	TESTOSTERONE	AS	RX
TETRACOR	LEPTAZOL	CN	RX
TETRAHYDROZOLINE	TETRAHYDROZOLINE HCL	SA	RX
TETRAZOL	LEPTAZOL	CN	RX
TEVABOLIN	STANOZOLOL	AS	RX
TH 152	METAPROTERENOL	SA	RX
THEBACETYL	THEBACON	NA	RX
THEBACODON	THEBACON	NA	RX
THEBACON	THEBACON	NA	RX
THECODIN(UM)	OXOCODONE	NA	RX
THEOFEDRAL TABLETS	EPHEDRINE	SA	RX
THEOZINE SYRUP & TABLETS	EPHEDRINE	SA	RX
THEPTINE	AMPHETAMINE	PS	RX
THERANABOL	OXYMESTERONE	AS	RX
THIOMESTERONE	TIOMESTERONE	AS	RX
THOREXIN	DEXTROMETHORPHAN	NA	RX
TIBOLONE	TIBOLONE	AS	RX
TILENE	PROPOXYPHENE	NA	RX
TIMOLIDE TABLETS	TIMOLOL MALEATE	BB	RX
TIMOPTIC STERILE OPHTHALMIC SOLUTION	TIMOLOL MALEATE	BB	RX
TIOMESTERONE	TIOMESTERONE	AS	RX
TIONIDEL	ETHYLMORPHINE	NA	RX
TMV-17	METHANDROSTENOLONE	AS	RX
TONAZOL	NIKETHAMIDE	CN	RX
TONEDRON	METHYLAMPHETAMINE	PS	RX
TONOBOLIN-INJ.	NANDROLONE PHENYLPROPIONATE	AS	RX
TONOBOLIN-TABL.	METHANDROSTENOLONE	AS	RX
TONOCARD	NIKETHAMIDE	CN	RX
TONORMON	METHANDRIOL	AS	RX
TORA	PHENTERMINE HYDROCHLORIDE	PS	RX
TORFAN	DEXTROMETHORPHAN	NA	RX
TORNALATE (SPECIAL CONSIDERATION)	BITOLTEROL MESYLATE	SA	RX
TOSTRINA-M	METHYLTESTOSTERONE	AS	RX
TRADON "BEIERSDORF"	PEMOLINE	PS	RX
TRANDATE TABLETS	LEBETALOL HCL	BB	RX
TRELA	LEPTAZOL	CN	RX
TRENBOLONE	TRENBOLONE	AS	RX
TRENBOLONE ACETATE	TRENBOLONE ACETATE	AS	RX
TRENBOLONE HEXAHYDRO-BENZYLCARBONATE	TRENBOLONE HEXAHYDROBENZYLCARBONATE	AS	RX
TRESTOLONE	TRESTOLONE	AS	RX
TRESTOLONE ACETATE	TRESTOLONE ACETATE	AS	RX
TRI HISTIN EXPECTORANT	PHENYLPROPANOLAMINE HCL	SA	RX
TRIAFED-C EXPECTORANT	CODEINE PHOSPHATE	NA	RX
TRIAMINIC ALLERGY TABLETS	PHENYLPROPANOLAMINE HCL	SA	OTC
TRIAMINIC CHEWABLES	PHENYLPROPANOLAMINE HCL	SA	OTC
TRIAMINIC COLD SYRUP	PHENYLPROPANOLAMINE HCL	SA	OTC
TRIAMINIC COLD TABLETS	PHENYLPROPANOLAMINE HCL	SA	OTC
TRIAMINIC EXPECTORANT	PHENYLPROPANOLAMINE HCL	SA	OTC
TRIAMINIC EXPECTORANT WITH CODEINE	CODEINE PHOSPHATE	NA	RX
TRIAMINIC-DM COUGH FORMULA	PHENYLPROPANOLAMINE HCL	SA	OTC
TRIAMINIC-DM COUGH FORMULA	DEXTROMETHORPHAN HYDROBROMIDE	NA	RX
TRIAMINIC-12 TABLETS	PHENYLPROPANOLAMINE HCL	SA	OTC
TRIAMINICIN TABLETS	PHENYLPROPANOLAMINE HCL	SA	OTC
TRIAMINICOL MULTI-	PHENYLPROPANOLAMINE HCL	SA	OTC

Brand Name	Generic Name	Class	SRC
SYMPTOM COLD SYRUP			
TRIAMINICOL MULTI-SYMPTOM COLD SYRUP & TABLETS	DEXTROMETHORPHAN HYDROBROMIDE	NA	RX
TRIAMINICOL MULTI-SYMPTOM COLD TABLETS	PHENYLPROPANOLAMINE HCL	SA	OTC
TRIAMINICOL SYRUP	PHENYLPROPANOLAMINE HCL	SA	OTC
TRIENBOLONE	TRENBOLONE	AS	RX
TRIMCAPS	PHENDIMETRAZINE TARTRATE	PS	RX
TRIMEPERIDINE	TRIMEPERIDINE	NA	RX
TRIMERPERIDINE	TRIMERPERIDINE	NA	RX
TRIMNEED	AMPHETAMINE	PS	RX
TRIMSTAT TABLETS	PHENDIMETRAZINE TARTRATE	PS	RX
TRIMTABS	PHENDIMETRAZINE TARTRATE	PS	RX
TRINALIN	PSEUDOEPHEDRINE SULFATE	SA	RX
TRIND-DM	PHENYLPROPANOLAMINE HCL	SA	OTC
TRIPROLIDINE	PSEUDOEPHEDRINE	SA	OTC
TROFORMONE	METHANDRIOL	AS	RX
TROPATIL	DIPHENOXYLATE	NA	RX
TROXILAN	DEXTOMORAMIDE	NA	RX
TUBIL	OXYMESTERONE	AS	RX
TUCODIL	HYDROCODONE	NA	RX
TURANONE	METHADONE	NA	RX
TURBILIXIR LIQUID	PHENYLPROPANOLAMINE HCL	SA	RX
TURBISPAN LEISURECAPS	PHENYLPROPANOLAMINE HCL	SA	RX
TURINABOL	DEHYDORCHLORMETHYLTESTOS-TERONE	AS	RX
TURINABOL	CLOSTEBOL ACETATE (CHLORTESTOSTERONE)	AS	RX
TURINABOL (NEVEFORM)	NANDROLONE PHENYLPROPIONATE	AS	RX
TURINABOL-DEPOT	NANDROLONE DECANOATE	AS	RX
TUSCODIN	DIHYDROCODEINE	NA	RX
TUSILAN	DEXTROMETHORPHAN	NA	RX
TUSQUELIN SYRUP	PHENYLPROPANOLAMINE HCL	SA	RX
TUSS-ORNADE CAPSULES	PHENYLPROPANOLAMINE HCL	SA	RX
TUSSADE	DEXTROMETHORPHAN	NA	RX
TUSSAGESIC TABLETS & SUSPENSION	PHENYLPROPANOLAMINE HCL	SA	OTC
TUSSAL	METHADONE	NA	RX
TUSSAPHED	PSEUDOEPHEDRINE	SA	OTC
TUSSAR DM	PHENYLEPHRINE HCL	SA	RX
TUSSAR DM	DEXTROMETHORPHAN HYDROBROMIDE	NA	RX
TUSSAR SF AND TUSSAR-2	CODEINE PHOSPHATE	NA	RX
TUSSCAPS	PHENYLPROPANOLAMINE HCL	SA	RX
TUSSEND	PSEUDOEPHEDRINE	SA	OTC
TUSSEND EXPECTORANT	HYDROCODONE	NA	RX
TUSSEND LIQUID & TABLETS	HYDROCODONE	NA	RX
TUSSI-ORGANIDIN	CODEINE PHOSPHATE	NA	RX
TUSSI-ORGANIDIN DM	DEXTROMETHORPHAN HYDROBROMIDE	NA	RX
TUSSIN	DEXTROMETHORPHAN	NA	RX
TUSSIONEX TABLETS & CAPSULES & SUSPENSION	HYDROCODONE RESIN COMPLEX	NA	RX
TUSSIREX SUGAR FREE AND SYRUP	CODEINE PHOSPHATE	NA	RX
TUSSIREX SUGAR-FREE AND SYRUP	PHENYLEPHRINE HCL	SA	RX

TUSSTROL LIQUID	PHENYLPROPANOLAMINE HCL	SA	RX
TYLANDRIL	METHYLTESTOSTERONE	AS	RX
TYLENOL MAXIMUM STRENGTH SINUS MEDICATION TABLETS AND CAPSULES	PSEUDOEPHEDRINE HCL	SA	OTC
TYLENOL WITH CODEINE ELIXIR AND TABLETS	CODEINE PHOSPHATE	NA	RX
TYLOX CAPSULES	OXYCODONE	NA	RX
TYMPAGESIC OTIC SOLUTION	PHENYLEPHRINE HCL	SA	RX
TYZINE	TETRAHYDROZOLINE	SA	RX
TZBRAINE	METHYLEPHEDRINE	SA	RX
U.R.I. CAPSULES - LIQUID	PHENYLPROPANOLAMINE HCL	SA	RX
U-0441	BENZPHETAMINE	PS	RX
U-10997	MIBOLERONE	AS	RX
U-15614	TESTOLONE ACETATE	AS	RX
U-6040	FLUOXYMESTERONE	AS	RX
UFARON (VASOTON)	EPINEPHRINE	SA	RX
ULTANDREN	FLUOXYMESTERONE	AS	RX
UNABOL	NANDROLONE PHENYLPROPIONATE	AS	RX
UNIFAST UNICELLES	PHENTERMINE HYDROCHLORIDE	PS	RX
UNIGESIC	PROPOXYPHENE	NA	RX
UNITROL	PHENYLPROPANOLAMINE HCL	SA	OTC
UQUICODID	HYDROCODONE	NA	RX
UQUIFA	DEXTROMORAMIDE	NA	RX
URSINUS INLAY-TABS	PHENYLPROPANOLAMINE HCL	SA	OTC
VACON	PHENYLEPHRINE	SA	OTC
VAL-ATUX	DEXTROMETHORPHAN	NA	RX
VALBINE	OXOCODONE	NA	RX
VALLIMIDA	ETHAMIVAN	CN	RX
VANABOL	METHANDROSTENOLONE	AS	RX
VANDAR 65	PROPOXYPHENE	NA	RX
VANDID	ETHAMIVAN	CN	RX
VANIDIAM	ETHAMIVAN	CN	RX
VAPEDRINE	AMPHETAMINE	PS	RX
VAPO-ISO SOLUTION	ISOPROTERENOL HCL	SA	RX
VAPO-N-ISO	ISOPROTERENOL	SA	RX
VAPONEFRIN	EPINEPHRINE	SA	OTC
VASAZOL	LEPTAZOL	CN	RX
VASAZOL "KWIZDA"	NIKETHAMIDE	CN	RX
VASCARDYNE	PHENYLEPHRINE	SA	OTC
VASOCONSTRICTINE	EPINEPHRINE	SA	RX
VASOCORDRIN	PHENYLEPHRINE	SA	OTC
VASODRINE	EPINEPHRINE	SA	RX
VASOROME	OXANDROLONE	AS	RX
VASOROME-KOWA	OXANDROLONE	AS	RX
VASOTON (SOJIET. PRAP.)	PHENYLEPHRINE	SA	OTC
VASOTON "STAR"	NIKETHAMIDE	CN	RX
VASOTON "UFAROM"	EPINEPHRINE	SA	RX
VASOTONIN	EPINEPHRINE	SA	RX
VATRONOL NOSE DROPS	EPHEDRINE	SA	OTC
VEBONOL	BOLDENONE UNDECYLATE	AS	RX
VENTILONE	ETHAMIVAN	CN	RX
VENTOLIN (SPECIAL CONSIDERATION DRUG)	ALBUTEROL	SA	RX
VENTRAMINE	NIKETHAMIDE	CN	RX
VENTRASOL	LEPTAZOL	CN	RX
VENTRAZOL	LEPTAZOL	CN	RX
VEREGUAD	EPHEDRINE	SA	RX
VERNATE INJECTION & CAPSULES & TABLETS	PHENYLPROPANOLAMINE HCL	SA	RX

Brand Name	Generic Name	Class	SRC
VERONYL	METHADONE	NA	RX
VETANAMIN	PEMOLINE	PS	RX
VETAZOL	LEPTAZOL	CN	RX
VI-ANDRO	METHYLTESTOSTERONE	AS	RX
VICKS DAYCARE LIQUID	PHENYLPROPANOLAMINE HCL	SA	OTC
VICKS FORMULA 44D DECONGESTANT COUGH MIXTURE SYRUP	PHENYLPROPANOLAMINE HCL	SA	OTC
VICKS INHALER	DESOXYEPHEDRINE	SA	OTC
VICODIN	HYDROCODONE	NA	RX
VIDIL	PEMOLINE	PS	RX
VIGOREX	METHYLTESTOSTERONE	AS	RX
VILESCON-WIRKSTOFF	PROLINTANE	PS	RX
VILLESCON - PROMOTIL - KATOVIT AND RELATED COMPOUNDS	PROLINTANE	PS	RX
VILLESCON-WIRKSTOFF	PROLINTANE	PS	RX
VIRASTINE	ETHYLESTRENOL	AS	RX
VIREX	TESTOSTERONE	AS	RX
VIREX-ORAL	METHYLTESTOSTERONE	AS	RX
VIRILON CAPSULES	METHYLTESTOSTERONE	AS	RX
VIRORMOLOCOMPR.	METHYLTESTOSTERONE	AS	RX
VIRORMONE	TESTOSTERONE	AS	RX
VIRORMONE-ORAL	METHYLTESTOSTERONE	AS	RX
VIROSTERONE	TESTOSTERONE	AS	RX
VIROTEST MARIATHERMA	TESTOSTERONE	AS	RX
VISADRON	PHENYLEPHRINE	SA	OTC
VISKEN	PINDOLOL	BB	RX
VISTIMON	MESTEROLONE	AS	RX
VOLITAL	PEMOLINE	PS	RX
VORTEL	CHLOROPRENALINE	SA	RX
W 2426	CHLORPHENTERMINE	PS	RX
WEH-LESS	PHENDIMETRAZINE TARTRATE	PS	RX
WEHLESS 105 TIMECELLES	PHENDIMETRAZINE TARTRATE	PS	RX
WEIGHTROL	PHENDIMETRAZINE TARTRATE	PS	RX
WELLS (LIPOMIN)	PHENMETRAZINE	PS	RX
WICK-HUSTENSTILLER	DEXTROMETHORPHAN	NA	RX
WILLPOWER	PHENMETRAZINE	PS	RX
WILPOWR	PHENTERMINE HYDROCHLORIDE	PS	RX
WIN 14098	PIMINODINE	NA	RX
WIN 14833	STANOZOLOL	AS	RX
WIN 17757	DANAZOL	AS	RX
WIN 20228	PENTAZOCINE	NA	RX
WIN 3046	ISOETHARINE	SA	RX
WIN 5162	ISOPROTERENOL	SA	RX
WINOBANIN	DANAZOL	AS	RX
WINSTROID	STANOZOLOL	AS	RX
WINSTROL	STANOZOLOL	AS	RX
WINSTROL V.	STANOZOLOL	AS	RX
WINTHROP	PIMINODINE	NA	RX
WY 3475	NORBOLETONE	AS	RX
WYANOIDS HEMORRHOIDAL SUPPOSITORIES	EPHEDRINE	SA	OTC
WYGESIC TABLETS	PROPOXYPHENE HCL	NA	RX
X-TROZINE CAPSULES AND TABLETS	PHENDIMETRAZINE TARTRATE	PS	RX
X-TROZINE LA-105 CAPSULES	PHENDIMETRAZINE TARTRATE	PS	RX
XENAGOL	PHENAZOCINE	NA	RX

XILATIL	DIPHENOXYLATE	NA	RX
XYLOMETAZOLINE HCL	XYLOMETAZOLINE HCL	SA	OTC
YDROCOD	HYDROCODONE	NA	RX
YETRAZOL	LEPTAZOL	CN	RX
YETRIUM	DEXTOMORAMIDE	NA	RX
YONCHLON-SYR.	MESTANOLON	AS	RX
YOSHITOMI (CENTRAMIN)	PEMOLINE	PS	RX
ZEDRINE	AMPHETAMINE	PS	RX
ZEFALGIN	METHADONE	NA	RX
1ZEMPHRINE	PHENYLEPHRINE	SA	OTC
ZEMSOXYN	METHYLAMPHETAMINE	PS	RX
ZENALOSYN	OXYMETHOLONE	AS	RX
ZENTRALEPTIN	BEMIGRIDE	CN	RX
ZEPH	PHENYLEPHRINE	SA	OTC
ZEPHROL	EPHEDRINE	SA	RX
ZORI (METAMINE)	METHYLAMPHETAMINE	PS	RX
ZORI (OBESIN)	PHENTERMINE	PS	RX
ORALDRINA	AMPHETAMINE	PS	RX
1-DEHYDROTESTOSTERONE	BOLDENONE	AS	RX
1A-METHYLANDROSTAN- OLON	MESTEROLONE	AS	RX
17-ENT	NORETHANDROLONE	AS	RX
17A-METHYLANDROSTAN- OLON	MESTANOLON	AS	RX
2166 R.P.	DEMEROL	NA	RX
8022 C.B.	NORETHANDROLONE	AS	RX
914 F	METHYLAMPHETAMINE	PS	RX

■

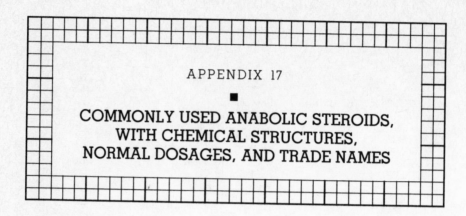

Please note that the dosages listed on the enclosed table are for sick patients; these are *far* below the quantities now being abused by normal, healthy athletes.

Testosterone, U.S.P.
 ANDROID-T
 ORETON
Aqueous suspension: 25, 50, and 100 mg/ml
for i.m. use (50 mg three times weekly)
Pellets: 75 mg for s.c. use (300 mg every 4 to 6 months)

Testosterone Propionate, U.S.P.
 ORETON PROPIONATE
Tablets: 10 mg (buccal; 10 to 20 mg daily)
Oily solution: 25, 50, and 100 mg/ml for i.m.
use (25 mg two to four times weekly)

Testosterone Enanthate, U.S.P.
 DELATESTRYL
Oily solution: 100 and 200 mg/ml for i.m.
use (100 to 400 mg every 2 to 4 weeks)

Testosterone Cypionate, U.S.P.
 DEPO-TESTOSTERONE
Oily solution: 50, 100, and 200 mg/ml for i.m.
use (100 to 400 mg every 2 to 4 weeks)

Methyltestosterone, U.S.P.
 METANDREN
 ORETON METHYL

Tablets: 5, 10, and 25 mg (buccal: 5 to 25 mg daily)
Capsules: 10 mg (10 to 50 daily)

Fluoxymesterone, U.S.P.
  HALOTESTIN
  ORA-TESTRYL
Tablets: 2, 5, and 10 mg (2 to 30 mg daily)

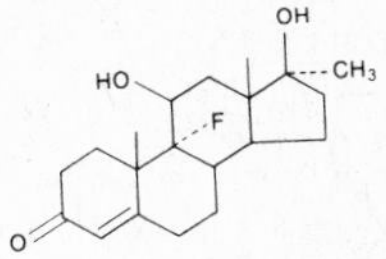

Danazol, U.S.P.
  DANOCRINE
Capsules: 50 mg (200 to 800 daily)

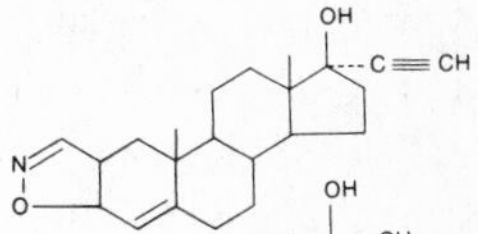

Calusterone
  METHOSARB
Tablets: 50 mg (200 mg daily for breast carcinoma*)

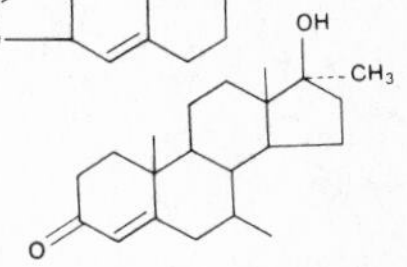

Dromostanolone Propionate, U.S.P.
  DROLBAN
Oily solution: 50 mg/ml for i.m. use (100 mg
three times weekly for breast carcinoma*)

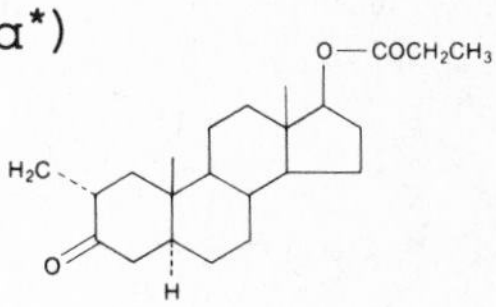

Ethylestrenol
  MAXIBOLIN
Elixir: 2 mg/5 ml
Tablets: 2 mg (4 to 8 daily)

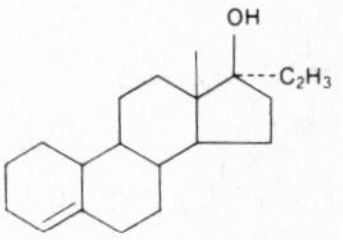

Methandriol
  ANABOL
Aqueous and oil solutions: 50 mg/ml for i.m.
use (50 to 100 mg once or twice weekly)

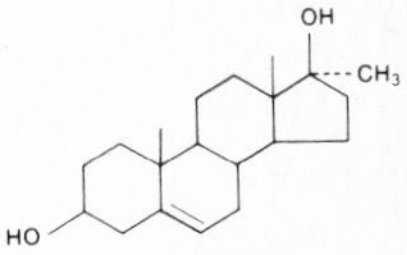

Methandrostenolone, U.S.P.
  DIANABOL
Tablets: 2.5 and 5 mg (5 mg daily)

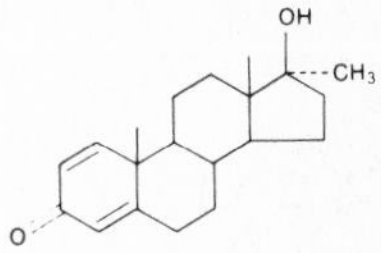

Nandrolone Decanoate, U.S.P.
  DECA-DURABOLIN
Oily solution: 50 and 100 mg/ml for i.m.
use (50 to 100 mg every 3 to 4 weeks)

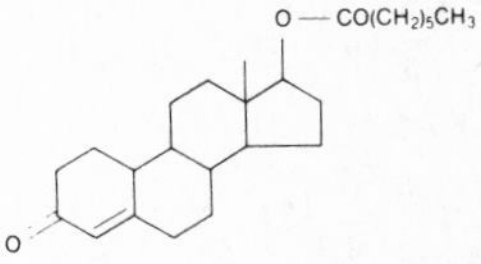

Nandrolone Phenpropionate, U.S.P.
  DURABOLIN
Oily solution: 25 and 50 mg/ml for i.m.
use (25 to 50 mg weekly)

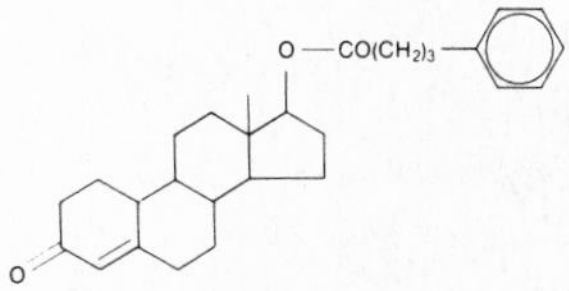

504   APPENDICES

Oxandrolone, U.S.P.
  ANAVAR
Tablets: 2.5 mg (5 to 10 mg daily)

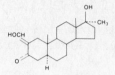

Oxymetholone, U.S.P.   ADROYD
  ANADROL
Tablets: 5, 10, and 50 mg (5 to 15 mg daily;
as much as 50 to 100 mg daily for anemia)

Stanozolol, U.S.P.
  WINSTROL
Tablets: 2 mg (6 mg daily)

Testolactone, U.S.P.
  TESLAC
Tablets: 50 and 250 mg (150 mg daily)
Aqueous suspension: 100 mg/ml for i.m.
use (100 mg three times weekly for
breast carcinoma*)

*Dosage schedules for breast carcinoma in females are generally two to three times those for androgen replacement. Reprinted with permission from Goodman and Gilman's *Pharmalogical Basis of Therapeutics*, 6th ed. (New York: Macmillan Publishing Co., 1980).

APPENDIX 18

■

STRUCTURES, NAMES, AND MANUFACTURERS OF ANABOLIC STEROIDS*

Structure	Systematic name[a]	Trivial and/or generic name	Trade name	Manufacturer
1. Testosterone-derived protein anabolic steroids				
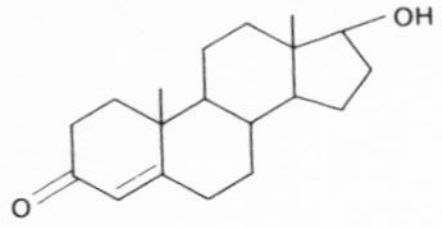	17β-Hydroxyandrost-4-en-3-one	Testosterone	Geno-cristaux	Gremy
			Malestrone	Kirk, N. Y.
			Orquisteron/Frosst	(Columbia)
			Primotest	Schering A. G.
			Oreton	Schering
		-acetate	Aceto-Sterandryl	Roussel
			Aceto-Testoviron	Schering A. G.
			Perandrone A	CIBA
		-propionate	Oreton	Schering
			Perandren	Ciba-Geigy
			Sterandryl	Roussel
			Testoviron	Schering
			Anertan	Boehringer (M)
			Enarmon	Takeda (Japan)
		-(3-p-hexyloxiphenyl)-propionate	Androdurin	Leo (Helsingborg)
		-heptanoate (enanthate)	Delatestryl	Squibb
			Androtardyl	Schering-Sepps
			Testoenant	Geymonod
		-cyclopentyl propionate	Depot testosterone cypionate	Upjohn

Structure	Systematic name[a]	Trivial and/or generic name	Trade name	Manufacturer
	4-Chloro-17β-hydroxyandrost-4-en-3-one	Chlorotestosterone-acetate	Steranabol Macrobin Turinabol Turinabol inj.	Farmitalia Teikoku Jenapharm Jenapharm
	17β-Hydroxy-17-methyl-androst-4-en-3-one	-capronate Methyltestosterone	Macrobin-depot Metandren Anertan Oreton Android	Teikoku Ciba Boehringer (M) Schering Brown
	9α-Fluoro-11β, 17β-dihydroxy-17-methylandrost-4-en-3-one	Fluoxymesterone	Halotestin Ultandren Androfluorene Fluotestin Orateston	Upjohn Ciba Midy Roter Hoechst
	4,17β-Dihydroxy-17-methyl-androst-4-en-3-one	Oxymesterone, 4-Hydroxymethyltestosterone	Oranabol Samaboral Theranabol	Farmitalia Kabi Lipfa May & Baker Ikapharm Theraplix
	11α,17β-Dihydroxy-17-methyl-androst-4-en-3-one	11α-Hydroxymethyl-testosterone	—	—

Structure	Chemical name	Trade name	Manufacturer
17β-Hydroxy-17-methyl-androst-4-ene-3,11-dione	11-Oxomethyltestosterone	—	—
4-Chloro-17β-hydroxy-17-methyl-androst-4-en-3-one	Chloromethyltestosterone	Turinabol tabl.	Jenapharm
1α,7α-Bis(acetylthio)-17β-hydroxy-17-methyl-androst-4-en-3-one	Thiomesterone	Emdabol	Merck A.G.
17β-Hydroxy-17-methyl-androsta-1,4-dien-3-one	Methandrostenolone Methandienone 1-De-hydromethyltestosterone	Dianabol Abirol Geabol Nabolin Nerobil Vanabol	Ciba Takeda Gea Eisai Richter Vitrum
	-cyclopentenyl ether (gen.) Quinbolon	Anabolicus	Vister
4-Chloro-17β-hydroxy-17-methyl-androsta-1,4-dien-3-one	Chloro-1-dehydromethyl-testosterone	Oral-Turinabol	Jenapharm
17β-Hydroxy-7α,17α-dimethyl-androst-4-en-3-one	Bolasterone, Dimethyltestosterone Callusterone	Myagen Methosarb	Upjohn Upjohn

II. 19-Nortestosterone-derived protein anabolic steroids

Structure	Systematic name[a]	Trivial and/or generic name	Trade name	Manufacturer
17β-Hydroxyestr-4-en-3-one	19-Nortestosterone Nandrolone		Nerobolil Nortestonate	Medimpex Upjohn
		-n-capronate	Methybol-depot	Mepha
		-propionate	Norybol Anabolicus-Serono	Serono Ausonia
		-phenylpropionate	Activin Durabol Durabolin Nerobolil Neutrosteron	Aristegui Pharmacia Organon Richter Organon
		-furylpropionate -hexahydrobenzoate -hexyloxyphenylpropionate	Demolon Nor-Durandon Anadur	Mochida Ferring Leo-Lundbeck
		-laurate -undecylate	Laurabolin Dynabolon	Organon (Vet.) Theramex
		-decanoate	Abolon Deca-Durabol Deca-Durabolin Eubolin Nordecon Retabolil	Benzon Pharmacia Organon Futerapica IBSA Richter
		-hemisuccinate -cyclohexylpropionate	Menidrabol Fherbolico Sanabolicum	Menarini Fher Sanabo

Chemical name	Common name / ester	Trade name	Company
	-cyclopentylpropionate	Sterocrinolo	Orma
		Depo-Nortestonate	Upjohn
		Pluropon	Boehringer
	-4-methylbicyclo[2.2.2]oct-2-ene-1-carboxylate	—	Syntex
4,17β-Dihydroxyestr-4-en-3-one	Oxabolone 4-hydroxy-19-nor-testosterone-cyclopentylpropionate	Steranabol-depot	Farmitalia
4-Chloro-17β-hydroxyestr-4-en-3-one	Chloro-19-nortestosterone-acetate	Steranabol	Farmitalia
17β-Hydroxy-17-methyl-estr-4-en-3-one	Methyl-19-nortestosterone	Methalutin	Syntex
		Orgasteron	Organon
17β-Hydroxy-19-nor-pregn-4-en-3-one	Norethandrolone Ethylnortestosterone -propionate	Nilevar	Searle
		Nor-Neutrormone	ICI
		Pronabol	Isis
		Solevar	Byla
		—	—
17β-Hydroxy-19-nor-pregna-4,9-dien-3-one	Ethyldienolone	—	—
(dl)-17β-Hydroxy-13β,17α-di-ethylgon-4-en-3-one / (dl)-13-Ethyl-17-hydroxy-18,19-dinor-17α-pregn-4-en-3-one	Norbolethone	Genabol	Wyeth

III. Androstane-derived protein anabolic steroids

Structure	Systematic name[a]	Trivial and/or generic name	Trade name	Manufacturer
	3β-Hydroxy-5α-androstan-17-one	Epiandrosterone Isoandrosterone	—	—
	17β-Hydroxy-5α-androstan-3-one	Androstanolone Stanolone Dihydrotestosterone	Anaboleen Anabolex Androlone Proteina Protona Apeton Apeton depot	B.A.G. Uni Chemie Lloyd-Hamol Samil Orma Gremy Gremy Fujisawa Fujisawa
	3α-Hydroxy-5α-androstan-17-one	-valerianate Androsterone	—	—
	17β-Hydroxy-2α-methyl-5α-androstan-3-one	Drostanolone 2α-Methylandrostanolone	Drolban Masterone	Lilly Recovdati Sarva Syntex
	2α-Methyldihydrotestosterone-propionate		Metorman Mastizol	Latino Shionogi
	17β-Hydroxy-1α-methyl-5α-androstan-3-one	Mesterolone	Mestoran Proviron	Schering (Denmark) Schering A.G.
	5α-Androstane-3β,17β-diol-3-n-octyl-enol ether	Androstanediol-3-n-octyl-enol ether	Ectovis Ectovister	Vister Drovyssa

Structure / chemical name	Generic name	Brand names	Manufacturers
17β-Hydroxy-17-methyl-5α-androstan-3-one	Mestanolone	Ermalon Androstalone	Roussel Roussel
(Methylandrostanolone-enanthoyl-acetate)	Methylandrostanolone-enanthoyl-acetate	Notandron-depot	Boehringer (M)
17β-Hydroxy-17-methyl-2-(hydroxy-methylene)-5α-androstan-3-one	Oxymetholone	Adroyd	Parke-Davis Samkyo Shionogi Syntex
		Anadrol	Parke-Davis
		Anadroyd	ICI
		Anapolon	Syntex
		Anasterone	Latino
		Anasterona	Cassenne
		Nastenon	Recordati
		Protanabol	
		Synasterobe	Sarva

IV. Heterocyclic protein anabolic steroids

Structure / chemical name	Generic name	Brand names	Manufacturers
17-Methyl-5α-androstano-[3,2-c]-pyrazol-17β-ol	Stanozolol	Winstrol	Yamanouchi Winthrop Zambon
		Stromba	Winthrop
		Tevabolin	Teva
17-Methyl-5α-androstano-[3,2-c]-isoxazol-17β-ol	Androisoxazole	Androxan	Leo-Lundbeck
		Neo-Ponden	Serono
		Neo-Pondus	Ausonia
2′,17-Dimethylandrost-5(10)-eno[3,2-d]-thiazol-17β-ol	—	—	—

Structure	Systematic name[a]	Trivial and/or generic name	Trade name	Manufacturer
	3-Azi-17-methyl-5α-androstan-17β-ol	Methyldiazirinol	—	—
	17β-Hydroxy-2α,17-dimethyl-5α-androstan-3,3'-azine	Dimethazine	Roxilon Dostalon	Richter Richter
	17β-Hydroxy-17-methyl-2-oxa-5α-androstan-3-one	Oxandrolone	Anavar	Searle

V. Miscellaneous structure protein anabolic steroids

Structure	Systematic name[a]	Trivial and/or generic name	Trade name	Manufacturer
	17β-Hydroxy-1-methyl-5α-androst-1-en-3-one	Methenolone -acetate -enanthate	Nibol Primobolan Primobolan-Acetate Primobolan-Depot	Squibb Schering A.G. Schering A.G. Schering A.G.
		—	—	—
	17-Methyl-3-methylene-5α-androst-1-en-17β-ol	Methylandrostenediol	Crestabolic	Nutrition Control Products
	17-Methyl-androst-5-ene-3β,17β-diol	Methandriol	Diamdrin Megabion Metilandrostendiol Neosteron	Astra Teikoku Schering A.G. Organon Pharmacia

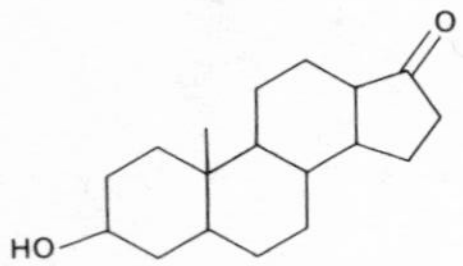

3β-Hydroxyandrost-5-en-17-one

	Trade name	Manufacturer
	Neutrormone	ISI
	Notandren	Boehringer (M)
-3-propionate	Protandren	Ciba
	Stenediol	Organon
-dipropionate	Metilbisexovis	Vister
	Methilbisexovister	Drovyssa
	Metildiolo	Orma
-dienanthoylacetate	Anabolin	Rafa
Dehydroepiandrosterone	Metandiol	Roussel
Dehydroisoandrosterone	Notandren-depot	Boehringer (M)
-acetate	Psicosterone	ICI

19-Norpregn-4-en-17β-ol

	Trade name	Manufacturer
Ethylestrenol	Diamdrone	Organon
	17-Chetovis	Vister
	Duraboral	Organon
	Maxibolin	Organon
	Orabolin	Organon
	Orgaboral	Organon
	Durabolin-0	Organon
	Orgabolin	Organon

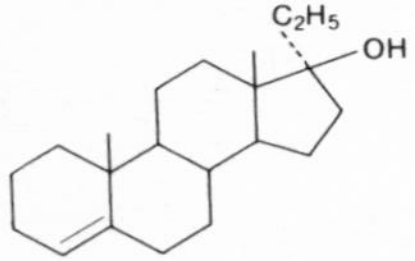

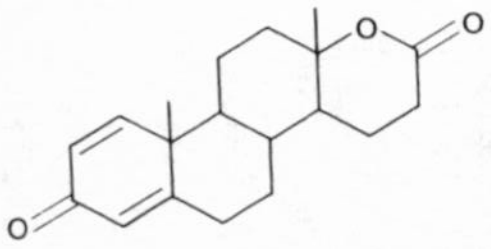

17α-Oxo-D-homo-androsta-1,4-diene-3,17-dione

1,2,3,4,4a,4b,7,9,10,10a-decahydro-2-hydroxy-2,4b-dimethyl-7-oxo-1-phenanthrene propionic acid

	Trade name	Manufacturer
Δ'-testololactone	Teslac	Squibb

*From Anabolic-Androgenic Steroids, by Charles D. Kochakiam (New York: Springer-Verlag, 1976) pp. 627–36. Prepared by ARNOLD, A., POTTS, G.O., and BEYLER, A.L.
a Chemical Abstracts Systemic Name, Collective Subject Indices, Chemical Abstract.

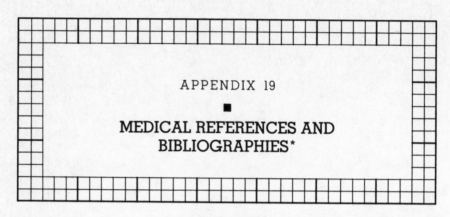

APPENDIX 19

■

MEDICAL REFERENCES AND
BIBLIOGRAPHIES*

CAFFEINE

Alles, G. & Feigen, G. The influence of benzedrine on work decrement and patellar reflex. *American Journal of Physiology*, 1942, **136**, 392–400.

Anderson, J., Hollefiedl, G., & Owen, J. A. Effects of caffeine on the epididymal fat pad in vitro. *Clinical Research*, 1966, **14**, 60–67.

Arushanyan, E. B., Belozertsev, A. Y., & Arvazov, K. G. Comparative effect of amphetamine and caffeine on spontaneous activity of sensorimotor cortical units and their responses to stimulation of the caudate nucleus. *Bulletin of Experimental Biology and Medicine*, 1974, **78**, 776–779.

Asmussen, E., & Boje, O. The effects of alcohol and some drugs on the capacity to work. *Acta Physiologica Scandinavica*, 1948, **15**, 109–118.

Atuk, N. O., Blaydes, M. C., Westervelt, P. O., & Wood, J. E. Effect of aminophylline on urinary excretion of epinephrine and norepinephrine in man. *Circulation*, 1967, **35**, 745–753.

Axelrod, J., & Reichenthal, J. The fate of caffeine in man and a method for its estimation in biological material. *Journal of Pharmacology and Experimental Therapeutics*, 1953, **107**, 519–523.

Baldwin, K. M., Klinkerfuss, G. H., Terjung, R. L., Molé. P. A., & Holloszy, J. O. Respiratory capacity of red, white and intermediate muscle: Adaptive response to exercise. *American Journal of Physiology*, 1972, **222**, 373–378.

Beavo, J. A., Rogers, N. L., Crofford, O. B., Hardman, J. G., Sutherland, E. W., & Newman, E. V. Effects of xanthine derivatives on lipolysis and on adenosine 3'5'-monophosphate phosphodiesterase activity. *Molecular Pharmacology*, 1970, **6**, 597–603.

Bellet, S., Kershbaum, A., & Aspe, J. The effect of caffeine on free fatty acids. *Archives of Internal Medicine*, 1965, **116**, 750–752.

Bellet, S., Kershbaum, A., Finch, E. Response of free fatty acids to coffee and caffeine. *Metabolism*, 1968, **17**, 702–707.

Bellet, S., Roman, L., DeCastro, O., Kim, K. E., & Kershbaum, A. Effect of coffee ingestion on catecholamine release. *Metabolism*, 1969, **18**, 288–291.

Berkowitz, B., & Spector, S. Effect of caffeine and theophylline on pheripheral catecholamines. *European Journal of Pharmacology*, 1971, **13**, 193–196.

*References and bibliography reprinted with permission from Human Kinetics Publishing, Box 5076, Champaign, IL 61820.

Berkowitz, B., Tarver, J. H., & Spector, S. Release of norepinephrine in the central nervous system by theophylline and caffeine. *European Journal of Pharmacology*, 1970, **10**, 64–71.

Berthet, J., Sutherland, E. W., & Rall, T. W. The assay of glucagon and epinephrine with use of liver homogenates. *Journal of Biological Chemistry*, 1957, **229**, 351–354.

Bertrand, C. A., Pomper, I., Hillman, G., Duffy, J. G., & Micheli, I. No relation between coffee and blood pressure. *New England Journal of Medicine*, 1978, **299**, 315–316.

Bianchi, C. P. Effect of caffeine on radiocalcium movement in frog sartorius. *Journal of General Physiology*, 1961, **44**, 845–858.

Bianchi, C. P. Kinetics of radiocaffeine uptake and release in frog sartorius. *Journal de Pharmacologie*, 1962, **138**, 41–47.

Bianchi, C. P., & Narayan, S. Muscle fatigue and the role of transverse tubules. *Science*, 1982, **215**, 295–296.

Blayney, L., Thomas, H., Muir, J., & Henderson, A. Action of caffeine on calcium transport by isolated fractions of myofibrils, mitochondria, and sarcoplasmic reticulum from rabbit heart. *Circulation Research*, 1978, **43**, 520–526.

Boje, O. Doping. *Bulletin of the Health Organization of the League of Nations*, 1939, **8**, 439–469.

Bowman, W. C., & Nott, M. W. Actions of sympathomimetic amines and their antagonists on skeletal muscle. *Pharmacological Reviews*, 1969, **21**, 27–72.

Bowman, W. C., & Raper, C. The effects of adrenaline and other drugs affecting carbohydrate metabolism on contractions of the rat diaphragm. *British Journal of Pharmacology*, 1964, **23**, 184–200.

Breckenridge, B. M., Burn, J. H., & Matshinsky, F. M. Theophylline, epinephrine and neostigmine facilitation on neuromuscular transmission. *Proceedings of the National Academy of Science (Washington)*, 1967, **57**, 1893–1897.

Bremer, J. The effect of acylcarnitines on the metabolism of pyruvate in rat heart mitochondria. *Biochimica et Biophysica Acta*, 1965, **104**, 581–590.

Bunker, M. I., & McWilliams, M. E. Caffeine content of common beverages. *Journal of the American Dietetic Association*, 1979, **74**, 28.

Burg, A. W. Effects of caffeine on the human system. *Tea and Coffee Trade Journal*, 1975, **147**, 40. (a)

Burg, A. W. Physiological disposition of caffeine. Drug *Metabolism Reviews*, 1975, **4**, 199–228. (b)

Butcher, R. W., & Baird, C. E. The regulation of cAMP and lipolysis in adipose tissue by hormones and other agents. In W. Holmes, L. A. Carlson, & R. Paoletti (Eds.), *Drugs Affecting Lipid Metabolism*. New York: Plenum, 1969.

Butcher, R. W., Ho, R. J., Meng, H. C., & Sutherland, E. W. Adenosine 3',5'-monophosphate in biological materials. II. The measurement of adenosine 3',5'-monophosphate in tissues and the role of the cyclic nucleotide in the lipolytic response of fat to epinephrine. *Journal of Biological Chemistry*, 1965, **240**, 4515–4523.

Butcher R. W. & Sutherland, E. W., Adenosine 3',5' phosphate in biological materials. *Journal of Biological Chemistry*, 1962, **237**, 1244–1255.

Carlson, L. A., Liljedahl, S. W., & Wirsen, C. Blood and tissue changes in the dog during and after excessive free fatty acid mobilization: A biochemical and morphological study. *Acta Medica Scandinavica*, 1965, **178**, 81–107.

Cheema-Dhadli, S., & Halperin, M. L. The effect of palmitoyl-CoA and β oxidation of fatty acids on the kinetics of mitochondrial citrate transporter. *Canadian Journal of Biochemistry*, 1976, **54**, 171–177.

Cheney, R. Comparative effect of caffeine per se and a caffeine beverage (coffee) upon the reaction time in normal young adults. *Journal de Pharmacologie*, 1935, **53**, 304–313.

Cheraskin, E., Ringsdorf, W. H., Setyaadmadja, A., & Barrett, R. Effect of caffeine versus placebo supplementation on blood glucose concentration. *Lancet*, 1967, **i**, 1299–1300.

Cheung, W. Y. Properties of cyclic 3',5' nucleotide phosphodiesterase from rat brain. *Biochemistry*, 1967, **6**, 1079–1087.

Chuck, L.H.S., & Parmley, W. W. Caffeine reversal of length-dependent changes in myocardial contractile state in the cat. *Circulation Research*, 1980, **47**, 592–598.

Clements, R. L., & Deatherage, F. E. A chromatographic study of some of the compounds in roasted coffee. *Food Research*, 1957, **22**, 222–225.

Clutter, W. E., Bier, D. M., Shak, S. D., & Cryer, P. E. Epinephrine plasma metabolic clearance rates and physiologic thresholds for metabolic and hemodynamic actions in man. *Journal of Clinical Investigation*, 1980, **66**, 94–101.

Coleman, A. W., & Coleman, J. R. Characterization of the methylxanthine-induced propagated wave phenomenon in striated muscle. *The Journal of Experimental Zoology*, 1980, **212**, 403–413.

Colton, T., Gosselin, R. E., & Smith, R. P. The tolerance of coffee drinkers to caffeine. *Clinical Pharmacology and Therapeutics*, 1968, **9**, 31–39.

Costill, D. L., Coyle, E., Dalsky, G., Evans, W., Fink, W., & Hoopes, D. Effects of elevated plasma FFA and insulin on muscle glycogen usage during exercise. *Journal of Applied Physiology*, 1977, **43**, 695–699.

Costill, D. L., Dalsky, G., & Fink, W. Effects of caffeine ingestion on metabolism and exercise performance. *Medicine and Science in Sports*, 1978, **10**, 155–158.

Costill, D. L., Jansson, E., Gollnick, P. D., & Saltin, B. Glycogen utilization in leg muscles of men during level and uphill running. *Acta Physiologica Scandinavica*, 1974, **91**, 475–481.

Crass, M. F. Exogenous substrate effects of endogenous lipid metabolism in the working rat heart. *Biochimica et Biophysica Acta*, 1972, **280**, 71–81.

Crass, M. F. Heart triglyceride and glycogen metabolism: Effects of catecholamines, dibutryl cAMP, theophylline and fatty acids. *Recent Advances in the Study of Cardiac Structure and Metabolism*, 1973, **3**, 275–290.

Dagenais, G. R., Tancredi, R. G., & Zierler, K. I. Free fatty acid oxidation by forearm muscle at rest, and evidence for an intramuscular lipid pool in the human forearm. *Journal of Clinical Investigation*, 1976, **58**, 421–431.

Davis, I. In vitro regulation of the lipolysis of adipose tissue. *Nature*, 1968, **218**, 349–352.

Dole, V. P. Effect of nucleic acid metabolites on lipolysis in adipose tissue. *Journal of Biological Chemistry*, 1961, **236**, 3125–3128.

El-Nady, A., Halfez, T. A., Lofty, R. A., & El-banna, M. Interrelationship between the stimulant effect of caffeine on lipolysis and its effect on glucose utilization and respiration of adipose tissue. *Egyptian Journal of Physiological Sciences*, 1976, **3**, 105–110.

Essig, D., Costill, D. L., & Van Handel, P. J. Effects of caffeine ingestion on utilization of muscle glycogen and lipid during leg ergometer cycling. *International Journal of Sports Medicine*, 1980, **1**, 86–90.

Essig, D. A., & White, T. P. Effects of caffeine on glycogen and triglyceride concentration in the soleus and plantaris muscles of the exercising rat. *Federation Proceedings*, 1981, 513. (Abstract)

Fabiato, A., & Fabiato, F. Dependence of the contractile activation of skinned cardiac cells on the sarcomere length. *Nature (London)*, 1975, **256**, 54–56.

Fain, J. N. Cyclic nucleotides in adipose tissue. In H. Cramer & J. Schultz (Eds.), *Cyclic 3',5' nucleotides: Mechanisms of action*. London: J. Wiley and Sons, 1977.

FDA Fact Sheet. Rockville, MD: U.S. Dept. HEW (PHS), Food and Drug Administration, July 1971. (FDA) 72-3003.

Fischbach, E. Coffee and sports. *Minerva Medica*, 1970, **61**, 4367–4369.

Fischbach, E. Problems of doping. *Medizinische Monatsschrift für Pharmazeuten*, 1972, **26**, 377–381.

Fitzgerald, G. A., Hossmann, V., Hamilton, C. A., Reid, J. L., Davis, D. S., & Dollery, C. T. Interindividual differences in the kinetics of infused norepinephrine in man. *Clinical Pharmacology and Therapeutics*, 1979, **26**, 669–675.

Fox, E. L. *Sports physiology*. Philadelphia: W.B. Saunders, 1979.

Fox, E. L., & Mathews, D. K. *The Physiological Basis of Physical Education and Athletics*. Philadelphia: Saunders College Publishing, 1981.

Fredholm, B. B. Are methylxanthine effects due to antagonism of endogenous adenosine? *Trends in Pharmacological Research*, 1980, **1**, 129–132.

Froberg, S. O., Rossner, S., & Ericsson, M. Relation between triglycerides in human skeletal muscle and serum and the fractional elimination rate of exogenous plasma triglycerides. *European Journal of Clinical Investigation*, 1978, **8**, 93–97.

Ganslen, R. V., Balke, B., Nagle, F., & Phillips, E. Effects of some tranquilizing analeptic and vasodilating drugs on physical work capacity and orthostatic tolerance. *Aerospace Medicine*, 1964, **35**, 630–633.

Gemmill, C. L. The effects of caffeine and theobromine derivatives on glycolysis in muscle. *Journal of Pharmacology and Experimental Therapeutics*, 1947, **91**, 292–296.

Goldstein, A., Kaizer, S., & Whitby, O. Psychotropic effects of caffeine in man. IV. Quantitative and qualitative differences associated with habituation to coffee. *Clinical Pharmacology and Therapeutics*, 1969, **10**, 489–497.

Goldstein, A., Warren, R., & Kaizer, S. Psychotropic effects of caffeine in man. I. Interindividual differences in sensitivity to caffeine-induced wakefulness. *Journal of Pharmacology and Experimental Therapeutics*, 1965, **149**, 156–159.

Gollnick, P. D., Armstrong, R. B., Saubert, C. W., Sembrowich, W. L., Shephard, R. E., & Saltin, B. Glycogen depletion patterns in human skeletal muscle fibers during prolonged work. *Pfluegers Archiv. European Journal of Physiology*, 1973, **344**, 1–12.

Goodman, L. S., & Gilman, A. *The pharmacological basis of therapeutics.* New York: 1965.

Gordon, A. M., Huxley, A. F., & Julian, F. J. The variation in isometric tension with sarcomere length in vertebrate muscle fibers. *Journal of Physiology,* 1966, **184,** 170–192.

Gould, L., Manoj Duman Goswami, C. V., Ramana, R., & Gomprecht, R. The cardiac effects of tea. *Journal of Clinical Pharmacology,* 1973, **13,** 469–474.

Grollman, A. The action of alcohol, caffeine and tobacco on the cardiac output (and its related functions) of normal man. *Journal of Pharmacology and Experimental Therapeutics,* 1930, **39,** 313–327.

Guthrie, J. R., & Nayler, W. G. Interaction between caffeine and adenosine on calcium exchangeability in mammalian atria. *Archives of International Pharmacology and Therapeutics,* 1967, **170,** 249–255.

Hagenfeldt, L., & Wahren, J. Metabolism of free fatty acids and ketone bodies in skeletal muscle. In B. Pernow & B. Saltin (Eds.), *Muscle metabolism during exercise.* New York: Plenum, 1971.

Haldi, J., & Wynn, W. Action of drugs on the efficiency of swimmers. *Research Quarterly,* 1946, **17,** 96–101.

Hartree, W., & Hill, A. V. The heat production of muscles treated with caffeine or subjected to prolonged discontinuous stimulation. *Journal of Physiology,* 1924, **58,** 441–454.

Hawk, P. A study of the physiological and psychological reactions of the human organism to caffeine drinking. *American Journal of Physiology,* 1929, **90,** 380–381.

Henderson, A. H., Claes, V. A., & Brutsaert, D. I. Influence of caffeine and other inotropic interventions on the onset of unloaded shortening velocity in mammalian heart muscle. *Circulation Research,* 1973, **33,** 291–302.

Hennekens, C. H., Drolette, M. E., Jesse, M. J., Davies, J., & Hutchison, G. Coffee drinking and death due to coronary heart disease. *New England Journal of Medicine,* 1976, **294,** 633–636.

Herxheimer, H. Zur Wirkung des Koffeins auf die Sportliche Leistung. *Moenchen Medizinische Wochenschrift,* 1960, **21,** 140–149.

Hess, M. E., & Haugaard, N. The effects of epinephrine and aminophylline on phosphorylase activity of perfused, contracting heart muscle. *Journal of Pharmacology and Experimental Therapeutics,* 1958, **122,** 169–175.

Hicks, M. J., Shigekawa, M., & Katz, A. M. Mechanism by which cyclic adenosine 3'5'-monophosphate-dependent protein kinase stimulates calcium transport in cardiac sarcoplasmic reticulum. *Circulation Research,* 1979, **44,** 384–391.

Hickson, R. C., Rennie, M. J., Conlee, R. K., Winder, W. W., & Holloszy, J. O. Effects of increased plasma free fatty acids on glycogen utilization and endurance, *Journal of Applied Physiology: Respiratory, Environmental and Exercise Physiology,* 1977, **43,** 829–833.

Himms-Hagen, J. Sympathetic regulation of metabolism. *Pharmacological Reviews,* 1967, **19,** 367–461.

Hoffman, W. W. Oxygen consumption by human and rodent striated muscle in vitro. *American Journal of Physiology,* 1976, **230,** 34–40.

Hollingsworth, H. The influence of caffeine on mental and motor efficiency. *Archiv für Psychologie (Frankfurt am Main)*, 1912, **3**, 1–166.

Horst, K., & Jenkins, W. L. The effect of caffeine, coffee and decaffeinated coffee upon blood pressure, pulse rate and simple reaction time of men of various ages, *Journal of Pharmacology and Experimental Therapeutics*, 1935, **53**, 385–400.

Huddart, H., & Oates, K. Localization of the intracellular site of caffeine on skeletal muscle. *Comparative Biochemistry and Physiology*, 1970, **36**, 677–682.

Isaacson, A., & Barany, M. Effects of caffeine on water content, sucrose space and 3-0-methyl glucose uptake of frog semitendinosus muscle. *Federation Proceedings*, 1973, **32**, 346.

Isaacson, A., & Sandow, A. Quinine and caffeine effects on 45 Ca movements in frog sartorius muscle. *Journal of Physiology*, 1967, **50**, 2109–2128.

Ivy, J. L., Costill, D. L., Fink, W. J., & Lower, R. W. Influence of caffeine and carbohydrate feedings on endurance performance. *Medicine and Science in Sports and Exercise*, 1979, **11**, 6–11.

Jick, H., Mittinen, O. S., Neff, R. K., Shapiro, S., Heinonen, O., & Slone, D. Coffee and myocardial infarction. *New England Journal of Medicine*, 1973, **289**, 63–67.

Kalsner, S., Mechanism of potentiation of contractor responses to catecholamines in aortic strips. *British Journal of Pharmacology*, 1977, **43**, 379–388.

Katz, A. Contractile proteins of the heart. *Physiological Reviews*, 1970, **50**, 63–158.

Kavaler, F., Anderson, T. W., & Fisher, V. J. Sarcolemmal site of caffeine's inotropic action on ventricular muscle of the frog. *Circulation Research*, 1978, **42**, 285–290.

Kavinsky, P. J., Shechosky, S., & Fletterick, R. J., Synergistic regulation of phosphorylase a by glucose and caffeine. *Journal of Biological Chemistry*, 1978, **253**, 9102–9106.

Kubovetz, W. R., & Poch, G. The action of imidazole on the effects of methylxanthines and catecholamines on cardiac contraction and phosphorylase activity. *Journal of Pharmacology and Experimental Therapeutics*, 1967, **156**, 514–521.

Lee, S. H., & Davis, E. J. Carboxylation and decarboxylation reactions. Anaplerotic flux and removal of citric acid cycle intermediates in skeletal muscle. *Journal of Biological Chemistry*, 1979, **254**, 420–430.

Little, J. A., Chanoff, H. M., Csima, A., & Yano, R. Coffee and serum-lipids in coronary heart disease. *Lancet*, 1966, **i**, 732–734.

Maccornack, R. A. The effects of coffee drinking on the cardiovascular system; Experimental and epidemiological research. *Preventive Medicine*, 1977, **6**, 104–119.

Macintosh, B. R., Barbee, R. W., & Stainsby, W. N. Contractile response to caffeine of rested and fatigued skeletal muscle. *Medicine and Science in Sports and Exercise*, 1981, **13**, 95.

Manchester, K. L., Bullock, G., & Roetzscher, U. M. Influence of methylxanthines and local anesthetics on the metabolism of muscle and associated changes in mitochondrial morphology. *Chemical-Biological Interactions*, 1973, **6**, 273–296.

Mansour, T. E., Phosphofructokinase. *Current Topics in Cellular Regulation*, 1972, **5**, 1–46. (a)

Mansour, T. E. Phosphofructokinase activity in skeletal muscle extracts following administration of epinephrine. *Journal of Biological Chemistry*, 1972, **247**, 6059–6066. (b)

Margaria, R., Aghemo, P., & Rovelli, E. The effect of some drugs on the maximal capacity of athletic performance in men. *Internationale Zeitschrift für Angewandte Physiologie Einschliesslich Arbeitsphysiologie*, 1964, **20**, 281–287.

Means, J. H., Aub, J. C., & DuBois, E. F. The effect of caffeine on the heat production. *Archives of Internal Medicine*, 1947, **19**, 832–839.

Medical Commission of the British Commonwealth Games. Prevention and detection of drug taking (doping) at the IX British Commonwealth Games. *Scottish Medical Journal*, 1971, **16**, 364–368.

Merkel, A. D., Wayner, M. J., Jolicoeur, F. B., & Mintz, R. Effects of caffeine administration on food and water consumption under various experimental conditions. *Pharmacology, Biochemistry & Behavior*, 1981, **14**, 235–240.

Merritt, M. C., & Proctor, B. E. Effects of temperature during the roasting cycle on selected components of different types of whole bean coffee. *Food Research*, 1959, **24**, 672–676.

Molé, P. A., Baldwin, K. M., Terjung, R. L., & Holloszy, J. O. Enzymatic pathways of pyruvate metabolism in skeletal muscle: Adaptations to exercise. *American Journal of Physiology*, 1973, **224**, 50–54.

Mustala, O. Improvement of athletic performance by drugs. *Suomen Laakarilehti*, 1967, **22**, 690–695.

Neely, J. R., Bowman, R. H., & Morgan, H. E. Conservation of glycogen in the perfused rat heart developing intraventricular pressure. In W. J. Whelan (Ed.), *Control of Glycogen Metabolism*. New York: Academic Press, 1968.

Novotony, I., & Bianchi, C. P. The effect of xylocaine on oxygen consumption in the frog sartorius. *Journal of Pharmacological and Experimental Therapeutics*, 1967, **155**, 450–462.

Oldendorf, W. H. Brain uptake of metabolites and drugs following carotid arterial injections. *Transactions of the American Neurological Association*, 1971, **96**, 46–50.

Olivecrona, T., Hernell, O., & Egelrud, T. Lipoprotein lipase. *Advances in Experimental Medicine and Biology*, 1975, **52**, 269–279.

Patwardhan, R. V., Desmond, P. V., Johnson, R. F., Dunn, G. D., Robertson, D. H., Hoyumpa, A. M., & Schenker, S. Effects of caffeine on plasma free fatty acids, urinary catecholamines and drug binding. *Clinical Pharmacology and Therapeutics*, 1980, **28**, 398–403.

Paul, P., Issekutz, B., & Miller, H. I. Interrelationship of free fatty acids and glucose metabolism in dogs. *American Journal of Physiology*, 1966, **211**, 1313–1320.

Perkins, R., & Williams, M. H. Effect of caffeine upon maximum muscular endurance of females. *Medicine and Science in Sports*, 1975, **7**, 221–224.

Pickering, J. W. Observations on the physiology of the embryonic heart. *Journal of Physiology (London)*, 1893, **14**, 383–466.

Porte, D., Graber, A., Kuzuya, T., & Williams, R. The effect of epinephrine on immunoreactive insulin levels in man. *Journal of Clinical Investigation*, 1966, **45**, 228–236.

Prineas, R. J., Jacobs, D. R., Crow, R. S., & Blackburn, H. Coffee, tea and VPB. *Journal of Chronic Diseases*, 1980, **33**, 67–72.

Pruett, E.D.R. Glucose and insulin during prolonged work stress in men living on different diets. *Journal of Applied Physiology*, 1970, **28**, 199–208.

Randle, P. J. Endocrine control of metabolism. *Annual Reviews of Physiology*, 1963, **25**, 291–324.

Randle, P. J., Newsholme, E. A., & Garland, P. B. Regulation of glucose uptake by muscle: Effects of fatty acids, ketone bodies and pyruvate and of alloxan diabetes and starvation on the uptake and metabolic rate of glucose in rat heart and diaphragm muscles. *Biochemical Journal*, 1964, **93**, 652–665.

Reimann, H. A. Caffeinism: A cause of long-continued, low-grade fever. *Journal of the American Medical Association*, 1967, **202**, 131–132. (December 18, 1967)

Rennie, M., Winder, W. W., & Holloszy, J. O. A sparing effect of increased free fatty acids on muscle glycogen content in exercising rat. *Biochemical Journal*, 1976, **156**, 647–655.

Rivers, W., & Webber, H. The action of caffeine on the capacity for muscular work. *Journal of Physiology*, 1907, **36**, 33–47.

Robertson, D., Johnson, G. A., Robertson, R. M., Nies, A. S., Shand, D. G., & Oates, J. A. Comparative assessment of stimuli that release neuronal and adrenomedullary catecholamines in man. *Circulation*, 1979, **59**, 637–643.

Robertson, D., Wade, D., Workman, R., Woosley, R. L., & Oates, J. A. Tolerance to the humoral and hemodynamic effects of caffeine in man. *Journal of Clinical Investigation*, 1981, **67**, 1111–1117.

Schirlitz, K. Über caffein bei ermüdender Muskelarbeit. *Internationale Zeitschrift für Angewandte Physiologie Einschliesslich Arbeitsphysiologie*, 1930, **2**, 273–277.

Second International Caffeine Workshop. Special Report. *Nutrition Reviews*, 1980, **38**, 196–200.

Somlyo, A. V., & Somlyo, A. P. Electromechanical and pharmacomechanical coupling in vascular smooth muscle. *Journal of Pharmacology and Experimental Therapeutics*, 1968, **159**, 129–145.

Spitzer, J. J., & Gold, M. Free fatty acid metabolism by skeletal muscle. *American Journal of Physiology*, 1964, **206**, 159–163.

Stankiewicz-Choroszucha, B., & Gorski, J. Effect of decreased availability substrates on intramuscular triglyceride utilization during exercise. *European Journal of Applied Physiology and Occupational Physiology*, 1978, **40**, 27–35.

Steiner, R. F., Greer, L., Bhat, R., & Oton, J. Structural changes induced in glycogen phosphorylase b by the binding of glucose and caffeine. *Biochimica et Biophysica Acta*, 1980, **611**, 269–279.

Stephenson, P. E. Physiologic and psychotropic effects of caffeine on man. *Journal of the American Dietic Association*, 1977, **71**, 240–247.

Strubelt, O. The influence of respirine, propanolol and adrenal medullectomy on the hyperglycemic actions of theophylline and caffeine. *Archives Internationales de Pharmacodynamie et de Therapie*, 1969, **179**, 215–224.

Studlar, M. Über den Einfluss von Caffein auf den Fett- und Kohlenhydratestoffwechsel des Menschen. *Zeitschrift fu/ur Ernaehrungswissenschaft*, 1973, **12**, 109–120.

Syed, I. B. The effects of caffeine. *Journal of the American Pharmaceutical Association*, 1976, **16**, 568–572.

Taylor, W. A., & Halperin, M. L. Regulation of pyruvate dehydrogenase in muscle: inhibition by citrate, *Journal of Biological Chemistry*, 1973, **248**, 6080–6083.

Thetapandha, A., Maling, H. M., & Gilette, J. R. Effects of caffeine and theophylline on activity of rats in relation to brain xanthine concentrations. *Proceedings for Experimental Biology and Medicine*, 1972, **139**, 582–586.

Thornton, G. The effects of benzedrine and caffeine upon performance in certain psychomotor tasks. *Journal of Abnormal and Social Psychology*, 1939, **34**, 96–113.

Truitt, E. B. The xanthines. In J. R. DePalma (Ed.), *Drill's pharmacology in medicine*. New York: McGraw-Hill, 1971.

Ugol, L. M., Hammack, M. J., & Hays, E. T. Caffeine contractures in rat soleus muscle. *Federation Proceedings*, 1981, **40**, (3 part 1), 513.

Van Handel, P. J., Burke, E., Costill, D. L., & Cote, R. Physiological responses to cola ingestion. *Research Quarterly*, 1977, **48**, 436–444.

Varagic, V. M., & Zugic, M. Interactions of xanthine derivatives, catecholamines and glucose-6-phosphate on the isolated phrenic nerve diaphragm preparation of the rat. *Pharmacology*, 1971, **5**, 275–286.

Venerando, A. Doping: Pathology and ways to control it. *Medicine dello Sport*, 1963, **3**, 972–993.

Victor, B. S., Lubetsky, M., & Greden, J. F. Somatic manifestations of caffeinism. *Journal of Clinical Psychiatry*, 1981, **42**, 185–188.

Villa, R., & Panceri, P. Action of some drugs on performance time in mice. *Farmaco, Edizione Pratica*, 1973, **28**, 43–48.

Wachman, A., Hattner, R. S., George, B., & Bernstein, D. S. Effects of decaffeinated and nondecaffeinated coffee ingestion on blood glucose and plasma radioimmunoreactive insulin responses to rapid intravenous infusion of glucose in normal men. *Metabolism*, 1970, **19**, 539–546.

Waldeck, B. Sensitization by caffeine of central catecholamine receptors. *Journal of Neural Transmission*, 1973, **34**, 61–72.

Weber, A. The mechanism of the action of caffeine on sarcoplasmic reticulum. *Journal of General Physiology*, 1968, **52**, 760–772.

Weber, A., & Herz, R. The relationship between caffeine contracture of intact muscle and the effect of caffeine on reticulum. *Journal of General Physiology*, 1968, **52**, 750–759.

Weiss, B., & Laties, V. Enhancement of human performance by caffeine and the amphetamines. *Pharmacological Reviews*, 1962, **14**, 1–36.

Wenzel, D., & Rutledge, C. Effects of centrally acting drugs on human motor and psychomotor performance. *Journal of Pharmaceutical Science*, 1962, **51**, 631–644.

White, B. C., Lincoln, C. A., Pearce, N. W., Reeb, R., & Vaida, C. Anxiety and muscle tension as consequences of caffeine withdrawal. *Science*, 1980, **209 (4464)**, 1547–1548.

Wilcox, A. The effects of caffeine and exercise on body weight and adiposity in the rat. *Medicine and Science in Sports and Exercise*, 1981, **13**, 122.

Williamson, J. R., Ford, C., Illingsworth, J., & Safer, B. Coordination of citric acid cycle activity with electron transport flux. *Circulation Research*, 1976, **38**, 139–151. (Supplement 1)

Wolman, W. Instant and decaffeinated coffee. *Journal of the American Medical Association*, 1955, **159**, 250.

Wood, D. S., Human skeletal muscle: Analysis of Ca++ regulation in skinned fibers using caffeine. *Experimental Neurology*, 1978, **58**, 218–230.

Zierler, K. L. Fatty acids as substrates for heart and skeletal muscle. *Circulation Research*, 1976, **38**, 459–463.

AMPHETAMINES

Adler, H. F., Burkardt, W. L., Ivy, A. C., & Atkinson, A. J. Effects of various drugs on psychomotor performance at ground level and simulated altitudes of 18,000 feet in a low pressure chamber. *Journal of Aviation Medicine*, 1950, **21**, 221–236.

Alles, G. A., & Feigen, G. A. The influence of benzedrine on work decrement and patellar reflex. *American Journal of Physiology*, 1942, **136**, 392–400.

Axelrod, J., Whitby, L. G., & Hertting, G. Effect of psychotropic drugs on the uptake of H3-norepinephrine by tissue. *Science*, 1961, **133**, 383–384.

Bättig, K. The effect of training and amphetamine on the endurance and velocity of swimming performance of rats. *Psychopharmacologia*, 1963, **4**, 15–27.

Beckman, H. *Drugs—Their nature, action, and use*. Philadelphia: W. B. Saunders, 1958.

Bhagat, B., & Wheeler, N. Effect of amphetamine on the swimming endurance of rats. *Neuropharmacology*, 1973, **12**, 711–713. (a)

Bhagat, B., & Wheeler, N. Effect of nicotine on the swimming endurance of rats. *Neuropharmacology*, 1973, **12**, 1161–1165. (b)

Blum, B., Stern, M. J., & Melville, K. I. A comparative evaluation of the action of depressant and stimulant drugs on human performance. *Psychopharmacologia*, 1964, **6**, 173–177.

Blyth, C. S., Allen, M., & Lovingood, B. W. Effect of amphetamine (Dexedrine) and caffeine on subjects exposed to heat and exercise stress. *Research Quarterly*, 1960, **31**, 553–559.

Borg, G., Edström, C. G., Linderholm, H., & Marklund, G. Changes in physical performance induced by amphetamines and amobarbital. *Psychopharmacologia*, 1972, **26**, 10–18.

Bouton, J. *Ball four*. New York: World Publishing, 1970.

Bradley, P. B., & Elkes, J. The effects of some drugs on the electrical activity of the brain. *Brain*, 1957, **80**, 77–117.

Bujas, Z., & Petz, B. Utjecaj fenamina na ekonomicnost staticnog rada. *Arhiz za Higijenu Rada*, 1955, **6**, 205–208.

Burger, A. (Ed.). *Drugs affecting the central nervous system* (Vol. 2). New York: Marcel Dekker, 1968.

Campbell, D. B. A method for the measurement of therapeutic levels of (+)-amphetamine in human plasma. *Journal of Pharmacy and Pharmacology*, 1969, **21**, 129–130.

Chandler, J. V., & Blair, S. N. The effect of amphetamines on selected physiological components related to athletic success. *Medicine and Science in Sports and Exercise*, 1980, **12**, 65–69.

Chatterjee, A. K., Jacob, S. A., Srivastava, R. K., Pabrai, P. R., & Ghose A. Influence of methylamphetamine on blood lactic acid following exercise. *Japanese Journal of Pharmacology*, 1970, **20**, 170–172.

Cooter, G. R., & Stull, G. A. The effect of amphetamine on endurance in rats. *Journal of Sports Medicine*, 1974, **14**, 120–126.

Costello, C. The effect of stimulant and depressant drugs on physical persistence. *American Journal of Psychology*, 1963, **76**, 698–700.

Costill, D. L., Coyle, E., Dalsky, G., Evans, W., Fink, W., & Hoopes, D. Effects of elevated plasma FFA and insulin in muscle glycogen usage during exercise. *Journal of Applied Physiology*, 1977, **43**, 695–699.

Cuthbertson, D. P., & Knox, J. A. The effects of analeptics on the fatigued subject. *Journal of Physiology*, 1947, **106**, 42–58.

Davis, D. R. Psychomotor effects of analeptics and their relation to fatigue phenomena in air crew. *British Medical Journal*, 1947, **5**, 43–45.

Dembert, M. L., & Harclerode, J. Effects of 1-Δ^9 - tetrahydrocannabinol, dl-amphetamine and pentobarbital on oxygen consumption by mouse brain and heart homogenates. *Biochemical Pharmacology*, 1974, **23**, 947–956.

Dimascio, A., & Buie, D. H. Psychopharmacology of chlorphentermine and d-amphetamine—A comparative study of their effects in normal males. *Clinical Pharmacology and Therapeutics*, 1964, **5**, 174–184.

Estler, C. J., Fickl, H.P.T., & Fröhlich, H. N. Substrate supply and energy metabolism of skeletal muscle of mice treated with methamphetamine and propranolol. *Biochemical Pharmacology*, 1970, **19**, 2957–2962.

Estler, C. J., & Gabrys, M. C. Swimming capacity of mice after prolonged treatment with psychostimulants. II. Effect of methamphetamine on swimming performance and availability of metabolic substances. *Psychopharmacologia*, 1979, **60**, 173–176.

Evans, W. O., & Jewett, A. The effect of some centrally acting drugs on disjunctive reaction time. *Psychopharmacologia*, 1962, **3**, 124–128.

Fitts, R. H., & Holloszy, J. O. Lactate and contractile force in frog muscle during development of fatigue and recovery. *American Journal of Physiology*, 1976, **231**, 430–435.

Foltz, E. E., Ivy, A. C., & Barborka, C. J. The influence of amphetamine (Benzedrine) sulfate and desoxyephedrine hydrochloride (pervitin) and caffeine upon work output and recovery when rapidly exhausting work is done by trained subjects. *Journal of Laboratory and Clinical Medicine*, 1943, **28**, 603–606.

Foltz, E. E., Schriffin, J. M., & Ivy, A. C. The influence of amphetamine (Benzedrine) sulfate and caffeine on the performance of rapidly exhausting work by untrained subjects. *Journal of Laboratory and Clinical Medicine*, 1943, **28**, 601–603.

Fowler, S. C., Filewich, R. J., & Leberer, M. R. Drug effects upon force and duration of response during fixed-ratio performance in rats. *Pharmacology Biochemistry and Behavior*, 1977, **6**, 421–426.

Fuch, F., Reddy, V., & Briggs, F. N. The interaction of cations with the calcium-binding site of troponin. *Biochemistry Biophysica Acta (Amsterdam)*, 1970, **221**, 407–409.

Fuller, R. W., & Hines, C. W. d-Amphetamine levels in brain and other tissues of isolated and aggregated mice. *Biochemical Pharmacology*, 1967, **16**, 11–16.

Fuster, J. M. Effects of stimulation on brain stem on tachistoscopic perception. *Science*, 1958, **127**, 150–153.

Gerald, M. C. Effects of (+)-amphetamine on the treadmill endurance performance of rats. *Neuropharmacology*, 1978, **17**, 703–704.

Gerald, M. C., & Hse, S. Y. The effects of amphetamine isomers on neuromuscular transmission. *Neuropharmacology*, 1975, **14**, 115–123.

Gilbert, B. Drugs in sport. *Sports Illustrated*, June 23, 1969, **30**, 64–72, (a).

Gilbert, B. Something extra on the ball. *Sports Illustrated*, June 30, 1969, **30**, 30–42. (b).

Gilbert, B. High time to make some rules. *Sports Illustrated*, July 7, 1969, **31**, 30–35, (c).

Golding, L. Drugs and hormones. In W. Morgan (Ed.), *Ergogenic aids and muscular performance*. New York: Academic Press, 1972.

Golding, L. A., & Barnard, J. R. The effect of d-amphetamine sulfate on physical performance. *Journal of Sports Medicine and Physical Fitness*, 1963, **3**, 221–224.

Goldstein, A., Searle, B. W., & Schimke, R. T. Effects of secobarbital and d-amphetamine on psychomotor performance of normal subjects. *Journal of Pharmacological Experimental Therapy*, 1960, **130**, 55–58.

Griffith, J. D., Canaugh. J., Held. J., & Oates, J. A. Dextroamphetamine: Evaluation of psychomimetic properties in man, *Archives of General Psychiatry*, 1972, **26**, 97–100.

Grinker, J. A., Drewnowski, A., Enns, M., & Kissileff, H. Effects of d-amphetamine and fenfluramine on feeding patterns and activity of obese and lean Zucker rats. *Pharmacology Biochemistry and Behavior*, 1980, **12**, 265–275.

Haldi, J., & Wynn, W. Action of drugs on efficiency of swimmers. *Research Quarterly*, 1946, **17**, 96–101.

Hart, J. B., & Wallace, J. The adverse effects of amphetamines. *Clinical Toxicology*, 1975, **8**, 179–180.

Hauty, G. T., & Payne, R. B. Effects of dextro-amphetamine upon judgment. *Journal of Pharmacology and Experimental Therapeutics*, 1957, **120**, 33–37.

Hickson, R. C., Rennie, M. J., Conlee, R. K., Winder, W. W., & Holloszy, J. O. Effects of increased plasma fatty acids on glycogen utilization and endurance. *Journal of Applied Physiology*, 1977, **43**, 829–833.

Hollister, L. E., & Gillispie, H. K. A new stimulant, prolintane hydrochloride, compared with dextroamphetamine in fatigued volunteers. *Journal of Clinical Pharmacology*, 1970, **10**, 103–109.

Hueting, J., & Poulus, A. Amphetamine, performance, effort and fatigue. *Pflügers Archives*, 1970, **318**, 260.

Hurst, P. M., Radlow, R., & Bagley, S. K. The effects of d-amphetamine and chlordiazepoxide upon strength and estimated strength. *Ergonomics*, 1968, **11**, 47–52.

Ikai, M., & Steinhaus, A. H. Some factors modifying the expression of human strength. *Journal of Applied Physiology*, 1961, **16**, 157–163.

Ivy, A. C., & Krasno, L. R. Amphetamine (Benzedrine) sulfate: A review of its pharmacology. *War Medicine*, 1941, **1**, 15–42.

Ivy, J. L., Costill, D. L., Van Handel, P. J., Essig, D. A., & Lower, R. W. Alteration in the lactate threshold with changes in substrate availability. *International Journal of Sports Medicine*, 1981, **2**, 139–142.

Jacob, J., & Michaud, G. Actions of various pharmacologic agents on the exhaustion time and behavior of mice swimming at 20°C. I. Description of the technic actions of amphetamine, cocaine, caffeine, hexobarbital and meprobamate. *Archives Internationales de Pharmacodymamie et de Therapie*, 1961, **133**, 101–105.

Johnson, L. A. *Amphetamine use in professional football.* Unpublished doctoral dissertation, United States International University, 1972.

Kalant, O. J. *The amphetamines: Toxicity and addiction* (2nd ed.). Toronto: University of Toronto Press, 1973.

Karpovich, P. V. Effect of amphetamine sulfate on athletic performance. *Journal of American Medical Association*, 1959, **170**, 558–561.

Kay, H., & Birren, J. E. Swimming speed of the albino rat. II. Fatigue, practice, and drug effects on age and sex differences. *Journal of Gerontology*, 1958, **13**, 378–285.

Kiplinger, G. F. The effects of drugs on the rate of development of fatigue in mice. *Texas Reports on Biological Medicine*, 1967, **25**, 531–540.

Kleinrok, Z., & Swiezynska, M. The effect on nialamid, pargylin, methylphenidan, amphetamine, carboethoxyphthalazinehydrazine, benzquinamide, and reserpine on the swimming speed of normal and weighted rats. *Acta Physiologica Polonica*, 1966, **17**, 549–556.

Knoefel, P. K. The influence of phenisopropyl amine and phenisopropyl methyl amine on work output. *Federation Proceedings*, 1943, **2**, 83.

Kornetsky, C. Effects of meprobomate, phenobarbital and dextroamphetamine on reaction time and learning in man. *Journal of Pharmacology and Experimental Therapeutics*, 1958, **123**, 216–219.

Kornetsky, C., Mirsky, A. F., Kessler, E. K., & Dorff, J. E. The effects of dextroamphetamine on behavioral deficits produced by sleep loss in humans. *Journal of Pharmacology and Experimental Therapeutics*, 1959, **127**, 46–50.

Laties, V. G., & Weiss, B. Performance enhancement by the amphetamines: A new appraisal. In H. Brill, J. O. Cole, P. Deniker, H. Hippins, & P. B. Bradley (Eds.), *Proceedings Vth International Congress of the Collegium Internationnale Neuropsychopharmacologium*, 1966, 1967, 800–808.

Latz, A., Kornetsky, C., Bain, G., & Goldman, M. Swimming performance of mice as affected by antidepressant drugs and baseline levels. *Psychopharmacologia*, 1966, **10**, 67–88.

Lehmann, G., Straub, H., & Szakáll. A. Pervitan als Leistungssteigernds Mittel. *Arbeitsphysiologie*, 1939, **10**, 680–691.

Lehmann, H. E., & Csank, J. Differential screening of phrentropic agents in man. *Journal of Clinical Psychopathology*, 1957, **18**, 222–235.

Lovingood, B. W., Blyth, C. S., Peacock, W. J., & Lindsay, R. B. Effects of d-amphetamine sulfate, caffeine, and high temperature on human performance. *Research Quarterly*, 1967, **38,** 65–71.

Maickel, R. P., Cox, R. H., Segal, D. S., & Miller, F. P. Studies on psychoactive drugs. I. Physiological disposition and time course of behavioral effects of d-amphetamine in rats. *Federation Proceedings*, 1966, **25,** 385.

Mandell, A. J. *The nightmare season.* New York: Random House, 1976.

Mandell, A. J. The Sunday syndrome: A unique pattern of amphetamine abuse indigenous to American professional football. *Clinical Toxicology*, 1979, **15,** 225–232.

Mantegazza, P., Müller, E. E., Naimzada, M. K., & Riva, M. Studies on the lack of correlation between hyperthermia, hyperactivity and anorexia induced by amphetamine. In E. Costa & S. Garattini (Eds.), *International Symposium on Amphetamines and Related Compounds.* New York: Raven Press, 1970.

Margaria, R., Aghemo, R., & Rovelli, E. The effect of some drugs on the maximal capacity of athletic performance in man. *Internationale Zeitschrift für Angewandte Physiologie Einschliesslich Arbeitsphysiologie*, 1964, **20,** 281–287.

Molinengo, L., & Orsetti, M. Drug action on the "grasping" reflex and on swimming endurance; an attempt to characterize experimentally antidepressant drugs. *Neuropharmacology*, 1976, **15,** 257–260.

Nakamura, Y., & Schwartz, S. The influence of hydrogen ion concentration on calcium binding and release by skeletal muscle sarcoplasmic reticulum. *Journal of General Physiology*, 1972, **59,** 22–32.

Opitz, K. Adipokinetic action of amphetamine—A study in the beagle dog. In E. Costa & S. Garattini (Eds.), *International Symposium on Amphetamines and Related Compounds.* New York: Raven Press, 1970.

Paul, P. FFA metabolism of normal dogs during steady-state exercise at different workloads. *Journal of Applied Physiology*, 1970, **28,** 127–132.

Pfeiffer, C. C., & Symthies, J. R. *Neurobiology* (Vol. 12). New York: Academic Press, 1970.

Pierson, W. R. Amphetamine sulfate and performance. A critique. *Journal of the American Medical Association*, 1961, **177,** 345–347.

Pierson, W. R., Rasch, P. J., & Brubaker, M. L. Some psychological effects of the administration of amphetamine sulfate and meprobamate on speed of movement and reaction time. *Medicina Dello Sports*, 1961, **1,** 61–66.

Pinter, E. J., & Pattee, C. J. Fat-mobilizing action of amphetamine. *Journal of Clinical Investigation*, 1968, **47,** 394–402.

Pirnay, F., Petit, J. M., Dujardin, J., Deroanne, R., Juchmes, J., & Bottin, R. Influence de l-amphetamine sur quelques exercices musculaires effectues par l' individu normal. *Internationale Zeitschrift für Angewandte Physiologie Einschliesslich Arbeitsphysiologie*, 1960, **18,** 280–284.

Quinn, G. P., Cohn, M. M., Reid, M. B., Greengard, P., & Weiner, M. The effect of formulation on phenmetrazine plasma levels in man studied by a sensitive analytic method. *Clinical Pharmacology and Therapeutics*, 1967, **8,** 369–373.

Ray, O. S. *Drugs, society, and human behavior.* St. Louis: C. V. Mosby, 1972.

Rennie, M. J., Winder, W. W., & Holloszy, J. O. A sparing effect of increased plasma fatty acids on muscle and liver glycogen content in the exercising rat. *Biochemistry Journal*, 1976, **156**, 647–655.

Seashore, R. H., & Ivy, A. C. Effects of analeptic drugs in relieving fatigue. *Psychological Monographs*, 1953, **67**, 1–16.

Singh, S. D. Effects of stimulant and depressant drugs on physical performance. *Perceptual and Motor Skills*, 1962, **14**, 270.

Smith, G. M., & Beecher, H. K. Amphetamine sulfate and athletic performance. I. Objective effects. *Journal of the American Medical Association*, 1959, **170**, 542–557.

Smith, G. M., Weitzner, M., & Beecher, H. K. Increased sensitivity of measurement of drug effects in expert swimmers. *Journal of Pharmacology and Experimental Therapeutics*, 1963, **139**, 114–119.

Sommerville, W. The effect of benzedrine on mental and physical fatigue in soldiers. *Canadian Medical Association Journal*, 1946, **55**, 470–476.

Stone, E. A. Swim—stress-induced inactivity: Relation to body temperature and brain norepinephrine, and effects of d-amphetamine. *Psychosomatic Medicine*, 1970, **32**, 51–59.

Thornton, G. R., Holck, H.G.O., & Smith, E. L. The effect of Benzedrine and caffeine upon performance in certain psychomotor tasks. *Journal of Abnormal Social Psychology*, 1939, **34**, 96–113.

Tyler, D. B. The effect of amphetamine sulfate and some barbiturates on the fatigue produced by prolonged wakefulness. *American Journal of Physiology*, 1947, **150**, 253–262.

Uyeda, A. A., & Fuster, J. M. The effects of amphetamine on tachistoscopic performance in the monkey. *Psychopharmacologia*, 1962, **3**, 463–467.

Uyeno, E. T. Hallucinogenic compounds and swimming response. *Journal of Pharmacology and Experimental Therapeutics*, 1968, **159**, 216–221.

Van Rossum, J. Mode of action of psychomotor stimulant drugs. *International Review of Neurobiology*, 1970, **12**, 307–383.

Venerando, A., Gesmundo, F., & Dal Monte, A. Azione dell' amfetamina sul rendimento del lavoro muscolare nell' uomo. I. Osservazioni sul consumo di ossigeno. *Bollenttino Della Societa Italiana Di Biology*, 1966, **42**, 613–616.

Weiss, B., & Laties, V. G. Enhancement of human performance by caffeine and the amphetamines. *Pharmacological Review*, 1962, **14**, 1–36.

Wenzel, D., & Rutledge, C. Effects of centrally acting drugs on human motor and psychomotor performance. *Journal of Pharmaceutical Science*, 1962, **51**, 631–644.

Williams, M. H. *Drugs and athletic performance*. Springfield, IL: C. C. Thomas, 1974.

Williams, M. H., & Thompson, J. Effect of variant dosages of amphetamine upon endurance. *Research Quarterly*, 1973, **44**, 417–422.

Wyndham, C. H., Rogers, G. G., Benade, A.J.S., & Strydom, N. B. Physiological effects of the amphetamines during exercise. *South African Medical Journal*, 1971, **45**, 247–252.

BLOOD DOPING

Amdur, N. Effect of drugs to aid athletes studied by U.S. *The New York Times*, August 22, 1976.

Balke, B., Grillo, G., Konecci, E., & Luft, U. Work capacity after blood donation. *Journal of Applied Physiology*, 1954 **7**, 231–238.

Berne, R., & Levy, M. *Cardiovascular physiology*. St. Louis. C. V. Mosby, 1967.

Blood bankers probe for the answer to oxygen release problem. *Medical Laboratory*, 1972, **8**, 14–15.

Blood doping. *Track and Field News*, November 1971, pp. 2–3.

Buick, F., Gledhill, N., Froese, A., Spriet, L., & Meyers, E. Effect of induced erythrocythemia on aerobic work capacity. *Journal of Applied Physiology*, 1980, **48**, 636–642.

Bunn, H., Forget, B., & Ranney, H. *Human hemoglobin*. Philadelphia: W. B. Saunders, 1977.

Cottrell, R. British Army tests blood doping. *The Physician and Sportsmedicine*, 1979, **7**, 14–16.

Devries, H. A. *Physiology of exercise for physical education and athletics*. Dubuque: W. C. Brown, 1974.

Edington, D., & Edgerton, V. *The biology of physical activity*. Boston: Houghton Mifflin, 1976.

Ekblom, B., Goldbarg, A., & Gullbring, B. Response to exercise after blood loss and reinfusion. *Journal of Applied Physiology*, 1972, **33**, 175–180.

Ekblom, B., Wilson, G., & Astrand, P. O. Central circulation during exercise after venesection and reinfusion of red blood cells. *Journal of Applied Physiology*, 1976, **40**, 379–383.

Fahey, T., & Rolph, R. Venous and capillary blood hematocrit at rest and following submaximal exercise. *European Journal of Applied Physiology*, 1975, **34**, 109–112.

Frye, A., & Ruhling, R. RBC infusion, exercise, hemoconcentration and VO_2. *Medicine and Science in Sports*, 1977, **9**, 69.

Gledhill, N., Spriet, L., Froese, A., Wilkes, D., & Meyers, E. Acid-base status with induced erythrocythemia and its influence on arterial oxygenation during heavy exercise. *Medicine and Science in Sports and Exercise*, 1980, **12**, 122.

Goforth, H., Campbell, N., Hodgdon, J., & Sucec, A. Hematologic parameters of trained distance runners following induced erythrocythemia. *Medicine and Science in Sports and Exercise*, 1982, **14**, 174.

Gregersen, M., & Chien, S. Blood volume, In V. B. Mountcastle (Ed.), *Medical physiology*. St. Louis: C. V. Mosby, 1968.

Gullbring, B., Holmgren, A., Sjostrand, T., & Strandell, T. The effect of blood volume variations on the pulse ratio in supine and upright positions and during exercise. *Acta Physiologica Scandinavica*, 1960, **50**, 62–71.

Guyton, A. *Textbook of medical physiology*. Philadelphia: W. B. Saunders, 1981.

Guyton, A., & Richardson, T. Effect of hematocrit on venous return. *Circulation Research*, 1961, **9**, 157–164.

Horstman, D., Weiskopf, R., Jackson, R., & Severinghaus, J. The influence of polycythemia, induced by 4 weeks sojourn at 4300 M(HA), on sea level (SL) work capacity. In C. Bard, M. Fleury, & E. Waghorn (Eds.), *Abstracts of the International Congress of Physical Activity Sciences*, 1976.

Howald, H. Blut-Doping. *Schweiz Zeitschrift Sportmedizin*, 1975, **23**, 201–203.

Howell, M., & Coupe, K. Effect of blood loss on performance in the Balke-Ware Treadmill Test. *Research Quarterly*, 1964, **35**, 156–165.

Huestis, D., Bove, J., & Busch, S. *Practical blood transfusion*. Boston: Little, Brown, 1976.

Itzchak, Y., Silverberger, A., Modan, M., Adar, R., & Deutsch, V. Hematocrit, viscosity and blood flow velocity in men and women. *Israel Journal of Medical Science*, 1977, **13**, 80–82.

Karpovich, P., & Millman, N. Athletes as blood donors. *Research Quarterly*, 1942, **13**, 166–168.

Klein, H. *Polycythemia*. Springfield, IL: C.C. Thomas, 1973.

Leavell, B., & Thorup, O. *Fundamentals of clinical hematology*. Philadelphia: W. B. Saunders, 1976.

Mollison, P. *Blood transfusion in clinical medicine*. Oxford: Alden and Mowbray, 1972.

Oscai, L., Williams, B., & Hertig, B. Effect of exercise on blood volume. *Journal of Applied Physiology*, 1968, **24**, 622–624.

Pace, N., Lozner, E., Consolazio, W., Pitts, G., & Pecora, L. The increase in hypoxia tolerance of normal men accompanying the polycythemia induced by transfusion of erythrocytes. *American Journal of Physiology*, 1947, **148**, 152–163.

Pate, R., McFarland, J., Van Wyk, J., & Okocha, A. Effects of blood reinfusion on endurance performance in female distance runners. *Medicine and Science in Sports*, 1979, **11**, 97.

Replogle, R., & Merrill, E. Experimental polycythemia and hemodilution: Physiological and rheologic effects. *Journal of Thoracic and Cardiovascular Surgery*, 1970, **60**, 582–588.

Robertson, R., Gilcher, R., Metz, K., Bahnson, H., Allison, T., Skriner, G., Abbott, A., & Becker, R. Effect of red blood cell reinfusion on physical working capacity and perceived exertion at normal and reduced oxygen pressure. *Medicine and Science in Sports*, 1978, **10**, 49.

Robertson, R., Gilcher, R., Metz, K., Casperson, C., Abbott, A., Allison, T., Skriner, G., Werner, K., Zelicoff, S., & Krause, J. Central circulation and work capacity after red blood cell reinfusion under normoxia and hypoxia in women. *Medicine and Science in Sports*, 1979, **11**, 98.

Robinson, B., Epstein, S., Kahler, R., & Braunwald, E. Circulatory effects of acute expansion of blood volume. *Circulation Research*, 1966, **29**, 26–32.

Shephard, R. *Frontiers of Fitness*. Springfield IL: C.C. Thomas, 1971.

Spriet, L., Gledhill, N., Froese, A., Wilkes, D., & Meyers, E. The effect of induced erythrocythemia on central circulation and oxygen transport during maximal exercise. *Medicine and Science in Sports and Exercise*, 1980, **12**, 122–123.

Videman, T., & Rytömaa, T. Effect of blood removal and autotransfusion on heart rate response to a submaximal workload. *Journal of Sports Medicine and Physical Fitness*, 1977, **17**, 387–390.

Von Rost, R., Hollman, W., Liesen, H., & Schulten, D. Uber den Einfluss einer Erthrozyten-Retransfusion auf die Kardio-pulmonale Leistungsfahigkeit. *Sportarzt und Sportmedizin*, 1975, **26**, 137–144.

Weisse, A., Calton, F., Kuida, H., & Hecht, H. Hemodynamic effects of normovolemic polycythemia in dogs at rest and during exercise. *American Journal of Physiology*, 1964, **207**, 1361–1366.

Williams, M., Bocrie, J., Goodwin, A. R., & Perkins, R. Effect of blood reinjection upon endurance capacity and heart rate. *Medicine and Science in Sports*, 1973, **5**, 181–186.

Williams, M., Lindhjem, M., & Schuster, R. The effect of blood infusion upon endurance capacity and ratings of perceived exertion. *Medicine and Science in Sports*, 1978, **10**, 113–118.

Williams, M., & Ward, A. J. Hematological changes elicited by prolonged intermittent aerobic exercise. *Research Quarterly*, 1977, **48**, 606–616.

Williams, M., Wesseldine, S., Somma, T., & Schuster, R. The effect of induced erythrocythemia upon 5-mile treadmill run time. *Medicine and Science in Sports*, 1981, **13**, 169–175.

Williams, W., Beutler, E., Ersley, A., & Rundles, R. *Hematology*. New York: McGraw-Hill, 1972.

OXYGEN

Asmussen, E., & Nielsen, M. The cardiac output in rest and work at low and high oxygen pressure. *Acta Physiologica Scandinavica*, 1946, **35**, 73–83.

Banister, E. W., Taunton, J. E., Patrick, T., Oforsagd, P., & Duncan, W. R. Effect of oxygen at high pressure, at rest and during severe exercise. *Respiration Physiology*, 1970, **10**, 74–84.

Bannister, R. G., & Cunningham, D.J.C. The effects on the respiration and performance during exercise of adding oxygen to the inspired air. *Journal of Physiology*, 1954, **125**, 118–137.

Briggs, H. Physical exertion, fitness, and breathing. *Journal of Physiology*, 1920, **54**, 292–318.

Buskirk, E. R., Kollias, J., Piconreatigue, E., Akers, R., Prokop, E., & Baker, P. Physiology and performance of track athletes at various altitudes in the United States and Peru. In R. Goddard (Ed.), *The effects of altitude on physical performance*. Chicago: The Athletic Institute, 1967.

Cunningham, D. A. Effects of breathing high concentrations of oxygen on treadmill performance. *Research Quarterly*, 1966, **37**, 491–494.

deVries, H. A. *Physiology of exercise*. Dubuque, IA: Wm. C. Brown, 1980.

Douglas, C. E., & Haldane, J. S. The effects of previous forced breathing and oxygen inhalation on the distress caused by muscular work. *Journal of Physiology*, 1909, **39**, 1–4.

Dressendorfer, R. H., Wade, C. E., & Bernauer, E. M. Combined effects of breathing resistance and hyperoxia on aerobic work tolerance. *Journal of Applied Physiology*, 1977, **42**, 444–448.

Ekblom, B., Huot, R., Stein, E. M., & Thorstenson, A. T. Effect of changes in arterial oxygen content on circulation and physical performance. *Journal of Applied Physiology*, 1975, **39**, 71–75.

Elbel, E. R., Ormond, D., & Close, D. Some effects of breathing oxygen before and after exercise. *Journal of Applied Physiology*, 1961, **16**, 48–52.

Fagraeus, L. Cardiorespiratory and metabolic functions during exercise in the hyperbaric environment. *Acta Physiologicia Scandinavica*, 1974, **92**, 1–40. (Supplement 414)

Feldman, I., & Hill, L. The influence of oxygen inhalation on the lactic acid produced during hard work. *Journal of Physiology*, 1911, **42**, 439–443.

Hagerman, F. C., Bowers, R. W., Fox, E. L., & Ersing, W. W. The effects of breathing 100 percent oxygen, during rest, heavy work, and recovery. *Research Quarterly*, 1968, **39**, 965–975.

Hill, A. V., Long, C.N.H., & Lupton, H. Muscular exercise, lactic acid and the supply and utilization of oxygen. *Proceedings of the Royal Society*, 1924, **97**, 155–167.

Hill, L., & Flack, M. The influence of oxygen on athletes. *Journal of Physiology*, 1909, **38**, 28–36.

Hill, L., & Flack, M. The influence of oxygen inhalations on muscular work. *Journal of Physiology*, 1910, **40**, 347–372.

Hill, L., & McKenzie, J. The effect of oxygen inhalation on muscular exertion. *Journal of Physiology*, 1909, **39**, 33–38.

Hughes, R. L., Clode, M., Edwards, R.H.T., Goodwin, T. S., & Jones, N. L. Effect of inspired O_2 on cardiopulmonary and metabolic responses to exercise in man. *Journal of Applied Physiology*, 1968, **24**, 336–347.

Kaijser, L. Physical exercise under hyperbaric oxygen pressure. *Life Sciences*, 1969, **8**, 929–932.

Kaijser, L. Limiting factors for aerobic muscle performance: The influence of varying oxygen pressure and temperature. *Acta Physiologica Scandinavica*, 1970, **79**, 1–96. (Supplement 346)

Kaijser, L. Oxygen supply as a limiting factor in physical performance. In J. Keul (Ed.), *Limiting factors of physical performance*. Stuttgart: Georg Thieme, 1973.

Karpovich, P. V. Effects of oxygen inhalation on swimming performance. *Research Quarterly*, 1934, **5**, 24–28.

Keul, J. (Ed.). *Limiting factors of physical performance*. Stuttgart: Georg Thieme, 1973.

Mathews, D. K., & Fox, E. L. *The physiological basis of physical education and athletics*. Philadelphia: W. B. Saunders, 1976.

McArdle, W. D., Katch, F. I., & Katch, V. L. *Exercise physiology: Energy, nutrition, and human performance*. Philadelphia: Lea & Febiger, 1981.

Miller, A. T., Jr., Perdue, H. L., Teague, E. L., Jr., & Fereber, J. A. Influence of oxygen administration on cardiovascular function during exercise and recovery. *Journal of Applied Physiology*, 1952, **5**, 165–168.

Morris, A. F. Comparing and contrasting two similar sports: Swimming and track. *Journal of Sports Medicine and Physical Fitness*, 1978, **18**, 409–415.

Nielsen, M., & Hansen, O. Maximale Körperliche Arbeit bei Atmung O_2-reicher Luft. *Scandinavia Archives of Physiology*, 1937, **76**, 37–59.

Spirduso, W. W. Physical fitness, aging, and psychomotor speed: A review. *Journal of Gerontology*, 1980, **35**, 850–865.

Stainsby, W. N. Critical oxygen tensions in muscle. In J. Keul (Ed.), *Limiting factors of physical performance*. Stuttgart: George Thieme, 1973.

Taunton, J. E., Banister, E. W., Patrick, T. R., Oforsagd, P., & Duncan, W. R. Physical work capacity in hyperbaric environments and conditions of hyperoxia. *Journal of Applied Physiology*, 1970, **28**, 421–427.

Welch, H. G., Bonde-Petersen, F., Graham, T., Klausen, K., & Secher, N. Effects of hyperoxia on leg blood flow and metabolism during exercise. *Journal of Applied Physiology*, 1977, **42**, 385–390.

Welch, H. G., Mulin, J. P., Wilson, G. D., & Lewis, J. Effects of breathing O_2-enriched gas mixtures on metabolic rate during exercise. *Medicine and Science in Sports*, 1974, **6**, 26–32.

Weltman, A., Katch, V., & Sady, S. Effects of increasing oxygen availability on bicycle ergometer endurance performance. *Ergonomics*, 1978, **21**, 427–432.

Weltman, A. L., Stamford, B. A., Moffatt, R. J., & Katch, V. L. Exercise recovery, lactate removal, and subsequent high intensity exercise performance. *Research Quarterly*, 1977, **48**, 786–796.

Wilmore, J. H. Oxygen. In W. P. Morgan (Ed.), *Ergogenic aids and muscular performance*. New York: Academic Press, 1972.

Wilson, B. A., Welch, H. G., & Liles, J. N. Effects of hyperoxic gas mixtures on energy metabolism during prolonged work. *Journal of Applied Physiology*, 1975, **39**, 267–271.

Wilson, G. D., & Welch, H. G. Effects of hyperoxic gas mixtures on exercise tolerance in man. *Medicine and Science in Sports*, 1975, **7**, 48–52.

Wilson, G. D., & Welch, H. G. Effects of varying concentrations of N_2/O_2 and He/O_2 on exercise tolerance in man. *Medicine and Science in Sports and Exercise*, 1980, **12**, 380–384.

Wyndham, C. H., Strydom, N. B., Van Rensburg, A. J., & Rogers, G. G. Effects on maximal intake of acute changes in altitude in a deep mine. *Journal of Applied Physiology*, 1970, **29**, 552–555.

MUSCLE GLYCOGEN SUPERCOMPENSATION

Ahlborg, B. G., Bergström, J., Brohult, J., Ekelund, L. G., Hultman, E., & Maschio, G. Human muscle glycogen content and capacity for prolonged exercise after different diets. *Foersvarsmedicin*, 1967, **3**, 85–99.

Asmussen, K., Klausen, K., Nielson, L. E., Techow, O.S.A., & Tonder, P. J. Lactate production and anaerobic work capacity after prolonged exercise. *Acta Physiologica Scandinavica*, 1974, **90**, 731–742.

Astrand, P. O., & Rodahl, K. *Textbook of work physiology*. New York: McGraw-Hill, 1977.

Baldwin, K. M., Fitts, R. J., Booth, F. W., Winder, W. W., & Holloszy, J. O. Depletion of muscle and liver glycogen during exercise: Protective effect of training. *Pflugers Archives*, 1975, **354**, 203–212.

Bergström, J. Muscle electrolytes in man: Determined by neutron activation analysis in needle biopsy specimens. A study on normal subjects, kidney patients, and patients with chronic diarrhea. *Scandinavian Journal of Clinical and Laboratory Investigation*, 1962, **14**, (Supplement 68)

Bergström, J., Hermansen, L., Hultman, E., & Saltin, B. Diet, muscle glycogen, and physical performance. *Acta Physiologica Scandinavica*, 1967, **71**, 140–150.

Bergström, J., & Hultman, E. A study of the glycogen metabolism during exercise in man. *Scandinavian Journal of Clinical and Laboratory Investigation*, 1967, pp. 218–228. (a)

Bergström, J., & Hultman, E. Muscle glycogen synthesis after exercise: An enhancing factor localized to the muscle cells in man. *Nature*, 1967, **210**, 309–310. (b)

Bergström, J., Hultman, E., & Roch-Norlund, A. E. Muscle glycogen synthase in normal subjects. Basal values, and effect of glycogen depletion by exercise and of a carbohydrate-rich diet following exercise. *Scandinavian Journal of Clinical and Laboratory Investigation*, 1972, **29**, 231–236.

Blom, P., Vaage, O., Kardel, D., & Hermansen, L. Effect of increasing glucose loads on the rate of muscle glycogen resynthesis after prolonged exercise. *Acta Physiologica Scandinavica*, 1980, **108**, C11. (Abstract)

Borg, G. A. Perceived exertion: A note on history and methods. *Medicine and Science in Sports*, 1973, **5**, 90–93.

Brown, J. H., Thompson, B., & Mayer, S. E. Conversion of skeletal muscle glycogen synthase to multiple glucose-6-phosphate dependent forms by cyclic adenosine monophosphate dependent and independent protein kinases. *Biochemistry*, 1977, **16**, 5501–5508.

Christensen, E. H., & Hansen, O. Respiratorischer Quotient and O_2-Aufnahme. *Scandinavian Archives of Physiology*, 1939, **81**, 180–189.

Cohen, P., Nimmo, H. G., & Proud, C. G. How does insulin stimulate glycogen synthesis? *Biochemical Society Symposia*, 1979, **43**, 69–95.

Costill, D. L., Blom, P., & Hermansen, L. Influence of acute exercise and endurance training on muscle glycogen storage. *Medicine and Science in Sports and Exercise*, 1981, **13**, 90. (Abstract)

Costill, D. L., Coyle, E. F., Dalsky, W., Evans, W., Fink, W. J., & Hooper, D. Effects of elevated plasma FFA and insulin in muscle glycogen usage during exercise. *Journal of Applied Physiology*, 1977, **43**, 695–699.

Costill, D. L., Gollnick, P. D., Jansson, E., Saltin, B., & Stein, B. Glycogen depletion in human muscle fibers during distance running. *Acta Physiologica Scandinavica*, 1973, **89**, 374–383.

Costill, D. L., Jansson, E., Gollnick, P. D., & Saltin, B. Glycogen utilization in leg muscle of men during level and uphill running. *Acta Physiologica Scandinavica*, 1974, **94**, 475–481.

Costill, K. L., Sherman, W. M., Fink, W. J., Maresh, C., Witten, M., & Miller, J. M. The role of dietary carbohydrate in muscle glycogen resynthesis after strenuous running. *American Journal of Clinical Nutrition*, 1981, **34**, 1831–1836.

Cureton, K. G., Sparling, P. B., Evans, B. W., Johnson, S. M., King, O. D., & Purvis, J. W. Effect of experimental alterations in excess weight on aerobic capacity and distance running performance. *Medicine and Science in Sports*, 1978, **10**, 194–199.

Danforth, W. H. Glycogen synthase activation in skeletal muscle. Interconversion of two forms and control of glycogen synthesis. *Journal of Biological Chemistry*, 1965, **240**, 588–593.

Embden, G., & Habs, H. Ueber chemische und biologische Veraenderunger der Muskulator nach oefters wiederholter faradischer Reizung. I. Mitteilung. *Zeitschrift für Physiologische Chemie*, 1927, **171**, 16–39.

Essen, B., & Hendriksson, J. Glycogen content of individual muscle fibers in man. *Acta Physiologica Scandinavica*, 1974, **90**, 645–647.

Essen, B., Pernow, B., Gollnick, P. D., & Saltin, B. Muscle glycogen content and lactate uptake in exercising muscles. In H. Howald & J. R. Poortmans (Eds.), *Metabolic adaptation to prolonged physical exercise*. Basel: Birkhauser Verlag, 1975.

Essig, D., Costill, D. L., & Van Handel, P. J. Effects of caffeine ingestion on utilization of muscle glycogen and lipids during leg ergometer cycling. *International Journal of Sports Medicine*, 1980, **1**, 86–90.

Fell, R. D., McLane, J. A., Winder, W. W., & Holloszy, J. O. Preferential resynthesis of muscle glycogen in fasting rats after exhausting exercise. *American Journal of Physiology*, 1980, **238**, 328–332.

Fitts, R. J., Kim, D. H., & Witzmann, F. A. The development of fatigue during high intensity and endurance exercise. In F. J. Nagle & H. J. Montoye (Eds.), Madison: University of Wisconsin Press, 1979.

Galbo, H., Holst, H. H., & Christensen, N. J. The effect of different diets and insulin on the hormonal response to prolonged exercise. *Acta Physiologica Scandinavica*, 1980, **107**, 19–32.

Gollnick, P. D., Pernow, B., Essen, B., Jansson, E., & Saltin, B. Availability of glycogen and plasma FFA for substrate utilization in leg muscle of man during exercise. *Clinical Physiology*, 1980, **1**, 1–22.

Gollnick, P. D., Piehl, K., Saubert, C. W., Armstrong, R. B., & Saltin, B. Diet, exercise, and glycogen changes in human muscle fibers. *Journal of Applied Physiology*, 1972, **33**, 421–425.

Gorski, J., Palka, P., Puch, P., & Kiczka, K. The post-exercise glycogen recovery in tissues of trained rats. *Acta Physiologica Polonica*, 1976, **27**, 47–53.

Hermansen, L., Hultman, E., & Saltin, B. Muscle glycogen during prolonged severe exercise. *Acta Physiologica Scandinavica*, 1967, **71**, 129–139.

Hodges, R. E., & Krehl, W. A. The role of carbohydrates in lipid metabolism. *American Journal of Clinical Nutrition*, 1965, **17**, 334–346.

Holloszy, J. O., & Booth, F. A. Biochemical adaptations to endurance exercise. *Annual Review of Physiology*, 1976, **18**, 273, 291.

Hultman, E. Studies on muscle metabolism of glycogen and active phosphate in man with special reference to exercise and diet. *Scandinavian Journal of Clinical and Laboratory Investigation*, 1967, **19**. (Supplement 94)

Hultman, E., Bergström, J., & Roch-Norlund, A. E. Glycogen storage in human skeletal muscle. *Advances in Experimental Medicine and Biology*, 1971, **11**, 273–288.

Hultman, E., & Nilsson, L. H. Liver glycogen in man. Effect of different diets and muscular exercise. *Advances in Experimental Medicine and Biology*, 1971, **11**, 143–154.

International Journal of Sports Medicine, 1982, **3**, 22–24.

Jacobs, I. Lactate, muscle glycogen and exercise performance in man. *Acta Physiologica Scandinavica*, 1981. (Supplement 495)

Jansson, E. Diet and muscle metabolism in man with special reference to fat and carbohydrate utilization and its regulation. *Acta Physiologica Scandinavica*, 1980. (Supplement 487)

Karlsson, J., & Saltin, B. Diet, muscle glycogen and endurance performance. *Journal of Applied Physiology*, 1971, **31**, 203–206.

Kelman, G. R., Maughan, R. J., & Williams, C. The effect of dietary modifications on blood lactate during exercise. *Journal of Physiology*, 1975, **251**, 34–35P.

Keul, J., Doll, E., & Keppler, D. *Energy metabolism of human muscle.* Baltimore: University Park Press, 1972.

Klausen, K., Piehl, K., & Saltin, B. Muscle glycogen stores and capacity for anaerobic work. In H. Howald & J. R. Poortmans (Eds.), *Metabolic adaptation to prolonged physical exercise.* Basel: Birkhauser Verlag, 1975.

Klausen, K., & Sjogaard, G. Glycogen stores and lactate accumulation in skeletal muscle of man during intense bicycle exercise. *Scandinavian Journal of Sports Sciences*, 1980, **2**, 7–12.

Kochan, R. G. *Glycogen synthase control of skeletal muscle glycogen resynthesis following exercise in humans.* Unpublished doctoral dissertation, University of Toledo, 1978.

Kochan, R. G., Lamb, D. R., Lutz, S. A., Perrill, C. V., Reimann, E. M., & Schlender, K. K. Glycogen synthase activation in human skeletal muscle: Effect of diet and exercise. *American Journal of Physiology*, 1979, **236**, E660–666.

Maehlum, S., Felig, P., & Wahren, J. Splanchnic glucose and muscle glycogen metabolism after glucose feeding during postexercise recovery. *American Journal of Physiology*, 1978, **235**, E255–260.

Maehlum, S., & Hermansen, L. Muscle glycogen concentration during recovery after prolonged severe exercise in fasting subjects. *Scandinavian Journal of Clinical and Laboratory Investigation*, 1978, **38**, 557–560.

Maehlum, S. Hostmark, A. T., & Hermansen, L. Synthesis of muscle glycogen during recovery after prolonged severe exercise in diabetic subjects. Effect of insulin deprivation. *Scandinavian Journal of Clinical and Laboratory Investigation*, 1978, **37**, 309–316.

Newsholme, E. A., & Crabtree, B. Theoretical approaches to control of metabolic pathways and their application to glycolysis in muscle. *Journal of Molecular Cellular Cardiology*, 1979, **11**, 839–856.

Newsholme, E. A., & Start, C. *Regulation in metabolism.* New York: John Wiley & Sons, 1973.

Olsson, K. E., & Saltin, B. Variations in total body water with muscle glycogen changes in man. *Biochemistry of Exercise, Medicine and Sports*, 1969, **5**, 159–162.

Olsson, K. E., & Saltin, B. Variations in total body water with muscle glycogen changes in man. *Acta Physiologica Scandinavica*, 1970, **80**, 11–18.

Pernow, B., & Saltin, B. Availability of substrates and capacity for prolonged heavy exercise. *Journal of Applied Physiology*, 1971, **31**, 416–422.

Piehl, K., Adolfsson, S., & Nazar, K. Glycogen storage and glycogen synthase activity in trained and untrained muscle of man. *Acta Physiologica Scandinavica*, 1974, **90**, 779–788.

Piehl, K., & Karlsson, J. Glycogen synthase and phosphorylase activity in slow and fast-twitch skeletal muscle fibers in man. *Acta Physiologica Scandinavica*, 1977, **100**, 210–214.

Plyley, M. J., Costill, D. L., & Fink, W. J. Influence of glycogen "bound" water on temperature regulation during exercise. *Canadian Journal of Applied Sport Sciences*, 1980, **5**, 5. (Abstract)

Saltin, B., & Hermansen, L. Glycogen stores and prolonged severe exercise. In G. Blix (Ed.), *Nutrition and physical activity*. Uppsala, Sweden: Almqvist & Wiksells, 1967.

Saltin, B., & Karlsson, J. Muscle glycogen utilization during work of different intensities. *Advances in Experimental Medicine and Biology*, 1971, **11**, 289–299.

Sherman, W. M. *Dietary manipulation to induce muscle glycogen supercompensation: Effect on endurance performance*. Unpublished master's thesis, Ball State University, 1980.

Sherman, W. M., Costill, D. L., Fink, W. J., & Miller, J. M. The effect of exercise and diet manipulation on muscle glycogen and its subsequent utilization during performance. *International Journal of Sports Medicine*, 1981, **2**, 114–118.

Sherman, W. M., Plyley, M. J., Sharp, R. L., Van Handel, P. J., McAllister, R. M., Fink, W. J., & Costill, D. L. Muscle glycogen storage and its relationship with water.

Yakovlev, N. N. The effect of regular muscle activity on enzymes of glycogen, and glucose-6-phosphate in muscles and liver. *Biochemistry*, 1968, **33**, 602–607.

SPORTS PSYCHOLOGY

Ammons, R. B. Effects of prepractice activities on rotary pursuit performance. *Journal of Experimental Psychology*, 1951, **41**, 187–191.

Atkinson, R. C., & Wickens, T. D. Human memory and the concept of reinforcement. In R. Glaser (Ed.), *The nature of reinforcement*. New York: Academy Press, 1971.

Barber, T., & Hahn, K. Experimental studies in "hypnotic behavior": Physiological and subjective effects of imagined pain. *Journal of Nervous & Mental Disease*, 1964, **139**, 416–425.

Bauer, R. M., & Craighead, W. E. Psychophysiological responses to the imagination of fearful and neutral situations: The effects of imagery instructions. *Behavior Therapy*, 1979, **10**, 389–403.

Bower, G. H. Mental imagery and associative learning. In L. Gregg (Ed.), *Cognition & learning in memory*. New York: Wiley, 1972.

Cautela, J. R. Covert conditioning: Assumptions and procedures. *Journal of Mental Imagery*, 1977, **1**, 53–64.

Clark, L. V. Effect of mental practice on the development of a certain motor skill. *Research Quarterly*, 1960, **31**, 560–569.

Corbin, C. B. The effects of covert rehearsal on the development of a complex motor skill. *Journal of General Psychology*, 1967, **76**, 143–150.

Corbin, C. B. Mental practice. In W. P. Morgan (Ed.), *Ergogenic aids & muscular performance*. New York: Academic Press, 1972.

Craig, K. Physiological arousal as a function of imagined, vicarious, and direct stress experiences. *Journal of Abnormal Psychology*, 1968, **73**, 513–520.

Desiderato, O., & Miller, I. B. Improving tennis performance by cognitive behavior modification techniques. *Behavior Therapist*, 1979, **2**, 19.

Dewitt, D. J. Cognitive and biofeedback training for stress reduction with university athletes. *Journal of Sport Psychology*. 1980, **2**, 288–294.

Epstein, M. L. The relationship of mental imagery and mental rehearsal to performance of a motor task. *Journal of Sport Psychology*, 1980, **2**, 211–220.

Gilmore, R. W., & Stolurow, L. M. Motor and "mental" practice of ball and socket task. *American Psychologist*, 1951, **6**, 295.

Girodo, M., & Wood, D. Talking yourself out of pain: The importance of believing that you can. *Cognitive Therapy & Research*, 1978, **3**, 23–34.

Highlen, P. S., & Bennett, B. B. Psychological characteristics of successful and nonsuccessful elite wrestlers: An exploratory study. *Journal of Sport Psychology*, 1979, **1**, 123–137.

Homme, L. E. Perspectives in psychology: XXIV. Control of coverants, the operants of the mind. *Psychological Record*, 1965, **15**, 501–511.

Jacobson, E. Electrical measurements of neuromuscular states during mental activities. *American Journal of Physiology*, 1930, **95**, 694–712.

James, W. *Principles of psychology*, (Vol. 1). New York: Holt, 1890.(a)

James, W. *Principles of psychology*, (Vol. 2). New York: Holt, 1890.(b)

Jones, J. G. Motor learning without demonstration of physical practice, under two conditions of mental practice. *Research Quarterly*, 1965, **36**, 270–276.

Kelsey, I. B. Effects of mental practice and physical practice upon muscular endurance. *Research Quarterly*, 1961, **32**, 47–54.

Lane, J. F. Improving athletic performance through visuo-motor behavior rehearsal. In R. M. Suinn (Ed.), *Psychology in sports: Methods & applications*. Minneapolis: Burgess, 1980.

Lang, P. J. A bio-informational theory of emotional imagery. *Psychophysiology*, 1979, **16**, 495–511.

Mahoney, M. J. *Cognitive & behavior modification*. Cambridge, MA: Ballinger, 1974.

Mahoney, M. J., & Avner, M. Psychology of the elite athlete: An exploratory study. *Cognitive Therapy & Research*, 1977, **1**, 135–141.

Mahoney, M. J., Thorensen, C. E., & Danaher, B. G. Covert behavior modification: An experimental analogue. *Journal of Behavior Therapy & Experimental Psychiatry*, 1972, **3**, 7–14.

Martiniuk, R. G. *Information processing in motor skills*. New York: Holt, Rinehart & Winston, 1976.

Meichenbaum, D. *Cognitive behavior modification: An integrative approach*. New York: Plenum, 1977.

Meichenbaum, D. Why does using imagery in psychotherapy lead to change? In J. L. Singer & K. S. Pope (Eds.), *The power of human imagination:*

New methods in psychotherapy. New York: Plenum, 1978.

Meichenbaum, D., & Cameron, R. The clinical potential of modifying what clients say to themselves. *Psychotherapy: Theory, Research & Practice,* 1974, **11,** 103–117.

Meichenbaum, D., & Goodman, J. The developmental control of operant motor responding by verbal operants. *Journal of Experimental Child Psychology,* 1969, **7,** 553–565.

Meyers, A., & Schleser, R. A cognitive behavioral intervention for improving basketball performance. *Journal of Sport Psychology,* 1980, **2,** 69–73.

Meyers, A., Schleser, R., Cooke, C. J., & Cuvillier, C. Cognitive contributions to the development of gymnastics skills. *Cognitive Therapy & Research,* 1979, **3,** 75–85.

Miller, N. E. *The influence of past experience upon transfer of subsequent training.* Unpublished doctoral dissertation, Yale University, 1935.

Ness, R. G., & Patton, R. W. The effects of beliefs on maximum weightlifting performance. *Cognitive Therapy & Research,* 1979, **3,** 205–212.

Noel, R. C. The effect of visuo-motor behavior rehearsal on tennis performance. *Journal of Sport Psychology,* 1980, **2,** 221–226.

Richardson, A. Mental practice: A review and discussion: Part I. *Research Quarterly,* 1967, **38,** 95–107.(a)

Richardson, A. Mental practice: A review and discussion: Part II. *Research Quarterly,* 1967, **38,** 263–273.(b)

Ryan, E. D., & Simons, J. Cognitive demand, imagery, and frequency of mental rehearsal as factors influencing acquisition of motor skills. *Journal of Sport Psychology,* 1981, **3,** 35–45.

Shick. J. Effects of mental practice on selected volleyball skills for college women. *Research Quarterly,* 1970, **41,** 88–94.

Silva, J. M. Performance enhancement in competitive sport environments through cognitive intervention. *Behavior Modification,* 1982, **6,** 443–463.

Singer, R. N. *Motor learning & human performance.* New York: Macmillan, 1971.

Skinner, B. F. *Science & human behavior.* New York: Macmillan, 1953.

Smyth, M. M. The role of mental practice in skill acquisition. *Journal of Motor Behavior,* 1975, **7,** 199–206.

Suinn, R. M. Behavior rehearsal training for ski racers. *Behavior Therapy,* 1972, **3,** 519–520.

Suinn, R. M. Body thinking: Psychology of Olympic champs. *Psychology Today,* 1976, **10,** 38–43.

Surburg, P. R. Audio, visual, and audio-visual instruction with mental practice in developing the forehand tennis drive. *Research Quarterly,* 1968, **39,** 728–734.

Titley, R. W. The loneliness of a long-distance kicker. *The Athletic Journal,* 1976, **57,** 74–80.

Twining, W. E. Mental practice and physical practice in the learning of a motor skill. *Research Quarterly,* 1949, **20,** 432–435.

Ulich, E. Some experiments on the function of mental training in the acquisition of motor skills. *Ergonomics,* 1967, **10,** 411–419.

Vandell, R. A., Davis, R. A., & Clungston, A. The function of mental practice in the acquisition of motor skill. *Journal of General Psychology*, 1943, **29**, 243–250.

Washburn, M. F. *Movement & mental imagery*. Boston: Houghton, 1916.

Watson, L. *Supernature*. New York: Doubleday, 1973.

Weinberg, R. S., Seabourne, T. G., & Jackson, H. Effect of visuomotor behavior rehearsal, relaxation and imagery on karate performance. *Journal of Sport Psychology*, 1981, **3**, 228–238.

White, K. D., Ashton, R., & Lewis, S. Learning a complex skill: Effects of mental practice, physical practice, and imagery ability. *International Journal of Sport Psychology*, 1979, **10**, 71–78.

Wolpe, J. *Psychotherapy by reciprocal inhibition*. Palo Alto, CA: Stanford University Press, 1958.

GENERAL PSYCHOLOGY

Angyal, A. *Neurosis and treatment: A holistic approach*. New York: John Wiley and Sons, 1965.

Bry, A. *Visualization*. New York: Barnes and Noble, 1978.

Ellis, A. *Humanistic psychotherapy: The rationale-emotive approach*. New York: Julian Press, 1973.

Gendlin, E. T. *Focusing*. New York: Everest House, 1978.

Herrigel, E. *Zen in the art of archery*. New York: Pantheon, 1953.

Hill, N. *The law of success*. Chicago: Success Unlimited, 1979.

Inge, W. An interview with William Inge. *Time*, December 16, 1957, **70**, 57–58.

Jacobson, E. Electrophysiology of mental activities. *American Journal of Psychology*, 1932, **44**, 677–694.

Jampolsky, G. G. *Love is letting go of fear*. Millbrae, CA: Celestial Arts, 1979.

Krause, D. R. *Peak Performance: Mental game plans for maximizing your athletic potential*. Englewood Cliffs, NJ: Prentice-Hall, 1980.

Korwin, L. *You can be good at sports*. Chicago: Sports Training Institute, 1980.

Leonard, G. *The ultimate athlete*. New York: Viking Press, 1975.

———. *The silent pulse*. New York: Dutton, 1978.

Libbey, B. O. J. New York: Putnam, 1974.

Lichtenberger, A. Faith and fear. *Anglican Digest*, Spring, 1962, **16**, 12–18.

Maltz, M. *Psychocybernetics*. New York: Pocket Books, 1969.

Maslow, A. H. *Toward a psychology of being*. New York: Van Nostrand, 1968.

———. *The farther reaches of human nature*. New York: Viking Press, 1971.

McCluggage, D. *The centered skier*. New York: Warner, 1977.

Morehouse, L. E., & Gross, L. *Maximum performance*. New York: Simon and Schuster, 1977.

Murphy, M., & White, R. *The psychic side of sports*. Reading, MA: Addison-Wesley, 1978.

Nicklaus, J. *Golf my way*. New York: Simon and Schuster, 1974.

Nideffer, R. M. *The inner athlete*. New York: Crowell, 1976.

Oxendine, J. B. Emotional arousal and motor performance. *Quest*, 1970, **13**, 23–30.

Richardson, A. Mental practice: A review and discussion. *Research Quarterly*, 1967, **38**, 95–107, 267–273.

Samuels, M., & Bennett, H. Z. *Be well*. New York: Random House/Bodyworks, 1974.

Samuels, M., & Samuels, N. *Seeing with the mind's eye*. New York: Random House/Bodyworks, 1975.

Shaw, W. A. The relationship of muscular action potentials to imaginal weight lifting. *Archives of Psychology*, 1940, **35**, 1–50.

Shealy, C. N. *90 days to self-health*. New York: Bantam Books, 1976.

Simonton, O. C., Matthews-Simonton, S., & Creighton, J. *Getting well again*. Los Angeles: J. T. Tarcher, 1978.

Singer, R. N. *Myths and truths in sports psychology*. New York: Harper and Row, 1975.

Vanek, M., & Cratty, B. J. *Psychology and the superior athlete*. London: Macmillan, 1979.

General Sport Psychology

Alderman, R. B. *Psychological behavior in sport*. Philadelphia: W. B. Saunders, 1974.

Bannister, R. *The four-minute mile*. New York: Dodd and Mead, 1955.

Beisser, A. R. (1967). *The madness in sports*. New York: Appleton-Century-Crofts, 1967.

Butt, D. S. *Psychology of sport*. New York: Van Nostrand Reinhold, 1976.

Cratty, B. J. *Psychology and physical activity*. Englewood Cliffs, NJ: Prentice-Hall, 1973.

———. *Psychology in contemporary sport*. Englewood Cliffs, NJ: Prentice-Hall, 1973.

Dickinson, J. *A behavioral analysis of sport*. Princeton, NJ: Princeton Book Company, 1976.

Fisher, A. C. *Psychology of sport: Issues and insights*. Palo Alto, CA: Mayfield, 1976.

Gallwey, W. T. *The inner game of tennis*. New York: Random House, 1974.

———. *Inner tennis*. New York: Random House, 1976.

———. *Inner golf*. New York: Random House, 1979.

Gallwey, W. T., & Kriegal, B. *Inner skiing*. New York: Random House, 1977.

Garfield, C. A. Mental skills for physical perfection. *Muscle and Fitness*, 1981, **42**, 47–49, 169, 172, 189, 190.

Glasser, W. *Positive addiction*. New York: Harper and Row, 1976.

Griffith, C. R. *Psychology and athletics*. Champaign, IL: University of Illinois Press, 1924.

Harman, B., with Monroe, K. *Use your head in tennis*. Port Washington, NY: Kennikat Press, 1950.

Harris, D. V. *Involvement in sport*. Philadelphia: Lea and Febiger, 1973.

Hendricks, G., & Carlson, J. *The centered athlete*. Englewood Cliffs, NJ: Prentice-Hall, 1982.

Jacklin, T. *Jacklin*. New York: Simon and Schuster, 1970.

Jerome, J. *The sweet spot in time*. New York: Avon, 1982.

Kostrubala, T. *The joy of running*. Philadelphia: Lippincott, 1976.

Llewellyn, L. H., & Blucker, J. A. *Psychology of coaching: Theory and application*. Minneapolis, MN: Burgess, 1982.

Luszki, W. A. *Psych yourself to better tennis*. Hollywood, CA: Creative Sports Books, 1971.

Morgan, W. P. (Ed.) *Contemporary issues in sport psychology*. Springfield, IL: Charles C. Thomas, 1970.

———. The mind of the marathoner. *Psychology Today*, 1978, **11**, 38–49.

———. The pain merchants. *Runner's World*, 1978, **13**, 64–69.

Murphy, M. *Jacob Atabet*. New York: Bantam, 1979.

Nideffer, R. M. *The ethics and practice of applied sport psychology*. Ann Arbor, MI: McNaughton Gunn, 1981.

Nieporte, T., & Sauers, D. *Mind over golf*. Garden City, NY: Doubleday, 1968.

Orlick, T. *Winning through cooperation*. Washington, D.C.: Acropolis, 1978.

———. *In pursuit of excellence*. Champaign, IL: Human Kinetics, 1984.

Reich, L. Try not to think about it. *Runner's World*, 1974, **9**, 17.

Rohé, R. *The zen of running*. New York: Random House/Bodyworks, 1974.

Rotella, R. J., & Bunker, L. K. *Mind mastery for winning golf*. Englewood Cliffs, NJ: Prentice-Hall, 1986.

Ryan, F. *Sports and psychology*. Englewood Cliffs, NJ: Prentice-Hall, 1981.

Schaap, D. *The perfect jump*. New York: New American Library, 1976.

Schwand, W. C. (Ed.) *The winning edge*. Washington, DC: AAHPER Publications, 1973.

Sheehan, G. *Dr. Sheehan on running*. Mountain View, CA: World Publications, 1975.

Silltoe, A. *The loneliness of the long-distance runner*. London: Pan Books, 1961.

Silva, J. M. III, & Weinberg, R. S. (Eds.) *Psychological foundations of sport*. Champaign, IL: Human Kinetics, 1984.

Simek, T. C., & O'Brien, R. M. *Total golf: A behavioral approach to lowering your score and getting more out of your game*. Garden City, NY: Doubleday, 1981.

Singer, R. N. *Coaching, athletics, and psychology*. New York: McGraw-Hill, 1972.

Spino, M. *Beyond jogging*. Millbrae, CA: Celestial Arts, 1976.

———. *Running Home*. Millbrae, CA: Celestial Arts, 1977.

Straub, W. F. (Ed.) *Sport psychology: An analysis of athlete behavior*. Ithaca, NY: Mouvement Publications, 1980.

Suinn, R. M. Body thinking: Psychology for Olympic champs. *Psychology Today*, 1976, **10**, 38–41.

Swartz, D., with Wayne, R. How to mentally prepare for better performances. *Runner's World*, 1979, **14**, 90, 93, 95.

Thomas, V. *Science and sport*. Boston: Little, Brown, 1970.

Tilden, B. *Match play and the spin of the ball*. Port Washington, NY: Kennikat, 1969.

Tutko, T., & Burns, W. *Winning is everything and other American myths*. New York: Macmillan, 1976.

Tutko, T., & Tossi, U. *Sports psyching*. Los Angeles: J. T. Tarcher, 1976.

Ullyot, J. *Women's running*. Mountain View, CA: World Publications, 1976.

Vanek, M., & Cratty, B. J. *Psychology and the superior athlete*. London: Macmillan, 1979.

Weber, D., & Alexander, R. *Weber on bowling*. Englewood Cliffs, NJ: Prentice-Hall, 1981.

General Performance Psychology

Garfield, C. A., & Bennett, H. Z. *Peak performance*. Los Angeles, CA: J. T. Tarcher, 1984.

Kriegel, R., & Harris Kriegel, M. *The C zone*. Garden City, NY: Anchor Press/Doubleday, 1984.

Kubistant, T. M. The psychology of peaking. *Muscle & Fitness*, 1984, **45**, 111, 211, 213, 214, 216, 219.

Peters, T. J., & Waterman, R. H., Jr. *In search of excellence*. New York: Harper and Row, 1982.

Smith, A. *Powers of the mind*. New York: Random House, 1975.

Thorenson, C. E., & Mahoney, M. J. (Eds.) *Self-control: Power to the person*. Monterey, CA: Brooks/Cole, 1974.

Vincent, L. M. *Competing with the sylph*. Kansas City: Andrews and McMeel, 1979.

Waitley, D. *The winner's edge*. New York: Berkley Books, 1980.

Positive Mental Attitude and Motivation

Hammond, D. J. *The fine art of doing better*. Phoenix, AZ: American Motivational Association, 1974.

Hill, N., & Stone, W. C. *Success through a positive mental attitude*. New York: Pocket Books, 1960.

Murphy, M. *Golf in the kingdom*. New York: Viking, 1972.

Peale, N. V. *The power of positive thinking*. Englewood Cliffs, NJ: Prentice-Hall, 1952.

Schwarzenegger, A., & Hull, D. K. *Arnold: The education of a bodybuilder*. New York: Simon and Schuster, 1977.

Sheehan, G. *Running and being: The total experience*. New York: Simon and Schuster, 1978.

Ziglar, Z. *See you at the top*. Gretna, LA: Pelican, 1983.

Relaxation and Visualization

Kubistant, T. M. Mental imagery and performance. *Imagery*, 1980, **3**, 4–5.

————. The uses of visualization in sportsmedicine. *Sportsmedicine Digest*, 1982, **4**, 6.

Richardson, A. *Mental imagery*. London: Rutledge and Kegan Paul, 1969.

Schultz, J., & Luthe, W. *Autogenic training*. New York: Grane and Stratton, 1959.

Suinn, R. M. *Psychology in sports*: Method and Application. Minneapolis, MN: Burgess, 1980.

Whiel, A. *Creative visualization*. New York: Greenwich Books, 1958.

White, J., & Fadiman, J. (Eds.) *Relax*. New York: Confucian Press, 1976.

Related Psychological Foundations

Adams, J. L. *Conceptual blockbusting*. New York: W. W. Norton, 1974.

Assagioli, R. *Psychosynthesis*. New York: Viking, 1965.

————. *The act of will*. Baltimore: Penguin Books, 1973.

Bosking-Lodahl, M., & Sirlin, M. The gorging purging syndrome. *Psychology Today*, 1977, **10**, 50–55.

Eisen, J., with Farley, P. *Powertalk!* New York: Cornerstone, 1984.

Huizinga, J. *Homo ludens*. Boston: Beacon Press, 1950.

James, W. *The principles of psychology*, volume 2. New York: Dove, 1890.

————. *The varieties of religious experience*. New York: Modern Library, 1902.

Kubistant, T. M. Bulimarexia. *Journal of College Student Personnel*, 1982, **23**, 333–339.

Spielberger, C. D. (Ed.) *Anxiety and behavior*. New York: Academic Press, 1966.

Basic Exercise Physiology

Bailey, C. *Fit or fat?* Boston: Houghton Mifflin, 1977.

Brody, J. *Jane Brody's nutrition book*. Toronto: Bantam, 1981.

Darden, E. *High-intensity bodybuilding.* New York: Perigee, 1984.

Hayden, N. *Everything you've always wanted to know about energy . . . but were too weak to ask.* New York: Pocket Books, 1977.

Samuels, M., & Bennett, H. Z. *The well body book.* New York: Random House/Bodyworks, 1973.

Schwartz, L. S. *Heavyhands.* Boston: Little, Brown, and Company, 1982.

Weider, J. *Bodybuilding: The Weider approach.* Chicago: Contemporary Books, 1981.

STRESS MANAGEMENT

Anderson, N. Algebraic models in perception. In E. C. Carterett & M. P. Friedman (Eds.), *Handbook of perception* (Vol.2). New York: Academic Press, 1974.

Anderson, N. Cognitive algebra. In L. Berkowitz (Ed.), *Advances in experimental social psychology* (Vol. 7). New York: Academic Press, 1974.

Anderson, N., & Shanteau, J. Weak inference with linear models. *Psychological Bulletin,* 1977, **84,** 1155–1170.

Antal, L. C., & Good, C. S. The effects of oxprenolol on pistol shooting under stress. In R. W. Elsdon-Dew, C.A.S. Wink, & G.F.B. Birdwood (Eds.), *The cardiovascular, metabolic, and psychological interface.* London: Royal Society of Medicine and Academic Press, 1979.

Astrand, P. O., & Rodahl, K. *Textbook of work physiology: Physiological bases of exercise* (2nd ed.). New York: McGraw-Hill, 1977.

Balog, L. The effects of exercise on muscle tension and subsequent muscle relaxation training. *Research Quarterly for Exercise and Sport,* in press.

Bandura, A. Self-efficacy: Toward a unifying theory of behavioral change. *Psychological Review,* 1977, **84,** 191–215.

Bard, C., & Fluery, M. Analysis of visual search activity during sport problem situations. *Journal of Human Movement Studies,* 1976, **3,** 214–222.

Beck, A. T. Cognitive therapy: Nature and relation to behavior therapy. *Behavior Therapy,* 1970, **1,** 184–200.

Bennett, B., & Stothart, C. The effects of a relaxation based cognitive technique on sport performances. In P. Klavora and K.A.W. Wipper (Eds.), *Psychological and sociological factors and sport.* Toronto: University of Toronto Press, 1980.

Benson, H. *The relaxation response.* New York: William Morrow, 1975.

Blais, M. *EMG biofeedback for control over precompetitive anxiety within a laboratory controlled environment.* Unpublished master's thesis, University of Ottawa, 1978.

Blanchard, E., & Epstein, L. The clinical usefulness of biofeedback. In M. Hersen, R. Eisler, & P. Miller, *Progress in behavior modification* (Vol. 4). New York: Academic Press, 1977.

Borg, G. Subjective aspects of physical and mental load. *Ergonomics,* 1978, **21,** 215–220.

Borkovec, T. D. Physiological and cognitive processes in the regulation of anxiety. In G. E. Schwartz & D. Shapiro (Eds.), *Consciousness and self-regulation: Advances in research.* New York: Plenum, 1976.

Bramwell, S., Masuda, M., Wagner, N., & Holmes, T. Psychosocial factors in athletic injuries: Development and application of the social and athletic readjustment rating scale (SARRS). *Journal of Human Stress*, 1975, 1, 6–20.

Caudill, D., Weinberg, R., Gould, D., & Jackson, A. The effects of the length of the psych-up interval on strength and endurance performance. *Psychology of Motor Behavior and Sport–1981* (Abstracts), NASPSA. Davis, CA: University of California, May 1981, p. 78.

Chance, J. P. The effects of thought stopping and covert assertion on performance of nine through eighteen year old swimmers (Doctoral dissertation, Mississippi State University, 1980). *Dissertation Abstracts International*, 1980, 41,(4-A), 3199.

Cliff, N. Scaling. *Annual Review of Pyschology*, 1973, 24, 473–506.

Daniels, F. S., & Landers, D. M. Biofeedback and shooting performance: A test of disregulation and systems theory. *Journal of Sports Psychology*, 1981, 4, 271–282.

Danish, S., & Hale, B. Toward an understanding of the practice of sport psychology. *Journal of Sport Psychology*, 1981, 3, 90–99.

Davidson, R. J. Specificity and patterning in biobehavioral systems: Implications for behavior change. *American Psychologist*, 1978, 33, 431–436.

Decaria, M. D. The effect of cognition rehearsal training on performance and on self-report of anxiety in novice and intermediate female gymnasts (Doctoral dissertation, University of Utah, 1977). *Dissertation Abstracts International*, 1977, 38,(1-B), 351.

Desiderato, O., & Miller, I. Improving tennis performance by cognitive behavior modification techniques. *The Behavior Therapist*, 1979, 2, 19.

deVries, H. A. Immediate and long term effects of exercise upon resting muscle action potential. *Journal of Sports Medicine*, 1968, 8, 1–11.

deVries, H. A., Wiswell, R., Bulbulian, R., & Moritani, T. Tranquilizer effect of exercise. *American Journal of Physical Medicine*, 1981, 60, 57–66.

De Witt, D. Cognitive and biofeedback training for stress reduction with university athletes. *Journal of Sport Psychology*, 1980, 2, 288–294.

Dishman, R. K. Contemporary sport psychology. In R. Terjung (Ed.), *Exercise and sport sciences reviews* (Vol. 10). Philadelphia: Franklin Institute Press, 1982.

Dorsey, J. A. The effects of biofeedback-assisted desensitization training on state anxiety and performance of college age male gymnasts (Doctoral dissertation, Boston University, 1976). *Dissertation Abstracts International*, 1977, 37(9-A), 5680.

Duffy, E. Activation. In H. Greenfield & R. Sternbach (Eds.), *Handbook of psychophysiology*. New York: Holt, Rinehart and Winston, 1972.

Durlak, J. A. Comparative effectiveness of paraprofessional and professional helpers. *Psychological Bulletin*, 1979, 86, 80–92.

Ekman, G., & Sjoberg, L. Scaling. *Annual Review of Psychology*, 1965, 16, 451–474.

Ellis, A. *Reason and emotion in psychotherapy*. New York: Stuart, 1962.

Etzel, E. F., Jr. Validation of a conceptual model characterizing attention among international rifle shooters. *Journal of Sport Psychology*, 1979, 1, 281–290.

Eysenck, H. F. *The biological basis of personality*. Springfield, IL: Charles C. Thomas, 1967.

Farmer, P., Olewine, D., Comer, D., Edwards, M., Coleman, T., Thomas, G., & Hames, C. Frontalis muscle tension and occipital alpha production in young males with coronary prone (type A) and coronary resistant (type B) behavior patterns: Effects of exercise. *Medicine and Science in Sports*, 1978, **10**, 51.

Farrell, P., Cates, W., Maksud, M., Morgan, W. P., & Tseng, L. Plasma beta-endorphin/beta lipotropin immunoreactivity increases after treadmill exercise in man. *Medicine and Science in Sports and Exercise*, 1981, **13**, 134.

Feltz, D. L., Landers, D. M., & Raeder, U. Enhancing self-efficacy in high-avoidance motor tasks: A comparison of modeling techniques. *Journal of Sport Psychology*, 1979, **1**, 112–122.

Fenz, W. D., & Epstein, S. Changes in gradients of skin conductance, heart rate and respiration rate as a function of experience. *Psychosomatic Medicine*, 1967, **29**, 33–51.

Fisher, A. C. Thurstonian scaling: Application to sport psychology research. *Journal of Sport Psychology*, 1980, **2**, 155–160.

Frankenhauser, M. Behavior and circulating catecholamines. *Brain Research*, 1971, **31**, 241–262.

French, S. N. Electromyographic biofeedback for tension control during fine and gross motor skill acquisition (Doctoral dissertation, Oregon State University, 1977). *Dissertation Abstracts International*, 1977, **37**(9-A), 5681.

Genov, F. Peculiarity of the maximum motor speed of the sportsman when in mobilized readiness. In G. S. Kenyon (Ed.), *Contemporary psychology of sport*. Chicago: The Athletic Institute, 1970.

Gerson, R., & Deshaies, P. Competitive trait anxiety and performance as predictors of pre-competitive state anxiety. *International Journal of Sport Psychology*, 1978, **9**, 16–26.

Gould, D., Weinberg, R., & Jackson, A. Mental preparation strategies, cognitions and strength performance. *Journal of Sport Psychology*, 1980, **2**, 329–339.

Gould, D., & Weiss, M. The effects of model similarity and model talk on self-efficacy and muscular endurance. *Journal of Sport Psychology*, 1981, **3**, 17–29.

Gravel, R., Lemieux, G., & Ladouceur, R. Effectiveness of a cognitive behavioral treatment package for cross-country ski-racers. *Cognitive Therapy and Research*, 1980, **4**, 83–89.

Griffiths, T. J., Steele, D. J., Vaccaro, P., & Karpman, M. B. The effects of relaxation techniques on anxiety and underwater performance. *International Journal of Sport Psychology*, 1981, **12**, 176–182.

Grossberg, J., & Grant, B. Clinical psychophysics: Applications of ratio scaling and signal detection methods to research on pain, fear, drugs and medical decision making. *Psychological Bulletin*, 1978, **85**, 1154–1176.

Gutmann, M., Squires, R., Pollock, M., Foster, C., & Anholm, J. Perceived exertion-heart rate relationship during exercise testing and training in cardiac patients. *Journal of Cardiac Rehabilitation*, 1981, **1**, 52–59.

Hamm, H. Competitive anxiety: Assessment and prescriptions. In T. Orlick, J. Partington, & J. Salmela (Eds.), *Mental training for coaches and athletes*. Ottawa, Canada: The Coaching Association of Canada, 1982.

Hanin, Y. (Ed.) *Stress and anxiety in sport*. Moscow: Physical Culture and Sport Publishers, 1981.

Harrison, R., & Feltz, D. The professionalization of sport psychology: Legal considerations. *Journal of Sport Psychology*, 1979, **1**, 182–190.

Highlen, P. S., & Bennett, B. B. Psychological characteristics of successful and nonsuccessful elite wrestlers: An exploratory study. *Journal of Sport Psychology*, 1979, **1**, 123–137.

Horton, A., & Shelton, J. The rational wrestler: A pilot study. *Perceptual and Motor Skills*, 1978, **46**, 882.

Ikai, M., & Steinhaus, A. Some factors modifying the expression of human strength. *Journal of Applied Physiology*, 1961, **16**, 157–161.

Ismail, A. H., & El-Naggar, A. M. Effect of exercise on multivariate relationships among selected psychophysiological variables in adult men. In J. Partington, T. Orlick, & J. Salmela (Eds.), *Sport in perspective*. Ottawa, Canada: The Coaching Association of Canada, 1982.

Jacobson, E. *Progressive relaxation*. Chicago: University of Chicago Press, 1938.

Jaremko, M. A component analysis of stress inoculation: Review and prospectus. *Cognitive Therapy and Research*, 1979, **3**, 35–48.

Kauss, D. An investigation of psychological states related to the psychoemotional readying procedures of competitive athletes. *International Journal of Sport Psychology*, 1978, **9**, 134–145.

Kazdin, A. *Research design in clinical psychology*. New York: Harper and Row, 1980.

Kendall, P. C., & Hollon, S. O. (Eds.) *Cognitive-behavioral interventions: Theory, research and procedures*. New York: Academic Press, 1979.

Kirschenbaum, D., & Bale, R. Cognitive-behavioral skills in golf: Brain power golf. In R. Suinn (Ed.), *Psychology in sports: Methods and applications*. Minneapolis: Burgess, 1980.

Klavora, P. Customary arousal for peak athletic performance. In P. Klavora & J. Daniels (Eds.), *Coach, athlete and the sport psychologist*. Champaign, IL: Human Kinetics, 1979.

Klavora, P., & Daniel, J. (Eds.) *Coach, athlete and the sport psychologist*, Champaign, IL: Human Kinetics, 1979.

Kolonay, B. *The effects of visuo-motor behavior rehearsal on athletic performance*. Unpublished master's thesis, Hunter College, The City University of New York, 1977.

Kroll, W. Competitive athletic stress factors in athletes and coaches. In W. Sime & L. Zaichkowsky (Eds.), *Stress management in sport*. Reston, VA: AAHPERD Publications, 1982.

Kukla, K. J. The effects of progressive relaxation training upon athletic performance during stress (Doctoral dissertation, Florida State University, 1976). *Dissertation Abstracts International*, 1977, **37**(12-B), 6392.

Lacey, J., & Lacey, B. Verification and extension of the principle of autonomic response-stereotypy. *American Journal of Psychology*, 1958, **71**, 50–73.

Landers, D. M. The arousal-performance relationship revisited. *Research Quarterly for Exercise and Sport*, 1980, **51**, 77–90.

Landers, D. M. Reflections on sport psychology and the Olympic athlete. In J.

Seagrave & D. Chu (Eds.), *Olympism*. Champaign, IL: Human Kinetics, 1981.

Landers, D., Furst, D., & Daniels, F. Anxiety/attention and shooting ability: Testing the predictive validity of the Test of Attentional and Interpersonal Style (TAIS). *Psychology of Motor Behavior and Sport—1981* (Abstracts), NASPSA. Davis, CA: University of California, 1981.

Langer, P. Varsity football performance. *Perceptual and Motor Skills*, 1966, **23**, 1191–1199.

Layman, E. M. Meditation and sports performance. In W. F. Straub (Ed.), *Sport psychology*. Ithaca, NY: Mouvement, 1978.

Lewis, S. A comparison of behavior-therapy techniques in the reduction of fearful avoidance behavior. *Behavior Therapy*, 1974, **5**, 648–655.

Mahoney, M. J. Cognitive skills and athletic performance. In P. C. Kendall & S. D. Hollon (Eds.), *Cognitive-behavioral interventions: Theory, research and procedures*. New York: Academic Press, 1979.

Mahoney, M. J., & Avener, M. Psychology of the elite athlete: An exploratory study. *Cognitive Therapy and Research*, 1977, **1**, 135–141.

Martens, R. Trait and state anxiety. In W. P. Morgan (Ed.), *Ergogenic aids and muscular performance*. New York: Academic Press, 1972.

Martens, R. Arousal and motor performance. In J. H. Wilmore (Ed.), *Exercise and sport science reviews* (Vol. 2). New York: Academic Press, 1974.

Martens, R. *Sport Competition Anxiety Test*. Champaign, IL: Human Kinetics, 1977.

Martens, R. How sport psychology can help Olympians. In J. Seagrave & D. Chu (Eds.), *Olympism*. Champaign, IL: Human Kinetics, 1981.

McGeer, P. L., & McGeer, E. G. Chemistry of mood and emotion. *Annual Review of Psychology*, 1980, **31**, 273–307.

Meichenbaum, D. H. *Cognitive-behavior modification*. New York: Plenum, 1977.

Messick, S. Constructs and their vicissitudes in educational and psychological measurement. *Psychological Bulletin*, 1981, **89**, 575–588.

Meyers, A. W., Cooke, C., Cullen, J., & Liles, L. Psychological aspects of athletic competitors: A replication across sports. *Cognitive Therapy and Research*, 1979, **3**, 361–366.

Meyers, A. W., & Schleser, R. A cognitive behavioral intervention for improving basketball performance. *Journal of Sport Psychology*, 1980, **2**, 69–73.

Meyers, A. W., Schleser, R., Cooke, C., & Cuvillier, C. Cognitive contributions to the development of gymnastic skills. *Cognitive Therapy and Research*, 1979, **3**, 75–85.

Meyers, A. W., Schleser, R., & Okwumabua, T. A cognitive behavioral intervention for improving basketball performance. *Research Quarterly for Exercise and Sport*, 1982, **53**, 344–347.

Miller, N. Biofeedback and visceral learning. *Annual Review of Psychology*, 1978, **29**, 373–404.

Morgan, W. P. Pre-match anxiety in a group of college wrestlers. *International Journal of Sport Psychology*, 1970, **1**, 7–13.

Morgan, W. P. Basic considerations. In W. P. Morgan (Ed.), *Ergogenic aids and muscular performance*. New York: Academic Press, 1972.

Morgan, W. P. Prediction of performance in athletics. In P. Klavora & J. V. Daniel (Eds.), *Coach, athlete and the sport psychologist.* Champaign, IL: Human Kinetics, 1979.

Morgan, W. P. Trait psychology controversy. *Research Quarterly for Exercise and Sport,*1980, **51**, 50–76.

Morgan, W. P. Psychological benefits of physical activity. In F. J. Nagle & H. J. Montoye (Eds.), *Exercise in health and disease.* Springfield, IL: Charles C. Thomas, 1981.

Morgan, W. P. Psychophysiology of self-awareness during vigorous physical activity. *Research Quarterly for Exercise and Sport,* 1981, **52**, 315–340.

Morgan, W. P., & Horstman, E. H. Psychometric correlates of pain perception. *Perceptual and Motor Skills,* 1978, **47**, 27–39.

Morgan, W. P., Horstman, D. H., Cymerman, A., & Stokes, J. Facilitation of endurance performance by means of a cognitive strategy. *Cognitive therapy and research,* in press.

Morgan, W. P., & Pollock, M. L. Psychologic characterization of the elite distance runner. *Annals of the New York Academy of Sciences,* 1977, **301**, 382–403.

Nelson, J. Investigation of effects of hypnosis, relaxation, and mental rehearsal on performance scores of golfers and runners (Doctoral dissertation, Louisiana State University and Agricultural and Mechanical College). *Dissertation Abstracts International,* 1980, **41**(4-B), 1484.

Nideffer, R. M. Test of attentional and interpersonal style. *Journal of Personality and Social Psychology,* 1976, **34**, 394–404.

Nideffer, R. M. *The ethics and practice of applied sport psychology.* Ithaca, NY: Mouvement, 1981.

Nideffer, R., Dufresne, P., Nesvig, D., & Selder, D. The future of applied sport psychology. *Journal of Sport Psychology,* 1980, **2**, 170–174.

Noel, R. C. The effect of visuo-motor behavioral rehearsal on tennis performance. *Journal of Sport Psychology,* 1980, **2**, 221–226.

Nunnally, J. *Psychometric theory,* New York: McGraw-Hill, 1978.

Orne, M., & Paskewitz, D. Aversive situational effects on alpha feed-back training. *Science,* 1974, **186**, 458–460.

Peele, S. Reductionism in the psychology of the eighties: Can biochemistry eliminate addiction, mental illness and pain? *American Psychologist,* 1981, **36**, 807–818.

Pinel, J., & Schultz, T. Effect of antecedent muscle tension levels on motor behavior, *Medicine and Science in Sports,* 1978, **10**, 177–182.

Pollock, M., Jackson, A. J., & Pate, R. Discriminant analysis of physiological differences between good and elite distance runners. *Research Quarterly for Exercise and Sport,* 1980, **51**, 521–532.

Richards, E. D., & Landers, D. M. Test of attentional and interpersonal style scores of shooters. In G. C. Roberts & D. M. Landers (Eds.), *Psychology of motor behavior and sport—1980.* Champaign, IL: Human Kinetics, 1981.

Rushall, B. S. Applied behavior analysis for sports and physical education. *International Journal of Sport Psychology,* 1975, **6**, 75–88.

Ryan, E. D., & Foster, R. Athletic participation and perceptual augmentation and reduction. *Journal of Personality and Social Psychology,* 1967, **6**, 472–476.

Ryan, E. D., & Kovacic, C. R. Pain tolerance and athletic participation. *Perceptual and Motor Skills*, 1966, **22**, 383–390.

Scanlan, T. K., & Passer, M. W. Factors influencing the competitive performance expectancies of young female athletes. *Journal of Sport Psychology*, 1979, **1**, 212–220.

Schultz, J. H., & Luthe, W. *Autogenic training: A psychophysiological approach in psychotherapy.* New York: Grune and Stratton, 1959.

Schwartz, G. E., Davidson, R. J., & Goleman, D. Patterning of cognitive and somatic processes in the self-regulation of anxiety: Effects of meditation versus exercise. *Psychosomatic Medicine*, 1978, **40**, 321–328.

Selye, H. *The stress of life*, New York: McGraw-Hill, 1976.

Shelton, T. O., & Mahoney, M. J. The content and effect of "psyching-up" strategies in weight lifters. *Cognitive Therapy and Research*, 1978, **2**, 275–284.

Silva, J. M. Behavioral and situational factors affecting concentration. *Journal of Sport Psychology*, 1979, **1**, 221–227.

Sime, W. E. A comparison of exercise and meditation in reducing physiological response to stress. *Medicine and Science in Sports*, 1977, **9**, 55.

Sime, W., & Zaichkowsky, L. (Eds.) *Stress management in sport.* Reston, VA: AAHPERD Publications, 1982.

Sjoberg, L., Svensson, E., & Persson, L. O. The measurement of mood. *Scandinavian Journal of Psychology*, 1979, **20**, 1–18.

Smith, R. E. A cognitive-affective approach to stress management training for athletes. In C. Nadeau, W. Halliwell, K. Newell, & G. C. Roberts (Eds.), *Psychology of Motor Behavior and Sport—1979.* Champaign, IL: Human Kinetics, 1980.

Stevens, S. S. *Psychophysics.* New York: Wiley & Sons, 1975.

Suinn, R. Behavior rehearsal training for ski racers. *Behavior Therapy*, 1972, **3**, 519–520.

Suinn, R. Stress management for elite athletes. In Y. Hanin (Ed.), *Stress and anxiety in sport.* Moscow: Physical Culture and Sport Publishers, 1981.

Suinn, R. Imagery and sports. In A. Sheikh (Ed.), *Imagery: Current theory, research and application.* New York: Wiley and Sons, 1982.

Suinn, R., & Deffenbacher, J. The behavioral approach. In I. Kutash & L. Schlesinger (Eds.), *Handbook on stress and anxiety: Contemporary knowledge, theory and treatment.* San Francisco: Jossey-Bass, 1980.

Tarter-Benlolo, L. The role of relaxation in biofeedback training: A critical review of literature. *Psychological Bulletin*, 1978, **85**, 727–755.

Teague, M. L. A combined systematic desensitization and electromyographic biofeedback technique for controlling state anxiety and improving gross motor skill performance (Doctoral dissertation, University of Northern Colorado, 1976). *Dissertation Abstracts International*, 1977, **37-04**, 2062-A.

Titley, R. The loneliness of a long distance kicker. *The Athletic Journal*, 1976, **57**, 74–80.

Tsukamoto, S. *The effects of EMG biofeedback-assisted relaxation as a self-control strategy for sport competition anxiety.* Unpublished master's thesis, University of Western Ontario, London, Ontario, 1979.

Vanek, M., & Cratty, B. J. *Psychology and the superior athlete.* New York: Macmillan, 1970.

Van Schoyck, S., & Grasha, A. F. Attentional style variations and athletic ability: The advantages of a sports-specific test. *Journal of Sport Psychology*, 1981, **3**, 149–165.

Weinberg, R. S. The effects of success and failure on the patterning of neuromuscular energy. *Journal of Motor Behavior*, 1978, **10**, 53–61.

Weinberg, R. S., & Genuchi, M. Relationship between competitive trait anxiety, state anxiety and golf performance: A field study. *Journal of Sport Psychology*, 1980, **2**, 148–154.

Weinberg, R. S., Gould, D., & Jackson, A. W. Expectations and performance: An empirical test of Bandura's self-efficacy theory. *Journal of Sport Psychology*, 1979, **1**, 320–331.

Weinberg, R. S., Gould, D., & Jackson, A. W. Cognition and motor performance: Effect of psyching-up strategies on three motor tasks. *Cognitive Therapy and Research*, 1980, **4**, 239–246.

Weinberg, R. S., Gould, D., & Jackson, A. W. Relationship between the duration of the psych-up interval and strength performance. *Journal of Sport Psychology*, 1981, **3**, 166–170.

Weinberg, R. S., & Ragan, J. Motor performance under three levels of trait anxiety and stress. *Journal of Motor Behavior*, 1978, **10**, 169–176.

Weinberg, R. S., Seabourne, T., & Jackson, A. W. Effects of visuo-motor behavior rehearsal, relaxation and imagery on karate performance. *Journal of Sport Psychology*, 1981, **3**, 228–238.

Weinberg, R. S., Yukelson, D., & Jackson, A. W. Effect of public and private efficacy expectations on competitive performance. *Journal of Sport Psychology*, 1980, **2**, 340–349.

Weingarten, P. Leistungsverhalten jugendlicher Sportler (unter Berucksichtigung der Ergopsychometrie). Wien: Forschungsauftrag des BMFUK, 1980.

Wolpe, J. *Psychotherapy for reciprocal inhibition*. Stanford: Stanford University Press, 1958.

Wolpe, J. The dichotomy between classical conditioned and cognitively learned anxiety. *Journal of Behavior Therapy and Experimental Psychiatry*, 1981, **12**, 35–42.

Zaichkowsky, L. Biofeedback for self-regulation of stress. In W. Sime & L. Zaichkowsky (Eds.), *Stress management in sport*. Reston, VA: AAHPERD Publications, 1982.

Zaichkowsky, L., Jackson, C., & Aronson, R. Attentional and interpersonal factors as predictors of elite athletic performance. In T. Orlick, J. Partington, & J. Salmela (Eds.), *Mental training for coaches and athletes*. Ottawa, Canada: The Coaching Association of Canada, 1982.

Zajonc, R. Feeling and thinking: Preferences need no inferences. *American Psychologist*, 1980, **35**, 151–175.

HYPNOSIS

Agosti, E., & Camerota, G. Some effects of hypnotic suggestion on respiratory function. *The International Journal of Clinical and Experimental Hypnosis*, 1965, **13**, 149–156.

Albert, I., & Williams, M. H. Effects of post-hypnotic suggestions on muscular endurance. *Perceptual and Motor Skills*, 1975, **40**, 131–139.

Arnold, J. Effects of hypnosis on the learning of two selected motor skills. *Research Quarterly*, 1971, **42**, 1.

Barber, T. X. The effects of hypnosis and suggestions on strength and endurance: A critical review of research studies. *British Journal of Social and Clinical Psychology*, 1966, **5**, 42–50.

Barber, T. X., & Calverley, D. S. Toward a theory of "hypnotic" behavior: Enhancement of strength and endurance. *Canadian Journal of Psychology*, 1964, **18**, 156–167.

Berman, R., Simonson, E., & Heron, W. Electrocardiographic effects associated with hypnotic suggestion in normal and coronary sclerotic individuals. *Journal of Applied Physiology*, 1954, **7**, 89.

Bevegård, S., Arvidsson, T., Åstrom, H., & Jonsson, B. Circulation effects of suggested muscular work under hypnotic state. *Proceedings of the International Union of Physiology*, 1968, **7**, 42.

Bier, W. [Contributions to the influence of psychic processes on the circulation.] *Zeitschrift fuer klinsche Medizin*, 1930, **113**, 762. (*Psychological Abstracts*, 1932, **6**, No. 4737.)

Blum, G. S., & Wohl, B. M. Monetary, affective, and intrinsic incentives in choice reaction time. *Psychonomic Science*, 1971, **22**, 69.

Borg, G.A.V. Perceived exertion: A note on "history" and methods. *Medicine and Sciences in Sports*, 1973, **5**, 90–93.

Burrows, G., & Dennerstein (Eds.) *Handbook of hypnosis and psychosomatic medicine*. Amsterdam: Elsevier/North Holland Biomedical Press, 1980.

Charcot, J. M. [*Lectures on diseases of nervous system.*] (T. Savill, trans.) London: New Syclenham Society, 1889.

Cobb, L. A., Ripley, H. S., & Jones, J. W. Role of the nervous system in free fatty acid mobilization as demonstrated by hypnosis. In M. J. Karvonen & A. J. Barry (Eds.), *Physical activity and the heart*. Springfield, IL: Charles C. Thomas, 1967.

Coyle, E. F., Feiring, D. C., Rotkis, T. C., Cote, R. W., Roby, F. B., Lee, W., & Wilmore, J. H. The specificity of power improvements through slow and fast isokinetic training. *Journal of Applied Physiology*, in press.

Crane, C. W. *Psychology applied*. Evanston, IL: Northwestern University Press, 1940.

Dudley, D. L., Holmes, T. H., Martin, C. J., & Ripley, H. S. Changes in respiration associated with hypnotically induced emotion, pain, and exercise. *Psychosomatic Medicine*, 1964, **26**, 46–57.

Edmonston, W. E., & Marks, H. E. The effects of hypnosis and motivational instructions on kinesthetic learning. *The American Journal of Clinical Hypnosis*, 1967, **9**, 252–255.

Evans, F. J., & Orne, M. T. Motivation, performance, and hypnosis. *The International Journal of Clinical and Experimental Hypnosis*, 1965, **13**, 103–116.

Eysenck, H. J. An experimental study of the improvement of mental and physical functions in the hypnotic state. *British Journal of Medical Psychology*, 1941, **18**, 304–316.

Fulde, E. [The influence of hypnotic states of excitation on gas exchange.]

Zeitschrift für die gesamte Neurologie und Psychiatrie, 1937, **159**, 761–766. (Psychological Abstracts, 1939, **13**, No. 3646.)

Garver, R. B. The enhancement of human performance with hypnosis through neuromotor facilitation and control of arousal level. American Journal of Clinical Hypnosis, 1977, **19**, 177–181.

Gorton, B. E. Physiologic aspects of hypnosis. In J. M. Schneck (Ed.), Hypnosis in modern medicine. Springfield, IL: Charles C. Thomas, 1959.

Graham, C., Olsen, R. A., Parrish, M., & Leibowitz, H. W. The effect of hypnotically induced fatigue on reaction time. Psychosomatic Science, 1968, **10**, 223–224.

Hadfield, J. A. The psychology of power. New York: Macmillan, 1924.

Ham, M. W., & Edmonston, W. E. Hypnosis, relaxation and motor retardation. Journal of Abnormal Psychology, 1971, **77**, 329–331.

Hanin, Y. L. A study of anxiety in sports. In W. F. Straub (Ed.), Sport psychology: An analysis of athlete behavior. Ithaca, NY: Mouvement Publications, 1978.

Hilgard, E. R. More about forensic hypnosis. American Psychological Association Division 30 Newsletter, April 1979.

Hilgard, E. R., & Boucher, R. G. Hypnosis research memorandum 59. Palo Alto, CA: Stanford University, Department of Psychology, 1967.

Hilgard, E. R., & Hilgard, J. R. Hypnosis in the relief of pain. Los Altos, CA: William Kaufmann, 1975.

Hull, C. L. Hypnosis and suggestibility: An experimental approach. New York: Appleton-Century-Crofts, 1933.

Hyvärinen, J., Komi, P. V., & Puhakka, P. Endurance of muscle contraction under hypnosis. Acta Physiologica Scandinavica, 1977, **100**, 485–487.

Ikai, M., & Steinhaus, A. H. Some factors modifying the expression of human strength. Journal of Applied Psychology, 1961, **16**, 157–163.

Ito, M. A mechanism of acquired anxiety and its effects on choice reaction time. Japanese Journal of Physical Education, 1978, **22**, 331–342.

Ito, M. The differential effects of hypnosis and motivational suggestions on muscular strength. Japanese Journal of Physical Education, 1979, **24**, 93–100.

Jackson, J. A., Gass, G. C., & Camp, E. M. The relationship between posthypnotic suggestion and endurance in physically trained subjects. The International Journal of Clinical and Experimental Hypnosis, 1979, **27**, 278–293.

Johnson, W. R. Body movement awareness in the non-hypnotic and hypnotic states. Research Quarterly, 1961, **32**, 263–264. (a)

Johnson, W. R. Hypnosis and muscular performance. Journal of Sports Medicine and Physical Fitness, 1961, **1**, 71–79. (b)

Johnson, W. R. The problem of aggression and guilt in sports, in F. A. Antonelli (Ed.), Proceedings, First International Congress of Sport Psychology, 1965.

Johnson, W. R., & Kramer, G. F. Effects of different types of hypnotic suggestions upon physical performance. Research Quarterly, 1960, **31**, 469–473.

Johnson, W. R. & Kramer, G. F. Effects of stereotyped nonhypnotic, hypnotic and posthypnotic suggestions upon strength, power, and endurance. Research Quarterly, 1961, **32**, 522–529.

Johnson, W. R., Massey, B. H., & Kramer, G. F. Effect of posthypnotic suggestions on all-out effort of short duration. *Research Quarterly*, 1960, **31**, 142–146.

Kosunen, K. J., Kuoppasalmi, K., Näveri, H., Rehunen, S., Närvänen, S., & Adlercreutz, H. Plasma renin activity, angiotensin II, and aldosterone during the hypnotic suggestion of running. *Scandinavian Journal of Clinical Laboratory Investigations*, 1977, **37**, 99–103.

Landers, D. M. Motivation and performance: The role of arousal and attentional factors. In W. F. Straub (Ed.), *Sport psychology: An analysis of athlete behavior*. Ithaca, NY: Mouvement Publications, 1978.

Langer, P. Varsity football performance. *Perceptual and Motor Skills*, 1966, **23**, 1191–1199.

Levin, S. L., & Egolinsky, I. A. [The effect of cortical functions upon energy changes in basal metabolism.] *Fiziologicheskii Zhurnal S.S.S.R.*, 1936, **20**, 979–992. (*Psychological Abstracts*, 1939, **13**, No. 4128.)

Levitt, E. E. President's message. *American Psychological Association Division 30 Newsletter*, August 1981.

Levitt, E. E., & Brady, J. P. Muscular endurance under hypnosis and in the motivated waking state. *The International Journal of Clinical and Experimental Hypnosis*, 1964, **12**, 21–27.

London, P., & Fuhrer, M. Hypnosis, motivation and performance. *Journal of Personality*, 1961, **29**, 321–333.

Manzer, C. W. The effect of verbal suggestions on output and variability of muscular work. *Psychological Clinic*, 1934, **22**, 248–256.

Marshall, G. D. Heart rate responses in real and hallucinated exercise. *Hypnosis research memorandum 113*. Palo Alto, CA: Stanford University, Department of Psychology, 1970.

Massey, B. H., Johnson, W. R., & Kramer, G. R. Effect of warm-up exercise upon muscular performance using hypnosis to control the psychological variable. *Research Quarterly*, 1961, **32**, 63–71.

Mead, S., & Roush, E. S. A study of the effect of hypnotic suggestion on physiologic performance. *Archives of Physical Medicine*, 1949, **30**, 700–704.

Mierke, K. [Directional and motivational forces in the execution of tasks.] *Zeitschrift für experimentelle und angewandte Psychologie*, 1954, **2**, 92–135. (*Psychological Abstracts*, 1956, **30**, No. 4044.)

Milvy, P. (Ed.) The marathon: Physiological, medical, epidemiological and psychological studies. *Annals of the New York Academy of Science*, 1977, **301**, 1-1090.

Moikin, Y. V., & Poberezhskaya, A. S. Mechanism of work refusal through fatigue reflected in electromyographic changes under hypnosis. *Bulletin of Experimental and Biological Medicine*, 1976, **80**, 862–864.

Moll, A. [Hypnotism] (A. F. Hopkirk, trans.). New York: Scribners, 1913.

Morgan, W. P. Oxygen uptake following hypnotic suggestion. In G. S. Kenyon (Ed.), *Contemporary psychology of sport*. Chicago: Athletic Institute, 1970.

Morgan, W. P. Hypnosis and muscular performance. In W. P. Morgan (Ed.), *Ergogenic aids and muscular performance*. New York: Academic Press, 1972.

Morgan, W. P. Hypnosis and sports medicine. In G. Burrows & L. D. Dennerstein (Eds.), *Handbook of hypnosis and psychosomatic medicine*. Amsterdam: Elsevier/North Holland Biomedical Press, 1980.

Morgan, W. P. The 1980 C. H. McCloy research lecture: Psychophysiology of self-awareness during vigorous physical activity. *Research Quarterly for Exercise and Sport*, 1981, **52**, 358–427.

Morgan, W. P., Hirota, K., Weitz, G. A., & Balke, B. Hypnotic perturbation of perceived exertion: Ventilatory consequences. *American Journal of Clinical Hypnosis*, 1976, **18**, 182–190.

Morgan, W. P., & Pollock, M. L. Psychologic characterization of the elite distance runner. In P. Milvy (Ed.), *Annals of the New York Academy of Science*, 1977, **301**, 382–403.

Morgan, W. P., Raven, P. B., Drinkwater, B. L., & Horvath, S. M. Perceptual and metabolic responsivity to standard bicycle ergometry following various hypnotic suggestions. *International Journal of Clinical and Experimental Hypnosis*, 1973, **31**, 86–101.

Naruse, G. The hypnotic treatment of stage fright in champion athletes. *International Journal of Clinical and Experimental Hypnosis*, 1965, **13**, 63–70.

Nemtzova, O. L., & Shatenstein, D. I. [The effect of the central nervous system upon some physiological processes during work.] *Fiziologicheskii Zhurnal S.S.S.R.*, 1936, **20**, 581–593. (*Psychological Abstracts*, 1939, **13**, No. 4129.)

Nevski, I., & Sryashchich, K. [Influence of hypnosis on muscular strength.] *Novoe V. Refleksologii fiziologii neronolsistemy*, 1929, **3**, 458–480. (*Psychological Abstracts*, 1930, **4**, No. 4290.)

Nicholson, N. C. Notes on muscular work during hypnosis. *Johns Hopkins Hospital Bulletin*, 1920, **31**, 89–91.

O'Leary, K. D., & Borkovec, T. D. Conceptual, methodological, and ethical problems of placebo groups in psychotherapy research. *American Psychologist*, September 1978, 821–830.

Orne, M. T. The nature of hypnosis: Artifact and essence. *Journal of Abnormal Psychology*, 1959, **58**, 277–299.

Pomeranz, D. M., & Krasner, L. Effect of a placebo on simple motor response. *Perceptual and Motor Skills*, 1969, **28**, 15–18.

Reitter, P. J. The influence of hypnosis on somatic fields of function. In L. M. LeCron (Ed.), *Experimental hypnosis*. New York: Macmillan, 1958.

Rosen, H. Hypnosis and drug abuse in sports. In T. T. Craig (Ed.), *The humanistic and mental health aspects of sports, exercise and research*. Chicago: American Medical Association, 1976.

Rosenhan, D., & London, P. Hypnosis: Expectation, susceptibility, and performance. *Journal of Abnormal Social Psychology*, 1963, **66**, 77–81.

Roush, E. S. Strength and endurance in the waking and hypnotic states. *Journal of Applied Physiology*, 1951, **3**, 404–410.

Ryde, D. A personal study of some uses of hypnosis in sports and sports injuries. *Journal of Sports Medicine and Physical Fitness*, 1964, **4**, 241–246.

Simonson, E. [Experiments on the physiology of foot racing.] *Travail humain*, 1937, **5**, 286–305. (*Psychological Abstracts*, 1938, **12**, No. 243.)

Slater, C. Expectancy and hypnotic performance. (Doctoral dissertation, Washington State University, 1967.) *Dissertation Abstracts International*, 1967, **28**, 2632B. (University Microfilms No. 67-15, 763.)

Slotnick, R., & London, P. Influence of instructions on hypnotic and nonhypnotic performance. *Journal of Abnormal Psychology*, 1965, **70**, 38–46.

Slotnick, R. S., Liebert, R. M., & Hilgard, E. R. The enhancement of muscular performance in hypnosis through exhortation and involving instructions. *Journal of Personality*, 1965, **33**, 36–45.

Smith, J. L., & Bozymowski, M. F. Effect of attitude toward warm-ups on motor performance. *Research Quarterly*, 1965, **36**, 78–85.

Unestähl, L. New paths of sport learning and excellence. *Proceedings of the Fifth World Sport Psychology Congress*, 1981.

Wallace, B., & Hoyenga, K. B. Performance of fine motor coordination activities with an hypnotically anesthesized limb. *The International Journal of Clinical and Experimental Hypnosis*, 1981, **29**, 54–65.

Weitzenhoffer, A. M. *Hypnotism: An objective study in suggestibility*. New York: John Wiley and Sons, 1963.

Wells, F. L. Reaction time and allied measures under hypnosis: Report of a case. *Journal of Abnormal and Social Psychology*, 1928, **24**, 264–275.

Whitehorn, J. C., Lundholm, H., & Gardner, G. E. The metabolic rate in emotional moods induced by suggestion in hypnosis. *American Journal of Psychiatry*, 1930, **9**, 661.

Williams, G. W. The effect of hypnosis on muscular fatigue. *Journal of Abnormal and Social Psychology*, 1929, **24**, 318–329.

Williams, G. W. A comparative study of voluntary and hypnotic catalepsy. *American Journal of Psychology*, 1930, **42**, 83–95.

Young, P. C. An experimental study of mental and physical functions in the normal and hypnotic states. *American Journal of Psychology*, 1925, **36**, 214–232.

■

INDEX

■

Acetylcholine, 118
Acid-citrate-dextrose (ACD), 63
Acne, anabolic steroids and, 407
Acromegaly as side effect of excess HGH, 52–53
Adrostenedione, 367
Adults, ACSM guidelines for exercising, 307–316
Aerobic dance-exercise, 275
Aerobic energy, 122, 124–129
  anabolic steroids' effect on, 350
Aerobics
  carbohydrate loading and, 4
  high-impact, x
Aerobic training devices, 173–182
  cross-country skiing, 179–180
  other devices, 180–182
  treadmills, 173–178
Aging
  cortisol and, 27–28
  death-hormone theory of, 25
  DHEA and, 26–27
  DNA repair theory and, 27
  free-radical theory of, 25
  Hayflick constant and, 26
  MHC and, 28
  thymic hormones and, 25–26
  See also Longevity; Longevity nutrients
AIDS Information Hotline, 25
Air Check-Alpha Energy Labs, 284
Air pollution, 96–97

Alactate energy, 120, 121, 123–124
  power and capacity of, 122
Alcohol, 71–81
  ACSM stand on usage of, 341–346
  drink equivalents, 73
  estimated deaths related to (U.S.—1977), 75
  mortality rate for alcoholics, 73–74
  myths and facts about, 77–81
  social implications of abuse of, 74
  USOC statement on, 435
Alcoholics Anonymous (AA), 85
Alexander, Dr. James, 64
Alkalies, 56–57
Allen, Woody, 24
Alpha-fetoprotein (AFP), 43
Altered carbohydrate metabolism, 408–409
Altitude training, 64–65
Aluminum cookware, 93, 94
Aluminum toxicity, 93–94
Alzheimer's disease
  aluminum toxicity and, 93, 94
  MHC and, 28
Amateur Athletic Union of the United States (AAU), 268–269
AAU House, 269
AAU/USA Junior Olympics, 268–269
American Aging Association, Inc., 284

American College of Advancement
    in Medicine, 286
American College of Sports
    Medicine (ACSM), 270–271
  exercise guidelines for healthy
    adults, 307–316
  on proper and improper weight-
    loss programs, 317–327
  on use of alcohol, 341–346
  on use of anabolic-androgenic
    steroids, 347–360
American Heart Association, 19
American International Health
    Industries, 259
American Longevity Association,
    283
American Longevity Research
    Institute, 35, 283, 284
*American Medical Athletic
    Association Newsletter*, 287
American Scientific Health and
    Fitness Products, 286
Amino-acetic acid, 57
Amino acids
  arginine and ornithine as, 20–21
  liver and, 42
Amino-acid supplements, 13
Amphetamines, 14, 36, 68–70
  half-life of, 87
D-Amphetamine, 14
Anabolic steroid factor, 40
Anabolic steroids, 36, 37–41,
    502–513
  ACMS on use of, 347–360
  acne and, 407
  altered carbohydrate metabolism
    and, 408–409
  body composition and, 348
  cancers associated with, 42–45
  cardiovascular system and,
    45–46, 352, 384–386
  chemical structures of, 368–369,
    502–504, 505–513
  effect on the body of, 39–41
  effect on women of, 47–48,
    352–353, 388
  general trade names of, 368–369
  hypertension and, 409
  IOC on
    banned-drug listing, 353–354,
      433

  testing for, 86
  length of stay in system, 86
  liver and, 44–45, 350–352,
    378–384, 410–411
  manufacturers of, 505–513
  medical uses of, 377
  muscular strength and, 349–350
  NCAA list of banned drugs (1986)
    and, 420
  nervous system and, 376
  normal dosages of, 502–504
  NSCA position paper on, 361–403
  prostatic enlargement and,
    411–412
  protein synthesis and, 377
  psychological effects of, 48–49,
    353, 388, 411
  reproductive systems and, 47–48,
    352–353, 386–387
  self-screening examination for
    male athletes, 404–413
  side effects of, 46–47, 48, 353,
    387–388
  testicular atrophy and, 46, 412
  trade names for, 502–504,
    505–513
  training and, 370–375
  urine testing for, 88–89
  USOC statement on, 435
Anadrol, 44
Androgenic steroid factor, 41
Angyal, Andras, 221
Annals of Internal Medicine, 44
Antabuse (Disulfiram), 72
ANTACHE (biofeedback
    instrument), 239
ANTENSE (biofeedback
    instrument), 239
Anthropomaximology, 222
Anthropometrics, 98
Antidoping laws, 86
Antiestrogens, 46–47
Antiinflammatories, 36
Antiinflammatory steroids, 40–41
Antioxidants, free-radical damage
    and, 11
Aqua Associates, Inc., 284
Arginine, 20–21
L-Arginine, 13
Arsenic in public water systems, 95
Arthritis, 21

pantothenic acid and, 18
Asbestos in public water systems, 95
Ascorbic acid, see Vitamin C (ascorbic acid)
Asopressin, 31
Aspirin, 36
    longevity and, 28–29
Association and Show Management Inc. (ASMI), 281
"Athletic acromegaly," 53–54
ATP, generation of, 119–129
    interaction of three energy pathways leading to, 127
Auditory subliminals, 230–232
Azoospermia, 352

Bach, Richard, 225
Baking soda (sodium bicarbonate), 8, 57
Bally Fitness
    exercise cycles, 166–167
    institutional-level exercise equipment, 209–210
    rowing machines, 146–148
Bannister, Roger, 225
Barbiturates, 36, 68
Barnziger, Dr. John, 90
Beckett, Dr., 86
Beef as source of iron and zinc, 12
Behavioral disorders, anabolic steroids and, 411
Behavior modification, flotation and, 249–251
Benzedrine, 69
Benzodiazepines, 68
Beta blockers, 54–55
    USOC statement on, 435
Beta-carotene as antioxidant, 11–12
Beta endorphins, 248
Beta oxidation, 125–129
Beta (β) receptors, 54
Beyer, Uwe, 49
Bias, Len, 83
Bicycles, stationary, 105
Biocycle, 164–166
Biodex isokinetic system, 216
Bioelectrical Impedance Analyzers (BIA), 100–101
Biofeedback, 235–239

flotation and, 250
Biomechanic evaluation of exercise equipment, 108–109
Biosig Instruments, 239
    pulse meters, 244–246
Biotechnology General, 51
Bloating, carbohydrate loading and, 5
Blood alcohol concentration (BAC), 76–77
Blood-chemistry tests, 292–306
Blood clotting, linoleic acid and, 19
Blood composition, normal, 414–415
Blood doping, 36, 61–63
    USOC statement on, 435
Blood glucose, liver and, 42
Blood hormone levels, 288–291
Body composition, 98–102
    analyzers for, 100–102
    effect of anabolic steroids on, 348
Body fat
    distribution in men and women of, 99
    methods used for measurement of, 99–100
    potential fat burners, 13–14
Bodyguard/Oglaend exercise cycles, 160–161
Bosch exercise cycles, 162–164
Boston Celtics, 83
Bradycardia, 59
Brain, hemisphericity factor of, 230–231
Brandy, 37
Brave New World (Huxley), 52
Bread, carbohydrate loading and, 5
Broccoli as source of pantothenic acid, 17
Bruns, Howard J., 282
Bull testicles, 37–38

Caffeine, 36, 58–61
Caffeine pills, 58
Calcium
    aluminum absorption and, 94
    as dietary supplement, x
Calorie (C), definition of, 109
Cam II system (Keiser exercise cycle), 208–209
Canadian Olympic Lab, 90

Cancer, 21
  anabolic steroids and, 42–45
  radon and, 97
  secondhand smoke and, 97
  warning signs for, 42
Cancer-hormone disturbance, five
    theories of, 41–42
Cannabis sativa hemp plant, 66
Capka, Donna, 232
Carbamates, 68
Carbohydrate metabolism, altered,
    408–409
Carbohydrates, 4–5
  carbohydrate loading, 4–5
  liver and, 42
Carbromal, 68
Carcinogens in public water
    systems, 94
Cardiac output, 240
Cardiac testing, cycle ergometry
    for, 162–163
Cardiovascular system
  anabolic steroids and, 45–46,
    352, 384–386
  beta blockers and, 54
  performance improvement and,
    131
D-Carnitine, 14
L-Carnitine, 13, 14
Catch (phase one of rowing
    technique), 138, 139
Cateye Ergociser (exercise cycle),
    169–170
Catlin, Dr. Donald, 86, 90
Cauliflower as source of
    pantothenic acid, 17
Cell therapy, longevity and, 34
Centers for Disease Control, 95
Central nervous system, muscle
    fibers connected to, 117–118
Central nervous system stimulants
  banned by IOC, 430
  banned by NCAA, 419
  USOC statement on, 434
Centrophenoxine, 33–34
Chelated iron, 12
Chlorine in sports drinks, 6
P-Chlorophenoxyacetic acid, 33
Cholestasis, 410
Choline loading, 14

Ciba Pharmaceutical Corporation,
    38
Citrate-phosphate-dextrose (CPD),
    63
Citric acid (Krebs cycle), 120, 123,
    124–125
City Sports, 287
Clean Water Act of 1986, 94
Clinique Paul Niehans
    (Switzerland), 34
Clip-on pulse meters, 247
Clomid (chlomiphene citrate), 47
Club Industry, 287
Cocaine, 36, 37, 58, 82–85
  half-life of, 87
  warning signs for, 84
Cocaine Anonymous, 85
Cocaine Hot Line, 85, 285
Coca plant, 68
Cocoa, 58
  caffeine in, 60
Coenzyme Q_{10}, antiaging
    properties of, 29
Coffee, caffeine in, 60
Coffey, Calvin, 148
Coffey rowing machines, 148–150
Cola drinks, caffeine in, 60
*Complete Health Club Handbook,
    The* (Dietrich and
    Waggoner), 255, 259
Complex carbohydrates, 4
Computer Instruments Corp. (CIC)
    pulse meters, 246–247
Computerized exercise cycles,
    164–167, 256
Computerized treadmills, 255–256
Concentric contraction, 111
Concept 2 Rowing Ergometer,
    150–151
Connolly, Olga Fikotova, 48
Cookware, aluminum, 93, 94
Cori Cycle, 128, 129
Corticosteroids, 48
Cortisol, 27–28
Cortisone, 41
Crack, 82, 83
Cristofallo, Vincent, 26
Cross-country skiing devices,
    179–180
CT scan, 43

Cushing's disease, 48
Cybex
    muscle-training system, 213
    upper-body ergometer (UBE), 172
Cyclists, sports drinks and, 7, 8
Czechoslovakia, 98

Dallas Cowboys, 260
Damiana, 34
Danazol, 47
Dance-exercise industry, 275
Dance Exercise Today, 275
Danocrine, 47
David Fitness exercise equipment,
        192, 193–194
Davis, Al, 68
Davis, Peter and Kathie, 275
DDT in public water systems, 95
Death-hormone theory of aging, 25
Death in the Locker Room: Steroids
        & Sports (Goldman), 39, 223
DECO (decreasing oxygen
        consumption) hormone, 25
De Merode, Prince, 86
Dencla, Dr. W. D., 25
Dexedrine, 69
DHEA (dehydroepiandrosterone),
        26–27
Diabetes, 21
Diagnostic muscle-training
        systems, 211–217
    Biodex, 216
    Cybex, 213
    Hydra-Fitness, 211
    Isotechnologies, 215
    Kin-Com, 213–215
    Loredan, 215–216
    Microfit, 217
    Universal Corp., 211–212
Dialysis, long-term, aluminum
        toxicity and, 93–94
Dianabol, 38
    psychological effects of, 48–49
Diapid, 31–32
Diastole, 240
Diathermy, shortwave, 263
Diazepam, 68
Dicarbamates, 68
Dieting programs, medical risks
        associated with, 319

Diet medications, caffeine in, 60
Dietrich, John, 255
    on flotation benefits, 259–260
Dioxin in water supplies, 96
Disassociative imagery, 226
Disulfiram, 72
Diuretics
    banned by NCAA, 420
    urine testing and, 87
DMAE (dimethylaminsesthanol), 33
    longevity and, 29–30
DMSO (dimethyl sulfoxide), 55–56
DMSO: The New Healing Power
        (Walker and Douglass), 55
DNA, 28
    repair theory, 27
Do-it-yourself subliminal training,
        233–234
Donike, Dr. Manfred, 86
Dopamine, 32–33
Doping, 36–37
    blood, 36, 61–63
        USOC statement on, 435
Doriden, 68
Douglass, U. C., 55
Dried beans, 4
Drug Control Hotline (USOC), 434,
        437
Drug detection, 86–92
    instrumentation for, 88–90
    IOC drug-testing labs, 90
    NCAA program for, 416–428
    procedures for, 90–92
Drugs
    IOC banned-drug list, 429–433
    NCAA banned-drug list (1986),
        419–421
    USOC banned-drug list (1986),
        434–501
    See also Anabolic steroids;
        Ergogenic drugs;
        Recreational drugs; names of
        drugs
Dual Piston Professional Rowers,
        140
Duration (training principle), 129
Dylan, Bob, 66

Eagle/Cybex exercise equipment,
        183–184

East Germany, 98–99
Eccentric contraction, 111
E. coli in manufacture of HGH,
    50–51
Ectomorphy (ectomorphs), 98
Egg white as source of amino
    acids, 13
Egg yolks as source of pantothenic
    acid, 17
Electrical stimulation in treatment
    of sports injuries, 264
Electrocardiography (ECG)
    biofeedback and, 237
    for monitoring heart rate, 242
Electroencephalography (EEG), 237
Electromyography (EMG)
    biofeedback and, 237
    integrated into muscle-training
        systems, 214
    muscle tension and, 236–237
Electronic exercise cycles, 164,
    169–170
Endomorphy (endomorphs), 98
Endorphins
    flotation and, 248, 251
    TENS stimulation and, 264
Energy systems
    for muscle training, 119–129
        alactate energy, 120, 121,
            123–124
        citric acid (Krebs cycle), 120,
            123, 124–125
        Cori Cycle, 128, 129
        glycolysis (lactic acid), 120, 121,
            123, 124
        oxidative phosphorylation, 120,
            123, 125–129
    performance improvement and,
        131
Engineering Dynamics Corp.
    exercise cycles, 164–166
Enrichment Enterprises Inc., 261
Entrepreneur, 254
Environmental Defense Fund, 285
Environmental Protection Agency
    (EPA), 285
    water pollution and, 94
Epinephrine, 69
Ergogenic aids, nutritional, 3–23
    amino-acid supplements, 13

arginine, 20–21
baking soda, 8, 57
carbohydrate loading, 4–5
neurotransmitter precursors, 14
niacin, 10, 19
oil of evening primrose, 19
ornithine, 20–21
PABA, 19
pantothenic acid (vitamin B_5),
    17–18
placebo effect of, 22
potential fat burners, 13–14
pregnancy and, 22–23
selenium, 18–19
sodium phosphate, 9, 57
sports drinks, 6–8
vitamin and mineral
    supplementation, 9–12
water, 5–6
Ergogenic drugs, 36–37
alkalies, 56–57
altitude training as, 64–65
beta-adrenergic blockers, 54–55
blood doping, 36, 61–63
caffeine, 36, 58–61
DMSO, 55–56
gelatin, 57–58
glycine, 57–58
human growth hormone (HGH)
    as, 49–54
marijuana as, 67
oxygen as, 63–64
phosphates, 57
testosterone as, 41–42
See also Anabolic steroids
Ergometers, 154
upper-body, 171–172
Erythorxylon coca plant, 82
Estrogen
conversion of testosterone into,
    46, 47
side effects of, 48
Estrogen supplements, x
Evans, H. M., 49
Excelsior Fitness Co. exercise cycle,
    167, 168
Exercise cycles, 154–172
Bally Fitness, 166–167
benefits of, 154
Biocycle, 164–166

Bodyguard/Oglaend, 160–161
Bosch, 162–164
Cateye Ergometer, 169–170
Exercycle, 168–169
Fitnron, 169
Monark, 161–162
Paramount, 170–171
Precor, 156–157
Protec Sports, 171
Schwinn, 167, 168
semirecumbant cycles, 155–156
Tunturi, 157–160
Universal Aerobicycle, 164
upper-body ergometers, 171–172
Exercise equipment
  guidelines for evaluation of,
    105–111
    biomechanic evaluation,
      108–109
    terminology overview, 109–111
  institutional-level, 183–210
    Bally Fitness, 209–210
    David Fitness, 192, 193–194
    Eagle/Cybex, 183–184
    Hunk Fitness, 202–203
    Hydra-Fitness, 188–191
    Keiser, 208–209
    Kinesi-Arc, 207–208
    Myotech/Muscle Dynamics,
      194–198
    Nautilus, 198–200
    Paramount, 184–188
    Polaris, 204–205
    Serious Lifting Systems,
      203–204
    Tygr USA, 201
    Universal Fitness, 205–207
  muscle-training systems, 111–114
    isokinetic contractions, 112–114
    isometric contractions, 111–112
    isotonic contractions, 112
    omnikinetics, 114, 115, 120
    physiology of, 115–135
  See also Aerobic training
      devices; Diagnostic muscle-
      training systems; Exercise
      cycles; Rowing machines
Exercise for maintaining fitness in
    healthy adults, ACSM
    guidelines for, 307–316

Exercycle, 168–169
Exersentry heart-rate monitor,
    246–247

Fad diets, medical risks associated
    with, 319
Fast-twitch muscle fibers, 117, 119
Fat burners, potential, 13–14
Fibromata mollusca, 53
Fine, Thomas, 251, 252
Fish, mercury level in, 96
Fitness Industry, 287
Fitness Master Inc. ski training
    devices, 180
Fitness Newsletter, 287
Fitnron cycle ergometer, 169
Flexibility, 111
Floatarium unit, 261
Flotation, 248–261
    as aid in behavior modification,
      249–251
    beneficial effects of, 251–256
    compared with other relaxation
      techniques, 249
    frequency of use, 249
Flotation centers, 255
Flotation REST response, 249
Flotation tanks, 255–256
    manufacturers of, 261
Fluidotherapy, 263
Fluoride, 94
Food of the Gods (Wells), 50
Football, sports drinks and, 8
Frankenstein Syndrome, 53
Free-radical damage
    selenium as barrier from, 18
    vitamin C and, 11
Free-radical theory of aging, 25
Frequency (training principle),
    129–130
FSH (follicle-stimulating hormone),
    47

Gallium-67 scan, 43
Galvanic skin resistance (GSR), 237
Galvanic stimulation, 264–265
Gas chromatography, 86
    for drug detection, 88–89
Gatorade, 7
Gelatin, 57–58

Genetech Inc., 51

Gerovital (GH-3), 30–31

Gigantism as side effect of excess
HGH, 52, 53–54

Glauberman, Dr. Lloyd, 253

Glucose concentration in sports
drinks, 7

Glutethimide, 68

Glycine, 57–58

Glycogen
carbohydrate loading and, 4, 5
fat burners and, 13
liver and, 42
sports drinks and, 7

Glycolysis (lactic-acid energy), 120,
121, 123, 124

Goals, setting, 225–226

Goldstein, Alan, 26

Growth hormones, see Human
growth hormones (HGH)

Gynecomastia, 46

Hachschild, Richard, 33

Handicapped, exercise equipment
designed for, 202–203

Hard work, definition of, 110

Harmon, Denham, 284

Harvey, John, Jr., 56, 70

Hayflick, Dr. Leonard, 26

Headaches, 59

Heart, effect of altitude training on,
64–65

Heart disease, anabolic steroids as
cause of, 45–46

Heart Mate Windracer Rower, 152–153

Heart rate (pulse), 240
biofeedback and, 237
calculating, 242–243
monitoring, 241–242, 243–244

Heartwatch (pulse meter), 247

Heat packs, 262–263

Heightened suggestibility, flotation
and, 253

Hematuria (blood in the urine), 45

Hemisphericity factor of brain,
auditory subliminals and,
230–231

Heroin, 37

High-density lipoproteins (HDLs),
45, 46

High Technology Fitness Research

Institute, x, 283
guidelines for exercise
equipment evaluation,
106–108

High-tech pulse monitoring,
240–247
calculating heart rate, 242–243
monitoring heart rate, 241–242,
243–244
pulse meters, 244–247

High-tech treatment of sports
injuries, 262–265
electrical stimulation, 264
fluidotherapy, 263
heat packs, 262–263
interferential current, 265
shortwave diothermy (SWD), 263
transcutaneous electrical nerve
stimulation (TENS), 263–264
ultrasound and galvanic
stimulation, 264–265

High-voltage galvanic stimulation,
264–265

Hormone drugs, see Anabolic
steroids; Steroids

Hormones
cellular activity altered by intake
of, 40
follicle-stimulating, 47
levels in blood and urine of,
288–291
luteinizing, 47
somatotrophic, 50
thymic-stimulating, 25–26

Hospital Practice, 50

Human chorionic gonadotropin
(HCG), 46–47

Human growth hormones (HGH),
49–54
amino-acid supplements and, 13
arginine and, 20–21
conditions caused by deficiencies
in, 20–21
half-life of, 87
L-Dopa as releaser of, 32
ornithine and, 20–21
physiology of, 51–52
side effects of, 21, 52–54

Human needs, basic, 221

Hunk Fitness exercise equipment,
202–203

Huxley, Aldous, 52
Hydergine, 25, 30
Hydra Fitness
  muscle-training system, 211
  omnikinetic machines, 114, 120,
    188–191
  rowing machines, 151–152
Hydrocollators (heat packs),
    262–263
Hydrostatic weighting, 99
Hyman, Albert S., 270
Hypercalcemia, 407–408
Hypercholesterolemia, 19
Hypercortisolemia, 408
Hyperglycemia, 21
Hyperlipidemia, 19
Hypertension, 409
Hypertriglyceridemia, 19
Hypnosis, see Subliminal training
Hypoglycemia, 54

Immune system
  linoleic acid and, 19
  vitamin C for, 11
Impotence, 54
Improper weight-loss programs,
    317–327
Impulse (training principle), 130
Injury prevention, flotation and, 251
INSTAPULSE heart-rate monitors
    (biofeedback instrument),
    239
Institutional-level exercise
    equipment, 183–210
  Bally Fitness, 209–210
  David Fitness, 192, 193–194
  Eagle/Cybex, 183–184
  Hunk Fitness, 202–203
  Hydra-Fitness, 188–191
  Keiser, 208–209
  Kinesi-Arc, 207–208
  Myotech/Muscle Dynamics,
    194–198
  Nautilus, 198–200
  Paramount, 184–188
  Polaris, 204–205
  Serious Lifting Systems, 203–204
  Tygr USA, 201
  Universal Fitness, 205–207
Intensity (training principle), 129
Interferential current for treatment

of sports injuries, 265
International Academy of Holistic
    Health and Medicine, The,
    283–284
International Cycling Federation,
    86
International Dance-Exercise
    Association (IDEA), 275–276
International Federation of Body
    Builders, 90–92
International Olympic Committee
    (IOC)
  on anabolic steroids
    banned-drug listing, 353–354,
      433
    testing for, 86
  banned-drug list of, 429–433
  on beta blockers, 55
  on blood doping, 63
  on caffeine, 58, 61
  drug-detection committee of, 86
  drug-testing labs of, 90
International Racket Sports
    Association (IRSA), 277–278
IRSA Club Business, 287
Interpretation of Diagnostic Tests
    (Wallach), 288, 292–293
Interval training, 105
Iron, 11, 12
Isokinetics, 112–114, 115
Isometrics, 111–112, 115
Isotechnologies muscle-training
    systems, 215
Isotonics, 112, 115
Ivanko Barbell Company, 197

Johansson ergograph, 72
Joki, Ernst, 270
Jones, Arthur, 198
Journal of Clinical Psychiatry, 49
Journal of Sports Science Research,
    272
Journal of the American
    Osteopathic Association, 44
Journals for the fitness trade, 287
Junior Olympics of the AAU/USA,
    268–269

Keiser Sports Health Equipment,
    208–209
Kenshan, 18

Kidney cancer, 45
Kilogram-meter, 110
Kin-Com muscle-training systems, 213–215
Kinesi-Arc exercise equipment, 207–208
Koch, Dr. Fred, 37
Kreb cycle (citric acid), 120, 123, 124–125
Kubistant, Tom, 224, 225
Kudinitz, Mark, 284
Kugler, Hans J., 284

Lactic acid, 8, 249
Lactic-acid energy, 120, 121, 123, 124
  power and capacity of, 122
Landice/BodyGuard treadmills, 177
Landon, E. Laird, 280
Landry, Tom, 260
Lange caliper, 99
Laradopa, 32
L-Dopa, 32–33
  side effects of, 33, 52
Left side of brain, auditory subliminals and, 230, 231
LH (luteinizing hormone), 47
LIDO (digital isokinetic rehabilitation system), 215–216
Lifecircuit, 209–210
Lifecycle, 166–167
Life Extension Foundation, 286
Life Extension Report, 283
Liferower, 147
LiftAmerica, 274
Linoleic acid, 19
Lipoproteins, 45, 46
Liver
  adverse effects of anabolic steroids on, 44–45, 350–352, 378–384, 410–411
  effect of HGH on, 51
  vital function of, 42
Liver cancer, 44–45
  physical signs of, 43
Long, J. A., 49
Longevity, 24–35
Longevity Letter, 283
Longevity nutrients

  arginine, 20–21
  niacin, 19
  oil of evening primrose, 19
  ornithine, 20–21
  PABA, 19
  pantothenic acid (vitamin B_5), 17–18
  placebo effects of, 22
  pregnant women and, 22–23
  selenium, 18–19
Loredan muscle-training systems, 215–216
Low-density lipoproteins (LDLs), 45, 46
Lung cancer, radon and, 97
Lupus cerebritis, 48

Magazines for the fitness trade, 287
Magnesium in sports drinks, 6
Male hormone, see Testosterone
Manual on Doping, 36
Manual pulse-taking, 241
MAO inhibitors, 33
Mariani, Angelo, 82
Marijuana, 66–67
  length of stay in system, 86–87
Marijuana Tax Act of 1937, 66
Market Watch, 280
Marquette Electronics, Inc. treadmills, 177–178
Maslow, Abraham, 221
Maximal oxygen uptake, see VO_2 max
Maximal work, definition of, 110
Maximum performance (peak experience), 222–225
Medical Commission of the British Commonwealth Games, 58
Medical uses of anabolic steroids, 377
Medicine and Science in Sports and Exercise (Percy), 64, 271
Medicine balls, 106
Memory capacity, hydergine and, 30
Men
  anabolic steroids and
    effect on reproductive system, 352, 386–387
    side effects, 387–388

body-fat distribution in, 99
impotence in, 54
self-screening examination for
    athletes taking anabolic
    steroids, 404–413
Mental imagery (visualization), 222,
    226
MERAC (Musculoskeletal
    Evaluation, Rehabilitation,
    and Conditioning) system,
    211–212
Mercury in water supplies, 96
Mesomorphy (mesomorphs), 98
Messenger RNA, effects of HGH on,
    51
N-Methamphetamine, 69
Methocarbamol, 68
Methylphenidate hydrochloride
    (Ritalin), 32
METS, definition of, 109–110
MHC (major histocompatibility
    complex), aging and, 28
MicroFit fitness-evaluation system,
    217
Miller, John A., 271
Mind-relaxation technique, 226–228
Mineral supplements, 9–12
    effect on pregnancy of, 23
Modeling, 221
Moderate work, definition of, 110
Monark exercise cycles, 161–162
Monoureides, 68
Morgan, Don, 232
Morphine, 36
Mueller, Grover W., 270
Muscle and Fitness/Shape/Flex,
    287
Muscle cells, 115
Muscle contraction (shortening),
    115–119
    aerobic energy for, 124–129
    alactate energy for, 123–124
    four factors determining strength
        of, 118–119
    isokinetic contraction, 112–114
    isometric contraction, 111–112
    isotonic contraction, 112
    lactic-acid energy for, 124
Muscle fibers, 115, 117, 119
Muscle growth, flotation and, 252

Muscle memory, 258
Muscle movement, basic terms for,
    111
Muscle pain, carbohydrate loading
    and, 5
Muscle relaxants, 36
Muscle tension, EMG levels and,
    236–237
Muscle-training systems, 111–114
    diagnostic, 211–217
        Biodex, 216
        Cybex, 213
        Hydra-Fitness, 211
        Isotechnologies, 215
        Kin-Com, 213–215
        Loredan, 215–216
        Microfit, 217
        Universal Corp., 211–212
    physiology of, 115–135
        energy systems, 119–129
        principles of training, 129–132
Muscular endurance, 110, 132–134
    measurement of, 132–134
Muscular power, 110–111, 134–135
    torque and, 135
Muscular strength, 110
    effect of anabolic steroids on,
        349–350
    performance improvement and, 131
Myofibrils, 115–116
Myosin, 115
Myotech/Muscle Dynamics exercise
    equipment, 194–198

Narcotic analgesics
    banned by IOC, 432
    USOC statement on, 434–435
Narcotics, 36
National Cancer Institute, 285
National Centers for Health and
    Medical Information, 283, 285
National Collegiate Athletic
    Association (NCAA)
    banned-drug list (1986), 419–421
    drug-testing program, 416–428
National Court Club Association
    (NCCA), 277
National Fitness Trade Journal, 197
National Health and Medical
    Trends, 283

National Institute of Drug Abuse,
      66, 71, 285
   cocaine-consumption estimates
      by, 83
National Pituitary Association, 50
National Scientific Research
      Center, 33
National Sporting Goods
      Association (NSGA), 279–281
NSGA Cost-of-Doing Business
      Survey, 280
National Strength and Conditioning
      Association (NSCA), 272–274
   on anabolic-steroids use, 361–403
   on prepubescent strength
      training, 328–340
National Strength & Conditioning
      Association Journal, 272, 287
National Tennis Association (NTA),
      277
National Testing Labs, Inc., 285
Nautilus exercise equipment,
      198–200, 255
Negatives (muscle movement), 111
Negative subliminal messages, 234
Nembutal, 68
Nervous system
   effects of anabolic steroids on,
      376
   muscle fibers connected to,
      117–118
Neuro-muscular programming, 254
   performance improvement and,
      132
Neurotransmitter precursors, 14
New Life Institute, 230
New Medical Science, 284
New York Health & Racquet Clubs,
      255, 259
New York Pioneer Club, 253
New York Times, The, 48, 56
Niacin, 10, 19
Nicotine, 70–71
Nitrates in water supplies, 96
Nolvadex, 47
Norepinephrine, 69, 71
Norisoephedrine, 68
Normal blood composition, 414–415
5'-Nucleotidase (5'-N), 306
Nutritional ergogenic aids, 3–23
   amino-acid supplements, 13

   arginine, 20–21
   baking soda, 8, 57
   carbohydrate loading, 4–5
   neurotransmitter precursors, 14
   niacin, 10, 19
   oil of evening primrose, 19
   ornithine, 20–21
   PABA, 19
   pantothenic acid (vitamin B_5),
      17–18
   placebo effect of, 22
   potential fat burners, 13–14
   pregnancy and, 22–23
   selenium, 18–19
   sodium phosphate, 9, 57
   sports drinks, 6–8
   vitamin and mineral
      supplementation, 9–12
   water, 5–6

Oakland Raiders, 68
Oatmeal as source of pantothenic
      acid, 17
Obesity, health-related problems
      associated with, 318
Octacosanol, 13–14
Oil of evening primrose, 19
Oligospermia, 352
Omnikinetic machines, 188–191
Omnikinetics, 114, 115, 120, 188–191
Omni-Tron muscle-training
      equipment, 211
Operation Everest Two, 64
Opium, 37
Ornithine, 20–21
L-Ornithine, 13
Overload, 129
"Overuse Syndromes in Young
      Athletes" (Harvey), 56
Oxidative phosporylation, 120, 123,
      125–129
Oxygen, 63–64
   as factor in sports performance, 109
   maximal oxygen uptake (VO_2),
      61–62, 109
Oysters as source of iron, 12

PABA (para-aminobenzoic acid),
      19, 31
Pacinian corpuscles, 117
Pain, 262

flotation and, 251
Pain-killers, 36
Pantothenic acid (vitamin B$_5$),
     17–18
Paramount Fitness Equipment
     exercise cycles, 170–171
     institutional-level exercise
          equipment, 184–188
Parkinson's disease, 52
     L-Dopa and, 32, 33
Parviainen, Arno, 194
Pasta, carbohydrate loading and, 4
PCBs in water supplies, 96
Peak experience (maximum
     performance), 222–225
Peak torque, 135
Peliosis hepatitis, 44, 382, 410
Pentobarbital, 68
Percy, E. C., 64
Performance improvement, 131–132
     flotation and, 252
Performing Your Best (Kubistant),
     224
Personal Exercise Planner (PEP),
     168
Pharmaceuticals, caffeine in, 60
Phosphates, 57
     in sports drinks, 6
Phosphatidycholine, 14
Photo-electric pickups for heart-rate
     monitoring, 241
Physical fitness, ACSM exercise
     guidelines for adults,
     307–316
Physician and Sports Medicine,
     100, 287
Piperidinedione, 68
Pituitary gland, HGH produced by,
     49, 50, 53
Placebos, 22
Pleythyein, 105
Plyometrics, 105–106
Polaris exercise equipment,
     204–205
Pollock, Dr. Mike, 100
Polycythemia, 411
Polymerized glucose in sports
     drinks, 7–8
Pork as source of iron, 12
Potassium, 6
     serum potassium, 298–300

Potassium citrate, 57
Potential fat burners, 13–14
Power, definition of, 109
Power lifting, definition of, 328
Power stroke or drive (phase two of
     rowing technique), 138, 139
Precor
     cross-country skiing devices,
          179–180
     exercise cycles, 156–157
     rowing machines, 140–142
     treadmills, 173–175, 178
Prednisone, 41
Pregnancy, effect of nutrient aids
     on, 22–23
Premature baldness, 46
Prepubescent athletes, definition
     of, 328–329
Prepubescent strength training
     (NSCA position paper),
     328–340
     available equipment, 331–332
     benefits, 329–330
     competition, 331
     guidelines for, 332–335
     risks, 330–331
Prescription medications, caffeine
     in, 60
Progesterones, 48
Propanolol (Inderal), 54
Proprioceptors, 117
Prostate cancer, 45
Prostatic enlargement, anabolic
     steroids and, 411–412
Protec Sports exercise cycles, 171
Protein synthesis, anabolic steroids
     and, 377
Protropin (synthetic HGH), 51
Psychological effects of anabolic
     steroids, 48–49, 353, 388, 411
Psychological Foundations of
     Sports (Mahoney et al.),
     221–222
Psychomotor stimulants
     banned by IOC, 429–430
     banned by NCAA, 419
     USOC statement on, 434
Puberty, increased androgen levels
     in, 367
Public water systems,
     contamination of, 94

Pulse meters, 244–247
Pulse monitoring, high-tech,
    240–247
  calculating heart rate, 242–243
  monitoring heart rate, 241–242,
    243–244
Pyloric valve, 4
Pyridoxine, 10

Quinton treadmills, 178

Radioimmunoassays (RIA), 86
Radon, 97
Raynaud's syndrome, 54
Recovery (phase three of rowing
    technique), 139
Recreational drugs, 66–85
  alcohol, 71–81
  amphetamines, 14, 36, 68–70
  cocaine, 36, 37, 68, 82–85
  marijuana, 66–67
  nicotine, 70–71
  sedatives, 68
Recresal, 57
Refined carbohydrates, 4
Relaxation, basic technique for,
    226–228
Relaxation response, 249
Reproductive systems, adverse
    effects of anabolic steroids
    on, 47–48, 352–353, 386–387
Resistance training, 328
Response-induction aids, 221
Restorative drugs, 36
Restricted environmental
    stimulation therapy (REST),
    248
Rheumatoid arthritis, pantothenic
    acid and, 18
Riboflavin, 10
RICE prescription for treatment of
    sports injuries, 262
Right side of brain, auditory
    subliminals and, 230–231
Ritalin, 32
RJL Systems Inc., 102
  body composition analyzer, 101
Robaxin, 68
Robert Bosch Medical Electronics,
    162

Roche Laboratories, 32
Rodgers, Don, 83
Rowing machines, 105, 136–153
  Bally Fitness, 146–148
  Coffey, 148–150
  Concept 2, 150–152
  Heart Mate, 152–153
  Hydra-Fitness, 151–152
  Precor, 140–142
  rowing technique, 138–139
  selection checklist, 137–138
  Tunturi, 142–143
  Universal Computerow, 144–146
  West Bend, 143–144, 145
Royal jelly as source of pantothenic
    acid, 17
Rumania, 98
Runners
  baking soda and, 8
  mineral supplements for, 12
  sodium phosphate and, 9
  sports drinks and, 7, 8
Runner's World, 287

Said, Bob, 258–259
St. Elizabeth's Hospital, 251
Samadhi Tank Co., 261
Sandbags, 106
Sarcolemma, 115
Sarcomeres, 117
Sarcoplasm, 115
Sarcoplasmic reticulum, 115
Saytzeff, Alexander, 55
Schmeltzer, David, 253
Schwartz, Dr. Arthur, 26–27
Schwarzenegger, Arnold, 20
Schwinn Air Dyne cycle, 167, 168
Scientific selection of athletes in
    Eastern Europe, 98–99
SCWL (subconscious to conscious
    way of learning) method,
    231, 232
Secondhand smoke, 96–97
Sedatives, 68
"Selective gigantism," 53–54
Selective Ion Monitoring (SIM) for
    drug detection, 90
Selenium, 18–19
  as antioxidant, 11–12
Self-actualization, 221

Self-efficacy statements, 222
Self-screening examination for male athletes taking anabolic steroids, 404–413
Selye, Hans, 27
Semirecumbant cycles, 155–156
Septien, Rafael, 250, 253
  on flotation benefits, 260
Serious Lifting Systems, 203–204
Serum alkaline phosphatase, 301–302
Serum cholesterol, 300–301
  selenium and, 18
Serum creatine, 295
Serum creatinine, 294–295
Serum gamma-glutamyl transpeptidase, 302–303
Serum lactic dehydrogenase (LDH), 304–306
Serum potassium, 298–300
Serum sodium, 297–298
Serum transaminase (SGOT), 303–304, 379–380
Serum urea nitrogen (BUN), 293–294
Serum uric acid, 296–297
Setting goals, 225–226
Shen Nung, 66
Shorter, Frank, 99
Shortwave diathermy (SWD), 263
Side effects
  of amphetamines, 68, 69–70
  of anabolic steroids, 46–47, 48, 353, 387–388
  of asopressin, 31
  of beta blockers, 54–55
  of blood doping, 62–63
  of caffeine, 59–60
  of cell therapy, 34
  of centrophenoxine, 34
  of DMAE, 30
  of estrogen, 48
  of HGH excess, 21, 52–54
  of hydergine, 30
  of L-Dopa, 33, 52
  of ritalin, 32
  of Zumba-Forte, 35
Skeletal muscle, 115
Skeletal system, flexibility of, 132
Skinfold thickness, measurement of, 99–100

Slow-twitch muscle fibers, 117, 119
SMAC (serum chemistry) test, 292–306
Smith, Willie, 83
Smoke, secondhand, 96–97
Smokeless tobacco, 71
Sniffing cocaine, 82
Sodium, 6
  serum sodium, 297–298
Sodium bicarbonate (baking soda), 8, 57
Sodium citrate, 57
Sodium phosphate, 9, 57
SomaTech, 102
  Ultrasonic Bodyanalyzer, 101
Somatic neurons, 117–118
Somatotrophic hormone (STH), 50
Somatotrophin, 50
Sonneborn, Dr. Joan, 27
Special Olympics of NSCA, 274
Specificity of training, 130
Speed, 36
Speedball (heroin-cocaine mixture), 37
Sperm count, 292
  drop in, 46
Sporting Goods Business, 287
Sporting Goods Manufacturers Association (SGMA), 282
Sporting Goods Market, The, 280
Sport Magazine, 287
Sports drinks, 6–8
Sports Foundation Inc., 281
Sports Illustrated, 287
Sports injuries, high-tech treatment of, 262–265
  electrical stimulation, 264
  fluidotherapy, 263
  heat packs, 262–263
  interferential current, 265
  shortwave diathermy (SWD), 263
  transcutaneous electrical nerve stimulation (TENS), 263–264
  ultrasound and galvanic stimulation, 264–265
Sports Medicine Bulletin, 271
Sports psychology, 221–228
  maximum performance, 222–225
  relaxation, 226–228

Sports psychology (*cont.*)
  setting goals, 225–226
  subliminal training, 229–234
    auditory subliminals, 230–232
    do-it-yourself training, 233–234
Sports Retailer, 279–280
StairMaster Sports/Medical
        Products, 181–182
Static muscle movement, 111
Stationary bicycles, 105
Stationary exercise cycles, *see*
        Exercise cycles
Steroid hormones, 37
Steroids
  ratio between androgenic and
        anabolic qualities in, 40
  two basic classes of, 40–41
  See also Anabolic steroids
Stima, Mike, 196, 197
Stitz, Lynn, 231
Stone, Michael H., 362
Strength training, definition of, 328
Stress, flotation and, 248–249
Stretch reflex, 106
Stroke volume, 240
Strychnine, 36, 37
Subliminal training, 229–234
  auditory subliminals, 230–232
  do-it-yourself training, 233–234
  effectiveness of, 234
Sugar in sports drinks, 7
Suggestibility, flotation and, 253
Superoxide dismutase (SOD), 28
Swanson, Don, 283
Sympathomimetic amines
  banned by IOC, 431
  banned by NCAA, 419
  USOC statement on, 434
Synthetic HGH, 50–51
Systole, 240

Tachycardia, 59
Tank Alternatives, 261
Taylor, Dr. Bill, 53
Tea, caffeine in, 60
Temperature, biofeedback and, 237
Tensionmeters, 200
Testicular atrophy, anabolic
        steroids and, 46, 412
Testosterone, 34, 41–42, 367

conversion to estrogen of, 46, 47
  therapeutic index value of, 40
Tetrahydrocannabinol (THC), 66–67
Therapeutic Index (TI), 40
Thiamine, 10–11
Thoreau, H. D., 248
Thymic-stimulating hormones,
        25–26
Thymosyns, 25–26
Thymus gland, 26
Timing (training principle), 130–131
Torque, 111, 135
Total body electrical conductivity
        (TOBEC) unit, 101
Total torque, 135
Toxicity
  of aluminum, 93–94
  of selenium, 18
Training, anabolic steroids and,
        370–375
Training diet, 4
Tranquilizers, 36
Transcutaneous electrical nerve
        stimulation (TENS), 263–264
Treadmills, 173–178
  computerized, 255–256
  Landice, 177
  Marquette Electronics, 177–178
  Precor, 173–175, 178
  Quinton, 178
  True Sports, 176–177
  Universal, 175–176
Tritech StairMaster, 181–182
Tropomyosin, 115, 116
Troponin, 116
True Sports Inc. treadmills, 176–177
T system tubules, 117
Tunturi
  exercise cycles, 157–160
  rowing machines, 142–143
Turner, Dr. John, 252
Tygr USA exercise equipment, 201

Ultrasound, 43, 264–265
Ultraviolet-light damage, PABA
        and, 19
Underground Steroid Handbook, 53
U.S. Figure Skating Association, 232
U.S. Olympic Committee (USOC)
  banned-drug list (1986), 434–501

drug-control hotline, 434, 437
U.S. World Cup Teams, 258
Universal Corp.
  Aerobicycles, 164
  Computerow, 144–146
  Fitnet system, 206–207
  institutional-level exercise
      equipment, 205–207
  muscle-training system, 211–212
  treadmills, 175–176
Upper-body ergometers, 171–172
Urine, hormone levels in, 289–291
Urine testing, 87, 292
  anabolic steroids and, 88–89

Valhalla Scientific bio-resistance
      body composition analyzer,
      101, 102
Valium, 68
Vasodilation, 54
  flotation and, 252
Vasopressin, 31–32
Veroshanski, Yuri, 105
VersaClimber/Heart Rate Inc., 181
  total-body climbing device,
      180–181
Visualization (mental imagery), 226
  flotation and, 253
Vitamin A, 22
Vitamin B$_5$ (pantothenic acid),
      17–18
Vitamin B$_6$, 23
Vitamin C (ascorbic acid), 25
  for boosting immune system, 11
Vitamin D, 23
Vitamin E, 25
  as antioxidant, 11
Vitamin K, 23
Vitamin supplements, 9–12
Volitionally Operant Exercise
      (VOE), 196
VO$_2$ max (maximal oxygen uptake),
      61–62
  definition of, 109
Voy, Dr. Robert, 90

Waggoner, Susan, 259
Walden (Thoreau), 248

Wallach, Jacques, 288, 292, 293
Warning signs
  for cancer, 42
  for cocaine usage, 84
Water, 5–6
Water pollution, 94–96
Watertest Corporation, 284
Watt, definition of, 109
Weight lifting
  definition of, 328
  sports drinks and, 8
Weight-loss programs, ACSM on,
      317–327
Weight training
  definition of, 328
  plyometrics and, 106
Wells, H. G., 50
West Bend rowing machines,
      143–144, 145
Whole grains, 4
Whole-wheat flour as source of
      pantothenic acid, 17
Wilms's tumor, 45, 383
Wolffe, Joseph B., 270
Women
  adverse effects of anabolic
      steroids on reproductive
      system, 47–48, 352–353,
      386–387
  body-fat distribution in, 99
  effect of nutrient aids on
      pregnancy, 22–23
Women's Sports & Fitness, 287
Work, definition of, 109, 110
Wright, James E., 362

Xanthine, 58, 59

Yohimbine, 34, 35
York Barbell Gym, 38

Zane, Frank, 257–258
Zane Haven (training facility), 258
Zane Nutrition (Zane), 257
Ziegler, Dr. John, 38–39
Zinc, 12
Zumba-Forte, 34–35